Get Writing: Paragraphs and Essays

with Readings--Eng 096

Mark Connelly | Robert P. Yagelski

CENGAGE
Learning™

Australia • Brazil • Japan • Korea • Mexico • Singapore • Spain • United Kingdom • United States

CENGAGE
Learning™

**Get Writing: Paragraphs and Essays
with Readings--Eng 096**

Mark Connelly | Robert P. Yagelski

Executive Editors:
 Maureen Staudt
 Michael Stranz
Project Development Manager:
 Linda deStefano
Senior Marketing Coordinators:
 Sara Mercurio

Senior Production / Manufacturing Manager:
 Donna M. Brown
PreMedia Services Supervisor:
 Joel Brennecke
Rights & Permissions Specialist:
 Kalina Hintz
 Todd Osborne

Cover Image:
 Getty Images*

For product information and technology assistance, contact us at
Cengage Learning Customer & Sales Support, 1-800-354-9706

For permission to use material from this text or product,
submit all requests online at **cengage.com/permissions**
Further permissions questions can be emailed to
permissionrequest@cengage.com

ISBN-13: 978-1-4240-8724-2

ISBN-10: 1-4240-8724-4

Cengage Learning
5191 Natorp Boulevard
Mason, Ohio 45040
USA

Cengage Learning is a leading provider of customized learning solutions with
office locations around the globe, including Singapore, the United Kingdom,
Australia, Mexico, Brazil, and Japan. Locate your local office at:
international.cengage.com/region

Cengage Learning products are represented in Canada by Nelson Education, Ltd.

For your lifelong learning solutions, visit **custom.cengage.com**

Visit our corporate website at **cengage.com**

Printed in the United States of America

BRIEF CONTENTS

CONTENTS

Part 2   Developing Paragraphs   33

Part 4   Improving Essays   287

Part 8   Readings for Writers   611

The Goals of Get Writing: Paragraphs and Essays

Get Writing helps students improve the writing skills needed to succeed in college and their future careers by engaging them in their own writing. *Get Writing* assumes that students have things to say about their jobs, their friends, their families, their college experience, their career goals, and the world around them. Throughout the book, students are given opportunities to express themselves on a variety of issues, then examine and improve their choice of words, sentences, and paragraphs. Above all, *Get Writing* connects critical thinking (what students are trying to say) with grammar and mechanics (what they have written).

This second edition incorporates suggestions taken from a survey of more than a hundred writing instructors and extensive reviews by instructors who teach developmental writing and who have used *Get Writing* in the classroom. Their practical advice and professional experience have enhanced *Get Writing*, making it a highly flexible teaching tool that meets the needs of developmental writers. In particular, instructors requested greater emphasis on improving essays.

Approach

Instructors have found *Get Writing*'s approach to be highly successful because it provides a simple system to improve student writing. *Get Writing* encourages students to think critically and sharpen their editing skills by asking them two basic questions:

1. **What are you trying to say?**
   - Why did you select this topic?
   - Why is it important?
   - What do you want readers to know about it?
   - What details should you include?
   - What is the best way to organize your ideas?

2. **What have you written?**
   - Are your words accurate and effective?
   - Do your sentences clearly express what you want to say?
   - Can readers follow your train of thought?
   - Are there mechanical errors that detract from your message?

Get Writing meets the needs of a variety of students, including recent high school graduates, working adults returning to school, and those for whom English is not their native language. Writing exercises and prompts cover an array of interests—history, politics, popular culture, jobs, education, science, and current events.

Get Writing does not teach writing in isolation. It assists students with the writing tasks they encounter in other courses and their jobs. Writing assignments ask students to comment on their progress in college, to identify upcoming challenges, and to consider strategies for improving their writing skills, study habits, and time management.

Focus on Writing

Get Writing **offers students a range of writing opportunities.**

What Are You Trying to Say?/ What Have You Written?

Chapters open by asking students to express their thoughts on a range of topics. After completing a writing assignment, they are asked to examine what they have written. By analyzing their word choices, their use of details, and their critical-thinking skills, they learn to improve their writing and link what they are studying with their own work.

Analyzing Images

Living in a media-driven age, students are accustomed to seeing images in ads, in commercials, in blogs, in movies, and on their cell phones. *Get Writing* opens and closes chapters with visual prompts, encouraging students to analyze rather than simply respond to images that depict jobs, family, school life, popular culture, and social issues. Photos are often paired to encourage students to examine similar or contrasting images. Analyzing Images introduces students to critical thinking by getting to them to move beyond immediate reactions and to question what they see.

Critical Thinking

Assignments direct students to write about personal experiences and express their opinions on issues ranging from national security to their favorite television show.

Real-World Writing

Throughout *Get Writing*, students write, revise, and edit documents they will encounter beyond the classroom: e-mail, letters, reports, and résumés. Instructors have repeatedly stressed that having students work with "real-world" documents demonstrates the practical value of writing skills and prepares students for tasks they will face in their careers. Adult students will recognize many of the writing challenges encountered in the workplace.

Working Together

Collaborative writing and editing exercises demonstrate the value of peer review and provide practice working in groups.

Organization

Get Writing consists of eight parts, which can be taught in different sequences to meet the needs of instructors and courses.

Part 1: Getting Started introduces students to the importance of writing and presents strategies for succeeding in composition courses. The writing process, from prewriting to final editing, is explained in practical steps.

Part 2: Developing Paragraphs shows students how to build paragraphs by creating clear topic sentences supported by details. These chapters cover nine patterns of development: description, narration, example, definition, comparison and contrast, division and classification, process, cause and effect, and argument.

Exam Skills demonstrate how students use different patterns of development to answer essay questions. Teaching students how to answer essay exams makes developmental writing a cornerstone of their education, providing valuable tips that aid them in other courses.

Student Paragraphs illustrate how students use a particular pattern of development to build paragraphs for personal essays, college assignments, and examinations.

Putting Paragraphs Together shows how separate paragraphs work together to create a short essay.

Writing at Work shows how patterns of development are used to create letters, e-mail, announcements, and reports.

Part 3: Writing Essays explains how to create thesis statements and develop outlines to organize supporting details and guide the first draft. Students are shown methods to create essays with clear transitions and effective introductions and conclusions. Step-by-step directions explain how to write essays in nine patterns of development: description, narration, example, definition, comparison and contrast, division and classification, process, cause and effect, and argument. Annotated student essays demonstrate how writers frequently use more than one pattern to develop an essay.

Part 4: Improving Essays provides students with guidelines for enhancing the focus, consistency, and style of essays, the clarity and variety of sentences, and the effectiveness of word choices. Students are shown how to overcome shifts in person and tense, choppy or unclear sentences, wordy phrases, and errors in usage. This new unit provides greater emphasis on revising essays.

Part 5: Special Writing Assignments instructs students on using MLA style to document sources and prepares them for writing in the workplace, focusing on e-mail, reports, résumés, and cover letters.

Parts 6 and 7: Understanding Grammar and Understanding Punctuation and Mechanics demonstrate that grammar is not simply a set of arbitrary rules but a tool to express ideas and prevent confusion. *Get Writing* connects grammar with critical thinking, so students understand that decisions about sentence structure depend on what they are trying to say. Students are given practical tips for detecting and repairing common sentence errors.

What Do You Know? exercises open each chapter, offering a short quiz with answers so students can test themselves to see how much they know about each unit.

Sequenced exercises direct students to identify and repair individual sentences, then detect and repair errors in context.

Writing exercises guide students to develop their own sentences and paragraphs, then look for and correct errors in their own writing. Exercises cover diverse topics, including popular culture, recent events, academic concerns, and professional issues, to meet the needs of a range of developmental students. The content of exercises is selected to attract attention and connect what students learn in composition with other courses and their future careers.

Cumulative exercises combine errors from previous chapters, providing students with realistic editing and revising challenges.

What Have You Learned? exercises conclude each chapter, offering a short quiz with answers so students can test themselves, identifying areas that need continued review.

Points to Remember provide main points for quick review and reference.

Part 8: Readings for Writers outlines strategies for critical reading and presents two professional essays for each pattern of development. The annotated readings include new and classic pieces by Anna Quindlen, Janice Castro, Maya Angelou, and Cornel West. The topics discussed include race relations, the environment, homelessness, and reality TV. Each reading is followed by questions that guide students to analyze the writer's meaning, strategy, and use of language. Writing prompts direct students to express their views and incorporate new techniques in their own writing.

Other Features

The **Handbook** summarizes grammar and mechanics for easy reference, reducing the need for handouts. Placing grammar rules with simple examples in single lists helps students quickly locate information while writing and revising and eliminates the need for a separate handbook.

Writing at Work offers practical advice on the most common writing tasks that students encounter after they leave college—writing e-mail, reports, cover letters, and résumés.

Using Sources and MLA Documentation demonstrates how to document essays to assist students not only in composition but also in other college courses requiring research papers.

Writing on the Web guides students to use the Internet to locate online writing resources.

Tips on Writing provide students with thumbnail guides and reminders that reinforce major points. Easily skimmed, these tips help students review chapters and locate information when revising.

Strategies give students step-by-step guidelines to succeed in composition courses and increase critical thinking.

New in This Edition

The second edition, which incorporates information gleaned from a survey of more than a hundred writing instructors and from reviewers in two- and four-year institutions from around the country, includes the following new features:

- **Chapter Goals** open each chapter, giving students a quick overview of what they will be learning.
- **Improving Essays** includes three revised chapters to devote greater attention to the essay.
- **Top Twenty** boxes alert students to the most common writing problems identified by a national survey of developmental writing instructors.
- **Knowing English,** revised with the help of Anne-Marie Schlender, Assistant Department Chair of ESOL at Austin Community College, presents ESL content to reinforce grammar and mechanics to benefit all developmental students.
- **Six new readings,** including "Why Schools Don't Educate" by John Taylor Gatto and Luis Alberto Urrea's "Border Story."
- **Writing at Work** documents accompany professional essays to illustrate how writers use the patterns of development in the workplace.
- **More exercises using student papers and real-world documents** rather than standard drills.

Ancillaries

The *Annotated Instructor's Edition* provides answers to exercises found in the student version of the textbook.

The *Instructor's Manual/Test Bank* is an inclusive supplement written by Jill Emerick of Indiana Business College.

The *Instructor's Manual* section contains a variety of teaching aids, including directions on how to use the integrated features of *Get Writing,* such as the Working Together activities, visual writing prompts, Critical Thinking assignments, and What Are You Trying to Say?/ What Have You Written? exercises. The manual also discusses how to incorporate the professional and student model paragraphs in class and provides additional writing assignments, collaborative activities, and teaching tips for every chapter. The *Instructor's Manual* offers ESL information for many chapters as well as suggestions for teaching to various learning styles.

The *Test Bank,* which includes diagnostic and mastery tests, consists of almost six hundred items. The tests are a combination of generative testing items, which ask students to write their own sentences within guided parameters, and objective questions that cover the skills and concepts presented in the textbook.

WriteSpace is a flexible, interactive, and customizable program that assesses students of English at all skill levels. *WriteSpace* motivates and assists students with varying skill levels by providing tutorial support. *WriteSpace* includes: 1) *Diagnostic skills assessments in writing and grammar skills.* Test results are linked to individualized concept reviews and study paths for self-remediation, helping motivate and prepare students for coursework; 2) *Exercises and Writing Modules* (tutorials) that give students additional practice beyond the classroom; 3) *Associated Press Interactives & NewsNow* that allow you to incorporate current events, critical thinking, and visual literacy into your course; 4) *Plagiarism Prevention Zone* that helps you keep plagiarism problems to a minimum; 5) *Online Tutoring;* 6) an *Online Handbook;* and a *Gradebook.*

The *Companion Website* (www.cengage.com/english/connelly) contains study resources, including information on the writing process, writing paragraphs, a grammar review, and sample essays. Online quizzes are also available.

PowerLecture is an easy-to-use CD-ROM provides a variety of teaching tools, including the Instructor's Resource Manual with Test Bank. *PowerLecture* also features ExamView ® Windows/Macintosh), an assessment and tutorial system that covers the skills and concepts presented and allows you to create, deliver, and customize tests and study guides(both print and online) in minutes.

Acknowledgments

All books are a collaborative effort. My special thanks goes to Lyn Uhl, Publisher; Annie Todd, Director of Developmental English; Laurie Runion Dobson, Development Editor, and Kyley Caldwell, English Editorial Assistant, for their support, vision, and enthusiasm for *Get Writing.* I would also like to thank the talented Cengage Learning production and marketing team: Corinna Dibble, Content Production Manager; Kirsten Stoller, Marketing Manager; and Emily Ryan, Technology Project Manager.

Get Writing: Paragraphs and Essays benefited greatly from comments and suggestions made by a dedicated group of reviewers:

Zoe Ann Cerny, *Horry-Georgetown Technical College*

Sandra Chumchal, *Blinn College*

Eileen DeFreece, *Essex County College*

Jill Emerick, *Indiana Business College*

Curtis Harrell, *NorthWest Arkansas Community College*

Jonathan Howle, *Plaza College*

Jill A. Lahnstein, *Cape Fear Community College*

Jennifer Ratcliff, *North Central Texas College*

I also wish to thank the reviewers of the first edition, whose insights continue to impact this textbook:

Caryl Terrell-Bamiro, *Chandler-Gilbert Community College*

Jeff Carney, *Snow College*

Zoe Ann Cerny, *Horry-Georgetown Technical College*

Sandra Chumchall, *Blinn College*

Beth Conomos, *Erie Community College*

Linda Conry, *Collin County Community College*

Carol Cooper, *Jackson State University*

Catherine Decker, *Chaffey College*

Rita Delude, *New Hampshire Community Technical College*

Terese Derballa, *Asheville-Buncombe Technical Community College*

Joy Ferkel, *Terra State Community College*

Rebecca Frier, *South Georgia College*

Judy Harris, *Tomball College*

Elaine Herrick, *Temple College*

Eric Hibbison, *J. Sargeant Reynolds Community College*

Peggy Hopper, *Walters State Community College*

Deborah Johnson, *Prince George's Community College*

Ann Lewald, *Tennessee Technical University*

Joan Mauldin, *San Jacinto College*

Jack Miller, *Normandale Community College*

Raymond Orkwis, *Northern Virginia Community College*

Teresa Prosser, *Sinclair Community College*

Dee Pruitt, *Florence Darlington Technical College*

Melissa Rankin, *Richland Community College*
David Robson, *Delaware County Community College*
Lawrence Roy, *Madisonville Community College*
Virginia Smith, *Carteret Community College*
Wendy Jo Ward, *Miami-Dade College*
Janet Wasson, *Hinds Community College*

Getting Started

CHAPTER 1

Why Write?

CHAPTER GOALS

- Learn Why Writing Is Important
- Understand Writing in Context
- Learn How to Succeed in Writing Courses

Lucidio Studio Inc./CORBIS

Get Writing

How much writing have you done in the last year? Did you write papers in high school or college courses, prepare reports at work, or e-mail friends?

Write a paragraph that describes your recent writing experiences. List any problems you have faced, from organizing your thoughts to grammar and spelling.

Few students plan to become writers. Most people think of writers as men and women who write for a living—newspaper reporters, screenwriters, historians, playwrights, and novelists. In the information age, however, writing is an important part of any career.

When you think of your life after college, you probably see yourself in action—a contractor working on a construction site, a nurse treating patients, a teacher in the classroom, or a police officer investigating an accident. All these professionals are writers. They may not publish books or write newspaper articles, but they communicate in writing. Contractors write reports, e-mail, and letters to investors, suppliers, customers, and managers. Nurses maintain detailed charts. Teacher draft lesson plans. Police officers record their observations in reports that may become evidence in court. Whatever profession you enter, your success will depend on your ability to express yourself in writing.

"Put It in Writing"

In school you write papers, reports, and essay examinations to demonstrate your knowledge and skills. A badly written assignment will result in a poor grade. Outside the classroom, however, badly written documents have more serious consequences. The e-mail, letters, contracts, and reports you write may make you responsible for decisions that can cost you or your employers millions of dollars. Poorly written documents can undo years of hard work. **When told to "put it in writing," make sure what you write clearly expresses what you are trying to say.**

Get Writing

WRITING ACTIVITY

What career do you want after graduation? What writing tasks do people face in that job? Whom do they write to? What kinds of problems or issues do they have to deal with? Why is writing important for their success?

_____

_____

_____

_____

_____

_____

_____

_____

_____

_____

_____

Read what you have written, and list the most important way writing will shape your future:

_____

_____

_____

Goals Of This Book

Get Writing has been created to help you:

- appreciate the importance of writing
- understand the writing process
- write effective paragraphs and essays
- overcome common writing problems
- prepare for the writing challenges in college and in your future career

Using *Get Writing*

At first glance, textbooks can be intimidating. Look through *Get Writing* to become comfortable with it. Highlight useful passages with bookmarks or Post-it notes for quick reference. Look at the handbook at the back of the book for help with common writing errors. Remember to use *Get Writing* as a resource not only in English courses but also in any writing you do in or out of school.

WORKING TOGETHER

Discuss writing with three or four other students, and ask them to list problems and questions they have—from getting started to using commas. List your own top five problems:

1. _____

2. _____

3. _____

4. _____

5. _____

Examine the table of contents and the index in *Get Writing,* and mark pages that address these problems.

What Is Good Writing?

Sometimes students feel confused about what is considered "good writing." Papers that would receive good grades in high school may be unacceptable in college. English teachers urge you to be creative and express yourself, whereas business instructors insist that you avoid making personal comments and only present facts. Writing that works in one situation maybe inappropriate in another.

Good writing expresses what you want to say, meets the readers' needs, and uses the appropriate style and format.

The Writing Context

What is considered "good writing" depends on context. Writing takes place in a context that has four parts:

1. the writer's goal

2. the readers' needs, expectations, beliefs, and knowledge

3. the discipline, situation, occupation, or event in which the writing takes place

4. the nature of the document

Context explains why a school fund-raising letter mailed to parents differs from a formal proposal sent to a government agency. A letter to people familiar with the school can explain the need for a new roof or more computers in a few paragraphs and motivate readers to write checks for fifty or a hundred dollars. A proposal seeking a million-dollar grant from the government, on the other hand, might run twenty pages and include statistics, audited balance sheets, and a formal mission statement.

Before you write, establish the context by asking yourself four key questions:

What Is Your Goal?

Are you writing to explain an idea, complete an assignment, answer a question, or apply for a job? Do you want to share ideas or motivate readers to take action?

Who Are the Readers?

Are you writing to an individual or a group? Are readers familiar with your subject, or do they require background information? Are they likely to be sympathetic, neutral, or hostile to your ideas? What evidence will they need to accept your views?

What Is the Discipline or Situation?

Disciplines, professions, corporations, and communities have unique traditions, standards, and values. A literature teacher expects students to write personal interpretations of a story or novel. Science instructors, on the other hand, demand that students follow uniform standards in conducting objective research. An ad agency depends on creativity, whereas an accounting firm demands accuracy. One company may believe that the best way to increase its profits is by improving its sales, whereas another may concentrate on lowering costs.

What Is Expected in the Document?

People expect newspaper articles, memos, and e-mail to be written in simple words and short sentences for easy reading. Résumés, ads, and brochures have to communicate at a glance and may use bulleted points to highlight important information. However, business reports and research papers may be written in highly technical or sophisticated language and devote pages to discuss a single detail. Your word choices, sentences, and paragraphs should suit the document.

Get Writing

WRITING ACTIVITY

A computer malfunction causes an airline to cancel more than a hundred flights on Christmas Eve, stranding thousands of passengers in airports across the country. Following industry guidelines, the airline attempts to place passengers on other flights, provides bus and train tickets for commuters, and offers hotel rooms to those who will have to wait until the following day to get a flight.

Briefly describe the context of the following documents.

A college student sending a text message to her parents explaining why she will miss her flight:

Writer's goal _____

Reader _____

Discipline _____

Document _____

A statement posted on the airline's website informing passengers of the delays and explaining steps being taken to assist with their travel plans:

Writer's goal _____

Reader _____

Discipline _____

Document _____

Comments on the blog of a travel writer who has consistently rated this airline as one of the nation's worst carriers:

Writer's goal _____

Reader _____

Discipline _____

Document _____

An airline e-mail to its employees urging them to handle passenger complaints with patience and respect:

Writer's goal _____

Reader _____

Discipline _____

Document _____

To appreciate the variety of writing contexts, examine websites, newspapers, and magazines. Notice how the writing style of *Seventeen, People,* and *Cosmopolitan* differs from that of the *New York Times, Newsweek,* and *Foreign Affairs.* How do your college textbooks differ from the ones you read in high school? How do car or computer ads in the *Wall Street Journal* differ from those in the *Star* or *National Enquirer*?

Strategies for Succeeding in Writing Courses

1. **Review your syllabus and textbooks carefully.** Make sure that you know the policies for missed classes, late papers, and incompletes. *Note due dates on your calendar.*

2. **As soon as possible, read descriptions of all assignments listed in the syllabus.** Looking at assignments before they are due lets you think ahead and get ideas for upcoming papers.

3. **Make sure that you fully know what your instructor expects on each assignment.** Study the syllabus, sample papers, and handouts for guidance. If you have any questions about an upcoming paper, ask your instructor.

4. **Locate support services.** Many colleges have computer labs, tutoring facilities, and writing centers to assist students.

5. **If you don't already write on a computer, learn.** Most colleges offer short courses in word processing. Once you graduate, you will be expected to work on a computer. Though a bit cumbersome at first, writing on a computer makes your job as a student much easier.

6. **Read papers aloud before turning them in.** The fastest and easiest way to edit papers is to read them aloud. It is easier to "hear" than to "see" missing and misspelled words, awkward phrases, fragments, and illogical statements.

7. **Keep copies of all assignments.**

8. **Study returned papers, especially ones with poor grades.** When you get an F or a D– on an assignment, you might want

to throw it away or bury it under some books. Although they are painful to look at, these papers hold the key for success. Read the instructor's comments and suggestions. Find the chapters in *Get Writing* that can help you overcome these problems in future assignments.

9. **Never copy or use the work of others without informing your readers.** Borrowing words or ideas from other sources without telling your readers is called plagiarism, a serious offense. See page 26 for strategies to avoid this problem.

10. **Write as often as you can.** Writing, like anything else, takes practice. Keep a journal or a blog, e-mail friends, and take notes in class. Record your thoughts while you watch television. Any of these activities will help you get used to expressing yourself in writing.

Get Thinking and Writing

CRITICAL THINKING

Write a paragraph describing your writing experiences in past courses or at a recent job. What assignments or tasks were the most difficult? What comments did teachers make about your writing? What work documents gave you the most trouble?

_____

_____

_____

_____

_____

_____

_____

_____

_____

_____

_____

_____

_____

_____

_____

_____

Read your paragraph, and identify the most important ideas you discovered. Summarize your most important point in one sentence:

_____

_____

What two or three things would you want to change about your writing?

1. _____

2. _____

3. _____

WHAT HAVE YOU WRITTEN?

Read your statement aloud. What changes would you make if you had to turn it in for a grade?

- Are there sentences that are off the topic and should be deleted?
- Could you add more details and examples?
- Could you choose words with more meaning?
- Would a teacher or other readers understand your main point?

Get Writing

ALAMY LIMITED

What challenges do you face this semester? Look at the syllabus for each of your classes. What assignments do you have?

Write a paragraph describing your greatest challenge. Are you taking a demanding course this semester? Do you have to balance work and school? Do you need to organize your time better? How can you improve your chances of success?

WRITING ON THE WEB

Exploring Writing Resources Online

The Internet contains numerous resources for student writers: dictionaries, encyclopedias, grammar exercises, databases, library catalogs, editing tips, and research strategies.

1. Review your library's electronic databases, links, and search engines. Locate online dictionaries and encyclopedias that can assist you with upcoming assignments.

2. Using a search engine such as Yahoo! or Google, enter key words such as *prewriting, proofreading, thesis statement, editing strategies,* and other terms that appear throughout the book, the index, or your course syllabus. In addition to formal databases, many schools and instructors have constructed online tutorials that can improve your writing, overcome grammar problems, and help with specific assignments.

POINTS TO REMEMBER

1. Writing is important not only in college but also in any career that you choose.

2. Writing takes place in a context formed by the writer's goal, the reader, the discipline or situation, and the document.

3. You can improve your writing by studying past efforts.

4. Writing improves with practice. Write as often as you can.

CHAPTER 2

The Writing Process

PATRIK GIARDINO/CORBIS

CHAPTER GOALS

- Understand the Writing Process
- Use Prewriting, Writing, and Editing Techniques
- Avoid Plagiarism
- Learn to Write Under Pressure

Get Writing

How do you write? Do you write with pen and paper or on a computer? Do you make notes or outlines to organize ideas? Do you write a complete draft and then make revisions, or do you work paragraph by paragraph? How do you decide what information to include? Do you edit your work for errors in grammar and spelling?

Write a paragraph describing your writing method. Identify areas you would like to improve.

This chapter explains the basic steps writers use to choose a subject, develop supporting details, organize ideas, create a first draft, make revisions, and edit a final copy. Follow these steps in your first writing assignments; then try other ways of writing that work with the way you think and the assignments you face.

The Writing Process

Step 1   Prewrite: Explore ideas with critical thinking.
Step 2   Plan: Establish context, develop a thesis, outline ideas.
Step 3   Write: Get your ideas down on paper.
Step 4   Cool: Put your writing aside.
Step 5   Revise: Review and rewrite your paper.
Step 6   Edit: Check the final document for mechanical errors.

POINT TO REMEMBER

You can improve your writing by asking yourself two questions:
What am I trying to say?
What have I written?

Although writing can be separated into different steps, it is often a *recursive* or repeated process. Writers don't always work step-by-step but instead write, revise, and edit as they go along. They may edit and polish the first paragraph before starting the rest of the essay. On another assignment, they may write the conclusion first. Writing on a computer allows you to move easily from writing to editing so that you can come up with new ideas and fix errors as you work.

Step 1: Prewrite

Good writing does more than record what you "feel" or repeat what you have heard from friends, seen on television, or read online. To write something meaningful, you first have to engage in *critical thinking*. You need to look at your subject carefully, ask questions, collect facts, and avoid making snap decisions. Good writing shares more than facts and dates, first impressions, or immediate reactions. **A good paper is never "about" a topic—it has a purpose and makes a point.**

Strategies for Increasing Critical Thinking

1. **Study subjects carefully—don't rely on first impressions or make snap judgments.** If your car is stolen and your neighbor's house is broken into, you may quickly assume that crime is

increasing in your community. But until you study police reports, you really know only that you are one of two victims. It could be that crime is actually dropping but that you and your neighbor happened to fall into the shrinking number of victims.

2. **Know the difference between facts and opinions.** Don't mistake people's opinions, attitudes, or feelings with facts. *Opinions express a point of view.* They can be valid, but they are not evidence. *Facts are objective statements that can be verified by others.* You can factually report that your sister sleeps until ten, doesn't make her bed, and won't look for a summer job. But calling her "lazy" states an opinion, not a fact.

3. **Don't rely on limited evidence.** Dramatic events or moving personal experiences may be interesting, but they lack the authority of objective research. The fact that your great-grandfather smoked three packs of cigarettes a day and lived past ninety does not prove that tobacco is harmless. No matter how striking, examples need to be supported by other evidence, such as statistics and expert testimony.

4. **Avoid relying on weak comparisons.** No two situations are ever identical. Because a health-care program works in Europe does not mean it will work in the United States. Study techniques that worked in high school might not be effective in college. Comparisons can be compelling arguments, but only if they are supported by facts.

5. **Don't mistake a time relationship with cause and effect.** Events take place over time. If you develop headaches after a car crash, you might assume they were caused by the accident. But the headaches could be caused by lack of sleep or a food allergy and have nothing to do with your recent accident.

6. **Judge ideas, not personalities.** Don't be impressed by celebrity endorsements or reject an idea because you don't like the person supporting it. Judge ideas on their own merits. Unpopular people often have good ideas, and popular people can be wrong.

7. **Avoid making absolute statements.** If you make absolute statements such as "all politicians are corrupt" or "people always regret buying a used car," your argument can be rejected if a reader can provide a single exception.

8. **Question quotations and statistics used as support.** People often try to influence us with quotations by famous people or impressive statistics. But until you know where the quotation came from or how the statistics were collected, they have little value. Statistics may be based on biased research and easily distorted. Even accurate numbers can be misinterpreted.

9. **Above all—think before you write.**

TIPS FOR BRAINSTORMING

1. **Focus brainstorming by keeping the final paper in mind.** Review the assignment instructions.

2. **Use full sentences to write out important ideas you may forget.**

3. **Use key words for a quick Internet search.** Glancing at a list of websites may stimulate new ideas.

4. **Think of the brainstorming list as a funnel leading from broad subjects to defined topics.** Avoid creating a list of random ideas.

Prewriting Techniques

Writers put critical thinking into action with *prewriting*. The goal of prewriting is not to create a rough draft but to explore a subject, discover ideas, and identify questions. Prewriting can help you save time by showing which topics are better suited for an assignment and which ones may be too complex or require too much research.

Writers use a variety of prewriting techniques. As a writing student, experiment with as many as you can. Feel free to switch or combine methods to discover which ones you find the most productive. A student planning a paper about globalization might use a variety of techniques to explore ideas, identify a topic, and develop details needed to support a thesis.

Brainstorming lists ideas. You can list ideas on a number of topics until you find one worth writing about or create a chain of related ideas that moves from general observations to specifics. This student begins with the general issue of globalization and explores a list of ideas until identifying a topic suited for a college paper:

GLOBALIZATION

Rapid transportation

Millions traveling by air

Import and export of food

Increased immigration

Fast spread of infectious diseases/international epidemics

International export of contaminated or toxic products/worldwide poisoning cases

TOPIC: *Potential health hazards of globalization*

Freewriting records ideas, observations, opinions, impressions, and feelings by writing as quickly as possible. Freewriting is not an attempt at a rough draft but a way to identify what you already know about your subject and discover new ideas. Freewriting is like talking into a tape recorder to capture everything you know about a topic. When you freewrite, don't stop to check spelling, worry about writing in complete sentences, or prevent yourself from going off topic. *Remember, you are not writing an essay but exploring ideas.*

To freewrite, sit with a blank page or computer screen and write as fast as you can about a subject.

Here a student begins writing about the global economy and the problem of outsourcing that sends American jobs overseas to foreign countries:

All across the country factories and offices are closing. Jobs are being outsourced, and highly-skilled people find themselves jobless. The global economy has many men and women concerned about their ability to find and hold onto careers and occupations. Everything is changing. One of the oldest furniture companies in the US now makes all it's products in Asia. Wehn you call your phone company or credit card company for service you talk to someone in India. Why pay a enigneer 75k when someone in India or Pakistan will do the job for 18 or 20k? Immigration brings in both high skilled and low silled workers so the college kid who has to compete for a summer job with a immigrant willing to work for minimum wage can find themself comptiting for a highly motivated immigrant when they graduate for a high skillled job. Except maybe for nurses, cops, and firefighters we all have to survive and thrive in a universal global market that has everyone competing with everyone. The Internet makes it possible to send media and information all over the world. The need for oil and worry about global warming will change our economy to. New energy sources will create new jobs in the world. The main thing is that graduates will have to flexible and able to adjust and constantly keep pace with demands for high tech skills to get jobs and command decent paychecks.

The paragraph contains unclear and awkward sentences, misspelled words, and unrelated observations. But the student has discovered a topic for an interesting paper—*competing for jobs in a global economy.*

Asking questions is an effective way to identify what you already know, what new words or ideas need to be defined, and which ideas require explanation. Questions start the critical-thinking process because they require answers, leading you to analyze your ideas and views rather than just list them. A student exploring the global economy might develop a paper that contains only superficial and obvious facts he or she has heard on television or read online. However, asking questions can help a writer develop new ideas and discover a topic:

What is the global economy?

What jobs are being outsourced?

What jobs can't be outsourced?

Does globalization create any jobs in the United States? Why or why not?

What can Americans sell to the rest of the world?

What do people in other countries want to buy from the United States?

How can intellectual property be protected from piracy so it can be exported?

TOPIC: *How can U.S. artists and producers take advantage of the foreign demand for movies, music, and computer games without having their products being illegally copied?*

Clustering (also called **diagramming, mapping,** and **webbing**) uses symbols such as circles, columns, boxes, and arrows to list and arrange ideas. If you are visually minded, this technique may be easier to use than freewriting or asking questions. It can be very helpful if you are looking at relationships between ideas or searching for a common link:

TIPS FOR FREEWRITING

1. **Use freewriting for personal essays and open-topic assignments.** Freewriting allows you to explore what you already know and believe. However, this method may not help you respond to highly structured assignments or to develop business documents.

2. **Use a question to focus freewriting.** Asking yourself "Why do teenagers drop out of school?" is a better starting point than a general idea of "writing a paper about public schools."

3. **Don't feel obligated to write in complete sentences.** Making lists or jotting down key words can save time.

4. **Save your freewriting for future assignments.** Ideas that do not work for one paper might prove useful in a future assignment.

5. **Highlight important ideas by underlining or circling them.** This can identify key ideas and distinguish them from minor details.

TIPS FOR ASKING QUESTIONS

1. **Keep the assignment in mind as you pose questions.**

2. **Avoid questions that call for simple yes or no answers.** Use questions that ask "why?" or "how?"

3. **Remember, the goal of asking questions is to identify a topic and prompt critical thinking.**

TIPS FOR CLUSTERING

1. **Clustering is helpful when you have complex or conflicting ideas.** You can put related ideas together and place pro and con items in separate columns.

2. **Keep the artwork simple.** Don't spend too much time on the appearance of your notes. Remember, you are not creating a visual aid for a formal presentation, just a rough diagram.

Global Economy

Global manufacturing

GM sells more Buicks in China than in the US
Major firms outsourcing jobs for cheaper labor overseas

Global services

US telemarketing, billling, banking, and accounting services contracted to India

Global information

Globalization requires fast, efficient communication.
Phones, satellites, computers
The INTERNET!

Global energy

Opec/world depends on oil and gas from a few countrie s
Energy demand from China driving up oil prices worldwide

Global government

Increasing role of UN and international organizations
Worldwide private agencies and charities

Notes: Everything in the global economy—energy sales, manufacturing by international companies, overseas information services, and global cooperation depends on the Internet.

TOPIC: The global economy could be paralyzed by a major failure of the Internet

POINTS TO REMEMBER

1. The goal of prewriting is to explore ideas, discover a topic, and organize points—not write a rough draft.
2. Try using more than one prewriting technique to discover the best way to develop and organize your thoughts.
3. Save prewriting notes. Ideas that may not work for one paper may be helpful in other assignments.
4. Keep prewriting simple. Avoid elaborate notes that may be hard to follow.

Get Writing

WRITING ACTIVITY

Select one of the following topics or a topic from the list on pages 705-706, and prewrite for ten minutes. You may use one or more techniques. If you have an upcoming assignment in any of your classes, use this opportunity to get started.

- RV1 reality TV shows
- your first boss
- immigration
- favorite band
- women in combat
- cost of day care

- school vouchers
- first apartment
- drinking age
- fad diets
- job interviews
- most challenging course

Step 2: Plan

Moving from Topic to Thesis

Narrowing Your Topic and Developing a Controlling Idea

After using prewriting to discover a topic, you may have to narrow it to develop one suited for your paper. It would be difficult to write anything meaningful about a broad topic such as the Internet in five hundred words, but you could write something interesting about online college courses or cyberterrorism. In narrowing a topic, it is important to develop a **controlling idea** that directs your paper to discuss something specific. What do you plan to say about cyberterrorism? What do you want readers to know about it?

Developing a Thesis Statement

After you limit the topic and develop a controlling idea, the next step is stating a **thesis,** or main point. Good papers are not "about" a topic. They make a point, pose a question, express an opinion, or make a declaration. The thesis states your goal, expressing what you want readers to understand about your topic. A **thesis statement** expresses your goal in a single sentence. A clearly worded thesis statement gives your paper focus and helps keep your writing on track.

Topic	Globalization
Narrowed topic	Global economy requires international communications
Controlling idea	The global economy depends on the Internet
Thesis	*A major failure in the Internet could weaken or paralyze the ability of governments and corporations to function and citizens to carry out everyday transactions.*

POINT TO REMEMBER

Don't confuse a thesis statement with a narrowed topic. A thesis does more than focus the subject of a paper—it has to express an opinion and make a statement.

WORKING TOGETHER

Select one of the following general topics or one from the previous exercise, and develop a narrowed topic, a controlling idea, and a thesis. When you are finished, share your work with other students. Make sure that each person in the group develops a thesis and not just a narrowed topic.

General Topics

campus parking	part-time jobs	online shopping
downloading music	cable news	voting
gas prices	shopping malls	worst job
favorite restaurant	dream job	Social Security
health insurance	makeover shows	veterans' benefits

General topic: _____

Narrowed topic: _____

Controlling idea: _____

Thesis: _____

Organizing Support

After developing a thesis statement, you need to organize your ideas by outlining the paper's introduction, body, and conclusion. Taking a few minutes to develop an outline before you begin to write can save time in the end. In planning your paper, consider your goal, your readers, the discipline, and the nature of the document.

Your goal	What idea or opinion do you want to express? What information, facts, or observations do you need to support your thesis?
Your reader	What attitudes do your readers have about your subject? What evidence will they find most convincing—statistics, expert testimony, eyewitness reports? Do readers have any prejudices or misconceptions that you must deal with or correct?
The discipline	Will your writing use the accepted approach, style, and support expected in this discipline or profession? Will your teachers or supervisors approve of the way you state your ideas and present evidence?
The document	What is the appropriate format for this paper? Does your instructor require footnotes? Does a supervisor expect you to follow company standards for e-mail, letters, or reports?

Developing an Outline

An outline does not have to use Roman numerals or capital letters. Even a rough sketch can organize ideas and save time by creating a road map of your first draft. It should list the beginning, middle, and end of your essay.

It is subject to change. As you write, new thoughts will come to you, and you may decide to expand or narrow the paper.

The kind of outline you use depends on your assignment. To plan an essay about a personal experience, you may need only a simple time line to organize ideas. Other papers may be more complex and require more detailed plans to arrange your thoughts, balance conflicting ideas, organize complicated evidence, or place confusing events in a logical order. Most outlines cover three basic parts of a document: introduction, body, and conclusion.

Introduction	grabs attention presents the topic addresses reader concerns prepares readers for what follows
Body	organizes supporting details in a logical pattern
Conclusion	ends with a brief summary, a final thought or observation, question, call for action, or prediction

POINT TO REMEMBER

You can place your thesis statement at the beginning, middle, or end of the paper. If your audience is opposed to your opinion, you may wish to present facts or tell a story before expressing your point of view.

A student planning to write about the role of the Internet in a global economy could use a simple outline to list and arrange ideas to create a road map to guide a first draft:

Introduction	Global economy's dependence on the Internet Thesis: *A major failure in the Internet could weaken or paralyze the ability of governments and corporations to function and citizens to carry out everyday transactions.*

Body	History of Internet
	   online economy
	   e-mail
	   financial and government transactions
	Vulnerability
	   Failure of Internet could be devastating Causes:
	   labor unrest, war, terrorism, or technical failure

Conclusion	Governments, corporations, institutions must recognize vulnerability & protect the Internet.

Get Writing

WRITING ACTIVITY

Develop an outline for a topic and thesis you created in the previous exercise. You may also use this opportunity to organize your next assignment.

Topic: _____

Introduction: _____

Body: _____

_____

_____

_____

Conclusion: _____

Step 3: Write

After going over your outline, write as much as you can in one sitting. Your goal at this point is not to attempt a final draft of your paper but to get your ideas on paper. Don't feel that you have to write complete sentences—to save time, use phrases or key words to list ideas that you might forget. Don't worry about spelling or grammar at this point. If you stop to look up a word in a dictionary or check a grammar rule in a handbook, you may break your train of thought. Instead, highlight errors for future reference as you write:

```
The global world economy is run on information and
communications. Consider that in one single day you
might order a DVD from Amazon on the Internet, pay a
bill, buy airline tickets, or e-mail a resume applica-
tion online. Thousands of companies use the Internet
to check inventories, exchange data, process orders,
and schedule deliveries. Airlines, hospitals, govern-
ment agencies, and fire and security services depend
on the Internet for communications. A major failure in
the Internet could paralyze governments, corporations,
and individual people.
    In the past twenty years a global economy has
developed that requires dependable high speed comm-
unications. Orders and payments for customers and
businesses are sent electronically. Banks and govern-
ments transfer billions of dollars every hour elec-
tronically. Once used to link government agencies,
research facilities, and military bases, the Internet
has replaced the telephone as the most common method
of human communication. Stores in shopping malls
process orders online, as do schools, churches, res-
taurants, even pizza delivery drivers.
    The Internet has created the world we live in. A
major failure of the Internet could be caused by labor
unrest, sabotage, terrorism, or technical failure. In
a future war, the most valuable targets will be com-
munications satellites, servers, and cell phone tow-
ers. Without the Internet a country could face a fro-
zen economy that would halt financial transactions,
payroll, production, Hospitals, factories, colleges,
911 systems, banks, and stores could find themselves
```

unable to access needed data or process the simplest
transaction. Within days millions of people would be
unable to buy food because they cannot withdraw money
from a bank or use a credit card.

To prevent this disaster nations, corporations,
and interational organizations will have to insure
the security of the Internet. Two hundred years ago
the navies of the world had to coopearte to free the
oceans of pirates that disrupted interational trade.
Today we must make sure cyberspace is free of threats.

Get Writing

WRITING ACTIVITY

*Write a draft of the paper you planned in the previous exercise or of an up-
coming assignment.*

Step 4: Cool

This is an easy—but important—step. After you finish writing, put your work
aside to let it "cool." When you complete a draft, your first impulse might be
to immediately check your work for mistakes. However, it is hard to revise
what you have just written because the ideas are still fresh in your mind.
Take a walk, run an errand, or work on another assignment. Then look at
your writing. If you have an e-mail to send today, plan to write a draft in the
morning so you can set it aside, then read and revise it in the afternoon.

Step 5: Revise

Revising means "to see again." Revising consists of more than just correcting spelling mistakes or adding missing commas. First, read your prewriting
notes and thesis statement carefully. If you are writing a paper for school,
review the assignment and any guidelines your instructor provided. Then
take an overall look at your rough draft. Does it meet the needs of the assignment? Have you proved your thesis statement? Did you give readers the
information they need to accept your point of view? Did your writing get off
track? What ideas did you forget to include? Are there any irrelevant details
or repetitious ideas that should be deleted?

The global ~~world~~ economy is ~~run on information and~~   *driven by*
communications. Consider that in ~~one~~ single day you   *A*
might order a product from Amazon ~~on the Internet~~,   *Delete*
pay a bill, buy airline tickets, or e-mail a resume
application online. Thousands of companies use the
Internet to check inventories, exchange data, process   *more examples*
orders, and schedule deliveries. Airlines, hospitals,
government agencies, and fire and security services
depend on the Internet for communications. — A major

failure in the Internet could paralyze governments, corporations, and individuals ~~people~~.

In the past twenty years a global economy has developed that requires dependable high speed communications. Orders and payments for customers and businesses are sent electronically. Banks and governments transfer billions of dollars every hour *repetitious* <u>electronically</u>. Once used to link government agencies, research facilities, and military bases, the Internet has replaced the telephone as the most common method of human communication. Stores in shopping malls process orders online, as do schools, churches, restaurants, even pizza delivery drivers.

reorganize details
Vague

The Internet has created the <u>world we live in</u>. A major failure of the Internet could be caused by labor unrest, sabotage, terrorism, or technical failure. In a future war, the most valuable targets will *SP* be communications <u>sattellites</u>, servers, and cell phone towers. Without the Internet, a country could face a frozen economy that would halt financial transactions, *Awkward* payroll, production, Hospitals, factories, colleges, 911 systems, banks, and stores could find themselves unable to access needed data or process the simplest transaction. Within days millions of people would be unable to buy food because they cannot withdraw money from a bank or use a credit card.

To prevent this disaster nations, corporations, *SP* and <u>interantional</u> organizations will have to insure the security of the Internet. Two hundred years ago the navies of the world had to coopearte to free the *SP* oceans of pirates that disrupted <u>interantional</u> trade. Today we must make sure cyberspace is free of threats.

NOTES
—Reorganize, stronger opening
—Add facts, more examples
—Revise sentences
—Edit spelling

Strategies for Revising

1. **Print a copy of your draft.** Revising on a computer can be difficult because the screen does not allow you to see the entire page.

2. **Review the assignment and your goal.** Does your draft meet the requirements and express what you want to say?

3. **Examine the thesis statement.** Is it clearly and logically stated? Would it be more effective if placed in another part of the essay?

4. **Make sure that the introduction gains attention and prepares readers for the body of the essay.**

5. **Determine if the body contains enough details to support your thesis.** Are your facts and ideas clearly organized? Can readers follow your train of thought?

6. **Look for mistakes in critical thinking.** Do you need to include additional evidence to support your views or restate your opinions?

7. **Eliminate unrelated facts, thoughts, or details.**

8. **End the essay with a strong conclusion that does more than repeat the introduction.** Provide readers with a fact, quotation, question, or call to action they will remember.

Using Peer Review

Many students think that asking for help with assignments is cheating. It is not cheating to have others read something you have written, make comments, and respond to questions you ask. **Never let others *write* a paper for you, but you can benefit from their criticisms and suggestions.**

Strategies for Using Peer Review

1. **Explain the assignment to reviewers.** Writing is difficult to evaluate unless people know who is going to read it or what it is supposed to accomplish. Before asking people to check your work, describe the assignment and show them any instructor's directions.

2. **Let your paper speak for itself.** Don't prompt readers by telling them what you are trying to say. Explain the assignment; then let them read your draft so they can evaluate the words on the page. After hearing their first comments, you might explain what you want to say, then ask if they think you accomplished your goals.

3. **Ask for detailed responses.** Questions such as "Is this any good?" or "What do you think?" may prompt only vague comments. Instead, ask readers if the thesis is clear, if the introduction is effective, if you present enough details, and if your arguments make sense.

4. **Encourage readers to be critical.** Friends and other students may be afraid to say anything negative. Let them know you need their honest feedback to improve your paper.

5. **When reviewing other people's writing, be objective and make constructive criticisms.** Don't just point out errors. Suggest ways to overcome mistakes or make improvements.

Get Writing

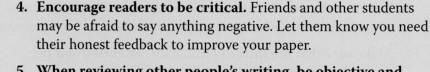
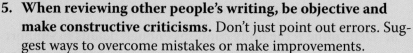

REVISING ACTIVITY

Revise the draft you have written. You may wish to share your work with other students and ask them for suggested improvements.

Step 6: Edit

The last step in the writing process is editing the final document. In editing, make sure that you not only correct spelling and capitalization errors but also eliminate wordy phrases and rewrite confusing or weak sentences:

```
                  Saving the Net
     In 1981 the Internet connected a few hundred re-
searchers. Today 1.4 billion people—twenty percent of
the world's population—have Internet access. The rapid
growth of cyberspace has helped create a global econo-
my that relies on instant international communication.
Corporations, governments, private institutions, and
individuals depend on the Internet to make electronic
transfers, manage production, bill clients, process
orders, and communicate with employees and customers.
In a single day a college student might buy a DVD, pay
a credit card bill, purchase an airline ticket, e-mail
a résumé, chat with a friend, and download articles
for a research paper online.
     The Internet has replaced the telephone as the
primary means of communication. Banks, hospitals,
schools, department stores, supermarkets, airlines,
hotels, city governments, and charities could not
function without the Internet. Political campaigns are
fueled by daily online contributions. Retailers keep
track of orders and inventories in thousands of stores
on an hourly basis. Attorneys, physicians, brokers,
bankers, and professors routinely access information
online.
     The Internet has made the world we live in. A major
Internet failure could weaken or paralyze governments,
```

corporations, and individuals, preventing them from functioning or carrying out the most routine transactions. In World War II the Allies targeted Germany's rail lines and oil supplies to disrupt the Nazi economy and cripple Hitler's war machine. In future wars cyberspace will be targeted. In 2007 Estonia moved a Soviet-era memorial, angering their Russian neighbors. In response, the Russians used a million computers to overload key Estonian government and corporate websites, forcing them to be closed down. Estonian citizens were unable to communicate or even pay their bills. NATO researchers see cyberspace as a future battleground. Cyberterrorists could use the Internet to disrupt key computers, hack into sensitive data, disrupt operations, and shut down or slow online communications.

Two hundred years ago the navies of the world had to clear the oceans of pirates who threatened world trade. Today nations, scientists, and corporations must cooperate to keep the Internet safe and secure from technical failures, sabotage, and attack.

Strategies for Editing

1. **Read your paper out loud.** It is often easier to "hear" than to see errors such as misspelled or missing words, awkward phrases, clumsy sentences, and fragments (see chapters 18 and 23).

2. **Make sure that your sentence structure is appropriate to the document.** An e-mail should be written in short, easy-to-read sentences. However, a long essay or research paper can include long and complex sentences (see chapters 18 and 22).

3. **Replace unnecessarily wordy phrases—for example, change "at this point in time" to "now" and "blue in color" to "blue" (see Chapter 19).**

4. **Make sure that your final document meets the required format.** Should it be single- or double-spaced? Do you need documentation such as endnotes and a works cited page? Check the original assignment or speak with your instructor before turning in your paper for a grade.

EDITING ACTIVITY

Get Writing

Edit the paper you have written and revised. Share your paper with other students. Refer to the index or table of contents of this book for help with grammar problems.

Avoid Plagiarism

Never copy or use the work of others in your writing without informing your readers. Using the work of others without telling your readers is a form of cheating called plagiarism. Faced with a tough assignment, you may be tempted to download an article from the Internet, copy a friend's paper, or take paragraphs from a magazine to put into your paper. Students caught copying papers are often failed or expelled. If you use an outside source such as a website or a magazine, just changing a few words does not make your writing original. You can quote important statements or use statistics and facts if you tell readers where they came from. You don't always need detailed footnotes to prove you are not stealing. Just make sure that you mention sources as you use them:

> *Newsweek* reported that fourteen leading economists agree that unless something is done, the Social Security system will go bankrupt in less than forty years.

Use quotation marks when you copy word for word what someone has said or written:

> In a recent address, Senator Claire Wilson stated, "Our national security depends on ending our dependence on foreign oil."

Mention the author when you *paraphrase* and use your own words to express the same idea:

> According to Senator Claire Wilson, national security requires eliminating the need for imported oil.

See Chapter 20 for guidelines on using and documenting outside sources.

Writing Under Pressure: The Essay Exam

Ideally, writing is done in stages so that you have enough time to think about what you want to say, develop a plan, write, revise, and edit over a few days. But often you will be forced to go through all these stages to answer an exam question in less than an hour. Instructors use multiple-choice and true-and-false questions to measure your memory of facts. Essay questions are designed to

- measure your understanding of facts by asking you to restate them in your own words
- see how well you evaluate and organize information
- test your critical-thinking skills
- measure your ability to apply knowledge and solve problems

Many students find essay examinations intimidating. However, there are strategies you can follow to both study for and write essay exam questions.

Strategies for Studying for Essay Examinations

1. **Ask your instructor what the exam will cover.** Make sure that you know what units will be on the test.

2. **Ask your instructor the best way to study for the exam.** Find out if you should focus on the textbook, lecture notes, online material, or handouts.

3. **Begin studying at once.** Don't attempt to cram the night before. Two hours of studying spread over a few days is more effective than four hours of last-minute cramming.

4. **Talk to other students about the upcoming examination.** Discuss possible topics, methods of studying, and lecture notes. When you talk to classmates, you may find out that you forgot important information or did not understand an instructor's directions.

5. **Consider the nature of the course.** The type of response that instructors expect depends on the course. In English or history, students are free to write personal interpretations of a book or historical event. Creative essays, provided they are well supported, are highly valued. However, in law, psychology, sociology, and nursing, students are expected to follow well-established rules.

6. **Review your syllabus, notes, textbooks, and handouts.** Highlight important passages for a quick review just before the exam.
   - Take notes as you study. Essay exams require that you state ideas in your own words, not simply identify what you have read. If definitions are important, close your book and write a brief version in your own words, and then compare it to the text. Writing about the material is the best way to prepare for an essay test.
   - If you are taking an open-book examination, highlight passages and use Post-its so you can quickly locate information while writing. Familiarize yourself with the book's index.

7. **Recall the types of questions your instructor has asked in class.** The kinds of questions asked to prompt class discussion may provide a clue about the way the instructor will word questions on essay examinations.
   - Does your instructor focus on comparing issues, analyzing problems, or debating alternative interpretations or theories?
   - Does he or she concentrate on presenting in-depth analysis of narrow topics or on providing a sweeping, inclusive overview of the subject?

8. **Think in terms of patterns of development.** Most essay questions ask students to *define* elements, *compare* related topics, *explain* a process, or list *causes* or *effects.*

   - In reviewing your notes and textbook, consider what major items require definition, which subjects are often compared, and what ideas are presented as causes or effects.

9. **Prewrite possible responses.** Select the key issues or topics you expect to appear on the examination, and freewrite, cluster, or brainstorm possible essays. List possible thesis statements.

   - Remember that an essay test requires that you express what you know in writing. Fifteen minutes of prewriting can help you collect facts, generate ideas, and reveal knowledge you have overlooked more quickly than hours of reading and memorizing. *Prepare yourself to write.*

10. **Get as much rest as possible the night before.** Late-night cramming may help you identify facts and figures that appear on multiple-choice tests, but essay questions demand thinking. If you are not rested, you may find yourself unable to analyze issues, generate ideas, make connections, and present your thoughts in an organized fashion.

Strategies for Writing Essay Examinations

Writing under pressure can frustrate even the most prepared student. If you tend to become nervous, you may wish to take a walk between classes, call a friend, eat a high-energy snack, or listen to your favorite song just before the test to put yourself in a positive mood.

1. **Come to the examination prepared to write.** Bring two pens, paper, and, unless prohibited, a dictionary and handbook.

2. **Read all the questions before writing.** Go over all the questions carefully before starting to write. Determine how much each question is worth. Some instructors will indicate the point value of each question.

3. **Budget your time.** Determine how much time you should devote to each question. Give yourself enough time for planning and editing each question.

4. **Answer the easiest questions first while thinking about the more difficult ones.** The easiest questions will take less time to answer and help stimulate ideas that may help you confront more challenging ones. If you run out of time, you will be skipping questions you may have been unable to answer.

5. **Read each question twice.** Students often miss points by failing to fully read the question. They respond to a word or phrase out of context and begin writing an essay that does not address the question.

6. **Study the verbs or command words that direct your response.** Most essay questions contain clues to the kind of response the instructor expects.

Question:	Desired Answer:
List reasons for the rise of labor unions in the 1930s.	A series of reasons rather than an in-depth analysis of a single factor
Distinguish the differences between gasoline and diesel engines.	A comparison/contrast, highlighting differences
What led to the collapse of the Soviet Union?	A cause-and-effect essay, perhaps presented in a narrative or organized by division or classification
Describe three common forms of depression.	Three short definitions or descriptions organized by division
Discuss the effects of global warming on the environment.	An essay consisting of cause and effect, process, description, or division

7. **Study questions that require more than a single response.** Some essay questions contain more than one command and require a two- or three-part response.

Question:	Desired Response
Provide a definition of chemical dependency, and *explain why* treatment remains problematic.	1. Define term 2. List causes for problems in treatment
Select three key economic proposals made by the president in the State of the Union address, and *predict how they will affect both the trade deficit and unemployment.*	1. Describe or define three points 2. Discuss each point, listing effects on trade deficit and unemployment

8. **Write a clear thesis statement.** Your essay should do more than just list facts and ideas. A strong thesis statement will give your response direction and can help organize points. This is very important if instructors present you with general questions or topics.

Question:
How has the concept of separation of church and state affected U.S. society?

Possible Thesis Statements:
The separation of church and state has allowed U.S. public schools to accommodate students from diverse religious backgrounds with little of the conflict found in other countries.

Unlike state-supported religious institutions in other nations, U.S. churches are independent and able to take active roles in criticizing government policies regarding discrimination, capital punishment, foreign policy, and abortion.

9. **Explain or justify your response to broad questions.** Sometimes instructors ask sweeping questions that cannot be fully addressed with a brief response.

Question:
What caused the American Civil War?

(If you write a short essay about slavery, an instructor may think you believe that it was the only cause for the conflict. If, on the other hand, you list a dozen reasons, an instructor may feel that your essay is superficial and without depth. You can earn a higher grade by explaining your answer.)

There were numerous political, social, economic, philosophical, and moral causes of the Civil War. But clearly the most significant and enduring cause for the conflict was the problem of slavery. . . .

Although most Americans cite slavery as the main reason for the Civil War, it is difficult to isolate a single factor as a cause for the conflict. To understand why the states went to war, one must appreciate the full range of social, economic, commercial, foreign policy, and moral disputes that separated North and South. . . .

10. **Keep an eye on the clock.** Pace yourself. Don't "overdo" a response simply because you are knowledgeable about the topic. Provide enough information to address the question, and then move on.

11. **Keep writing.** If you become blocked or stalled on a question and can't think, move on to other questions or review what you have answered. Often, rereading the response to one question will spark ideas that aid in another.

12. **Provide space for revisions.** Write on every other line of the page, or leave wide margins. You will not have time to write a full second draft, but you can make neat corrections and slip in ideas if you give yourself space for changes and additions.

Chapters 5–13 contain sample essay questions and student responses.

CRITICAL THINKING

How well did your high school courses prepare you for college? Do you wish that instructors devoted more time to certain subjects? Were you given the basic reading, writing, and math skills you believe you need to succeed? Write a paragraph stating your views. Use revision and editing to improve your comments.

Get Thinking and Writing

Get Writing

TIM BROWN/GETTY IMAGES

Do you consider how your words will be read? Do you try to visualize the person reading your work? In expressing something you want to say, why is it important to consider who you are writing to?

If you were assigned to create a fund-raising letter for a charity, what would you want to know about the readers? Write a paragraph describing why it would be important to analyze the audience to be successful in motivating people to make donations.

WRITING ON THE WEB

1. Using a search engine such as Yahoo! or Google, enter terms such as *writing process, writing strategies, prewriting techniques, revising papers, improving college writing,* and *proofreading skills* to locate sites that might assist you in this course.

2. Write an e-mail to a friend. Notice the writing process you use to create an informal document. How many times do you revise, edit, and rewrite a simple message?

POINTS TO REMEMBER

1. Writing is a process—it does not occur in a single burst of inspiration.

2. Good writing has a purpose: a *thesis statement,* or controlling idea. It is not a collection of random thoughts, first impressions, or feelings. Good writing reflects *critical thinking*—close observation, research, and analysis.

3. Prewriting techniques help explore ideas. Brainstorming, freewriting, and asking questions are useful tools to identify topics, discover new ideas, narrow a topic, and develop a thesis.

4. Outlines, whether formal or informal, organize ideas and identify missing information or unnecessary details.

5. First drafts serve to get ideas on paper—they are not expected to be perfect.

6. Reading papers aloud while revising and editing can help you detect missing details, awkward sentences, misspelled words, and grammar errors.

7. Avoid plagiarism. Never use the work of others without informing readers.

Blend Images/MediaBakery

PART 2

Developing Paragraphs

CHAPTER 3

Developing Topic Sentences and Controlling Ideas

CHAPTER GOALS

- Understand the Role of Paragraphs
- Write Topic Sentences
- Develop Controlling Ideas
- Revise Paragraphs for Clarity

Frederick M Brown/Getty Images

Get Writing

Write one or more paragraphs describing your reactions to this photograph. Do you believe that celebrities have too much influence on teenagers? Does the emphasis on style, fashion, and consumerism distort young people's values?

What Is a Paragraph?

Paragraphs form the building blocks of writing. Like chapters in a book, paragraphs work to emphasize important ideas and help readers follow your train of thought.

A paragraph is a group of related sentences that express a main idea.

Writing without paragraphs is difficult to read. Important ideas are hard to identify, and transactions are lost in the block of text:

> In 1898 a struggling author named Morgan Robertson concocted a novel about a fabulous Atlantic liner, far larger than any that had ever been built. Robertson loaded his ship with rich and complacent people and then wrecked it one cold April night on an iceberg. This somehow showed the futility of everything, and in fact, the book was called *Futility* when it appeared that year, published by the firm of M. F. Mansfield. Fourteen years later a British shipping company named the White Star Line built a steamer remarkably like the one in Robertson's novel. The new liner was 66,000 tons displacement; Robertson's was 70,000. The real ship was 882.5 feet long; the fictional one was 800 feet. Both vessels were triple screw and could make 24–25 knots. Both could carry about 3,000 people, and both had enough lifeboats for only a fraction of this number. But, then, this didn't seem to matter because both were labeled "unsinkable." On April 10, 1912, the real ship left Southampton on her maiden voyage to New York. Her cargo included a priceless copy of t he *Rubaiyat of Omar Khayyam* and a list of passengers collectively worth two hundred fifty million dollars. On her way over she too struck an iceberg and went down on a cold April night. Robertson called his ship the *Titan;* the White Star Line called its ship the *Titanic.* This is the story of her last night.

Presented in its original form, the foreword to Walter Lord's book *A Night to Remember* is far more dramatic and easier to read:

> In 1898 a struggling author named Morgan Robertson concocted a novel about a fabulous Atlantic liner, far larger than any that had ever been built. Robertson loaded his ship with rich and complacent people and then wrecked it one cold April night on an iceberg. This somehow showed the futility of everything, and in fact, the book was called *Futility* when it appeared that year, published by the firm of M. F. Mansfield.
> *introduction*
>
> Fourteen years later a British shipping company named the White Star Line built a steamer remarkably like the one in Robertson's novel. The new liner was 66,000 tons displacement; Robertson's was 70,000. The real ship was 882.5 feet long; the fictional one was 800 feet. Both vessels were triple screw and could make 24–25 knots. Both could carry about 3,000 people, and both had enough lifeboats for only a fraction of this number. But, then, this didn't seem to matter because both were labeled "unsinkable."
> *transition*
>
> On April 10, 1912, the real ship left Southampton on her maiden voyage to New York. Her cargo included a priceless copy of the *Rubaiyat of Omar Khayyam* and a list of passengers collectively worth two hundred fifty million
> *transition*

dollars. On her way over she too struck an iceberg and went down on a cold April night.

conclusion

Robertson called his ship the *Titan;* the White Star Line called its ship the *Titanic.* This is the story of her last night.

Paragraphs play an important part in organizing essays:

- Paragraphs work as building blocks.
- Paragraphs usually present a single main idea expressed in a *topic sentence.*
- Paragraph breaks signal transitions, moving readers from one main idea to another.
- Like chapters in a book, paragraph breaks provide pauses, allowing readers to absorb ideas before moving to new material.
- Paragraph breaks in dialogue indicate shifts between speakers.

What Do You Know?

Answer each question about paragraphs True or False.

1. _____ Paragraphs arrange information.
2. _____ Paragraphs help readers follow a writer's ideas.
3. _____ Paragraphs must contain at least five sentences.
4. _____ Long essays about complex topics always have long paragraphs.
5. _____ Introductions and conclusions must always be placed in separate paragraphs.

Answers appear on the following page.

Get Writing

WHAT ARE YOU TRYING TO SAY?

Write a two- or three-paragraph response to one of the following topics:

- Compare your best and worst jobs, college courses, cars, or apartments.
- Describe the greatest challenge you face this semester and how you plan to meet it.
- Review the best or worst movie you have seen.
- Explain the most serious problems facing this country.
- Describe your ideal job.

_____

_____

_____

_____
_____
_____
_____
_____
_____
_____
_____
_____
_____
_____

WHAT HAVE YOU WRITTEN?

*Examine what you have written. Are your ideas clearly stated and easy to
follow? Are important ideas organized in paragraphs? Do paragraph breaks
make logical pauses and demonstrate transitions from one main point to another? Are there short, choppy paragraphs that could be combined to join
related ideas?*

Topic Sentences and Controlling Ideas

Most paragraphs contain a topic sentence *that expresses what the paragraph
is about* and conveys a **controlling idea** *that states a main point or opinion.* The remaining sentences support the topic sentence with facts, details,
comments, and observations. Topic sentences generally open paragraphs to
introduce the main idea and indicate the support to follow:

> **Revenue sharing has benefited professional football, allowing
> NFL teams to survive in smaller cities.** Unlike baseball, basketball, and
> hockey, professional football teams share money from television and memo-
> rabilia sales. Each team gets $100 million annually, allowing teams in smaller
> cities such as Green Bay and Minneapolis to compete with teams in major
> markets such as New York and Chicago. As a result, NFL teams are more bal-
> anced, having the money to hire players and invest in team development and
> coaching. Other sports, which suffer declining ticket sales and lowered profits
> in smaller media markets, may consider moving to revenue sharing to keep
> teams competitive and maintain fan interest.

Topic sentences can appear anywhere in a paragraph:

> In Milwaukee, the castle-like brick buildings that once housed the Pabst
> Brewing Company are being renovated into an upscale community of shops,
> apartments, offices, and condominiums. In Camden, New Jersey, the mammoth
> RCA factory has been transformed into loft apartments. In Manhattan, old

tanneries, cutting mills, and packing houses are being turned into apartments, art galleries, coffee shops, and gourmet restaurants. **Throughout the country, formerly run-down slums are being transformed into fashionable neighborhoods for young professionals who want to live in suburban comfort without a two-hour commute.**

Topic sentences serve key roles in a paragraph:

- Topic sentences explain what the paragraph is about.
- Topic sentences make a general statement supported by the rest of the paragraph.
- Topic sentences indicate the kind of detail that readers should expect in the paragraph.
- Topic sentences signal shifts in the writer's train of thought.
- Topic sentences dramatize a writer's main points, making writing easier to read and remember.

EXERCISE 1 Identifying Topic Sentences in Paragraphs

Underline the topic sentences in each paragraph.

1. People must take responsibility for their own health. The biggest killers today are lifestyle related—smoking, drinking, and overeating. One-fourth of American adults still smoke. A third of college students binge drink, and many admit to driving drunk. Obesity has become a national problem, especially among children and young adults. Although Americans have a right to complain about the high cost of health insurance, they should also help lower costs and improve their own well-being by healthy living. Basic changes in our lifestyles could dramatically lower rates of preventable disease and reduce the cost of health care.

2. Las Vegas is the last Detroit. It is the one city where someone can find a good-paying job and support a middle-class lifestyle without any technical skills. Eighty years ago immigrants and small-town boys could journey to Detroit and work on the line. Back then the assembly line required few technical skills. The work was hard, hot, and boring. But it paid well. If you were willing to tighten lug nuts on Buicks or screw headlights into Model T's nine hours a day, you could afford to own a home and send your children to college. Today people move to Las Vegas. You can make good money here with few skills. If you are willing to open and close car doors and lug suitcases in hundred-degree heat in a black suit and tie, you can make a hundred thousand a year in tips. The work is hot, boring, repetitive, and, at times, demeaning. But, as in Detroit eighty years ago, if you put in the hours, you can afford a home and give your children a better life.

3. Today parents blame teenage misbehavior on computer games, violent television shows, and bad-girl celebrities. The antics and reckless behavior of Britney, Lindsay, and Paris, they argue, lead girls to become mean, petty, and vindictive. Gangsta rap, they claim, encourages young black men to abuse women and to associate guns with manhood. In the

Sixties, parents blamed rock music for the youth rebellion and the sexual revolution. A decade earlier, TV executives showed Elvis only from the waist up, believing that his hip-twisting moves were obscene. In the Forties, parents were shocked when their teenage daughters swooned over Sinatra. Decades earlier, clergymen and women's groups blamed Valentino for luring impressionable girls into a life of sin. A century ago, the dime novel was cited as a cause for teenagers running away from home. Throughout history, adults have identified popular culture as the cause of juvenile delinquency.

4. I now have to work two part-time jobs and still borrow money from my parents to pay my bills. I never knew how much parking and utilities would cost. I did not realize how much I would end up spending on household items such as paper towels and cleaning supplies. Moving off campus my freshman year was a big mistake. My dorm room was small but affordable. I could walk to class and never had to spend money on gas or parking. I worked on weekends but could spend every night studying. Now I work three nights a week just to buy gas. I am exhausted and falling behind in two subjects.

Reading Topic Sentences

No doubt by this point in the semester you have read textbooks in this and other courses. If you have underlined or highlighted as you studied, look at your textbooks.

1. **Examine the sentences you highlighted.** How many of them are topic sentences? Do they state a controlling idea supported by the rest of the paragraph?

2. **Skim through a few pages in your textbooks.** How important are topic sentences in communicating ideas? Would it be harder to read and remember information if authors did not use topic sentences?

When you read, notice how writers use topic sentences to emphasize important ideas.

Writing Topic Sentences

Topic sentences have to be clearly and carefully worded to be effective. General or abstract statements might announce a topic but not express a controlling idea. The more clearly defined a topic sentence is, the easier it is for readers to understand what you are trying to say:

| General statement | Students need self-discipline to succeed in college. |
| Defined topic sentence | Students need self-discipline to concentrate on their studies, avoid distractions, and manage their time. |

EXERCISE 2   Identifying Topic Sentences and Controlling Ideas

Select the best topic sentence in each group.

1. a. _____ Television soap operas began airing in the late 1940s.

  b. _____ Many early soap operas were based on earlier radio programs.

  c. _____ Soap operas have remained popular for sixty years because they tap into the most basic challenges humans face: finding love and overcoming obstacles to happiness.

  d. _____ Daytime dramas are called "soap operas" because early programs were sponsored by detergent companies.

2. a. _____ In 1919 Congress passed the Volstead Act, which prohibited the manufacture, sale, and distribution of alcohol.

  b. _____ Supporters of Prohibition were nicknamed "drys," and their opponents called themselves "wets."

  c. _____ Prohibition was unpopular with ethnic groups that considered wine part of household meals.

  d. _____ Passed in a spirit of idealism that followed the First World War, Prohibition was widely ignored, gave birth to organized crime, and seemed to have little effect on the problems of alcohol abuse.

3. a. _____ Throughout the twentieth century, the supply and price of oil had profound effects on the world economy.

  b. _____ As oil wells began to run dry in Pennsylvania, many feared a coming gasoline famine in the 1920s, driving prices up.

  c. _____ A few years later, prices collapsed when huge oil deposits were found in Oklahoma and Texas.

  d. _____ Increases in oil prices in the 1970s fueled inflation in Europe, the United States, and Japan.

4. a. _____ A tsunami is caused by an earthquake on the ocean floor.

  b. _____ *Tsunami* is a Japanese word that is considered more accurate than the term *tidal wave*.

  c. _____ Tsunamis are not associated with tides.

  d. _____ Tsunamis are mammoth waves that can devastate low-lying coastal areas, killing thousands and destroying billions of dollars in property.

5. a. _____ Once produced on Hollywood back lots and mammoth sound-stages, motion pictures are now made on location all over the world.

  b. _____ Modern film equipment is smaller and more mobile.

c. _____ Today's audiences expect the natural realism of films shot on actual locations rather than sets.

d. _____ An increasing number of filmmakers find it cheaper to make movies in Canada.

EXERCISE 3   Developing Topic Sentences

Write a topic sentence for each subject, inventing details or opinions to express a controlling idea.

EX: Subject   **Home foreclosures**

Topic sentence   <u>Home foreclosures are devastating neighborhoods by lowering property values and leaving streets full of empty houses that become targets for arson and vandalism.</u>

1. **Subject**   **Your favorite television show**

   Topic sentence   _____

   _____

2. **Subject**   **Paying for school**

   Topic sentence   _____

   _____

3. **Subject**   **Camera phones**

   Topic sentence   _____

   _____

4. **Subject**   **Car insurance**

   Topic sentence   _____

   _____

5. **Subject**   **High school sports**

   Topic sentence   _____

   _____

Paragraphs Without Topic Sentences

Not all paragraphs have a topic sentence you can underline. However, all paragraphs should have a controlling idea or a main point.

In October, Patton Industries was sued by a group of investors who claimed the company owed them money. Two months later, a fire destroyed its main warehouse in San Diego. Unable to meet customer demands, Patton Industries lost several highly profitable contracts. Facing the loss of commissions and lowered bonuses, nearly 20 percent of the sales force left the firm. Several leading catalog companies dropped Patton products in the fall.

The list of problems faced by Patton Industries states a clear controlling idea, so the paragraph does not need a topic sentence such as "Patton Industries faces several serious problems."

POINT TO REMEMBER

Paragraphs may not have a topic sentence, but they must have unity and purpose. All the ideas in a paragraph should relate to a clear point that readers will easily understand. *All paragraphs should have a controlling idea.*

EXERCISE 4   Identifying Controlling Ideas and Creating Topic Sentences

Read each paragraph, and describe in your own words its controlling idea—its main idea. Then supply a possible topic sentence.

1. I grew up in Cherrywood. It has no town square, city hall, or business district. Fifty thousand people live in half a dozen subdivisions connected by miles of strip malls. The main streets are almost identical. North Avenue, West Avenue, South Avenue, and East Avenue present visitors with an unchanging pattern of billboards, fast-food restaurants, muffler shops, taco stands, gas stations, laundromats, and cell-phone stores. Even longtime residents can forget what street they're on. For a while North Avenue stood out from the rest when Bill Franco opened Napoli Pizza on the corner of North and Tenth. But this distinction did not last long. The restaurant proved so popular that Franco soon opened duplicates on West Avenue and South Avenue.

Controlling Idea _____

_____

Possible Topic Sentence _____

_____

2. Working parents can obtain day care from community organizations, churches, their employers, even their neighbors. Children need a clean, safe environment. But they also need a place that helps them grow as people. Children's lives are complicated and too often disrupted. They benefit from continuity and consistency. Parents should look for centers that have a low staff turnover. They should also look for centers that have steady clients. This way children can form relationships and friendships, as they would in their own neighborhoods. Avoid drop-in

centers where each day a child is put into the uncomfortable situation of having to meet strangers. Parents should network and invite day-care center playmates to their children's birthday parties and other family events so they can form true friendships.

Controlling Idea _____

_____

Possible Topic Sentence _____

_____

3. Millions of people earn commissions instead of salaries. Being paid a percentage of what they sell, some sales representatives will earn a paycheck bigger than their bosses or even the owner of the company in a good week. But a big commission check can be followed by weeks with little or no money coming in. A blizzard can keep malls and showrooms empty for days. A hike in interest rates can make consumers delay buying a car or new furniture. People who make commissions can be tempted to splurge and buy high-ticket items, then find it hard to keep up with their bills during the slow weeks. Some businesses are seasonal, and employees can expect a busy Christmas or summer season to be followed by slow months where long hours result in few sales and small commissions. A sales professional who earns a hundred thousand in commissions one year might face making half that the next. Car and mortgage payments can be a challenge when future income is hard to predict.

Controlling Idea _____

_____

Possible Topic Sentence _____

_____

4. When considering a job offer, many college graduates look only at the starting salary. They like to boast to their friends how much they are getting. First-year salary offers can be deceiving. Some dead-end positions have to pay well to attract applicants because there is no chance for advancement. The best companies sometimes pay employees low wages for the first year because they offer them valuable training they can obtain nowhere else. High-profile organizations and individuals may pay less but offer employees valuable contacts that could lead to promotions in the future. Employment at a prestigious firm can be more valuable for someone's future career than an MBA. Startup businesses and employers working with cutting-edge technology may pay little but offer employees a chance to start on the ground floor of the next Microsoft or Google.

Controlling Idea _____

_____

Possible Topic Sentence _____

_____

Revising Paragraphs

Even if you have created a detailed outline, you may have some trouble making logical paragraph breaks when you write the first draft. New ideas will come to you as you write. You may include new points without being sure where to place them in the text. Out of habit, you may discover that your first draft is written in a single block of text or as a series of choppy two- or three-sentence paragraphs:

> Students need self-discipline to concentrate on their studies, avoid distractions, and manage their time.
> Too often, first-year students get swept up in campus events, sports, and other extracurricular activities. They get excited about meeting new people and making new friends. They need to remember why they came to college and focus on their education.
> They have to learn to turn off the TV, shut off the cell phone, and close the door in order to study.
> Managing time is essential, especially for students who have jobs or children. They have schedule their day carefully and make sure that school remains a priority in their busy lives.

Revised

> Students need self-discipline to concentrate on their studies, avoid distractions, and manage their time. Too often, first-year students get swept up in campus events, sports, and other extracurricular activities. They get excited about meeting new people and making new friends. They need to remember why they came to college and focus on their education. They have to learn to turn off the TV, shut off the cell phone, and close the door in order to study. Managing time is essential, especially for students who have jobs or children. They have to schedule their day carefully and make sure that school remains a priority in their busy lives.

In revising a draft, look at your notes and consider new ideas you may have added. What ideas are the most important? What are your main points? Paragraphs should organize main points and demonstrate transitions.

WORKING TOGETHER

Working with a group of students, read over this student essay, and indicate where you would make paragraph breaks to make the essay easier to read.

Rochell Patterson   English 101
                        College Challenges

    Many students find the first year of college extremely
challenging. First, the transition from high school to
college can be difficult. High school students attend
class seven hours a day, doing most of their work in
school. Their teachers closely monitor their attendance
and remind them of missing assignments. In college, students attend class a few hours a week. They are expected
to complete most of the work on their own. Instructors
often do not take attendance or chase after students for
late work. They hand out a syllabus and expect students
to turn in their assignments on time. Students have to
develop the discipline to work independently. In addition, they have to learn to schedule their time and
avoid temptations. Balancing studying, jobs, and family responsibilities takes careful planning. Too often,
students can let their social lives crowd out time for
study. It takes a lot of discipline to turn down invitations from friends to go shopping or see a movie in
order to study. Friends who are not in school may not
appreciate how much homework a college student faces.
Because some assignments may not be due for several
weeks, it can be easy for students to procrastinate,
putting off working on a research paper or studying for
an exam until the last minute. Students can also face
financial pressures that add stress to their lives and
force them to make painful choices. In addition to tuition, which is rising all the time, students have to
pay for books, lab equipment, and parking fees. These
costs can force students to go deeply into debt or ex-
haust themselves by working overtime. Because so much of
their income is absorbed by college expenses, they may
be unable to afford car repairs or health insurance. For
all these reasons most people look back on their college
careers and agree that the first year is the toughest.

_____
_____
_____
_____
_____
_____
_____
_____
_____
_____
_____
_____
_____
_____
_____
_____
_____
_____
_____
_____
_____
_____
_____
_____
_____

EXERCISE 5   Revising Paragraphs

Examine this draft of a student essay. Identify its main ideas, and then rewrite the essay in no more than six paragraphs.

Communication Skills 151   Luis Alba
              The Changing Face of Education

    Today, college students have many alternatives to the
traditional three-day-a-week lecture. Across the country, a growing number of students are taking advantage
of new delivery systems.
    Many of these students are working adults with families
whose schedules prevent them from taking standard courses.
    Some work during the day or travel, making it
difficult to even sign up for night school courses.
    Other students live at great distance from the
nearest college offering the programs they need.
    To meet the needs of these nontraditional
students, colleges offer a variety of distance-
learning opportunities.
    For decades many colleges have broadcast telecourses
on cable or local PBS stations, allowing students to
watch educational programs and mail in assignments.
    These courses are being supplemented with newer tele-
vision technology that lets students interact with the
instructor or other students.
    The most popular new delivery system is the Internet,
which allows instructors to reach a global audience.
A noted professor of rare art in New York can offer a
highly specialized course to students nationwide.
    Internet courses are becoming more sophisticated as
websites now offer video.
    Online courses enable students to post comments and
questions and use chat rooms for discussions.
    These new delivery systems do have critics.
    Some educators question if students will find it
easier to cheat because instructors cannot tell who
is e-mailing assignments or taking online tests.
    Defenders of new delivery systems point out that
cheating has always been a problem in colleges.
    New technology, they argue, will eliminate much of the
problem.
    Internet courses are winning over many traditional
teachers who now supplement lectures with online study
guides and links to research material.

_____
_____
_____
_____
_____
_____
_____
_____
_____
_____
_____
_____
_____
_____
_____
_____
_____
_____
_____
_____
_____
_____
_____

Using Paragraph Breaks in Dialogue

Dialogue repeats what people have said word for word by using direct quotations. If you write a conversation in direct quotations, paragraphs play a critical role in showing the back-and-forth nature of dialogue. Paragraph breaks show when one person stops talking and another begins:

I shall never forget the day she scolded me into reading *Beowulf*.

"But Miss Bessie," I complained, "I ain't much interested in it."

Her large brown eyes became daggerish slits. "Boy," she said, "how dare you say 'ain't' to me! I've taught you better than that."

"Miss Bessie," I pleaded, "I'm trying to make first-string end on the football team, and if I go around saying 'it isn't' and 'they aren't,' the guys are gonna laugh me off the squad."

"Boy," she responded, "you'll play football because you have guts. But do you know what really takes guts? Refusing to lower your standards to those of the crowd. It takes guts to say you've got to live and be somebody fifty years after all the football games are over."

CARL ROWAN, "UNFORGETTABLE MISS BESSIE"

EXERCISE 6   Using Paragraph Breaks in Dialogue

Rewrite this student paragraph to separate the direct quotations between the two speakers. Remember to start a new paragraph each time a person starts speaking:

"Are you going to the library?" Mika asked.
"I can't," said Jane.
"Why not?"
"I have to take my car in for new tires. I had a flat last week. Today I noticed another tire is losing air."
"If I find anything that might help with your paper, I'll e-mail you."

Last summer I had what I thought would be an ideal summer job, working at a local cable TV station. I was fascinated with the high-tech control room and seeing the reporters and sportswriters for the evening news. I even hoped to see some athletes and celebrities who did interviews on *News at Nine*. But I had no idea I would have a boss like Cynthia Peterson to work with. "Just do what I say, when I say it, and everything will work out," she told me sternly at our interview. "Great," I told her. "I've never worked in TV and want to learn as much as I can." "Good," she told me with a tight-lipped smile. "First thing, take the webcast footage down to the control room for me," she said, handing me a CD and walking out of the room. I took the CD downstairs and opened the door to the control room. Instantly, three or four people began shouting at me. "What the hell are you doing?" the floor director yelled. "Ms. Peterson told me to bring this down to the control room," I answered, shaking with embarrassment. "Didn't she tell you never to come in here during a broadcast?" "No," I replied. This would be the first of a stream of mistakes I would make trying to follow Cynthia Peterson's incomplete orders.

_____

_____

_____

_____

_____

_____

_____

_____

_____

_____

_____

_____

_____

_____

_____

_____

_____

_____

_____

_____

_____

Get Writing

CRITICAL THINKING

Write two or three paragraphs describing a difficult decision you had to make in the last year. Did you decide to quit a job, return to school, sell a prized possession, quit smoking, or end a relationship?

WHAT HAVE YOU WRITTEN?

Write out the topic sentence or controlling idea for each paragraph. Is each one clearly stated? Do the details in each paragraph support the controlling idea?

Do the paragraphs clearly organize main points? Do the paragraphs demonstrate clear transitions? Should any paragraphs be separated for greater clarity? Are there any choppy paragraphs stating related ideas that should be combined?

Review your sentences for spelling errors (see Chapter 35), fragments (see Chapter 23), comma splices and run-ons (see Chapter 25), and errors in agreement (see chapters 28 and 30).

Get Writing

Do you see a connection between this photograph and the one on page 34? Does the image that celebrities present affect the way young people see themselves? Do the media give teenagers unrealistic and distorted views of adult life? Are teens driven to measure themselves too much on how they look and dress? Does our society stress glamour, fashion, and celebrity over knowledge, values, and spirituality?

Write one or more paragraphs describing what this image symbolizes to you. Does it simply capture a lighthearted and enjoyable part of growing up? Or do you see it as evidence of a serious social problem?

What Have You Learned?

Answer each question about paragraphs True or False.

1. ____ Every paragraph must have a controlling or main idea.

2. ____ Paragraphs usually consist of details supporting a topic sentence.

3. ____ Paragraph breaks signal transitions.

4. ____ Topic sentences always open a paragraph.

5. ____ An essay always has at least five paragraphs.

Answers appear on the following page.

WRITING ON THE WEB

Using a search engine such as Yahoo! or Google, enter terms such as *paragraphs, topic sentences, controlling ideas,* and *writing paragraphs* to locate current sites of interest.

1. Review recent articles in online journals, and note how writers use topic sentences to state main ideas and paragraphs to organize articles.

2. Write an e-mail to a friend; then review your use of paragraphs. How can paragraphs make even a short e-mail easier to read? Do you use paragraph breaks to reproduce dialogue?

POINTS TO REMEMBER

1. **Paragraphs are the building blocks of an essay.**

2. **Every paragraph must have a controlling idea supported by details.**

3. **Paragraph breaks signal transitions between main points.**

4. **Paragraph breaks are used to separate direct quotations in dialogue.**

5. **Precisely worded topic sentences guide writing, helping you decide which details to include in paragraphs and which details to leave out.**

Answers to What Have You Learned? on page 51

1. True (pages 37–39)   2. True (page 37)   3. True (page 36)
4. False (page 37)   5. False

CHAPTER 4

Supporting Topic Sentences with Details

JEFF J MITCHELL/STAFF/GETTY IMAGES

CHAPTER GOALS

- Support Topic Sentences with Relevant Details

- Recognize Different Types of Support

- Blend Supporting Details to Create Effective Paragraphs

Get Writing

How have websites such as YouTube changed society? Do people post images that would not be broadcast by TV networks? Can an embarrassing video clip ruin a celebrity's reputation or destroy a politician's career? Should there be more control or censorship of what is posted online?

Write a paragraph describing the influence of YouTube and explaining whether or not you think it should be censored.

What Are Supporting Details?

For a paragraph to be effective, the topic sentence and controlling idea must be supported by details—facts, statistics, testimony, personal experiences, and observations.

Without enough support, a topic sentence is unproven. Irrelevant details can confuse and distract readers and weaken the paragraph.

Topic Sentence	**The chemistry building must be renovated if the college wants to compete with other universities.**	
Supporting details	*facts:*	Building never renovated since it opened in 1967.
		Newest computer is three years old.
	statistics:	45% of equipment obsolete by national standards.
		50% of pre-med students transfer in sophomore year.
	testimony:	Chemistry professors' complaints to dean.
	personal experience:	students' inability to conduct experiments.
	observations:	numbers of students seen waiting to use equipment.
Irrelevant details		Style of the chemistry building.
		Price of textbooks and lab fees.
		Reasons why students major in chemistry.
		Professors who don't keep office hours.

What Do You Know?

Underline the topic sentence in the following paragraph; then cross out sentences that do not support the controlling idea.

U.S. students should be required to learn at least one foreign language. The United States is the greatest superpower in the world. It is the richest nation on the planet. However, its power and prosperity depend on maintaining good relations with other countries and participating in the global economy. With the collapse of the Soviet Union, the United States became the leading military power in the world. This has caused many people in other countries to see America as an imperial power bent on building a modern version of the British Empire. Millions of U.S. jobs now depend on exports. Yet few U.S. executives are able to converse in languages other than English. U.S. forces are operating in Afghanistan and Iraq, but few military officers speak Urdu or Arabic. Surprisingly, many public schools and colleges are dropping foreign language requirements just when we must be able to communicate with the rest of the world for our survival. We must make the study of foreign languages a requirement for graduating. Computer courses should be required as well because nearly every job now requires people to send e-mail and access online data.

Answers appear on the following page.

WHAT ARE YOU TRYING TO SAY?

Select one of the topics below or develop one of your own, and make a few notes before writing.

- job interviews
- talk shows
- voting machines
- underage drinking
- racial profiling
- health clubs
- campus parking
- first dates
- bloggers
- current fashions
- role models
- cell phone etiquette

Write a clear topic sentence, and then write a paragraph that supports it with meaningful details.

_____

_____

_____

_____

_____

_____

_____

_____

_____

_____

_____

_____

Answers to What Do You Know? on Page 54

<u>U.S. students should be required to learn at least one foreign language.</u>
Cross out the following: With the collapse of the Soviet Union, the United States became the leading military power in the world. This has caused many people in other countries to see America as an imperial power bent on building a modern version of the British Empire. Computer courses should be required as well because nearly every job now requires people to send e-mail and access online data.

WHAT HAVE YOU WRITTEN?

Read your paragraph carefully.

1. Underline the topic sentence. Does it express a focused controlling idea? Could it be more clearly stated?

2. Do the other sentences support the controlling idea, or do they contain unrelated details?

Steps to Building Effective Paragraphs

Start with a Clear Topic Sentence and Focused Controlling Idea

In Chapter 3 you learned the importance of developing a topic sentence. When you revise paragraphs, examine the topic sentences to make sure that they state a clear controlling idea.

Weak Topic Sentence	Improved Topic Sentence
College is tough.	My college courses are more difficult than I expected.
High school sports benefit students.	High school sports teach students the importance of teamwork, discipline, and self-reliance.
The United States needs more tools to fight terrorism.	The United States needs greater intelligence, more cooperation from foreign governments, improved diplomatic relations with Islamic countries, and enhanced security technology to fight terrorism.

EXERCISE 1   Improving Topic Sentences

Revise each of the following weak topic sentences, adding details to create a more focused controlling idea.

EX: Exercise is important.

Regular exercise improves cardiovascular function, reduces stress, and helps those who need to lose weight.

1.   Cable television can be bad for young children.

_____

_____

2.   College students misuse credit cards.

_____

_____

3.   Recycling is a good idea.

_____

_____

4.   Communicating with teenage children is hard.

_____

_____

5.   Junk e-mail is a headache.

_____

_____

Distinguish Between Supporting Detail and Restating Topic Sentences

A topic sentence expresses a controlling idea. The remaining sentences in the paragraph should provide evidence that supports, explains, or proves the controlling idea, not simply repeats it. In writing a first draft, you may find yourself repeating general ideas rather than providing detailed evidence:

> The new stadium is a disappointment. After spending nearly $250 million, fans and taxpayers expected a lot more. Those who anticipated Opening Day this year were dismayed. The new stadium does not measure up to what the public wanted. More and more people are expressing their unhappiness with the situation. A quarter of a billion dollars should have given the city a landmark facility, not one that has disappointed fans and upset taxpayers. The new stadium is just a disaster.

The first sentence states a controlling idea. However, the following sentences do not support or explain it but simply restate the idea in different words. The paragraph provides no reasons why the stadium is a disappointment. Deleting repetitions and supporting the topic sentences with facts and observations will create a stronger, more convincing paragraph:

> The new stadium is a disappointment. After spending $250 million, taxpayers expected a state-of-the-art venue with ample parking, comfortable seating, appealing shops, and decent refreshments. Those attending Opening Day soon discovered the same parking problems they faced at the old stadium. The seats are small and uncomfortable. Several sections are poorly lit and have blocked views. Vendors operate from pushcarts rather than stores. Most of the refreshments consist of microwaved hot dogs and frozen pizza. The public expected a lot more for a quarter-billion dollars.

Support Topic Sentences with Adequate and Relevant Details

Topic sentences state an opinion or observation that requires adequate and relevant support. The other sentences should contain details that directly support the topic sentence—not simply list everything you know or can remember about the topic. A topic sentence is not a writing prompt to inspire you to write everything you can think of, but a clear statement requiring specific evidence:

Vague

> The college needs a new bookstore. The current store was built in 1967 and is outdated. It no longer meets the needs of this growing college. Two years ago the library received a ten-million-dollar renovation. But the bookstore remains unchanged since the sixties. Enrollment has increased as have the number of courses offered. The bookstore computer system is inadequate. Book orders cannot be tracked. Students can often get a book faster by ordering it on the Internet than going to the bookstore on campus. This is the same with athletic uniforms as well. The athletic department requires six weeks to order something you can have mailed to your dorm room in ten days. The bookstore causes headaches every semester. Until a new bookstore is built, getting books will remain a chore that students dread.

This paragraph opens with a clearly worded topic sentence. The sentences that follow basically repeat the topic sentence, adding only minor details. Comments about the library and athletic department are interesting but provide no direct support for the need for a new bookstore. Sentences contain words such as *inadequate* and *headache* but few details. Eliminating repetition and adding more specific detail can create a more effective paragraph:

Improved

The college needs a new bookstore. Built in 1967, the current store no longer meets the needs of a college with a growing student enrollment and expanding list of course offerings. In the sixties the college needed to supply books for less than a hundred courses. Last semester the college offered over 250 separate courses, each with a unique book list. The outdated computer system cannot track book orders. Books are ordered from publishers and distributors by phone, mail, or fax. Every semester, students can expect long lines, misplaced book orders, mislabeled books, and clerks who cannot help because they cannot access computer data. Students find it easier, cheaper, and faster to order their books online, denying the college a source of income. The college has renovated the library, the swimming pool, and a faculty garage in the last two years. It is time to renovate the forty-year-old bookstore.

EXERCISE 2   Recognizing Relevant Supporting Details

After reading each topic sentence, check those sentences that provide relevant support. Ignore sentences that simply restate the topic sentence or contain irrelevant details.

1. Political campaigns are increasingly expensive.

    a. _____ It costs more and more money for a candidate to run for office.

    b. _____ In 2008 presidential candidates spent as much as a million dollars a day.

    c. _____ To have a chance of being elected, candidates must buy expensive airtime for commercials, maintain websites, hire communications experts, and pay media consultants.

    d. _____ Supplying donuts and coffee to its phone-bank volunteers cost one campaign two thousand dollars a day.

    e. _____ Anyone thinking of running for office will face major expenses.

2. Popular television shows have the power to influence social and cultural change.

    a. _____ Because TV shows are popular, they can influence behavior.

    b. _____ The 1970s show *The Love Boat* is credited for the increased demand for ocean cruises.

    c. _____ A decade later, applications to law school increased after *LA Law* became a hit.

    d. _____ When television started, many Hollywood stars thought appearing on the small screen would hurt their careers.

e. _____ Italian newspapers called that country's legal reforms the Perry Mason law after the popular U.S. TV show that led Italians to question their nation's old-fashioned justice system.

3. **Global warming could have disastrous effects on agriculture, wildlife, the economy, and political stability.**

   a. _____ Rising temperatures will cause droughts and famines, especially in the poorer nations of Africa.

   b. _____ Environmental change could kill rare species throughout the world.

   c. _____ Climate change caused by the Earth's warming will cause economic, social, and farming problems.

   d. _____ Some scientists and politicians question whether global warming is taking place at all.

   e. _____ Ironically, global warming may cause ocean currents to shift, making Northern Europe colder.

4. **Owning a restaurant requires a major commitment of time, money, and energy.**

   a. _____ Restaurant ownership demands hard work and dedication.

   b. _____ Restaurant owners typically work sixty to eighty hours a week.

   c. _____ Many owners are forced to work holidays, and many forgo vacations.

   d. _____ Many people dream of owning their own business.

   e. _____ Restaurants have a high failure rate; half of newly opened restaurants will go out of business within five years.

5. **Childhood obesity is becoming a major health crisis in America.**

   a. _____ Children are getting heavier, and more of them are developing health problems once associated with middle age.

   b. _____ Americans spend billions on exercise programs, diet plans, and weight-loss spas.

   c. _____ More children are eating at fast-food restaurants.

   d. _____ Worried about their children using drugs or joining gangs, some parents overlook poor eating habits.

   e. _____ In a desire to look like their favorite stars, some teenage girls go on binge diets and risk their health.

Types of Support

Personal Observations and Experiences

Personal observations include thoughts and memories about a person, place, thing, or situation. A paragraph about your first days of military basic training would include memories of your drill instructor, the barracks, the other recruits, and training. A topic sentence which stated that boot camp was tougher than you expected could be supported by focusing on how demanding the exercises were and how tired you were at the end of the day. A topic sentence which declares that your apartment building needs repair could be supported by your observations about faulty wiring, uncollected trash, broken elevators, and damaged windows.

Like personal observations, experiences from your own life can supply rich details to support a topic sentence. Writing about your experiences as a student, parent, resident of a particular neighborhood, or employee can make an issue more real and provide gripping evidence. Nathan McCall uses personal experiences to illustrate the problems black students faced when bused to previously all-white schools:

> The daily bus ride home brought its own set of fears. A group of white boys got on our bus regularly for the sole purpose, it seemed, of picking fights. I was scared to death of them. With older brothers to fight at home, I was confident I could whip any white boy my age and size, but many of the white guys who got on that bus were eighth graders, and they looked like giants to me. Others were older, white, leather-jacket-wearing hoods who I was certain were high school dropouts.
>
> *MAKES ME WANNA HOLLER*

Examples

Examples are specific people, things, places, or events that illustrate an idea or provide supporting evidence. Examples may be individual items, but they are not isolated. They represent something larger. You can support a topic sentence describing the dangers of fad diets with examples of one or more people who became sick or died attempting to lose weight. In writing about a high school teacher who gave him valuable lessons that changed his life, Carl Rowan supports his opening topic sentence with a specific example:

> Miss Bessie noticed things that had nothing to do with schoolwork, but were vital to a youngster's development. Once a few classmates made fun of my frayed, hand-me-down overcoat, calling me "Strings." As I was leaving school, Miss Bessie patted me on the back of that old overcoat and said, "Carl, never fret about what you don't have. Just make the most of what you do have—a brain."
>
> *"UNFORGETTABLE MISS BESSIE"*

Facts and Opinions

Facts are objective details that can be observed, analyzed, and documented by others. A personal observation might reflect the writer's opinion, such as "The Ramones lived in a spacious home in one of the most exclusive communities in El Paso." The terms "spacious" and "exclusive" are personal impressions, not facts. "The Ramones lived in a five-bedroom home in a subdivision where house prices begin at $800,000" is a statement of facts that can be verified. Facts are not opinions, but they serve as evidence to support opinions. Opinions reflect a personal impression, viewpoint, or attitude. Opinions can be used as support (see pages 62–63) but should never be confused with facts.

Opinion	Fact
Sid wants too much for his '92 Mustang.	Sid wants $9,500 for his '92 Mustang.
Tredway is a great investment.	Tredway stock has risen 35% in two years.
The Aviator is a great movie.	*The Aviator* was nominated for eleven Academy Awards.

Facts provide strong support for topic sentences. In some instances writers allow facts to speak for themselves and list them without a general topic sentence. To inform readers about the devastating impact of the Great Depression on New York City in the 1930s, Robert Caro developed a paragraph that includes numerous facts. Although there is no topic sentence you can underline, the paragraph has a clearly defined controlling idea:

> More than 10,000 of New York's 29,000 manufacturing firms had closed their doors. Nearly one of every three employables in the city had lost his job. An estimated 1,600,000 New Yorkers were receiving some form of public relief. Many of those fortunates who had kept their jobs were "underemployed," a euphemism for the fact that they worked two or three days a week or two weeks a month—or, if they worked full time, were paid a fraction of their former salaries; stenographers, earning $35 to $40 per week in 1928, were averaging $16 a week in 1933; Woolworth's was paying salesladies $7 a week.
>
> *THE POWER BROKER*

TIPS FOR USING EXAMPLES AS SUPPORT

1. **Make sure that your examples are not exceptions.** Listing a half-dozen smokers who lived past eighty does not adequately support the idea that tobacco is harmless.

2. **Use examples that readers will recognize.** Avoid using events or people that require lengthy explanations as examples.

3. **Provide more than one example, if possible.**

4. **Blend examples with factual support.** To prove that your example is not an isolated case, provide statistics or expert testimony.

TIPS FOR USING FACTS AS SUPPORT

1. **Facts should directly support the topic sentence or controlling idea, not bring up other issues.**

2. **Use facts from reliable sources that readers will recognize and respect.** Facts taken from government publications, encyclopedias, and mainstream magazines will be more convincing than facts from someone's home page or an advertisement.

3. **Use facts to balance personal observations and examples to add credibility to your opinions.**

4. **Make sure that you use representative facts.** Don't just pick facts that support your opinion. Try to get the big picture and use facts fairly. Don't take facts out of context.

Statistics

Statistics are facts stated in numbers. Statistics can provide powerful support because they are easy for readers to understand and remember:

Eighty-five percent of our students work full or part time.

One in eight trucks on the road has faulty brakes.

This year 25 percent of our employees earned bonuses.

Used properly, statistics are convincing evidence to support a topic sentence. Arguing that the criminal justice system is unfair to African Americans, Manning Marable offers statistics as support:

> In criminal justice, African Americans constitute only one-seventh of all drug users. Yet we account for 35 percent of all drug arrests, 55 percent of drug convictions and 75 percent of prison admissions for drug offenses.
>
> *"An Idea Whose Time Has Come"*

TIPS FOR USING STATISTICS AS SUPPORT

1. **Make sure that the items being counted are clearly defined.** Statistics about juvenile delinquents, for example, are not accurate if people use different definitions of *delinquency*.

2. **Use statistics from reliable government sources, such as academic institutions, respected writers, or major magazines, such as *Time*, *Newsweek*, and *Fortune*.**

3. **Make sure that you present enough statistics.** Stating that "over 80 percent of Acme workers own stock in the company" makes the firm sound employee owned—until you learn the average worker only has a dozen shares. Ninety percent of the stock could be held by outsiders or even a single investor.

4. **Consider alternative interpretations of statistics.** Often, numbers can be interpreted differently. If reports of child abuse have risen 50 percent in two years, does this mean that more children are being abused or that more cases are being reported?

Testimony (Quotations)

Testimony includes the words, experiences, opinions, ideas, and observations of others. They can be participants in an event, witnesses, or experts. Testimony can be given in direct quotations that repeat word for word what someone wrote or said or in indirect summaries. The words or observations of real people add life to a paragraph. Stanley Karnow describes the initial optimism that U.S. soldiers had in the early days of the Vietnam War, supporting his point with the testimony of a young officer:

> All this power intoxicated the Americans who initially went to Vietnam with a proud and overwhelming sense of confidence. Whatever the objective of the war—and many could not define its purpose with any precision—they were certain that U.S. omnipotence would triumph. Philip Caputo, then a young marine lieutenant, recalled the feeling that he and his buddies shared as their battalion splashed ashore at Danang in the spring of 1965: "When we marched into the rice paddies on that damp March afternoon, we carried, along with our packs and rifles, the implicit convictions that the Vietcong would be quickly beaten."
>
> *Vietnam: A History*

TIPS FOR USING TESTIMONY AS SUPPORT

1. **Avoid using quotations from famous people unless they directly support your topic sentence.** Adding quotations by Shakespeare or Martin Luther King, no matter how impressive, will only distract readers unless such quotations clearly support your controlling idea.

2. **Make sure that you quote people accurately.** Don't rely on your memory of what someone said. Try to locate the original source and copy it exactly.

3. **Place direct quotations in quotation marks.** Remember to use quotation marks when you copy word for word what someone else has said or written (see pages 359–361).

4. **Do not take quotations out of context.** Make sure that the quotations you use don't distort someone's point of view.

5. **If needed, explain who you are quoting.** Testimony will be effective only if readers understand the speaker's knowledge or value. Just adding quotations to a paragraph will not impress readers.

   The rising crime rate is ruining the Southside. Joe Long said, "I can't take it anymore, so I'm moving."

   Improved
   The rising crime rate is ruining the Southside. Joe Long, who has lived here for thirty-eight years, said, "I can't take it anymore, so I'm moving."

6. **Verify the accuracy and validity of opinions.** Opinions can be powerful evidence as long as the person you are quoting is a respected expert or authority. Avoid biased opinions or those based on little factual support.

Blending Support

Because each type of support has strengths and weaknesses, writers often use more than one to provide evidence for a topic sentence:

> **Online gambling has become a major problem, especially on college campuses.** Gambling has always posed a problem for college students. Edgar Allan Poe dropped out of the University of Virginia when he was unable to pay his gambling debts. A few years ago several New York colleges intervened when fraternities began renting vans for weekly gambling runs to Atlantic City. Now online gambling poses a new threat. According to Dr. Myra Godell, a therapist who treats compulsive gamblers, "One in ten college students surveyed gambled online at least once in his or her freshmen year." Over 15% of students seeking help at NYU's counseling center cite online gambling as a major distraction to their studies. For the troubled student far from home, the rush and thrill of gambling are as close as a laptop. He or she does not have to travel to a casino or even interact with other people. One sophomore admitted, "I gambled day and night whenever I felt lonely or depressed. Only after I maxed out two credit cards to the tune of nine thousand dollars did I realize I was hooked and had to stop."

topic sentence

examples

testimony

statistics

testimony/example

POINT TO REMEMBER

In selecting details, ask yourself, "Does this support my controlling idea?" In writing the first draft, you may remember facts or experiences. New ideas about your subject may come to mind. But unless these details directly support the topic sentence, they do not belong in the paragraph.

EXERCISE 3   Developing Supporting Details

Supply supporting details for each topic sentence. Make sure that the details directly support the controlling idea expressed by the topic sentence.

1. **Cars are safer than they used to be.**
   a. Testimony _____
   b. Example _____
   c. Fact _____
   d. Personal observation _____

2. **Young people benefit from summer jobs.**
   a. Statistics _____
   b. Testimony _____
   c. Example _____
   d. Fact _____

3. **Television makeover shows give the public unrealistic expectations about cosmetic surgery.**
   a. Testimony _____
   b. Fact _____
   c. Personal observation _____
   d. Example _____

4. **Americans do not save enough money.**
   a. Statistics _____
   b. Fact _____
   c. Example _____
   d. Personal experience _____

5. **Public schools don't provide skills that students need to succeed in college.**
   a. Example _____
   b. Fact _____
   c. Statistics _____
   d. Personal observation _____

EXERCISE 4   Revising the Paragraph

Revise this e-mail, deleting repetitive and irrelevant details and adding your own ideas that support the topic sentence.

May 1, 2009
From: Leland Hawkes
To: Carol Hayes

TALKING POINTS FOR PTA APPEARANCE MAY 14, 2009

Excessive television watching can damage children's health, social development, and education. Children who watch too much TV spend their free time on a couch, often eating junk food instead of playing outside. Junk food is too easily available these days. Neighborhoods that once had one fast-food restaurant now have four or five. In addition, the servings have gotten larger. Children usually watch television in isolation. They are not learning the social development skills that come from interacting with others. They are not getting the lessons you can learn by playing and working with other children. The fast pace of television may limit children's attention spans and make it harder for them to have the concentration needed to read. Studying requires attention and concentration.

EXERCISE 5   Writing Organized Paragraphs

Write a well-organized paragraph that builds on one or more of the following topic sentences and uses one or more types of supporting details.

1. It is difficult to quit smoking.

2. People who use cell phones are often inconsiderate.

3. Reality television shows are extremely popular.

4. Many families find health insurance unaffordable.

5. The media spends too much time focusing on celebrities.

WORKING TOGETHER

Working with a group of students, edit this paragraph from a student paper to eliminate repetition and irrelevant details. Review sentences for fragments (see Chapter 23), run-ons and comma splices (see Chapter 25), and misspelled words (see Chapter 35).

I never considered my self "prosperous" or "afluent" until I visited my father's hometown in Mexico. I grew up in a ranch house that seemed too small for four kids, my parents' cars were always second hand. No way did I feel priviledged. Last summer my Dad took us to Mexico on vacation were we usually go. But we did visit our usuall destanations like Cancun or Acapulco. Instead, he took us to the village where he was born. A village with no electricity or running water. The streets were dirt, the houses were tin shacks. The people did not have phones, never saw TV, or went to doctors. They had to wash clothes in steel tubs and cook on wood fires. I could not believe people lived like this in the 21st century. Looking at the way my cousins lived, I felt guilty. How could a eigteen-year old with a TV, DVD player, air-conditioned bedroom, camera phone, palm pilet, and a car feel he wasn't rich next to them?

_____
_____
_____
_____
_____
_____
_____
_____
_____
_____
_____
_____

Get Thinking and Writing

CRITICAL THINKING

Would you buy a hybrid car that used less energy and caused less pollution even if it cost more than a regular car? Why or why not? Write one or more paragraphs stating your opinion, supported by details.

WHAT HAVE YOU WRITTEN?

Read your paragraphs out loud. Is there a clear controlling idea? Have you stated it in a topic sentence? Do you provide enough supporting detail? Are there irrelevant details that should be deleted? Edit your sentences for run-ons and comma splices (see Chapter 25), agreement errors (see Chapter 28), and misplaced modifiers (see Chapter 26).

Get Writing

The first computers, constructed with thousands of vacuum tubes and miles of wire, cost millions of dollars and were the size of a small house. Few scientists then could imagine that computers would shrink to the size of a phone book and cost a few hundred dollars. How do you think computers will change in the next fifty years? Will computers improve education, expand business opportunities, and give individuals greater influence? Will they invade personal privacy, provide terrorists with new weapons, and rob people of their identity?

Write two or more paragraphs describing the positive and negative ways that computers could change the world in the next fifty years.

What Have You Learned?

Read the following paragraph carefully, and underline the topic sentence; then cross out sentences that do not support the controlling idea.

The Internet has increased the amount of information students can access, but it has not made them smarter. Today, a student in a small, remote school can easily log on and obtain information from the most famous and well-stocked libraries in the world. The Internet lets people order clothes, invest in stocks, and buy airline tickets without leaving home. Despite all this information flashing on their computer screens, students are not getting much of an improved education. Education is essential for our kids to get good jobs in a high-tech world and global economy. There is a lot of adult material on the Internet that endangers children as well. The problem with the Internet is that it just provides raw data. Students need to develop skills to interpret, analyze, evaluate, and compare sources. They need sophisticated intellectual skills to make use of all the data at their fingertips. Schools and parents don't always face the fact that the Internet spews out information. It does not teach students how to think.

Answers appear at the top of this page.

WRITING ON THE WEB

Using a search engine such as Yahoo! or Google, enter terms such as *paragraph design, modes of development, revising paragraphs,* and *topic sentences* to locate current sites of interest.

1. Review recent online articles, and notice how writers select and organize details to support a topic sentence and express a controlling idea.
2. Note how authors use the modes of development to organize paragraphs.

POINTS TO REMEMBER

1. **Paragraphs must have clearly stated controlling ideas.**
2. **Topic sentences must be supported with facts, statistics, personal observations and experiences, and/or testimony.**
3. **Avoid simply restating the topic sentence.**
4. **Details should directly support the topic sentence, not introduce new or irrelevant ideas.**
5. **Each type of support has limitations, so use more than one.**

Developing Paragraphs Using Description

CATHERINE KARNOW/CORBIS

CHAPTER GOALS

■ Understand the Elements of Description

■ Distinguish Between Objective and Subjective Description

■ Appreciate the Importance of Creating Dominant Impressions

Write a paragraph describing what children learn by playing sports. Consider your own experiences or those of children you know.

Get Writing

What Is Description?

Description presents facts, images, and impressions of people, events, things, and ideas. Description records what we see, hear, feel, taste, touch, and smell.

Description can be **objective** or **subjective**. Objective description presents factual details that others can see or verify, such as the height of building or the population of a city. This type of description is used in college papers, news articles, business letters, and professional reports:

> Cullen, Georgia, population four thousand, was formerly the site of four major linen mills. Since 2000 the population has dropped 35% as laid-off workers have sought jobs in Atlanta, Memphis, and Chattanooga. The current unemployment rate is 25%. Alcohol and drug-related offenses have increased 44% in five years. City and state officials have been unable to attract new industry or other development to the region. After announcing the third budget cut in a single year, the town's part-time mayor resigned.

Subjective description expresses feelings, images, and personal observations rather than facts or statistics, such as the style of a building or the mood of a city. This type of description is found in personal letters and essays:

> In Cullen, Georgia, it's *Grapes of Wrath* all over again—without the hope of a New Deal. The great old linen mills are silent and empty. Jobless men wander hopelessly down aching streets lined with vacant shops. Others sit in doorways and drink. Now and then a rusty pickup or dusty SUV, its windows blocked with plastic bags full of clothes, heads north, taking another family from the dying town. The part-time mayor, a broken man, resigned in despair.

The type of description you use depends on your purpose, your readers, and the writing context. Popular books and magazine articles often blend subjective impressions with objective facts:

> Cullen, Georgia, is a relic of the nearly dead American linen industry. One by one, the crumbling nineteenth-century red-brick mills closed their doors, unable to compete with Asian imports. Hundreds of families have left the dying town, seeking jobs in the cities. The once-thriving working-class community has become a mini-ghetto with its share of drunks and drug addicts loitering around empty storefronts and Cullen's lone tavern. After announcing yet another budget cut, the town's part-time mayor announced his resignation.

Get Writing

WHAT ARE YOU TRYING TO SAY?

Select one of the following topics:

- your first apartment
- a local restaurant or club
- a popular band
- the last movie you saw

- your first school
- your last boss
- your co-workers
- a celebrity

Write a description paragraph that includes objective, factual details about your topic.

_____

_____

_____

_____

_____

_____

Write a description paragraph that includes subjective details expressing your personal impressions and feelings about your topic.

_____

_____

_____

_____

_____

_____

WHAT HAVE YOU WRITTEN?

Read your paragraphs carefully. Underline words that provide details about your topic. Does your objective description give readers facts and not personal impressions? Does your subjective description use words and details that reflect personal impressions and feelings?

Creating Dominant Impressions

Whether you are writing objective description for a research paper or subjective description for a personal essay, your goal is not to list every fact and detail you can remember. Good descriptions have a focus. They make a point. If you attempt to include everything you can think of to describe a restaurant, for instance, you can create a collection of trivial and obvious details:

> The Pride of Athens is located at 2844 West Greenfield Avenue between a dry cleaner and a hardware store. There is only street parking. It used to be a shoe store. There is a small oak bar that looks like something from a Wild West saloon. The kitchen doors are screened off with black and red screens with Chinese symbols on them. They came from the old Cathay House that closed last year. The booths along the bar came from a Wendy's. The second-hand menu holders have pictures of pizzas on them. The only Greek décor

comes from a large homemade tacky mural of the Acropolis painted on one wall. The place is popular. The food is great. The owner plans to expand and begin catering. It's the most Greek place in town.

The paragraph provides a lot of facts and observations but fails to make a clear point. No connection is made between the non-Greek décor and the statement that it is the "most Greek place in town." The restaurant is described as being "popular" and having "great food," but with little explanation. The most important ideas are not developed, but minor details about parking and menu holders are included. A more effective description deletes trivial details and creates a **dominant impression** that highlights the most important things you want your readers to know about your subject:

> The Pride of Athens is an unlikely place to win restaurant awards. Wedged between a hardware store and a dry cleaners, the one-time shoe store is furnished with an assortment of secondhand items from a Wendy's, a Chinese restaurant, and a bankrupt pizzeria. Cups and saucers do not match. The only décor clue to the restaurant is a tacky homemade mural behind the bar. However, the owner spares no expense on the food. Patrons come from Chicago, ninety miles away, to savor his dishes of broiled lamb and genuine moussaka. Visiting Greek officials have asked him for his recipes. In the last two years, four national restaurant magazines have run feature articles about the Pride of Athens, which the famed *Gourmet Guide to America* rates with four stars.

By creating a dominant impression and adding specific details about why the restaurant is special, the description becomes lively and effective.

POINT TO REMEMBER

The dominant impression is the controlling idea of a description paragraph.

EXAM SKILLS

Many examination questions call for writing one or more description paragraphs. As with any exam, read the question carefully and make sure that your paragraph directly responds to it.

From American History

What Was the Underground Railroad?

general description

The Underground Railroad was a system of safe houses and escape routes used by abolitionists to help slaves flee the South before the Civil War.

details	*Because their actions were illegal, the abolition-ists had to operate in secret. They used railroad terms as a code. The people who led the escaping slaves from point to point were called "conductors." Hiding places, usually barns or attics and cel-lars in private homes, were called "stops" or "sta-tions." Some people built secret rooms to hide slaves in case their homes were searched. The work was dangerous. Slaves risked being tortured or killed.*
general description	*Whites caught helping escaping slaves faced jail. Often their homes were burned in reprisal. The Underground Railroad was loosely organized and did not keep records, but historians believe that it helped thousands of slaves flee North to free states.*

The paragraph opens with a general description of the Underground Rail-road and adds details explaining its name and how it operated. The stu-dent closes the paragraph by noting the lack of documents and historians' estimates.

Like an encyclopedia article, the student's response offers a brief but thorough description of the topic.

EXERCISE 1   Recognizing Dominant Impressions and Supporting Details

Read the following descriptive paragraph, identify the dominant impression and controlling idea, and list the supporting details. Circle key words that express the writer's point of view and make an impression on readers.

As soon as you enter Weldon Machine Tool, you are overwhelmed by the noise. Stamping presses thunder so loudly that the aluminum walls of the building shud-der. At the end of the conveyor line, metal parts are fired out like machine gun bullets into huge plastic bins that wobble from the vibration. Injection molding ma-chines spit out gaskets like a firehose. All around, workers in yellow helmets and headphones yell at each other and make wild gestures. Runners dash from machine to machine, wheeling out full barrels of hot parts and scrambling to replace them with empty ones. Trolleys, old golf carts, even a kid's red wagon have been pressed into service. Exhausted by mandatory overtime, workers gulp sodas to keep going. Hot coffee takes too long to drink. Lunch breaks are nonexistent. People munch chips and peanuts while racing from machine to machine. The owner runs up and down the line shouting, "Faster! Faster!" Looking up at him, workers pump the air with their fists. Everyone is energized. If the production goal is met on time, GM will keep the plant open and a hundred people will keep their jobs.

Dominant impression

_____

_____

Supporting details

1. _____

2. _____

3. _____

4. _____

Key words

1. _____   6. _____

2. _____   7. _____

3. _____   9. _____

4. _____   9. _____

5. _____   10. _____

EXERCISE 2   Creating Dominant Impressions

Create a dominant impression for each subject.

1. **A local shopping mall**

_____

2. **The coach of a college or professional sports team**

_____

3. **A local news anchor**

_____

Chapter 5   Developing Paragraphs Using Description   75

4. Your favorite childhood television show

_____

5. The best or worst car you have had

_____

EXERCISE 3   Supporting Dominant Impressions

Select a topic from Exercise 2, and list examples of details that would support the dominant impression.

Dominant impression

_____

_____

Supporting details

1. _____

2. _____

3. _____

4. _____

Improving Dominant Impressions and Supporting Details

Dominant impressions are developed by details. To be effective, these details have to be precisely stated. Vague and abstract words and phrases lack impact and fail to give readers strong impressions of your topic. In writing descriptive paragraphs, avoid using general words such as "great," "terrible," or "wonderful." Select words that are concrete and specific.

General Description

My mother's optimism is boundless and inspiring. Although she faced many terrible things in her life, my mother managed to always stay positive. She had to overcome many obstacles to finish her education. She worked hard, but just when things were going well, we faced both a family and economic crisis. But my mother managed to create a whole new career that allows her to balance her growing demands for child care and desire to succeed in her career.

Improved

My mother's optimism is boundless and inspiring. After the divorce, my mother, a high school dropout, was left with three children and no income. She waited tables fifty hours a week, went to night school to get her GED, and later earned an associate degree in data processing. She was hired by an insurance firm and received four promotions in two years. We had just moved into a nice condo when she was laid off and my younger brother was diagnosed with autism. Refusing offers to move in with relatives, my mother started her own online consulting business, which allows her to pursue a growing career at home, where she can look after my brother.

EXERCISE 4 Revising Dominant Impressions and Supporting Details

Revise the following descriptions by inventing details and adding more precise and effective word choices (see pages 338–345 about word choice and connotations).

1. Bill's car is terrible to drive. The tires are in bad shape. The steering is not good, especially on icy roads. The heater does not work. The seats are old. The radio is not good. The engine makes terrible noises. The muffler is bad, and you have to keep a window open to get air even in winter.

2. The new dorms are perfect. There is plenty of space for students to store things. The desks are very modern. They are perfect for computers, monitors, and printers. The view from the windows is very nice. In fact, these dorm rooms remind many visitors of a resort hotel.

3. Last night's Music Awards were awful. The show took too long. The performers were not at their best. The presenters seemed confused. The winners gave speeches that were too long and hard to understand. There were many commercials. Some of the best groups did not even make an appearance.

4. The new women's basketball coach is great. She looks like she can take the team all the way to the state finals this season. She is an inspiring leader. She keeps the players positive by her example. Her unique training program builds on her players' strengths. She has taught players how to respond to bad situations.

5. The bridesmaids' dresses my sister chose for her wedding were awful. They had the worst colors you could imagine. They looked terrible. They looked like something in a bad movie. Plus they were very uncomfortable. The skirts were so badly designed you had trouble sitting down. Just the expressions on their faces in the video shows how much the bridesmaids hated what my sister made them wear.

Writing at Work: Description

Business and technical documents, like this announcement, use objective description to inform readers.

AS YOU READ

Notice the importance of the document's format in creating a clear, easy-to-read message.

Majeski Electric

260 East Highland Avenue
Milwaukee, Wisconsin 53202
(414) 555-2727
www.majeskielectric.com

PROPERTY WANTED

Majeski Electric, a manufacturer of industrial and commercial electronic monitoring devices, is seeking to purchase or lease warehouse space in northern New Jersey. The ideal facility will meet or exceed the following specifications:

- Located within five miles of Newark International Airport with easy access to Garden State Parkway.
- Contains 25,000 square feet of clean, climate-controlled warehouse space with 2,500 square feet of office space suitable for inside sales and product display.
- Provides secure enclosed parking for ten cars and four semi trailers.
- Security cameras and space for expansion highly desirable.

Interested parties should contact Joe Lee Park at (414) 555-2727, Ext. 234, or at park.joelee@majeski.com.

Student Paragraphs

Description of a Person

Usually the class clown is some hyperactive kid who might be bright and witty but not focused enough to pay attention to lessons or disciplined enough to study hard. Ben Mandelstein was different. He was half Einstein, half Seinfeld. He brought every class to life. In French he corrected the teacher's pronunciation, and when she reprimanded him, he would pout like Jean Paul Belmondo, puff an imaginary cigarette, and talk back to her in Parisian slang that reduced her to tears. He buzzed through geometry tests in ten minutes, then spent the rest of the hour making paper airplanes. While we struggled to finish the test before class ended, he sailed off a dozen paper planes that swooped over our heads and crashed into the trash can. The day we started reading *Death of a Salesman* in English, he came to class in one of his father's old suits bearing a suitcase, which he parked by his desk and began an Oscar-worthy imitation of an exhausted Willy Loman.

Description of a Place

Café Norde, located below a florist shop on Brady Street, has been an eastside venue of the offbeat, the angry, and the artistic since its beatnik days of the late 1950s. The beatniks are long gone, as are the hippies and Gen Xers who followed them. But the coffeehouse still carries that air of left-wing defiance. Protest posters are taped haphazardly on the scarred wooden walls along with poems and concert flyers. The coffee is strong, the air thick with illegal cigarette smoke. The stone floor is strewn with trash. Bearded college students bend over chipped wooden tables to shout politics over the blare of reggae folk music. As the haven of the young and the hip, Café Norde, in many ways, has not changed in fifty years.

Description of a Concept

Just-in-time production, popularized by the Japanese, is now used by many companies to lower warehousing costs. Years ago, factories maintained huge warehouses full of raw materials waiting to be processed and more warehouses full of finished products waiting to be shipped. With just-in-time production, raw materials are delivered as needed to the plant, and finished products are shipped out as soon as they leave the assembly line. The system is highly efficient and saves money. However, it is very dependent on reliable transportation. Any delay in shipping at either end can shut down the whole operation. Still, many businesses believe that the overall savings can make up for any temporary interruptions.

PUTTING PARAGRAPHS TOGETHER

Pompeii

Most cities evolve over the centuries, with old buildings being torn down to make way for the new, so their history is lost. Ironically, the Roman city of Pompeii was both destroyed and preserved by one of the deadliest natural disasters in history. In 79 CE Mount Vesuvius erupted, spewing hot ash and cinders onto the thriving Roman city of 20,000. The torrent of hot wet ashes buried the city, smothering many in their homes. Others died from breathing poisonous fumes and collapsed in the streets, their bodies encased in ash. Soon only the tallest columns stood above sixty feet of ash covering the town.

introduction

topic sentence

supporting details

1. How does this paragraph introduce readers to the topic?
2. How does the student describe the disaster?

Survivors returned to the city to dig for valuables and personal possessions, but soon these efforts were abandoned. Later eruptions toppled those ruins protruding from the surface, and all traces of the city vanished. Over the centuries, local peasants dug tunnels to locate items of value, but few outsiders remembered the city at all. In 1500, workers discovered the lost city's amphitheater and forum. Later excavations unearthed artifacts that were placed in museums. Systematic archaeological digs began in the late 1800s and continued for over a hundred years. Slowly, the city that was destroyed emerged nearly intact from its protective cover of hardened ash.

description of city's loss and rediscovery

topic sentence

1. How does this paragraph build on the first one?
2. What details does the student include to describe how the city vanished and was later rediscovered?
3. The student places the topic sentence last. Is this effective? Why or why not?

Today, Pompeii is a great outdoor museum that transports visitors to first-century Rome. Tourists can walk the streets that were hidden from view for over a thousand years, providing remarkable glimpses into the daily life of Romans. They can visit the temples, the homes of the wealthy, the public

topic sentence

descriptive details

lavatories, the sporting arenas, and the brothels.
Guides point out that just before the eruption, an
election was being held. Many of the ancient walls
still bear campaign slogans. Artifacts such as eating
utensils, coins, earrings, and statues are on display
in a nearby museum. However, tourists are easily reminded of the tragedy that preserved this city. Among
the most memorable exhibits are the plaster casts
taken of the ash-coated bodies of men, women, and
children unearthed 2,000 years after their death. The
hot wet ash coated them as they died, preserving forever their last agonized expressions. Few visitors
will forget the faces of those who died with their
mouths open, evidently crying for help as the burning
ash enveloped them.

1. How does this paragraph follow the previous ones?
2. How do the details support the topic sentence?
3. What impact does the last line have?

Steps to Writing a Descriptive Paragraph

1. **Study your subject and apply critical thinking by asking key questions:**

   Why did I choose this subject?

   What does it mean to me?

   What is important about it?

   What do I want other people to know about it?

2. **List as many details as you can, keeping your main idea in mind.**

3. **Review your list of details, highlighting the most important ones, especially those that create a dominant impression.**

4. **State a controlling idea or topic sentence for your paragraph.**

5. **Write a first draft of your paragraph.**

6. **Read your paragraph aloud and consider these questions:**

   Is my subject clearly described?

   Do I provide enough details?

   Are there minor or irrelevant ideas that can be deleted?

Do I use clear, concrete words that create an accurate picture of my subject?

Do I create a clear dominant impression?

Does my paragraph tell readers what I want them to know about my topic?

Selecting Topics

Consider the following topics for writing descriptive paragraphs:

People
- your favorite relative
- a celebrity you consider a role model
- your supervisors or managers
- fans at sports events or concerts
- a homeless person
- the teacher, boss, or coach who helped you make an important decision
- the person you consider your exact opposite

Places
- your ideal workplace
- a bus stop or subway station
- a place you would like to visit on vacation
- the place that symbolizes what you consider right or wrong about U.S. society or values
- a favorite store or mall
- a place that inspires you
- a place you would take a first date
- a place you want your children to see

Things
- your cell phone
- a musical instrument
- a car, house, or other object you believe represents success
- clothes you love or hate
- tattoos
- something in your home or car you want to replace
- a lost object you wish you could replace

EXERCISE 5   Planning and Writing Paragraphs

Select a topic from the previous lists or choose one of your own, and develop details and a topic sentence.

Subject:

Possible supporting details:

1. _____

2. _____

3. _____

4. _____

5. _____

Circle the most important details to create a dominant impression.

State your controlling idea, and write a topic sentence:

_____

_____

Write your first sentence: topic sentence, first detail, or introductory statement.

_____

_____

Supporting details:

1. _____

2. _____

3. _____

4. _____

5. _____

Write your last sentence: final detail, concluding statement, or topic sentence.

_____

_____

Write out your paragraph, and review it by reading it out loud.

WORKING TOGETHER

Working with a group of students, revise this description from a report to delete irrelevant or obvious details that do not support the dominant impression and controlling idea.

Riverton Project-2

Riverton Gardens is the city's most successful attempt at building a "green community." The five ten-story condominium towers were constructed largely of recycled materials and are 50% more energy efficient than the apartment buildings they replaced. Nearly 20% of the residents are employed within half a mile of their homes, meaning that many of them walk to work, reducing carbon emissions, wear and tear on downtown streets, and rush-hour traffic jams. The community has seen a dramatic rise in property values, caused in part by both a dramatic drop in street crime and its proximity to the lake and nearby yacht club. Visitors to Riverton Gardens are struck by the views of the lakefront to the east and city skyline to the west. In addition, Riverton Gardens uses solar panels to generate 18% of the electricity used in heating and cooling. Rock gardens with trees and shrubs have reduced the need for watering and grass cutting. Builders and designers from New York, Los Angeles, and Chicago have visited Riverton, many of them impressed by the architect's use of skylights to reduce the need for inside lighting.

_____

_____

_____

_____

_____

_____

_____

_____

_____

_____

Get Thinking and Writing

CRITICAL THINKING

In one or more paragraphs, describe the most important skill needed to succeed in your career.

WHAT HAVE YOU WRITTEN?

Read your paragraph(s) carefully. Do you clearly describe the skill's significance to your future? Do you include specific details? Are the supporting details clearly organized?

Write out the topic sentence or implied controlling idea.

_____

_____

List the details that support your topic sentence or implied controlling idea.

_____

_____

_____

- *Do the details support your controlling idea and create a dominant impression?*
- *Could you improve your description by adding more details?*
- *Are there minor facts or trivial details that could be deleted?*

Get Writing

In a paragraph, describe your reaction to this photograph. How does it differ from the image on page 69? Have societies used children's interest in teamwork, uniforms, recreation, and achievement to manipulate and indoctrinate them? Can you think of current examples?

ASSOCIATED PRESS/AP PHOTO

Children's March in Fascist Italy.

WRITING ON THE WEB

Using a search engine such as Yahoo! or Google, enter terms such as *description, writing description,* and *rhetorical mode description* to locate current sites of interest.

1. Review online articles that describe a recent event, person, or situation. Notice how the writers develop controlling ideas, create dominant impressions, use supporting details, and use word choice. Examine liberal and conservative websites to read opposing descriptions of a current controversy or personality.

2. Write an e-mail to a friend describing a recent event on campus, at work, or in your life. Revise your paragraphs to create controlling ideas, build dominant impressions, and organize supporting details.

POINTS TO REMEMBER

1. Description paragraphs present images and impressions of places, people, things, and events.

2. Effective description paragraphs create dominant impressions that state the writer's most important points.

3. Dominant impressions and controlling ideas are supported with specific details.

4. Not all description paragraphs contain a topic sentence, but they should express a clear controlling idea.

CHAPTER 6

Developing Paragraphs Using Narration

CHAPTER GOALS

- Understand the Elements of Narration
- Use Clear Transitions
- Appreciate the Use of Dialogue in Narration

ADAM GAULT/DIGITAL VISION/GETTY IMAGES

Get Writing

Have you ever used a cell phone in an emergency?

Write a paragraph about an incident where having a cell phone prevented you from becoming lost, wasting time, or missing an important appointment.

What Is Narration?

Narration tells a story or explains a chain of events. Narration can be fiction or nonfiction. Novels, short stories, fables, screenplays, and many comedy routines are narration, as are biographies, police reports, history books, and most newspaper articles. Many of the papers you write in college use narration:

English

It began snowing at ten, and the principal canceled afternoon classes so we could get home before the blizzard blocked the roads.

Economics

The Security and Exchange Commission was established in the 1930s to regulate the stock market and prevent the wild speculation that occurred in the 1920s.

Psychology

Fifteen of the twenty-six patients treated with the new medication reported fewer symptoms of depression and anxiety.

WHAT ARE YOU TRYING TO SAY?

Write a paragraph that relates one of the following events:

- moving into your first apartment or dorm room
- the surprise ending of a favorite movie or TV show
- a key play in the best or worst game you have seen recently
- an event that led you to make a decision
- an incident that changed your opinion of someone or something

_____

_____

_____

_____

_____

_____

_____

_____

_____

WHAT HAVE YOU WRITTEN?

Get Writing

Read your paragraph carefully. Does your narrative highlight the most important events, or is it cluttered with minor details? Is your paragraph clearly and logically organized?

Writing Narration: Making a Point

Effective narratives have a clear purpose. They not only state what happened but also explain why the events are important. Narrative paragraphs do not always have a topic sentence, but they should have a controlling idea and dramatize a clearly focused point.

Narrative Lacking Focus

It was December 26, 2008. It was cold and snowy. The streets were icy, and there were not many places to park with all the snow banks. It was the day I had to help my grandmother move out of her house on 28th and National. The house was being sold on the first of the year, and she was moving into a nursing home. Walking into the house was sad. It was empty. All her belongings were in boxes heading to storage. She had two bags. Her whole life was in those bags. I could see how sad she looked. I picked up her bags, and I slowly helped her down the sidewalk to my uncle's SUV. I borrowed his car because my Neon was too small for everything. I drove her away from National Avenue for the last time. She looked so sad. I hit the expressway and headed west to the nursing home. This was the hardest thing I have ever done. I could not wait for this day to be over. I just did not know what to say to her. She was so sad but never spoke.

The paragraph explains an important event in the life of the student, but its impact is weakened because it is cluttered with unimportant details such as the address, the weather, the car, and directions to the nursing home. Deleting these minor details and stressing the significance of this event can create a more moving and interesting narrative:

I was home for Christmas vacation, so the task of moving my grandmother into a nursing home fell to me. She was no longer able to maintain the house she had lived in for fifty-six years. She was leaving the small house she first entered as a young bride, the house where she raised children and visited with grandchildren. With my grandfather dead and her vision failing, she sadly accepted the fact that she had to move. I knew this was coming. We all did. But as I walked into her house that last day, the blank emptiness of the rooms hit me like a hammer. I was unprepared to see all the pictures, books, china, and souvenirs I had known since childhood packed into boxes for storage. She had only two bags and a photo album she was unable to see. I helped her to the car, and we left her home for the last time. I expected that she might want one last look, but she stared straight ahead into the winter sun, her face wet with tears.

TIPS FOR MAKING POINTS

1. **Guide your writing by keeping in mind the most important thing you want your reader to know.**
2. **Delete minor details that do not support your main point.**
3. **Focus on conflict or contrast to create tension or drama.**
4. **Organize details to create strong impressions.**
5. **Use concrete words rather than general or abstract terms to provide dramatic but accurate depictions of events.**

Abstract
The new student service lounge areas have become popular places for commuter students to spend time on campus between classes.

Concrete
The new coffee bar, salad bar, and Internet café have become popular places for commuter students to meet, relax, nap, and study between classes.

6. **Avoid shifting point of view (from "I" to "you" or "they") unless there is a clear change in focus.**

Awkward Shift
Whether **I** drive or take the bus, it takes **you** almost an hour to get to school.

Improved
Whether **I** drive or take the bus, it takes **me** almost an hour to get to school.
or
Whether **you** drive or take the bus, it takes **you** almost an hour to get to school.

Acceptable Change in Point of View
When **I** worked in the mail room last year, **I** never had to deal with problems **you** face every day.

7. **Use tense shifts to show logical changes between past and ongoing or current events.**

I **drove** a cab in Manhattan, which **takes** a lot of patience.
Sandy **sings** the songs she **wrote** when she worked at MGM.
The physics lab **is** in Carroll Hall, **constructed** in 1910.

EXERCISE 1   Making a Point

Select one of the following subjects, narrow the topic, and establish a controlling idea.

- an argument or scuffle you witnessed
- the most dramatic event that happened in high school or at your job
- the way someone delivered bad news
- an accident or medical emergency
- an event that changed U.S. society
- a turning point in your life or the life of a friend

Narrowed topic: _____

Point or controlling idea: _____

Now develop a narrative paragraph that uses details to support the controlling idea.

After completing your paragraph, review your subject and your main point. Does your paragraph tell readers what you want them to know? Should minor details be deleted and important details emphasized?

EXAM SKILLS

Many examination questions call for writing one or more narrative paragraphs. As with any exam, read the question carefully and make sure that your paragraph directly responds to it. In writing a narrative, remember that your goal is not to tell everything that happened or every detail you can remember but to concentrate on an important point. Your narrative should have a clearly stated goal and topic sentences to guide the events you select.

From American Institutions

What caused the rise and eventual collapse of the Know-Nothing Movement?

introduction and summary of events

details

controlling idea

"Know-Nothing" is an unofficial term for a number of anti-immigrant secret societies that formed in the 1840s on the East Coast. Many native-born Americans feared and resented the influx of immigrants, especially Catholics, whom they saw as a threat to their values. Their nickname came from the fact that when members were questioned about their groups or activities, they claimed to "know nothing." The Know-Nothing organizations grew rapidly but were soon eclipsed by the Mexican War in 1845. The various groups regained influence when the war ended. They argued that people should vote only for people born in the United States and that immigrants should have to reside in America for 25 years before becoming citizens. The major Know-Nothing groups split over the issue of slavery, and the movement died out by the time of the Civil War. The Know-Nothing movement was one of many anti-immigrant movements that sought to restrict the rights of people they perceived as threats to American social order. The Know-Nothings targeted Irish Catholics. Later groups would attack Asian, Jewish, and Hispanic immigrants.

Writing Narration: Using Transitions

A narrative paragraph relates events over a period of time. To prevent readers from becoming confused and to help them follow the actions, it is important to signal shifts in time with transitional words and phrases:

> **Two nights ago** the fire alarm went off in my building. This is the third time this has happened this year. **Last month** the alarm went off at two in the morning. I had a midterm exam **the following day** and ended up standing in the parking lot **until almost five a.m.** while the fire department searched for the cause of the alarm. **Yesterday** I ran into the manager and asked her if something could be done to fix the problem. She agreed that false alarms were a common complaint. The system that the owner installed **two years ago** is very sensitive and is sometimes set off by smoke from a cigarette or even heat from a candle. She agreed false alarms were a headache but reminded me of the apartment fire in Nashville last winter that killed sixteen people while they slept. **After hearing that,** I agreed that the occasional false alarm is a small price to pay for safety.

KEY TRANSITIONS

before	now	first
after	later	finally
after a while	immediately	suddenly
next	the following day	hours, days, weeks later
following	in the meantime	that morning, afternoon
while	then	

EXERCISE 2   Identifying Transitions

Underline transitional statements in the following student paragraph.

The American oil industry began when Colonel Drake struck oil in Pennsylvania in 1858. Within a few decades, companies like Standard Oil became some of the richest and most powerful corporations in the country. John D. Rockefeller, who owned Standard Oil, became the first American billionaire. Just as it was reaching its peak, the oil industry faced a threat to its existence. At that time oil was mostly used to make kerosene or lamp oil. In 1876 Edison invented the light bulb. By the turn of the century, electric lights had replaced oil lamps in the cities and larger towns. Oil companies continued to sell kerosene to farmers and people in small towns without electric power. Standard Oil exported lamp oil to China, but even in Asia electricity was beginning to lessen the demand for this product. It seemed only a matter of time before the powerful oil industry would shrink into insignificance. But just as the demand for kerosene was dropping, the demand for gasoline to power the rapidly growing number of cars rose. Oil companies once threw away gasoline as a useless by-product. Now the need for gasoline would keep them in business throughout the twentieth century.

Writing Narration: Using Dialogue

If you are explaining an event that involves people talking, using direct quotations can advance the story better than an indirect summary of a conversation.

Indirect Summary

    I was taking a nap on the patio when I heard Mrs. Gomez next door screaming for help. I woke up and jumped over the small hedge between our yards. I asked her what the problem was, and she said her son had fallen into their pool. Timmy was lying on the ground. His face was puffy and bluish white. I told her to call 911 and get a blanket. I rubbed his wrists and ankles, trying to remember what I had learned in first-aid class. Mrs. Gomez asked me if he was breathing. I told her I was not sure. I turned him over, and water came out of his mouth. I laid him out straight and started doing mouth to mouth. His mother kept asking me if he was breathing. I motioned with my hand, not wanting to stop. He coughed up more water and moved his legs. Mrs. Gomez began crying. As the paramedics arrived, Timmy pulled away and coughed up more water. A paramedic told us he was breathing, but they needed to take him to the hospital to be examined by doctors. Mrs. Gomez sank to her knees and kept thanking God.

Narrative with Direct Quotations

    I was taking a nap on the patio when I heard Mrs. Gomez next door scream, "Help me! Help!"

    I jumped over the small hedge between our yards. "What's wrong?" I asked.

    "Timmy fell in the pool. I found him floating in the pool," she said, sitting next to Timmy, who was lying on the ground. His face was puffy and bluish white.

    "Call 911 and get a blanket!" I shouted to her. I rubbed his wrists and ankles, trying to remember what I had learned in first-aid class.

    "Is he breathing?" Mrs. Gomez asked.

    "I don't know. I'm not sure," I told her. I turned him over, and water came out of his mouth. I laid him out straight and started doing mouth to mouth.

    "Is he breathing? Is Timmy breathing? Can he breathe?" Mrs. Gomez kept asking.

    Not wanting to stop mouth to mouth, I motioned with my hand. He coughed up more water and moved his legs. Mrs. Gomez began crying.

As the paramedics arrived, Timmy pulled away and coughed up more water. A paramedic said, "He's breathing on his own, but we need to get him to the hospital to be checked out. Just to make sure. But he looks good right now."

Mrs. Gomez sank to her knees, moaning, "Thank God, thank God, thank God."

- Dialogue brings people to life by having them speak directly. Their tone, attitude, and lifestyle can be demonstrated by the words they choose.
- Because dialogue is stated in short paragraphs, it is faster and easier to read than a long block of text. In addition, direct quotations can reduce the need for statements like "he said" or "she told me."

POINT TO REMEMBER

In writing dialogue, start a new paragraph each time a new person speaks. Because dialogue may include many short paragraphs, including one-word responses, your essay may appear to be longer than the assigned length. Use a computer word count. A three-page essay with dialogue is often no longer than a page and a half of description.

EXERCISE 3   Writing Narration Using Dialogue

Write a narrative paragraph that uses dialogue—direct quotations—to relate an event in which two people have an argument, someone tells friends a funny story, or a boss gives employees some bad news.

Writing at Work: Narration

Business and technical documents, like this incident report, use narration to report events.

AS YOU READ

Notice the importance of the document's format in creating a clear, easily read message.

Keller, Loman, and Maxon

Rockefeller Center
1230 Avenue of the Americas
New York, New York 10020

SECURITY ALERT

NOTICE TO ALL MANAGERS:

On May 5, 2009, at approximately 3:35 p.m. a twenty-seven-year-old former employee entered the lobby and left a package addressed to senior management at the front desk. Five minutes later a telephone call to the receptionist stated that the package contained a bomb. The receptionist, following corporate and building safety procedures, called 911, alerted the firm's security chief, and contacted Rockefeller Center security.

The office and entire 27th floor were fully evacuated by 3:45. The NYPD bomb squad removed the package, which contained two toy hand grenades. Following a thorough security sweep, personnel were allowed to return to the offices at 5:25 p.m.

At no time were any personnel in danger. All safety procedures were followed. The former employee has been questioned by authorities and is currently detained for a psychiatric evaluation.

Contrary to rumors, the individual in question resigned last October and was not terminated for failing to meet a sales quota. No weapons or explosives were found in his apartment, and NYPD reports he had no known ties to organized crime or terrorist organizations. According to his parents, the individual in question has been treated for psychiatric disorders in the past.

Please remind personnel that Keller, Loman, and Maxon strives to provide its employees with a safe, secure work environment. We fully believe this incident to be an isolated one. There should be no cause for alarm, but employees should be reminded to review emergency procedures in their staff manuals.

Leslie McMahon
Director of Security and Emergency Operations

Student Paragraphs

Personal Narrative

Growing up in a Duluth suburb, I was usually seen as being Hispanic. I joined a Latino organization, took Spanish, and listened to a lot of Mexican music. Last December, however, my first visit to Mexico was an awakening. I went to visit my grandfather. Despite three years of high school Spanish, I found it almost impossible to hold a conversation. I was unprepared for the poverty of my grandfather's mountain village. The food was like nothing I ate in a Mexican restaurant in America. The villagers celebrated Christmas without carols, trees, or a Santa. I never felt so American in my life. My grandfather evidently felt the same way because he jokingly introduced me to his friends, telling them my name was George Bush.

Narrative in a History Paper

The Tet Offensive in early 1968 was the turning point in the Vietnam War. Although college students had been protesting against the draft and the war for several years, most Americans believed the United States was making progress in the fight against the Vietcong. Then during the Tet New Year's holiday, Communist forces stormed into Saigon and nearly overran the U.S. embassy. Battles erupted throughout South Vietnam. Americans saw the fierce house-to-house fighting on TV and sensed that the war could not be won. Public opinion shifted, and many famous Americans began to call for an end to the war. Facing pressure from the demonstrators and critics in his own party, President Johnson announced he would not run for re-election. Ironically, the Tet Offensive was a major defeat for the Communists, who failed to create a popular uprising and lost so many men and supplies that it took them years to recover.

Narrative in an Earth Science Research Paper

In the 1770s Joseph Priestly conducted a series of experiments using bell jars. He noticed that a candle placed under a glass jar soon went out. He placed a mouse under a glass jar and watched as the mouse stopped moving and eventually died. Clearly, some substance necessary for the flame to burn and the mouse to live was being absorbed or lost. He also noticed that if he placed a green plant under the jar, the candle could be relit. A mouse placed under the jar with a green plant lived longer. Whatever substance the flame and mouse absorbed was being refreshed by the plant. Without fully realizing it, Priestly had discovered oxygen and carbon dioxide and the basic nature of the Earth's atmosphere.

PUTTING PARAGRAPHS TOGETHER

A Vital Lesson

introduction

> Most of us are luckier than we know. Occasionally, however, we run into a reminder. Two summers ago I got a job at Victor's. I was not twenty-one and could not

details about job

> get a bartender's license and earn good tips. The only job I could do was wash dishes. It was hot, dirty, and depressing work. But it was the only job I could find near my house. All the jobs I wanted were too far to take the bus. It looked like it was going to be long, boring, and lonely summer. My girlfriend was taking summer courses in New York. My car was sitting in my uncle's garage with a cracked block and more oil leaks than I could count. Leaving work each night with wet clothes and sore hands,I went home to watch TV in my empty apartment, feeling very sorry for myself. Every-

details about writer's mood

> one else I knew seemed to be having a great time hitting the beach, cruising in cars, and partying. I felt so down sometimes I wished I was dead.

1. What is the controlling idea of this paragraph?
2. How does the student organize the details?
3. How effective is the last sentence? Is it a good place to make a break in the narrative? Why or why not?

incident at bank

> One Friday afternoon I went to the bank to cash my measly paycheck. I was very depressed. I was angry. My whole summer was going to be a waste. I kept looking at my check. After I paid my bills, I would have thirty-six dollars to last two weeks. I'd have to use my credit card again to buy groceries, getting deeper in debt when I should have been saving for college. I was getting madder and madder; then I heard a crash and a teller say, "Someone should help him."

1. How does this paragraph advance the narrative?
2. How does it build on the first paragraph?

> I turned and saw a person on crutches caught in the revolving door. I was closest to the door, so I walked over and helped him. I was about to turn back, when I noticed it was Erik Thoma from high school. He had been our quarterback and class president. He was an honor student who dated the head cheerleader and got a full scholarship to Yale. He had rich parents and drove a Boxster. In short, he was the kind of guy I loved to hate. Fumbling on his crutches, he said,

"Thank you." Then looking up, his eyes met mine, and
he nodded feebly, saying, "Hi, sorry but I . . .
I don't do well with names these days." The weakness
of his voice shocked me. He sounded like an old man.

1. How does this paragraph follow the preceding one?
2. What is the paragraph's controlling idea? Does the paragraph have a topic sentence? Is one needed? Why or why not?
3. What details does the student highlight? How do they differ from those in the preceding paragraphs?

After we cashed our checks, Erik offered to drive
me home. "I'm just getting back to driving," he said
as he painfully worked his way behind the wheel of his
car. As he drove, he filled me in on what had happened. It seemed almost as if he was getting rid of
something painful by talking. "It was just before
Christmas. Sandy and I were making a snowman in the
park. This kid on a snowmobile lost control on some
ice, hit a snow bank, and flipped over right on top
of us. I was in intensive care for a week and had two
operations. I lost a kidney, and they had to put in a
plastic hip joint. But I'm lucky. Sandy's still in a
coma. We were going to get married in June. But she
doesn't even recognize me now."

1. How does this paragraph advance the narrative?
2. What role do direct quotations play in the paragraph?
3. What is the impact of the last line? Is it a good place to end the paragraph? Why or why not?

When I got out of the car, my knees were shaking.
I was almost ready to cry, not only because of Erik
but because of my childish selfishness. I went to my
apartment and sent my girlfriend a long e-mail. I told
her what had happened to Erik and Sandy and asked her
to ignore all the whiny letters I had sent her over
the weeks. We were apart. I had an unpleasant summer
job. My car was trashed. However, all these problems
were temporary and could be overcome by gifts that
money can never buy—a sound mind and healthy body.

1. How effective is this final paragraph? Does it bring the narrative to a logical close?
2. How does the last line relate to the opening line?
3. How important are final paragraphs in a narrative? How can writers highlight or demonstrate an idea or detail they want readers to remember?

Steps to Writing a Narrative Paragraph

1. **Study your topic and use critical thinking by asking key questions:**

   Why did I choose this event to write about?
   What did it mean to me?
   Why do I remember it?
   What is significant about it?
   What do I want other people to know about it?
   What is my most important point?

2. **List your point or message as a topic sentence to guide your writing (the topic sentence does not have to appear in the finished paragraph).**

3. **List supporting details that establish your point.**

4. **Review your list, deleting minor details and highlighting significant ones.**

5. **If people speak in your narrative, consider using dialogue rather than indirect summaries of conversations.** Remember to use paragraph breaks to indicate a shift in speakers (see pages 48–49).

6. **Write a first draft of your paragraph.**

7. **Read your paragraph aloud, and consider these questions:**

   Does my paragraph make a clear point?
   Does it tell readers what I want them to know?
   Do I provide sufficient details?
   Are there unimportant details that could be deleted?
   Do I use concrete words, especially verbs, to create action?
   Do I avoid illogical shifts in point of view or tense?
   Do I provide clear transitions to advance the narrative and explain the passage of time?

Selecting Topics

Consider these topics for writing narrative paragraphs:

- renting your first apartment or buying your first home
- the most memorable event that happened when you were a child
- an event that changed the life of a close friend or co-worker
- the best or worst party you've attended

- how someone you know overcame a problem
- the story of how a false rumor got started
- being lost
- enduring a blizzard, hurricane, or some other natural disaster
- an incident that placed you in danger
- an event that led you to end a relationship, quit a job, or return to school
- a story your parents or grandparents told you about their childhood
- how you responded on September 11, 2001
- the most amazing play you saw an athlete or team make recently
- the history of your neighborhood, school, or employer
- preparing for an unpleasant task
- being caught doing something you regretted
- a telephone call that changed your life
- the moment you felt you became an adult
- a brief history of a local scandal or sensational crime
- a news story that affected you personally

EXERCISE 4   Planning and Writing Paragraphs

Select a topic from the previous list or choose one of your own, and develop details and a topic sentence that states the point of your narrative.

Topic _____

Possible supporting details:

1. _____

2. _____

3. _____

4. _____

5. _____

Circle the most important details that explain the event.

State the point of your narrative, and write a topic sentence:

_____

_____

Organize your supporting details chronologically, using transitional statements to advance the narrative.

First sentence: topic sentence, first detail, or introductory statement

_____

_____

Supporting Details:

1. _____

2. _____

3. _____

4. _____

5. _____

Last sentence: final detail, concluding statement, or topic sentence

_____

_____

Write out your paragraph, and review it by reading it out loud.

WORKING TOGETHER

Working with a group of students, revise this accident report to delete irrelevant details, illogical shifts in tense and person, and awkward transitions. Edit the paper for fragments (see Chapter 23), run-ons and comma splices (see Chapter 25), and misspelled words (see Chapter 35).

March 19, 2009
Sidney Carton

RE: Accident March 19, 2009 Cherry Hill, NJ SUV #12

Dear Sidney:

I was told to send you an e-mail as soon as I could. This morning at 7:55 I had an accident on Route 70 and Breckinridge Road in Cherry Hill. I had picked up some flyers at the Kinkos on Saukville Road and stopped at the post office before heading back to Philadelphia to meet Maynard Sloate about a loan package. I am driving just under the speed limit on Route 70 (45 m.p.h.) when a white florist van pulled out of gas station and hits my rite rear fender. I skid sideways and struck a light poll that smashed in the grille and broke a headlight. No one was hurt and the police gave the driver of the florist truck a citation for reckeless driving. Witnesses on the scene backing up my version of the event. I had the SUV towed to Garden State Auto Repair at 1818 Blackhorse Pike. I contact the insurance company and I e-mailed a claim. Let me know if there anything else I should do. I can drive my own car until a company vehicle is provided, I will not miss any other sales calls.

Trinity Mitchell

_____

_____

_____

_____

_____

_____

_____

_____

_____

_____

_____

_____

_____

Get Thinking and Writing

CRITICAL THINKING

Write one or more paragraphs that relate an encounter you had with a stranger. Did talking to someone you sat next to on a plane or met waiting in line teach you something about people, yourself, or the world around you? Have you ever encountered racist or sexist behavior? Did anyone challenge your sense of right and wrong? Have you ever had to ask a stranger for help or had someone ask you for a favor? Remember, you can include dialogue if you wish.

WHAT HAVE YOU WRITTEN?

Read your paragraph carefully.

Write out your topic sentence or implied controlling idea:

_____

_____

List the main supporting details in your paragraph:

_____

_____

_____

- Do these details support your controlling idea and provide evidence for your point of view?
- Could you improve your paragraph by adding more details?
- Are there minor facts or trivial details that could be deleted?
- Does your paragraph explain the significance of this encounter?

Get Writing

Have you seen people talking on a cell phone while driving? Have you ever felt unsafe when the person driving the car you were riding in picked up a phone?

Write a narrative paragraph about a driver using a cell phone. Include dialogue if you wish.

JIM CRAIGMYLE/CORBIS

WRITING ON THE WEB

Using a search engine such as Yahoo! or Google, enter terms such as *narration, writing narration, narrative techniques,* and *first-person narratives* to locate current sites of interest.

1. Review news articles in online versions of magazines such as *Time* and *Newsweek,* and notice how writers explain events. How do they organize paragraphs, use dialogue, and signal transitions?

2. Write an e-mail to a friend describing something you saw or experienced. Revise your paragraphs to delete minor details and highlight important points.

POINTS TO REMEMBER

1. **Narration paragraphs should make a clear point, not simply summarize events.**

2. **Narratives can be written in first person ("I"), second person ("you"), or third person ("they"). Avoid illogical shifts.**
   I climbed to the top of the hill, where you *can see for miles.*

   Correct
   I climbed to the top of the hill, where I could see for miles.

3. **Narration can be stated in past or present tense. Avoid illogical shifts.**
   I drove to the library, where I study all night.

   Correct
   I drove to the library, where I studied all night.

4. **Paragraphs should have clear transition statements to advance the narrative, indicate the passage of time, and prevent confusion.**

5. **Dialogue—direct quotations—can be more effective than summaries of conversations. Remember to use quotation marks and to begin a new paragraph to indicate a shift in speakers.**

CHAPTER 7

Developing Paragraphs Using Example

TONY ARRUZA/CORBIS

CHAPTER GOALS

■ Understand How Writers Use Examples

■ Distinguish Between Descriptions of One Subject and Examples Representing a General Type

■ Appreciate the Different Types of Examples

Get Writing

What does this photograph represent? Is it an example of creative advertising or a growing social problem?

Write a paragraph commenting on the way companies should and should not advertise alcoholic beverages. Support your views with clear examples.

What Is an Example?

Examples illustrate ideas, issues, problems, situations, theories, or behaviors. Examples explain something or provide evidence to support a point of view. You can explain that a felony is "a serious crime" by giving readers examples—*murder, robbery, sexual assault.* To argue that your landlord is not taking care of your apartment building, you can list examples of uncut grass, burnt-out lights, broken pipes, missing locks, and peeling paint. **Examples are specific items that represent something greater:**

Colleges are cutting support to sports that generate little revenue—**track and field, swimming, boxing,** and **fencing.**

New York, Minneapolis, Milwaukee, and **San Francisco** are examples of cities that have seen a dramatic drop in violent crime.

Over-the-counter medications such as **cold pills, cough syrup,** and **aspirin** are often abused.

POINT TO REMEMBER

Descriptions provide details about one subject. Examples provide details about a type.

Get Writing

WHAT ARE YOU TRYING TO SAY?

Write a paragraph that uses one or more examples to explain an idea or support a point of view about one of the following topics:

- self-destructive behavior
- people who overcome obstacles
- television shows that you consider inappropriate for children
- fad diets
- products that have made your life easier
- potential problems that you will face this semester

_____

_____

_____

_____

_____

_____

_____

_____

WHAT HAVE YOU WRITTEN?

Read your paragraph carefully. Underline the topic sentence. Does it clearly describe your subject? Do the examples illustrate or support your topic sentence? Will readers understand the examples you include? Can you think of better ones?

Writing Example Paragraphs

Example paragraphs provide specific illustrations for ideas or concepts that readers might find abstract or confusing:

> In order to get a loan, you must have enough **collateral** the bank can take in case of nonpayment. Ideally, **collateral** consists of items with fixed values that can be easily seized and used to pay for a loan in case of default. These include *savings accounts, stocks, bonds,* and *mutual funds.* Other forms of **collateral,** such as *cars, artwork, stamps, coins,* and *jewelry,* are less desirable because their value is harder to determine and they take time to convert to cash.

The examples of *stocks, bonds,* and *mutual funds* illustrate what is meant by **collateral.**

Writers also use examples as evidence, giving readers specific facts or incidents to support an argument:

> **Pacific Air is violating federal security procedures.** On three occasions in March, *passengers were allowed to board flights out of San Jose without boarding passes.* In San Antonio, *Pacific Air employees allowed vendors to service aircraft without checking their credentials.* In San Francisco, *two Air Pacific charter jets were left untended for two hours with their cargo doors open.* On a flight from Dallas to Los Angeles, *an Air Pacific pilot failed to secure the cockpit door.*

The list of specific security violations supports the writer's claim that the airline violates federal regulations.

TIPS FOR USING EXAMPLES

1. **Create a strong topic sentence or state a clear controlling idea to prevent examples from being a list of random facts or narratives.**
2. **Choose examples that readers can identify and understand.**
3. **Provide more than one example to support a point of view.** A single example could be an exception and would not provide enough evidence for readers to accept your ideas.
4. **Supply additional forms of support such as statistics and facts.** Even a long list of examples does not always provide sufficient proof. Clips of a quarterback making spectacular passes does not prove he is a great player or that his team has a winning record.

Types of Examples

You can develop a paragraph using single or multiple examples.

A **single extended example** provides details about a person, place, or thing that illustrates something larger. The fact that many Americans do not have health insurance can be illustrated by one family's situation:

> **Medical crises cause 46% of personal bankruptcies in the United States.** Like most Americans, Erika Perez had health insurance through her employer, an Arizona trucking company. After losing that job, she found work selling lawn-care services on commission. Although she earned as much as a

topic sentence starting a point of view

single example

thousand dollars in a good week, she could not afford health insurance. Rushed to the hospital with excruciating back pains, Perez learned she needed emergency surgery to repair a slipped disc. Postoperative therapy and costly prescription drugs erased her savings and left her with $65,000 in medical expenses. No longer able to drive, she began telemarketing from home but rarely earned more than a few hundred dollars a week. After selling her car and borrowing thousands from her retired parents, Perez sought advice from a lawyer, who informed her that her best option was to declare bankruptcy.

TIPS FOR USING A SINGLE EXAMPLE

1. **Choose the example that best illustrates or supports your main idea.**

2. **Explain the significance of your example to prevent readers from seeing it as an isolated situation.** You can demonstrate the significance of an example by adding a fact or statistic:

   Erika Perez is just one of 2,300 Arizonians to declare bankruptcy because of a medical crisis this year.

3. **Focus on those details that directly support your point.** Delete minor items. Remember, your goal is not to tell a story but to present an example.

You can also develop a paragraph using **multiple examples:**

topic sentence stating
general idea
example 1
example 2
example 3

example 4

example 5

     Product placement, the use of motion pictures to promote products, has a long history. One of the first movies ever made, an 1896 French silent film, included boxes of soap supplied by a sales rep. In the 1930s Bell Telephone supplied movie studios with their new "French phones" free of charge. They assumed that the movie-going public would want to replace their old phones with the new models they saw used by Clark Gable and Jean Harlow. In the 1940s DeBeers promoted diamonds by providing movie studios with jewelry to be worn by leading ladies. In *The Seven Year Itch,* Marilyn Monroe is seen eating a bag of Bells potato chips, which was then beginning a national sales campaign. Car makers have supplied vehicles for television programs and movies. Product placement has proven so successful that many companies that once supplied products without cost in exchange for free publicity are now being charged hundreds of thousands of dollars for an actor to drink their soft drink, eat their cereal, or pull into one of their gas stations on film.

TIPS FOR USING MULTIPLE EXAMPLES

1. **Choose a range of examples.** A list of specific examples can simply provide a number of exceptions and not provide significant evidence. Offer examples that include facts, statistics, or expert testimony to create a broad base of support.

2. **Avoid examples that are too complicated or require too much explanation.**

3. **Choose examples that readers will recognize and understand.**

4. **Place the examples in a logical order—by time or by importance.**

5. **Make sure that your examples directly support your topic sentence or controlling idea.**

Using Hypothetical Examples

Most writers use real examples to illustrate an idea. In some cases, however, you can create a **hypothetical,** or fictional, example to explain a subject:

Make sure you report all injuries, no matter how minor, to your supervisor immediately. Do not delay. For example, you fall from a stepladder and twist your knee. It feels stiff and sore but does not seem serious. You complete your shift and punch out, without informing anyone of your accident. You take some aspirin and go to bed. You wake up in the middle of the night, your swollen knee throbbing in pain. You have someone drive you to the emergency room, where tests reveal you have torn ligaments and tendons that require surgery and weeks of rehabilitation. Because you failed to report the accident before leaving work, you cannot prove you injured your knee on the job and may be unable to claim benefits. Many serious injuries do not manifest themselves for hours or even days after an accident. Remember to report all work injuries immediately.

topic sentence
hypothetical example

TIPS FOR USING HYPOTHETICAL EXAMPLES

1. **Hypothetical examples are useful to illustrate ideas, but because they are not real, they are not effective support for an argument.**

2. **Use hypothetical examples that are simple and easy to understand.**

3. **Add facts or statistics to demonstrate the significance of hypothetical examples:**

   Last year 45 percent of disputed worker's compensation claims involved unreported on-the-job injuries.

EXERCISE 1   Identifying Examples

Read this student paragraph carefully, and answer the questions that follow it.

Laws often have unintended consequences. In Australia a requirement in the 1990s that bicyclists wear helmets to prevent head injuries proved to have a dramatic impact on the incidence of brain trauma. Teenagers considered the helmets so ugly that many stopped riding bikes altogether. Tough drunk driving laws in the United States initially led to more hit-and-run accidents as drunk drivers tried to outrace the police. A law to ban smoking in the workplace, for instance, might lead to more fires as employees sneak off to light up in storerooms and stairwells.

1. **What is the topic sentence?**

   _____

   _____

2. **How many examples are given?**

   _____

   _____

3. Are any examples hypothetical?

_____

_____

4. What facts or statistics could be added to create additional support?

_____

_____

_____

Writing Example: Using Transitions

Paragraphs containing examples need clear transitions to keep them from becoming just lists of unrelated items. Examples have to directly support the topic sentence or main idea they are illustrating:

> My new car is a lemon. One month after I bought it, **for example,** the muffler fell off.

Key Transitions

It is helpful to introduce examples and link them to your topic sentence with transitional words or phrases:

For example, . . .	For instance, . . .
Consider the case of . . .	To illustrate, . . .
To demonstrate, . . .	Another example is . . .
Recent experiences reveal . . .	A case in point is . . .
An example is . . .	Examples could include . . .
The best example is . . .	One of the worst cases is . . .

EXERCISE 2   Creating Examples to Explain an Idea

Select one of the following ideas, and write a paragraph that uses one or more real or hypothetical examples to illustrate your topic sentence.

- best ways to study for an exam
- the best sitcoms
- undesirable jobs
- people's fear of becoming old
- challenges that parents with small children face when traveling
- overrated vacation spots
- problems faced by students with jobs

After completing your paragraph, review the topic sentence and the example or examples you developed. Do the examples clearly illustrate your ideas, or do they simply tell stories or offer descriptions?

EXERCISE 3   Creating Examples to Support a Point of View

Select one of the following ideas, and write a paragraph that uses one or more factual or hypothetical examples to support your point of view.

- why students drop out of high school
- why teenagers take risks
- why older people have difficulty changing careers
- why trials should or should not be televised
- why a sports team is having a winning or losing season
- why some communities are suspicious of the police
- why a recent movie succeeded or failed with audiences

After completing your paragraph, review your topic sentence and the example or examples you developed. Do the examples support your point of view, or do they tell related stories or offer descriptions?

EXAM SKILLS

Many examination questions call for writing one or more example paragraphs. As with any exam, read the question carefully, and make sure that your paragraph directly responds to it. Create a clear topic sentence, and develop one or more examples that illustrate an idea or provide proof.

From Abnormal Psychology

Explain the disabling consequences of bipolar depression.

topic sentence giving explanation   Patients with bipolar depression experience severe mood swings from elated excitement to deep depression. Both extremes can lead to behavior that can have devastating consequences. In their "high" state, **examples** patients feel all powerful and have an elevated self-esteem that leads them to make irrational and destructive decisions. For example, they will buy expensive gifts they cannot afford, quit their jobs to become movie stars, decide to run for office, or announce they are going to the United Nations to propose a solution to terrorism. In their "low" state, patients feel de- **examples** pressed, lonely, and powerless. For example, they will withdraw from friends or family, quit work or school because they feel inadequate, and abuse drugs or alcohol. Because symptoms may develop slowly, people **conclusion** have gone bankrupt, lost careers, and ruined families before their irrational behavior was diagnosed as bipolar depression. New drugs and therapy have helped patients cope with this disabling disorder.

Writing at Work: Example

Business and technical documents, like this notice, use example to explain concepts.

AS YOU READ

Notice the importance of the document's format in creating a clear, easily read message.

Triton Academy

www.tritonacademy.org

TO ALL FACULTY:

CLARIFICATION: PERSONAL LEAVE DAYS

Current policies allow faculty members up to three "personal leave days" per academic year. Personal leave days are granted to allow faculty to attend to "compelling personal needs" and should not be abused.

Compelling personal needs include funerals and hospital visits to immediate family members; court appearances as a defendant, plaintiff, or witness; consultation with an attorney, therapist, or other professional that cannot be scheduled during after-school hours; or emergency home repairs when one's home or property cannot be left unattended.

Compelling personal needs DO NOT include weddings; appointments with travel agents, wedding planners, or realtors; picking up family, friends, or relatives at the airport; or routine home repairs.

Heidi Froman
Vice Principal

Student Paragraphs

Single, Extended Example

Freshman courses are the most demanding ones that students take. For example, in my macroeconomics course I was bombarded with new terms, theories, and concepts I was totally unprepared for. I spent two to three hours a night cramming just to get B's on the ten-question quizzes the professor gave us each week. In order to write a research paper, I had to do a lot of background work before I could select a topic. When I began looking up articles on the Internet, I discovered I had to constantly refer to my dictionary of economics terms just to figure out what the article was about.

Multiple Examples

A few years ago movie studios made money primarily on ticket sales and television rights. Today there is an increasing variety of additional markets that provide new sources of income. Video and DVD sales, for example, sometimes exceed the amount the studio makes in theaters. Cable networks such as HBO and Cinemax offer studios markets for movies that might not be suited for ABC or NBC. Websites are used to sell movie memorabilia such as T-shirts, coffee mugs, posters, and caps. Soundtracks and book versions of a film generate additional sources of cash. Ancillary sales can make cult films with a small but dedicated fan base highly profitable.

Hypothetical Examples

Anyone who has studied or worked with family members of addicts has probably run into what experts call "enabling." Although they are angry and hurt by the addict's behavior, family members often unconsciously allow it to continue. For example, the parents of a drug-addicted teenager who calls home asking for money because her purse was stolen send her money even though they suspect she will spend it on drugs. The wife of an alcoholic accepts her husband's excuse that he had to work late when it is obvious to her that he has been drinking. The children of a drug abuser make excuses to relatives why Mom or Dad is unable to attend a wedding or come to Thanksgiving dinner. Because they are afraid to confront the problem, people allow the addict to continue his or her life of abuse. They cover up for loved ones out of shame or embarrassment. Often they fear that confrontation will only lead to arguments or the addict leaving home. In order to cope with this problem, many therapists believe that treatment must involve the whole family, not just the person with a substance abuse problem.

PUTTING PARAGRAPHS TOGETHER

Working at Home

introduction

explanation

Computers and the Internet make it possible for more and more professionals to work from home offices. Accountants, editors, analysts, lawyers, and salespeople can conduct business at home, accessing corporate records online and using virtual meetings to discuss issues with colleagues in a dozen different cities.

topic sentence

Working from home has proven to have advantages for both employers and employees.

1. What is the controlling idea of this paragraph?
2. How does the student explain why the number of people working at home has increased?

example 1 topic sentence

Nearly half the claims adjusters for Great Lakes Casualty, for example, now work at home. Previously, the company had eighty adjusters working in cubicles in a Chicago office tower sending e-mail, making phone calls, and filing reports on computers. Realizing that most of this work could be done elsewhere, the company encouraged adjusters to work at home. Great Lakes Casualty has cut its need for office space, employee lounges, and electricity. Last year when a blizzard shut down the city, most of its key people could still get their jobs done without leaving home. Great Lakes Casualty also found it easier to recruit and retain employees, especially those with small children. The firm also believes that it helps the environment by cutting back on the number of employees who drive to work.

1. What is the controlling idea of this paragraph?
2. How does it connect to the first paragraph?
3. How does the example support the writer's main idea?

example 2 topic sentence

New companies are formed around people who expect to work at home. Firms that once would rent several floors of office space now rent space for just a few offices, work stations, and conference rooms. San Diego Design was able to save nearly a million dollars its first year by hiring employees with home offices. In some cases it was able to hire talented designers

in Los Angeles and San Francisco without asking them
to relocate.

> 1. What is the controlling idea of this paragraph?
> 2. How does the example support the topic sentence?
> 3. How does this paragraph build upon the preceding one?

Employees find that working at home saves them both
time and money. Vicki Bert, a claims adjuster for
Great Lakes Casualty, found that working at home saved
her an hour-and-twenty-minute commute in and out of
Chicago each day. By working at home, she also saved
sixty dollars a week in gas and parking. She used to
get up at six in order to dress and hit the expressway to make it downtown by nine. She normally took an
hour lunch, then faced a ninety-minute commute home.
Today she often gets out of bed at six, jumps behind
her computer, and completes a day's worth of filing by
noon. Other employees find that working at home lowers
day-care costs or the need for a second car.

example 3 topic sentence

> 1. What is the controlling idea of this paragraph?
> 2. How does the example support the topic sentence?
> 3. How does this paragraph support the topic sentence of the first
>   paragraph?

Not all people find working at home desirable,
however. Some managers find it difficult to coordinate
operations handled by a dozen people working different schedules in different locations. Emergency meetings are difficult to arrange. Sometimes companies
have trouble responding to customer questions and
complaints because employees are not in one location.
Employees can find working at home isolating and
lonely. Many miss the interaction and informal help
they get from co-workers in a traditional workplace.
Family members do not always respect the home office
or resent the home worker who interrupts a meal to
take a business call.

conclusion examples

> 1. What is the controlling idea of this paragraph?
> 2. How do the examples support the topic sentence?
> 3. How does this paragraph contrast with the preceding ones?

Steps to Writing an Example Paragraph

1. **Clearly establish your topic, and describe it accurately.** Examples will work only if they provide proof for a clearly stated point of view.

2. **Consider your readers when you choose examples.** Will they recognize the people, events, or situations that you provide as support?

3. **Avoid examples that are too complicated or require too much explanation.**

4. **Organize examples in a clear pattern.** You might arrange events by time or group people by their age or profession. Avoid creating a jumble of examples that readers may find confusing.

5. **If you use a single example, delete minor details and focus on those that clearly support your main point.**

6. **Write a draft of your paragraph.**

7. **Read your paragraph aloud, and ask yourself these questions:**

    Do I have a clear topic sentence that defines my subject?

    Do the examples illustrate or represent my subject?

    Will readers make the connection between my examples and the larger topic they are supposed to represent?

    Can I think of better examples?

Selecting Topics

There are two ways to develop topics for an example paragraph.

One option is to select a specific person, place, thing, or idea that you think represents something greater:

- A local political scandal provides a perfect example of a good person corrupted by power.
- The appearance of fifty e-mails in less than an hour provides examples of spam.
- A friend's loss of a job provides a perfect example of downsizing.

Another option is to select a topic or state an opinion, then think of examples that best illustrate your idea or provide evidence for your point of view:

- Describe a problem in your community and provide examples.

- Outline your definition of good day care; then illustrate it with one or more examples.
- Argue for a change in a law or policy, such as immigration, drinking age, airport security, bankruptcy, unemployment insurance, or health care, and support your opinion with examples.

EXERCISE 4 Planning and Writing Paragraphs

Establish a topic, and define it carefully. Determine what you want readers to understand about it by listing the most important points you want to dramatize.

Topic _____

Details, things readers should know:

1. _____

2. _____

3. _____

4. _____

Example or examples that represent the topic:

1. _____

2. _____

3. _____

4. _____

First sentence: topic sentence, first example, or introductory statement:

_____

_____

_____

Examples:

1. _____

2. _____

3. _____

4. _____

Last sentence: final example, concluding statement, or topic sentence:

_____

_____

WORKING TOGETHER

Working with a group of students, revise the following e-mail by adding examples to make it clearer. Invent any details you need.

Attn: South Florida Productions staff
RE: Use of company vehicles

South Florida Productions provides cars to sales and repair personnel in order to service accounts. Company vehicles are not meant for personal use except in some circumstances.

It is not permissible for employees to use company cars for nonbusiness use on holidays or vacations. Employees cannot loan company cars to others, except family members in an emergency.

To save personnel time, South Florida Productions does allow employees to use a company car for limited personal reasons on the way to or from work.

If you have any questions about the use of company cars, call Bill Hewett at (786) 555-7100.

Kelly Rodriguez

Get Thinking and Writing

CRITICAL THINKING

Do you believe that movies and television programs have the power to change society? State your position, and support it with examples of films or shows that you believe caused or failed to cause social change.

WHAT HAVE YOU WRITTEN?

Read your paragraph carefully. Write out your topic sentence:

_____

Is it clearly worded? Could it be revised to better state your controlling idea?

- Do your examples illustrate the topic sentence?
- Are there unrelated details that could be deleted?
- Can you supply better examples?

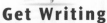

Get Writing

PHOTODISC/ALAMY LIMITED

What is your reaction to this image? Do you see it as an example of a social problem, law enforcement, youthful behavior, or an issue of personal responsibility? How does it relate to the photograph on page 103?

Write a few sentences or a brief paragraph to accompany this image to create an ad warning young people about drinking and driving. Use words and phrases that will grab the attention of youthful drivers.

WRITING ON THE WEB

Using a search engine such as Yahoo! or Google, enter terms such as *example, writing example paragraphs,* and *example techniques* to locate current sites of interest.

1. Review news articles in online versions of magazines such as *Time* and *Newsweek,* and notice how writers use examples to illustrate ideas.

2. Write an e-mail to a friend, and use examples to explain your ideas. If you are having problems at school, provide specific examples.

POINTS TO REMEMBER

1. Examples are *not* descriptions. Descriptions provide details about one person, place, or thing. Examples provide details about a person, place, or thing that represents a general type or supports a point of view.

2. Example paragraphs need strong, clearly worded topic sentences that identify the main idea the examples represent or support.

3. Readers may reject examples as random events or exceptions. Support your point of view with other types of evidence such as facts, expert opinions, and statistics.

CHAPTER 8

Developing Paragraphs Using Definition

CHAPTER GOALS

- Understand How Writers Use Definitions

- Recognize the Difference Between Definition and Description

- Write Different Types of Definitions

JIM BOURG/CORBIS

Get Writing

How do you define marriage? Do you believe that marriage licenses should be issued to gay couples? Why or why not?

Write one or more paragraphs stating your definition of marriage and the reasons for your views.

What is Definition?

Definition probably makes you think of a dictionary. When you hear a new word or come across a term you find confusing, you look it up in a dictionary to find out what it means. Many of your college textbooks include glossaries, which are lists of definitions of important terms. **Definitions limit or explain the meaning of a word or idea.** To communicate effectively, people must use terms with shared meanings. Doctors, lawyers, auto mechanics, stockbrokers, police officers, software designers, and health-care professionals use specialized vocabularies to communicate with others in their field. Introductory courses in subjects such as psychology, business law, sociology, or health sciences often focus on definitions of key terms.

Definition applies not only to technical terms you might learn in a physics or computer class, but to everyday words as well. If you and your landlord have different definitions of *excessive noise* or *normal wear and tear,* you may find yourself being evicted or losing your security deposit. In one company, a *rush delivery* might mean a week; in another, it might mean ten minutes. One health insurance policy may consider liver transplants *standard care* and pay for them. Another policy may define liver transplants as *experimental* and deny coverage.

POINT TO REMEMBER

Descriptions provide details about a single person, place, or thing. Definitions establish details about a personality type, kind of place, or class of things.

WHAT ARE YOU TRYING TO SAY?

Write a paragraph that establishes and explains your definition of one of the following topics:

- a role model
- an educated person
- an ideal job
- sexual harassment
- a drama queen
- stalking

Get Writing

_____

_____

_____

_____

_____

_____

_____

_____

_____

_____

_____

_____

WHAT HAVE YOU WRITTEN?

Read your paragraph carefully. Underline the topic sentence. Does it provide a clear definition of your subject, or does it just list descriptive details? Do you illustrate your definition with examples?

Writing Definition: Establishing Meaning

There are different types of definition:

Standard definitions are widely accepted and usually do not change. Words such as *aluminum, circle,* and *dyslexia* have exact meanings that are understood and shared by experts. Most professional and technical terms in law, biology, business, and engineering have standard definitions.

Qualifying definitions are not as precise or as widely accepted as standard definitions. They limit the meaning of complex, abstract, or controversial words or ideas. For example, doctors and therapists have different definitions of *obesity* or *depression.* Economists use varying definitions of *recession.* Because qualifying definitions differ, it is important to explain which one you are using.

Personal definitions express an individual's values, views, or opinions. Your definitions of a *good parent, love,* or *success* may differ from those of your friends, classmates, or relatives. Personal definitions rely on accurate descriptions and effective examples.

Invented definitions are created by writers to explain some object, characteristic, behavior, or situation that has been previously unnamed. The term *road rage* was invented to describe a driver's overly aggressive reaction to a minor traffic incident. *Spanglish* defines a blend of English and Spanish spoken by bilingual people. When people began using the Internet to harass, follow, or threaten people, it was defined as *cyberstalking.* Writers often invent a definition to help readers recognize and understand a new issue. You might invent a term like *cybercourtship* to define the way people date on the Internet or *parking pig* to define drivers who take up two parking spaces in crowded parking lots.

EXERCISE 1   Establishing Meanings

Select a term you have learned this semester or one of those listed below, and write a clear definition in your own words. You can refer to a dictionary or encyclopedia for details. After developing your definition, determine whether it is a standard, qualifying, personal, or invented definition.

- smog
- jobs that no one wants
- glacier
- the American Dream
- tornado

- genius
- computer virus
- air rage
- cyber junkie
- shopaholic

Term _____

Definition _____

_____

_____

Type _____

The Purpose of Definition

Writers use definition for two basic purposes: to explain or to convince.

The goal of most definitions is to *explain* words or ideas to prevent confusion. Terms such as *exculpatory evidence, cirrhosis,* and *altimeter* have specific meanings for lawyers, doctors, and pilots. Writers also use definitions to *convince* people to accept a point of view. Drug addiction can be defined as a *crime* deserving punishment or a *disease* needing treatment. Graffiti has been defined as *vandalism* by some and *street art* by others. Some parents define spanking as a form of *discipline,* whereas others define it as *child abuse.*

EXERCISE 2   Creating Definitions to Convince

Select one of the terms below or use one of your own, and state a definition that will persuade readers to accept your interpretation of the term.

- racism
- binge drinking
- poverty
- job security
- police brutality

- rap music
- anxiety
- obesity
- child neglect
- capital punishment

EXAM SKILLS

Many examination questions call for writing one or more definition paragraphs. As with any exam, read the question carefully, and make sure that your paragraph directly responds to it. In writing a definition, remember that your goal is not simply to describe details or provide examples, but to clearly state general principles that characterize a kind or type. Your definition paragraph should have a clearly stated thesis that states a basic definition in one sentence.

From Police Science

What is an arraignment?

definition statement

details

An arraignment is an initial court appearance where charges are presented to a defendant who enters a plea or asks for a continuance to plea at a later date. During this appearance the court establishes whether the defendant has a lawyer. The judge may set bail and schedule future court appearances. Although often a formality, the arraignment is an important part in the criminal justice process. Errors made at arraignment will complicate cases later on and sometimes lead to charges being dismissed.

Writing at Work: Definition

Business and technical documents, like this announcement, use definition to explain ideas.

AS YOU READ

Notice the importance of the document's format in creating a clear, easily read message.

Capitol Motors

2700 West Capitol Drive
Cherry Hill, New Jersey 08033
(856) 555-1500
www.capitolmotors.com

24 March 2009

To All Sales Personnel:

Beginning April 1st the term "executive-driven" will be applied only to those cars that are less than one year old with fewer than ten thousand miles that have been permanently assigned to full-time Capitol Motors employees. Cars used as loaners, assigned to part-time or contract employees, or provided as courtesy cars for VIPs, parades, or special events will be considered "used" cars. Vehicles with damage or wear and tear that cannot be removed through detailing will no longer be deemed executive driven.

If you have a personally assigned vehicle reaching the age or mileage limit, call Sid Loman.

Larry C. Reilly
Executive Vice President

Student Paragraphs

Standard Definition

"Homicide" is the killing of a human being by another. It is not the same thing as "murder." Murder is one type of homicide. In fact, not all homicides are considered crimes. A person who kills someone in self-defense commits a homicide but may not be charged with a crime. A construction worker might cause a homicide by accidentally dropping a heavy object that strikes and kills a passerby. Homicides become crimes when they involve malicious intent or recklessness. The person who kills for money or revenge may be guilty of murder, the most serious kind of homicide. A drunk driver who kills a pedestrian did not intend to harm anyone but showed reckless disregard for others and may be charged with manslaughter, a less serious type of homicide.

Homicide detectives investigate suspicious deaths. In nearly every case they will agree that a "homicide" has taken place. Their job is to define which kind of homicide it is and if criminal charges are warranted.

Qualifying Definition

Experts disagree over the precise definition of what is commonly called obsessive-compulsive disorder, or OCD. However, most agree that it is a real psychological disorder that can be managed with therapy and, in some cases, medication. Obsessive-compulsive disorder is an involuntary and overwhelming need to engage in abnormally repetitive and unnecessary behaviors that can be socially disabling. A person who lives in a high crime area and checks the locks two or three times before going to bed is probably cautious. A person who checks the locks ten or twenty times and wakes up three or four times a night to check them again is clearly abnormal. People who wash their hands before and after meals are hygienic. People with OCD might wash their hands twenty or thirty times a day and panic when they are away from soap and water. Psychiatrists and psychologists can generally identify extreme cases but often disagree on whether those with less severe symptoms have mild OCD or are simply eccentric.

Invented Definition

Today many parents have discovered that their children have become Twixters, young adults who do not leave home, either because they cannot afford a home of their own or because they refuse to give up the conveniences of living with their parents. They often have low-paying jobs or no job at all, settling into a permanent teenage existence of borrowing Dad's car and expecting Mom to do their laundry. This is not simply an American phenomenon. Twixters exist in Canada, where they are called "Boomerang Kids" because they bounce back home after they graduate. Germans call this generation "nesthockers" or "nest squatters." In Britain, Twixters are called KIPPERS, which stands for "Kids in Parents' Pockets Eroding Retirement Savings."

PUTTING PARAGRAPHS TOGETHER

True Heroes

The word *hero* is used a lot in today's society. Celebrities, athletes, and elected officials have been called "heroic" for making an edgy movie, hitting home runs, or taking a stand on an issue. We see "heroes" shaking hands with the president, getting awards, and giving speeches, usually while touting some book or movie deal.

introduction and background

1. What is the main point of this paragraph? How does it open the essay?
2. How does the writer use examples to build the paragraph? Do they give you a clear idea of the kinds of people the student sees as being celebrated as heroes in our society?

But these people are not true heroes. They may be famous and successful, but they are not heroic. The millionaire athlete who scores touchdowns or the actress who gains weight to look ugly for a controversial film may be bold or daring but not heroic. Heroes don't do things because they have their eyes on the Super Bowl or an Academy Award. We should not confuse heroism with celebrity.

transition contrast, what heroes are not

examples

1. What is the purpose of this paragraph? How does it relate to the previous paragraph?
2. How does the writer use examples to support the topic sentence?

A hero is a person who risks his or her life, status, or security for others without seeking anything in return. The man who runs into a burning building to save a stranger's child is a hero. The woman who volunteers to help refugees in a war-torn country is a hero. The executive or government official who refuses to participate in corruption and leaves a powerful, well-paying, high-status job to work in a factory or to teach school is a hero. Sacrifice, not success, is the mark of a hero. Heroes should not be measured by what they gain but by what they lose. The actress who refuses to play a role she feels is demeaning to women even though it would further her career and the athlete who won't use

definition statement

examples

steroids and loses honestly are far more heroic than the celebrities who get headlines. The real test for heroes is their desire for anonymity and self-denial. Many of the war heroes of World War II shunned publicity and preferred to keep their acts of heroism to themselves.

1. How clearly stated is the definition statement? Can you express it in your own words? What key words state the writer's meaning?
2. How does this paragraph relate to the previous one?
3. What role do examples play in establishing the definition?

conclusion and final considerations

Today, however, there seems to be too little interest in true heroes. There is a strong desire for "role models" who can inspire young people by achieving fame and success. Heroes are not always going to be popular role models, especially in a consumer society. True heroes sacrifice and suffer. Often their lives end tragically or in anonymity, poverty, and unhappiness, with only a few aware of their good deeds.

1. What is the purpose of this paragraph? How does it relate to the previous ones?
2. Why does the writer believe that true heroes do not make popular role models?

Steps to Writing A Definition Paragraph

1. **Determine whether your goal is to explain or convince.**

2. **Determine whether you are writing a standard, qualifying, personal, or invented definition.**

3. **Make sure that your paragraph has a clear definition statement, usually contained in a single topic sentence that summarizes your meaning.**

4. **Avoid defining a word by using the same word, such as "a diffusion pump diffuses" or "a cheapskate is a person who is cheap."**

5. **Establish meaning by explaining what your subject is *not* to eliminate confusion or common misconceptions:**

   A cheapskate is a person who has money but refuses to spend it.
   A poor person who cannot afford anything but necessities is not a cheapskate.

6. **Define using description to provide details about what your subject looks, sounds, or feels like.** Try to help readers visualize your subject by describing it in action:

    An airbag is a rapidly inflated cushion that protects the occupants of a car in a collision.

7. **Define using examples that readers can identify:**

    An adjective is a word that describes nouns: a *red* car, a *new* bus, a *cold* drink, a *broken* door, or a *popular* movie.

    Examples are useful to qualify abstract terms. People are likely to have different interpretations of a term such as "minor theft." Examples can help establish your meaning of the term:

    Only inmates convicted of minor thefts, such as shoplifting items under twenty dollars, snatching a neighbor's newspaper, or stealing hubcaps, were given an early release.

8. **Define using comparisons.** You can explain an abstract or technical term or idea by comparing it with something more common that people can recognize:

    When picked up on radar, an airplane has a **signature** indicating its size and shape, much like a flashlight casting someone's shadow on a wall.

    Because comparisons can oversimplify a subject, use them carefully.

Selecting Topics

Consider these topics for writing definition paragraphs:

- a good boss
- loyalty
- a healthy lifestyle
- depression
- self-respect
- a best friend
- beauty
- civil rights
- censorship
- child neglect
- talent

EXERCISE 3   Planning and Writing Definition Paragraphs

Select a topic from the previous list or choose one of your own, and develop details that support a clearly stated topic sentence that makes a definition statement.

Subject _____

Definition statement:

_____

_____

Supporting details:

1. _____

2. _____

3. _____

4. _____

5. _____

Write out your paragraph, and review it by reading it out loud. Does your paragraph state a definition or provide only descriptive details?

WORKING TOGETHER

Revise the following e-mail to make it clearer by creating definitions that use examples.

October 1, 2009
Attn. sales representatives

Please remind clients that luxury items are not covered by standard homeowner policies. Typical kitchen appliances, furniture, clothing, and consumer electronics are fully covered. However, expensive luxury items and collectibles are insured up to one thousand dollars only. Remind clients that these items can be easily and affordably protected by purchasing additional coverage.

Sari Goldman
Vice President, Sales and Marketing

CRITICAL THINKING

Should alcoholism or addiction be defined as a "disability"? Do you believe that addiction is a disease like diabetes or schizophrenia? Should alcoholics or addicts who are unable to work receive disability benefits? Why or why not? Write a paragraph stating your opinion. Your paragraph should contain your definitions of both alcoholism/addiction and disability.

Get Thinking and Writing

WHAT HAVE YOU WRITTEN?

Read your paragraph carefully. Do you establish clear definitions, then explain why alcoholism or addiction is or is not a disability?

Write out the topic sentence stating your definition:

_____

_____

_____

List the details that support the topic sentence or further explain your definition:

_____

_____

_____

- • Do these details directly support your definition?
- • Could you improve your definition by adding more details?
- • Are there minor or irrelevant details that should be deleted?

Get Writing

How do you define patriotism? Can someone protest against the government in a time of war and be considered a patriot? Why or why not?

WRITING ON THE WEB

Using a search engine such as Yahoo! or Google, enter terms such as *definition, writing definition paragraphs, establishing definitions,* and *controversial definitions* to locate current sites of interest.

1. Review news articles in online magazines, and notice how writers use definitions of key terms to both inform and persuade readers.

2. Examine websites by groups taking sides on controversial issues such as the war in Iraq, Social Security, capital punishment, and abortion, and notice how each offers different definitions of terms such as *security, family values, rights,* and *justice.*

3. Select terms you have learned this semester in one or more courses, and use a search engine to locate alternative definitions.

POINTS TO REMEMBER

1. **Definitions are *not* descriptions. They do not provide details about one person, place, thing, or idea—they characterize a type.**

2. **Definition paragraphs should have a clear definition statement that summarizes your characterization of the subject.**

3. **Definition statements can be supported with description, examples, and comparisons.**

4. **There are different types of definition: *standard definitions* with universal and fixed meanings, *qualifying definitions* that limit the meaning of a complex or controversial subject, *personal definitions* that express an individual interpretation, and *invented definitions* that create a name or label for a personality type, behavior, situation, or place.**

5. **Definitions can be used to inform or persuade readers.**

CHAPTER 9

Developing Paragraphs Using Comparison and Contrast

CASTLE ROCK/NELSON/COLUMBIA / THE KOBAL COLLECTION

CHAPTER GOALS

■ Understand How Writers Use Comparison and Contrast

■ Distinguish Between Using Comparison to Explain and Using Comparison to Convince

■ Understand the Subject-by-Subject and Point-by-Point Methods of Organizing Comparisons

Get Writing

Do you think that men and women communicate differently? Do they use language differently? Do you see differences in the way they deliver bad news, express anger, give orders, or make suggestions?

Write a paragraph comparing the ways that men and women communicate.

What Are Comparison and Contrast?

Comparison illustrates how two topics are alike. **Contrast** demonstrates how they are different. College courses use comparison and contrast to explain how a federal law differs from a state law, how one infection is different from another, or how two presidents dealt with a similar crisis. You probably have used comparison and contrast to make decisions at work, determining which method to use to solve a problem, how to make a repair, or decide which supervisor to call for assistance. Consumers use comparison and contrast when they consider which car to purchase, which apartment to rent, or how to pay for a vacation. Many college papers and business documents use comparison and contrast:

> The FBI handles domestic investigations of terrorism; the CIA handles overseas counterterrorism operations.
> After World War II, the United States constructed freeways, unlike Europe, which concentrated on building public transportation.
> Midwest National provides better insurance coverage for our employees than Pacific Mutual.

Get Writing

WHAT ARE YOU TRYING TO SAY?

Write a paragraph that compares or contrasts one of the following pairs:

- married and single friends
- two popular comedians
- civilian jobs and government jobs
- Democratic and Republican views on taxes, terrorism, education, or Social Security
- two football, baseball, or basketball teams, players, or coaches
- your attitudes about school, marriage, success, or jobs and those of a friend or family member

_____

_____

_____

_____

_____

_____

_____

_____

_____

_____

_____

_____

_____

_____

WHAT HAVE YOU WRITTEN?

Read your paragraph carefully. Underline your topic sentence. Does it clearly state the two topics? What are the important details you listed for the first topic?

1. _____

2. _____

3. _____

What are the important details you listed for the second topic?

1. _____

2. _____

3. _____

Can you think of better details to add? Are there any unrelated details that could be deleted?

How could you revise this paragraph to improve its impact?

The Purposes of Comparison and Contrast

Comparison and contrast is used for two reasons: to explain and to convince.

Writing to Explain

Comparisons can explain similar topics, showing the differences between high school and college, U.S. and European laws, or warm- and cold-blooded animals. You can think of these comparisons as pairs of descriptions or definitions. The goal of these paragraphs is to teach readers something or clear up common misunderstandings:

> Many people use the terms "fire truck" and "fire engine" interchangeably. In fact, some dictionaries and city governments make no distinction between the two terms. But in many fire departments, including ours, there are distinct differences. Fire engines carry water and are used to fight fires, especially where hydrants are not available, such as wooded areas, expressways, and airports. Fire trucks carry ladders and other equipment used in fighting fires and other emergencies, especially rescuing people from burning buildings or vehicles. Our department has three engine companies and five ladder or truck companies. Fire engines and fire trucks have separate crews and command structures. Engine companies and ladder companies respond to separate emergencies, although they often work together on major fires or disasters.

TIPS FOR WRITING COMPARISON PARAGRAPHS TO EXPLAIN

1. **Create direct, clearly worded sentences that describe both items.**

2. **Use details and examples to illustrate each type.**

3. **Point out key similarities and key differences.**

4. **Use concrete words rather than general or abstract words.**

5. **Avoid details that require too much explanation.**

EXERCISE 1 Using Comparison and Contrast to Explain

Write a paragraph using comparison or contrast to explain the similarities and differences of one of the following topics:

- classic and punk rock
- credit and debit cards
- two fast-food restaurants
- satellite versus cable television
- two pension plans

- football and baseball fans
- two day-care centers
- two popular diets
- film and digital cameras
- two sitcoms

- two cars
- two teachers
- Mexican and Puerto Rican dialects of Spanish
- two sisters

Writing to Convince

Comparison can be useful when you want to convince readers that one thing is better than another. You might convince readers to lease rather than buy their next car or support or reject a change in Social Security or tax law. Comparison paragraphs designed to convince readers need a clear topic sentence:

> **In order to grow, Vincennes County Community and Technical College should expand its humanities offerings rather than its technical programs.** Although Vincennes began as a vocational school and built its reputation as a leading technical college, the local economy and student demand indicate that the college's future depends on teaching general education and college transfer liberal arts courses. Supporters of technical programs insist that Vincennes focus on high-tech programs such as fiber optics and robotics to attract students. These programs are extremely expensive to set up. The three largest manufacturing companies that once hired nearly half our technical students have closed. The biggest employers are now insurance companies, health-care facilities, and social service agencies that require college degrees. Vincennes can maintain its enrollment only by meeting the needs of students who intend to get bachelor degrees. As a two-year school, we can serve this market by offering more college-level courses in English, history, sociology, psychology, and economics. Last semester, for example, four technical programs were canceled because of lack of enrollment, whereas both the English Department and the Math Department filled all their classes in one week and had to turn away nearly two hundred students.

TIPS FOR WRITING COMPARISON PARAGRAPHS TO CONVINCE
1. **Create a strong topic sentence that clearly states your choice.**
2. **Provide readers with concrete evidence and examples to support your topic sentence, not just negative comments.**

Ineffective
Technical programs are a total waste. Young people today don't want to get their hands dirty or work in factories.

Improved

> Technical programs are less popular. Young people today want to develop general education skills they can use in a variety of future occupations rather than specific skills they fear may become obsolete in a few years.

3. Support your topic sentence with examples, facts, quotations, and statistics.

EXERCISE 2   Using Comparison and Contrast to Convince

Write a paragraph using comparison or contrast to convince readers that one option is better than another:

- alternative fuels
- ways of punishing criminals
- union jobs and nonunion jobs
- study techniques
- solutions to illegal immigration
- views of the United Nations
- online and traditional classes

- working for yourself versus working for others
- renting versus owning a home
- treatments for addiction
- parenting styles
- two types of day care
- ways of preventing terrorism

Organizing Comparison Paragraphs

Because comparison paragraphs contain two subjects, they must be clearly organized to prevent confusion.

Confusing

> Right now the city is considering two plans to rebuild downtown and improve the economy and employment opportunities. Mayor Bolan supports granting $50 million in tax breaks for corporations and developers. Aldermen Marks and Spens want to build new low-income housing, job training centers, and community health centers. Bolan supporters believe that we need to increase the tax base by building high-rise condos and townhouses to attract wealthy people to the city. Marks and Spens believe that without skills and day care, few poor people will be able to fill any newly created jobs. Bolan believes that upper-income residents will shop and dine downtown, creating entry-level jobs in stores and restaurants. New housing, Marks and Spens argue, should benefit the homeless, not the rich. Bolan has said the city needs a thriving, upscale downtown to attract tourists and investors. Marks and Spens insist that money spent on restoring a few blocks for the rich will never help the poor. Marks and Spens believe that the first step in making the city attractive is spending $200 million to clear the slums that line the river and border the expressway. However, everyone agrees that massive investment is needed to bring the ailing downtown back to life.

The paragraph contains a number of details, but it shifts back and forth between the two proposals and is hard to follow.

There are basically two methods of organizing comparison paragraphs: **subject by subject** and **point by point.**

Subject by Subject

Subject by subject divides the paragraph into two parts. The first sentences generally introduce the two topics and state the controlling idea. The paragraph describes the first subject, then the second. Most of the actual comparison occurs in the second part of the paragraph:

> Right now the city is considering two plans to rebuild downtown and improve the economy and employment opportunities. Mayor Bolan supports granting $50 million in tax breaks for corporations and developers. Bolan supporters believe that we need to increase the tax base by building high-rise condos and townhouses to attract wealthy people to the city. They believe that upper-income residents will shop and dine downtown, creating entry-level jobs in stores and restaurants. Mayor Bolan has said the city needs a thriving, upscale downtown to attract tourists and investors. Aldermen Marks and Spens believe that the first step in making the city attractive is spending $200 million to clear the slums that line the river and border the expressway. They want to build new low-income housing, job training centers, and community health centers. Marks and Spens believe that without skills and day care, few poor people will be able to fill any newly created jobs. New housing, they argue, should benefit the homeless, not the rich. Marks and Spens insist that money spent on restoring a few blocks for the rich will never help the poor. However, everyone agrees that massive investment is needed bring the ailing downtown back to life.

- Subject-by-subject paragraphs are simple to organize because they divide the paragraph into two parts.
- You can avoid repetition by mentioning facts and details that are found in both subjects in a single statement:

> The mayor and his opponents both agree that the city must create jobs and higher revenues to overcome two decades of urban decay.

Point by Point

Point by point develops a series of comparisons, showing specific similarities and differences:

> Right now the city is considering two plans to rebuild downtown and improve the economy and employment opportunities. Mayor Bolan supports granting $50 million in tax breaks for corporations and developers. Aldermen Marks and Spens believe that the first step in making the city attractive is spending $200 million to clear the slums that line the river and border the expressway. Bolan supporters believe that we need to increase the tax base by building high-rise condos and townhouses to attract wealthy people to the city. New housing, Marks and Spens argue, should benefit the homeless, not the rich. They want to build new low-income housing, job training centers, and community health centers. Bolan believes that upper-income residents will shop and dine downtown, creating entry-level jobs in stores and restaurants. Marks and Spens believe that without skills and day care, few poor people will be able to fill any newly created jobs. Bolan has said the city needs a thriving, upscale downtown to attract tourists and investors. Marks and Spens insist that money spent on restoring a few blocks for the rich will never help the poor. However, everyone agrees that massive investment is needed to bring the ailing downtown back to life.

- Point-by-point comparisons place specific facts, numbers, dates, or prices side by side for easier reading.
- Point-by-point comparisons are useful to demonstrate advantages and disadvantages because each point is presented separately.

EXAM SKILLS

Many examination questions call for writing one or more comparison paragraphs. As with any exam, read the question carefully, and make sure that your paragraph directly responds to it. In writing a comparison paragraph, make sure that you organize details clearly by using either a subject-by-subject or point-by-point approach.

From Allied Health Occupations

What are the main differences between bacterial and viral infections?

general
comparison
first subject

second subject

The main differences between bacterial and viral infections are the agents that cause them. Both produce mild to fatal contagious and non-contagious infections. Bacterial infections are caused by single-cell organisms that can be seen with a microscope. They exist throughout the environment. Most bacteria are harmless, and some aid digestion in humans and animals. Harmful bacteria invade the body and release enzymes that destroy or damage living cells. Tuberculosis, anthrax, and diphtheria are bacterial infections. Viral infections are caused by capsules of genetic material. Much smaller than bacteria, they can be seen only with electron microscopes. Unlike bacteria, viruses cannot live outside a host. After entering the body, viruses take over cells and direct them to produce the material needed for the virus to grow. The common cold, influenza, HIV, and polio are viral infections. It is important to distinguish between infections because they respond to different drugs. Overuse of antibiotics to treat viruses has been blamed on creating drug-resistant germs.

Writing at Work: Comparison

Business and technical documents, like this announcement, use comparison to organize information.

AS YOU READ

Notice the importance of the document's format in creating a clear, easily read message.

WESTERN GRAINS

March 27, 2009

Western Grains is announcing a new product line in its breads, cereals, and snack division to be called From the Heartland. From the Heartland products will be produced in two varieties:

ALL-NATURAL

All-Natural From the Heartland products will feature gold packaging. These products will consist of all-natural ingredients and additives. They will contain no synthetic or artificial colorings, sweeteners, binders, or preservatives. The grains, nuts, sugars, and fruits used in manufacture will be purchased worldwide. Although the ingredients will be all-natural, chemical fertilizers and pesticides may have been used by farmers. In addition, some packaging used in shipping may contain preservatives to prevent spoilage.

ORGANIC

Organic From the Heartland products will feature green packaging. Like All-Natural products, they will contain only natural ingredients and additives. However, organic products will be purchased only from growers and farmers who do not use synthetic fertilizers or chemical pesticides. In addition, no preservatives are applied in shipping and storage. Organic products will be refrigerated to retard spoilage.

We feel that given the increased demand for natural and organic products, our new line will be highly successful.

Leslie Cowlins

Marketing and Product Development

Student Paragraphs

Subject by Subject

Over the past five years I have rented both apartments and flats. Apartments have the advantage of being low maintenance. I never had to carry out trash, shovel snow, or cut the grass. Trash and recycling chutes were located on every floor, so I never had to go outside in winter to take out trash. Both buildings had heated underground parking, laundry facilities, vending machines, and a community room I could rent for parties. However, apartments were confining. The rooms were small, and the windows could not be fully opened. Flats, on the other hand, were spacious and homey. I lived in duplexes with spacious front lawns and backyards. I had large balconies where I could sunbathe or grill a steak. On the other hand, the flats had no garages. There was no building manager, so I had to shovel my walk, change light bulbs in the hall, and lug trash outside. Although I enjoy the homey atmosphere of a flat, I prefer an apartment because between going to school and working two jobs, I have little time for household chores.

Point by Point

New York City and Los Angeles both have police departments with colorful and sometimes controversial histories that have made them popular subjects for movies and TV shows. However, there are major differences in their size and organization. New York has 39,000 police officers, making it larger than some European armies. In contrast, the entire city of Los Angeles is protected by only 9,000 officers. Police officers are paid well in both cities, though New York City officers earn more. The median pay for a police sergeant in New York is about $91,000 a year; sergeants in Los Angeles receive a median pay of $84,000. Because of the density of Manhattan and the crowded streets, officers and detectives often work on foot. An officer's beat can be a few blocks or a single high-rise. In contrast, Los Angeles police officers operate out of cars and respond to calls. New York cops have been celebrated in shows such as *Kojak* and *Law and Order* and shown as corrupt and violent in movies such as *Serpico* and *Prince of the City.* Los Angeles officers have been depicted as heroes in programs such as *Dragnet* and *Adam-12* and portrayed as racist and brutal in movies such as *L.A. Confidential.* No doubt both departments will continue to inspire future generations of moviemakers and television writers.

Point by Point

The majority of Hispanic students at Ocala Community College are from Mexico and Cuba. Most of the Mexican students are recent immigrants, unlike the Cubans, nearly all of whom are the children or grandchildren of those who left Cuba after Castro assumed power in 1959. The majority of Mexican students are low income, and many work full time in order to pay for college. Most of the Cuban Americans are middle class, and some come from very affluent families. For nearly all the Mexican students, English is a second language, and many are enrolled in ESL classes. For most of the Cubans, English is their primary language. Some do not speak Spanish at all, and only a few are truly fluent in both languages. Mexican students tend to support Democratic candidates and are concerned about poverty and social justice issues. Although not as fiercely anti-Castro as their parents, Cuban students generally support Republican candidates and are interested in maintaining a strong economy and low taxes.

PUTTING PARAGRAPHS TOGETHER

Shia and Sunni

introduction
topic sentence

Since the Iraq War, Americans have heard a lot about Shia and Sunni Muslims, but few understand what the terms mean or the events that led Muslims to split into two groups.

1. What is the goal of this paragraph?
2. Is a one-sentence introduction helpful or distracting?

topic sentence

historical explanation
definition of "Sunni"

The split between Shia and Sunnis dates back to the death of Muhammad. There was a dispute over who would assume leadership. Sunnis (Arabic for "one who follows the traditions of the Prophet") accepted Abu Bakr, one of Muhammad's most trusted advisors, as the rightful successor. Not all Muslims agreed with this position.

Some believed that the successor should come from Muhammad's family. They asserted that the true successor should have been Muhammad's cousin and son-in-law, Ali. Shia (Arabic for "Party of Ali") view Ali as Muhammad's true successor. Over the centuries, Sunni and Shia Muslims have developed different traditions, interpretations of the Koran, and legal systems.

definition of "Shia"

1. What are the main ideas in this paragraph?
2. How does the student organize this paragraph?
3. How does this paragraph answer questions raised in the first paragraph?

A major difference between Sunni and Shia Muslims concerns their view of imams, or spiritual leaders. Sunnis believe that imams should earn the trust of the people by demonstrating skills and knowledge. Shia Muslims, on the other hand, follow a line of imams they believe were appointed by Muhammad or God. Imams are viewed as infallible and are often revered as saints. Shia Muslims make pilgrimages to shrines and tombs of imams. Sunnis reject the idea of a hereditary class of leaders and do not view them as having the power of divine intervention.

topic sentence

contrasting views of leadership

1. How does this paragraph build on the previous one?
2. How does the student organize the details?

Sunnis make up 85 percent of all Muslims and dominate most Muslim nations. Shia live mostly in Iran and Iraq, the only two countries with Shia majorities. Although Shia and Sunni Muslims have engaged in violent conflicts, both groups share basic Islamic values and beliefs. Many Muslims prefer to identify themselves simply as "Muslims" rather than belonging to either group.

conclusion

topic sentence

1. How does this paragraph serve to end the comparison?
2. Does the topic sentence relate to the ideas in the opening paragraph?
3. Why is the last sentence important?

Steps to Writing A Comparison and Contrast Paragraph

1. **Narrow your topic and identify key points by creating two lists of details.**

2. **Determine the goal of your paragraph.** Do you plan to explain differences or argue that one subject is better or more desirable than the other?

3. **Develop a topic sentence that clearly expresses your main point.**

4. **Determine whether to use subject by subject or point by point to organize your details; then make a rough outline.**

5. **Write a draft of your paragraph; then consider these questions:**

   Is my topic sentence clearly stated?

   Are there minor details that should be deleted or replaced?

   Is my paragraph clearly organized?

   Do I provide enough information for readers to understand my comparison or accept my point of view?

Selecting Topics

Consider these topics for developing comparison-and-contrast paragraphs:

- two people you have worked with
- satellite and cable TV
- the way television, music, an industry, or neighborhood has changed over time
- differences between generations
- contrasting ways that people confront bad news
- film and digital cameras
- American and Asian customs
- U.S. and Canadian health-care systems
- conventional wars versus wars against terrorism
- pros and cons of welfare reform, school choice, legalizing marijuana, banning handguns, or other issues

- two ways of commuting to work or school
- advantages and disadvantages of buying a new car, owning a home, investing in the stock market, getting married at a young age, staying home to raise children, or owning a pet

PLANNING AND WRITING COMPARISON AND CONTRAST PARAGRAPHS

Get Thinking and Writing

Select a topic from the previous list or choose one of your own, and develop details and a topic sentence that states the goal of your paragraph.

Topic:_____

Possible supporting details:

Subject 1   *Subject 2*

1. _____   1. _____

2. _____   2. _____

3. _____   3. _____

4. _____   4. _____

Topic sentence:

_____

Organization (Subject by Subject or Point by Point):

First sentence: topic sentence, first detail, or introductory statement:

_____

Supporting details in order:

1. _____

2. _____

3. _____

4. _____

Last sentence: final detail, concluding statement, or topic sentence:

_____

Write your paragraph, and review it by reading it aloud.

WORKING TOGETHER

Working with a group of students, revise this e-mail message to make it easier to read by organizing it in a subject-by-subject or point-by-point pattern. Consider why comparison-and-contrast writing depends on clear organization to be effective.

District Managers:

Please remind your staff about corporate communications policies. Employees should use e-mail for ALL internal communications. Communications directed to individual employees involving pensions, medical benefits, terminations, promotions, hiring, or disciplinary actions must be sent by first-class mail to their home address. E-mail is appropriate for personnel announcements intended for all employees. Deliveries of hard-copy reports or shipments should be announced and acknowledged by e-mail. Customer questions sent by e-mail should be answered by e-mail. If managers believe that the question requires a response in letter form, an e-mail should inform the customer of the letter response.

If there are any questions about the use of e-mail and first-class mail, contact Cara Malina at ex. 5656.

Shannon O'Donoghue

Get Thinking and Writing

CRITICAL THINKING

In past wars the government urged the public to buy bonds and accept sacrifices such as rationed gasoline and higher taxes. Do you think our government should ask Americans to make sacrifices to fight the war on terrorism? Write a paragraph stating your views.

WHAT HAVE YOU WRITTEN?

Read your paragraph carefully.

Write out your topic sentence below:

_____

_____

_____

Could it be stated more clearly or directly? Do the details in the rest of the paragraph support your topic sentence? Can you add more ideas? Are there irrelevant or minor details that could be deleted?

Get Writing

PICTORIAL PRESS LTD/ALAMY LIMITED

Write a paragraph comparing and contrasting male and female attitudes about relationships. What do men value in a relationship? What do women think is important? Use either subject by subject or point by point to organize your ideas.

WRITING ON THE WEB

Using a search engine such as Yahoo! or Google, enter terms such as *writing comparison, comparison contrast essays, organizing comparison essays, subject-by-subject comparison,* and *point-by-point comparison* to locate current sites of interest.

1. Search for news articles using comparison and contrast, and review how writers organized their ideas.

2. Review websites hosted by organizations with opposing views on controversial issues such as abortion, gun control, or the war in Iraq. Notice how their statements use comparison to influence others to share their ideas.

3. Write an e-mail to a friend using comparison to discuss how something has changed, the difference between two classes, two concerts you attended, or two jobs you are considering.

POINTS TO REMEMBER

1. Comparison points out similarities; contrast points out differences.

2. Comparison can be used to explain differences or argue that one subject is superior to another.

3. Comparison paragraphs should have a clear topic sentence expressing your goal.

4. Comparison paragraphs can be organized *subject by subject* to discuss one topic then the other or *point by point* to discuss both topics in a series of comparisons.

5. Comparison paragraphs depend on clear transitions to prevent confusion.

CHAPTER 10

Developing Paragraphs Using Division and Classification

PICTORIAL PRESS LTD/ALAMY LIMITED

CHAPTER GOALS

- Understand How Writers Use Division and Classification

- Distinguish Between Official and Personal Divisions and Classifications

- Appreciate the Role of Organization in Developing Division and Classification

Get Writing

Write a paragraph explaining the careers you are interested in. What is most important to you—income, security, helping others, a sense of personal accomplishment, or owning your own business?

What Are Division and Classification?

Division separates a subject into types. Many of your college textbooks use division to organize information. A biology text divides animals into birds, mammals, fish, and reptiles. A finance text divides investments into stocks, bonds, and mutual funds. A first-aid manual might divide burns into those caused by fire, chemicals, and electrical shock. A business could divide products into those sold in department stores, discount outlets, and online catalogs. If you got a job as a cashier in a retail store, you might be trained how to handle customers paying with cash, those paying with checks, and those using credit cards.

Division separates a subject into parts, types, or regions, much like cutting a pie into slices:

Division

A balanced diet includes fruits and vegetables, protein, and whole grains.

Our employees include students, homemakers, and recent immigrants.

My neighborhood is made up of ranch houses, two-story colonials, and split-levels.

Classification ranks subjects on a scale. A biology text might classify species from the most to least endangered A finance text could classify investments from the safest to the riskiest. A first-aid manual will classify burns as first, second, or third degree depending on how serious they are. A business might classify its products from the cheapest to the most expensive. A retail store might have three levels of employees, such as clerks, shift supervisors, and store manager.

Classification ranks things on a scale, much like a teacher grading quizzes from A to F:

Classification

These diets include 1,200-calorie, 1,500-calorie, and 2,000-calorie-per-day programs.

Our employees are paid hourly, weekly, or monthly.

My neighborhood is made up of houses with two, three, and four bedrooms.

Division and classification both contain lists of descriptions or definitions of related subjects, but it is important to remember how they differ.

POINT TO REMEMBER

Division separates a subject into parts; classification ranks types on a scale.

Get Writing

WHAT ARE YOU TRYING TO SAY?

Write a paragraph that uses division to discuss different types of one of the following subjects:

- students at your college*

- your neighbors
- cliques or groups of students at your high school
- off-campus housing
- useful websites
- local restaurants
- problems caused by poverty
- health problems related to poor diet
- ways people cope with stress
- music groups

Example: Divide students by their major, their ethnic background, their residence, or the way they study.

or

Write a paragraph that uses classification to rank types of one of the following subjects:

- students at your college*
- bosses
- diets
- new cars
- consumers
- disabilities
- careers
- recent movies
- Internet search engines

Example: Classify students from youngest to oldest, best to worst, those who work full time, part time, or not at all, or poorest to richest.

_____

_____

_____

_____

_____

_____

_____

_____

_____

_____

_____

WHAT HAVE YOU WRITTEN?

For a division paragraph:

1. What is your subject? _____

2. Underline your topic sentence. If you find it unclear, revise it.

    _____

    _____

3. How do you divide your topic? _____

4. What types do you discuss?

    a. _____   **c.** _____

    b. _____   **d.** _____

5. Could you add other types? Could some of the divisions be combined?

6. Does your paragraph clearly describe or define each type?

For a classification paragraph:

1. What is your subject? _____

2. Underline your topic sentence. If you find it unclear, revise it.

    _____

    _____

3. How do you classify or measure your topic? _____

4. What levels or ranks do you discuss?

    a. _____   **c.** _____

    b. _____   **d.** _____

5. Are the classifications easy to understand? Do you clearly organize the ranks in order: A, B, C; 1–10; by age; or by price range?

6. Does your paragraph clearly describe or define each level?

Writing Division Paragraphs

Paragraphs that explain a subject by breaking it into types or parts have to be carefully organized to prevent confusion:

1. **Write a clear topic sentence that explains your method of division.** Tell readers how you are dividing your subject, such as separating

cars into sedans, SUVs, and compacts or dividing movies into dramas, comedies, and action adventures.

2. **Define each type clearly.** Give readers detailed descriptions and examples of each type.

3. **Let readers know about possible exceptions.** If some items may not fit into your categories, explain that exceptions exist. For example, maybe not all movies can be placed into the groups you created. Beginning your paragraph with a statement such as *"Most* of today's movies belong to one of three types" lets readers know that exceptions exist.

Official and Personal Divisions

You can develop a paragraph using either an **official** or a **personal** division. **Official divisions use widely known and accepted categories created by the government, a company, or an organization.** The National Football Conference, for example, divides its football teams into four official divisions: East, North, West, and South. **Personal divisions are created by writers to express their individual view of a subject.** A sportswriter looking at the NFC might divide the teams into three types: those that emphasize offense, those that stress defense, and those that depend on special teams.

A corporate brochure, for example, uses **official division** to describe the company's three units:

> Triplex Data Processing has three divisions. Triplex National, headquartered in Boston, manages account information for banks, insurance companies, and mutual funds. It creates financial statements for individual and corporate account holders. Triplex Credit, located in Houston, is the second largest data-processing center for credit card companies. It uses state-of-the-art technology to process millions of credit card purchases an hour. Triplex Atlantic works only with government agencies. It has contracts with several cities, states, and the U.S. military to issue payroll and pension checks.

A former employee uses a **personal division** to describe the people she worked with:

> After working at Triplex Atlantic for two years, I noticed that most of the workers fit into one of three distinct groups. There were the lifers, mostly glum-looking, overweight middle-aged men and women in drab business suits who drank a lot of coffee and spent their break time talking about early retirement. There were the part-timers, nearly all of whom were college students. They generally worked second shift and considered themselves lucky to be making $20 an hour banging out computer reports while they listened to hip hop on their headphones. They drank Diet Coke and sent out for pizzas. The interns formed a small but noticeable group. These were fresh business-school graduates. They were here to work for six weeks to learn the ropes before being sent on for further training. They were the same age as the part-timers but dressed in stylish suits and took their jobs and themselves very seriously. The part-timers admired them, hoping to join their ranks someday. The lifers gave them a grudging, resentful respect, knowing that these kids were on the fast track and would soon be their bosses.

TIPS FOR WRITING A DIVISION PARAGRAPH

1. **Announce the number of categories in your division.** It can be easier for readers to remember your ideas if you let them know there are "three kinds of insurance" or "four types of alternative fuels."

2. **Avoid misleading readers about the size of the groups.** If you state that "there are three types of teachers," many readers will assume that each group represents about a third of the faculty. Let readers know how large or significant each category is. You might tell readers, for example, that "80 percent of the teachers work full time, 15 percent work part time, and 5 percent have full-time temporary contracts."

3. **Give each category a number, title, or name that readers can remember.** Avoid introducing categories with general statements, such as "another group is. . . ."

EXERCISE 1   Writing Division Paragraphs

Write a paragraph using division to explain different types of one of the following topics:

• movies	• co-workers	• college courses
• teachers	• hobbies	• credit cards
• actors or singers	• talk shows	• women's magazines
• pet owners	• drivers	• student jobs

Writing Classification Paragraphs

Paragraphs that classify subjects have to be carefully organized to prevent confusion:

1. **Write a clear topic sentence that explains your method of classification.** Tell readers how you are rating your subjects. You can rank football teams by wins and losses or rate cell phone plans from the cheapest to most expensive.

2. **Define each rating clearly.** Give readers detailed descriptions and examples of each ranking.

3. **Let readers know about possible exceptions.** Are there some items that cannot fit on your scale? Can subjects change ratings over time? If you rate college students by their GPA, point out that such ratings can change. The student who gets D's this semester can work hard and earn B's next semester. The A student might burn out or take harder courses and slip to a B average.

Official and Personal Classifications

As with division, you can organize a paragraph using an **official** or a **personal** classification. **Official classifications use widely known and accepted ranks or categories created by the government, a business, or an organization.** For example, the Motion Picture Association of America rates movies G, PG, PG-13, R, and NC-17. This official rating will appear on DVD cases, in previews, and all newspaper listings. **Personal classifications are created by writers to express their individual view of a subject.** The newspaper movie listing that shows a film is officially rated PG-13 might also display one to five stars. These reflect the opinion of a local critic. Although officially classified PG-13 nationwide, a film might get a poor review by the *New York Times* and receive one star in its movie listings but be given four stars by the *Chicago Tribune,* which gave it a rave review.

A company brochure, for example, uses an **official classification** to describe the three grades of power cables that the company produces:

Reynolds Electric produces power cords and cables in three grades. *Consumer grade* consists of extension cords, printer cables, telephone cords, and other devices designed for home or small office use. They are widely sold in hardware and wholesale outlets such as Office Depot, Staples, Wal-Mart, Home Depot, and Ace Hardware. *Commercial grade* includes heavier power cords used in the construction of commercial properties such as restaurants, strip malls, motels, and some high-rise office and apartment buildings. *Industrial grade* consist of cables used in aircraft carriers, generator plants, and high-tension power lines.

A former employee uses a **personal classification** to rate her supervisors from best to worst:

> When I worked at Reynolds, I ran into three types of supervisors. The best ones had superior knowledge about the plant, products, and industry, and had great human relations skills. Ed Norton and Sally Deptford were perfect examples. You could go to them with any problem and get not only the information you needed but also some support and maybe a tip on getting a promotion. They were fun to be around, and you could learn a lot by just sharing a cup of coffee with them. The next group had superior knowledge and would help when you had a problem, but they were cold and distant. They always acted like you were interrupting something important, and they made you feel guilty for not knowing some arcane serial number or computer code. They stayed in their offices or work cubicles and never spent free time with the rank and file. The worst supervisors were either brand new and just as clueless as you were or nearing retirement and would rather calculate their pension than keep up on the new codes. Both types were useless. They may have been friendly, but they never had any answers to the questions I had.

TIPS FOR WRITING A CLASSIFICATION PARAGRAPH

1. **Clearly define a single method of classifying your subject.** For example, you can classify cars by price, fuel efficiency, or size. However, you cannot mix classifications and write a paragraph about expensive cars, fuel-efficient cars, and small cars.

2. **Give each category a number, title, or name that readers can remember.**

3. **Establish clear ranks or classes that do not leave any gaps.** A grading scale, for instance, should establish clear categories for each grade to prevent confusion of what test score receives an A and what score receives a B.

4. **Illustrate each class with specific examples.**

EXERCISE 2   Writing a Classification Paragraph

Write a paragraph using classification to explain different types of one of the following topics:

- football or baseball standings
- hotels or cruise ships
- salary schedules
- car engines
- restaurants
- musicians
- fractures or other injuries
- health insurance plans
- addictive drugs
- sitcoms
- home security systems

EXAM SKILLS

Many examination questions ask for writing one or more paragraphs that use division or classification. As with any exam, read the question carefully, and make sure that your paragraph directly responds to it. In writing a division paragraph, make sure that you clearly explain how and why you are breaking the subject into parts. In writing a classification paragraph, remember to use a single method to measure or evaluate your subject. In both cases, explain possible exceptions or situations in which someone or something could fit more than one category or move from one to another.

From Metal Working

Explain the different types of stainless steel and their common uses.

topic sentence	There are four basic kinds of stainless steel, made with different alloys and carbon levels to
explaining four types	serve different purposes. Austenitic stainless steel has a low carbon content and contains at least
type 1	16 percent chromium. It is tough and resists corrosion and is used in shafts, pipes that transport salt water, and equipment used in chemical plants and dairy food production. Ferritic stainless steel con-
type 2	tains 10.5 to 27 percent chromium. It is less tough and less resistant to corrosion than austenitic steels.
type 3	It is used in automotive trim and exhaust systems. Martensitic steels have higher carbon content and contain 11.5 to 18 percent chromium. They are magnetic. They are hard but less resistant to corrosion. They are used to make medical instruments,
type 4	knives, aircraft parts, and bearings. Precipitation-hardening steels are similar in alloy content to austenite or martensite steels but are heat-treated to make them very strong. They are used in shafts, high-pressure pumps, fasteners, and springs.

Writing at Work: Division and Classification

Business and technical documents, like this announcement, use division and classification to present information.

AS YOU READ

Notice the importance of the document's format in creating a clear, easily read message.

Northern Machine Tool

120 South Maine Street Suite 225
Seattle, WA 98104
(206) 555-3400
www.northernmachinetool.com

PERSONNEL

There has been recent confusion about the revised benefits package. Northern Machine Tool provides three forms of coverage to all its employees: life, disability, and health. All employees have a life insurance benefit equal to their previous year's salary. Disabled employees are eligible to receive a maximum of 75% of their base salary. Health insurance is provided based on employment status:

Full-time employees	$500 annual deductible/10% co-payment
Full-time temporary employees	$1,000 annual deductible/15% co-payment
Part-time employees	$1,500 annual deductible/20% co-payment

If you have any questions about your benefits, please give me a call at ext. 3939.

Karen Gomez

Student Paragraphs

Division

The music industry is dominated today by three types of performers. First, there are the classic recording artists whose CDs sell millions and who get a lot of airtime on both AM and FM radio. These performers are known for their strong vocal presence and distinctive style. Video artists are a more recent type. Their high-production films get a lot of play on MTV and VH1, but they command a much smaller presence on radio. Without their visual imagery and glossy fashion-model looks, their sound is often weak and unappealing. Finally, there are the performance artists. They don't produce videos or appear high on the sales charts, but they sell out stadiums and have tens of thousands of loyal fans who will follow them from concert to concert. They offer the public a cross between a Broadway show and a revival meeting. People pay seventy-five dollars or more for a ticket to share an experience as much as listen to a concert. Some singers and bands, of course, do all three. Others will start in one format, then change their delivery as they find their voice and determine the best way to connect with an audience.

Classification

People usually divide cars into two types, American and import. In today's global economy, however, you really have to classify cars by the degree they benefit the U.S. economy. First, you have American/American cars, such as Buicks built in Detroit. Even though they probably contain a large portion of imported parts, these cars are made here, creating jobs for American workers, and an American corporation gets the profits. Then there are American/foreign cars, such as Chryslers assembled in Mexico or Canada. Although an American company makes a sale and gets the profits, it has outsourced jobs to foreign workers. Foreign/American cars, such as Toyotas built in Tennessee, create jobs for Americans, but the profits go to a foreign company. Finally, there are the foreign/foreign cars, such as BMWs imported from Germany or Kias from Korea. The only Americans benefiting from these cars are sales reps and service personnel. The manufacturing jobs and profits go overseas.

Division and Classification

In most states convicted criminals are assigned to maximum-, medium-, and minimum-security facilities based on four criteria: the nature of their offense, their flight risk, past criminal behavior, and potential for violence against themselves, staff, and other inmates. In maximum-security facilities, inmates spend

up to 23 hours a day in locked cells. They are given
few privileges and allowed little movement within
the prison. In medium-security prisons, inmates often
have the ability to lock and unlock their doors. Except at night, they can freely move about within the
prison. They eat in mess halls, attend classes, or
work in shops. They are counted several times a day
and locked in at night. Many minimum-security facilities have no high walls or even a fence. They resemble
college campuses or military bases. Inmates are often
allowed to go outside or even enjoy weekend passes.
These convicts are usually guilty of nonviolent crimes
or are deemed nonflight risks. Occasionally, major
crime figures serve time in these facilities because
they have plea bargained, accepting a two-year sentence for testifying against others rather than facing
twenty years. Fear of reprisals from other criminals
make them highly unlikely to escape. In some minimum-
security facilities, the dormlike facilities have no
locked doors and only a white line on the lawn to indicate the boundary of the prison.

PUTTING PARAGRAPHS TOGETHER

Types of Businesses

Like many people, you may dream of going into business for yourself. **Before you get started, though, it
is important to understand the four basic kinds of
businesses: sole proprietorship, general partnership,
limited partnership, and corporation.** Each type has
advantages and disadvantages. One issue you have to
consider is just how much risk you are willing to
assume.

introduction

**division into four types of
classification issue**

1. How does the student introduce the subject?
2. How does the paragraph use division?
3. Why is the opening paragraph important for division and classification essays? What must it include?

A sole proprietorship is the simplest business and
is the easiest to set up. Basically, you and the business are one in the same. The business does not file
taxes. As business owner, you report all income on
your personal income-tax return. The main disadvantage
is that as owner you have unlimited personal liability
for any business losses. Sole proprietorships expose
you to great risk.

type 1

details
definition

1. How does this paragraph build upon the first paragraph?
2. What details does the student use to explain sole proprietorship?
3. Does this paragraph supply enough information? Can you define "sole proprietorship" in your own words?

type 2

details

A general partnership is an association of two or more people engaged in making a profit. It is a bit more complicated to set up. Because you work with other people, you can benefit by adding their start-up capital, time, energy, and talent to the business. Like a sole proprietorship, the partnership does not pay taxes. Profits are split among the partners, who report them on their personal income-tax returns. The major drawback to a partnership is risk. As a partner, you are liable not only for your own actions but for the actions of your partners as well. Because of this risk, it is essential to choose potential partners carefully.

1. How does this paragraph build upon the first paragraph?
2. How does the student distinguish a general partnership from a sole proprietorship?
3. What transitions does the student use?

type 3

definition

In a limited partnership, you go into business with a general partner and receive a split of the profits, which you report on your personal income-tax return. The general partner or partners operate the day-to-day operations of the business while you serve as an investor. The arrangement is more complex to set up than a general partnership but has a clear advantage. As a limited partner, your liability is limited to the amount of your investment.

1. How does this paragraph relate to the others?
2. Why does this paragraph appear after the previous one?
3. Why does a limited partnership have less risk than a general partnership?

type 4

definition

details

Corporations are the most complex businesses to set up and usually require the services of a lawyer or an accountant. A corporation is unlike a sole proprietorship or partnership because you and the business are considered separate entities. You can create a corporation and then hire yourself as an employee, usually as the president, and set up tax-deductible pension

```
and benefit plans. Because the corporation is sepa-
rate from your personal finances, it exposes you to
the least personal liability. However, corporations
must file taxes quarterly and adhere to more regula-
tions than other businesses. But tax advantages and
the limited personal liability can make corporations
attractive even if you intend to operate a one-man or
one-woman enterprise.
```

1. Why does a corporation expose business owners to the least risk?
2. How does this paragraph relate to the first paragraph?
3. Why does this paragraph come last? Does it make a logical conclusion?

Steps to Writing A Division or Classification Paragraph

1. **Determine whether your goal is to divide your subject into types or classify subjects on a single scale.**

2. **Consider your readers.** Do you need to provide background information or define terms before readers can understand your division or classification?

3. **Clearly explain the method you are using to divide your subject into parts or measure the parts on a single scale.**

4. **Consider numbering types or classes. It is easier for readers to remember divisions and classifications if you state at the beginning that there are three types of students or four classes of car insurance.**

5. **Use examples to illustrate each type or class.**

6. **Explain any exceptions, especially if it is possible for a subject to belong to more than one category at the same time or change categories.**

7. **Write a draft of your paragraph.**

8. **Read your paragraph aloud, and ask yourself these questions:**

   Have I clearly defined my topic?

   Do I clearly explain how I am dividing or classifying my subject?

   Do I illustrate each category with clear examples my readers can understand?

   Is there anything misleading about my division or classification? Do I need to explain exceptions?

Selecting Topics

1. Select a topic with which you are familiar, such as a subject you are studying in college, a job you have had, a sport or hobby, people you know, or a place you are familiar with.

2. Determine the best way to explain differences or complexities about this topic.

3. Use division to explain types of infections you studied in a nursing class or methods of auditing in an accounting course, types of sporting equipment, or groups of people you live or work with.

   or

   Use classification to rate mild to serious medical problems, simple to complex audits, price ranges of sporting equipment, or best to worst co-workers or neighbors.

EXERCISE 3   Planning and Writing Paragraphs

Select a topic, and explain it by using division or classification. Make sure that you provide clear descriptions or examples for each category.

Topic _____

Method of division or classification: _____

_____

First sentence: topic sentence, introductory statement, or method of division and classification:

_____

_____

Types or classes:

1. _____

2. _____

3. _____

4. _____

Possible exceptions or changes: _____

_____

Last sentence: final type or class, concluding statement, comment about exceptions, or topic sentence:

_____

_____

WORKING TOGETHER

Working with a group of students, revise the following announcement by establishing clearer organization of the classifications. Invent any details that you need. Develop new titles or a number or lettering system to clarify types.

Attn: Service Staff
RE: Vehicle Repair Priority

To ensure that vehicles are serviced and repaired in the proper order, follow these new priority guidelines: General service vehicles such as staff cars, general delivery vans, tractors, and pickup trucks should be serviced only after all Class B emergency vehicles.

Class A emergency vehicles include ambulances, paramedic and fire vehicles, and bomb squad trucks. These must be serviced before all other vehicles.

Class B emergency vehicles include first-aid vans, general police cars, and fire trucks. These should be serviced after all Class A vehicles.

Power mowers, street cleaners, and trash trucks are serviced last.

There is one important seasonal consideration. From April 15 to November 30, snowplows are classified in the group with trash trucks. From December 1 to April 14, they are considered Class A emergency vehicles.

CRITICAL THINKING

At any given time the United States faces a range of domestic and foreign policy problems, ranging from health care to terrorism. Write one or more classification paragraphs describing the most to least important problems on which you think the president and Congress should concentrate.

Get Thinking and Writing

WHAT HAVE YOU WRITTEN?

Read your paragraph carefully. Write out your topic sentence:

_____

Is it clearly worded? Could it be revised to better state your controlling idea?

• Have you established clear classes and organized them in a logical pattern from most to least serious?

• Do you explain why you consider some problems more serious than others?

• Do you provide examples that readers can understand? Can you think of additional or better examples?

Get Writing

Write a paragraph that classifies what you consider the best to worst bosses. Establish clear classifications, and provide examples of each type that clearly demonstrate why you consider them desirable or undesirable.

PICTORIAL PRESS LTD/ALAMY LIMITED

WRITING ON THE WEB

Using a search engine such as Yahoo! or Google, enter terms such as *writing division and classification, division paragraphs,* and *classification paragraphs* to locate current sites of interest.

1. Look up online articles using search terms such as *types of* or *classification* to locate articles that use division or classification.

2. Look for articles using *types of* or *classes of* as title search terms.

3. Write an e-mail to a friend about your current experiences at college or work. Use division to discuss recent types of problems or assignments, and use classification to organize them from easiest to most difficult.

POINTS TO REMEMBER

1. Division separates a subject into parts; classification ranks subjects on a scale.

2. Divisions and classifications can be official or personal.

3. Division and classification paragraphs need details and examples to clearly define each type or class.

4. Readers should be alerted to possible exceptions.

CHAPTER 11

Developing Paragraphs Using Process

CHAPTER GOALS

■ Understand How Writers Use Process to Explain How Things Work and to Give Directions

■ Appreciate the Importance of Precise Wording and Numbered Steps in Writing Instructions

PHOTODISC/ALAMY LIMITED

Get Writing

What processes have you learned in previous jobs or courses? Can you describe how to create a web page, apply for a job, or take someone's blood pressure? Have you studied how the heart functions, how a bill becomes a law, or how a hybrid engine works?

Write a paragraph explaining step-by-step how a process, such as registering for classes or buying a car, takes place. Be sure to define terms and explain background information.

What Is Process?

Process paragraphs explain how things work or **give directions to accomplish a specific task.** College textbooks use process to explain how interest rates are set, how earthquakes occur, how a disease affects the body, or how police book a criminal suspect.

Recipes, repair manuals, and instructional booklets give readers step-by-step directions to bake a cake, change a tire, install new software, or operate a power tool. Consumer magazines use process to give readers advice on how to lose weight, choose a doctor, start an exercise program, buy a used car, or save for retirement. To be effective, a process paragraph has to be directed to specific readers, whether they are students, employees, or consumers.

Explaining How Things Work

The bacteria grows in warm wet places, then spreads to dry areas in direct sunlight.

The personnel staff examines the résumés, selects ten candidates, conducts a round of interviews, then chooses three finalists to be interviewed by the managers.

As tires lose air, they flatten, placing more of their surface on the road, which increases friction and reduces fuel efficiency.

Giving Directions

To prevent bacteria growth, clean your lab bench carefully and fully dry all cloths, test tubes, and instruments.

At the interview, greet each member of the committee, provide five copies of your résumé, answer questions directly and positively, and be prepared to give a five-minute presentation on why you want to work at National Electric.

To improve gas mileage, make sure that your tires are fully inflated.

Get Writing

WHAT ARE YOU TRYING TO SAY?

Write a paragraph that uses process to explain something you learned in college or at work:

- how cell phones work
- how aluminum or paper is recycled
- how the NFL draft works
- how the electoral college functions
- how exercise builds muscle
- how digital cameras work
- how computer viruses are spread
- how people become citizens

or

Write a paragraph that explains how readers can accomplish a task:

- how to study for a test
- how to cook with a wok

- how to send a text message
- how to select a good day-care center
- how to operate a power tool
- how to drive in snow
- how to improve a golf swing

_____

_____

_____

_____

_____

_____

_____

_____

_____

_____

_____

_____

WHAT HAVE YOU WRITTEN?

1. What is your subject? _____

2. Do you provide background information or define terms that readers need to know in order to understand the process or follow directions?

3. Do you use numbered steps so readers can follow your explanation or instructions?

4. Write down the three or four most important things readers need to know about the process you describe:

a. _____   **c.** _____

b. _____   **d.** _____

Does your paragraph clearly explain these points? Have you forgotten details or created sentences that readers may find confusing?

5. Read your paragraph aloud; then rewrite it to include any details you have forgotten and revise awkward or confusing sentences.

Writing Paragraphs That Explain

Process paragraphs explain how something works by breaking it down into a series of steps. Like a slow-motion scene in a movie, it slows down a process so readers can understand how it takes place. In explaining how something works, it is important to consider how much your readers know about the subject. Make sure that you provide necessary background information, define key terms, and clear up any common misunderstandings people may have about the subject:

> Contrary to what some people think, tornados don't suddenly appear out of a clear sky. They are actually created by thunderstorms that contain updrafts of warm, moist air. This warm, humid air rises and forms clouds in the higher, colder atmosphere, creating ice crystals, which explains why hail often precedes a tornado. Downdrafts of cold air can also occur as the thunderstorm gets stronger. If the winds are powerful, the updraft of air begins to spin. Along the ground, a horizontally rotating column of air rises vertically. If the rotation becomes strong enough, a spinning cloud descends from the thunderstorm, creating a funnel-shaped cloud. When this funnel-shaped cloud touches the ground, it officially becomes a tornado. Moving at speeds of 300 m.p.h. or greater, tornados can cause tremendous damage. Because they appear with little warning and can move erratically, tornados are extremely dangerous, and people should seek immediate shelter.

TIPS FOR EXPLAINING HOW THINGS HAPPEN

1. **Study the process carefully, and emphasize key points.**
2. **Separate the process into logical steps.** Avoid emphasizing minor points by making them single steps or crowding too much information in one stage.
3. **Alert readers to possible exceptions to or variations in the process.**
4. **Use transitional words and phrases to link steps,** such as "after preheating the oven. . . ."
5. **Stress the importance of time.** Because process explains things in slow motion, it can mislead people about the amount of time involved. You can prevent confusion by opening with a "real-time" description of the process:

   The test car struck the barrier at thirty-five miles an hour. In less than a tenth of a second, the bumper crumpled, sending shock waves through the vehicle as the fenders folded back and the hood flew off, shattering the windshield.

   The rest of the paragraph can repeat the process, slowly relating each stage in greater detail.
6. **Use images, details, and examples to explain steps.**

EXERCISE 1   Writing Paragraphs That Explain

Write a paragraph that explains one of the following processes:

- how things are sold on eBay
- the hiring process at your job
- how children learn to walk or talk
- a method used to complete a task at work
- how computer viruses damage computers
- how a lottery operates
- how wages or salaries are set at your job
- how playoffs work in the NFL
- how people lose weight
- how people look for jobs
- how something is made, sold, or repaired
- how winners are chosen on *American Idol* or *Project Runway*

Writing Paragraphs That Give Directions

Directions are step-by-step instructions that tell readers how to accomplish a specific task. Process paragraphs that provide advice or suggestions can be written in a standard paragraph:

> During a tornado watch, pay attention to the sky. Tornados are formed by thunderstorms, especially those with frequent thunder and lightning. Look for an extremely dark sky highlighted with green or yellow clouds. Listen for a steady rumbling noise that might sound like a distant freight train or jet engine. If these conditions occur, do not wait for the approach of a funnel cloud; take shelter immediately.

If you are giving readers precise, step-by-step instructions, consider using numbered steps or bulleted points rather than a traditional paragraph. Recipes and repair manuals are used as references while people are working at something, and numbered steps make them easier to read. Numbered steps highlight key information and eliminate the need for transitional phrases such as *the next thing you should do is* and *once this is done, now it is time to. . . .* To emphasize action, begin each numbered point with a clear action verb that tells people what to do:

> In case of a tornado warning, which means that a funnel cloud has been reported, take these steps immediately:
>
> 1. Turn off all computers and lab equipment. *Make sure that all Bunsen burners and other gas flames are turned off.*
> 2. Place microscopes on the floor under the bench.
> 3. Secure all documents in lab bench drawers.
> 4. Turn out the lights, leave the lab, and close both doors.
> 5. Take shelter in the basement of the main building.
> 6. Do *NOT* take shelter in the cafeteria, gym, or garage.
> 7. Remain in the shelter until the warning is declared over by your instructor.

TIPS FOR GIVING DIRECTIONS

1. **Consider your readers' level of knowledge.** Define key terms.

2. **Make sure that directions are self-contained.** Your paragraph should include all the information readers need.

3. **Consider using numbered steps, graphs, diagrams, and other visual aids for easier reading.**

4. **Provide precise, complete instructions.** Avoid vague directions such as "put the cake in the oven for thirty minutes or until done." Someone baking the cake for the first time will have no idea what it is supposed to look like when "done." Stating "put the cake in the oven for thirty minutes or until the center is firm and the edges are dark brown" gives readers a clear idea of what to expect.

5. **Tell readers what not to do.** Give negative directions to prevent readers from making common mistakes such as skipping a step or substituting cheaper materials.

6. **Inform readers of possible events they may misinterpret as mistakes.** If at some point in the process a machine can overheat or a mixture changes color or a computer slows down, let readers know this is normal.

7. **Keep sentences short and direct.**

8. **Warn readers of any hazards to their health and safety or risks to their property, other people, or the environment.**

9. **Use peer review to test your directions.** Other readers may be able to spot missing or confusing steps.

EXERCISE 2   Writing Paragraphs That Give Directions

Write a paragraph that provides instructions on how to do one of the following processes. You may use numbered steps if appropriate.

- how to service or repair an appliance
- how to plan a wedding
- how to teach a child to walk
- how to quit smoking
- how to operate a machine
- how to respond to a fire or other emergency

- how to rent an apartment
- how to care for a pet
- how to avoid foreclosure
- how to treat a minor injury
- how to send a text message
- how to stay on a diet

EXAM SKILLS

Many examination questions call for writing process paragraphs that either explain how something works or provide specific directions. As with any exam, read the question carefully, and make sure that your paragraph directly responds to it. Explain your subject step-by-step, and provide transitional words or phrases or numbered points to organize details.

From Economics

How does the Federal Reserve set monetary policy?

general description

description

step-by-step process

The Federal Reserve System's monetary policy, which controls the supply of money, is determined by its Federal Open Market Committee, or FOMC. This group has 12 voting members, which include 7 from the Federal Reserve Board of Governors and 5 Reserve Bank presidents. The FOMC is headed by the Chairman of the Reserve Board and meets 8 times a year. At these meetings, the members determine to lower, maintain, or increase the discount rate (the rate that the Reserve charges member banks for overnight loans). The FOMC can also influence the money supply by buying and selling government securities that affect the federal funds rate. These changes in interest rates cause banks,

effects of the process	credit card companies, and other lenders to raise or lower the interest that they charge consumers.
goal of the process	The Federal Reserve lowers interest rates to stimulate the economy and raises them to prevent inflation. The actions of the FOMC are designed to maximize employment while keeping prices stable.

Writing at Work: Process

Business and technical documents, like these guidelines, use process to present directions.

AS YOU READ

Notice the importance of the document's format in creating a clear, easily read message.

Stein and Cassell Career Consultants

CONDUCTING A SELF-ASSESSMENT

Transitioning to a new career after losing a job can be stressful. You may feel bitter, confused, and anxious. Stein and Cassell specializes in helping displaced professionals find new and rewarding employment opportunities. Before meeting with your assigned consultant, follow these guidelines to identify your strengths and weaknesses. The more you know about yourself, the better prepared you will be to benefit from our services.

1. **Examine your work history, and ask yourself these two questions:**
   What three things did I like about my past jobs?
   What three things did I hate?

2. **Identify your strengths and weaknesses:**
   List three of your greatest strengths or abilities.
   List three of your greatest problems or weaknesses.

3. **Create a priority list of the following items you want in a new career. Think carefully, and add comments about each one.**

   a income
   b job security
   c the ability to work independently
   d chance for advancement

   e personal satisfaction
   f opportunity to learn new skills
   g pension and benefits
   h status

4. **Write a paragraph describing your ideal job.**

5. **List five things you will have to accomplish to get this job.**

Student Paragraphs

Explaining How Something Works

San Francisco cable cars operate without any steering or engines. They are propelled by a cable under the streets that moves at a constant speed of 9.5 miles an hour. To move the car, the operator uses a lever that grips the cable, much like a skier grabbing onto a towline on a ski lift. Heading downhill, operators often release the car and allow gravity to pull it forward. To slow or stop the car, the operator uses a complex system of brakes. The brake shoes are made of long blocks of soft pine that are replaced every three days. Because the cars cannot turn themselves, huge turntables at the end of each line are used to reposition the cars to head in the opposite direction.

Giving Directions

There are over 50,000 known computer viruses, with almost 500 new ones being created each month. To protect your computer from viruses, there are a number of steps you can take. First, use a good, up-to-date antivirus system that will block viruses and allow you to scan and delete potentially infected files. Make sure to scan your computer at least once a week and update your system regularly. Most viruses today are spread through e-mail. Do not open e-mail from someone you do not know. Be especially careful about opening attachments, especially if you do not know the sender. Back up your important files on discs, CDs, or an external drive.

Giving Directions Using Numbered Steps

If you fail to get the job after a good interview, you are bound to feel angry, discouraged, or depressed. Not getting a job you really wanted and felt you were perfect for can weaken your self-esteem. If you really want the job, you should send a letter or e-mail to the person who interviewed you:

1. Thank the person for the opportunity of being interviewed, and express continued interest in the organization or the position.
2. Maintain a positive tone. Don't suggest that you would have been a better candidate than the person hired or that the employer made a mistake.

3. Briefly restate the strong points highlighted on your résumé and at your interview.
4. Close by saying how and where you can be contacted for future interviews.

If the firm is small and not likely to have additional openings, consider e-mailing or calling the interviewer and ask her if she knows any other employers who might be looking for someone with your skills.

PUTTING PARAGRAPHS TOGETHER

Boosting Your FICO

introduction

definition

topic sentence

Most students know their SAT score and their GPA. But few have even heard of a FICO score or how it can affect their lives. FICO scores (which come from a system created by Fair Isaac & Co) are credit ratings. Anyone who plans to borrow money to buy a car or a house should know how FICOs are determined and how to boost his or her score. Lenders use FICO scores to determine what interest rate you should pay or even whether you deserve a loan at all.

1. What is the function of this paragraph?
2. How does the student explain what a FICO is and why it is important?

explanation of how scores are determined

numbered parts of process

FICO scores are determined by five main factors that are given different values:

1. Payment History (35%)
   The number of accounts you have and the number of late or missing payments are counted.
2. Amounts Owed (30%)
   The amount you owe and the types of loans or credit accounts you have are measured.
3. Credit History (15%)
   The length of your credit history and age of your credit accounts are measured.
4. Types and Use of Credit (10%)
   The number and types of accounts (mortgage, car loan, school loans, credit cards) are evaluated.
5. New Credit (10%)
   Recent requests for credit or newly opened accounts are considered.

explanation of scoring system

Because evaluations and values can vary, lenders usually use scores from three agencies and use the middle score. Scores range from 300-900. Half of American consumers have scores between 700-800. Anyone with a score lower than 620 will have problems getting credit.

1. How do these directions relate to the explanation paragraphs?
2. Would this paragraph be effective if written without numbered steps? Why or why not?
3. How does the student highlight important points?

You can boost your score by taking some important steps that will make it easier for you to get loans and save money by getting lower interest rates:

directions to increase scores

1. Plan ahead.
   It can take three to six months to change your credit rating, so start the process as soon as you can.
2. Get your credit report.
   You can order your credit report from three agencies: Equifax (www.equifax.com), Experian (www.experian.com), and TransUnion (www.transunion.com).
3. Study your report for errors.
   Report mistakes to creditors and credit agencies as soon as possible.
4. Pay bills promptly.
   Pay at least the minimum due on credit cards. Avoid late payments at all costs.
5. Avoid going over your credit limit even if your creditors automatically extend your limit without penalty.
6. Cancel cards you are not using, and avoid acquiring new ones.
7. Pay down credit cards with high balances, and don't consolidate credit cards.
   Having balances over 50% of your credit limit lowers your score. It is better to owe $1,500 on two cards with $5,000 limits than $3,000 on a single card with a $5,000 limit.

numbered steps

1. What is the purpose of this paragraph? How does it explain the process?
2. How does this paragraph build upon the first paragraph?
3. Why does the student use numbered points? Would the list of factors be harder to read if placed in a standard paragraph?

You can obtain additional information from your
bank, credit union, and a number of nonprofit credit
organizations listed in the Yellow Pages.

> 1. What does this paragraph add? Why is it important?
> 2. How should writers address readers' desire or need for additional information or questions?

Steps to Writing a Process Paragraph

1. **Determine whether your goal is to explain how something happens or to give readers directions to accomplish a task.**

2. **Consider your readers' existing knowledge.** Do you need to define terms or explain background information for people to understand the process?

3. **Address common misconceptions or confusions.** In some cases the first thing your paragraph should do is establish clear definitions or separate fact from fiction.

4. **Use examples to illustrate steps in the process.**

5. **Explain any exceptions to or variations in the process.** Recipes, for example, might give different directions for people using conventional and microwave ovens.

6. **Write a draft of your paragraph.**

7. **Read your paragraph aloud, and ask yourself these questions:**

   Have I clearly defined my topic?

   Is my description of the process self-contained? Is it complete? Did I forget any steps?

   Do I break the process into logical steps?

   Do I use numbered steps or transitional words and phrases to link steps in the process?

   Is there anything misleading in my paragraph that my readers may not understand?

Selecting Topics

1. Select a topic with which you are familiar, such as a subject you have studied, something you have worked with, or something you have learned about as a consumer.

2. Determine whether you want to explain how the process works or direct readers to accomplish a process step-by-step.

3. Consider your readers. Are you writing to people familiar with your topic or to the general public?

EXERCISE 3 Planning and Writing Process Paragraphs

Select a topic, and explain it or give directions. Make sure that you divide the process into clear steps.

Topic _____

Goal—to explain or to give directions: _____

First sentence—topic sentence, introduction, definition, or background information:

_____

_____

Steps in the process:

1. _____

2. _____

3. _____

4. _____

5. _____

Possible exceptions or changes: _____

_____

_____

Potential hazards: _____

_____

Last sentence—final step, suggestions about further information, or final comment:

_____

_____

WORKING TOGETHER

Working with a group of students, revise the following e-mail by establishing clearer steps and adding missing information. List questions you have about these instructions. Refer to a car repair or car owner's manual or a website to evaluate the quality of these directions. Note missing steps and safety warnings.

Note to all drivers of company vehicles.

Because sales staff often travel on remote roads far from possible assistance, all drivers should know how to change a tire.

1. Park the car.
2. Remove the jack from the trunk.
3. Loosen lug nuts.
4. Use the jack to raise the car and remove lug nuts.
5. Remove old tire from axle and replace with spare.
6. Tighten lug nuts and lower car.
7. Remove jack and firmly tighten lug nuts.

Get Thinking and Writing

CRITICAL THINKING

Write a paragraph giving suggestions to high school seniors heading to college or adults returning to school. Based on your own experiences, give them step-by-step directions that will prepare them not only for classes but also for adjustments that they may have to make in their personal lives to succeed in college.

WHAT HAVE YOU WRITTEN?

Read your paragraph carefully. Write out your topic sentence or controlling idea:

_____

Is it clearly stated? Could it be revised to better state your goal?

- Have you organized the paragraph in clear steps?
- Do you number steps or use clear transitions to move readers from step to step?
- Do you emphasize your most important suggestions by placing them first or last on your list?
- Do you give people information that will really help?
- Do you give readers practical examples that they can understand?
- Is there anything else you can add that would help readers prepare for college?

Get Writing

Write one or more paragraphs that relate an experience in which you tried to teach someone how to do something or give directions. Why is giving instructions difficult? Looking back, can you spot errors you made?

WRITING ON THE WEB

Using a search engine such as Yahoo! or Google, enter terms such as *how to, how things work, how things happen, process writing, writing explanations, writing directions,* and *writing instructions* to locate current sites of interest.

1. Read online advice articles or websites giving directions to see how writers organize instructions and explain complex or abstract ideas.

2. Explore websites about hobbies or interests you have to see how these sites give advice, inform readers, or state directions.

3. Write an e-mail to a friend explaining step-by-step something you learned at work or in college.

POINTS TO REMEMBER

1. Process explains how something happens or gives directions to accomplish a task.
2. Readers may need background information or definitions of key terms to fully understand the process.
3. Process paragraphs can include numbered steps for easy reading and reference.
4. Examples and clear details are important to explain steps.
5. Directions should inform readers of any potential hazards.
6. Peer review can detect missing steps and confusing directions.

CHAPTER 12

Developing Paragraphs Using Cause and Effect

CHAPTER GOALS

- Understand How Writers Use Cause and Effect
- Appreciate the Value of Critical Thinking
- Realize the Importance of Organization

IMAC/ALAMY LIMITED

Get Writing

What causes people to gamble? Is gambling a harmless pastime, an exciting challenge, or a dangerous habit? Do you ever gamble? Why or why not?

Write a paragraph stating your views on gambling.

What Is Cause and Effect?

Why are reality shows popular? What motivates suicide bombers? How will global warming damage the planet? Why are health-care costs rising? How effective are crash diets? How does outsourcing affect the job market? The answers to all these questions call for **cause-and-effect writing that explains reasons why things happen or analyzes or predicts results:**

> I dropped my evening classes because I transferred to the second shift.

> Hybrid cars are selling well because people fear rising gas prices and are concerned about the environment.

> If you keep smoking, you will ruin your lungs.

> After ten years of effort, Mayor Ramon's plan to attract business to downtown created 150 new jobs.

WHAT ARE YOU TRYING TO SAY?

Write a paragraph that explains the causes or effects of one of the following topics.

Causes why:
- students suffer from stress
- few Americans learn foreign languages
- people immigrate to the United States
- a candidate won or lost a recent election

Effects of:
- dropping out of school
- violent video games
- terrorism
- 24-hour cable news channels

Get Writing and Revising

_____

_____

_____

_____

_____

_____

_____

_____

_____

_____

_____

_____

_____

_____

WHAT HAVE YOU WRITTEN?

Read your paragraph carefully. Underline the topic sentence. List the main causes or effects in your paragraph:

1. _____

2. _____

3. _____

Do these causes or effects logically relate to your topic sentence?
Can you think of better causes or effects? To revise this paragraph, what changes would you make?

Critical Thinking for Writing Cause-and-Effect Paragraphs

Writing about causes and effects requires careful observation and critical thinking. Experts on terrorism, for example, disagree about its causes—poverty and the lack of opportunities for young men in poor countries, U.S. foreign policy, religious extremism, or authoritarian regimes in the Middle East. Economists argue whether cutting taxes will create jobs or just increase the national debt. Even when you write about your own life, you may be unable to define the reasons for decisions you have made. For instance, why did you choose this college? Which factor influenced you the most: course offerings, the campus, the location, your family, or the cost?

Strategies for Critical Thinking

1. **Look beyond first impressions and assumptions.** Make sure that you collect enough evidence and examine it carefully before making any judgments. *Don't jump to conclusions.*

2. **Don't mistake a time relationship for cause and effect.** If your transmission fails the day after you had an oil change, does it prove that the mechanics were responsible? The mechanics may have never touched your transmission, which was bound to fail with or without an oil change. If car sales soar after a big ad campaign, does it prove that the commercials worked? Could auto sales have increased for other reasons—lower interest rates, better employment, or price increases by other carmakers? *Don't mistake coincidence with cause.*

3. **Don't confuse an association with a cause.** For years some experts claimed that marijuana led to heroin addiction because nearly every addict had smoked marijuana before trying heroin. The evidence seemed convincing. But because addicts also probably drank beer, smoked cigarettes, and chewed gum, it did not prove that use of one substance caused addiction to another.

4. **Don't assume that past performance can predict the future.** Just because prices of real estate, gold, or oil have increased dramatically in recent years does not mean they will continue to rise in the future. *Don't assume that trends will continue.*

5. **Don't mistake an effect for a cause.** If children who read poorly spend a lot of time watching TV, you might assume that it interferes with their reading ability. But instead of causing the problem, it could be an effect. Because they have problems reading, they watch spend more time in front of television than with books and magazines.

EXERCISE 1 Critical Thinking and Cause and Effect

Read each statement, and evaluate how effectively the writer uses critical thinking to identify a cause-and-effect relationship. Write C for a probable cause-and-effect relationship and X for a mistake in critical thinking.

1. _____ I flunked my math exam. I should have known something bad was going to happen today. I saw a black cat this morning.

2. _____ SAT scores at our school have increased steadily. It may be because more students are using the library and computer labs.

3. _____ My baseball card collection doubled in value in two years. In ten years I can sell it and buy a car.

4. _____ Green Bay will beat Chicago on October 15. So far this season they have won every game played on an odd day of the week.

5. _____ Every student getting A's in my physics class watches the Discovery Channel. Parents should make sure that their children watch educational TV if they want them to do well in school.

6. _____ Since we hired security guards to patrol the store on weekends, shoplifting has dropped 45 percent on Saturdays and Sundays. We should consider using guards seven days a week.

7. _____ My grandmother had a stroke three months after moving to Miami. Her neighbor had a heart attack right after she moved to Palm Beach. Old people just can't take the Florida heat.

8. _____ Movie attendance has dropped 8 percent this year. High ticket prices are likely to blame.

9. _____ Three big-budget movies about 9/11 failed at the box office. Two television specials about Osama bin Laden and Al Qaeda had low ratings. The public does not want to be reminded of terrorism.

10. _____ Eighty percent of teenagers arrested for drug use listen to hip hop. Parents need to keep their children away from this music if they want to keep them drug free.

EXERCISE 2   Identifying Causes

Read the following paragraph; then answer the questions that follow.

We can expect oil prices to increase over the next decade. First, oil reserves are steadily dwindling. As oil producers have to use more expensive technology to locate oil and bring it to the surface, it will cost more. Production will be hampered because of political instability in Iraq. Russia has large oil fields, but its pipelines are decayed and will take years to replace in order to develop an efficient delivery system. Second, demand is rising sharply throughout the world. India and China are booming. They are increasing their industrial production, and hundreds of millions of their citizens are becoming consumers. China, for example, has seen a surge in two-car families, something that was almost unheard of just ten years ago. With a growing demand for a limited amount of oil, petroleum prices will definitely rise.

1. **What is the topic sentence?**

2. **What are the causes? Restate them in your own words:**

    a. _____

    b. _____

    c. _____

    d. _____

    e. _____

EXERCISE 3   Identifying Effects

Read the following paragraph; then answer the questions that follow.

The likely increase in oil prices will have dramatic effects on the economy, consumer behavior, and scientific research. First, we can expect higher fuel prices will drive up the cost of living. Almost everything that is sold in this country is shipped by truck. Airfares and bus tickets will likely rise to pay for the higher cost of fuel. Housing prices will rise because roof shingles and plastic pipes are made from petroleum. Rising gas prices will lessen demand for SUVs and spark interest in smaller, more fuel-efficient cars. Hybrid cars will no doubt increase in sales. Interest in alternative sources of energy, ranging from wind to nuclear, will increase as well. Rising transportation costs will lead businesspeople to use video conferences and e-mail to reduce the need for face-to-face meetings. Rather than fly across the country to attend conventions, more professionals may prefer to participate online. Rising oil prices will cause inflation and unemployment. As consumers have to spend more on gas and heating oil, they will have less money to spend on other goods and services. These economic problems will cause greater pressure on Congress to fund research to find new energy sources.

1. **What is the topic sentence?**

2. **What are the effects? Restate them in your own words:**

   a. _____

   b. _____

   c. _____

   d. _____

   e. _____

EXAM SKILLS

Examination questions often call for cause-and-effect answers. Given the time limit of most exams, it is important to identify key causes or effects. Because any answer you give will likely be incomplete, you can qualify your answer with a strong introduction or conclusion.

From Introduction to Literature

Why does Willy Loman commit suicide at the end of *Death of a Salesman?*

introduction, rejects other possible causes	Many readers assume that Willy Loman commits suicide because he is depressed over losing his job. Willy <u>is</u> a defeated and angry man, but he does not kill himself out of despair. Willy is not facing an economic crisis. His house is paid off, and
topic sentence	his friend Charley offers to give him a job. <u>Instead, Willy Loman views taking his life not as an escape from his problems but a victory over them.</u> Willy
cause 1	imagines he will have a massive funeral that will finally prove to his son Biff that he was well-known
cause 2	and respected. In addition, he plans to leave his insurance money to Biff. With this money, Biff, who has been making a dollar an hour as a farmhand, will finally become a success. For Willy, suicide is not an act of desperation but his last big business deal that will prove to everyone that he was right all along.

Writing at Work: **Cause and Effect**

Business and technical documents, like this report, use cause and effect to present ideas.

AS YOU READ

Notice the importance of the document's format in creating a clear, easily read message.

CAMPUS HEALTH OFFICE

TO ALL STAFF

SHARING OF PRESCRIPTION MEDICATION

Background

Recent studies have shown that one in four Americans share prescriptions with others. A campus survey revealed that 18% of students reported sharing prescription medication with friends. The most commonly shared drugs included painkillers and anti-depressants.

Causes

- Peer pressure.
- Desire to help friends in distress, provide immediate relief, spare friends cost of physician or hospital visits.
- Lack of understanding of potential risks.
- General belief that prescription medications are safer than illegal or "street drugs."

Effects

- Accidental overdoses.
- Allergic reactions and interactions with other medications.
- Masking of symptoms delaying needed medical evaluation and treatment.
- Fraudulent requests for additional medication.

Recommendations

The college must educate students about the dangers of sharing prescription medication.

- Include a unit on sharing prescription medications in freshman orientation.
- Add banner message on Student Life website with link to Campus Health.
- Remind coaches, health instructors, biology instructors, therapists, and counselors who have contact with students to instruct them about the dangers of sharing prescription medication.
- Post warnings in dorms, classroom buildings, locker rooms, and student union.

Student Paragraphs

Cause Paragraph

Our football team had another disappointing season. We remain a campus joke. Of course, a technical college does not draw serious players. The gifted high school players are recruited by the state universities and big schools with generous athletic programs. We do have good players. We do have a good coach. But we have a hard time building a winning team for two main reasons. First, most of our players are older men with jobs and families. They may love the game, but it cannot be a priority in their lives as it is for a teenager on an athletic scholarship. Second, all of our players live off campus. We don't have team housing or have players who can walk across the street between classes to hit the weight room. Some of our players have to commute fifty miles to practice and arrive tired and stressed out. We are never likely to have a winning season, but we play for one reason: We play because we love the game.

Effect Paragraph

Learning I had high blood pressure last May, I decided to begin exercising. I joined a health club, which I visit three times a week, and I take a morning run every day. This routine was tough at first. But after two months, I lost fifteen pounds and became firmer. I also found that my concentration and energy improved. I no longer needed a nap after I came home from work to stay awake in night school. It took me less time to complete assignments, and I remembered more of what I read. The main effect of my exercise program has been a more positive attitude. I feel more optimistic, more enthusiastic about doing new things, and more confident about my future. I no longer feel overwhelmed and no longer take comfort in junk food.

Cause-and-Effect Paragraph

In the last decade, infection has become a serious problem in our nation's hospitals. In some institutions, one-third of patients leave the hospital with an infection they did not have when they were admitted. There are many causes, but the most important two are the rise in drug-resistant germs and poor hand-washing habits. Some studies show that only 10 percent of doctors follow the approved sanitation standards. As a result, thousands of people die needlessly, and tens of thousands require longer hospitalization and expensive drugs to recuperate. The proper use of soap and water can shorten hospital stays, reduce complications, and save billions of dollars annually.

PUTTING PARAGRAPHS TOGETHER

Insecurity Cams

topic sentence

Consumers of an inexpensive electronic device have discovered something strange and dangerous. Costing about a hundred dollars, license plate cams are widely sold in discount stores and car supply shops. Mounted at the rear of a vehicle, a small video camera sends a signal to a dashboard screen, giving drivers an unobstructed view of objects behind them. This is especially helpful to owners of SUVs and vans when backing into garages or out of driveways, especially where cars or small children might be hidden by blind spots. Driving through some neighborhoods, owners of license plate cams have been surprised by what appears on their dashboard screens. Instead of seeing the cars behind them, they find themselves looking into stores, restaurants, bars, bowling alleys, even people's bedrooms.

1. What is the purpose of this paragraph?
2. What factual details does it contain?

topic sentence

The cause of this phenomenon is very simple. Millions of homes and businesses contain wireless security cams. Small cameras broadcast a signal to a monitor elsewhere in the building. A mother can keep her eye on a child sleeping upstairs while preparing a meal in the kitchen. Business owners can check on employees and customers in the front of stores without leaving their desks in the back office. Although short range, the signals are strong enough to penetrate the walls of homes and most commercial buildings. Someone outside with a similar monitor can pick up the signal and observe what is going on inside.

1. What cause does the paragraph describe?
2. How does this paragraph build upon the first one?
3. What is the purpose of this paragraph?

The effects of this are obvious and disturbing. **topic sentence**
Thieves can now park outside a store and survey the
business without exposing themselves to potential witnesses. They can see if the location has a security
guard or a metal detector. They can wait until the
store empties of customers or for a clerk to walk away
from the cash register before entering the premises.
Stalkers and predators can watch their victims in
their homes and wait for a person to undress or leave
a child unattended. Embarrassing or incriminating activities can not only be secretly monitored but also
recorded and placed online. The cameras that people
have installed to ensure their privacy and heighten
their security are now exposing them to the very
dangers they fear.

1. How does this paragraph build upon the previous one?
2. What effects does it list?

Owners of wireless video camera systems should **topic sentence**
consult security professionals to eliminate this risk.
Although more expensive, hard-wired systems do not
broadcast signals but connect a camera directly to
a monitor the way a cable connects a computer with a
printer. Existing wireless systems can be recalibrated
and fitted with scramblers to limit unauthorized
monitoring.

1. What is the purpose of this paragraph?
2. How does it relate to the previous paragraphs?
3. What details does it include?

Steps to Writing A Cause-And-Effect Paragraph

1. **Study your topic and use critical thinking by asking key
   questions:**

   Am I going to explain causes, effects, or both?

   *What is the most important cause or effect I want readers to
   know?*

   Are there any terms I need to define?

Do readers need any background information?

What evidence such as facts, examples, or quotations can support my ideas?

2. **Develop a topic sentence that clearly states your controlling idea.**

3. **Review your list of causes or effects, and delete minor or confusing details.** Organize your ideas by time or by order of importance.

4. **Write a draft of your paragraph.**

5. **Read your paragraph aloud, and consider these questions:**

    Does my paragraph have a clear topic sentence?

    Are causes or effects clearly stated and supported by facts, examples, and other evidence?

    Is the paragraph clearly organized?

6. **Use peer review to check your paragraph.** Other readers may be able to detect mistakes in critical thinking or awkwardly stated ideas you have missed.

Selecting Topics

Consider the following topics for cause-and-effect paragraphs.

Explain the causes of one of the following topics:

- low voter turnout
- racism
- student cheating
- popularity of a TV show
- the breakup of a band
- popularity of a fad

Measure the effects of one of the following topics:

- unemployment
- a death in the family
- living away from home
- having a baby
- cost of health-care insurance

EXERCISE 4   Planning and Writing Cause-and-Effect Paragraphs

Select a topic from one of the previous lists, or choose one of your own. Develop a topic sentence that states your point of view.

Topic:

Causes or effects:

1. _____

2. _____

3. _____

4. _____

First sentence—topic sentence, first cause or effect, or introductory statement:

_____

_____

Causes or effects:

1. _____

2. _____

3. _____

4. _____

Last sentence—final cause or effect, concluding statement, or topic sentence:

_____

_____

Write out your paragraph, and review it by reading it aloud.

WORKING TOGETHER

Working with a group of students, revise this e-mail to shorten and clarify directions. You may wish to create numbered points.

Dorm Resident Advisors:

Security guards have again reported that students are breaking the rules regarding the underground parking garage in the dorms. Remember that under no circumstances are students allowed to store gasoline cans or other flammable products in the garage. Several students with motorcycles have been placing cans of gas in their parking spaces or on homemade tool benches. Also, parking spaces must be kept clear. They are getting cluttered with spare tires and toolboxes. In addition, remind students not to work on their cars in the garage, especially to change tires using jacks or to change oil. Students are not allowed to wash cars in the garage. The hose is for maintenance use only. Remind students that for insurance reasons we cannot have students working on cars in the garage. Also it is a fire hazard to have gasoline stored in cans in an underground garage. Please make sure you inform all students of these rules, which are listed in the student handbook.

Cindy Rosales

Get Thinking and Writing

CRITICAL THINKING

What effects have cell and camera phones had on society? Have they improved communications, making our jobs and lives better and easier? Or have they robbed us of privacy and created a new source of annoyance in theaters, restaurants, and other public places? Write a paragraph outlining the positive and/or negative effects of cell and camera phones. Support your points with examples.

WHAT HAVE YOU WRITTEN?

Read your paragraph carefully.

Write out your topic sentence or controlling idea:

_____

_____

_____

List the effects you identify:

_____

_____

_____

- Are they significant effects? Can you think of more important ones?
- Could you place them in a different order to make your paragraph stronger and easier to read?

Get Writing

MICHAEL DWYE/ALAMY LIMITED

What effects does gambling have? Does it lead people to spend money they cannot afford? Can it cause compulsive behavior? Do you know anyone with a gambling problem?

Write a paragraph outlining the effects of gambling.

WRITING ON THE WEB

Using a search engine such as Yahoo! or Google, enter terms such as *writing cause and effect, cause-and-effect essays, organizing cause-and-effect essays,* and *critical thinking and cause and effect.*

1. Search for news articles using cause and effect to examine issues such as terrorism, global warming, unemployment, tax cuts, or a recent controversy in your area.

2. Write an e-mail to a friend using cause and effect to explain a decision you have made or to give reasons for a problem.

POINTS TO REMEMBER

1. Cause-and-effect paragraphs need clear topic sentences.

2. Cause-and-effect paragraphs depend on critical thinking and evidence. Readers will expect you to prove your points. Make sure that you avoid errors such as jumping to conclusions or confusing an association with a cause.

3. Peer review can help detect mistakes in critical thinking and awkwardly stated ideas.

CHAPTER 13

Developing Paragraphs Using Argument

CHAPTER GOALS

- Understand the Goal of Argument and Persuasion

- Use Evidence to Support Arguments

- Appeal to Readers' Interests, Values, and Concerns

- Overcome Readers' Objections

ASSOCIATED PRESS/AP PHOTO

Hijacker Mohammed Atta passes through airport security, September 11, 2001

Get Writing

What can be done to protect our nation from terrorists? The 9/11 hijackers were able to enter the country, obtain driver's licenses, take flying lessons, and board planes with weapons.

Write a paragraph arguing how to increase our security.

What Is Argument?

Argument paragraphs convince readers to accept an idea, adopt a solution, change their opinions, or take action. Writers use reason and facts to support their positions, often challenging other points of view. Lawyers prepare written arguments stating why a client deserves a new trial. Scientists present test results to prove that a drug is unsafe. Economists collect data to support arguments to raise or lower taxes. Campaign commercials encourage voters to support a candidate. Pop-up ads on your computer urge you to upgrade your software. As a student, you develop arguments in essays and research papers to demonstrate your skills and knowledge. In your career, you will have to impress clients, motivate employees, justify decisions, defend actions, and propose new ideas with well-stated arguments.

To write effective argument paragraphs, it is important to understand what an argument is *not*. First, the word *argument* does not mean a fight. Calling people names, using stereotypes, making accusations, and using facts taken out of context is not likely to be convincing:

> Mayor Jack Swanson's plan to build a light-rail system downtown is totally insane. Only an idiot would suggest spending over $500 million to build a streetcar line. They ripped out the streetcar tracks almost a hundred years ago when they invented buses. Evidently Swanson does not realize we already have public transportation. It is called the bus line. Maybe he could look out the window of his city limo and notice the lines of people waiting for the bus on every corner. How about spending just maybe $10 million to buy a few more buses and save us all a lot of trouble? Swanson must be on the take from the contractors bidding on the biggest waste of city money in history.
>
> *LETTER TO THE EDITOR*

Effective argument is based on facts and reason and does not use insults or accusations to try to change people's minds.

Improved

> Mayor Jack Swanson has proposed spending $500 million to build a streetcar line to reduce downtown congestion. Construction would take three years and disrupt traffic on major intersections just when the city is trying to attract major conventions to the expanded Civic Center and new Hyatt Hotel. The city already operates a highly effective bus system that carries more than 25,000 riders downtown every day. We can achieve many of Mayor Swanson's goals by simply spending $10 million on more buses.

WHAT ARE YOU TRYING TO SAY?

Get Writing

Write a paragraph that uses argument to state your opinion on one of the following topics. You may narrow the topic to focus on a key point. Make sure that you have a strongly stated topic sentence and give readers reasons to accept your point of view.

- why a school policy should or should not be changed
- why drivers should always wear seat belts
- why illegal aliens should or should not be given driver's licenses
- why women should or should not be required to register for the draft

- why everyone should know his or her cholesterol level and blood pressure
- why high schools should or should not teach sex education
- why a recent film, band, or television show is under- or overrated
- why a choice in roommate can affect your success in college
- why the state should or should not limit the number of hours that high school students may work

WHAT HAVE YOU WRITTEN?

Read your paragraph carefully.
What is the topic sentence or controlling idea?

_____

_____

Can you rewrite it to make it more precise or convincing?
What examples, reasons, evidence, or observations do you include to support your topic sentence?

1. _____

2. _____

3. _____

4. _____

Do these items directly support your topic sentence? Should any be deleted or revised? Can you think of better types of support?

Critical Thinking for Writing Argument Paragraphs

Argument paragraphs require clearly stated topic sentences. Your goal is not to simply provide information or express your feelings but to direct readers to accept a specific point of view, take a particular action, or become aware of a problem or situation:

The college must increase security in the Student Union to stop purse snatchings.

Students should support the History Department's demand for expanded computer lab and library hours during exam weeks.

The city must invest in new roads, sewers, and water lines if it wants to expand.

TIPS FOR WRITING TOPIC SENTENCES FOR ARGUMENT PARAGRAPHS

1. State your argument precisely; avoid vague generalized statements.

Vague
They should do something about all this trash on campus.

Improved
The maintenance department should clean the campus by removing litter and installing more trash cans.

2. Avoid emotionally charged, insulting, or exaggerated arguments.

Emotionally Charged

These sick child molesters should be shot on the spot.

Improved

People convicted of multiple sexual assaults against children should be given the maximum sentence the law allows.

3. Create topic sentences that can be supported with specific facts, examples, statistics, and other evidence. Avoid topic sentences that simply make a comment or state an observation.

Mere Observation

The automotive services program has not been upgraded since 1994.

Improved

The automotive services program is outdated and needs new equipment to train students to work on hybrid engines.

Topic sentences must be supported with evidence:

Facts are objective details that can be directly observed or collected from reliable sources. A student arguing for greater campus security can describe unguarded entrances he or she has noticed and use police reports to document an increase in thefts, assaults, and break-ins.

Testimony (quotations) are observations or statements made by witnesses, participants, or experts. A call for additional security could be supported by quotations from victims or police officers.

Examples are specific persons, events, or situations that illustrate a writer's point. The need for security on campus could be demonstrated with examples of recent break-ins, carjackings, and muggings.

Statistics are facts expressed in numbers. The argument for more security could include numbers of reported crimes or statistics showing an increase in 911 calls.

TIPS FOR USING EVIDENCE

It is important to use evidence that is effective. In writing and revising an argument paragraph, ask yourself the following questions about the support you include:

1. Is the evidence accurate? Can you verify that the facts, statistics, and quotations you present are correct? Use library databases to locate current and accurate information.

2. Are the sources reliable? Did you collect information from objective sources such as encyclopedias, recognized authorities, government agencies, and professional journals found in libraries, or did it come from gossip magazines, blogs, or special interest groups?

3. Does the evidence suit your topic sentence? An argument for a change in immigration policy or tax laws requires factual or statistical support, not merely quotations from individuals stating personal opinions.

4. Do you provide evidence that your readers will understand and accept? Quotations from unknown people, long lists of statistics, or facts taken from little-known magazines or websites may not impress readers. Explain what your evidence means and why it is important.

EXERCISE 1   Identifying Topic Sentences and Supporting Evidence

Read the following student paragraph, and answer the questions that follow.

Last year, President Neiman told the school paper "we must dramatically increase our enrollment or face severe cuts in state funding." He approved a $150,000 increase in television, radio, and print advertising to attract new students. To spare enrolling students from standing in endless lines, the school promoted its touchtone and online system. In theory, students can avoid a trip downtown and register by phone or online from home 24 hours a day. In reality, nearly one-third of students who registered off campus never appeared on official college rosters. Many were mailed packets of forms that arrived too late to sign up for needed courses. Twenty-six nursing students who received e-mail confirmations discovered they were never actually registered in clinical programs and had to delay graduation. The registrar claims that in-person registration is the only reliable way of signing up for classes. This is an unacceptable attitude in a technical college. Every method of registration must be equally reliable or should not be offered. The college must overhaul its obsolete registration software if it wants to serve its students, project a good image to the community, and achieve President Neiman's enrollment goals.

1. What is the student's topic sentence?

_____

_____

2. How does the student demonstrate the need for his or her position?

_____

3. What evidence does the student provide to support the topic sentence?

_____

_____

_____

_____

4. What additional evidence might be included to support the student's position?

_____

_____

_____

_____

5. How does the student use the evidence to support his or her point of view?

_____

_____

6. How does the college president's quotation support the student's argument?

_____

_____

_____

EXERCISE 2   Developing Evidence to Support Topic Sentences

Describe the evidence needed to support each of the following topic sentences:

1. The college should offer more sections of math and English.

_____

_____

_____

_____

2. Car insurance must be made mandatory for all drivers in this state.

_____

_____

_____

_____

3. The stadium should stop beer sales after halftime.

_____

_____

_____

_____

4. Parents must limit their children's consumption of junk food.

_____

_____

_____

_____

EXERCISE 3   Evaluating Evidence

To provide effective support, the evidence that you present must be accurate, be reliable, and meaningfully relate to your topic sentence. Read each topic sentence carefully, and rate the value of the supporting evidence. Is the evidence likely to convince readers to accept the writer's argument?

1. *The campus fire alarm system must be repaired.* **Last month classes were disrupted six times by false alarms while a fire in the Chemistry Building failed to trigger the sprinkler system.**

Type of evidence: _____

Value of evidence:

Very reliable____Reliable____Somewhat reliable____Unreliable____

Comments or suggestions for additional evidence:

_____

_____

_____

2. *Smoking is harmless.* **Churchill smoked cigars and lived to be ninety. My eighty-year-old grandfather smokes two packs a day and is in great shape.**

Type of evidence: _____

Value of evidence:

Very reliable____Reliable____Somewhat reliable____Unreliable____

Comments or suggestions for additional evidence:

_____

_____

_____

3. *The government should approve plans to build a nuclear power plant on the Boyle River.* **The president of Southern Power and Light says we need the electricity.**

Type of evidence: _____

Value of evidence:

Very reliable____Reliable____Somewhat reliable____Unreliable____

Comments or suggestions for additional evidence:

_____

_____

_____

4. *The college needs additional parking.* **Last year 72 percent of students polled complained about the lack of parking. Of 85 complaints sent to Student Services this semester, 39 concerned parking.**

Type of evidence: _____

Value of evidence:

Very reliable____Reliable____Somewhat reliable____Unreliable____

Comments or suggestions for additional evidence:

_____

_____

_____

Understanding Your Audience

Whenever you write, you need to consider your readers. This is especially true when you write an argument. In description or narration, you are simply sharing ideas and experiences with readers. In argument, you are asking people to change the way they think or behave. To be effective, you have to target your argument to address your readers' concerns, feelings, knowledge, values, and attitudes. An argument to lower the drinking age to eighteen targeted to college students may not convince their parents, state legislators, or law enforcement professionals. They may not be impressed by student polls or quotations from eighteen-year-olds insisting they are mature enough to drink responsibly. On the other hand, they might be influenced by evidence supplied by psychologists, government reports, research studies, and statistics from experts in alcohol abuse. Above all, it is important to address readers' potential objections to your ideas.

Appealing to Hostile Readers

Perhaps the most challenging problem you can face is trying to convince a hostile audience to accept your ideas—readers you know or expect will have negative attitudes about you, the organization you represent, or the ideas you advocate. There is no way to magically make people change their beliefs and feelings, but there are techniques you can use to influence readers to consider your point of view.

TIPS FOR ADDRESSING HOSTILE READERS

1. **Openly admit differences.** Instead of trying to pretend that no conflict exists, frankly state that your view may differ from that of your readers.

2. **Responsibly summarize opposing viewpoints.** By describing your opponents' views in their own words, you show that you understand their position and that you can argue fairly and responsibly.

3. **Avoid insults and accusations.** Don't call people who disagree with you stupid or immoral. Insulting readers will only make them resist your arguments and make it harder for them to change their minds.

4. **Respect readers' concerns and objections.** Don't dismiss readers' concerns as being wrong, uninformed, or selfish. If people object to building low-income housing in their neighborhood because they are concerned about crime and congestion, acknowledge and address their issues directly. Don't reject their objections by calling them racist or narrow-minded.

5. **Ask readers to maintain an open mind.** Don't demand or expect to convert readers, but keep in mind that almost everyone will agree to try to be open-minded and receptive to new ideas.

6. **Overcome negative stereotypes.** Determine what negative stereotypes your readers might have about you, the organization you represent, or your thesis. Use examples, references, evidence, and stories to create positive impressions about your point of view.

EXERCISE 4   Overcoming Readers' Objections

Describe how the writers in the following situations could approach readers to overcome their objections. What facts, statistics, quotations, or other evidence would they need to provide to convince readers to accept their point of view? What objections would they have to address?

1. A student group urging alumni football fans to donate to the library instead of the stadium.

Strategy _____

_____

Evidence _____

_____

2. A tenant urging a landlord to spend money on roof and window repairs.

Strategy _____

_____

Evidence _____

_____

3. A scientist from the Food and Drug Administration explaining why a new drug needs more testing before it can be approved for AIDS patients.

Strategy _____

_____

Evidence _____

_____

4. A student organization defending its decision to invite a controversial figure to speak on campus despite complaints from parents, alumni, and the public.

Strategy _____

_____

Evidence _____

_____

5. A mayor arguing to homeowners why property taxes have to be increased to pay for new schools.

Strategy _____

_____

Evidence _____

_____

EXAM SKILLS

Examination questions often call for argument paragraphs. Given the time limit of most exams, it is important to develop a clearly defined topic sentence that expresses your point of view and to support it with reliable evidence. If needed, you may have to address common objections to your views.

From Fire Science

What is the most important way that fire professionals can educate the public about fire safety?

introduction	Many fire departments have programs to educate the public about smoke alarms, but they do little to explain the reasons why. Unlike fire pro-
common misconception	fessionals, most of the public has no direct experience and little knowledge about the dynamics of fires. From watching TV and movies, people have a tremendous fear of being burned in fires but little
topic sentence	understanding of how deadly smoke is. Fire professionals must educate the public to appreciate that the true killer in most fires is smoke, not flame,
example	in order to prevent needless death and injury. For example, in a Chicago hotel fire in 2004, 180 people were overcome by smoke inhalation. They remained in the smoky lobby because they saw
statistics	no flames and felt safe. According to a survey of homeowners, only 15 percent knew that plastics and other building materials release poisonous
testimony	chemicals when burned. Smoke killed more people than fire at the World Trade Center in 2001, according to Fire Chief Andrews. The best public service that fire professionals can provide is to educate the public about the fact that when rescuers pull out burned bodies from a fire, most of the victims were killed by smoke long before flames ever touched them.

Writing at Work: Argument

Business and technical documents, like this letter, use argument to influence readers.

AS YOU READ

Notice the importance of the document's format in creating a clear, easily read message.

River West Association

March 18, 2009
Nancy Kwan
Supervisor of Zoning and Regulations
City Hall Room 241
100 Tampico Street
Tampico, CA 94710

RE: Proposed Zoning Change at 27th Street and Santa Rosita Avenue

Dear Ms. Kwan:

In 2004 Mayor Rosa Rodriguez declared that the empty lot on 27th and Santa Rosita Avenue (former site of A-1 Motors) would be turned into park space. In the last five years, twenty-two homes and six condominiums have been constructed on Santa Rosita Avenue, creating a vibrant, family-friendly neighborhood that has added to the city's tax base and helped reverse the trend of middle-class residents leaving the city.

Last month our organization, which represents Santa Rosita Avenue homeowners, learned that Calco Drugs is asking the city to rezone the park on 27th and Santa Rosita Avenue in order to build a big-box superstore. Calco Drugs already six outlets in the city. We fully appreciate its desire for a location on 27th Street. However, there are vacant commercial lots six blocks to the north and eight blocks to the south of Santa Rosita Avenue that are better suited to the company's needs.

We strongly urge that your committee maintain the current zoning status. The small park on 27th and Santa Rosita Avenue creates not only a popular recreation area for families but also a gateway to a new residential neighborhood. Realtors and developers tell us that construction of a big-box outlet store would depreciate home values. Six homes that now face the park would view the loading docks and dumpsters of the proposed Calco Drug store.

We will call you early next week to set up a meeting to discuss this issue. We are willing to work with other members of the zoning board, Mayor Rodriguez, and representatives of Calco Drugs to resolve this issue to the benefit of all concerned.

Sincerely,

Carla Montoya

President, River West Association

Student Paragraphs

Argument to Accept an Idea

I found out about the programs offered by the state's technical college system only by accident. I found a website listing programs I never knew existed. Like most people, I thought people went to community college to learn to be an auto mechanic or a welder. I had no idea these colleges offered computer programming, accounting, banking and finance, business law, and travel and tourism. My high school counselor, the school's Career Week, and parent/teacher conferences mentioned only the state university system. The technical colleges now offer college transfer courses, many of which are taught by Ph.D.s with professional experience. The same introductory courses at the university are taught by teaching assistants working on master's degrees. The tuition at a technical college is a fraction of that at the university. Unfortunately, most people learn about the technical college only by word of mouth. We have to realize that higher education is not limited to universities and that technical schools have a lot to offer.

Argument to Take Action

The U.S. Congress must address rising health-care costs not only for those without insurance but also for the companies that provide it. Our corporations must compete in a global economy, and rising health-care costs are inflating the cost of doing business in this country. In 2004, for example, Ford and GM paid $9 billion for health care. These costs are reflected in the sticker price of their cars, making it harder for them to compete with imports. Politicians who worry about the forty million Americans without health insurance have to think about the companies that have to pay billions to insure their workers. High health-care costs are making it harder for U.S. companies to keep their prices down and are a major reason that many are trying to lower their insurance costs by sending jobs overseas. Write your congressman and senators, and demand they take action!

Argument to Arouse Interest

Teasing and gossip have always been a part of high school life. The Internet has given teens a new way of harassing and persecuting unpopular students. In Cincinnati, several girls started a blog that posted rumors, unflattering pictures, and obscene jokes about a student they dubbed Patty the Pig. The overweight girl was stalked in hallways by students using camera phones to take pictures of her eating or trying to squeeze into a chair. Her parents transferred her to a private school. On her first day she found a Patty the Pig cartoon taped to her locker. The school changed her e-mail address after she was bombarded with Patty the Pig jokes sent from as far away as Texas and Toronto. Gossip and taunts that once had a limited audience are now spread worldwide. The anonymity of the Internet encourages teens to be vicious while concealing their identity. Schools teach driver safety, and many have dress codes. Today they must teach Internet ethics and develop a code of online conduct.

PUTTING PARAGRAPHS TOGETHER

Toxic Trash

introduction When personal computers appeared on the market twenty-five years ago, they were so expensive that most consumers thought of them as a once-in-a-lifetime purchase, not unlike a piano or a Jacuzzi. Few could foresee that computers would become low-cost, disposable items that people replace faster than their cars or slipcovers. **topic sentence** As a result, Americans are contributing to two serious problems by improperly discarding old computers.

1. What is the purpose of this paragraph?
2. How important is the topic sentence?

topic sentence Each year, ten million computers are dumped into landfills, where they have become a major environmental hazard. Computers contain over 700 chemicals, many of which are harmful. A single computer monitor contains two to eight pounds of lead, along with mercury **factual support** and other heavy metals. When monitor screens are broken or pulverized, these toxic elements leach into the soil and contaminate groundwater.

1. What is the purpose of this paragraph?
2. How does it build upon the first paragraph?
3. What evidence does the student use to support the topic sentence?

The improper disposal of computers also exposes millions to identity theft. Consumers often throw away, sell, or donate computers without removing sensitive data from their hard drives. Simply deleting files or emptying trash bins does not erase information from a computer. Many computer owners assume that because they can no longer see files listed in a word processing program, their documents have been destroyed. In fact, all the data they entered remain on the hard drive and can be retrieved. One woman bought a used computer and found the prescription records of two thousand customers from a local drugstore. An accountant upgraded his computer and gave his old one to his son, who later sold it to a friend for fifty dollars, not realizing that it still contained income tax returns of three hundred of his father's customers. Thieves have caught on to the value of old computers. Last year police arrested a Michigan man who had purchased eighty-seven old computers on eBay and recovered enough data to make fraudulent charges on 1,250 credit cards and transfer $450,000 from a car dealer's payroll account to an offshore bank.

examples as support

1. How does this paragraph relate to the first paragraph?
2. What evidence does the student include?

Consumers need to protect their data by removing and destroying the hard drive before taking a computer to a recycling center. Before selling or donating computers they must wipe the entire hard drive with software recommended by the manufacturer. **Most importantly, the federal government must establish regulations mandating the proper cleaning and disposal of old computers.** And even if you safeguard your hard drive, can you assume that your doctor, drugstore, dentist, accountant, or bank will properly clean your personal information from a computer before discarding it?

argument, call to action

1. How does this paragraph conclude the essay?
2. What role does the last sentence have?

Steps to Writing an Argument Paragraph

1. **Determine the goal of your argument—to convince readers to accept an idea or motivate them to take action.**

2. **Consider your readers' existing knowledge, attitudes, and possible objections to your views.**

3. **Develop a precisely worded topic sentence that expresses a point of view that can be supported by logic and evidence.**

4. **Support your topic sentence with evidence that is accurate, is reliable, and addresses your readers' needs, interests, and objections.**

5. **Avoid insults and accusations that will offend readers and make it harder for them to change their minds and accept your point of view.**

6. **Write a draft of your paragraph.**

7. **Read your paragraph aloud, and ask yourself these questions:**

   Have I developed a clearly worded topic sentence that accurately expresses my point of view?

   Do I provide enough evidence that is reliable and that readers will understand and accept?

   Do I avoid using questionable evidence or emotional statements that may alienate readers?

   Is my topic sentence placed in the best position in the paragraph? Should it come first or after some explanation and supporting evidence?

8. **Consider using peer review.** Other people may be able to detect missing evidence, weak arguments, or awkward statements you have overlooked.

Selecting Topics

1. Select topics that you can handle. The word *argument* leads many students to think that they have to write about controversial or political issues such as abortion, gun control, or the death penalty. But you can convince readers to exercise, support a change in a local law, recycle trash, wear seat belts, register to vote, or sign a petition to urge legislation to solve a social problem.

2. Consider your readers' attitudes and possible objections.

3. Develop a well-stated topic sentence, and list the type of evidence needed. You may wish to conduct some library research or search the Internet for facts, statistics, examples, and expert testimony.

Consider these topics for argument paragraphs:

- school uniforms
- global warming
- labor unions
- speed dating
- tattoos and piercings
- pension plans
- personal responsibility for health and fitness
- using cell phones while driving
- violent video games and children
- companies that hire illegal immigrants
- campus day-care services
- health-care costs
- bilingual education

EXERCISE 5   Planning and Writing Argument Paragraphs

Select a topic from the preceding list, or choose one of your own. Develop a topic sentence that states your point of view, addresses readers' concerns, and lists supporting details.

Topic: _____

Topic sentence: _____

_____

Readers' concerns or possible objections: _____

_____

First sentence—introductory fact, topic sentence, or example:

_____

Supporting evidence—facts, quotations, statistics, or examples:

_____

_____

_____

_____

Last sentence—final detail, topic sentence, or concluding remark: _____

_____

_____

Write out your paragraph, and review it by reading it out loud.

WORKING TOGETHER

Working with a group of students, revise the following e-mail asking small business owners to support the Junior Entrepreneur Program. Invent support such as quotations, facts, statistics, and examples.

Dear Ms. Sandoval:

As a Northside business owner and employer, you know the value of hard work and discipline, especially in our young people. Please consider donating this month to the Junior Entrepreneur Program. It is a good program. It helps high school students learn by running their own businesses. The students learn a lot. They work hard. Many famous people support it. It is a good idea to let students learn how to run a business. It is popular with students, but the program needs your support. Please donate generously by calling 1-800-555-9700 today. We really need your support.

Get Thinking and Writing

CRITICAL THINKING

Select a problem you see in your community, college, or workplace. State a clear topic sentence that convinces readers to accept your point of view or motivates them to take action. Support your topic sentence with relevant evidence such as facts, examples, statistics, or quotations.

WHAT HAVE YOU WRITTEN?

Read your paragraph carefully. Write out your topic sentence or controlling idea:

_____

_____

Does it clearly express your point of view or direct readers to take specific actions? Could it be revised to make it clearer and more precise?

List the main supporting details:

_____

_____

_____

_____

- Is this evidence relevant? Does it directly support your topic sentence?
- Is the evidence accurate and reliable? Are you relying on memory or something you saw on TV? Can you recall the source of the support?
- Do you address objections readers might have?
- Can you think of additional evidence?

If possible, conduct an Internet search to locate additional support.

Russell Lee/Bettmann/CORBIS

In April 1942, four months after the attack on Pearl Harbor, Japanese Americans, many of them born in the United States, were placed in internment camps. Many were forced to sell their businesses and houses at a great loss. Recognizing the unfairness of this action, Congress granted each survivor $20,000 in compensation in 1988.

Write a paragraph arguing how the government can fight terrorism without racial profiling, discrimination, or civil rights violations.

WRITING ON THE WEB

Using a search engine such as Yahoo! or Google, enter terms such as *writing argument, analyzing readers, argument essays, developing arguments, using evidence, reader objections,* and *hostile audiences.*

1. Search for online editorials about controversial issues, and examine how writers developed topic sentences, used evidence, and addressed reader objections.
2. Write an e-mail to a friend using argument to express your point of view on a current issue.

POINTS TO REMEMBER

1. Argument paragraphs convince readers to accept an idea or motivate them to take action.
2. Argument paragraphs need clearly stated topic sentences.
3. Topic sentences must be supported with facts, examples, statistics, and quotations.
4. Readers' concerns, needs, and possible objections to your point of view must be addressed.
5. Arguments are not fights but logical assertions. Avoid making accusations, insults, or emotional claims that cannot be supported with facts.
6. Peer review can help you refine your topic sentence, examine the quality of evidence, and identify reader objections.

Writing Essays

CHAPTER 14

Planning Essays

CHAPTER GOALS

- Write Effective Thesis Statements

- Understand the Main Parts of an Essay

- Organize Essays Using Outlines.

STEPHEN CERNIN/AP PHOTO

Get Writing

In recent years several politicians have resigned following a sex scandal. Do you believe that immoral behavior disqualifies people from holding public office? Why or why not?

Write one or more paragraphs stating your views.

What Is an Essay?

Throughout your college career you will be assigned essays or essay examinations. To develop effective essays, it is important to first know what an essay is *not:*

An essay is <u>not</u> just a collection of paragraphs.

An essay is <u>not</u> a list of everything you know about a subject.

An essay <u>does</u> not simply provide facts or ideas "about" a topic.

An essay is a group of paragraphs that support a thesis. Formal essays inform readers about an idea or persuade them to accept a point of view. Informal essays share a writer's personal feelings, thoughts, or experiences. Whether written to inform, entertain, motivate, or express an opinion, **essays must have a clear goal, address a specific subject, and logically organize supporting details.**

The Thesis Statement

The most important part of any essay is the **thesis statement,** or main idea. Just as the topic sentence expresses the controlling idea of a paragraph, a thesis statement explains the controlling idea of an essay. The **thesis statement presents the writer's position and serves as the essay's mission statement.** A thesis is not simply a narrowed topic—a thesis expresses a point of view. It is a declaration of purpose.

Topic	Narrowed Topic	Thesis Statement
TV shows	quiz shows	Quiz shows remain popular because they allow viewers to match wits with contestants.
being a smart consumer	using credit cards wisely	Credit cards should be used for emergencies and necessities, not meals, fashion items, or impulse purposes.
public schools	charter schools	Charter schools need accurate methods to measure student performance.

Elements of A Thesis Statement

Effective thesis statements share common elements:

- **The thesis statement forms the core of the essay.** It states the writer's most important idea.
- **Thesis statements are usually stated in a single sentence.** Most writers create a single sentence to summarize their main idea.

- **Thesis statements help limit the topic.** Part of the job of a thesis statement is to focus the topic. The thesis statement "Speed dating is an effective way for busy professionals to meet each other" expresses a point of view and narrows the essay to a single method of meeting new people.
- **Thesis statements organize supporting details.** The thesis statement "Running burns calories, exercises the heart, and reduces stress" suggests that the essay will be divided into three parts.
- **Thesis statements indicate the kind of support that follows.** The thesis statement "The airport must be expanded to reduce congestion" implies a cause-and-effect argument based on factual details. The thesis statement "The loneliness of road sales led me to choose a job where I could work with people" suggests an essay expressing personal observations and experiences.

EXERCISE 1 Developing a Thesis Statement

Narrow the topic and develop a thesis statement for each of the following subjects. Remember that your thesis should express a point of view and not simply narrow the topic.

1. Used cars

Narrowed topic: _____

Thesis statement: _____

2. Day care

Narrowed topic: _____

Thesis statement: _____

3. Quitting smoking

Narrowed topic: _____

Thesis statement: _____

4. Student loans

Narrowed topic: _____

Thesis statement: _____

5. Immigration

Narrowed topic: _____

Thesis statement: _____

Organizing Essays

Essays generally consist of three main parts:

title and introduction

body

conclusion

Each part is important in developing an effective essay.

The Title and Introduction

The Title

Titles play a vital role in creating effective essays. A strong title announces what the essay is about, attracts attention, can express a thesis, and prepares readers to accept your ideas. Don't think you have to decide on a title right away. As you write, you may discover an interesting word or phrase that captures the essence of your essay and can serve as an effective title.

Writers use a variety of titles.

Labels announce what the essay is about:

Education Reform in Ohio

Campus Day Care

Thesis statements declare a point of view:

We Must Stop Child Abuse

Racial Profiling Does Not Prevent Terrorism

Note: Even if presented in the title, thesis statements should always appear in the main text of the essay.

Questions arouse reader interest and create suspense because the writer does not announce his or her point of view:

Should We Lower the Drinking Age?

Do You Know Your Credit Score?

Creative phrases generate curiosity:

Dodging the Audit Bullet

Facelifts and Mine Fields

The title you select should match your purpose, audience, and context. Creative titles and questions should be avoided in research papers and formal business reports but can be very effective to generate attention in personal essays.

The Introduction

The introduction should make a strong, clear statement that arouses the readers' attention and prepares them for the details that follow. Avoid weak introductions that serve as titles, only announcing the topic.

Weak

> This paper is about property taxes. Property taxes are too high. This is hurting the city.

There are several ways of creating strong introductions:

Open with a Thesis Statement

> To prevent more businesses from leaving the city, property taxes must be lowered.

Open with a Fact or Statistic

> In a 2009 survey of two hundred business owners, nearly a third cited high property taxes as the main reason they moved to the suburbs.

Open with a Quotation

> Speaking before the Common Council, Ivan Bettelheim, president of the American Management Association, warned that "high property taxes are costing the city ten thousand jobs a year."

Open with a Short Example or Narrative

> After sixty-five years in operation, Midland Tool and Die decided to move its main plant, employing three hundred workers, to the suburbs, where lower taxes would help the business compete with low-cost imports from China.

The Body

The paragraphs that make up the body or main part of the essay contain details—facts, observations, personal experiences, statistics, and quotations—that support the thesis statement. Just as all the sentences in a paragraph should relate to the topic sentence, all the paragraphs in an essay should support the thesis statement.

The body paragraphs may be organized by one or more patterns of development. For instance, an essay describing your first apartment might contain a paragraph comparing living at home with living on your own and another using cause and effect to explain your reasons for moving out.

The body should present paragraphs in a logical way so readers can follow your train of thought. **There are three common methods of organizing details: by time, parts, or importance.**

Organize by Time

Essays can be organized as a chain of events. A formal essay could discuss the Internet by explaining its rapid growth in its first ten years. An informal essay about your sister could discuss your relationship from early childhood to the present. An essay in a history class might examine immigration from the 1920s to the present. A psychology paper can trace the effects of a mental illness by telling the story of a single patient.

- Readers find essays organized as narratives or stories easy to follow.
- Important events in an essay can be highlighted with flashbacks and flashforwards. An essay about high school might open with your graduation, then flash back to explain the challenges you had to overcome and flashforward to college.

Organize by Parts

The supporting details of an essay can be organized by grouping them into parts or subdivisions. An essay about professional athletes might discuss football, baseball, and basketball players. An essay analyzing job opportunities could be organized by region, industry, or starting salaries. A personal essay might classify three kinds of employees you have worked with.

- Complex issues are easier to explain part by part.
- Organizing an essay in parts helps people follow your train of thought step-by-step, letting them pause to understand details before moving on to the next section.

Organize by Importance

If you think that some ideas or details are more significant than others, you can arrange them by order of importance. Because reader attention is greatest at the beginning and end of an essay, you should open or close your essay with your most important ideas.

- You can start with a minor point and move on to more important ideas, then end the essay with your most significant point to create a dramatic conclusion.
- You can also open with your most significant point to get your readers' attention, then follow it with additional supporting details.
- Avoid placing your most important ideas in the middle of the essay, where readers may overlook them.

The Conclusion

The conclusion of an essay should state a memorable fact, final thought, or observation; pose a question; or call for action. In a short essay, there is little need to repeat or summarize what readers have just read.

Weak
> In conclusion, the city must lower property taxes.

There are several ways of creating strong conclusions:

Conclude with a Significant Fact or Statistic That Readers Will Remember
> Because of high property taxes, the city has been unable to convince a single major employer to locate here since 1996.

End with a Meaningful Quotation
> Former mayor Karen Lopez told reporters last week, "I supported higher property taxes fifteen years ago, but today for every dollar we raise through property taxes, we lose three dollars in payroll revenue."

Pose a Final Question
> If we want to generate more money for the city and create more jobs, can we afford to chase businesses out of town?

End with a Call to Action
> If you want to keep jobs from leaving the city, vote Yes on the proposition to lower property taxes this November.

EXERCISE 2   Evaluating the Essay

Underline the thesis statement twice and each topic sentence once in the following essay; then answer the questions that follow it.

Terry Jackson   English 101

Life Lessons

introduction

I played football in high school. I spent most of my time on the bench. I never scored a touchdown or made a play anyone will ever remember. But it changed the rest of my life. Football taught me discipline, teamwork, and maturity.

body paragraph

Until my father urged me to play football, I was disorganized and lazy. I got C's in school, spent my free time lying on the couch watching TV, and never exercised. Once on the team, however, I had to show up at practice on time and be prepared to work. The drills were tough and left me sore and exhausted. The coach put us all on a rigid schedule, which forced me to structure my time and give up TV. I stopped eating junk food and began working out at home. Football taught me how to take charge of my life and use my time and energy to accomplish goals.

body paragraph

Football made me appreciate the importance of working with others. I had been pretty much a loner before playing sports. In drills, in practice games, and on the field I learned how important it was to connect with others. We got to the point that we could communicate with a hand signal or a number and work together like a well-oiled machine. Making plays depended on each of us knowing his part. We began to think like a group and worked to keep each other motivated when someone got hurt or frustrated with a bad play.

body paragraph

Perhaps the most important thing football did was help turn me into an adult. I had always been an impulsive and emotional person. I used to blow up at minor insults or get depressed and withdrawn when something disappointed me. I played in many tough games. We often lost. In September I would throw my helmet on the ground, curse, or slam a locker door. By December, when the season ended, I had learned to control my emotions, accept my limits, recognize the strengths of others without jealousy, and take responsibility for my actions.

conclusion

Parents and teachers often criticize high school sports for stressing athletics over academics and giving teenagers false hopes of turning pro. I was a terrible football player, but football made me a better student, equipped me for the rigors of college, and prepared me for the tough decisions that come with adult life.

1. State the thesis in your own words.

_____

_____

2. What points does the student make in the introduction?

_____

_____

3. What is the main idea of the second paragraph?

_____

_____

4. What is the main idea of the third paragraph?

_____

_____

5. What is the main idea of the fourth paragraph?

_____

_____

6. What is the most important point of the conclusion?

_____

_____

Putting It All Together: Developing an Outline

To plan an essay you do not have to create a *formal outline* with Roman numerals and capital letters. A *working outline* can be a simple list of ideas, key words, and facts. Think of it as a rough sketch, a blueprint, or a road map to guide your first draft. Taking a few minutes to plan your essay can help you discover new ideas, organize your thoughts, and save time once you start writing:

```
            Preparing for a Job Interview
Intro—Valuable tips lead to success

Par #1—Preparation
            learning about company
            reviewing past
            dry runs

Par #2—Interview
            do's and don'ts
            attitudes
            tough questions
            questions to ask

Par #3—Thank-you letter
            what to say
            what to add

Conclusion—What to do if you don't get the job
```

Topic Sentence Outlines

Topic sentence outlines are useful planning tools because they clearly establish the controlling idea of each paragraph in the essay. By writing out the thesis statement and each topic sentence before beginning to write your essay, you establish a clear blueprint to guide the first draft:

```
            Preparing for a Job Interview
Intro/Thesis    Job applicants can improve their
                chances of success through prepara-
                tion, honesty, and persistence.
```

Par #1	Applicants should research employers, rehearse for interviews, and conduct a dry run to build confidence.
Par #2	Maintaining a positive attitude and demonstrating genuine interest in the employer as well as the job are essential in making you stand out from other applicants.
Par #3	Although often overlooked, the thank-you letter is critical to securing a job offer.
Conclusion	Don't become discouraged if you don't get the job.

Having written out the thesis and topic sentences, you can complete the essay by adding details to support each topic sentence.

Preparing for a Job Interview

Job applicants can improve their chances of success through preparation, honesty, and persistence. Many talented people fail to get hired because they make common interview errors. They arrive late, are disorganized, appear selfish or defensive, and often show little interest in the employer's goals or problems. Following these simple tips can help improve your chances of getting a job.

Applicants should research employers, rehearse for interviews, and conduct a dry run to build confidence. Learn as much as you can about the company you are going to interview with. Search the Internet for information about the company's history, products, problems, goals, and organization. Rehearse what you want to stress about your skills, experience, and education. Think of three or four key accomplishments you can explain in detail. Consider making a dry run of the interview. Make sure that you know how to get to the employer's office, where to park, and what to wear. Visit the employer a few days before, if you can, to become familiar with the environment. The more you know about the location, the more confident you will feel.

Maintaining a positive attitude and demonstrating genuine interest in the employer as well as the job are essential in making you stand out from other applicants. A job interview is a sales presentation. Don't simply discuss your skills and experience, but suggest how they can benefit the employer. Avoid being boastful or defensive. Answer questions directly and honestly. If you lack a skill or do not know the answer to a question, admit your lack of knowledge, but point out situations in the past that demonstrate your ability to learn quickly. Don't focus only on the job, but show interest in the employer by asking about the company's overall aims and current challenges. Demonstrate how your background or interests will help the company achieve its goals.

Although often overlooked, the thank-you letter is critical to securing a job offer. As soon as you leave the interview, plan a letter or e-mail. Thank the interviewer for taking time to meet you, and stress why you believe you can benefit the company. Include any details you forgot to mention during the interview. Less than 10 percent of applicants send a thank-you letter, so even a brief note will make you memorable.

Don't become discouraged if you don't get the job. Don't allow yourself to become angry, disappointed, or depressed if a seemingly successful interview does not lead to a job offer. The job may have been filled by a transfer or promotion. The fact that you were not hired does not mean that you may not be hired in the future. Send a letter or e-mail to the employer reminding them of your skills and suggesting that you are willing to consider other positions. Call the employer, and ask for suggestions about finding other jobs. Use this person as a contact to find other job openings you may not know about. If you don't get the job, at least use the interview to learn something.

POINT TO REMEMBER

Outlines should guide the first draft. As you write, however, new ideas may come to you. You may discover that your essay needs to be expanded or realize that you are attempting to address too many ideas in a single essay. Be willing to make changes to your outline to improve the focus of your essay. Review the assignment and your goals to ensure that any changes or additions you make will improve your paper.

EXERCISE 3   Developing an Outline

Select a topic from the following list or develop one of your own, and pre-write for a few minutes to develop ideas. Organize your ideas on the following form.

  how high school students should prepare for college

  reasons why you admire or dislike someone

  reasons why you decided to attend this college

why men and women have different attitudes about relationships, marriage, or dating

two types of bosses, employees, or customers

your prediction for a sports team's success or failure next season

your worst day in the last month

a person you worry about

the hardest thing about quitting smoking, losing weight, saving money, or studying for exams

Topic/title _____

Introduction and thesis _____

_____

Topic sentence for supporting paragraph _____

_____

_____

Topic sentence for supporting paragraph _____

_____

_____

Topic sentence for supporting paragraph _____

_____

_____

Conclusion _____

_____

WORKING TOGETHER

Work with a small group of students, and exchange outlines. Make copies so each person can make notes. Discuss what you want to say, and ask if they think your outline makes sense. Does your introduction grab the readers' attention and state a clear thesis? Do the paragraphs in the body directly support the thesis? Are they arranged in a logical order? Does the conclusion make a final, memorable point or just repeat the introduction?

Get Thinking and Writing

CRITICAL THINKING

If you saw a co-worker stealing from your employer, would you tell your boss, confront the employee, or look the other way?

Write two or more paragraphs explaining the actions you would take. Would your actions depend on the value of the property taken, the person involved, or the type of job you had?

WHAT HAVE YOU WRITTEN?

Read your paragraphs carefully. Do you clearly explain the action you would take and why?

- How effective is your opening sentence? Does it engage readers or simply announce what you are writing about?
- How do you organize your main ideas? Do you use paragraphs to signal transitions or shifts in your train of thought?
- Do all the sentences in the paragraph support the paragraph's controlling idea? Do all the paragraphs support the thesis?
- How do you end your final paragraph? Does it simply repeat what you have written, or does it make a final, memorable point?

Get Writing

Michael Tweed/Reuters/CORBIS

Actor Robert Blake after his trial

Do juries treat celebrities differently? Do you think a jury would find it hard to convict a popular movie star of a serious crime? Do people excuse acts committed by celebrities that they might condemn in others?

Prewrite for a few minutes to develop ideas; then create an outline to guide a short essay of three or four paragraphs. After writing a draft, review your outline. Could your plan have been easier to follow? Could it have helped organize your ideas better or helped save time?

WRITING ON THE WEB

Using a search engine such as Yahoo! or Google, enter terms such as *writing essays, types of outlines,* and *planning essays* to locate current sites of interest.

1. Read news articles online, and notice how writers develop introductions, create conclusions, and use paragraphs to organize their ideas.

2. Write a multi-paragraph e-mail to a friend. Make sure that your message has a clear introduction and conclusion.

POINTS TO REMEMBER

1. An essay states a main idea supported by related paragraphs that provide details.

2. Essays consist of three parts:

Title and introduction:	Grabs attention
	Announces the topic
	Addresses reader concerns
	Prepares readers for what follows
	States a clear thesis or main idea
The body:	Organizes paragraphs in a clear, logical pattern
The conclusion:	Ends with a brief summary, final thought or observation, question, call for action, or prediction

3. Essays often use different types of paragraphs—for example, comparison, narration, cause and effect, and description—to support a thesis.

4. In writing essays, consider your readers when presenting ideas, selecting details, and choosing words.

CHAPTER 15

Developing Essays

DIGITAL VISION/ALAMY LIMITED

CHAPTER GOALS

■ Understand the Patterns of Developing Essays

■ Develop Organized Essays

Get Writing

Television commercials advertise prescription drugs that promise to cure depression, reduce anxiety, improve sexual performance, and eliminate the effects of aging. Do these ads send the wrong message to the public?

Write one or more paragraphs stating your view of the way that prescription drugs are advertised. Do these ads inform or mislead the public?

How Do Writers Develop Essays?

College assignments and business documents often call for specific kinds of writing. An essay for an English course might *compare* two short stories, a psychology exam might ask students to *define* a mental illness, and an e-mail from the sales department might demand to know *causes* for delays in shipping. Chapters 5–13 show how to develop paragraphs using the **modes,** or **patterns of development.** These same methods can be used to develop whole documents, such as essays, research papers, business letters, and reports. However, these patterns of development are more than just ways of organizing material. They refer to your main purpose of writing—the goal of your essay.

The pattern of development that you choose depends on what you are trying to say:

Description—*Presents facts, observations, and impressions about persons, places, objects, or ideas. It records what you see, hear, feel, taste, and touch.*

Narration—*Tells stories or relates a series of events, usually in chronological order.*

Example—*Illustrates ideas, issues, events, or personality types by describing one or more specific events, objects, or people.*

Definition—*Explains or limits the meaning of a word or idea.*

Comparison and contrast—*Examines similarities and differences.*

Division/classification—*Separates a subject into parts or measures subjects on a scale.*

Process—*Explains how something occurs or provides step-by-step instructions to accomplish a specific task.*

Cause and effect—*Explains reasons and results.*

Argument—*Directs readers to accept a point of view or take action.*

 POINT TO REMEMBER

Writers often use several patterns of development to create an essay. In making an argument, you may include narrations, examples, and definitions to support your thesis.

Description

Description presents facts, observations, and impressions about persons, places, objects, or ideas. It records what you see, hear, feel, taste, and touch.

The goal of a description essay is to explain a subject to readers by providing meaningful details. These details can be objective facts or the writer's personal impressions. Good descriptions bring people, places, and things to life by highlighting interesting details and creating dominant impressions.

Steps to Writing A Description Essay

Planning

1. **Determine your purpose.** Is your goal to provide readers with facts or personal impressions? What do you want readers to know about your subject?

2. **Consider your readers.** What type of description best suits your audience? Are you writing a personal essay for an English class or an objective description for a business or technical course?

3. **Narrow your topic.** In a two-page essay, it is easier to develop interesting facts and details about a concert in Central Park than to attempt to describe New York City.

4. **Select key details.** Avoid minor facts such as dates, addresses, or people's height or ages, unless they are important for readers to know.

5. **Organize details in a clear pattern.** Consider using comparison, narration, or process paragraphs to arrange your ideas.

Writing the First Draft

1. **Create dominant impressions.** Good descriptions do not simply list details but instead create an overall picture of a topic. Instead of describing your apartment by telling readers about the furniture in each room, let them know why the apartment is important to you. Does it make you happy or sad? Does it make you feel secure or homesick?

2. **"Show" rather than "tell."** Descriptions can be brought to life by using short narratives or examples to show people and objects in action. Instead of telling readers simply what someone looks like, show them how they behave. Describe them driving, talking, working, or playing. Show readers why this person is important to you. What did he or she teach you?

3. **Include dialogue to add action to descriptions of people.** Letting people speak in their own words is an effective way of revealing their education, attitudes, and personalities.

Revising—Questions to Ask About a Description Essay

1. **Does my essay have a thesis or controlling idea, or is it only a loose collection of facts and observations?**

2. **Do I create dominant impressions supported by interesting and accurate details?**

3. **Are there details that should be deleted because they are repetitive or off topic?**

4. **Are details clearly arranged so readers can follow my train of thought?**

> 5. **Can I add action or dialogue to bring life to my description?**
>
> 6. **Does my essay tell readers what I want them to know?**

Henri Troyat   English 212
                             My Bug

introduction   My father was in first grade when my Bug rolled off
an assembly line in West Germany thirty-eight years
ago. I have no idea what its original color was, but
it has gone from gray to rust to black during my time.
thesis   **My '69 VW is not just a car but a family artifact.**
narration: family   My grandfather bought it in May 1969 as a second
history of car   car for his wife. She drove it along the Jersey shore
selling real estate for six years. The car followed
the family west to San Francisco in 1975. My uncle
then got the car and drove it to college in New
Mexico. After graduating and getting a new car, he
gave it to my dad, who was just learning to drive.
By now, the car bore the tattoos of college bumper
stickers, bent fenders, and rusted chrome. My dad had
the car painted a light cream color and invested in
new tires. During a ski trip his freshman year, the
Bug skidded off an icy mountain road in Colorado and
rolled over. He had the dents pounded out and the car
painted gray. It took my parents on their honeymoon.
Two years later the battered Bug carried me home from
the hospital. After my parents bought a van, the Bug
was relegated to being a backup vehicle. When my mom
got a new car, the Bug was retired to the garage.
description: details   Now it is mine. The fenders, though repainted,
about car   still bear the shallow depressions from the Colorado
rollover. The windshield is pitted from stones that
flew off a a speeding gravel truck that nearly ran me
off the road in Nevada last year. The door handles
are replacements I found on eBay. The car seats are
patched with tape. Rust holes in the floorboards have
been covered with cookie sheets. The dashboard sports
the compass that my mother glued on ten years ago so
she would not get lost taking me to soccer games. The
glove compartment is jammed with rumpled maps and
snapshots from three decades of family vacations and
road trips.
conclusion   My Bug is not the most glamorous vehicle in the
college parking lot, but it has to be the most loved.
It looks like a rolling homeless shelter to many. But

to me it is a moving family album. I love every
ding and dent.

Understanding Meaning: What Is the Writer Trying to Say?

1. Can you state the student's thesis in your own words?

_____

_____

2. What is the student's dominant impression about the car? Does it support the thesis?

_____

_____

3. What details does the student select to support the dominant impression?

_____

_____

Evaluating Strategy: How Does the Writer Say It?

1. Which details are subjective, and which are objective?

<u>Subjective</u>   <u>Objective</u>

_____   _____

_____   _____

_____   _____

_____   _____

2. How does the student use narrations to develop the description of the car? What do these stories add?

_____

_____

3. How does the student organize the description? How effective are the introduction and conclusion?

_____

_____

4. How does the student organize the body of the essay?

_____

_____

Appreciating Language: What Words Does the Writer Use?

1. Which words most effectively describe the car?

_____

_____

2. How would you describe the student's tone and style?

_____

_____

WORKING TOGETHER

Working with a group of students, discuss this essay, and consider how you might improve it.

1. What are the essay's strong points?

_____

_____

2. What are the essay's weak points?

_____

_____

3. How would you revise this essay? What other information do you wish the student had added? Are there details that could be deleted? Would you rearrange or rewrite any of the paragraphs? Can you think of a more effective introduction or conclusion?

_____

_____

4. List your group's primary suggestion or a question you wish you could ask the writer.

_____

_____

Get Writing

WRITING ACTIVITY

Write a descriptive essay about one of the following topics or one your instructor suggests. Remember to build dominant impressions and include details to support your points. You may use contrast, narrative, or other methods of development to create your essay.

- your first car
- your room

- a recent date
- best or worst YouTube

- a favorite possession
- a fashion, behavior, or social trend you disapprove of
- most interesting person on campus
- a student clique in high school
- your dream home

- best or worst job
- best or worst neighborhood in town
- best or worst actor or singer
- a favorite store, café, or park

Narration

Narration tells stories or relates a series of events, usually in chronological order.

The goal of a narration essay is to tell a story. It could relate a personal experience and highlight your thoughts and feelings or present an accurate and objective narrative of a historical event or scientific experiment. Narration essays can be written in first person ("I") or third person ("they"). As a writer, you can be the main character, relating everything from your point of view, or an objective reporter of events.

Steps to Writing a Narration Essay

Planning

1. **Define the purpose of your narrative.** What is the point of your narrative? What do you want your readers to understand about your story?

2. **Consider your readers.** How much background information or definitions do you need to supply so readers can appreciate the significance of your narrative?

3. **Limit the scope of your narrative.** Your job in writing a narrative essay is not to recall everything that happened. If you try to describe everything that happened the day your grandmother died, for example, you might create a superficial list of events. However, you could create a moving narrative by focusing on a single incident that occurred that day, such as greeting a mourning relative or making a difficult phone call.

4. **Select key details.** Avoid minor facts, such as dates and addresses, unless they provide information that readers need to know.

5. **Create a clear time line to organize events and details.** Make sure that readers will not be confused about the sequence of events.

Writing the First Draft

1. **Use transitional statements to show the passage of time and advance the narrative.** Phrases such as *an hour later* or *the next day* help readers follow the time line and understand the flow of events.

2. **Add dialogue to advance the narrative.** If people exchange words in your narrative, consider using direct quotations rather than summaries. Direct quotations express what people really said, revealing their attitudes, personalities, and moods.

3. **Avoid awkward shifts in tense.** Keep the narrative in past or present tense unless there is a clear change in time.

   AWKWARD
   I drive all night and got to Miami by noon.

   Improved
   I drove all night and got to Miami by noon.

Revising—Questions to Ask About a Narration Essay

1. **Does my narration have a thesis or controlling idea, or is it only a list of events?**

2. **Do I spend too much time on minor incidents or fail to develop important events?**

3. **Am I trying to cover too much? Should I narrow the focus of the narrative?**

4. **Are there details that can be deleted because they are repetitive or off topic?**

5. **Are events clearly arranged so readers can follow my train of thought?**

6. **Can I add action or dialogue to bring life to my narration?**

7. **Does my narration create the impact I want?**

Mahoud Kassem   English 112

Law and Order and Me

introduction   When I got a summer intern job working for a television show, I could not believe my luck. I was just out of high school and had sent in a résumé almost as a joke. But a production assistant called me back, and soon I was working for the hit series *Law and Order*.

description: expectations   Learning that I would be helping the location manager, I visualized myself standing behind the cameras watching actors, stuntmen, and directors at work. I imagined the stars arriving in limos, signing autographs for tourists, and nodding at me as one of the crew.

The reality was very different. My job was to help scout and set up locations. Most of the time I held a tape measure or climbed ladders to measure ceilings for the manager, who drove a battered Volvo station wagon full of secondhand tools. We spent our days checking out dumpy bars, cabstands, street corners, filthy tenement lobbies, and stuffy subway stations. We had to take measurements and set up diagrams so other crews knew what lighting equipment they would need and where to place the cameras.

contrast: realities

My summer dragged on. Every day I would squeeze into the battered Volvo with no air-conditioning and windows that couldn't open. We would rattle up to Harlem to look at a nightclub and wait for an hour for the manager to show up, only to realize his club was too classy to match the script's call for a seedy drug den. Then we would hit the second club on our list, a dingy dive in the Bronx that reeked of stale beer and bug killer. But that club wouldn't work either, so we moved on to check the third spot, a grimy tavern on Second Avenue. The next day we might be scouting a warehouse or a landfill. Later in the week I would be pacing off spots on a rooftop parking lot in 98°F heat and putting down X's in masking tape.

narration

After a few weeks, something began to bother me. I had seen enough episodes of *Law and Order* to know many of the scenes are shot in upscale clubs, art galleries, townhouses, office suites, and mansions. One day while eating our usual lunch of French fries and cheeseburgers, I asked my boss why we never visited those locations. "Oh," he said casually, "I let Lou stake out places like Tiffany's and Trump Tower. Those people expect you to dress nice, and I hate wearing ties. But Lou doesn't seem to mind."

conclusion

Understanding Meaning: What Is the Writer Trying to Say?

1. What is the student's main point about the job?

_____

_____

2. How did the student's expectations contrast with the reality of the job?

_____

_____

3. What details does the student use to characterize the job?

_____

_____

4. The student does not provide a thesis statement for this narrative. Can you summarize the essay's main point in a sentence?

_____

_____

Evaluating Strategy: How Does the Writer Say It?

1. How does the student organize the essay and advance the narrative?

_____

_____

2. The student states that the reality of the job was different from what he expected, but the student never states what his feelings were. What words or details about the job suggest the student's attitude?

_____

_____

3. How effective is the conclusion? Is the dialogue effective?

_____

_____

Appreciating Language: What Words Does the Writer Use?

1. Circle the words that reflect the student's attitude about the job. What impressions do they create?

2. Do you find the tone and style of the essay to be effective?

_____

_____

WORKING TOGETHER

Working with a group of students, discuss this essay, and consider how you might improve it.

1. What are the essay's strong points?

_____

_____

2. What are the essay's weak points?

_____

_____

3. How would you revise this essay? What other information do you wish the student had added? Are there details that could be deleted? Would you rearrange or rewrite any of the paragraphs? Can you think of a more effective introduction or conclusion? Would you add more dialogue?

_____

_____

4. List your group's primary suggestion or a question you wish you could ask the writer.

_____

_____

WRITING ACTIVITY

Get Writing

Write a narrative essay about one of the following topics or one your instructor suggests. Remember to use transitions and paragraph breaks to advance the narrative. You may use description, comparison, or other methods of development to create your narrative.

- a job interview
- a controversial event
- story told by your parents or other relatives
- story behind making a tough decision
- your first day at college
- an event that changed someone's life

- an emergency
- plot of your favorite movie
- biography of someone you admire
- an event that taught you a lesson
- a historical event you think was important

Example

Example illustrates ideas, issues, events, or personality types by describing one or more specific events, objects, or people.

One way to explain a topic is to provide readers with specific items, events, or people they can recognize. You can explain that a verb is a _word that expresses action,_ then illustrate it with examples—_run, buy, sell, build, drive._ The achievements of a movie director can be demonstrated by describing scenes from his or her films. Lawyers filing a discrimination claim will list examples of illegal actions. Students demanding better dorms might use examples of leaking pipes, broken windows, and peeling paint to support their views.

POINT TO REMEMBER

Examples differ from descriptions or narrations, which provide details about a single subject or tell one story. Examples represent something larger. The story of one coach could provide an example of a role model. The success of one business could illustrate an economic trend.

An example essay can tell a single story, describe a single person, or provide a number of examples. Examples can be **real** or **hypothetical:**

Real

The Internet has created a generation of female entrepreneurs. For example, Miranda Ocara started an online interior design service in her home that, in a single year, grew into a multi-million-dollar business with sixteen employees.

Hypothetical

The Internet has created a generation of female entrepreneurs. For example, imagine a housewife taking her knowledge of interior design and creating an online business selling her advice to homeowners all over the country.

Steps to Writing an Example Essay

Planning

1. **You can plan an example essay in two ways. You can examine a specific person, situation, object, or event, and explain how it illustrates something larger:**
    *   A power failure in your building illustrates our dependence on electric power.
    *   A friend's dedication to a disabled child illustrates your concept of devotion.

    Or you can select a topic and use one or more examples to illustrate it or provide evidence for your point of view:
    *   You explain cyberstalking, then provide one or more examples of victims.
    *   You state that the college needs better student advising and support your views with examples of students being assigned the wrong classes or given the wrong schedules.

2. **Consider your readers.** Select examples your readers can relate to. For instance, teenagers may not understand historical examples from the Great Depression or World War II.

3. **Determine if your essay would benefit from one extended example or a series of examples.**

4. **Develop a well-stated thesis statement that links the specific example with the general subject it illustrates.**

5. **Organize examples in a clear pattern.** Consider using comparison, narration, or process paragraphs to arrange details.

Writing the First Draft

1. **Create a strong thesis statement that explains the purpose of your essay and what the examples illustrate.**

2. **Introduce examples with phrases such as** *for example,* *for instance,* **and** *to illustrate.*

3. **Highlight the important details of examples, and delete minor details that do not directly support your thesis, such as dates, addresses, and physical descriptions of people.**

Revising—Questions to Ask About an Example Essay

1. **Does my essay include examples that illustrate a general idea or just describe specific subjects or tell isolated narratives?**

2. **Do I keep the examples in the same tense, tone, and voice? Do I shift from first to third person or past to present tense when there is no clear change in time?**

3. **Are there examples that can be deleted because they are repetitive or off topic?**

4. **Are examples clearly arranged so readers can follow my train of thought?**

5. **Do my examples tell readers what I want them to know?**

Carol Dorsey   Study Skills 101

Falling Through the Cracks

On Valentine's Day last year, Chris Day, a 58-year-old Vietnam veteran, froze to death in a cardboard box under Wacker Drive. He had been mentally ill for years and homeless for months. Day had been living in a Southside rooming house until neighbors, complaining about his disruptive behavior, demanded that the landlord evict him. He was getting over a thousand dollars a month in Social Security disability and veterans benefits. His sister and mother sent him money every month. He had been visited by a social worker and was being treated at a veterans' hospital. Day stopped taking his medicine, lost or threw away the cell phone his mother gave him, and dropped out of sight.

introduction

narration

description

Some people think that a homeless veteran dying of exposure is a sign of an uncaring society. But I think Chris Day is an example of someone who falls through

transition

thesis

the cracks and gets lost despite the best efforts to help him. He received enough money from the government to afford a room and food. He was entitled to free medical care and received free medication. His family tried to help when he avoided social workers. But even his mother was unable to control him. He created arguments, played his boom box all night, and frightened his sister's small children. He refused or forgot to take his medication and repeatedly walked off, leaving hundreds of dollars stuffed in envelopes or old coffee cans.

transition

Chris Day is just one of thousands of people who are not sick enough to be placed in a hospital against their will but not really able to live on their own.

additional example

In Boston a schizophrenic who lived in a halfway house stopped taking his medication and fell or jumped from a rooftop. Five homeless people froze to death in 2008 on a single subzero night in Manhattan. One of the victims, who had been sleeping in a doorway, had three uncashed disability checks and a city hotel voucher in her purse.

conclusion

It might sound cold to say that these things happen. But even when people are willing to help, there are those in need who just can't be reached.

Understanding Meaning: What Is the Writer Trying to Say?

1. State the student's thesis in your own words.

_____

_____

2. How do the examples illustrate the student's thesis?

_____

_____

3. How does the opening example illustrate the student's last line?

_____

_____

Evaluating Strategy: How Does the Writer Say It?

1. How effective is the opening example? Would you want to see more details about Chris Day?

_____

_____

2. How does the student use narration and description to develop this example essay?

_____

_____

3. Would the inclusion of facts, statistics, or quotations from experts strengthen this essay? Why or why not?

_____

_____

4. How does the student organize the essay? Are the introduction and conclusion effective?

_____

_____

Appreciating Language: What Words Does the Writer Use?

1. How would you describe the tone and style of this essay?

_____

_____

2. Do any words or phrases suggest that the student is uncaring about the victims?

_____

_____

WORKING TOGETHER

Working with a group of students, discuss this essay, and consider how you might improve it.

1. What are the essay's strong points?

_____

_____

2. What are the essay's weak points?

_____

_____

3. How would you revise this essay? What other information do you wish the student had added? Are there details that could be deleted? Would you rearrange or rewrite any of the paragraphs? Can you think of a more effective introduction or conclusion?

_____

_____

4. List your group's primary suggestion or a question you wish you could ask the writer.

_____

_____

Get Writing

WRITING ACTIVITY

Write an essay using one or more examples to illustrate a point. Choose one of the following topics or one suggested by your instructor. Remember that examples have to illustrate something or provide support for a point of view. Your examples can be real or hypothetical.

- a role model
- the loss of privacy
- the way women are portrayed on television
- terrorist threats
- differences between men and women

- bad habits
- an environmental problem
- racial profiling
- dangers posed by the Internet
- job opportunities
- people's ability to overcome challenges

Definition

Definition explains or limits the meaning of a word or idea.

The goal of a definition essay is to give readers a precise understanding of a concept or persuade them to accept the writer's interpretation of an idea. A definition essay can take several forms:

- **Standard definitions,** often found in encyclopedias and textbooks, explain a widely accepted understanding of a term or concept.
- **Personal definitions** express your individual interpretation of a subject, such as who is a "hero" or what you consider "child abuse."
- **Persuasive definitions** influence readers to share your interpretation of a subject. You might suggest that violent video games be defined as "adult material" like pornography and should not be sold to anyone under eighteen or that drug addicts be seen as "victims of a disease" rather than criminals.
- **Invented definitions** explain the meaning of a previously unnamed attitude, behavior, or situation that you have observed. You might define someone who always seems to introduce her single friends to the wrong people as a "toxic matchmaker" or call those who habitually gather at upscale coffee shops as "coffeeholics."

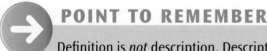

POINT TO REMEMBER

Definition is *not* description. Description provides details about one person, item, idea, or place. Definition provides details about a class or type of people, items, ideas, or places. A *description* essay might *describe* your uncle as being a cheapskate because he refuses to buy items he can easily afford. However, a *definition* essay would *define* what a "cheapskate" is and use your uncle as an example.

Steps to Writing a Definition Essay

Planning

1. **Determine your purpose.** Is your goal to define a standard term, share a personal interpretation, persuade readers to accept your opinion, or create a new definition?

2. **Develop a clear thesis statement summarizing your definition.**

3. **Consider your readers.** How much do they know about the subject? Do you need to provide background information or define other terms so that they can understand your essay? What is the best way to explain your definition? What examples would they be able to understand?

4. **Organize details in a clear pattern.** Consider using comparison, narration, or process paragraphs to arrange your ideas.

Writing the First Draft

1. **Make sure that you *define* and not just *describe* your topic.** Remember that your goal is to establish meaning about a general type, not just list details about a single person, place, or thing.

2. **Clear up misconceptions by explaining what your topic is *not*.** If you write an essay defining "felonies," list crimes that are felonies, then also include examples of crimes that are not felonies.

3. **Use comparisons, examples, and descriptions carefully.** In establishing a definition, you can use comparisons, examples, and descriptions, but be careful to point out exceptions to avoid misleading readers. In defining a computer virus, for example, you could compare it to a human infection. To be accurate, however, you would have to point out how an electronic virus is different from a human disease.

Revising—Questions to Ask About a Definition Essay

1. **Does my essay have a clearly stated thesis statement summarizing my definition?**

2. **Do I use examples that readers can understand?**

3. **Are there details that can be deleted because they are repetitive or off topic?**

4. **Are details clearly arranged so readers can follow my train of thought?**

5. **Does my essay tell readers what I want them to know?**

Asa Cooper   Earth Science 175
                              Tsunami

introduction and background
    The 2004 tsunami that ravaged Southwest Asia killed 250,000 people and did billions of dollars of damage. It drew worldwide interest to this form of natural disaster.

what a tsunami is not
Massive destructive ocean waves were commonly called "tidal waves." But this term is misleading because these waves have nothing to do with the tides, which are controlled by the moon.

thesis stating definition
    Tsunamis are catastrophic waves caused by volcanic eruptions, landslides, comparison or earthquakes

comparison
under the ocean. Like a swimmer kicking his or her legs under the water in a pool, these underwater movements cause ripples that roll outward in concentric circles.

description
Out at sea, tsunamis may travel over 400 miles an hour and move hundreds of miles outward in all directions. Because they are often less than three feet high, tsunami waves can pass under a ship without being noticed. As they reach land, however, tsunami waves become higher.

process
    The first indication of a major series of tsunami waves is a sudden outrush of water. This is soon followed by the first large wave that covers the exposed beach and surges inland. Subsequent waves are often larger, forcing huge volumes of water onto the land, turning streets into rivers.
    The amount of destruction that tsunamis cause depends on their intensity and geography. Waves that crash against high cliffs may cause minimal damage. However, similar waves striking low-level areas can flood hundreds of square miles. Motion pictures often depict tsunamis as towering waves hundreds of feet high that crash down on shorelines. In reality, it is not the height of a single monster wave that causes destruction but the massive volume of water in a series of waves that pushes inland.

The death toll from tsunamis can be very high for a number of reasons. The waves can hit suddenly with little warning and can occur on a clear, sunny day. In contrast, floods caused by rainstorms give ample warning, allowing people to evacuate to higher ground. In addition, tsunamis are uncommon events. People do not always appreciate the impending danger. In 2004 many people on the beach stood and watched as the water rushed out to sea just before the first wave hit.

cause and effect

Given the terrible death toll caused by tsunamis in 2004, the international community must take steps to create warning systems in the Indian Ocean that would at least give a few hours' notice of a coming disaster.

conclusion

Understanding Meaning: What Is the Writer Trying to Say?

1. Can you restate the student's definition in your own words?

_____

_____

2. Why is "tidal wave" an inaccurate term for tsunamis?

_____

_____

3. What creates tsunamis, and why can they be so destructive?

_____

_____

Evaluating Strategy: How Does the Writer Say It?

1. How does the student use description, comparison, cause and effect, and process to develop this definition essay?

_____

_____

2. How does the student organize the essay?

_____

_____

3. How effective are the introduction and conclusion?

_____

_____

Appreciating Language: What Words Does the Writer Use?

1. Which words does the student use to express the force and power of tsunamis?

_____

_____

2. How would you describe the essay's tone and style?

_____

_____

WORKING TOGETHER

Working with a group of students, discuss this essay, and consider how you might improve it.

1. What are the essay's strong points?

_____

_____

2. What are the essay's weak points?

_____

_____

3. How would you revise this essay? What other information do you wish the student had added? Are there details that could be deleted? Would you rearrange or rewrite any of the paragraphs? Can you think of a more effective introduction or conclusion?

_____

_____

4. List your group's primary suggestion or a question you wish you could ask the writer.

_____

_____

Get Writing

WRITING ACTIVITY

Write a definition essay about one of the following topics or one suggested by your instructor. Remember that a definition essay does not describe a single subject but establishes details about a type. You may use example, narrative, comparison, or other methods of development to create your essay.

- a best friend
- a just society
- loyalty
- responsibility
- sportsmanship
- road rage

- stalking
- an educated person
- wealth
- addiction
- a good relationship
- sexism

Comparison and Contrast

Comparison and contrast examines similarities and differences.

The goal of a comparison-and-contrast essay is to point out the similarities and differences of two subjects. Your comparison essay can be informative, presenting a pair of descriptions or definitions, or persuasive, arguing that one subject is better than the other.

Because comparison essays deal with two subjects, they have to be carefully organized to prevent confusion. There are two standard patterns for organizing comparisons:

- **Subject by subject** divides the essay into two parts, fully describing the first subject, then showing how it differs from the second.
- **Point by point** divides the essay into a series of comparisons, discussing both subjects in each paragraph.

A comparison of two hotels, for example, could be organized either way:

Subject by Subject	Point by Point
Introduction	Introduction
Hyatt Hotel	Hotel size
1. Size	**1.** Hyatt Hotel
2. Location	**2.** Marriott Hotel
3. Banquet facilities	Hotel location
4. Convention facilities	**1.** Hyatt Hotel
5. Room rates	**2.** Marriott Hotel
Marriott Hotel	Banquet facilities
1. Size	**1.** Hyatt Hotel
2. Location	**2.** Marriott Hotel
3. Banquet facilities	Convention facilities
4. Convention facilities	**1.** Hyatt Hotel
5. Room rates	**2.** Marriott Hotel
Conclusion	Room rates
	1. Hyatt Hotel
	2. Marriott Hotel
	Conclusion

Steps to Writing a Comparison/Contrast Essay

Planning

1. **Determine your purpose.** Is your goal to explain similarities and differences or to argue that one subject is better than the other?

2. **Select key details about both subjects.**

3. **Determine the best way to organize your comparison—subject by subject or point by point.**

4. **Consider your readers.** Define key terms, and clear up any misconceptions that your readers may have.

Writing the First Draft

1. **Write clear, concise descriptions of both subjects.**

2. **Choose words carefully.** Be aware how connotations can shape meaning. A small home can be labeled a "cottage" or a "shack." A person focused on achieving a goal can be called "determined" or "stubborn." Make sure that the words you use, whether positive or negative, reflect your meaning.

3. **Use similar patterns to organize comparisons.** Comparisons are easier to follow if you present facts or ideas in the same format:

   Nancy Adams, who supports school vouchers, is a 26-year-old lawyer from Maryland with two children. Her opponent, LaToya Green, who opposes vouchers, is a 35-year-old sales manager from Delaware with one child.

4. **Include a conclusion only if it adds new information or makes a final point.** Your essay may not need a conclusion that simply summarizes what readers have just read.

Revising—Questions to Ask About a Comparison-and-Contrast Essay

1. **Are my two topics clearly described or defined?**

2. **Do I devote sufficient attention to both subjects, or is my essay lopsided, devoting eight paragraphs to one subject and two paragraphs to the other?**

3. **Is my essay easy to follow?**

4. **Are there details that can be deleted because they are repetitive or off topic?**

5. **Does my comparison essay tell readers what I want them to know?**

Rita Roxas   Business Management

Entrepreneurial and Family Businesses

Small businesses generate many of the entry-level jobs open to recent graduates. **Entrepreneurial start-ups and long-established family businesses both offer job seekers advantages and disadvantages, so it pays to understand how they operate.** Choosing the right one can give you the career and lifestyle you seek. Choosing the wrong one can lead to constant frustration and often the need to quit and start over.

introduction
thesis

Entrepreneurs are people who create a new business venture. By nature they are people with a dream. They are gamblers. They gamble that their product or service will beat the established competition.

definition

They gamble their own fortunes, their credit ratings, their reputations, and their employees. They can be bold, intelligent, and inspiring. They can also be narrow-minded, selfish, and stubborn.

description

Working for an entrepreneur has many risks and potential rewards. If you are lucky, you may be getting in on the ground floor of a booming business and sharing in the company's growth and expansion. On the other hand, many new ventures fail, and you may find yourself looking for a job after the entrepreneur has gone bankrupt. Before working for anyone starting a new enterprise, make sure that his or her business plan is realistic. Make sure that your values match his or hers. In negotiating for a job, consider asking for potential shares as part of your salary. If you own stock, your boss will see you as more of a partner than an employee. If the company succeeds, a few shares of an initial stock offering could be worth several years' salary.

advantages
disadvantages

process:
suggestions

Long-established family-owned businesses tend to offer greater stability. The advantage is that a family-owned business often has a greater chance of success. The partners are related and share a sense of responsibility for the company's success. They are more willing to invest personal capital or forgo a paycheck to help the business in tough times.

description
advantages

On the other hand, working for a family-owned business places you at a disadvantage. You will always be an outsider. You may find yourself working with or even supervising relatives who can easily go over your head because the boss is also their father or grandfather. Because they are accustomed to being treated as children rather than employees, they may expect special treatment.

disadvantages

process:
suggestions

It is not uncommon for workers to be fired in order to give a job to an unemployed family member. In negotiating for a job, ask if the company has promoted nonrelatives. Be honest about your concerns about working in a family-owned business.

In looking at any job opening, consider the merits of the organization and your long-term goals.

Understanding Meaning: What Is the Writer Trying to Say?

1. Can you restate the student's thesis in your own words?

_____

_____

2. What are the main advantages and disadvantages of working for an entrepreneur?

_____

_____

3. What are the main advantages and disadvantages of working for a long-established family business?

_____

_____

4. Based on what you have read, which business would better suit you when you graduate? Why?

_____

_____

Evaluating Strategy: How Does the Writer Say It?

1. How does the student use definition and description to establish the comparison?

_____

_____

2. How does the student organize the essay?

_____

_____

3. What evidence does the student provide to support the main points?

_____

_____

Appreciating Language: What Words Does the Writer Use?

1. How does the student define *entrepreneur?*

_____

_____

2. Do you detect any bias in words or phrases which suggests that one form of small business is better than the other?

_____

_____

WORKING TOGETHER

Working with a group of students, discuss this essay, and consider how you might improve it.

1. What are the essay's strong points?

_____

_____

2. What are the essay's weak points?

_____

_____

3. How would you revise this essay? What other information do you wish the student had added? Are there details that could be deleted? Would you rearrange or rewrite any of the paragraphs? Can you think of a more effective introduction or conclusion?

_____

_____

4. List your group's primary suggestion or a question you wish you could ask the writer.

_____

_____

Get Writing

WRITING ACTIVITY

Write a comparison or contrast essay about one of the following topics or one your instructor suggests. You can use either the subject-by-subject or point-by-point method to organize details. You may use the essay to explain differences or to suggest that one topic is better than the other.

- a difference between men and women
- two sports teams
- best and worst jobs
- two friends
- buying versus leasing cars
- high school and college

- contrasting attitudes toward a recent controversy
- best and worst bosses
- two popular TV shows
- Republican versus Democratic view of a problem or issue

Division and Classification

Division and classification separates a subject into parts or measures subjects by a standard.

Division essays make complicated or abstract subjects easier to understand or work with by separating them into parts. You might write an essay about terrorism and use division to discuss different threats—biological, chemical, radiological, and hijacking—or causes—poverty, resentment of the West, and religious fundamentalism. An essay about diets could discuss low-carbohydrate diets, low-calorie diets, and low-fat diets.

Classification essays rank subjects by one standard. You might classify terrorist risks from the most to least likely or from most to least destructive. Diets could be classified by the most to least successful or from most to least healthy. Remember to use a single standard to measure your subject and to define each category or level clearly. You can write an essay classifying new cars by their price, their fuel efficiency, or their cost to insure. But you cannot write a classification essay that discusses expensive cars, fuel-efficient cars, and hard-to-insure cars.

Steps to Writing a Division or Classification Essay

Planning

1. **Determine your purpose.** Is your goal to divide your subject into parts (division) or to rank subjects on a scale (classification)?

2. **Consider your readers.** How much background information do your readers have? Are there terms you need to explain or define?

3. **In writing division, establish clear types.** Consider your division essay a series of short descriptions or definitions. Each item should be fully explained.

4. **In writing classification, establish clear categories on a well-defined scale.** Explain that you are ranking cars by those costing $20,000–30,000, $30,000–40,000, and $40,000–50,000

or grouping students by those who are not working, those who are working part time, and those who are working full time.

Writing the First Draft

1. **Develop a clear introduction explaining your purpose and method of division or classification.**

2. **Explain possible exceptions.** If not all items can fit in the categories you establish, point this out to readers. Simply stating "most students belong to three types . . ." indicates that not all students fit your division or classification.

3. **Explain possible changes.** If it is possible for a person or situation to change over time and switch categories, point this out to readers. For example, a student classified as an "A student" might do poorly on midterms and slip into the "B student" category. A student earning A's in chemistry could receive C's in history.

4. **Use examples to illustrate each type.**

Revising—Questions to Ask About a Division and Classification Essay

1. **Does my essay establish clear categories?**

2. **Is my thesis clearly stated?**

3. **Are there any categories that are not clearly defined or could be confused with others?**

4. **Are my categories clearly organized by paragraph breaks and transitional statements? Can readers follow my train of thought?**

5. **Do I explain possible exceptions?**

6. **Does my essay tell readers what I want them to know?**

Communications Skills 151   Jack Rodriguez

Blog America

America has become a nation of bloggers. Right now some eight million Americans blog. Some blog every day. Bloggers are people who use the Internet to share their thoughts, feelings, opinions, and experiences with the world. Blogs, which come from the words "web logs," are as varied as the people who use the Internet, but four distinct types have emerged.

The cyber diary. Thousands of blogs record the thoughts, feelings, and experiences of ordinary people ranging from high school students writing about prom dates to desperate housewives detailing their latest

introduction: definition of blogger

thesis

type 1

description sexual fantasy. Most go unread, but some bloggers have developed fans who love to follow the lives of people like them. These blogs are a blend of reality TV and the age-old wish to read someone else's diary. Most are boring, but some are witty and moving.

type 2
description

The therapy room. For some, the blog has become an anonymous way of speaking out about some of the most troubling and devastating life situations. Blogs are maintained by parents of autistic children, addicts struggling to stay straight, battered women, downsized executives looking for work, or people with eating disorders. These blogs range from confessions to cries for help. Some become self-help networks, with readers posting responses, adding links to online resources, research, and professional help.

type 3

description

The shadow media. Blogs have created a new form of media. Blogs are produced by amateur reporters, columnists, and researchers. An earthquake in California will generate dozens of blogs by eyewitnesses, scientists, and local reporters whose stories never made the papers. Blogs may contain more direct, accurate, and in-depth information than provided by mainstream media, whose reporters are generalists limited to brief articles or sound bites. Bloggers are credited with generating major news stories and undoing the career of CBS anchor Dan Rather.

type 4

description

The conspiracy web. Conspiracy theories are not new, but they used to be broadcast slowly by fringe publications and radio call-in shows. Now bloggers instantly respond to events, post videos and links, and broadcast to the world the latest theory about UFOs, 9/11, Iraq, global warming, or terrorism. The ability to link one fringe website to another can create an instant network of people trying to convince the world of their latest theory.

conclusion

Blogs are emerging all over the Middle East, creating an online democracy. As with the Internet itself, only time will tell whether blogs will be a major force shaping the politics, society, and art of the twenty-first century.

Understanding Meaning: What Is the Writer Trying to Say?

1. What is a blog?

_____

_____

2. What four types of blog does the student describe?

_____

_____

3. What social impact have bloggers had?

_____

_____

Evaluating Strategy: How Does the Writer Say It?

1. Which method does the student use to write about blogs—division or classification?

_____

_____

2. How does the student use description and definition to develop the essay?

_____

_____

3. What role do paragraph breaks play in organizing the essay?

_____

_____

Appreciating Language: What Words Does the Writer Use?

1. Why is it important for the student to explain "blog" and "blogger"? Are these terms clearly defined?

_____

_____

2. What do the tone, style, and word choice reveal about the student's intended readers?

_____

_____

WORKING TOGETHER

Working with a group of students, discuss this essay, and consider how you might improve it.

1. What are the essay's strong points?

_____

_____

2. What are the essay's weak points?

_____

_____

3. How would you revise this essay? What other information do you wish the student had added? Are there details that could be deleted? Would you rearrange or rewrite any of the paragraphs? Can you think of a more effective introduction or conclusion?

_____

_____

4. List your group's primary suggestion or a question you wish you could ask the writer.

_____

_____

Get Writing

WRITING ACTIVITY

Write a division or classification essay about one of the following topics or one suggested by your instructor. Remember to clearly establish categories and to provide examples to illustrate each type. You may use definition, comparison and contrast, or other methods of development to create your essay.

<u>Division</u>	<u>Classification</u>
Divide students by . . .	*Classify students by . . .*
• ethnic background	• grade point average
• favorite sports	• income level
• majors	• hours worked per week
Divide houses by . . .	*Classify houses by . . .*
• style	• price
• homeowner	• distance from downtown
• landscaping	• cost to insure
Divide TV shows by . . .	*Classify TV shows by . . .*
• type (talk show, sitcom, soap opera)	• ratings
• appeal (entertainment, information)	• amount of adult content
• source (network, basic cable, premium channel)	• education level of viewers

Process

Process explains how something occurs or provides step-by-step instructions to accomplish a specific task.

Many textbooks use process to explain how to write a speech, how a diesel engine works, how a bill becomes a law, how rising interest rates affect the economy, or how a disease affects the body.

Manuals, repair books, recipes, lab books, and first-aid instructions use process to provide readers with step-by-step instructions on how to install software, change a tire, bake a cake, conduct an experiment, or treat a sprained ankle.

Steps to Writing A Process Essay

Planning

1. **Determine your purpose.** Is your goal to explain or instruct?

2. **Consider your readers.** Are you writing to the general public or to people familiar with your subject? Do you need to provide background information or define important terms?

3. **Separate the process into logical stages.** Don't crowd too many actions in a single step or devote a step to a minor task.

4. **Consider using numbered steps, especially in giving instructions.** Process essays do not have to be written in standard paragraphs. Numbered steps, paragraph breaks, and visual aids can help inform readers and make your ideas easier to follow.

Writing the First Draft

1. **Create a clear introduction that announces the subject and explains your purpose.**

2. **Use transitional statements to advance the essay step-by-step.** Statements such as "after the bill passes the Senate" or "once you agree on the price" can help readers follow your train of thought.

3. **Make sure that instructions are self-contained.** Directions should include all the information that readers need to accomplish the task, not refer readers to another document to complete the process.

4. **Give negative instructions.** To prevent readers from making common mistakes, tell readers not only what they should do but also what they should not do.

5. **Provide complete instructions.** Avoid vague directions. Readers should be given clear descriptions so they know when one stage ends and the next begins:

Vague
Place the cake in the oven at 300 degrees for 30 minutes or until it is done.

Improved

Place the cake in the oven at 300 degrees for 30 minutes or until the center is firm and the edges are golden brown. (*Note:* If the center remains soft, microwave for one minute.)

6. **Warn readers of any hazards to their health, safety, or property.** If instructions direct people to use stoves, cleaning products, or machinery, alert them to any possible dangers.

Revising—Questions to Ask About a Process Essay

1. **Does my essay clearly explain a process or provide clear instructions?**

2. **Would numbered steps make my essay easier to read?**

3. **Have I included all relevant information?**

4. **Have I warned readers of any possible dangers?**

5. **Are there details that can be deleted because they are repetitive or off topic?**

6. **Does my essay tell readers what I want them to know?**

Jennifer Bukowski   English 112
                    Securing Your Home

introduction
background information

Homeowners frequently think of security only when planning a vacation. Leaving home for a week or two, they install additional locks, set timers to trigger lights, purchase sophisticated monitoring systems, alert neighbors, and hope that their homes will not be robbed in their absence. But most homes are robbed before 9 p.m., often while their owners are near or inside the residence. Your house is more likely to be robbed while you are grilling in the backyard or watching a football game in a basement rec room than when you are on a cruise or camping trip.

thesis

Although it is impossible to make any home "burglar proof," there are some actions you can take to protect your home and property:

numbered steps

1. Document your assets.
   Make a list of your valuables. Photograph or videotape each room in your home. Keep receipts of major purchases. Store these and other important records in a safe-deposit box so you can prove any losses. Review your insurance policies

to see if special items such as furs, artwork, or coin collections are covered.

2. **Identify valuables.**
Engrave computers, televisions, cameras, stereos, and DVD players with your name or an identifying number. Police often discover stolen property but have no way of contacting the owners.

3. *Always* **lock your doors.**
Nothing attracts a thief more than an open garage or unlatched screen door. Lock up even when you plan to visit a neighbor for "just a minute." That "minute" can easily become half an hour, plenty of time for a burglary to occur. Don't leave doors open if you are going to be upstairs or in the basement.

4. **Install only security systems you will use.**
Many homeowners invest in expensive, high-tech security systems that are so cumbersome that they leave them off most of the time. A cheap alarm system used twenty-fours a day provides more protection than a state-of-the-art system used randomly.

5. **Trim shrubbery around entrances and windows.**
Don't provide camouflage for burglars. Thieves can easily conceal themselves behind foliage while jimmying doors and windows.

6. **Network with neighbors.**
Let neighbors know if you expect deliveries, houseguests, or contractors. Thieves have posed as moving crews, casually looting a house and loading a truck while neighbors look on.

7. **Store valuables in attics and basements.**
Thieves are reluctant to venture beyond the ground floor, which usually offers numerous exits in case of detection. Therefore, attics and basements provide more security for valuable or hard-to-replace items.

Finally, call the police the moment you discover a burglary has occurred. If you return home and find evidence of a break-in—*do not go inside!* The thieves, who could be armed, might still be on the premises. Use a cell phone or ask a neighbor to call the police. Never attempt to confront a burglar yourself. No personal possession is worth risking death or a disabling injury.

warning and negative instruction

Understanding Meaning: What Is the Writer Trying to Say?

1. When do most robberies occur?

_____

_____

2. Why should people refrain from entering a house if they detect evidence of a break-in?

_____

_____

3. Summarize the student's directions in your own words.

1. _____   **5.** _____

2. _____   **6.** _____

3. _____   **7.** _____

4. _____

Evaluating Strategy: How Does the Writer Say It?

1. How does the student use description and example to develop this process essay?

_____

_____

2. The student uses numbered points in this essay. Is this effective in giving directions? Why or why not?

_____

_____

3. How does the student organize paragraphs? Are they easy to follow?

_____

_____

Appreciating Language: What Words Does the Writer Use?

1. What do the tone, word choice, and style suggest about the student's intended audience?

_____

_____

2. How does the student use verbs in the numbered steps to stress action?

_____

_____

WORKING TOGETHER

Working with a group of students, discuss this essay, and consider how you might improve it.

1. What are the essay's strong points?

_____

_____

2. What are the essay's weak points?

_____

_____

3. How would you revise this essay? What other information do you wish the student had added? Are there details that could be deleted? Would you rearrange or rewrite any of the paragraphs? Can you think of a more effective introduction or conclusion?

_____

_____

4. List your group's primary suggestion or a question you wish you could ask the writer.

_____

_____

Get Writing

WRITING ACTIVITY

Write a process essay about one of the following topics or one your instructor suggests. You can either explain how a process works or give readers step-by-step instructions to accomplish a specific task. Remember, numbering directions can make them easier to follow.

- how to apply for a car loan
- how a disease is spread
- how a tornado or earthquake occurs
- how to teach something to small children
- how to prepare for a job interview
- how a machine operates
- how to protect your computer against viruses
- how to change a tire
- how to save money

Cause and Effect

Cause and effect explains reasons and results.

Cause-and-effect essays explain the reasons why something happens or discusses the results that something creates. History books explain the causes of the Great Depression and the effect of Roosevelt's New Deal programs. Medical courses discuss the causes of arthritis and the effects of new treatments. Business professors present the causes of globalization and then predict its effects.

Critical thinking is important in writing cause-and-effect essays. Be sure to avoid three common errors:

- **Hasty generalizations or jumping to conclusions.** Don't make snap judgments based on what you think you know. If you hear that someone you know had a car accident, don't assume that it was caused by drunken driving simply because you know this person consumes a lot of alcohol. Don't instantly assume that a fatal explosion at an army base in Iraq was caused by terrorists. Make sure that you base conclusions on evidence.

- **Mistaking a time relationship for a cause-and-effect relationship.** Just because one event came before another does not mean that it was the cause. The fact that you became ill an hour after lunch does not mean it was caused by something you ate.

- **Confusing an association for a cause-and-effect relationship.** Just because two things are closely related does not mean that one causes the other. You might notice that every member of a youth gang has tattoos. There is a strong *association* but no real proof that getting tattoos *causes* juvenile delinquency.

Steps to Writing a Cause-and-Effect Essay

Planning

1. **Determine your purpose.** Your essay can discuss causes, results, or both.

2. **Develop a clear thesis statement that expresses the goal of your essay.**

3. **Explain the methods of establishing causes or measuring results.** If you write that outsourcing causes the loss of skilled jobs, explain how you measure the loss of these jobs.

4. **Organize causes or effects from least to most important or most to least important.** Don't place your most important points in the middle of the essay, where reader attention is weakest.

5. **Offer logical, accurate evidence.** Present facts, observations, examples, and statistics from standard, reliable sources that readers will trust.

Writing the First Draft
1. **Develop a strong introduction outlining the goal of your essay and providing background information.**

2. **Use example, comparison, process, and definition to explain causes and outline results.**

3. **Use transitional statements and paragraph breaks to signal shifts between separate causes and effects.**

4. **Point out possible exceptions or alternative interpretations.**

Revising—Questions to Ask About a Cause-and-Effect Essay
1. **Does my essay have a thesis or controlling idea?**

2. **Do I explain causes and results clearly with comparisons, examples, and narratives?**

3. **Do I provide enough evidence to convince readers?**

4. **Do I avoid making mistakes in critical thinking such as hasty generalizations or mistaking a time relationship for a cause?**

5. **Are there details that can be deleted because they are repetitive or off topic?**

6. **Are details clearly arranged so readers can follow my train of thought?**

7. **Does my essay tell readers what I want them to know?**

Kay Neumann   American History
                    Why Do They Hate Us?

   In the months following 9/11, many shocked Americans wondered why people hated the United States. The horror of watching planes flying into buildings was matched by the disbelief and anger that many felt while watching people in the Middle East dancing in the streets, honking car horns, and passing out candy to children like it was a holiday. Polls taken in the Middle East revealed that vast numbers of Arabs and Muslims approved of Osama bin Laden, whose image appeared on posters and T-shirts. As President Bush prepared for war in Iraq, many people in Europe began to criticize the United States. The anti-American feeling in countries such as Britain, France, and Germany troubled many Americans.

*introduction
description*

suggested causes

Why do they all seem to hate us? Scholars, reporters, and diplomats have given us many reasons. They suggest that anti-Americanism is caused by jealousy, resentment over the way American culture is eroding traditional cultures, America's support for Israel, and the exploitation of workers and resources.

But none of these reasons is new. America has been making movies that offend foreign tastes for eighty years. The United States has supported Israel since 1948.

thesis
causes

The main cause for rising anti-Americanism, I think, is the end of the Cold War. For almost fifty causes years the world was controlled by two superpowers—the United States and the USSR. This conflict made America look less threatening and violent in contrast to a Communist dictatorship that killed and jailed millions.

examples
comparisons

People in West Germany may have grumbled about being under America's shadow, but they only had to look over the Berlin Wall to realize it was a lot better than being in East Germany under Communist rule. There was no comparison between living in South and North Korea, either. The Arabs may have resented America's support for Israel, but they knew the United States believed in freedom of religion. The Soviets were atheists and denounced all religion. The spread of American influence may have weakened Islamic values, but the growth of Soviet-sponsored Communist movements in Pakistan, Iran, and Egypt threatened to abolish Islam.

causes

The Cold War made America look like the lesser of two evils. We were the good cop in the good cop/bad cop scenario. People resented American influence, but they had reasons to fear the Communists.

effects

Now that the Cold War is over, the world has one superpower. We no longer look like the good cop or the lesser evil. To many people in other countries, the United States is a global bully, an economic giant, and a cultural titan—all of which make other nations feel intimidated and second-rate. And no one likes feeling second-rate.

conclusion

Understanding Meaning: What Is the Writer Trying to Say?

1. What is the student's thesis? Can you state it in your own words?

_____

_____

2. Why does the student dismiss many of the causes for anti-Americanism suggested by others?

_____

_____

3. What does the student mean by "the good cop/bad cop scenario"?

_____

_____

4. How did the end of the Cold War create problems for the United States?

_____

_____

Evaluating Strategy: How Does the Writer Say It?

1. How does the student use example and comparison to develop this cause-and-effect essay?

_____

_____

2. How does the student organize the essay? What role do paragraphs play in arranging details?

_____

_____

3. How effective are the introduction and conclusion?

_____

_____

Appreciating Language: What Words Does the Writer Use?

1. Are expressions like "good cop/bad cop" appropriate in an essay about a serious subject such as foreign policy? Why or why not?

_____

_____

2. What do the tone, style, and word choice suggest about the student's intended audience?

_____

_____

WORKING TOGETHER

Working with a group of students, discuss this essay, and consider how you might improve it.

1. What are the essay's strong points?

_____

_____

2. What are the essay's weak points?

_____

_____

3. How would you revise this essay? What other information do you wish the student had added? Are there details that could be deleted? Would you rearrange or rewrite any of the paragraphs? Can you think of a more effective introduction or conclusion?

_____

_____

4. List your group's primary suggestion or a question you wish you could ask the writer.

_____

_____

Get Writing

WRITING ACTIVITY

Write a cause-and-effect essay about one of the following topics or one your instructor suggests. Your essay may present causes, effects, or both. You may use description, example, definition, or other methods of development to create your essay.

<u>**Causes of:**</u>

- childhood obesity
- high school dropouts
- drug abuse
- low voter turnout
- a team's recent victory or defeat
- divorce
- a TV show's popularity
- changes in a local neighborhood
- problems with Social Security

<u>**Effects of:**</u>

- violent video games
- domestic violence
- having a child
- 24-hour cable news networks
- losing a job
- online gambling
- cheap imported products
- school vouchers
- tougher child-support laws

Argument

Argument directs readers to accept a point of view or take action.

The goal of argument is to influence the way that readers think about something or motivate them to change their behavior. Writers use

three appeals to influence readers. Each appeal has advantages and disadvantages:

Logical Appeal—Uses facts, statistics, scientific evidence, expert opinions, surveys, and interviews.
>   *Advantages*
>>   provides compelling, objective support
>>   offers evidence needed for major or group decisions
>   *Disadvantages*
>>   requires a high degree of reader attention
>>   can be boring and undramatic

Emotional Appeal—Uses images, sensations, or stories to stir readers
to respond based on their fears, loves, dislikes, biases, and hopes.
>   *Advantages*
>>   has instant impact
>>   requires little reader preparation or attention
>   *Disadvantages*
>>   has a temporary effect
>>   offers little hard evidence to support major decisions

Ethical Appeal—Uses shared values, ideals, and beliefs.
>   *Advantages*
>>   provides compelling motivation
>>   calls upon readers' core beliefs
>   *Disadvantages*
>>   depends on readers sharing the writer's values
>>   provides no hard evidence for major decisions

Because each appeal has limitations, writers often use more than
one. An argument calling for a change in mortgage practices might use all
three:

Emotional appeal using human-interest story of one person:

In 2007 Sheri Naboti's dream came true. She bought her first house,
putting down twenty percent, more than her bank required. She paid every
mortgage payment on time, maintained her property, and added to its value.
Then in late 2008 she received a notice stating that her interest would jump
from 6.25% to 12.5%. She searched for a second job, cashed in savings bonds,
and worked overtime to meet the increased payments. When her daughter
was hospitalized, she fell behind in her house payments. She borrowed from
her mother and was only one payment behind when she received her eviction
notice.

Logical appeal presenting facts and evidence:

Naboti is just one of nearly a million Americans who lost their homes
in the last two years. According to a *Wall Street Journal* report, 18 percent
of those evicted had missed only three house payments. Jane Newman, a
Harvard economics professor, argues, "In many instances, borrowers saw
mortgage interest rates rise because of problems with a credit card or an auto
loan even though they made their house payments on time. Lenders have to
realize that the one bill most people will pay is the one that keeps a roof over
their head."

Ethical appeal calling upon fairness and common sense:
>   We must take steps to reform lending practices to prevent responsible homeowners from being penalized because of unrelated debts. As long as families pay their mortgage on time, their homes should not be threatened. The loss of homes devastates families, lowers neighborhood property values, and weakens our financial markets. The current policy is unfair and self-defeating. Instead of protecting their interests, lending institutions are hurting their customers, eroding their own assets, and weakening the entire economy.

Steps to Writing an Argument Essay

Planning

1. **Determine your purpose—to persuade readers to accept your opinion or motivate them to take action.**

2. **Consider your readers' existing beliefs, attitudes, and knowledge.**

3. **Determine which appeals best suit your purpose.**

4. **Don't confuse propaganda with persuasion.** Calling people names, using inflated or biased statistics, hurling accusations, and making unfair comparisons create weak and unconvincing arguments.

5. **Organize ideas from most important to least important or least important to most important.** Avoid placing your most important details in the middle of the essay, where reader attention is the weakest.

6. **Develop an introduction that grabs attention, explains your approach, and addresses readers' concerns.**

7. **Create a conclusion that ends the essay with a final thought, meaningful fact, call to action, or thought-provoking question.**

Writing the First Draft

1. **Present facts in ways that readers can understand.** Explain what statistics mean or the qualifications of people you quote.

2. **Use a variety of appeals.** Emotional appeals can add human interest to an essay largely supported by facts and statistics. Personal experiences may be moving but may require factual support to convince readers to accept your thesis.

3. **Use paragraph breaks and transitional statements to signal shifts between main points.**

4. **Recognize and comment on possible alternative opinions.**

5. **Address possible reader objections to your views.**

> **Revising—Questions to Ask About an Argument Essay**
> 1. **Does my essay have a clearly stated thesis?**
> 2. **Do I provide enough support to convince readers?**
> 3. **Is my argument easy to follow?**
> 4. **Are there details that can be deleted because they are repetitive or off topic?**
> 5. **Does my essay tell readers what I want them to know?**

Cheryl Jackson   Written Communications
            Curbing Our Enthusiasm: Cutting Down on
                    Off-Campus Drinking

Last semester fifty-two students were charged with underage drinking at an off-campus St. Patrick's Day party at a "fraternity house." That weekend four students were seriously injured when a drunk senior ran a stop sign in the main parking lot. This fall's Homecoming Weekend saw police shutting down four illegal keg parties. — *introduction / examples*

North Central Community College does not serve alcohol anywhere on campus. It has no dorms. But in the last few years, several duplexes on Interbay Avenue have become de facto "fraternity houses" populated by mostly male students right out of high school. In the last few years, keg parties in these houses have led to minors drinking and some students binge drinking to the point of needing the paramedics. As many as two hundred students have crowded into these houses. Photos taken at these parties show as many as fifty students crowded on flimsy wooden decks and balconies. Balconies like these have collapsed in other cities, leading to deaths and serious injuries. — *description*

In the last two years, these "fraternity houses" have posted invitations on campus and on websites urging students to buy a ten-dollar ticket that allows them to enter the house and eat and drink for free. The students evidently believe this makes the distribution of liquor legal since they are not actually "selling" it on-site.

These parties have attracted very negative media attention. Local residents have repeatedly filed complaints. Given the college's desire to expand next year, the administration cannot afford to alienate the community. — *effects*

thesis

definition

details

factual support

conclusion

North Central Community College must take steps to curb off-campus drinking parties. Although they don't take place on school property, students are involved, and it reflects badly on the school's image.

First, the college must ban illegal fraternities. True fraternities are independent corporate organizations that have to have a charter from a college to operate. They have to promise to follow all college rules and local regulations. Groups calling themselves fraternities without charters should not be allowed to advertise parties on campus. The Student Union should not allow them to post ads on college bulletin boards or take out ads in the school paper.

Second, the administration must work with Alderman Secora, the police, and landlords to make sure that student tenants obey laws regarding alcohol, occupancy, and parking regulations. Clearly, the last few parties were fire hazards. A two-story duplex was never meant to hold hundreds of people.

Third, college organizations should offer nonalcohol activities. At Piedmont College, the Irish Club stages a St. Patrick's Day festival featuring Irish food, dancing, music, limerick contests, and sporting events, providing students with fun and recreation that has greatly reduced binge drinking. There is no reason why North Central can't stage a similar event. Cinco de Mayo, another favorite day for off-campus parties, could feature events hosted by any number of Chicano organizations.

Fourth, the college has to educate students about the dangers of drunk driving, binge drinking, and alcohol abuse in general. The National Institute of Alcohol Abuse and Alcoholism reports that each year 1,400 college students die and 500,000 are injured by hazardous drinking. No North Central student has died so far. We should not wait for a fatality and perhaps a major lawsuit to make the college take action.

Understanding Meaning: What Is the Writer Trying to Say?

1. Can you state the student's thesis in your own words?

2. Why does the student believe the college must regulate off-campus student activities?

_____

_____

3. What steps does the student suggest the college take to reduce student drinking?

_____

_____

4. Why does the student call the fraternities illegal?

_____

_____

Evaluating Strategy: How Does the Writer Say It?

1. What reasons and support does the student provide to support the thesis? Is it effective?

_____

_____

2. The student includes statistics from the National Institute of Alcohol Abuse and Alcoholism. Should the essay contain more factual detail?

_____

_____

3. How does the student organize the essay?

_____

_____

Appreciating Language: What Words Does the Writer Use?

1. Many students, no doubt, consider these parties to be fun and harmless. How does the student's choice of words, tone, and style reveal the writer's attitude?

_____

_____

2. Why is it important for the student to define _fraternity?_

_____

_____

WORKING TOGETHER

Working with a group of students, discuss this essay, and consider how you might improve it.

1. What are the essay's strong points?

_____

_____

2. What are the essay's weak points?

_____

_____

3. How would you revise this essay? What other information do you wish the student had added? Are there details that could be deleted? Would you rearrange or rewrite any of the paragraphs? Can you think of a more effective introduction or conclusion?

_____

_____

4. List your group's primary suggestion or a question you wish you could ask the writer.

_____

_____

Get Writing

WRITING ACTIVITY

Write a persuasive essay for or against one of the following topics or one your instructor suggests. You may use contrast, example, cause and effect, or other methods of development to create your essay.

- school choice
- raising the minimum wage
- taxing online sales
- tougher gun laws
- requiring women to register for the draft
- right-to-die laws
- granting driver's licenses to undocumented workers

- investing in alternative energy
- requiring welfare recipients to work for benefits
- censoring cable television
- admitting lie-detector evidence in court
- working while attending college

Get Thinking and Writing

CRITICAL THINKING

The Internet and computers have allowed an increasing number of people to work from their homes. For some, this means they can schedule work around family errands, save time and money by not having to commute, and limit day-care costs. For others, working at home is lonely and isolating and erases a needed boundary between a job and their personal life.

Write a short essay stating whether or not you would want to work from your home. Would it make you more productive? Would you miss working with others? Would your family understand?

WHAT HAVE YOU WRITTEN?

Read your essay carefully.

- What is your thesis? Is it clearly focused and precisely worded?
- What kind of essay did you write—narration, comparison, or argument?
- What kinds of paragraphs did you use to support your thesis? What patterns of development do they represent—definition, description, or cause and effect?
- How effective is the introduction? Does it arouse attention, include your thesis, or pose a question, or does it only announce what the paper is about?
- Does the conclusion end the essay on a strong point or simply repeat what you have already stated?

If possible, use peer review to improve your essay.

Get Writing

Before doctors understood its addictive properties, cocaine was used as an ingredient in over-the-counter medicines, including those given to children. Do you think there is a danger that many of the popular drugs advertised on television today may prove dangerous in the future? Do consumers assume that anything endorsed by doctors is safe?

Write a short essay that expresses your views on drug safety. Do drugs require more testing? Do commercials fully inform people about potential side effects?

Bettmann/CORBIS

COCAINE TOOTHACHE DROPS
Instantaneous Cure!
PRICE 15 CENTS.
Prepared by the
LLOYD MANUFACTURING CO.
219 HUDSON AVE., ALBANY, N. Y.
For sale by all Druggists.
(Registered March 1885.)   See other side.

WRITING ON THE WEB

Using a search engine such as Yahoo! or Google, enter terms such as *developing essays, writing essays, writing comparison, using cause and effect, argument,* and *composing essays* to locate current sites of interest.

1. Read online news articles, and notice how writers use different patterns of development to organize an essay. Notice which appeals are used in persuasive essays, editorials, and opinion pieces.

2. Write a multi-paragraph e-mail to a friend. Practice using different methods of development such as comparison, definition, or process in telling a story or describing a situation.

POINTS TO REMEMBER

1. An essay states a main idea supported by related paragraphs that provide details.

2. Writers generally use more than one pattern of development in creating an essay. A narration essay might include paragraphs consisting of definitions, cause and effect, or example.

3. Essays should have a defined topic and clear purpose.

4. Consider your readers' attitudes, background knowledge, and interests as you define new terms, clarify misconceptions, and present evidence that readers can appreciate.

Revising Essays

CHAPTER GOALS

- Appreciate the Importance of Revising

- Understand That Revising Differs from Editing

- Practice Revision Strategies

Get Writing

Arnold Schwarzenegger, an Austrian immigrant, body builder, and movie star, became governor of California. Ronald Reagan, another Hollywood actor, served as governor of California before becoming the fortieth president of the United States. Do you think celebrities have an advantage when they enter politics? Why or why not?

Write a brief essay stating your opinion on whether celebrities have an advantage when running for public office.

What Is Revision?

When you complete the draft of an essay, your first thought might be to look for misspelled words, verify names and facts, and check punctuation. These steps are called *editing*—making final repairs. Before editing, however, you should **revise** your essay.

Revision is different from editing. **Revision means *to see again.***

Before editing your essay for minor mistakes, you need to revise it by looking at the big picture.

Strategies for Revising an Essay

1. **Let your writing "cool."** Before you can look at your writing objectively, set it aside. Trying to revise your work just after you finish writing is hard because the ideas are still fresh in your mind. Let some time pass between writing and revising. Work on other assignments, run an errand, or check your e-mail before looking at your essay.

2. **Print your draft.** Some students can revise on a computer, but you may find it easier to work with a hard copy. Printing the draft lets you spread out the pages and see the whole essay at once. Double- or triple-space the hard copy to leave room for notes and corrections.

3. **Review your goal.** Before reading your essay, go over the assignment and any instructor guidelines:
    *   Look at samples of the essay you are writing.
    *   If your essay does not fit the assignment, it may be easier to review your notes, create a new outline, and write a new essay than to rewrite a failed attempt.

4. **Examine the big picture.** Revising is *not* editing. Don't immediately begin to correct spelling and punctuation. Instead, focus on the larger elements of the draft:
    *   Does the introduction get your readers' attention and prepare them for what follows?
    *   Is the thesis clearly stated?
    *   Are paragraphs logically organized?
    *   Do paragraph breaks organize the whole essay by showing clear transitions between main ideas?
    *   Are sections "off topic" or repetitive? Are there unimportant details that could be deleted?
    *   Is there enough supporting evidence?
    *   Does the conclusion leave readers with a strong final impression, question, or call to action?

- Does your essay meet the requirements of the assignment?
- What are the strong and weak points of the essay? What problems are the most serious?

5. **Read the essay with a "reader's eye."** Consider how your readers' knowledge, experiences, values, or attitudes will shape their responses to your essay:
   - Do you think readers are likely to be supportive, indifferent, or hostile to your thesis?
   - Do you anticipate reader objections? Do you provide evidence to encourage readers to change their minds? Do you try to reason with those who have different points of view?
   - Do readers need background information to understand your ideas? Are there misconceptions that need to be cleared up? Do you need to define any terms?
   - Will readers respond favorably to your essay's style and tone?

6. **Read your essay out loud.** Illogical statements, awkward sentences, repeated ideas, and missing details are far easier to "hear" than read.

7. **Have others read your draft.** Many instructors encourage students to use peer review. If you have the chance to work with a group, ask other students to read your essay:
   - Let others read your essay "cold." If you tell them what you are trying to say before they read it, they will have a harder time evaluating your essay objectively.
   - If you ask people who are not in your class to read the essay, first explain the assignment. People cannot give you good advice unless they know what the essay is supposed to accomplish. The more they know about your goal and the intended audience, the more valuable their responses will be.
   - Don't be defensive. Ask for people to give you their honest opinion of your essay.
   - Ask students what they consider the paper's strong and weak points.
   - Make notes of their remarks, and ask how your draft could be improved.

8. **Revise and rewrite:**
   - Revising is a continuing process. If you write on a computer, it is easy to make minor improvements every time you read your essay.
   - As you make changes to your essay, keep your goal and the assignment in mind.

Peer Review

Many writing instructors encourage students to work in small groups and engage in peer review of writing assignments. Sharing your essay with other students can give you fresh views about your topic as well as tips for filling in missing details and repairing errors. When you read the work of other students, you become an editor. There are several things you can do to make peer review helpful for everyone in the group.

Strategies for Peer Review

1. **Understand the role of editors.** An editor is not a writer. Your job as editor is not to tell other students how you would write their essays but to help them improve their work.

2. **Understand the writer's goal and the assignment.** If you are not familiar with the assignment, ask to see any directions the student received from the instructor. Read the directions carefully to offer valuable suggestions.

3. **Review the essay globally; then look at specifics.** Before pointing out grammar and spelling errors, focus on the big picture:
   - Does the topic fit the assignment?
   - Does it need to be more clearly focused or limited?
   - Does the paper have a clear thesis?
   - Is the thesis supported by details?
   - Are there irrelevant details that can be deleted?
   - Do paragraph breaks adequately organize the paper? Could the paragraph structure be more effective?
   - Can you detect sentences that are unclear, illogical, or awkward?
   - Does the paper need proofreading for spelling and grammar errors? As a peer editor, your job is not to correct mechanical errors, but you should indicate to the writer if the paper needs proofreading.

4. **Be positive.** Make constructive, helpful comments. Don't simply point out errors, but show how they can be corrected or avoided.

5. **Ask questions.** Instead of stating that a sentence or paragraph does not make sense, ask the student what he or she was trying to say. Asking questions can prompt a writer to rethink what he or she wrote, remember missing details, or consider new alternatives.

6. **When you submit work to peer editors, seek their advice.**
Don't be defensive. Allow editors to read and speak freely.
Encourage feedback by asking targeted questions. If you simply
ask "Do you like it?" or "Is my paper any good?" you are likely
to get polite compliments or vague comments that your work
is "OK." To get advice you can use, ask other students specific
questions:

- Is the thesis clear?
- Does the essay need more support?
- Should I put in more statistics? Are the quotations effective?
- Should I add some more details in the introduction?

Revising Elements of an Essay

Although you can correct spelling and punctuation mistakes whenever you
spot them, remember that your main goal in revising is examining the larger
elements of your essay, especially paragraphs.

Look at the Big Picture

Review the Entire Essay

Read your essay out loud. How does it sound? What ideas or facts are missing, poorly stated, or repetitive? Highlight areas needing improvement, and
delete paragraphs that are off topic or repetitive.

- Does your essay meet your goal and the needs of the assignment?
- What are the most serious problems?
- Is the essay clearly organized? Should you open with your strongest
  point or state it in the conclusion?

Examine the Thesis Statement

Does your essay have a clearly written thesis statement or controlling
idea—or is it simply a collection of facts and observations? Does the essay
have a point?

- If your essay has a thesis statement, read it aloud. Is it clearly
  worded? Is it too general? Can it be adequately supported?
- Where have you placed the thesis? Would it be more effective if
  placed before or after you presented evidence, defined a term, or
  explained some background information? Remember, the thesis does
  not have to appear in the opening paragraph.

Review the Topic Sentence and Controlling Idea of Each Paragraph

Each paragraph should have a clear purpose and support the thesis:

- Review the controlling ideas for each paragraph.
- Do all the paragraphs support the thesis?
- Are there paragraphs that are off topic? You may have developed some interesting ideas, included an important fact or quotation, or told a moving story, but if these elements don't support the thesis, they do not belong in the essay.

Review the Order of Paragraphs

As you write, you may add new ideas. Look at the topic sentence in each paragraph to see if the order of ideas should be revised:

- Should paragraphs be rearranged to maintain a clear time line or build greater emphasis?
- Does the order of paragraphs follow your train of thought? Should some paragraphs come after those containing definitions and background information?
- Are there paragraphs that would make a better introduction or conclusion?

Revise the Introduction

The opening sentences and paragraphs of your essay are important. They set the tone, announce the topic, get readers' attention, and establish how the rest of the essay is organized.

Introduction Checklist

1. Does the introduction clearly announce the topic?

2. Does the opening paragraph arouse interest?

3. Does it limit the topic, preparing readers for what follows?

4. If the thesis appears in the opening, is it precisely stated?

5. Does the language of the opening paragraph set the proper tone for the paper?

6. Does the introduction address reader concerns, correct misconceptions, or provide background information so readers can understand and appreciate the evidence that follows?

Because you cannot always predict how you will change the body of an essay, you should always return to the introduction and examine it before writing a new draft.

Revise Body Paragraphs

The paragraphs in the body of the essay should support the thesis, develop ideas, or advance the chronology.

Body Paragraph Checklist

1. **Does the paragraph have a clear focus?**

2. **Is the topic sentence supported with enough evidence?**

3. **Is the evidence easy to follow?** Does the paragraph follow a logical organization? Would a different pattern of development be more effective?

4. **Are there irrelevant ideas that should be deleted?**

5. **Are there clear transitions between ideas and within paragraphs?**

6. **Do paragraph breaks signal major transitions?** Should some paragraphs be combined and others broken up?

Revise the Conclusion

Not all essays require a separate conclusion. A narrative may end with a final event. A comparison may conclude with the last point.

Conclusion Checklist

1. **Does the conclusion end the paper on a strong note? Will it leave readers with a final image, question, quotation, or fact that will challenge readers and lead them to continue thinking about your subject?**

2. **Does the conclusion simply repeat the introduction or main ideas? Is it necessary? Should it be shortened or deleted?**

3. **If your purpose is to motivate people to take action, does the conclusion provide readers with clear directions?**

Revising an Essay

After attending a campus forum on legalizing drugs, a student decided to respond to one of the speakers in an argument paper for an English class.

First Draft

```
           Why Legalizing Drugs Won't Work
     For thirty years various people have been say-
ing that drugs should be legalized for a lot of rea-
sons. They believe legalizing drugs would eliminate
drug gangs and the crimes caused by desperate junkies
because the legal drugs would be cheaper. These ar-
guments make a lot of sense until you begin to think
about it.
     The only way drugs would be legalized is if they
were treated like alcohol so nobody under 21 could buy
them. So we still would have illegal drugs. Mostly
people start using drugs in high school so we would
still have that problem.
     Another thing people who support legalization don't
talk about is just who is going to sell legal drugs.
I don't think that Walgreens or Rite Aid is going
to sell grass and crack. If the idea is making drugs
cheaper, then there won't be enough profit for any
established business to want to sell them. Drugstores
make their profit selling prescription drugs and
beauty products. Customers with kids would avoid any
store that would have druggies walking around.
     The whole idea of treating addicts like people with
a problem and not criminals makes sense. I agree with
that. So letting these people have access to cheap
drugs and clean needles might help stop the spread of
AIDS and lower crime a little. But people are only go-
ing to step forward for legal programs when they are
really dope sick. So for years before they did drugs
and maybe stole to get money to buy them. We treat
alcoholics like people with a disease but that has
not stopped drunk driving from killing people. People
don't wake up one day and decide to take heroin so
they sign up to be legal addicts. Only after years of
abuse do they hit bottom and want help.
     So legalizing drugs is not going to fix everything.
It might work. But it won't have the great results its
supporters predict.
```

Revision Notes

```
           Why Legalizing Drugs Won't Work
     For thirty years various people have been say-
ing that drugs should be legalized for a lot of rea-
```

vague: needs strong thesis statement

sons. They believe legalizing drugs would eliminate drug gangs and the crimes caused by desperate junkies because the legal drugs would be cheaper. These arguments make a lot of sense until you begin to think about it.

limit essay

The only way drugs would be legalized is if they were treated like alcohol so nobody under 21 could buy them. <u>So we still would have illegal drugs.</u> Mostly people start using drugs in high school so we would still have that problem.

number points

rewrite topic sentence

<u>Another thing people who support legalization don't talk about is just who is going to sell legal drugs.</u> I don't think that Walgreens or Rite Aid is going to sell grass and crack. If the idea is making drugs cheaper, then there won't be enough profit for any established business to want to sell them. Drugstores make their profit selling prescription drugs and beauty products. Customers with kids would avoid any store that would have druggies walking around.

weak transition

improve wording

The whole idea of treating addicts like people with a problem and not criminals makes sense. I agree with that. So letting these people have access to cheap drugs and clean needles might help stop the spread of AIDS and lower crime a little. But people are only going to step forward for legal programs when they are really dope sick. So for years before they did drugs and maybe stole to get money to buy them. We treat alcoholics like people with a disease but that has not stopped drunk driving from killing people. People don't wake up one day and decide to take heroin so they sign up to be legal addicts. Only after years of abuse do they hit bottom and want help.

revise topic sentence

make comparison stronger

So legalizing drugs is not going to fix everything. It might work. But it won't have the great results its supporters predict.

need stronger conclusion

Revised Essay

Why Legalizing Drugs Won't Work

For thirty years advocates of legalizing drugs have argued that legalization would make drugs cheaper, eliminating violence associated with drug gangs and crimes committed by desperate junkies. **However, legalizing drugs will have a minimal impact on crime and violence for three main reasons.**

thesis listing three points

First, most people who take drugs begin using them in high school. It is unlikely that any state will allow the legal sale of addictive drugs to anyone under twenty-one. We would still see drug gangs and an underground drug culture supplying drugs to minors.

topic sentence	Legalizing drugs will have no effect on teenage drug abuse.
	Second, advocates of legalization never explain how addicts will be able to buy drugs. Because the goal of legalization is to lower prices to stem crime, sales of drugs will not generate substantial profits. Drugstores such as Walgreens and Rite Aid make their money selling prescription drugs and beauty supplies. They are not going to alienate their customers and community leaders by selling addictive recreational drugs.
topic sentence	Legalizing drugs will eliminate crime only if they are easy to obtain. Because it is unlikely legal businesses will want to sell them, legalizing drugs will have no impact on crime and violence.
topic sentence	Third, making drugs and clean needles available to addicts may help stop the spread of AIDS but will have little impact on crime and violence. Advocates have suggested that drug addicts be treated like patients, not criminals, and be allowed to register for programs that would give them inexpensive or free drugs. But people do not become addicts overnight. They begin experimenting with drugs, then become casual users, then move to full-blown addiction. Along the way, under the influence of drugs, they commit crimes, abuse their partners, lose jobs, and ruin families. Only when they hit rock bottom are addicts likely to step forward to register. Alcohol is legal. Alcoholics are not treated like criminals and can obtain treatment whenever they want. Those without insurance can enter free programs or join AA. But that does not stop violence committed by those under the influence of alcohol or prevent thousands of people from being killed by drunk drivers every year.
conclusion topic sentence	Legalizing drugs, despite the promises of its advocates, will realistically have only a limited impact on the problem of crime and violence caused by drug addicts.

EXERCISE 1   Revising Essays

Improve the following essay by revising the thesis statement, topic sentences, and organization of paragraphs. Delete details that are off topic, and add facts, ideas, and examples that support the thesis.

English 101   Damon Ramon

Volunteering

Many college students suffer a dilemma. They know that education alone will not help get them a good job in the career they seek. They need experience. Some will be lucky enough to get a part-time job in their field. Some may get internships. The rest wait tables, deliver pizzas, and cram for exams hoping their degree alone will convince an employer to hire them. Students need to recognize that in addition to helping others, being a volunteer can help them as well.

College students can use volunteer work in two very important ways. First, they can demonstrate skills needed in the career they intend to enter. The person who wants to become a sales representative can help with a fund drive for the symphony, an alumni organization, or charity. He or she can run a phone bank, write direct mail appeals, or make personal presentations. In raising money for a non-profit without pay, a student can get real professional experience and build a track record of sales that can make a résumé stand out. The person who wants to go into social work can impress an employer by listing real experience helping the elderly, serving disabled children, or working with recovering addicts. Volunteering is also a good way to relieve stress. College work is often abstract and theoretical, with the only reward being a good grade. Volunteer work can bring the meaningful gratification of making a difference.

Secondly, volunteer work can be used to build a network. Nearly every profession has an organization or association that needs volunteers. Even if you just end up stuffing envelopes or updating mailing lists, working a few hours a week can bring you into contact with the architects, attorneys, physicians, or restaurant owners you someday hope to work for. The student who wants to work in local government can help work on a political campaign.

In conclusion, volunteering can be helpful for students to achieve their career goals. Volunteering can teach students a lot, and besides it serves a good cause.

EXERCISE 2 Revising Essays

Select an essay you wrote this semester. Review the assignment and your original notes; then examine your essay carefully. Determine how you could improve your writing by revising the thesis statement, topic sentences, supporting details, and organization. Pay attention to the introduction and conclusion.

WORKING TOGETHER

Work with a group of students, and exchange copies of recent essays you have written. Make copies so each person can make corrections and comments. Discuss what you want to say, and ask how what you have written could be improved.

Get Thinking
and Writing

CRITICAL THINKING

Should the United States bring back the draft and require all eighteen-year-olds to serve in the military? Why or why not? If the armed forces do not need troops, should young people be required to serve some other form of national or community service? Why or why not?

Write a short essay stating your opinion about requiring eighteen-year-olds to serve their country.

WHAT HAVE YOU WRITTEN?

1. Does your essay have a clearly written thesis expressing your opinion?

2. Does each paragraph's topic sentence support the thesis statement?

3. Do the details in each paragraph support its topic sentence?

4. Are there details that are off topic or repetitive and could be deleted?

5. Do some points require further development? Should you add facts, ideas, or examples to support your points?

6. Does the introduction arouse attention, explain background information, state your thesis, and prepare readers for what follows in the rest of the essay?

7. Are the paragraphs in the body clearly organized? Do paragraph breaks and transitional statements help readers follow your train of thought?

8. Does the conclusion bring the essay to a logical end, or does it simply repeat the introduction?

Get Writing

Former president Ronald Reagan played heroes in several movies before entering politics. Do you think that an actor who played evil, violent, or comic characters would be taken seriously by voters? Could a stand-up comedian or a rap artist who made explicit music videos enter politics? Can voters separate an artist's image from his or her personal character?

Write an essay stating your views; then review your thesis, topic sentences, and paragraph structure.

ASSOCIATED PRESS/AP PHOTO

WRITING ON THE WEB

Using a search engine such as Google or Yahoo!, enter terms such as *revising essays, the writing process, writing essays,* and *developing essays* to locate current sites of interest.

1. Read news articles online, and study how writers develop introductions, use conclusions, and organize paragraphs.

2. Write some e-mails to friends. Before sending them, review the way you have used paragraphs to organize ideas. Revise your message to strengthen the introduction and conclusion, improve transitions, and add necessary details.

POINTS TO REMEMBER

1. Revision is an important part of the writing process.

2. Before revising an essay, review your plan, the needs of the assignment, and your readers.

3. In examining your essay, look at the "big picture" first. Determine if your essay has a clear thesis supported by sufficient details.

4. The introduction should announce your topic, arouse reader attention, supply background information, and prepare readers for what follows in the rest of the essay.

5. The paragraphs in the body of the essay should follow a logical pattern of development using clear transitions so readers can follow your train of thought.

6. The conclusion should end the essay with a memorable fact, call to action, quotation, or question.

7. Peer review can help detect errors and provide suggestions for improving your essay.

PART 4

Improving Essays

CHAPTER 17

Improving Style and Consistency

CHAPTER GOALS

- Appreciate the Importance of Style and Consistency
- Avoid Illogical Shifts in Tense
- Revise Awkward Shifts in Person
- Use Consistent Organization
- Maintain Clear Transitions

EVERETT COLLECTION

Get Writing

Do you think movies and television present stereotypes about Arabs?

Write a short essay analyzing the way popular culture has shaped attitudes toward people from the Middle East. Include examples of movies, characters, images, and themes to support your point of view.

Good writing takes readers on a journey. For readers to follow your train of thought and understand what you are trying to say, your essay should use **consistent tense, consistent person, consistent organization, and clear transitions.**

Get Writing

WHAT ARE YOU TRYING TO SAY?

Write a paragraph describing an experience that changed your life. Discuss the past event and the way it continues to shape your attitudes or behavior today.

_____

_____

_____

_____

_____

WHAT HAVE YOU WRITTEN?

Review your paragraphs for the use of tense. Do you clearly distinguish between past and present? Do you make any awkward shifts from first person ("I") to second person ("you") or third person ("they")? (See Chapter 30.)

Using Consistent Tense

Tense refers to time—*past, present, or future.* Readers depend on your use of tense to understand the events you describe:

Samira *worked* at WKTJ, which *was* the only all-jazz station in Chicago.
[Samira was once employed at Chicago's former only all-jazz station.]

Samira *worked* at WKTJ, which *is* the only all-jazz station in Chicago.
[Samira was once employed at Chicago's only all-jazz station.]

Samira *works* at WKTJ, which *was* the only all-jazz station in Chicago.
[Samira is employed at Chicago's former only all-jazz station.]

Samira *works* at WKTJ, which *is* the only all-jazz station in Chicago.
[Samira is employed at Chicago's only all-jazz station.]

Using Past and Present

In revising essays, make sure that your use of tense clearly reflects your meaning. Use past tense to describe actions or situations that occurred in the past or have been completed:

It rained yesterday.
The drug damaged my uncle's red blood cells.
Chicago dug the canal in 1912.

Use present tense to describe actions that are happening now, are on-going, or began in the past and continue into the present:

It is raining.
Red blood cells carry oxygen.
Chicago is building a new public library.

In writing a narrative, for example, you can relate events either in past or present. Most writers relate an event that has happened in the past tense:

Ben *went* out with a twisted ankle, and Coach Jackson *called* me in. It *was* my first scrimmage of the season. The ball *was snapped*. I *dodged* past the defense and *raced* down the field. The field *was* slippery with wet leaves. I *turned* to catch the ball. The impact *knocked* me off balance, and I *tripped* into the end zone, scoring my one and only touchdown in high school.

However, writers sometimes write about a past event using present tense to create a sense of immediate action. Present tense can dramatize an event by making it appear that the action is happening now rather than in the past:

Ben *goes* out with a twisted ankle, and Coach Jackson *calls* me in. It *is* my first scrimmage of the season. The ball *snaps*. I *dodge* past the defense and *race* down the field. The field *is* slippery with wet leaves. I *turn* to catch the ball. The impact *knocks* me off balance, and I *trip* into the end zone, scoring my one and only touchdown in high school.

You can use both tenses to show logical shifts between past and present action:

I *love* playing football. I *enjoyed* my high school experiences, even though I *scored* only one touchdown. Coach Jackson *is* one of the best coaches in the state. He *won* state honors in two of the last five years. He *has* a website that *provides* high school athletes with valuable advice about everything from getting better grades to avoiding steroids. When I *played* ball, he *encouraged* us to study hard, reminding us that our education *came* first. He *is* just as proud of his players who *have gone* onto Harvard and Yale as he *is* of the players who made it to the NFL.

Avoid confusing readers with illogical shifts between past and present:

The field *was* covered with wet leaves. Everyone *was* slipping. Somehow I *manage* to dodge past the defense, and I *was* racing toward the end zone. I *turn* and *caught* the ball. The impact *knocks* me off my balance. I *tripped* into the end zone and *score* a touchdown.

EXERCISE 1   Revising for Consistent Tense

Revise the paragraphs in this essay to avoid awkward and illogical shifts in tense by changing the tense of verbs. Remember to shift tense only when there is a logical change from past to present.

Damon Ruiz   Communications 212

The Flag of Our Fathers

The most widely reproduced photograph in history is the flag raising on Iwo Jima taken by Joe Rosenthal on February 23, 1945. This photograph inspires the

Marine Corps War Memorial in Washington, D.C. Initial confusion about how the picture is taken causes controversy that lasted to this day. Some people have discredited the photograph, insisting that the picture was posed and not really a news photo of a genuine historical event. They point out that it was not a picture of the original flag raising but a reenactment. Others insist that the photograph is genuine.

Much of the confusion stemmed from the photographer's initial comments. On February 23, 1945, a small American flag is flying atop Mt. Suribachi on the embattled island of Iwo Jima. The sight of the flag rallied the Marines locked in the bloodiest campaign in their history. It was decided to replace this flag with a larger one.

Joe Rosenthal, an AP photojournalist, trudges up the mountain with military photographers, one of whom carried a color movie camera. The Marines carefully time the changing of the flags so that the second, larger one would be raised just as the smaller flag is lowered. Five Marines and a Navy corpsman began to raise the bigger flag, and Rosenthal scrambles to catch the moment. He swings his bulky camera into position and snapped a picture without having time to look through the viewfinder. Thinking he misses shooting the event, he asks the Marines to pose at the base of the flagpole. The Marines cluster around and wave at the camera.

Rosenthal sends his film to be developed. A Navy technician immediately spots the dramatic picture of the Marines raising the flag, crops off the edge to center the image, and wired it to the United States. Within days the photo appeared on the front pages of hundreds of newspapers. President Roosevelt orders millions of copies to be printed to boost morale and promote the sale of war bonds.

However, some people suspected that the photo was a fake. It looks too dramatic and too perfect to be real. A reporter asked Rosenthal, who had no idea that his accidental picture had become nationally famous, if he posed the shot. Thinking the reporter is referring to his second photo, Rosenthal said yes. A radio program then reported that the famous photo was posed, starting a legend that the whole event is just a piece of wartime propaganda.

Sixty years later, historians still debate the issue. Many agree that the photograph, taken by accident, depicted a genuine event, the raising of the second flag on Iwo Jima. The heroism of the Marines raising the flag was genuine as well. Of the six flag raisers, three lose their lives on Iwo Jima.

_____

_____

_____

_____

_____

_____

_____

_____

_____

_____

_____

_____

_____
_____
_____
_____
_____
_____
_____
_____
_____
_____
_____
_____
_____
_____
_____
_____
_____
_____
_____
_____
_____
_____
_____
_____
_____
_____
_____
_____

Summaries of plays, movies, novels, and stories can be written in past or present tense.

Past

In "The Cask of Amontillado," Edgar Allan Poe presented the gleeful confession of a psychotic murderer. Montresor delighted in retelling his story of taking revenge against a friend who had insulted him. Knowing his friend's love of wine, Montresor lured his victim to his underground vaults and entombed him in a crypt.

Present

In "The Cask of Amontillado," Edgar Allan Poe presents the gleeful confession of a psychotic murderer. Montresor delights in retelling his story of taking revenge against a friend who insulted him. Knowing his friend's love of wine, Montresor lures his victim to his underground vaults and entombs him in a crypt.

In any narrative or description, you can include both past and present tense to indicate the difference between past and current or ongoing action:

> In "The Cask of Amontillado," Edgar Allan Poe *presented* the gleeful confession of a psychotic murderer. Poe's character *represents* something rare in literature, a man who *kills* without remorse. Montresor *lured* his victim to an underground vault and *entombed* him in a crypt. The murder *was* never discovered. Poe's hero *celebrated* the fact that after fifty years no one *had discovered* the body. This attitude *reminds* modern readers of recent serial killers.

EXERCISE 2   Maintaining Consistency in Tense

Revise these paragraphs from an e-mail to avoid awkward and illogical shifts in tense by changing the tense of verbs. Remember to shift tense only when there is a logical change from past to present.

DATE: May 25, 2009
TO: Sharon Thomson

FROM: Kari Neils

RE: Health and Safety: Food Storage and Preparation

Last month outbreaks of food-borne illnesses struck three Atlanta restaurants. In order to prevent problems in our outlets, I am reminding all managers to follow company food safety procedures. Yesterday fresh food is found left on loading docks for up to four hours. This is unacceptable. Fresh produce must be refrigerated on delivery. Last week inspectors find employees preparing food without washing their hands after clearing dirty dishes. When asked, the workers explain no one told them they had to wash their hands before entering food prep areas. The inspectors also find most of the hand sanitizers were empty. We suggest that at this month's employee meeting you show all staff the food safety video. The video is only fifteen minutes but gave a full, easy-to-understand explanation of hazards and how to prevent them. The video is shot in one of our outlets and showed step-by-step how to easily avoid food spoilage and disease. I strongly urge you to make sure that all employees follow company guidelines.

Kari

_____
_____
_____
_____
_____
_____
_____
_____
_____
_____
_____
_____
_____
_____
_____

Using Consistent Person

Essays can be written in first, second, or third person:

First person: _I_ (singular) or _we_ (plural)

Second person: _you_ (singular and plural)

Third person: _he_ or _she_ (singular) or _they_ (plural)

Use **first person** when you write about things you have seen or experienced or to state a personal opinion:

_I_ was born in Brooklyn but grew up in Great Neck, where _my_ father taught high school English and _my_ mother managed a bookstore.

As _we_ waited to cross the street, _we_ saw a cab run the stop sign and slam into a parked delivery van.

_I_ am convinced that capital punishment does not deter criminals from committing violent crimes. After all, _I_ doubt if anyone contemplating committing a crime expects to get caught.

Avoid using first person in formal reports and research papers.

Use **second person** to directly address your reader, especially when giving directions or suggestions:

You must scan computers for viruses at least once a week.

Keep _your_ canceled check as a receipt.

Avoid using second person in making general statements rather than ones directed to specific readers.

Awkward

The new show will air this fall on Comedy Central, one of _your_ basic cable channels.

Her car needs a transmission overhaul, which is *your* most expensive
repair job.

They forgot to file a flight plan, *your* most common pilot mistake.

Revised

The new show will air this fall on Comedy Central, a basic cable channel.

Her car needs a transmission overhaul, which is the most expensive
repair job.

They forgot to file a flight plan, the most common pilot mistake.

Use **third person** to describe the actions of other people or organizations:

He drove to Philadelphia last night.

She moved to France.

They raised prices twice last year.

Switch persons to show logical changes in point of view:

They flew to Boston, where *I* went to school.

I went to the accountant to get *your* taxes.

Avoid awkward and illogical shifts between persons:

Awkward

Sara went to the top of the Eiffel Tower, where *you* could see for miles.

People often gain weight when *you* quit smoking.

You get a fifty-dollar discount when *customers* pay in cash.

Improved

Sara went to the top of the Eiffel Tower, where *she* could see for miles.

People often gain weight when *they* quit smoking.

You get a fifty-dollar discount when *you* pay in cash.

or

Customers get a fifty-dollar discount when *they* pay in cash.

EXERCISE 3   Revising Shifts in Person

Revise the following paragraphs from a report to avoid awkward shifts in person.

History of Television   17

For fifty years, television news was dominated by your network evening broadcasts. Tens of millions of Americans rushed home from work to see the day's events reported on television. With only three networks, your anchormen such as Walter Cronkite and Huntley and Brinkley were popular and highly influential. Their coverage of civil rights demonstrations, assassinations, and moon landings shaped the way Americans thought of the country and themselves. The power of news anchors was summed up by President Johnson's comment: "If I've lost Cronkite, I've lost middle America." Infuriated by Cronkite's coverage of the Vietnam War, Johnson sometimes called CBS, demanding to speak to Cronkite during a commercial break. Cronkite was so powerful that he refused to take calls from the White House.

Today the influence of the network evening news has dwindled. Cronkite had as many as 22 million viewers in 1968. When Dan Rather retired in 2005, he drew only 7 million viewers. Only 8 percent of people under 40 now watch the network broadcasts. Today TVs carry CNN, CSPAN, or Fox News in your waiting rooms, hotel lobbies, bars, gyms, schools, and offices. We see the news as it happens throughout the day and feel no need to see it when you get home. Every time you log on to the Internet, we get headlines of breaking news stories and can easily click to online news sources to track stories in detail.

With so many news sources bombarding us all day long, some people still see the evening news as your official summary of current events.

_____

_____

_____

_____

_____

_____

_____

_____

_____

_____

_____

_____

_____

_____

_____

_____

_____

_____

_____

EXERCISE 4 Revising Shifts in Person

Revise the following paragraph from a student paper to eliminate awkward shifts in person.

We reached San Francisco by noon and checked in to our hotel. We walked to Chinatown, where you can find silk dresses, inlaid boxes, Chinese coins, and exotic prints at great prices. We then took a cab to Fisherman's Wharf. One can take a boat to Alcatraz, where you can tour the old prison, which is now a national park. The trip is so popular that you should make reservations. We were lucky because it was a weekday, and you could get tickets. The trip is worth it. The prison is one of the most fascinating places one can visit. We really felt the island was haunted by the ghosts of all the prisoners who were held there. I kept remembering the movie *Escape from Alcatraz* with Clint Eastwood. People still wonder if the prisoners depicted in the film managed to get to the mainland or were swept out to sea.

_____
_____
_____
_____
_____
_____
_____
_____
_____
_____
_____
_____

Using Consistent Organization

One way to improve comparison, division, classification, and cause-and-effect essays is to use consistent organization. When you describe or define more than one topic, you can help readers follow your train of thought by presenting ideas in the same order. An essay comparing Franklin Roosevelt and Winston Churchill might begin by explaining Roosevelt's family background, his education, his attitude toward the Nazis, and his most important wartime decisions. In discussing Winston Churchill, the paragraphs would follow the same pattern, first describing his family background, then discussing his education, his attitude toward the Nazis, and his most important wartime decisions. Using a consistent order makes your essay easier to read and the information easier to remember. A student writing about three colleges, for example, organizes details about each one in the same order: first, stating the school's name and location; second, describing its faculty and student body; and third, explaining its most noted program:

Most of our high school seniors attend one of three local community and technical colleges.

name and location

faculty and students

most noted program

Brixton County Technical College in Mayfield offers associate degrees in business, technology, and aviation mechanics. It has a faculty of 150 and an enrollment of 2,000. The college is best known for its FAA-approved aviation mechanic program, which trains students to service aircraft used by Delta, Midwest, United, and other major airlines.

name and location

faculty and students

most noted program

Martin Luther King College in Patterson offers diplomas and associate degrees in business, health occupations, and social services. It has a faculty of 75 and an enrollment of 1,100. The college's most popular program is pre-nursing, which trains about 400 students a year, who transfer to nursing programs at the state university.

name and location

faculty and students

most noted program

Payton Technical Institute in Plymouth provides certificates in auto mechanics, electronic repair, carpentry, and welding. It has a faculty of 50 and 500 students. The new robotics welding program is very popular and trains graduates for work in the local Ford assembly plant.

EXERCISE 5   Revising for Consistent Organization

Revise the following paragraphs to develop a consistent organization.

Jackson -4

Three of the most significant black leaders to emerge following the emancipation of the slaves were Frederick Douglass, Booker T. Washington, and W. E. B. DuBois.

Frederick Douglass was best known for his impassioned oratory against slavery. He was born a slave in 1817 and fled to freedom in 1838. He began a career in public speaking, denouncing not only slavery but also discrimination and segregation in the North. After publishing his autobiography, *Narrative of the Life of Frederick Douglass,* he went to England, where he continued to campaign against slavery. Friends raised money to purchase his freedom. Douglass returned to America and founded an anti-slavery newspaper called *The North Star.* During the Civil War, Douglass met with Lincoln several times and helped recruit blacks to serve in the Union Army. He served as the U.S. Minister to Haiti from 1889 to 1891. He died in 1895.

Booker T. Washington is best known for his interest in education. He founded the Tuskegee Institute, which stressed vocational skills, and the National Negro Business League, which encouraged black enterprise. Washington advised several presidents and addressed Southern politicians, urging them to provide jobs for blacks. Washington was born a slave in 1856 and taught himself to read. His position that economic opportunities were more important than civil rights led to criticism from other black leaders. His organizations began to lose support after 1910. Washington died in 1915.

W. E. B. DuBois died in Ghana in 1961 after nearly eighty years of work dedicated to the advancement of African Americans. A Pan Africanist, he believed that blacks in America should view themselves as Africans rather than Americans. He opposed Booker T. Washington's approach, which he thought kept blacks as second-class citizens. DuBois was a world traveler, visiting Russia and China, as well as several African nations. He was born in Massachusetts in 1868. In 1895 he became the first African American to receive a Ph.D. from Harvard.

The three leaders often had divergent views, but their impact has shaped African American culture, politics, and art into the twenty-first century.

_____

_____

_____

_____

_____

_____

_____

_____

_____

_____

_____

_____

_____

_____

_____

_____

_____

_____

_____

_____

_____

_____

_____

_____

_____

_____

_____

Using Clear Transitions

When you write, you often make transitions, changing your train of thought by introducing examples, comparisons, references, quotations, or definitions. For transitions to be clear and effective, make sure that you provide enough information so readers understand the full meaning of a reference, the value of a quotation, or the significance of a comparison:

Unclear

> My first year of college was a shock. My English teacher assigned us ten novels to read in one semester. My psychology teacher gave a weekly quiz. Both my history and business law instructors required twenty-page research papers. This was so different from high school. I had to give up my social life and quit my part-time job just to maintain a B- average.

The student mentions that high school was different from college but does not explain how. Adding more details about his or high school experiences gives readers a greater understanding of why the student found the first year of a college to be such a shock:

Revised

> My first year of college was a shock. My English teacher assigned us ten novels to read in one semester. My psychology teacher gave a weekly quiz. Both my history and business law instructors required twenty-page research papers. **In high school we read one novel a year, and no teacher gave weekly quizzes or required anything longer than a five-page paper.** I had to give up my social life and quit my part-time job just to maintain a B- average.

Link quotations to your own writing. When you include quotations in an essay, link them to your own words. Don't simply insert a quotation between sentences and let it stand alone in a paragraph:

Unclear

> Schizophrenia remains a devastating disease. "We have discovered new treatments, but we still have not found out what causes it" (Wilson 34). Many patients and their families find existing therapies only partially helpful, leading some to consider alternative medicine.

Connecting quotations to your own writing creates a clearer and smother transition. In addition, it is important to introduce a quotation by explaining why it supports your thesis, where it comes from, or who said it:

Improved

> Schizophrenia remains a devastating disease. **George Wilson, director of the National Institute of Mental Health, notes,** "We have discovered new treatments, but we still have not found out what causes it" (34). Many patients and their families find existing therapies only partially helpful, leading some to consider alternative medicine.

EXERCISE 6 Improving Essays

Take one or more of your recent essays, and examine your paragraphs for awkward shifts in tense and person, inconsistent organization, and unclear transitions. Make a note of repeated errors, and keep these in mind when you revise and edit future assignments.

WORKING TOGETHER

Working with a group of students, revise this announcement to eliminate awkward shifts in tense and person, inconsistent organization, and unclear transitions. Invent necessary facts or details.

Attention All Sales and Service Personnel:

City of Angels Productions will introduce a new travel/expense policy on May 1st:

<u>Sales/Service Personnel, LA District</u>
Employees are allowed a maximum of $50 a day travel reimbursement. Employees issued company cars can still use your corporate charge cards for gas. Meal allowances remain at a maximum of $25 a day.

<u>Sales/Service Personnel, Western Region</u>
Your meal allowances have been increased to $40 a day.
    Employees are allowed a maximum of $150 a day travel reimbursement. Use of company cars for out-of-state travel is discouraged.

<u>Sales/Service Personnel, National Accounts</u>
Employees are allowed a maximum of $250 a day travel reimbursement. Airline tickets should be charged to your corporate charge card. Employee meal allowances have been increased to $60 a day.
    If you have any questions, please contact me at ext. 7403.

Jack Vincennes

City of Angels Productions

Get Thinking and Writing

CRITICAL THINKING

In the 1930s, when President Roosevelt wanted better relations with Latin America, his administration encouraged Hollywood to avoid making films with negative stereotypes of South Americans. Today we are trying to improve our relations with Arab nations. Should Hollywood, which makes movies seen around the world, avoid negative images of Arabs and Muslims? Would you consider this a good idea or censorship? Write a short essay stating your views.

WHAT HAVE YOU WRITTEN?

Write out your thesis statement or controlling idea:

_____

_____

Does this statement accurately express your point of view? Could it be revised to be more direct or less abstract?

Do you accurately use shifts in tense to show changes between past and present?

Which person do you use—first ("I/we"), second ("you"), or third ("he/she/they")?

Do you make any awkward or illogical shifts in person?

If you develop your essay with comparisons or examples, are details organized in a consistent pattern?

Read your essay aloud. Are there any unclear transitions? Do you explain references and examples so readers can follow your train of thought?

Get Writing

What impact does U.S. popular culture have on audiences in other countries? If all you knew about the United States came from watching U.S. movies, television shows, and music videos, what would you think about the country? What would seem to be its values, its ethics, its attitudes toward other nations?

Think of your favorite movies, television shows, and music videos, and write an essay describing the messages they send to people who have no other knowledge of the United States.

WRITING ON THE WEB

Using a search engine such as Yahoo! or Google, enter terms such as *improving essays, revising essays, parallel development, shifts in tense, consistent tense, shift in person, consistent use of person,* and *awkward transitions.*

POINTS TO REMEMBER

1. You can improve your essays by making it easier for readers to follow your train of thought and by avoiding awkward shifts.

2. Use consistent tense. Shift from past to present only when there is a logical change in time.

3. Use consistent person. Avoid illogical shifts from I to you or they.

4. Avoid unclear transitions. Fully explain examples and references, and link quotations to your own text.

5. Use consistent organization to present ideas in a common pattern.

CHAPTER 18

Improving Sentence Variety

CHAPTER GOALS

- Appreciate the Value of Sentence Variety
- Vary Sentence Length
- Use Questions and Exclamations to Increase Variety
- Vary Sentence Openings
- Combine Related Sentences

JOHN ROBERTSON/ALAMY LIMITED

Get Writing

Do you think that the news media is fair? Does it seem to take sides on many issues? Can you think of evidence of biased reporting?

Write a short essay expressing your views on the way that television presents the news. Support your opinions with examples.

You can make paragraphs and essays more effective and easier to read by increasing the variety of your sentences. Changing the usual sentence patterns can more clearly express what you are trying to say and prevent your writing from becoming dull and repetitive:

My family faced many problems last year. My grandmother died. She battled cancer for two years. My uncle was forced to close his bakery. He was deeply in debt. My cousins worked with him. They immediately lost their jobs. My sister left her husband. She needed a place to live. She moved in with me. She has two children. My apartment used to be quiet. Now it is so noisy I cannot study at home.

Revised

My family faced many problems last year. **After a two-year battle with cancer,** my grandmother died. **Deeply in debt,** my uncle was forced to close his bakery. My cousins worked with him**, and they** immediately lost their jobs. My sister left her husband**, and** she needed a place to live. **She and her two children moved in with me. Once quiet, my apartment is now so noisy I cannot study at home.**

Get Writing

WHAT ARE YOU TRYING TO SAY?

Describe something you would like to own, such as a house, boat, car, or guitar.

WHAT HAVE YOU WRITTEN?

Read your paragraph carefully. Notice the style and length of your sentences. Write out the shortest sentence:

_____

_____

Is the idea important enough to isolate in a single sentence? Could it be combined with another sentence?

Write out the longest sentence:

_____

_____

_____

What idea does it express? Does your sentence address a complex issue or include more than one complete idea? Does it contain wordy phrases that add little meaning? Would your ideas be clearer if stated in more than one sentence?

Do many of your sentences follow a repetitive pattern, such as "It has air-conditioning. It has power steering. It has a DVD player"?

Top 20

SENTENCE VARIETY
Varying the pattern of your sentences highlights important ideas and keeps readers interested in what you are trying to say.

Varying Sentence Length

The length and complexity of sentences should reflect the ideas they are trying to express. Short sentences stand out and command attention. They can be read at glance and should be used to express important ideas or signal transitions. Longer sentences allow you to demonstrate a train of thought, showing readers how ideas develop or connect with others. Blending longer and shorter sentences signals the importance of ideas, keeps your writing fresh, and maintains readers' attention.

Short Sentences

Short sentences can be effective because they are direct and dramatic. They can stress an important fact or idea that readers can easily understand and remember:

Her career is finished.
The jury voted guilty.
Never swim alone.

However, too many short sentences can make writing choppy and hard to understand because instead of connecting ideas to create a train of thought, they become a list of separate statements.

Choppy

Mayor Beam is running for reelection. He is seeking a third term. He faces a tough campaign. He is running against Elizabeth Holzer. She is a popular businesswoman. She owns the Hotel Metro. She built several condos downtown.

Improved

Mayor Beam is running for reelection, **seeking a third term.** He faces a tough campaign against Elizabeth Holzer, **a popular businesswoman.** She owns the Hotel Metro **and has built several condos downtown.**

You can reduce choppy writing by joining short, related sentences that better demonstrate the relationship of ideas.

Choppy

Talk shows dominate afternoon TV. Soap operas remain popular. They have had to change. The shows have to appeal to a younger generation. Soap stars now portray professional women. They also portray single mothers.

Improved

Talk shows dominate afternoon TV, **though soap operas remain popular. They have had to change to appeal to a younger generation. Soap stars now portray professional women and single mothers.**

You can also reduce choppiness by avoiding using complete sentences that simply add a single fact or detail that could be included in a related sentence.

Choppy

Cara bought a mint-condition 1965 Mustang. It is a convertible.
He was born in Chicago in 1978. His parents are Polish.
The demonstration led to a riot. The riot killed six people.

Improved

Cara bought a mint-condition 1965 **Mustang convertible.**
He was born in Chicago **to Polish parents** in 1978.
The demonstration led to a riot **that killed six people.**

EXERCISE 1   Increasing Sentence Variety by Reducing Choppiness

Revise the following sentences by joining related sentences. Eliminate sentences that simply add a detail that could be included in a related sentence.

1. Desi Arnaz was a band leader, singer, and actor. He was also the husband of Lucille Ball.

2. In 1951, Desi and Lucy agreed to star in a TV comedy. It was called *I Love Lucy.*

3. At that time, TV comedies were broadcast live from studios. The studios were in New York.

4. Lucy and Desi wanted to stay in California. They wanted to live at home.

5. They suggested recording the show on film. It would be like a motion picture.

_____

_____

6. The sponsor agreed with the plan but insisted on one change. The sponsor wanted a live audience.

_____

_____

7. Desi helped pioneer a new way of recording a live performance. It used three cameras.

_____

_____

8. This was expensive. CBS asked Lucy and Desi to accept a reduced salary.

_____

_____

9. Desi agreed in exchange for something he wanted. He wanted to own the rights to the films.

_____

_____

10. CBS accepted Desi's request. He would own the films after they were broadcast.

_____

_____

11. Television was new. Few people understood the value of reruns.

_____

_____

12. Lucy and Desi created a studio. It was called Desilu.

_____

_____

13. A few years later, Lucy and Desi sold the films back to CBS. They received four million dollars for them.

_____

_____

14. Desilu grew rapidly. It produced many hit shows. It bought RKO Movie Studios.

_____

_____

15. **For a while, Desilu was the largest studio in the world. Lucy and Desi divorced in 1960. They split the company when they divorced.**

_____

_____

EXERCISE 2   Improving Sentence Variety by Reducing Choppiness

Revise this paragraph from a student essay by combining related sentences. Eliminate those that simply add a detail that could be included in another.

Anderson-3

It was almost thirty years before 9/11. Samuel Byck planned to hijack a jet. He wanted to use it as a weapon. Samuel Byck was a failed salesman. He was emotionally unbalanced. He blamed President Nixon for his personal problems. He made threats against the president. He sent strange tapes to celebrities. The Secret Service took notice. He picketed the White House. He was arrested. He was denied a small business loan. Byck blamed Nixon. He tape-recorded an elaborate plan. He called it Operation Pandora's Box. He obtained a gun. He made a gasoline bomb. He planned to hijack a commercial airliner. He would force the pilot to fly over Washington. He would shoot the pilot. He would then crash the plane into the White House. He wanted to kill Nixon. On February 22, 1974, Byck drove to Baltimore/Washington International Airport. He shot a security guard. He stormed onto a Delta flight. He ordered the crew to take off. The pilots explained they could not. Byck shot them both. Police fired into the cockpit. Byck was wounded. He fell to the floor. He shot himself in the head. The assassination attempt drew little attention at the time. It was overshadowed by news about the Watergate scandal. It was almost forgotten. Byck's bizarre story did attract attention thirty years later. Historians and moviemakers were fascinated by Byck. Sean Penn played Byck in *The Assassination of Richard Nixon*. The film was released in 2004.

_____

_____

_____

_____

_____

_____

_____

_____

_____

_____

_____

_____

_____

_____

_____

_____

_____

_____

Long Sentences

Long sentences are useful to explain complicated ideas and demonstrate the relationship between ideas by placing them in a single sentence:

> Mayor Aronson has built a career on championing the need for low-income housing, but her challenger, June Avery, is gaining support by promising more jobs and better schools.

> In World War I, the United States fought Germany and was allied with Italy and Japan; in World War II, the United States fought Germany, Italy, and Japan.

Paragraphs containing too many long sentences can become difficult to read, even if the sentences are grammatically correct:

> A good college education provides students with the technical skills they need to obtain a job after graduation; however, many of these skills will become obsolete within a few years. Students also need to develop critical-thinking skills; the ability to learn new ideas, analyze problems, evaluate data, and communicate effectively will help them adjust to future changes in technology and the economy.

Improved

> A good college education provides students with the technical skills they need to obtain a job after graduation. **However, many of these skills will become obsolete within a few years.** Students also need to develop critical-thinking skills. **The ability to learn new things, analyze problems, evaluate data, and communicate effectively will help them adjust to future changes in technology and the economy.**

You can increase variety by breaking up long sentences and using short, dramatic sentences to highlight a single important idea:

> After watching her mother suffer a series of strokes when she was only fifty, Carla decided she had to change her lifestyle and began a vigorous routine of diet and exercise, losing twenty-five pounds in a single month.

After watching her mother suffer a series of strokes when she was only fifty, Carla decided she had to change her lifestyle and began a vigorous routine of diet and exercise. **She lost twenty-five pounds in a single month.**

Eric promised his parents he would do better this semester, but he soon fell back to his old habit of sleeping late and watching television all day, never opening a single book.

Eric promised his parents he would do better this semester, but he soon fell back to his old habit of sleeping late and watching television all day. **He never opened a single book.**

EXERCISE 3   Increasing Sentence Variety by Highlighting Ideas in Separate Sentences

Revise the following long sentences by breaking them up to highlight important ideas in a separate short sentence. You may have to add words or short phrases for clarity.

1. Science fiction writers have imagined inventions long before they became practical realities, such as Jules Verne, who wrote about submarines and moon rockets in the nineteenth century, and H. G. Wells, who described nuclear weapons in 1914.

   _____

   _____

   _____

2. In *The World Set Free,* Wells describes how scientists use a substance similar to plutonium to create a bomb that, when dropped from a small plane, destroys an entire city with a massive release of atomic energy at a time when most armies still relied on horses.

   _____

   _____

   _____

   _____

3. Harold Nicholson envisioned rockets, much like modern cruise missiles, delivering atomic bombs that create tidal waves causing global climate change in *Public Faces,* a novel he published in 1932.

   _____

   _____

   _____

4. J. B. Priestly's 1938 novel *The Doomsday Men* describes a conspiracy to use a cyclotron to unleash a colossal chain reaction that would tear open the Earth's crust and end all human life; the conspirators were religious terrorists.

   _____

   _____

   _____

5. In April 1944, *Astounding Science Fiction* published a story about an atom bomb that readers rated the worst story in that issue, but the story's details so closely resembled the top-secret atom bomb being developed by the Manhattan Project that the author was investigated by military intelligence.

_____

_____

_____

_____

EXERCISE 4   Revising to Create Sentence Variety

Revise this paragraph by breaking up overly long sentences. Highlight important or dramatic ideas by placing them in short sentences.

Ruiz-1

When it first appeared, the Internet was simply another way that news organizations broadcast their stories to the public; by the mid-1990s even small-town newspapers had online editions, which allowed them to reach a worldwide audience. The change was dramatic, and it presented publishers and broadcasters with a financial challenge. People could now read stories and see video online rather than buy a newspaper or watch a TV broadcast; media owners are dependent on advertising revenue, and they feared a loss of income. Now there is another challenge, and it has to do with content. Blogs have turned regular citizens into columnists and journalists; popular sites such as YouTube have become alternative networks where average citizens can post their camcorder clips of events. When dramatic statements and footage appear online, news organizations are faced with a dilemma. Professional journalists follow certain standards about collecting information, filming events, and verifying sources, but they cannot always know the sources of dramatic footage posted online. When a clip gets millions of hits on YouTube, however, news editors feel they cannot ignore the story; many worry that their credibility could suffer if they end up broadcasting fake or misleading videos.

_____

_____

_____

_____

_____

_____

_____

_____

_____

_____

_____

_____

_____

_____

_____

_____

_____

Increasing Sentence Variety with Questions and Exclamations

Most of the sentences you write are **declarative.** They state facts, present ideas, or describe actions:

> Austin is the capital of Texas.
> I think it might snow tonight.
> I sold my SUV.

Because most documents are written in declarative statements, you can arouse interest and create variety by using other types of sentences.

Questions engage readers by asking them to evaluate what they are reading or consider their own knowledge or attitudes:

> When will we end our addiction to foreign oil?
> Are you prepared for retirement?
> Is your child safe?

Exclamations express strong statements and have exclamation points for emphasis:

> Do it today!
> After seven months of bitter campaigning, Kim Sung lost the election by six votes!
> He's not raising taxes on the rich; he's raising taxes on the poor!

Because questions and exclamations are special effects, they should be used sparingly:

> The name William Durant is not as well-known as Henry Ford, but he was just as important to the development of the automobile industry. **Who was he?** Durant was the founder of General Motors, the largest carmaker in the world. He began his career as general manager of Buick in 1904. Four years later, he formed General Motors and acquired Oldsmobile. Over the next few years, he added Oakland (later Pontiac) and Cadillac. In 1915 he brought Louis Chevrolet's company into General Motors. Durant became a giant in the auto industry. The GM headquarters became known as the Durant Building. But Durant made reckless business decisions. In 1920 he was fired from the company he started. **Once the head of General Motors with a personal fortune of $50 million, Durant ended his career running a bowling alley!**

EXERCISE 5   Increasing Sentence Variety with Questions and Exclamations

Increase the sentence variety of this paragraph by turning one sentence into a question and one sentence into an exclamation.

Cinco de Mayo is widely celebrated by Mexican Americans throughout the United States. However, there is a great deal of confusion about what the holiday celebrates. It is not Mexican Independence Day. Mexico's equivalent of the Fourth of July is not the Fifth of May (Cinco de Mayo) but the Sixteenth of September. Cinco de Mayo celebrates the Mexican army's 1862 victory over the French, who invaded the country after Mexico was unable to repay its European loans.

_____

_____

_____

_____

_____

_____

Varying Sentence Openings

An effective way to increase sentence variety is to alter the common subject–verb–object pattern of most sentences:

> Most people in Detroit are unaware of the vast network of streets a thousand feet under them. These streets are as wide as four-lane highways. Truck headlights shine eerily as they illuminate the dazzling white floors, walls, and ceilings of this strange underground city. Detroiters worked aboveground making cars. Other Detroiters toiled invisibly beneath them digging and blasting salt. Scientists estimated that there was enough salt to operate the Detroit mines for millions of years. The mines closed in 1983. They were unable to compete with cheaper salt from Canada.

Opening Sentences with Adverbs

Adverbs (see Chapter 31) modify verbs, adjectives, and other adverbs. Many end in *-ly*. Because they can modify so many important words associated with the subject and verb, they can be used effectively to start a sentence:

> She **suddenly** announced she was quitting.
> **Suddenly,** she announced she was quitting.

> He **occasionally** played golf with old friends
> **Occasionally,** he played golf with old friends.

Opening sentences with adverbs can break up the monotony of standard sentence patterns and make writing more lively and interesting:

> Most people in Detroit are unaware of the vast network of streets a thousand feet under them. These streets are as wide as four-lane highways. **Eerily shining,** truck headlights illuminate the dazzling white floors, walls, and ceilings of this strange underground city. Detroiters worked aboveground making cars. **Invisibly** toiling beneath them, other Detroiters dug and blasted salt. Scientists estimated that there was enough salt to operate the Detroit mines for millions of years. **Surprisingly,** the mines closed in 1983. They were unable to compete with cheaper salt from Canada.

EXERCISE 6   Opening Sentences with Adverbs

Underline the adverb in each sentence; then revise the sentence by placing the adverb at the beginning. Remember that you may have to set off an opening adverb or adverbial phrase with a comma.

1. **Put your name at the top of the page always.**

   _____

2. **He carefully defused the timing mechanism of the bomb.**

   _____

3. **Terry reluctantly placed her badge and gun on the chief's desk.**

   _____

4. **He foolishly dropped out of school a month before graduation.**

   _____

5. **He bravely clung to the raft, waiting for help.**

   _____

6. **The team immediately lost hope of ever getting to the playoffs.**

   _____

7. **The overloaded plane slowly lifted off the ground.**

   _____

8. **The students gratefully accepted the extended deadline.**

   _____

9. The editor thoughtlessly failed to check the facts of the story.

_____

10. The mayor reacted immediately to the crisis.

_____

EXERCISE 7   Opening Sentences with Adverbs

Begin each sentence with an adverb. Remember to add a comma if needed.

1. _____ the parents confronted the coach.

2. _____ the Senate passed the bill after a ten-minute debate.

3. _____ we waited for the test results.

4. _____ the audience watched the last episode of *Everybody Loves Raymond.*

5. _____ the cast thanked their writers.

6. _____ the generals decided to respond to the surprise attack.

7. _____ Sandy called 911.

8. _____ crash investigators suspected sabotage.

9. _____ the coach decided to go for a touchdown.

10. _____ they bought the house without considering how much they would have to spend each month on utilities and property taxes.

Opening Sentences with Prepositions

Prepositions express the relationships between ideas, especially about time and space.

Common Prepositions

above	below	near	to
across	during	of	toward
after	except	off	under
along	for	over	with
around	from	past	within
before	like	since	without

Prepositions and prepositional phrases (often set off with a comma) can be used to open sentences:

He went to New York **without a dollar in his pocket.**
Without a dollar in his pocket, he went to New York.

She collapsed from exhaustion **on a public-speaking tour in New Mexico.**
On a public-speaking tour in New Mexico, she collapsed from exhaustion.

He mowed lawns **during the summer.**
During the summer he mowed lawns.

Opening sentences with prepositions can make writing lively by altering the standard pattern of words and ideas:

In Detroit most of the people are unaware of the vast network of streets a thousand feet under them. These streets are as wide as four-lane highways. Truck headlights shine eerily as they illuminate the dazzling white floors, walls, and ceilings of this strange underground city. **Aboveground,** Detroiters made cars. **Underground,** other Detroiters dug and blasted salt. Scientists estimated that there was enough salt to operate the Detroit mines for millions of years. **In 1983** the mines closed. They were unable to compete with cheaper salt from Canada.

EXERCISE 8 Opening Sentences with a Preposition

Underline the preposition or prepositional phrase in each sentence; then rewrite the sentence by placing the preposition at the beginning.

1. World leaders throughout history have been concerned about their public image.

_____

2. This has become increasingly important with the advent of photography.

_____

3. Stalin hid a deformed arm beneath his heavy uniforms.

_____

4. Roosevelt disguised the effects of polio during public appearances.

_____

5. He created the illusion that he could walk by leaning on the arm of an aide and using a cane.

_____

_____

6. Kennedy did not wish to be seen smoking his favorite cigars in public.

_____

7. He would slip the lit cigar into his pocket before leaving his car or *Air Force One.*

_____

8. Kennedy burned many of his suit jackets in this effort to avoid being seen as a cigar-smoking politician.

_____

_____

9. Kennedy hid his reading glasses from the public among other things because he felt they detracted from his image of youth and strength.

_____

_____

10. Romanian dictator Nicolae Ceausescu looked taller between body-guards selected for their short stature.

_____

_____

EXERCISE 9   Opening Sentences with a Preposition

Add a preposition or prepositional phrase to the opening of each sentence. Remember to add a comma if needed.

1. _____ wars have been fought over many issues.

2. _____ actors and actresses appear glamorous and attractive.

3. _____ makeup, lighting, and camera angles are used to show stars at their best.

4. _____ the design and color of clothing can make a person look slimmer or taller.

5. _____ high school athletes can feel overwhelmed by the competition they face in college athletic programs.

6. _____ they are confronted by dozens of other athletes from across the country.

7. _____ the competition becomes intense as students work to impress recruiters from the NBA and NFL.

8. _____ some students neglect their studies.

9. _____ the stress of performing well leads some students to take steroids.

10. _____ colleges bear some responsibility for the popularity of steroids.

EXERCISE 10   Opening Sentences with Adverbs and Prepositions

Rewrite this paragraph by using adverbs and prepositions to create variety. Add words and punctuation where needed.

Rahman George   Business 201

Crayola: An American Original

Every child in America has probably played with Crayola crayons. Edward Binney and Harold Smith founded the brand in 1903. They had previously developed dustless chalk that became a hit with schoolteachers and even received a gold medal at the St. Louis World's Fair. They visited schools and noticed the poor quality of wax crayons that children used for coloring. They added color to industrial wax markers and created an improved crayon for artwork. Binney's wife came up with the name "Crayola" by combining the French word *craie* ("chalk") and *oleaginous* ("oily"). Binney and Smith put eight of their oily chalks in a box and sold them for a nickel. The new crayons immediately became popular with children, teachers, and parents. The 100 billionth Crayola crayon was produced in 1996. That year the U.S. Post Office celebrated the company by issuing a stamp featuring a box of Crayola crayons.

Varying Methods of Joining Ideas

You can increase the variety of sentences by using different methods to combine ideas (see Chapter 24). You can join ideas using present and past participles, compound subjects and verbs, appositives, and relative clauses.

Combining Sentences with Present Participles

Present participles are *-ing* verbs such as *running, standing, selling, dancing,* or *thinking.* You can join two related sentences by turning the verb of one sentence into an *-ing* verb to open a sentence combining the ideas of both. This can reduce repetition and wordiness and create a more lively sentence pattern:

> I worked all night. I was exhausted by noon.
> The car failed to start. The car was towed to the garage.
> Sara studied for hours. She was determined to pass.

Improved

> **Working** all night, I was exhausted by noon.
> **Failing** to start, the car was towed to the garage.
> **Studying** for hours, Sara was determined to pass.

EXERCISE 11   Combining Sentences with Present Participles: *-ing* Verbs

Turn one of the verbs into an -ing verb, and use it to open a single sentence that combines the ideas of both sentences.

1. **I have worked in my father's waste management company for four years. I have learned a lot about business.**

   _____

   _____

2. **My father spotted a single missing word in an e-mail I wrote. He taught me a valuable lesson about the importance of writing in business.**

   _____

   _____

3. **I knew my father wanted to expand. I thought I would help him get new accounts.**

   _____

   _____

4. **I learned that Rockaway Construction was opening a new facility in Queens. I called and asked if they had contracted with anyone to haul their waste.**

   _____

   _____

5. I wanted to surprise my dad with a new account. I decided to work fast.

_____

6. I had read my father's contract offers. I thought I knew how to write one.

_____

7. I wrote up the offer. I hoped my dad would be proud of me.

_____

8. I was preparing to send the e-mail. I spotted my dad entering the office and asked him to read it over.

_____

_____

9. He looked over my shoulder. He tapped the screen.

_____

10. I forgot to add the word "nonhazardous" in one sentence. I made it seem like my father's company was violating federal environmental regulations.

_____

_____

Past participles are verbs in the past tense. Regular verbs end with -*ed* or -*d,* such as *worked, developed, painted, collapsed,* and *created.* Irregular verbs have different forms, such as *seen, bought, flown, sewn,* and *born* (see pages 498–500). Like present participles, they can be placed at the beginning of a sentence to combine ideas and eliminate wordiness and repetition:

> The home office was difficult to reach. It was located in Olathe, Kansas.
> The hotel was devastated by Hurricane Rita. It took years to recover.
> The museum was equipped with high-tech security devices. It was very safe.

Improved

> **Located** in Olathe, Kansas, the home office was difficult to reach.
> **Devastated** by Hurricane Rita, it took the hotel years to recover.
> **Equipped** with high-tech security devices, the museum was very safe.

EXERCISE 12 Combining Sentences with Past Participles

Turn one of the verbs into a past participle, and use it to open a single sentence that combines the ideas of both sentences.

1. Charles Goodyear was born in 1860. He is credited with developing vulcanization, the process that revolutionized the use of rubber.

_____

_____

2. **Rubber had been known for centuries. It had been widely studied because it was elastic and airtight.**

_____

_____

3. **Rubber became useless when subjected to cold or heat. It became brittle or melted.**

_____

_____

4. **Goodyear married at twenty-six. He started one of the first hardware stores in America.**

_____

_____

5. **Goodyear was imprisoned for not paying his bills after the store failed. He sought a new venture.**

_____

_____

6. **A businessman showed Goodyear a warehouse full of rubber products that had become worthless goo in the heat. He realized the need to overcome this problem.**

_____

_____

7. **Goodyear became obsessed with rubber. He endured poverty and illness to devote his time to experiments.**

_____

_____

8. **Goodyear was dedicated to finding a way of making rubber useful. Goodyear accidentally discovered that sulfur and heat could toughen rubber so it would not melt or crack.**

_____

_____

9. **Goodyear was brokenhearted by the death of his daughter and legal battles over his discovery. He died deeply in debt.**

_____

_____

10. **The Goodyear Tire and Rubber Company was founded by Frank Seiberling in 1898. The corporation has no tie to the Goodyear family.**

_____

_____

Combining Sentences Using Compound Subjects and Verbs

An effective way of increasing sentence variety and reducing repetitive statements is to create compound subjects and verbs to combine related sentences:

> Yale is a famous Ivy League university. Harvard is also a famous Ivy League university.
> **Yale and Harvard** are famous Ivy League universities. [compound subject]

> The company sold computers. It also serviced copiers.
> The company sold computers and serviced copiers. [compound verb]

EXERCISE 13   Combining Sentences with Compound Subjects

Rewrite the following pairs of sentences, using compound subjects to create a single sentence.

1. The 1919 World Series became embroiled in scandal. Eight players became embroiled in scandal.

   _____

   _____

2. Careers were changed forever. The game of baseball was changed forever.

   _____

   _____

3. Chick Gandil, first baseman for the Chicago White Sox, decided to fix the games. Joseph Sullivan, a professional gambler, decided to fix the games.

   _____

   _____

4. In 1919 sportswriters predicted that the Chicago White Sox would easily defeat the Cincinnati Reds. Gamblers also predicted that the Chicago White Sox would easily defeat the Cincinnati Reds.

   _____

   _____

5. Gandil resented White Sox owner Charles Comiskey, who was known for paying low salaries. Many other Chicago players resented White Sox owner Charles Comiskey, who was known for paying low salaries.

   _____

   _____

6. The players were motivated by greed and saw a unique opportunity. Gamblers were also motivated by greed and saw a unique opportunity.

_____

_____

7. Eight White Sox players conspired to fix the games so the underdog Reds would win an upset victory. Gamblers conspired to fix the games so the underdog Reds would win an upset victory.

_____

_____

8. After the highly favored White Sox lost, sportswriters became suspicious. Baseball officials also became suspicious.

_____

_____

9. The most famous player charged with throwing the games, Shoeless Joe Jackson, first confessed, then retracted his confession. Eddie Cicotte also first confessed, then retracted his confession.

_____

_____

10. Cleared of criminal charges, Shoeless Joe Jackson was banned from organized baseball for life. Seven other White Sox players were also banned from organized baseball for life.

_____

_____

EXERCISE 14   Combining Sentences with Compound Verbs

Rewrite the following sets of sentences, using compound verbs to create a single sentence.

1. Many scientific developments do not rely on a single person. They do not depend on a single discovery.

_____

_____

2. For centuries doctors knew basic anatomy. They understood the body's major functions.

_____

_____

3. Without a safe way of rendering a patient unconscious, however, doctors were limited to simple procedures. They had to operate fast to prevent shock.

_____

_____

4. Surgeons practiced speed rather than precision. They sought to end operations as quickly as possible.

_____

_____

5. In the 1840s the discovery of ether allowed doctors to put patients to sleep. They could take time to perform complicated operations.

_____

_____

6. During the Civil War, surgeons could repair serious wounds. They could even replace missing skull tissue with steel plates.

_____

_____

7. However, doctors at the time had no knowledge of germs. They rarely bothered to wash their hands between operations.

_____

_____

8. Patients were saved by new surgical techniques. They often died from infections days or weeks later.

_____

_____

9. Doctors began to accept the germ theory of disease in the late nineteenth century. They introduced sanitary operating room procedures. They sterilized their instruments.

_____

_____

_____

10. When the knowledge of anatomy came together with the discovery of anesthetics and understanding of germs, doctors could safely use surgery to treat disease. They could operate to repair injuries.

_____

_____

_____

Combining Sentences Using Appositives

An effective way to avoid choppy, repetitive writing is to combine sentences by turning one of them into an **appositive,** a word or phrase that describes, defines, or adds information about a noun or pronoun. Appositives, usually set off by commas, directly follow a noun or pronoun:

> George Washington, **the first president of the United States,** died in 1799.
> Juanita, **my best friend,** got a new job.

When a sentence just states a single fact, it can often be turned into an appositive and inserted into a related sentence:

Choppy Sentences

> Telly Savalas was the star of **Kojak.** He once worked for the U.S. State Department.
> MIT is a major research university. It is conducting the laser experiments.
> Penicillin is one of the oldest antibiotics. It is losing its ability to kill many germs.

Combined with Appositives

> Telly Savalas, **star of Kojak,** once worked for the U.S. State Department.
> MIT, **a major research university,** is conducting the laser experiments.
> Penicillin, **one of the oldest antibiotics,** is losing its ability to kill many germs.

POINT TO REMEMBER

Appositives are set off with commas and must come directly before or after the noun or pronoun they refer to:

> George Washington, **the first president of the United States,** served two terms.
> **The first president of the United States,** George Washington served two terms.

EXERCISE 15   Combining Sentences Using Appositives

Combine each pair of sentences by turning one of them into an appositive that describes a noun or pronoun. Remember to set the appositive off with commas and to place it directly before or after the word it refers to. The appositive may appear at the beginning, middle, or end of the sentence.

1. The Academy of Motion Pictures Arts and Sciences is a professional honorary organization. It has some 6,000 members.

_____

_____

2. The Academy was organized as a nonprofit corporation. It was organized in 1927.

_____

_____

3. **The organization is best known for awarding the Academy Award of Merit to directors, actors, writers, and technicians. The award is known as the Oscar.**

_____

_____

4. **The Academy Award was designed by Cedric Gibbons in 1928. He was chief art director of MGM.**

_____

_____

5. **Frederic Hope was Gibbons's assistant. He designed the original black marble base.**

_____

_____

6. **The Academy Award is one of the most famous awards in the world. The award weighs almost nine pounds.**

_____

_____

7. **There are many stories about how the award began to be called Oscar. It was a nickname.**

_____

_____

8. **Gold was a precious metal. Gold was hard to obtain during World War II.**

_____

_____

9. **From 1942 to 1944, the Academy presented winners with Oscars made of plaster. This was a wartime substitute.**

_____

_____

10. **At the end of the war, winners exchanged their plaster trophies for gold ones. They were mementos that stars treasured for a lifetime.**

_____

_____

Combining Sentences Using Relative Clauses

You can combine related sentences by turning one of them into a relative clause. **Relative clauses** begin with _which, who,_ or _that_ and describe or define a noun or pronoun. Relative clauses not only reduce choppy sentences but also more clearly express what you are trying to say by emphasizing main ideas:

> Kim Hsu speaks only Korean. She is nominated for a special effects award.
> George Miller was arrested just last week. He was caught shoplifting this morning.
> Brighton College is located in Maine. The college specializes in oceanography.

> Kim Hsu, **who speaks only Korean,** is nominated for a special effects award.
> George Miller, **who was arrested just last week,** was caught shoplifting this morning.
> Brighton College, **which is located in Maine,** specializes in oceanography.

POINTS TO REMEMBER

Use commas to set off a *nonrestrictive* relative clause that adds extra information about the word it modifies:

> Teddy Hughes, ***who won a scholarship,*** suddenly dropped out of school.

who won a scholarship adds only extra information about Teddy Hughes, who is defined by his name.

Restrictive relative clauses that describe or define a word are not set off with commas:

> The student ***who won a scholarship*** suddenly dropped out of school.

who won a scholarship restricts or limits the meaning of the general word *student* and is not simply extra information.

EXERCISE 16   Combining Sentences with Relative Clauses

Combine each pair of sentences by turning one of them into a relative clause. Remember to set off nonrestrictive clauses—those that add extra information—with commas.

1. **Daylight saving time is sometimes called Summer Time. It is designed to extend daylight during working hours.**

   _____

   _____

2. **The idea seems simple enough. It has caused controversy all over the world.**

   _____

   _____

3. **Advocates included economists, business leaders, and politicians. They argued that daylight saving time would help farmers and reduce traffic accidents.**

   _____

   _____

4. **Opponents felt that changing clocks was unnatural and inconvenient. They consisted of ministers, parents, and transport executives.**

_____

_____

5. **Daylight saving time was introduced during World War I. It was unpopular.**

_____

_____

6. **The federal daylight saving time law was signed by Woodrow Wilson. It was repealed in 1919.**

_____

_____

7. **Daylight saving time was again signed into law in 1942. It was supposed to save energy for the war effort.**

_____

_____

8. **Daylight saving time was suspended in September 1945 in the United States. However, it was imposed on Japan as part of the U.S. occupation.**

_____

_____

9. **Japanese citizens greatly resented being forced to change their clocks. They ended its use as soon as the U.S. occupation ended.**

_____

_____

10. **The Uniform Time Act was passed in 1966. It mandated national use of daylight saving time in the United States.**

_____

_____

EXERCISE 17   Combining Sentences

Use past and present participles, compound nouns and verbs, appositives, and relative clauses to revise the following paragraph to eliminate choppy and repetitive sentences.

Winslow Price   Film History 101

Oscar Micheaux

Few moviegoers have heard of Oscar Micheaux. He was a pioneer African American filmmaker. He overcame many odds. He was born in Illinois in 1884.

His parents were former slaves. Micheaux moved to South Dakota. He operated a homestead farm. He began writing stories. No one was interested in publishing his work. Micheaux created his own publishing company. He sold his books door to door. In 1919 he became the first African American to make a movie. His first movie was *The Homesteader*. It was based on his novel of the same name. He produced *Body and Soul* in 1924. The movie starred Paul Robeson. Over the next three decades, Micheaux made forty movies. His movies avoided the stereotyped black characters seen in Hollywood productions. Micheaux's films depicted black people positively. Micheaux's movies played in black theaters in the South. Micheaux made the first black film shown in white theaters. Micheaux died in 1951. His work had been celebrated by critics. It has been celebrated by scholars. Oscar Micheaux is now honored with a star on the Hollywood Walk of Fame.

EXERCISE 18　Improving Sentence Variety

Take one or more of the recent essays or paragraphs you have written in this book, and examine the variety of your sentences. Are there choppy, dull, or repetitive sentences that could be improved with greater variety? Are there sentences that could be combined using participles, compound subjects and verbs, appositives, or relative clauses?

WORKING TOGETHER

Working with a group of students, revise this e-mail to reduce choppy and repetitive sentences.

Attn: Clerical Staff
RE: Patient Records

State law requires total patient confidentiality. We do not release records to patient families. We do not release records to insurance companies. These records contain personal information. These records contain sensitive material.

If people call asking for records, tell them you can refer the request to the clinic director. If people e-mail asking for records, tell them the same thing.

Do not answer any questions about a patient's health. Do not answer any questions about which doctor a patient is seeing. It is important to be polite. It is important to maintain a professional attitude. Explain that you are not allowed to release patient information of any kind. Explain that you can pass requests on to the clinic director.

If you have any questions, call me at ext. 287.

Sandy LaFarve

CRITICAL THINKING

Get Thinking and Writing

What do you do to stay in shape? Do you diet, exercise, or play sports? Do you find it difficult to maintain a healthy lifestyle? Does your schedule prevent you from working out? Is it difficult to find healthy meals?

Write a paragraph describing your attempts at maintaining a healthy lifestyle.

WHAT HAVE YOU WRITTEN?

Write out your topic sentence or controlling idea:

_____

_____

Does it clearly express what you are trying to say? Could it be combined with other sentences to avoid choppy and repetitive writing?

Read the remainder of your paragraph. Can any sentences be combined using appositives, compound subjects and verbs, present and past participles, or relative clauses?

Get Writing

Do you think that female reporters are more likely to be judged by their appearance than males? Why or why not?

State your views in one or more paragraphs, and support your opinions with examples.

PAUL PRESCOT/ALAMY LIMITED

WRITING ON THE WEB

Using a search engine such as Yahoo! or Google, enter terms such as *combining sentences, increasing sentence variety, relative clauses, appositives, choppy sentences,* and *revising sentences* to locate current sites of interest.

POINTS TO REMEMBER

1. The length of your sentences should reflect the ideas you are trying to express.
2. Short sentences make dramatic, easy-to-remember statements. However, too many short sentences can create choppy and dull writing.
3. Long sentences can express complicated relationships between ideas. However, too many long sentences can be difficult to read and remember.
4. Avoid sentences that simply add a single word or minor idea that could be included in a related sentence.
5. Vary the way you open sentences to keep your writing lively and readers interested in what you are trying to say.
6. Combine related ideas to better express your train of thought and overcome choppy and repetitive sentences.

CHAPTER 19

Improving Word Choice

CHAPTER GOALS

- Appreciate the Power of Words

- Select Words That Are Correct, Effective, and Appropriate

- Avoid Deadhead Words

- Understand the Role of Connotation

RUI VALE DE SOUSA/USED UNDER LICENSE FROM SHUTTERSTOCK

Get Writing

How hard is it to choose the right word?

Write a paragraph describing a situation, such as applying for a job or writing a sympathy card to a friend, when you had problems finding words to express what you were trying to say.

The Power of Words

Words are the building blocks of paragraphs and essays. They have the power to inform, entertain, and persuade. When we talk, our word choices can be casual because we also communicate through eye contact, tone of voice, and gestures. Speech is interactive. We can repeat sentences for emphasis and reword awkward phrases as we talk. If our listeners cannot understand what we are saying, they can ask questions:

> "Going to that deal tonight?"
> "Which deal?"
> "The presentation by that computer guy."
> "You mean Phil Armstrong?"
> "Sure."
> "Wish I could. I have to work at six."
> "Six at night?"
> "No, I start at six a.m. tomorrow, so I have to get to bed early."

When we write, however, our readers can react only to the words on the page. They cannot ask us questions or give us a chance to repeat our ideas—we have to get things right the first time. Readers have to rely on the text to understand what we are trying to say. Readers will assume that our word choices will match the definitions they find in the dictionary.

What Do You Know?

Choose the appropriate word in each sentence.

1. ____ The (presents/presence) of foreign troops on the street sparked a riot.

2. ____ The camp is (further/farther) up the road.

3. ____ Can you (accept/except) an out-of-state check?

4. ____ That costs more (then/than) he can afford.

5. ____ She is tired and should (lie/lay) down.

6. ____ (It's/Its) going to snow tonight.

7. ____ The brain needs a (continual/continuous) supply of oxygen.

8. ____ Her grandmother (dyed/died) of a stroke last night.

9. ____ This is (to/too) heavy for one person to carry.

10. ____ Computer hackers now have (access/excess) to our credit card files.

Answers appear on the following page.

WHAT ARE YOU TRYING TO SAY?

Write a paragraph that describes something you regret doing or not doing. Do you regret buying a car without checking its engine? Do you wish you had helped a friend who asked for a favor? Did you turn down an opportunity you wish you had taken? Did anyone ever coax you into making a decision that you now regret? Write two paragraphs, the first describing the action or decision you did or did not make, the second explaining your current feelings. Choose words carefully to describe the decision you made and your present attitudes.

Get Writing and Revising

Answers to What Do You Know? on page 334

1. presence 2. farther 3. accept
4. than 5. lie 6. It's 7. continuous
8. died 9. too 10. access

_____

_____

_____

_____

_____

WHAT HAVE YOU WRITTEN?

Underline the key words in your paragraphs. Do they give readers a strong impression? Could you improve your statement by choosing different words? Read your paragraphs out loud. What changes would you make to increase their impact? Will readers appreciate why you regret the decision?

Improving Word Choices

To improve the effectiveness of your paragraphs and essays, it is important to examine the words you have chosen.

Guidelines for Choosing Words

1. **Use correct words**—make sure that you know a word's precise meaning.

2. **Use effective words**—use clear, specific language that your readers understand.

3. **Delete "deadhead" words**—eliminate words that add little meaning and wordy phrases that can be replaced with a single word.

4. **Use appropriate words**—use words suited to your purpose, subject, audience, and document. Be aware of connotations.

Top 20

EASILY CONFUSED WORDS
Make sure that you use the right word. See pages 700–703 to check words such as *hear* and *here* or *plane* and *plain*.

Using Correct Words

English has a number of words that are easily confused or misunderstood. Learn to recognize the difference between words that look and sound alike, especially ones you have had trouble with:

adopt	to take	They want to *adopt* a child.
adapt	to change	We will *adapt* the budget to include these new figures.
everyday	ordinary	You can't wear *everyday* clothes to a wedding.
every day	daily	Terri jogs six miles *every day*.
passed	successfully completed	We *passed* through the city at night.
past	history	His *past* remains a mystery.
who's	contraction of "who is"	*Who's* coming with me?
whose	possessive of "who"	*Whose* car is that?

(See pages 700–703 for other easily confused words.)

Top 20

SPELLING

Make sure that you spell words correctly! Use dictionaries and glossaries to check spelling. See pages 703–704 for a list of commonly misspelled words.

A Note On Spelling

An important part of using words is making sure you spell them correctly. Spelling errors confuse readers and make your work appear sloppy and unprofessional.

Tips for Improving Your Spelling

1. **Pronounce new words.** Reading them out loud can help you recall letters you might overlook, such as the *n* in "environment" or the *r* in "government."

2. **Write out new words you learn in school and at your job.**

3. **Make a list of words you repeatedly misspell, and refer to it whenever you write.** Keep copies of this list in your notebook, by your desk, or in your purse or briefcase.

See Chapter 35 for further help with spelling.

EXERCISE 1   Using the Correct Word

Underline the correct word in each sentence.

1. She should (wear/where) more conservative clothes in the office.

2. The embossed (stationery/stationary) was too expensive for a mass mailing.

3. The men were arrested for selling (illicit/elicit) drugs.

4. Whenever I lose my temper, my (conscience/conscious) bothers me for days.

5. We can't (rise/raise) wheat during a drought.

6. (Less/Fewer) students are taking advanced math this semester.

7. We can't afford to (lose/loose) any more games this season.

8. After inspection, the band will (precede/proceed) to the stadium.

9. Make sure that the children are (already/all ready) vaccinated.

10. (Everyone/Every one) of the cars had bad tires.

POINT TO REMEMBER

Words sometimes have special or specific meanings. One college might define a *full-time student* as someone who takes twelve credits, whereas another school requires students to take sixteen credits. The word *high rise* means one thing in New York City and another in Kansas City. Make sure that your readers understand the exact meanings of the words you use. Define terms with footnotes at the bottom of a page or with a glossary—a list of words and definitions—at the end of your paper to prevent confusion.

EXERCISE 2   Understanding Meaning

Define each of the words; then check your answers using a college dictionary.

1. alibi _____   6. irony _____

2. anecdotal _____   7. marital _____

3. caustic _____   8. nonplussed _____

4. defamation _____   9. orthodox _____

5. felon _____   10. sarcasm _____

How many words have you heard but could not define? How many did you get wrong? Which words have additional meanings you were unaware of?

Learning More About Words

1. Use a college dictionary to look up new or confusing words.

2. Study the glossaries in your textbooks to learn special terms and definitions.

3. Jot down unfamiliar words you hear at school or at work, and look them up in dictionaries or glossaries.

KNOWING ENGLISH

Dictionaries for ESL Students

If English is your second language, refer to dictionaries such as the *Longman Dictionary of American English* and the *Collins Cobuild Dictionary*. They not only give definitions but also explain rules for combining words. If you look up *future,* for example, you learn that it often appears in phrases such as *predict the future, plan the future,* and *face the future.* These dictionaries include sample sentences to show how a word is used in context.

EXERCISE 3   Editing Your Writing

Select one or more writing responses you completed in a previous chapter or in the draft of an upcoming assignment, and review your use of words. Look for errors in usage. Have you confused there *and* their *or* its *and* it's? *Have you written* affect *for* effect *or* adapt *for* adopt? *List words you have confused in the back of this book or in a notebook for future reference.*

Using Effective Words

To express your ideas effectively, choose words that are clear and concrete. Vague and general terms lack impact:

> I loved working at Lakeside Grill, one of the nicest restaurants in the Loop. It is a very attractive place with a lot of special customers. I met so many interesting people working there. The owner is nice and fun to work for. His wife is a great manager who really cares about the staff. Although they were busy, they treated employees well and made all of us feel special.

The words *attractive* and *interesting* are abstract. The paragraph simply lets us know that a student enjoyed working at Lakeside Grill but does not really tell us why. What made the customers *special?* Why was the boss *nice* and his wife a *great manager?* Concrete words create stronger impressions:

> I loved working at Lakeside Grill, one of the most exclusive steakhouses in the Loop. Its elegant turn-of-the-century brass and woodwork are striking, as are the regular customers, who include the mayor, professional athletes, foreign leaders, and visiting entertainers. I waited on Jennifer Lopez, George Clooney, and the Italian ambassador in one week. The owner is pleasant, witty, and always willing to support his employees in a tough situation. His wife is a caring manager who makes sure our work schedules do not conflict with school. Even though they run a multi-million-dollar business catering to the rich and powerful, they never forget an employee's birthday or fail to send flowers to anyone who gets sick.

Instead of *made all of us feel special,* this paragraph offers specific details such as *never forget an employee's birthday or fail to send flowers.* Readers can understand that seeing *Jennifer Lopez, George Clooney, and the Italian ambassador* would make an after-school job interesting.

Using Specific Nouns

Specific nouns create strong images that readers can identify and remember. As a college student or new employee, you may think that using big words will impress instructors or make you appear more professional. In many cases, however, a short word or phrase gives readers more information:

Abstract	Specific
protective headgear	helmet
highly caloric desserts	cake and ice cream
student residence	dorm
electronic communications device	cell phone

Using Strong Verbs

Verbs should emphasize action. Avoid weak verb phrases that use several words to describe action that could be expressed with a single word.

Weak Verb Phrase	Strong Verb
make a decision	decide
effect a transfer	transfer
offer an excuse	excuse
perform a test	test

Avoiding Clichés

Clichés are overused sayings. They may have been original, striking, or colorful when first used, but like jokes that have been told too often, they have become stale and meaningless.

Cliché	Improved
crack of dawn	dawn
at a snail's pace	slowly
out cold	unconscious
way bad	bad

EXERCISE 4   Improving Word Choices

Rewrite each of the following sentences, replacing abstract nouns, weak verb phrases, and clichés.

1. During the years of the Great Depression, people longed to find an escape from the problems of unemployment and business failures that seemed unrelenting.

_____

_____

2. Poverty had cut through the middle class like a knife, leaving people with few financial resources to pay for recreational endeavors.

_____

_____

3. Charles Darrow developed plans for a board game he called Monopoly, which allowed players to engage in fantasies about wheeling and dealing properties like the Rockefellers and Vanderbilts.

_____

_____

_____

4. Darrow made an attempt to sell his new game to Parker Brothers, who rejected it after making a determination that Monopoly had fifty-two design mistakes.

_____

_____

5. Not willing to give up, Darrow initiated a plan to manufacture Monopoly sets on his own, which began selling like hotcakes in a local department store.

_____

_____

6. With a success on his hands, Darrow went back to Parker Brothers, who had to eat their words and admit that his game was a hit.

_____

_____

7. Parker Brothers made the decision to purchase Darrow's game, and soon Monopoly was being played coast to coast.

_____

_____

8. During World War II, the Allies hid real money, maps, and compasses in Monopoly sets that were made available to POWs to facilitate their plans for escape.

_____

_____

9. Seventy years after its initial debut, Monopoly remains a popular way for people to pass their recreational time.

_____

_____

10. Today, Parker Brothers manages the production of Monopoly in twenty-six languages and facilitates the printing of 50 billion dollars in Monopoly money in a single year.

_____

_____

Deleting "Deadhead" Words

Deadhead is an old railroad term for a nonpaying passenger, usually an employee riding along with the crew on the way to another job. Deadhead words ride along with others in a sentence but add no meaning. They are empty words that clutter a sentence and should be deleted to make your writing easier to read:

Cluttered

> I went home and ***started*** to pack. Then ***all of a sudden*** George called and said he was ***beginning to get*** worried about missing the plane. I told him I was ***going to get*** ready as fast as I could so we could ***start to*** leave early.

Improved

> I went home to pack. George called and said he was worried about missing the plane. I told him I was getting ready as fast as I could so we could leave early.

Reading your writing aloud can help spot deadhead words and phrases.

EXERCISE 5   Deleting Deadhead Words

Rewrite each sentence by deleting deadhead words and replacing wordy phrases with a single word where possible.

1. After a long shift, I was getting tired and could not wait to be getting home so I could begin to relax and start getting dinner going.

   _____

   _____

2. I was trying to clean the house before my parents began to arrive.

   _____

   _____

3. Sara and Andy were working to paint the room, but they ended up running out of paint and had to quit.

   _____

   _____

4. This semester the college is beginning to charge a parking fee for student events that are being held in Parker Hall.

   _____

   _____

5. They were driving along to work when they got a flat tire and had to start to hitchhike the rest of way.

   _____

   _____

Using Appropriate Words

The words you choose should suit your purpose, your readers, and the document. Words, like clothing, can be formal or informal, traditional or trendy. Just as you dress differently for a business meeting or a picnic, you write differently to produce a research paper, a résumé, or an e-mail to your best friend. It is important to use the right level of diction or word choice.

Using the Appropriate Level of Diction

Professionals such as attorneys, accountants, and physicians use *formal* or *technical* terms that most people are not likely to understand. Most college textbooks contain glossaries of technical terms. Understanding these terms is essential for people to communicate without confusion. *Standard* words are widely known and used. They are the kind of words found in popular books, magazines, and most websites. *Informal* English can include slang, jargon, and local expressions. Police officers, pilots, athletes, software developers, stockbrokers, and entertainers all have their own words and phrases.

Levels of Diction

Informal/Personal

slang, regional expressions, colorful images, or text messaging ("u" for "you" or "brb" for "be right back") used to reflect a personal view or communicate with friends:

> *Why you get gangsta on me last night? What I do?*
>
> **IM** TO A FRIEND

> *Her new movie is a train wreck on steroids.*
>
> **ONLINE MOVIE REVIEW**

Standard/Academic

widely accepted words and phrases found in books, magazines, and newspapers used to communicate to an educated audience:

> *The Senate will debate the trade bill this session.*
>
> **NEWSPAPER ARTICLE**

> *I will seek a second term only if I can gain the support of the Common Council.*
>
> **POLITICAL SPEECH**

Business/Technical

scientific terms, jargon, and special expressions used to communicate within a discipline, profession, or specific workplace:

> *Stern Price has maintained steady P&E's this quarter by avoiding underfunded IPOs.*
>
> **CORPORATE REPORT TO INVESTORS**

> *Elevated SGOT levels indicate possible cirrhosis.*
>
> **PHYSICIAN'S NOTES**

The level of diction that writers use depends on their goal, their readers, and the document. Doctors use official medical terminology to fill out insurance forms, standard English to instruct patients, and technical jargon or specialized slang to inform other physicians and medical staff.

It is important to avoid inappropriate word choices that can confuse readers or weaken the impact of your writing. Slang in a research paper or business report will make a writer appear unprofessional. Formal language can make e-mail difficult to read at a glance.

EXERCISE 6   Replacing Inappropriate Words

Revise each sentence to replace inappropriate words for a formal research paper.

1. **In 1976 the Ebola virus <u>popped up</u> in the Sudan, signaling the presence of a previously unknown infectious agent.**

   _____

   _____

2. **Economists in the early 1970s coined the term "stagflation" to describe the conflation of rising consumer prices and <u>unemployment going hog wild</u>.**

   _____

   _____

3. **NASA engineers reported consistent computer failures in the Mars rover that will cost <u>an arm and a leg</u> to repair.**

   _____

   _____

Revise each sentence to remove inappropriate words for an informal memo.

4. **Inform sales representatives that their <u>personal vehicles do not qualify for corporate insurance coverage</u>.**

   _____

   _____

5. **All <u>electronic communications</u> directed to customers may be monitored for adherence to <u>corporate procedure and regulations</u>.**

   _____

   _____

Using Appropriate Idioms

Idioms are expressions or word combinations that state ideas. Idioms are not always logical. For example, you *get* **in a car** but *get* **on a plane.** You *hang* **up the phone** and *hang* **out with friends.** Idioms can be a challenge to understand for two reasons. First, some idioms, such as *pay respect to,* can't be easily understood by looking at the meaning of each word. Second, many idioms, such as *break the ice, over the hill,* and *take the gloves off,* don't mean what they literally suggest. Idioms are often difficult or impossible to translate word for word into other languages.

In college and business writing, you will be expected to use idioms accurately. If you are confused about the meaning of an idiom, refer to multilingual dictionaries such as the *Longman Dictionary of American English* or the *Collins Cobuild Dictionary.*

Commonly Misused Idioms

Incorrect	Correct
different **than** the others	different **from** the others
in/with **regards** to	in/with **regard** to
independent **to**	independent **of**
irritated **with**	irritated **by**
on accident	**by** accident
satisfied **in**	satisfied **with**
superior **than**	superior **to**
type **of a**	type **of**

EXERCISE 7   Using the Appropriate Idioms

Write sentences using each of the following idioms correctly.

1. drop on, drop off

_____

2. run up, run out

_____

3. wait for, wait on

_____

4. break away, break up

_____

5. play along, play up

_____

Being Aware of Connotations

When you choose words to express ideas, it is important to understand the role of **connotation.** All words have a **denotation,** or basic, literal meaning found in the dictionary. **Connotation** refers to a word's implied or suggested meaning. A small house can be called a *cottage,* a *cabin,* or a *shack.* They all have the same basic meaning but create different impressions. A person who spends money carefully can be *thrifty* or *cheap.* A skyscraper can be praised for its *clean, simple lines* or criticized for being *sterile* and *unimaginative.* A stand-up comic's performance could be described as *risqué* or *obscene.* A strict mother could be called *firm* or *unfeeling.*

The words you choose can paint very different pictures of what you describe:

The soldiers **secured** the village.

Anticipating an attack, they **withdrew.**

Caving into protestors, the mayor fired the **tough** chief of police.

The **suspects** were **detained** in a **public building** and provided **food** and **a place to sleep. until morning**

Wendy Smith comes from one of the **richest** and **most powerful** families in the state. Now she wants to **take over a scheme** to **destroy** our **struggling** schools.

The soldiers **occupied** the village.

Fearing an attack, they **fled.**

Responding to the people, the mayor fired the **brutal** chief of police.

The **victims** were **locked** in **government warehouse** and given **stale bread** and **forced to sleep on the floor the entire night.**

Wendy Smith comes from one of the **most successful** and **respected** families in the state. Now she wants to **head up a plan** to **reform** our **failing** schools.

Political debates often produce opposing lists of words as advocates try to use connotations to influence the public:

capital punishment	the death penalty
tax relief	tax break
illegal alien	undocumented worker
abortionist	abortion provider
gambling	gaming industry
negotiate with	give in to
bombing	air support
drilling for oil	exploring for energy
lobbyist	activist

Whenever you write, consider the impact that your choice of words will have on readers.

KNOWING ENGLISH

Learning Connotations

To make sure you understand a new word's connotation, study how it is used in context. If the word is used in a phrase or sentence that seems negative, the word's connotation is probably negative. If the phrase or sentence seems positive, the word's connotation is probably positive. You can also use a thesaurus to find a word's synonyms and antonyms. If you look up *stubborn,* for example, you will find it means the same as being *obstinate* and *pigheaded* and the opposite of *compliant* and *easygoing.*

WORKING TOGETHER

Working with a group of students, review the text of this e-mail to eliminate negative connotations. Write a more positive version of this message.

National Enterprises regrets to inform customers that orders placed after December 10 will not be shipped before Christmas. Because so many customers failed to include phone numbers or e-mail addresses, we were unable to verify orders. In the future, include your phone number and e-mail address if you want to receive your orders on time. We simply cannot send letters to every customer who fails to include information necessary for us to process orders.

Get Thinking and Writing

CRITICAL THINKING

Select a product—for example, cars, perfume, cell phones, computers, or airlines—and then review the words used in commercials, websites, and print ads that advertise it. Write a paragraph analyzing the use of connotations. What do word choices in ads reveal about the product, the intended consumer, and the appeals used to attract buyers?

Get Writing

Examine the connotations used to word this World War I poster. Underline key words that have positive and negative connotations. Why would the government choose to use the word "liberty" to name bonds it was selling to the public? Why do the words "buy freely" suit the poster better than "buy often"?

If you were going to create a web page to raise money to protect the country from terrorists, what images and words would you use? What picture would you want in the background? What phrases would you highlight? Write the text of your web page; then examine your sentences for accurate word choice, use of connotations, and the presence of deadhead words.

©Swim Ink 2, LLC/Corbis

What Have You Learned?

Choose the appropriate word in each sentence.

1. ___ The new law will (affect/effect) the way Medicare pays doctors.

2. ___ They never (accept/except) late payments.

3. ___ (They're/There) working late again.

4. ___ Some parents are not (conscious/conscience) of their children's drug use.

5. ___ Premature infants in intensive care require (continual/continuous) monitoring.

Choose effective words and phrases in the following sentences.

6. ___ Scientists (performed tests on/tested) the Martian rock samples.

7. ___ Her new dress is (blue/blue-colored).

8. ___ If a (strike situation/strike) takes place, our shipments may be delayed for weeks.

9. ___ You should (begin to plan/plan) your summer school schedule this week.

10. ___ The city required the agency to (perform an audit/audit) its financial records.

Choose the proper level of diction for a college research paper.

11. ___ During the Depression, people were (disheartened/ticked off) by growing unemployment.

12. ___ Oil reserves cannot be (racked up/considered) as wealth if terrorism prevents oil exports.

13. ___ The demand for $50 billion was thought (way too much/excessive) for Congress to approve.

14. ___ Consumers expected that these devices would work (immediately/from the get-go).

15. ___ Few scientists were able to (witness/eyeball) the volcano's first eruption.

Choose words with positive connotations.

16. ___ Heather Price (refused/declined) to make a statement.

17. ___ They hired the (veteran/old) stage actor Harold Green to play the lead.

18. ___ The soldiers (secured/occupied) the village.

19. ___ His popularity is based less on humor than his (antics/gestures) on stage.

20. ___ This drug may cause (blindness/visual impairment).

Answers appear on the following page.

WRITING ON THE WEB

1. Use a database or a search engine such as Yahoo! or Google to look up articles from a variety of magazines. What do you notice about the level of diction, the use of words? How do styles of *The New Yorker, The Village Voice, People, Time,* and your local newspaper differ? What does this say about the writers, the publication, and the intended readers?

2. Analyze the language used in chat rooms on America Online or other Internet services. Have these electronic communities produced their own slang or jargon? Do chat rooms of car enthusiasts differ from those dedicated to child care or investments? Do people with special interests bring their particular terminology and culture into cyberspace?

3. Use a search engine such as Yahoo! or Google, and enter terms such as *diction, connotation, usage, word choice, slang,* and *vocabulary* to locate current sites of interest.

4. Write two or three sentences using new words you discover on the web. Determine which are technical, standard, and informal.

5. Ask your instructors for useful websites. Keep a list, and update it when you find a useful source.

POINTS TO REMEMBER

1. The words that you choose shape the way that readers will react to your writing.

2. Choose correct words—check dictionaries to make sure that you have selected the right words and spelled them correctly.

3. Choose effective words—use words that are clear and specific; avoid wordy phrases, clichés, and abstract terms.

4. Consider connotations—be aware of the emotional or psychological impacts that words may have. Choose words that reflect your message.

5. Review the lists of commonly confused and misspelled words on pages 700–703.

6. Study glossaries in your textbooks to master new terms you encounter in college.

7. Select a good college-level dictionary, and get in the habit of referring to it several times a week. Use highlighters or Post-it notes to personalize your dictionary.

8. Practice using an online dictionary, especially if you write on a computer.

Answers to What Have You Learned? on page 347

1. affect 2. accept 3. They're
4. conscious 5. continuous (see pages 700–703) 6. tested 7. blue
8. strike 9. plan 10. audit (see pages 700–703) 11. disheartened
12. considered 13. excessive
14. immediately 15. witness (see pages 700–703) 16. declined
17. veteran 18. secured
19. gestures 20. visual impairment (see pages 700–703)

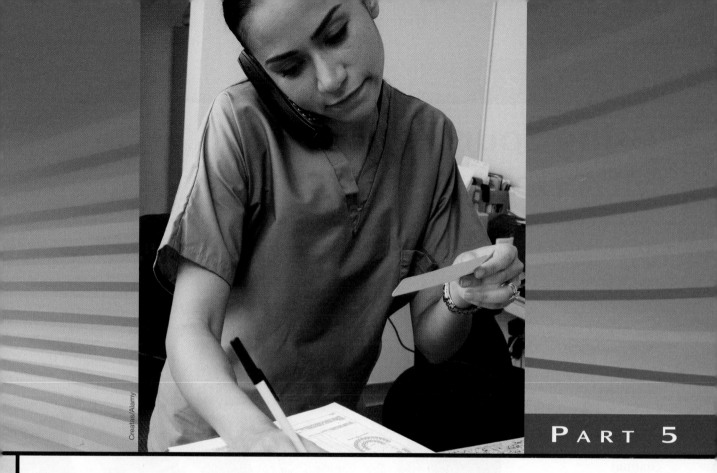

PART 5

Special Writing Assignments

CHAPTER 20

Using Sources and MLA Documentation

CHAPTER GOALS

- Understand the Role of MLA Documentation

- Document Sources to Avoid Plagiarism

- Use Quotations and Paraphrases to Support a Thesis

- Develop Works Cited Lists and Parenthetical Citations

Guy Call/Corbis

Get Writing

Lawyers support their arguments with scientific evidence, documents, eyewitnesses, and expert testimony. In some cases experts are paid thousands of dollars to testify.

Write a short essay expressing your opinion about paid experts. If you were on a jury, would you trust witnesses who were paid to testify? Why or why not?

Why Use and Document Sources?

Throughout your college career, you will probably be assigned papers that require using and documenting **sources,** such as facts, quotations, ideas, and statistics taken from books, magazines, websites, and interviews. When you include material from these sources in a paper, you need to **document** them, letting readers know what you are quoting and where it came from. Even if your instructor does not ask you to include sources, adding documented evidence can strengthen your essay:

Original

Too many students are dropping out of high school. The rate is alarming. This will make it hard for them to find jobs. It also threatens the nation's ability to compete in a global economy.

With Documented Sources

One in four American high school students will drop out this year. In Detroit the dropout rate is 40 percent (Brown 22). The National Association of Manufacturers has called the dropout rate "the nation's greatest challenge" (11). Speaking in New York last week, Bill Gates noted "if this dropout rate continues, we will not be able to compete in the global economy."

Outside sources give your essay greater authority by supporting your thesis with facts, statistics, and quotations from experts.

Using Sources

Whenever you use outside sources, it is important to remember your goal. The purpose of your essay is to state *your* thesis and *your* arguments and support them with evidence—not simply list facts and summarize what other people have written.

The sources you select should be **relevant, accurate, reliable,** and **representative:**

- **Relevant** sources relate directly to your thesis. The facts, statistics, and quotations you include should support your ideas, not simply supply additional information about a general topic.

- **Accurate** sources provide correct, recent, and objective information. Make sure that you copy quotations, numbers, and statistics carefully. Avoid confusing readers by taking facts out of context. The statement "In 2008 eighteen students from Marshall High School were expelled for gang activity" may be accurate but misleading if you fail to inform readers that this is the lowest number of expulsions in ten years and that the "gang activity" involved nonviolent crimes such as minor vandalism and dress code violations.

- **Reliable** sources include articles, books, speeches, interviews, and websites by widely respected authors, experts, and institutions. Use sources available in your college library or online databases. Avoid using websites, blogs, and publications that make exaggerated claims, advance conspiracy theories, or launch personal attacks.

If you are unsure about the reliability of a source, speak with your instructor or a reference librarian before using it in your paper.

- **Representative** sources provide examples, facts, statistics, and opinions that present a true and fair picture of a subject or situation. You might create a list of famous people who never finished high school. Your facts may be accurate and reliable, but they do not present a true and fair picture of the lives of dropouts.

Finding and Locating Sources

You can locate sources in the library, online, or on your own.

Library Sources

College and public libraries offer a range of sources, including books, magazines, videos, and databases.

- **Encyclopedias and reference books,** such as the Encyclopedia Britannica and Who's Who, provide background information and offer an overview of topics. Specialized encyclopedias, including An Encyclopedia of World History and Cassell's Encyclopedia of World Literature, offer in-depth articles about people, facts, events, and terms.
- **Online and card catalogs** list books and their call numbers in the library's collection. You can search books by author, title, or subject.
- **Periodical indexes** (also called **serials holding lists**) list magazines, newspapers, and journals held by the library.
- **Databases** such as InfoTrac College Edition and LexisNexis allow you to search thousands of magazines to locate articles. In most cases you can read, print, and e-mail articles.

If you have difficulty locating sources about your topic, ask the reference librarian for help. Telling the librarian about your assignment and the type of paper you are writing can help him or her direct you to the best sources.

Internet Sources

You can explore the Internet in the library or at home by using a number of search engines:

Google	www.google.com
Yahoo!	www.yahoo.com
AltaVista	www.altavista.com
Northern Light	www.northernlight.com
HotBot	www.hotbot.com

- **Check the spelling of search terms.**
- **Make search terms specific.**
- **Follow search engine directions to refine your search:**

  `prescription drugs AND addiction` *or* `prescription drugs + addiction` will list sites that include both terms.

  `prescription drugs NOT addiction` *or* `prescription drugs − addiction` will list sites about prescription drugs that do not mention addiction.

  `"Leopold and Loeb"` will list only sites that contain the whole phrase in quotation marks, eliminating sites about King Leopold or Loeb Realty.

Evaluating Online Sources

The Internet offers valuable sources, but remember that cyberspace is open to everyone. Much of the material you may encounter may be inaccurate, biased, and misleading. For example, Wikipedia is a popular website, but many college instructors do not accept it as a valid source. Library databases, such as InfoTrac College Edition, provide access to millions of articles from professional and peer-reviewed magazines that are better suited for college papers. When you use general search engines such as Google or Yahoo!, however, you must carefully evaluate items you find online before accepting them as reputable sources.

Strategies for Evaluating Online Resources

1. **Consider the source.** Who hosts the website? Is it a recognized news organization, such as CNN or the New York Times; a university; a major organization, such as the American Medical Association; or a government agency, such as NASA or the National Institute of Health? Avoid sources such as personal blogs, homepages, and sites sponsored by special interest groups that may have a political bias. If you are unsure about the reliability of a website, talk to your instructor or a reference librarian before using it as a source in your paper.

2. **Evaluate the author.** If an author is listed, check your library's online catalog or Amazon.com (www.amazon.com) to see if he or she has published any books. If so, were these published by major publishers? Amazon often lists reviews and other information that can establish the nature of the writer's reputation. Search a library database such as InfoTrac College Edition to see if the author has published articles in professional magazines. If so, do they appear in major news magazines such as Time or Newsweek, or special interest periodicals such as the Nation and National Review, which have a clear liberal or

conservative stance? Place the author's full name in quotation marks ("George Will"), and use it as a search term in Google or Yahoo! to locate biographical information. Your instructor or a reference librarian can help you evaluate authors.

3. **Examine the nature of the website.** Does the site present information in a professional, objective manner? Does it appear to have a clear bias or point of view? Does the site contain insulting and sarcastic language? Does it include editorial cartoons or images designed to provoke readers?

4. **Check links to blogs and other websites.** Does the site link to objective and professional sites, such as CNN, Newsweek, NASA, or only to a list of blogs with the same outlook?

5. **Verify claims.** Before accepting quotations, facts, or stories as being valid, check them online. Place key words in quotation marks, and use them as search terms in general search engines to see if these items appear in reliable news and academic sources.

6. **Evaluate the site for mistakes in critical thinking.** Does the site jump to conclusions on weak evidence or make unfair comparisons to prove a point? Does it present facts, statistics, and quotations out of context or without sources? (See Strategies for Increasing Critical Thinking on pages 12–13.)

7. **Verify claims using a library database such as InfoTrac that contains articles from recognized periodicals and newspapers.**

POINT TO REMEMBER

Whenever you use outside sources, take careful notes, and be sure to record information you will need to document your paper:

- **Books:** author or editor, title, city of publisher, publisher, edition, year, and page numbers of material you will use.
- **Articles:** author, article title, magazine or newspaper title, date, page numbers, and specific page numbers of material you will use.
- **Websites:** URL address (www.abc.com), owner of site, author, title, date of site, and date of access (date you looked at or printed the site).

Note: If you make photocopies of books or magazines, write the information on your copies to prevent confusion. Make sure if you print online material that your hard copies contain all the information you need.

EXERCISE 1   Locating Sources

Explore sources at your library or online to find information for the following questions.

1. What is the population of Chattanooga, Tennessee?

2. Who is the current mayor of New Orleans?

3. Does the University of Wisconsin—Milwaukee have a law school?

4. What is the library call number for Herman Melville's *Moby-Dick?*

5. Can you locate three articles on autism that came out in the last six months?

What Is MLA Documentation?

Whenever you include outside sources in a paper, you must document their use. Documentation is a way of showing readers which ideas are your own and which ideas come from another source. There are several documentation methods used in college courses. Most college English courses use the MLA style, developed by the Modern Language Association.

More Information On Documentation

This chapter covers the basics of MLA documentation. For additional help, refer to these websites:

Modern Language Association: Frequently Asked Questions About the MLA Handbook

http://www.mla.org/handbook_faq

The OWL at Purdue: MLA Formatting and Style Guide

http://owl.english.purdue.edu/owl/resource/557/01

MLA documentation consists of two parts:

citations that appear in parentheses in the essay whenever you use an outside source

a Works Cited list that appears at the end of your essay and lists all outside sources

Using Citations

As you include outside sources, note their use with **citations.** These citations should be brief but accurate. If you mention an author or source in your text, you need to add just a page number at the end in parentheses:

```
Winston Hachner has noted, "The Internet has provided
us with a dilemma of choice" (874).
```

(Note: Place the period after the parentheses. It is part of the sentence.)

If you do not mention the source, include the author's last name or the title with page numbers in the parentheses:

```
The Internet has given us more choices than we can
process (Hachner 874). The sheer volume of information
```

can overwhelm, confuse, and strangle businesses accustomed to defined channels of communication ("Internet Nation" 34-35).

Sources without page references do not require citations in parentheses if you mention them in your essay:

During a <u>60 Minutes</u> interview in 2008, George West argued, "A terrorist attack in cyberspace can cripple our economy."

You can avoid long, awkward notes in parentheses by mentioning the names of authors or titles in your essay:

As stated in the <u>Complete Directory of Modern Communication</u>, "The Internet has reshaped the way we think, communicate, and see our place in the world." Jacobson and Marley view the Internet as the greatest force in communications since the invention of the printing press (145-46).

You can shorten long titles by using one or two of the first key words. A newspaper article without an author called "The Dramatic Birth of a New Energy Source" could be cited as "Dramatic" or "Dramatic Birth":

The desire to reduce pollution and free the country from Middle Eastern oil is generating a range of new sources of power ("Dramatic" 15).

Do not shorten the title to "Birth" because that would lead readers to expect the full title of the article to be alphabetized under B rather than D.

Building a Works Cited List

As you write your essay, keep track of the outside sources you use. All sources that appear in the final paper will be listed alphabetically in a Works Cited list at the end of your essay:

<u>Complete Dictionary of Modern Communications</u>.
    Educational Network. 25 Apr. 2008 <http://www.
    ednetwork.com/modcom.dic./html>.

Hachner, Winston. <u>America and the Millennium</u>.
    New York: Atlantic, 2007.

——. "Internet Nation." <u>Chicago Magazine</u> Mar. 2004:
    32-41.

Jacobson, Max, and Jane Marley. <u>The Internet and the
    World</u>. New York: Random, 2008.

West, George. Interview. <u>60 Minutes</u>. CBS. WCBS,
    New York. 3 Apr. 2005.

Pages 363–371 show how to cite and list books, articles, television shows, and online material.

POINT TO REMEMBER

When an instructor in any class assigns a paper, ask two questions:

- Do I have to document outside sources?
- What documentation style should I use?

Why Document Sources?

Using documentation achieves three important goals:

1. **Avoiding plagiarism.** *Plagiarism* is using the words, ideas, or artistic work of others without giving them credit. It is considered cheating and stealing. Colleges have strict policies about plagiarism. Instructors often fail students who plagiarize papers. Many universities expel students who submit plagiarized assignments. *If you document your use of outside sources, no one can accuse you of cheating.*

2. **Supporting a thesis.** Citing sources not only protects you from charges of plagiarism but also makes your writing more effective. To convince readers to accept your thesis, it is important to provide them with evidence. *The more controversial your thesis, the more readers will demand supporting evidence from reliable sources.*

3. **Helping readers learn more.** Your citations show readers where they can obtain additional information by listing periodicals, books, and websites.

What *Not* to Document

Just because you include facts and statements you looked up in a book or found online does not mean they require documentation.

1. **Common expressions or famous quotations.** If you refer to statements readers are familiar with, such as Martin Luther King's "I have a dream" or John F. Kennedy's "Ask not what your country can do for you—ask what you can do for your country," you don't have to note their original source. *Less familiar statements, especially controversial ones, must be documented.*

2. **Common knowledge that doesn't change and is available in numerous sources.** You don't have to list the Encyclopedia Britannica as a source if you use it to look up where George Washington was born, when Death of a Salesman opened on Broadway, when Malcolm X died, or the height of Mount Everest. General facts such as these are not subject to change and are readily available in hundreds of books, almanacs, biographies, textbooks, and websites. No one will accuse you of stealing information that is considered standard and widely known

> by millions of people. *Facts subject to change or dispute, such as the population of Denver, the number of people on death row, or income tax regulations, must be documented.*

What You *Must* Document

In almost every other case, you must acknowledge the use of sources.

1. **Direct quotations.** When you copy word for word the spoken or written words of others, use quotation marks or indented paragraphs to distinguish them from your own words and indicate the source.

2. **Indirect quotations or paraphrases.** Even if you don't copy information but restate the author's ideas in your own words, you must list the source. Changing a few words in a quotation or summarizing several pages in a paragraph does not change the fact that you are using material from an outside source. Although you don't use quotation marks, indicate your use of other sources.

3. **Specific facts, statistics, and numbers.** Facts will be acceptable to readers only if they know where they came from. If you state, "Last year eighteen innocent men were sentenced to death for crimes they did not commit," readers will wonder where you got this figure and if it is true.

4. **Graphs, charts, photographs, and other visual aids.** Images, like facts or statistics, are valid sources only when you explain where you got them from. If you cut and paste a visual from the Web, list the website as you would for an a written quotation. Pay attention to dates. An interesting-looking graph or chart could be based on obsolete information. Make sure that your visuals are current.

EXERCISE 2　Documenting Sources

For each of the following sources, answer True if it must be documented or False if it does not need to be documented.

1. _____ Opening sentences of the Gettysburg Address.
2. _____ Names of Supreme Court justices nominated by President Johnson.
3. _____ Number of high school seniors in Chicago public schools in 2005.
4. _____ Quotation from a recent movie review in the New York Times.
5. _____ Original box-office figures for The Matrix.

Using and Documenting Sources

There are two basic ways of including outside sources:

- **direct quotations** that copy a source word for word.
- **paraphrases** (**indirect quotations**) that summarize a source in your own words

In both cases, you need to let readers know you are using outside material.

Using Direct Quotations

Direct quotations should be used sparingly. Remember, the goal of your paper is to express your thoughts and opinions, not present a collection of other people's ideas. However, there are times when direct quotations can be powerful additions to your essay.

Use direct quotations:

1. When they present a significant statement by an authority or eyewitness.
2. When the statement is unique or memorable.
3. When the idea expressed conflicts with common views.
4. When the original statement is well written and more compelling than a paraphrase or summary.
5. When readers may question a controversial point of view or question that a certain person made the statement.

Direct quotations should blend smoothly into your essay:

1. Indicate short direct quotations (1–4 lines) by placing them in quotation marks followed by a parenthetical citation:

   ```
   According to Lester Armstrong, "The university
   failed to anticipate the impact of state budget
   cuts" (17).
   ```

   Indicate long direct quotations (more than 4 lines) by placing them in indented paragraphs without quotation marks. Indent ten spaces (one inch) on the left side, and introduce with a colon. (*Note*: Place the period before the parenthetical citation.)

   ```
   According to Lester Armstrong, higher education
   suffered greatly during the recession:
           The university failed to anticipate the
           impact of state budget cuts. As a result,
           construction on the new stadium was halted.
           Twenty-five administrators were laid off.
   ```

```
Plans to expand the computer labs, bilin-
gual programs, and adult night school were
scrapped. The library budget was slashed by
24 percent, and two day-care centers were
closed. The century-old Main Hall, which was
scheduled for an extensive refurbishing, was
given only cosmetic repairs and painting. (17)
```

2. Link direct quotations with your text. Quotations should not stand alone in a paragraph. They should connect with your sentences:

Incorrect

```
Children are greatly affected by violence on
television. "By the time a child graduates from
high school, he or she has witnessed over 18,000
homicides on television" (Smith 10). Young people
come to view violence, even murder, as a reason-
able method of resolving conflicts.
```

Blend direct quotations into your text by introducing them:

Revised

```
Children are greatly affected by violence on
television. John Sanchez, author of Toxic TV,
notes that "by the time a child graduates from
high school he or she has witnessed over 18,000
homicides on television" (10). Young people come
to view violence, even murder, as a reasonable
method of resolving conflict.
```

Introducing quotations also allows you to explain the significance of what you are quoting or why it is important.

3. You may edit quotations to eliminate redundant or irrelevant material. Indicate deleted words by inserting an *ellipsis* (three spaced periods).

Original Text

```
George Washington, who was heading to New York to
confer with his leading advisors, agreed to meet
with Franklin in Philadelphia on June 10th.
```

Edited Quote

```
As Smith notes, "George Washington . . . agreed
to meet with Franklin in Philadelphia on June
10th" (12).
```

Deletions should remove only unnecessary information; they should not alter the meaning of the text by removing qualifications or changing a negative statement into a positive one. It is unethical to alter a quotation such as "We should, only if everything else fails, legalize drugs" to read "We should . . . legalize drugs."

4. Insert words or other information to prevent confusion or avoid grammatical errors. For instance, if a direct quotation refers to a World War II general named Samuel Roosevelt only by his last name and you are concerned that readers will confuse him with President Roosevelt, you may insert his first name, even though it does not appear in the original text:

Original Text

```
In 1944 Roosevelt was so desperate for more
troops, he urged lowering the draft age to
sixteen.
```

Edited Quotation

```
According to Sara Yen, "In 1944 [Samuel]
Roosevelt was so desperate for more troops, he
urged lowering the draft age to sixteen" (14).
```

If you delete words or phrases, you may have to insert words to prevent a grammatical error:

Original Text

```
Poe and other writers of his generation were
influential in shaping a new, truly American
literature.
```

Edited Quotation

```
According to Jenna Falco, "Poe . . . [was]
influential in shaping a new, truly American
literature" (64).
```

Using Paraphrases

Paraphrases are indirect quotations. Instead of copying word for word what someone said or wrote, you might **paraphrase** it by putting these ideas in your own words. For example, you might read three or four pages about the Civil War in a history book and summarize the points in a single paragraph. Even though you are not copying anything or using quotations marks, you are still using the work of others and have to document that source.

Original Text

Between 1945 and 1954, 9 million people moved to the suburbs. Millions more followed thereafter. Altogether, between 1950 and 1976, the number of Americans living in central cities grew by 10 million, the number in suburbs by 85 million. By 1976 more Americans lived in suburbs than either central cities or rural areas.

DANIEL YERGIN, THE PRIZE, PP. 550–551

Paraphrase

```
The suburbs exploded after World War II. Nearly ten
million people moved to the suburbs by 1954. By 1976
more Americans lived in suburbs than in the country or
in big cities (Yergin 550-51).
```

Parenthetical references should be placed immediately after the paraphrased material at an appropriate pause or at the end of the sentence.

EXERCISE 3   Documenting Direct Quotations and Paraphrases

Write one or two paragraphs about the job market, and use at least one direct quotation and one paraphrase from the following source.

GETTING AHEAD   187

Before you take a job, make sure you, your personality, and your goals match up with the prevailing corporate culture. There are three main cultures that dominate the corporate world today:

Basketball teams are new startups that reward risk takers and innovators. They offer high salaries and bonuses for star performers. Winning is everything for these outfits, and they care little for routine and red tape. Employees are encouraged to compete against each other. Winners can write their own tickets and rise quickly. Losers are quickly shown the door. This is a job for confident self-starters. These firms devote few resources to training and supervision. There is little patience with employees with problems. You will be expected to be independent and productive. Don't expect help with childcare or hope that long hours alone will prove your worth. Bottom line, bringing in the dollars is all that counts. Turnover is high. In most high tech companies 25% of people hired are fired in the first six months.

Examples: sales outfits, new high tech companies, Google and Yahoo in the early 2000's.

Clubs are long established firms that reward service and loyalty. Employees rise by putting in time and following the rules. Age and experience are highly regarded. Youthful innovators may be viewed as "reckless" and accused of "rocking the boat." Stability is important here. You will be expected to punch in and out on time, follow the corporate dress code, dot your i's, and do what you are told. These outfits offer solid careers and, unless there is a major financial crisis, layoffs are few and far between. Fifty percent of the Fortune 500 companies fit this category. Typically 65% of employees hired will work there until they retire.

Examples: the telephone company, utilities, the military, major banks, government agencies.

Bunkers are organizations under siege. They are preoccupied with survival. In their glory days they may have been basketball teams or clubs, but now they are threatened by a hostile takeover, foreign competition, regulation changes, scandal, or a financial crisis. With key personnel jumping ship, these organizations do offer job opportunities for problem solvers and turn around artists. Burnt out, overworked, and depressed, the top management is looking for "new blood" and may offer a beginner a great opportunity, if only out of desperation. Entering the bunker is a gamble, but it can pay off, especially if you can take credit for plugging the holes in the dike.

Examples: airlines, dot.coms and Enron in the early 2000's, subprime lenders.

Source: <u>Getting Ahead</u>, by Jerry Gomez, published by Prescott Books in New York in 2009.

MLA Guidelines for Listing Sources in Works Cited and Parenthetical Notes

When you include quotations and paraphrases from other sources, list them alphabetically in the **works cited** at the end of your paper. Whenever quotations and paraphrases appear in your paper, you show where they came from with a **parenthetical note.** This list shows how to set up **works cited** entries and **parenthetical notes** for a variety of sources. For more information, go to the MLA website (**http://www.mla.org/handbook_faq**).

Books

- Write the author's last name, first name, then any initial. Copy the name as written. "C. W. Brown" would appear as:

  ```
  Brown, C. W.
  ```

  Omit any degrees or titles such as Ph.D. or Dr.

- State the full title of the book. Place a colon between the main heading and any subtitle. Underline all the words and punctuation in the title, except for the final period:

  ```
  Brown, C. W. Sharks and Lambs: Wall Street in
        the Nineties.
  ```

- Record the city of publication, publisher, and date of publication. If the book lists several cities, use only the first. If the city is outside the United States, add an abbreviation for the country. If a U.S. city may be unfamiliar, you can include an abbreviation for the state. Record the main words of the publisher, deleting words such as "publishing" or "press" (**Monroe** for Monroe Publishing Company). However, if the publisher is called a "University Press," use the initials "UP" (**Yale UP** for Yale University Press). End the citation with the last year of publication.

Works Cited entry:

```
Brown, C. W. Sharks and Lambs: Wall Street in
      the Nineties. Kehoe, IL: Kellogg UP, 2003.
```

Parenthetical note:

> (Brown 12)

Book with Two or Three Authors

Works Cited entry:

> Smith, David, John Adams, and Chris Cook.
> Writing On-line. New York: Macmillan,
> 2008.

Parenthetical note:

> (Smith, Adams, and Cook 23-24)

Books with More Than Four Authors

Works Cited entry:

> Chavez, Nancy, et al. Mexico Today. New York:
> Putnam, 2008.

Parenthetical note:

> (Chavez et al. 87)

Book with Corporate Author

Works Cited entry:

> National Broadcasting Company. Programming
> Standards. New York: National Broadcasting
> Company, 2007.

Parenthetical note:

> (National Broadcasting Company 112)

To avoid a long parenthetical note, mention the author or title in the text:

According to the National Broadcasting Company's
Programming Standards, "No single executive should be
able to cancel a program" (112).

Book with Unnamed Authors

Works Cited entry:

> New Yale Atlas. New York: Random, 2008.

Parenthetical note:

> (New Yale 106)

Book with Multiple Volumes

Works Cited entry:

> Eisenhower, Dwight. Presidential
> Correspondence. Vol. 2. New York:
> Dutton, 1960. 6 vols.

Parenthetical note:

> (Eisenhower 77)

If you cite more than one volume in your paper, indicate the number.

> (Eisenhower 2:77)

Book in Second or Later Edition

Works Cited entry:

> Franklin, Marcia. <u>Modern France</u>. 3rd ed.
>   Philadelphia: Comstock, 1987.

Parenthetical note:

> (Franklin 12)

Work in an Anthology

Works Cited entry:

> Ford, John M. "Preflash." <u>The Year's Best Fan-</u>
>   <u>tasy</u>. Ed. Ellen Datlow and Terri Windling.
>   New York: St. Martin's, 1989. 265-82.

Parenthetical note:

> (Ford 265-66)

Book in Translation

Works Cited entry:

> Verne, Jules. <u>Twenty Thousand Leagues Under the</u>
>   <u>Sea</u>. Trans. Michel Michot. Boston: Pitman,
>   1992.

Parenthetical note:

> (Verne 65)

Book with Editor or Editors

Works Cited entry:

> Benson, Nancy, ed. <u>Ten Great American Plays</u>.
>   New York: Columbia UP, 2007.

Parenthetical note:

> (Benson 23)

Book with Author and Editor

Works Cited entry:

> Gissing, George. <u>Workers in the Dawn</u>. Ed. Jason
>   Day. London: Oxford UP, 1982.

Parenthetical note:

> (Gissing 78)

Book in a Series

Works Cited entry:

> Swessel, Karyn, ed. <u>Northern Ireland Today</u>. Modern Europe Ser. 3. New York: Wilson, 2008.

Parenthetical note:

> (Swessel 34)

Republished Book

Works Cited entry:

> Smith, Jane. <u>The Jersey Devil</u>. 1922. New York: Warner, 2008.

Parenthetical note:

> (Smith 23-25)

Periodicals

Newspaper Article

Works Cited entry:

> Chavez, Maria. "The Hispanic Century." <u>New York Times</u> 12 Mar. 2008: A13.

Parenthetical note:

> (Chavez)

Note: If an article has only one page, page numbers are not included in parenthetical notes.

Magazine Article

Works Cited entry:

> Janssen, Mary. "Iran Today." <u>Time</u> 25 Mar. 2009: 15+*.

*Note: In some publications an article might start on page 15, then jump to pages 24–26, and finally end on page 54. These are called **nonconsecutive pages**. If an article appears on nonconsecutive pages, list the first page followed by a "+" sign.

Parenthetical note:

> (Janssen 24)

Scholarly Article

Works Cited entry:

> Grant, Edward. "The Hollywood Ten: Fighting the Blacklist." <u>California Film Quarterly</u> 92 (2002): 14-32.

Parenthetical note:

> (Grant 21-23)

Newspaper or Magazine Article with Unnamed Author

Works Cited entry:

> "The Legacy of the Gulf War." <u>American History</u> 12 Mar. 2008: 23-41.

Parenthetical note:

> ("Legacy" 25)

Letter to the Editor

Works Cited entry:

> Roper, Jack. Letter. <u>Chicago Defender</u> Jan. 2002, sec. B: 12.

Parenthetical note:

> (Roper)

Other Print Sources

Encyclopedia Article with Author

Works Cited entry:

> Keller, Christopher. "Lisbon." <u>World Book Encyclopedia</u>. 2008.

Parenthetical note:

> (Keller, "Lisbon")

Note: Page numbers are not used with works in which items are arranged alphabetically.

Encyclopedia Article with Unnamed Author

Works Cited entry:

> "Lisbon." <u>Columbia Illustrated Encyclopedia</u>. 2008.

Parenthetical note:

> ("Lisbon")

Pamphlet with Author

Works Cited entry:

> Tindall, Gordon, ed. <u>Guide to New York Churches</u>. New York Chamber of Commerce, 2008.

Parenthetical note:

>   (Tindall 76-78)

Pamphlet with Unnamed Author

Works Cited entry:

>   Guide to New York Museums. New York: Columbia
>   UP, 2008.

Parenthetical note:

>   (Guide 176-82)

The Bible

Works Cited entry:

>   Holy Bible. New International Version. Grand
>   Rapids, MI: Zondervan, 1988.

Note: Titles of sacred texts are not underlined.

Parenthetical note:

>   (Mark 2:4-9)

Nonprint Sources

Motion Picture

Works Cited entry:

>   Casino. Dir. Martin Scorsese. Universal, 1995.

Note: You may wish to include names of performers or screenwriters if they are of special interest to readers.

Television Program

Works Cited entry:

>   "The Long Goodbye." Law and Order. Dir. Jane
>   Hong. Writ. Peter Wren. Perf. Rita Col-
>   letti, Diane Nezgod, and Vicki Shimi. NBC.
>   WTMJ, Milwaukee. 12 May 2003.

Videotape

Works Cited entry:

>   Colonial Williamsburg. Prod. Janet Freud.
>   American Home Video, 1996.

Note: You may include information about the director, performers, or screenwriters if these are important for readers.

Live Performance of a Play

Works Cited entry:

> <u>All My Sons</u>. By Arthur Miller. Dir. Anita
>   Dayin. Lyric Theater, New York. 10
>   May 2008.

Speech

Works Cited entry:

> Goode, Wilmont. "America in the Next Century."
>   Chicago Press Club. 12 Oct. 2008.

Personal or Telephone Interview

Works Cited entry:

> Weston, Thomas. Personal interview. 21 May 2008.

Parenthetical Notes for Nonprint Sources

Because nonprint sources often have long titles, parenthetical notes can be cumbersome and interrupt the flow of your sentences:

Cases of depression rise during periods of high unemployment (<u>National Mental Health Association's Annual
Address 2008</u>). Drug and alcohol abuse, divorce, and
suicide also increase (<u>Losing the American Dream</u>).

You can avoid long parenthetical notes by mentioning the source in your sentence. This also allows you to introduce or explain who or what you are quoting or paraphrasing:

The <u>National Mental Health Association's Annual Address 2008</u> observes that cases of depression rise
during periods of unemployment. The documentary film
<u>Losing the American Dream</u> notes that drug and alcohol
abuse, divorce, and suicide also increase.

Electronic Sources

CD-ROM

Works Cited entry:

> "Understanding <u>Macbeth</u>." <u>Master Dramas</u>. CD-ROM.
>   Educational Media: Microsoft, 2002.

E-mail

Works Cited entry:

> Ballard, Morton D. "Rental Cars." E-mail to
>   Germaine Reinhardt. 21 May 2008.

Electronic Journal

Works Cited entry:

> Smith, Perry. "Truman Capote and Kansas."
>   <u>Phoenix</u> 2.7 (2008). 15 Sep. 2008 <http://
>   www.englishlit./hts/phoenix/index>.

Article from Online Newspaper

Works Cited entry:

> "<u>Long Day's Journey Into Night</u> Production
>   Disappointing." <u>New York Times on the Web</u>
>   17 Mar. 2003. 22 Apr. 2009 <http://www
>   .nytimes.com/aponline/a/ap-play.html>.

Reference Database

Works Cited entry:

> <u>The Emerald Project: Irish Literature from
>   1500-2000</u>. Boston University. 21 Oct. 2008
>   <http://www/bostonuniv/emerald/>.

Electronic Texts

Many books are available online. Because they lack page numbers, mention the title within the text to avoid long parenthetical notes.

Works Cited entry:

> Gissing, George. <u>Demos</u>. London, 1892. <u>The
>   Electronic Text Center</u>. Ed. Jacob Korgman.
>   Aug. 2003. U of Michigan Lib. 5 Mar. 2000
>   <http//etext.lib.michigan.edu>.

Web Pages

Web pages vary greatly. In general, include the name of the person or organization that created the site, the title, descriptions, the date of creation, the date of access, and the URL.

Works Cited entry:

> Chicago Irish Center. Home page. 5 Apr.
>   2003. 10 May 2002 <http://www.chi.irish
>   .cent.org>.

Discussion Group Posting

Works Cited entry:

> Baker, Jordan. "Golf Today." Online posting.
>   2 Mar. 2000. Professional Sports Discus-
>   sion List. 15 Mar. 2000 <http://www
>   .prosports.com/posting>.

Linked Sources

MLA does not provide a method of citing hypertext links, but the following format allows readers to follow your search.

Works Cited entry:

```
Trainer, Lois. "F. Scott Fitzgerald." Online
        posting. 4 Aug. 2003. Ansaxnet. 10
        Oct. 2000 <http://www.amlit/edu>. Lkd.
        <http://www.yalelit.edu/biography>.
```

Sources and Sample Documented Essay

Read the excerpts taken from a book, a magazine article, and a website, and note how the student uses and documents these sources to write a paper about student credit card debt.

Book Excerpt

From: <u>How to Survive College</u> by Nancy Hughes, published by Academic Press, New York City, 2005.

HOW TO SURVIVE COLLEGE   176

Today credit card companies bombard incoming freshmen with credit card offers. Card companies operate on campuses, often in student unions and dorm lobbies. Giving out free hats, T-shirts, coffee mugs, and pizza coupons, they encourage students to sign up for cards. Companies generally issue cards to students over eighteen whether they have jobs or not. Faced with the need for books, clothes, computer supplies, and student fees, many students quickly apply for cards and ring up charges. At Northwestern University nearly 10% of incoming freshmen had maxed out at least one credit card by the end of their first semester.

Actual purchases, however, are often not the culprit. The ability to use a credit card to get cash from an ATM leads many students to live well beyond their means, getting into debt $40 or $60 at a time. Miranda Hayes, who graduated with $7,500 in credit card debts, had made only $2,000 in purchases. "I charged a computer my freshman year and all my books," she admits. "The rest was all cash from an ATM that went for movies, beer, pizzas, bus fare, my cell phone, health club dues, and interest."

Magazine Article

From: "University of Wisconsin Takes Up the Issue of Student Credit Card Debt" in <u>Cardline</u>, June 11, 2004, page 1.

Cardline, June 11, 2004   1

UNIVERSITY OF WISCONSIN TAKES UP THE ISSUE OF STUDENT CREDIT CARD DEBT

The Board of Regents for the University of Wisconsin System, which operates the state's 13 four-year schools and 14 two-year schools, was expected to discuss credit card solicitation today, a spokesperson for UW—Madison tells *CardLine.* The discussion was promoted by the release in May of a 15-page, UW-commissioned report, "Student Credit Card Debt and Policies on Credit Card Solicitation on the University of Wisconsin," which said that 40% of its students owe credit card balances of $1,000 or more. It's not clear what action the regents, who are meeting at the UW's Milwaukee campus, will take, but three of its campuses have adopted formal policies regarding credit card solicitations and others have informal ones. The report recommends that the regents adopt rules that are consistent system-wide. Some UW administrators take a much harsher attitude. They wanted credit card solicitation banned altogether, but the report said such a ban might violate the law. The UW commissioned the report following several national studies, including one by the General Accounting Office. Newspapers also regularly reported on the issue. The report gathered its data through telephone interviews with staff members, student surveys and anecdotal information. It found that between 62% and 71% of students had at least one credit card. A UW Student Spending and Employment Survey found that of those who responded to it, 40% of students owed credit card debts of $1,000 to $5,000, and 10% owed over $5,000. The high card debt takes a toll on some students. Although the campuses don't. . . .

A Website

From: "Top Ten Student Money Mistakes," by Blythe Terrell, on *Young Money,* updated at http://www.youngmoney.com/money_management/spending/020809_02, and accessed March 21, 2005.

Top Ten Student Money Mistakes

By Blythe Terrell, University of Missouri

For many students, college is the first major landmark on the path to independence. Moving away from home means no more curfews, no asking for permission, and no parents looking over their shoulders. It also means that the liberty-seeking college kid is now free to make his or her own mistakes.

In such an environment, money management often becomes an issue. Knowing how to avoid these problems is the key to beating them. Here are ten common mistakes students make, and how you can avoid them.

1. **Making poor choices about which credit cards to get.** Credit card companies set up booths on college campuses, offering T-shirts and other items to anyone who will sign up for a card. Although the deals can seem fantastic, students must look into the card's repayment terms carefully. "When students get credit cards, two things can happen," said Stephen Ferris, professor of finance at the University of Missouri—Columbia. "One, they don't read the fine print and see what they're paying. And they're paying a lot. Or they use it until it's maxed out." It is absolutely necessary to pay your credit cards on time each month, added Ferris.

2. **Letting friends pressure them into spending money.** College life is full of opportunities to spend money, finals-week smorgasbords, an evening out with friends, road trips and vacations. . . . Not knowing how to say "no" can cause students to spend money they just do not have. "If you can't afford it, just say no," says David Fingerhut, a financial adviser with Pines Financial in St. Louis.

3. **Not setting up a budget.** If they have a set amount of money, they must plan ahead and know how much they can spend each month. "It has to work on paper before it works in real life," Fingerhut said.

4. **Not seeking out the best bank rates.** Banks offer many different kinds of checking and savings accounts, but some charge fees that others do not. It is essential for students to do research and not simply go with the closest, most accessible bank, Ferris said.

Student Essay

College Students and Debt

Students graduating in debt is nothing new. Few students or their parents have enough money to pay as they go. Even students with scholarships take on debts to pay for college expenses. But in recent years tens of thousands of students have added to their financial burdens by amassing credit card debts. Colleges, which allow credit card companies to operate on campus, must regulate the way they advertise and educate students on managing their money.

student thesis

topic sentence
paraphrase

facts stating problem

citation showing author and page

specific fact cited

Arriving on campus, freshmen encounter credit card promoters in student unions and their dorms. Offering students free gifts, the various card companies urge students to sign up for credit cards. Card companies will issue cards to any college student who is at least eighteen (Hughes 176). Credit cards have become extremely popular with students. Currently 62-71% of college students have at least one credit card ("University" 1).

topic sentence

example supporting thesis

quotation within quotation cited

Many students are unsophisticated when it comes to using credit. Whether making a purchase or cash advance, they rarely calculate how interest charges or ATM fees will inflate their balance. In many cases, students get deep into debt not by making major purchases, but by withdrawing costly cash advances. Many students share the fate of Miranda Hayes, who amassed a $7,500 credit card debt, noting, "I charged a computer my freshman year and all my books. The rest was all cash from an ATM that went for movies, beer, pizzas, bus fare, my cell phone, health club dues, and interest" (qtd. in Hughes 1).

paraphrase

The University of Wisconsin, among others, is considering establishing new policies to regulate credit card promotions on campus ("University" 1).

topic sentence

quotation within cited
expert quotation

paraphrase

But the real service colleges can give students is to prepare them for the responsibilities of adult life by including financial planning seminars that focus on credit cards, budgets, and loans. Stephen Ferris, a finance professor, points out that when students sign up for cards, "they don't read the fine print and see what they are paying. And they're paying a lot" (qtd. in Terrell). Students don't consider interest rates, let peer pressure guide their spending, and fail to set up budgets (Terrell).

conclusion
restatement of thesis

Ultimately, students are responsible. Away from home for the first time, they have to learn to manage their time, ignore distractions and peer pressure, and use credit wisely. Parents and colleges can provide information and give advice, but as adults, college students must take responsibility for the decisions they make.

Works Cited

Hughes, Nancy. How to Survive College. New York: Academic, 2005.

```
Terrell, Blythe. "Top Ten Student Money Mistakes."
     Young Money. 21 Mar. 2005 <http://www.youngmoney
     .com/money_management/spending/020809_02>.
```

```
"University of Wisconsin Takes Up the Issue of Student
     Credit Card Debt." Cardline 11 June 2004: 1.
```

EXERCISE 4   Writing a Documented Essay

Using the three sources on pages 371–373, write your own essay about student credit card use. You may choose another topic and locate at least two outside sources to create a documented essay. Include both in-text citations and a Works Cited page.

WORKING TOGETHER

Working with a small group of students, exchange documented essays and source material. Refer to pages 359–361 to see if you have cited quotations and paraphrases correctly. Make sure that you avoid plagiarism—using but failing to cite facts, ideas, and quotations taken from outside sources.

Get Thinking
and Writing

CRITICAL THINKING

Select a controversial or highly debated topic such as abortion, gun control, the mortgage crisis, immigration, terrorism, or reparations for slavery. Conduct an Internet search, and locate at least three sources advocating different points of view.

Notice how different sources use facts, statistics, and quotations to support their opinions.

Develop a list of questions that would help you evaluate the strength and weaknesses of websites on the Internet. What should people consider before believing what they read in cyberspace?

WHAT HAVE YOU WRITTEN?

1. How have you defined or described the most serious concern that students should have in examining online sources? Could you restate it more clearly and directly?

   _____

   _____

2. List errors in logic or critical thinking you have detected in any of the sources you located.

   _____

   _____

Some attorneys argue that television shows such as *CSI* give the public and juries misconceptions about the quality of evidence that prosecutors can present in court. Do you think television dramas can mislead the public by creating unrealistic expectations of what evidence that law enforcement officers use to convict criminals?

Write a short essay examining whether or not television programs educate or mislead the public about the criminal justice system. You may wish to refer to episodes you have seen on television or conduct an Internet search on DNA evidence to obtain additional sources.

WRITING ON THE WEB

Using a search engine such as Yahoo! or Google, enter terms such as *plagiarism, avoiding plagiarism, MLA documentation, documenting Internet sources, using online sources, writing research papers, using quotations and paraphrases,* and *Works Cited page.*

1. Locate a documented article online, and notice how the author documents quotations and paraphrases.
2. Look up definitions and examples of plagiarism. Locate your college's policy on plagiarism.

POINTS TO REMEMBER

1. **Outside sources strengthen essays by adding facts, statistics, and quotations to support the thesis.**
2. **Using outside sources without acknowledging them is plagiarism, a serious offense.**
3. **Documentation distinguishes your ideas from those taken from outside sources.**
4. **Commonly known facts such as someone's birth date, the height of a mountain, or a state's capital do not have to be documented.**
5. **Document both direct quotations and paraphrases.**
6. **The goal of a documented essay is to express your thesis supported by sources. An essay is not a list of facts and quotations. Make sure that the paper expresses what you think, not what others have written.**

CHAPTER 21

Writing at Work

Comstock Select/CORBIS

CHAPTER GOALS

- Appreciate How Writing at Work Differs from Writing in College

- Learn Strategies for Writing E-mail, Business Reports, Résumés, and Cover Letters

- Realize the Importance of Format in Writing Business Documents

Get Writing

Why is writing different on the job than in school?

Write three or four paragraphs comparing and contrasting the kind of writing you have done in college with the kinds of writing tasks you might expect in your career.

Writing at work differs greatly from writing in college. Although memos, e-mail, letters, and reports follow the same rules of grammar and spelling as school assignments, they are developed in a very different environment, have different readers, and serve different needs:

Business writing takes place in a specific context. The tone, style, wording, and format of business writing are shaped by the history and standards of the profession, organization, readers, and subject.

Business writing is directed to specific readers. In college you write to a general academic audience. In business you address customers, employees, supervisors, and investors who have specific questions, concerns, and problems.

Business writing is action-oriented. In college you write papers to present ideas. At work you are more likely to direct people to take action—to buy a product, use a service, hire an employee, or make an investment.

Business writing is sensitive to legal implications. Letters, reports, and contracts are legal documents. Avoid making statements that can expose you to a lawsuit.

Business writing represents the views of others. In college your papers express personal ideas and opinions. At work the e-mails, letters, and reports you write should reflect the values, attitudes, and positions of your employer. Avoid stating personal opinions.

This chapter focuses on four of the most common business writing assignments you will face: e-mail, reports, résumés, and cover letters.

E-mail

Today almost every job uses e-mail to communicate. Some people confuse e-mail with "instant messages" or chat-room conversations. They write and answer e-mail without thinking, producing a stream of tangled ideas, missing details, grammar errors, and inappropriate comments. E-mail, like any kind of writing, takes thought and planning to be effective.

Strategies for Writing E-mail

1. **Realize that e-mail is *real mail*.** E-mail can be stored, distributed, and printed. Unlike a note or memo that can be retrieved or corrected, e-mail, once sent, becomes permanent. *Never send e-mail when you are tired or angry. Avoid sending messages that you will later regret.*

2. **Think before you write.** E-mail should have a clear goal. Consider whom you are writing to, what they need to know, and how you can persuade them to accept your ideas.

3. **Follow the prewriting, drafting, revising, and editing strategies you would use in writing a paper document.** Don't let an e-mail message simply record whatever comes into your head. E-mail should have a clear purpose and an easy-to-follow organization. Plan before you write.

4. **Understand what messages *should not* be expressed in e-mail.** E-mail is considered appropriate for short, informative messages. Do not attempt to send a fifteen-page report by e-mail, though it might be sent as an attachment. Do not send personal or sensitive information by e-mail. E-mail is seen as too informal and too public for confidential correspondence.

5. **Respond to e-mail carefully.** Often, e-mail messages will list multiple readers. Before sending a reply, determine whether you want everyone or just a few people to see your response.

6. **Make sure that you use the correct e-mail address.** E-mail addresses can be complicated and oddly spelled. Names are often shortened or reversed. Donald Peterson might appear as "donald. peterson," "dpeterson," or "petersond." Double-check addresses.

7. **Clearly label your e-mail in the subject line.** Spam—unwanted e-mail messages—uses misleading headings such as "Following your request" or "Next week's conference" to grab attention. To prevent your e-mail from being overlooked or deleted before it is read, use specific identifying details in the subject such as "RE: April 19th health insurance reminder" or "Smithkin Supplies Annual Audit."

8. **Include your full name, e-mail address, and the date on anything you attach to an e-mail.** Attachments are often saved or printed separately. If your name does not appear on the documents, readers may not remember who sent them.

9. **Keep e-mail direct and concise.** People expect e-mail to be brief and easy to read. Avoid complicated sentences and long paragraphs. Use short paragraphs and bulleted or numbered points to increase readability.

10. **End the e-mail with a clear summary, request, or direction.** Summarize important points. If you are asking for information or help, clearly state what you need, when you need it, and how you can be reached. If you want readers to take action, provide clear directions.

11. **Ask readers for an acknowledgment if you want to make sure they received your message.**

12. **Review, edit, and double-check e-mail before sending.** Check your spelling, addresses, names, prices, or figures for accuracy. Read your e-mail aloud to catch missing words, illogical statements, confusing sentences, or awkward phrases.

13. **Print hard copies of important e-mail for future reference.**

January 30, 2009

From: John Rio
To: Sales Staff
RE: Expense Account Reports

To all sales staff:

As of March 1, 2009, Pacific Mutual will no longer provide sales representatives with company cars or expense accounts. Instead, sales representatives will
be given a flat monthly grant to cover office, travel, and vehicle expenses:

Inside Sales Reps $250 per month
District Sales Reps $500 per month
Regional Sales Reps $750 per month

This policy affects only regular monthly expenses. Pacific Mutual will continue
to pay all expenses for those attending regional and national sales conventions.

If you have any questions about the new policy, please contact me at ext. 7689.

John Rio

EXERCISE 1   Revising E-mail

Revise this e-mail to create a clear, concise message.

Kim:

This e-mail is about the student enrollment problems we face with online courses.
Right now it seems many students sign up and cannot find the website for their
course and have no idea how the class is going to be run or what is expected of them.
This is causing a problem. I am getting a lot of complaints from students who seem
lost. I think we can do some things to improve this situation next semester. The
main college website should have a link to all online courses. Each online instructor must place on the course website an expanded syllabus that explains the nature
of the course, office hours, assignment due dates, readings, and online discussion
groups. In addition, each department website should list its online offerings.

Bijan Naboti

Reports

Business reports use the same methods of development found in college papers, such as definition, process, cause and effect, and comparison. However, there are key differences in the approach, style, and format of business
reports.

Business reports emphasize facts and actions rather than thoughts. Academic reports explore ideas, advance theories, and offer personal interpretations. Business reports deal with practical day-to-day realities. They are direct and to the point.

Business reports are generally written to multiple readers. Academic reports are written for one instructor, who is expected to read the entire document. Business reports often are sent to a number of people, who may read only the sections that deal with their concerns. In many cases, no one will read the entire report.

Business reports use subtitles or numbered points to signal transitions. Academic reports are double-spaced and might run ten pages without any breaks. Readers are expected to follow the writer's train of thought through subtle transition statements. Business reports are single-spaced and use visual markers to break up the text into labeled sections to make the document readable at a glance.

Business reports are generally objective and avoid using the first person ("I").

Business reports generally do not use formal documentation of outside sources. Instead, they may informally note sources:

```
According to Business Week, the deficit will not
affect interest rates.

Recent news reports indicate growing labor unrest
in China.
```

Business reports make greater use of visual aids such as graphs and charts.

Strategies for Writing Reports

1. **Determine a clear goal for your report.** Business reports either direct people to take action or provide them with information they will use to make decisions. Focus on facts and objective details.

2. **Focus on specific readers.** Consider the practical needs of the people who will read your report. What facts, figures, and concepts do they need to know to make decisions, resolve conflicts, prevent problems, or make money? Give readers information they can use.

3. **Include a table of contents in reports longer than three pages.** Tables of contents list headings and page numbers, helping readers to quickly locate information.

4. **Use an informational, direct title that clearly tells readers what the report is about.** Avoid simple labels or generalized titles you might use in a college paper.

5. **Open the report with a clear statement of purpose.** Introductions in college papers may tell a story or provide an example to arouse interest. Business reports open with a direct statement of a problem or the writer's goal.

6. **Organize ideas in a logical format that is clearly labeled.** Avoid transitional statements or subtle shifts in your train of thought.

7. **Use conclusions to explain findings, summarize key points, or list recommendations.**

Boylan Electric

DATE: January 12, 2009
TO: Mary Liotta, Property Manager
FROM: Saheeb Pradi, District Manager
SUBJECT: Property at 901 West Highland Avenue, Milwaukee

RELOCATION OF SALES OFFICE/ SALE OF 901 WEST HIGHLAND BLDG.

It is highly recommended that Boylan Electric sell its 901 West Highland building and rent offices near the airport to serve its sales staff.

BACKGROUND

The Boylan sales office in Milwaukee has been located at 901 West Highland Avenue since 1959. The building provided ample office and storage space and had easy freeway access. In 2005 freeway reconstruction and neighborhood redevelopment altered the environment. Freeway access is now limited. Parking, once available for a nominal fee across the street, is now limited to four spaces in front of the building and two spaces in the loading dock. The building, now nearly fifty years old, no longer serves the needs of Boylan's reduced sales staff. In 1959 Boylan manufactured small power tools widely sold in automotive, hardware, and department stores. Today this represents less than 10% of the product line, and sales are managed through catalog and online operations. Current sales representatives call on industrial accounts nationwide, 75% of whom make at least one flight from Mitchell Field a week.

RELOCATION NEEDS

The current sales and support staff of ten requires 1,500 square feet of office space. Several office complexes on Layton Avenue and Airport Drive have vacancies ranging from $1,100 to $1,950 a month. All provide sufficient parking and would reduce time and expense traveling to the airport. In addition, the majority of current employees live in the southern and western suburbs, so a relocation to this area would reduce their daily commuting time to a downtown office.

SALE OF HIGHLAND AVENUE PROPERTY

The Highland Avenue building, although in need of major roof and plumbing repairs, is currently valued at $395,000 (Shorewest estimate). Realtors report that the property is highly marketable because of major rehabilitation of the former Pabst Brewery properties. Prospective buyers include merchants seeking retail or restaurant space and developers seeking to raze the building to allow expansion of neighboring buildings.

RECOMMENDATIONS

- Boylan Electric to seek advice and current estimates from three real estate agents.
- Boylan Electric to secure appropriate office space near the airport.
- Boylan Electric to allocate $5,000–$10,000 for minor repairs, landscaping, painting, and carpeting the lobby of 901 West Highland to enhance its marketability.
- Boylan Electric to prepare photographs, blueprints, and building specifications for realtors and potential buyers.

Résumés and Cover Letters

Résumés and cover letters are the first professional documents you will write in your career.

Résumés

Before starting to write a résumé, it is important to know what a résumé is and what a résumé is not.

A résumé is *not* a biography or a list of jobs—it is a ten-second ad. Research shows that the average executive spends just ten seconds looking at each résumé before rejecting it or setting it aside for further reading. A résumé does not have to list every job you have had or every school you attended. It should not be cluttered with employer addresses or names of references. It should briefly but clearly present facts, experiences, skills, and training that relate to a specific job or profession.

The goal of a résumé is to get an interview, not a job. Few people are hired based on a résumé. Résumés show an employer only that you are worth talking to. The goal of a résumé is to generate enough interest to prompt someone to call you for an interview.

You may need several résumés. Companies create different ads to sell the same product to different people. You might need three or four résumés that target specific jobs. For example, a nurse might create one résumé highlighting her intensive-care experience and another focusing on her work with abused children. Because résumés are quickly screened, they have to communicate at a glance. A résumé that tries to cover too many areas will be vague or confusing.

Strategies for Writing Résumés

1. **Understand that there are no absolute "rules" for writing résumés, only guidelines.** You may have heard people say that a résumé should be only one page or must never include your age. Because careers vary, there are exceptions.

2. **Develop your résumé by focusing on the job description or company.** Study the wording of want ads or job announcements, and highlight skills and experiences that directly match those listed in the ad.

3. **Include your full name, address, telephone number with area code, and e-mail address.**

```
            Linda Chen
     842 California Street # A1
   San Francisco, California 94108
          (415) 555-8989
        l.chen@sfnet.com
```

4. **Provide a clear objective statement describing the job you seek.** Avoid vague objectives such as "a position making use of my skills

and abilities" or "sales, marketing, or public relations." If you have different interests, create separate résumés for each field or job.

```
OBJECTIVE    Restaurant management
```

5. **Use a brief overview or summary to highlight key skills and experience.**

```
OVERVIEW     Three years experience in restau-
             rant management. Proven ability to
             hire, train, and motivate wait staff.
             Highly skilled in customer relations,
             menu design, and loss prevention.

SUMMARY      Restaurant Management
             *  Assistant Restaurant Manager,
                Dio's, 2005-2009
             *  Banquet Manager, Dio's 2006-2009
             *  Banquet hostess, Lady of Shanghai,
                2006
             *  Completed Hyatt management seminar,
                2006
```

You may find it easier to write the overview last, after you have identified your most important skills and accomplishments.

6. **List your most important credentials first.** If you are a college graduate with no professional experience, list education first. If a current or recent job relates to the job you seek, list experience first.

7. **Arrange education and job experience by time, beginning with the most recent.**

8. **Avoid general job descriptions.**

General

Office manager responsible for greeting visitors, maintaining staff schedules, ordering supplies, scheduling appointments, and processing payroll and expense reports.

Focus on individual accomplishments, and demonstrate the significance of your experience.

Improved

Office manager for 26 attorneys and paralegals in state's largest law firm specializing in medical malpractice. Individually responsible for scheduling appointments and processing payroll and expense reports. Reported directly to senior partners on hiring and firing of office staff.

9. **List training seminars, volunteer work, hobbies, and military service only if they directly relate to the job you want.**

10. **Do not include addresses of employers, names of supervisors, or references.** These details can be supplied after you are called in for an interview.

Recent Graduate with Experience

LINDA CHEN
842 California Street #A1
San Francisco, California 94108
(415) 555-8989
l.chen@sfnet.com

GOAL	Restaurant management
OVERVIEW	Associate degree in hotel and hospitality management. Three years experience in restaurant management, supervision and training of wait staff, inventory control, loss prevention, menu design, scheduling, and vendor ordering.

EXPERIENCE
2007–2009

Assistant Manager, DIO'S, San Francisco, CA
Directly assisted manager and owner of 50-seat Italian restaurant with three banquet rooms.
* Supervised all special events and banquet operations, including business luncheons, wedding receptions, fundraisers, and annual meetings.
* Individually responsible for managing banquet staff of 15.
* Assisted owner in redesigning banquet menu, pricing, and scheduling.

2006

Banquet Hostess, LADY OF SHANGHAI, San Francisco, CA
Hosted over 50 banquets and special events, including weddings, holiday parties, fundraisers, and business seminars.

EDUCATION

CALTECH EXTENSION, San Francisco, CA
Associate Degree in Hotel and Hospitality Management, May 2009.
Completed courses in business management, accounting, food service, food science, human relations, and marketing.
* 3.5 GPA.
* One of six students selected to assist faculty in annual alumni fundraising dinner.

HYATT HOTEL, San Francisco, CA
Completed food service management course, 2006.
* Sponsored by owner of Lady of Shanghai Restaurant.
* Toured major restaurants, banquet halls, and hotels in San Francisco.
* Participated in national online discussion group hosted by Hyatt Hotel corporation.

LANGUAGES
Fluent in Chinese.

References available on request.

Recent Graduate with Unrelated Experience

THERESA ALBANESE
2744 South Prairie Avenue
Chicago, IL 60615
(312) 555-7862
albaneset@earthlink.net

OBJECTIVE   Property casualty insurance sales

OVERVIEW   Six years experience in direct sales and sales management. Skilled in direct sales. Proven ability in developing leads through cold calling and tele-marketing. Experienced in training and motivating sales staff. Adept at developing online training and management tools to enhance sales support and productivity.

EDUCATION   LASALLE COMMUNITY COLLEGE, Chicago, IL
Associate Degree, Marketing, 2009.
Completed courses in sales management, tele-marketing, business law, insurance law, and inland marine insurance.
* Attended Kemper insurance seminar.
* Assisted in design and production of college ad campaign.

NATIONAL SALES INSTITUTE
Completed sales training program, 2006.

SALES   UNITED STATES ARMY, Chicago, IL
EXPERIENCE   Sgt. in Chicago recruiting office responsible for
2005–Present   statewide recruiting.
* Supervised 29 recruiters.
* Achieved over 100% sales goal each year.
* Introduced new database system to trace prospects.
* Refined telemarketing procedures.
* Developed online training seminars for new recruiters.
* Reduced overhead 15% first year.

2003–2005   Sgt. Public Affairs Office, Fort Sheridan, IL
* Prepared press releases, newsletters, and person-nel announcements.
* Trained staff in public presentations.
* Assisted in design of crisis communications policies.
* Rehearsed press conferences and media appearances with base commander.

References and transcripts available.

Cover Letters

Cover letters can be as important as the résumés they introduce. Résumés submitted without letters are often discarded because employers assume that applicants who do not take the time to address them personally are not serious. Résumés tend to be lists of cold facts; cover letters allow applicants to present themselves in a more personalized way. The letter lets applicants explain a job change, a period of unemployment, or a lack of formal education.

Strategies for Writing Cover Letters

In most instances, cover letters are short sales letters using standard business letter formats.

1. **Avoid beginning a cover letter with a simple announcement.**

   ```
   Dear Sir or Madam:

   This letter is to apply for the job of office
   supply sales rep advertised in the Times Picayune
   last week. . . .
   ```

2. **Open letters on a strong point emphasizing skills or experiences.**

   ```
   Dear Sir or Madam:

   In the last two years I opened thirty-six new ac-
   counts, increasing sales by nearly $750,000.
   ```

3. **Use the letter to include information not listed on the résumé.** Volunteer work, high school experiences, or travel that might not be suited to a résumé can appear in the letter—if they are career related.

4. **Refer to the résumé, indicating how it documents your skills and abilities.**

5. **End the letter with a brief summary of notable skills and experiences and a request for an interview.** To be more assertive, state that you will call the employer in two or three days to schedule an appointment.

Cover Letter Responding to a Want Ad

LINDA CHEN
842 California Street #A1
San Francisco, California 94108
(415) 555-8989
l.chen@sfnet.com

May 25, 2009

Kim Sung
Royal Canton
835 Grant Avenue
San Francisco, CA 94108

RE: Banquet Management position advertised in the *San Francisco Chronicle*, May 24, 2009

Dear Ms. Sung:

In the past three years, I have supervised over 150 banquets and special events, including wedding parties of 500, political fundraisers, VIP luncheons, sales meetings, and three Chinatown Improvement Association Annual Awards dinners.

For the past two years, I was the assistant manager at Dio's on Fisherman's Wharf, where I managed three banquet rooms and supervised a staff of fifteen. I am fully familiar with all aspects of banquet operations, from promotion and planning to ordering and scheduling. By working closely with special events planners, I was able to improve services and lower Dio's overhead by 10% the first year.

As my résumé shows, I have just received an associate degree in Hotel and Hospitality Management. In addition, I completed a Hyatt Hotel food service management course. Given my education in restaurant management and my experience in banquet operations, I believe I would be an effective banquet manager for Royal Canton. I look forward to the opportunity of discussing this position with you at your convenience. I can be reached at (415) 555-8989, or you can e-mail me at l.chen@sfnet.com.

I can e-mail you samples of banquet plans, employee training memos, and letters of recommendation, if you wish.

Sincerely yours,

Linda Chen

Linda Chen

Cover Letter Responding to Personal Referral

THERESA ALBANESE
2744 South Prairie Avenue
Chicago, IL 60615
(312) 555-7862
albaneset@earthlink.net

May 25, 2009

John Stephens
Great Lakes Casualty
500 North Dearborn Suite 823
Chicago, IL 60610-4910

RE: Insurance Agent Position

Dear Mr. Stephens:

Phil Douglass mentioned to me that Great Lakes Casualty has openings for additional insurance agents to call upon small- and medium-sized businesses in the greater Chicago area.

As my résumé shows, I have just completed my associate degree in marketing and have six years experience in direct sales. I am fully familiar with all areas of sales, from developing leads through cold calls and telemarketing to closing sales.

Before deciding to go into insurance, I served with the United States Army in the state's largest recruiting operation. I supervised 29 recruiters who achieved over 100% of sales goals each year through advanced training, including online sales seminars I designed, which are now used service-wide.

Given my knowledge of current insurance law and my practical experience in sales, I believe I could be an effective agent for Great Lakes Casualty. I would appreciate the opportunity to discuss this position with you at your convenience. I can be reached by phone at (312) 555-7862 or by e-mail at albaneset@earthlink.net.

Sincerely yours,

Theresa Albanese

Theresa Albanese

WORKING TOGETHER

Working with a group of students, discuss this résumé and cover letter, and recommend changes. Delete needless information, reword awkward phrases, eliminate repetitions, and edit for spelling and other mechanical errors. List details you would ask the student to add to make the résumé more impressive.

KURT RUDEL
262 Peachtree Street
Atlanta, Georgia 30303
(404) 555-5687

GOAL To ultimately own my own business. In the meantime seeking a position in tool and die.

EDUCATION Westside Highschool
2851 Heath Road
Macon, Georgia 31216
Graduted 2007
Was actively in band, school yearbook printing, football team.
* Assisted football coach while recovering from major knee injury.

Atlanta Area Technical and Community College
2500 Western Avenue
Atlanta, Geogia 30320
Graduated 2009
Completed tool and die program with courses in tool and die making, machining, quality control, industral design, and shop managment.

EXPERIENCE Southern Machine and Tool
2009 6536 North Industrial Drive
Atlanta, Georgia 30320
worked part time

2005–2007 Becker & Houghton
1287 Brooklawn Road NE
Atlanta, GA 30319
worked part time

References George Adello   Francine Demarest   Maria Valadez
(404) 555-8989   (404) 555-9090   (404) 555-8987

KURT RUDEL
262 Peachtree Street
Atlanta, Georgia 30303
(404) 555-5687

May 25, 2009

Dear Mr. Bechmann:

This letter is to reply to the ad in the <u>Atlanta Consitution</u> that appeared May 22, 2009 last week.

I think I would make an excellant employe at your company because I know a lot about tool and die even before going to school.

I worked at Becker & Houghton and Southern Machine and Tool while going to school

Please call me this week.

Thanking you for your attention,

Kurt

Kurt

CRITICAL THINKING

When you graduate and enter the job market, you will have to evaluate job offers. Consider the following offers, and choose the one that you feel best suits your goals and lifestyle. Write two or three paragraphs explaining your choice. If you wish, you can use classification to rank these opportunities from the most to least desirable.

a. A major organization in your hometown offers an entry-level position that provides security but limited upward mobility.

b. A major organization offers an entry-level position with excellent opportunities for promotion. The job is located five hundred miles away.

c. A newly formed organization needs someone with your skills. There may be excellent chances of heading a department in a few years and earning a substantial salary and bonus. However, the organization is just as likely to fail.

WHAT HAVE YOU WRITTEN?

Do you clearly explain which opportunity best suits your needs? Do you use cause and effect, comparison, and description to explain why one job better suits your goals than another? Have you organized details clearly?

KEITH BROFSKY/PHOTODISC/GETTY IMAGES

Write three or four paragraphs comparing how readers of business documents (résumés, letters, e-mails, and business reports) differ from readers of college assignments. How will an employer examine your résumé compared to an instructor evaluating a term paper?

WRITING ON THE WEB

Use a search engine such as Google or Yahoo!, and enter terms such as *résumés, writing résumés, cover letters,* and *applying for jobs* to locate current sites of interest.

POINTS TO REMEMBER

1. Business writing occurs in a very different environment than college writing. Be sensitive to the tone, style, and format used in your field.

2. E-mail is real mail. Write e-mail messages with the professionalism you would use in writing a first-class letter.

3. E-mail should be clear, concise, and direct. Avoid long, rambling messages.

4. Realize the limits of e-mail. Longer documents should be sent as attachments.

5. Résumés should be written concisely so they can be scanned in seconds.

6. Résumés should stress important points in your career—avoid including hobbies, high school jobs, and other minor details.

7. Cover letters should emphasize skills and experience and link you to the job you want.

8. Cover letters give you the opportunity to explain unrelated experience and add information not suited for the résumé.

Stockbyte/Alamy

Understanding Grammar

CHAPTER 22

Understanding the Sentence

CHAPTER GOALS

■ Realize That Sentences
  Express Complete
  Thoughts

■ Know the Parts of
  Speech

■ Understand the Role of
  Subjects and Verbs

■ Recognize Dependent
  and Independent
  Clauses

Bettmann/Corbis

Get Writing

The Ford Motor Company faced bankruptcy following World War
II. In 1949 it introduced a streamlined model with many new features that
became so popular it was called "the car that saved Ford." Over a million
were produced.

Write a paragraph that describes the types of cars that U.S. companies have to
produce today to compete with imports and attract buyers.

What Is a Sentence?

Everything that happens in life—natural occurrences, historical events, conflicts, thoughts, feelings, opinions, ideas, and experiences—is expressed in sentences. A main idea is connected to an action or linked with other words to state a thought. Long before they learn to read, children talk in sentences. Unwritten languages are spoken in sentences. The sentence is basic to all human communication.

> *Yond Cassius has a lean and hungry look.*
> **SHAKESPEARE**

> *We have nothing to fear but fear itself.*
> **FRANKLIN DELANO ROOSEVELT**

> *You can't eat the orange and throw the peel away—a man is not a piece of fruit!*
> **ARTHUR MILLER**

> *At last, after a long silence, women took to the streets.*
> **NAOMI WOLF**

> *A mind is a terrible thing to waste.*
> **UNITED NEGRO COLLEGE FUND**

> A sentence is a group of words that contains a subject and a verb and states a complete thought.

What Do You Know?

Underline the subjects (main idea) and circle the verbs (action words) in each sentence.

1. Children eat too much candy.

2. The mayor signed the bill this morning.

3. You work too hard!

4. Carlos and Erica married in August.

5. Kim designs software for accounting and tests computer systems for viruses.

6. The mayor and the citizens group demanded federal aid and insisted on new state funding.

7. Although he lived in Mexico until he was seven, Hector speaks only a few words of Spanish.

8. Originally designed by NASA, this computer chip helps most airliners stay on course.

9. The director, assisted by her staff of attorneys, prepared a response to the lawsuit.

10. Las Vegas and San Jose, among other Western cities, attract new homeowners.

Answers appear on the following page.

Get Writing

WHAT ARE YOU TRYING TO SAY?

Write a one-sentence response to each of the following questions.

1. What is the toughest course you are taking this semester?

_____

2. Who was your best friend in high school?

_____

3. How do you try to stay healthy?

_____

4. What is your ideal job?

_____

5. If you could change one thing about yourself, what would it be?

_____

WHAT HAVE YOU WRITTEN?

Read each sentence out loud. Have you expressed a complete thought? Does your sentence make sense? Does it state what you were thinking, what you were trying to say?

This chapter explains the working parts of a basic sentence. By understanding how a sentence works, you not only avoid making mistakes but also create writing that is fresh, interesting, and easy to read. To understand how sentences function, it is important to understand the **parts of speech**—words that have special functions.

The Parts Of Speech

Nouns
name persons, places, things, or ideas:
doctor, basement, Iraq, car, honesty

Pronouns
take the place of nouns:
he, she, they, it, this, that, what, which, hers, his, their

Verbs
express action:
fly, jump, consider, evaluate, swim, walk, dream, sing

link ideas:
is, are, was, were

Adjectives
add information about nouns or pronouns:
a *new* hat, a *red* pen, a *rented* car

Adverbs
add information about verbs:
shouted *boldly, carefully* planned, *hotly* debated

add information about adjectives:
very old car, *poorly* edited letter

add information about other adverbs:
rather awkwardly stated

Prepositions
link nouns and pronouns, expressing relationships between related words:
in the attic, *around* the house, *between* classes, *through* the tunnel

Conjunctions
link related parts of a sentence:

Coordinating conjunctions link parts of equal value:
and, for, or, yet, but, so, nor
She bought a hat, *and* he bought a shirt.

Subordinating conjunctions link dependent or less important parts:
While she bought a hat, he bought a shirt.

Interjections
express emotion or feeling that is not part of the basic sentence and are set off with commas or used with exclamation points:
Oh, he's fired? *Wow!*

Words can function as different parts of speech:

I bought *oil* (noun).
I am going to *oil* (verb) those rusty hinges.
There's a leak in your *oil* (adjective) pan.

Parts of speech can be single words or phrases, groups of related words that work together:

Dr. Green and her nurses (noun phrase)
sang and danced (verb phrase)
during the evening (prepositional phrase)

Answers to What Do You Know?
on pages 395–396

1. Subject: Children, Verb: eat
2. Subject: mayor, Verb: signed
3. Subject: You, Verb: work
4. Subjects: Carlos, Erica, Verb: married 5. Subject: Kim, Verbs: designs, tests 6. Subjects: mayor, citizens group, Verbs: demanded, insisted 7. Subject: Hector, Verb: speaks 8. Subject: computer chip, Verb: helps 9. Subject: director, Verb: prepared 10. Subjects: Las Vegas, San Jose, Verb: attract

Subjects and Verbs

The two most important parts of any sentence are the subject and verb. The **subject** is the actor or main topic that explains what the sentence is about. Subjects, which generally appear at the beginning of the sentence, may be a single word, several words, or a phrase:

Tanya drives a school bus.
Tanya and Eric drive school buses.
Driving a school bus requires skill.

Note: **-ing** verbs are called **gerunds** and can be used as subjects:

Swimming is fun.
Smoking is unhealthy.
Playing the piano takes practice.

Subjects are usually **nouns** or **pronouns**.

What Are Nouns?

Nouns are names of people, places, ideas, or things:

People	Places	Ideas	Things
doctor	basement	liberty	television
parents	valley	greed	airplane
farmer	farm	fear	nickel
pilot	plane	generosity	steel

Count nouns refer to things that may be singular or plural:

Singular	*Plural*
car	cars
woman	women
house	houses

Spelling note: Most nouns become plural by adding an "s," but some nouns have a plural spelling. See Chapter 35 for further information.

Noncount nouns refer to things that have one form for both singular and plural:

deer   gymnastics

Nouns may be **common** or **proper.** Common nouns refer to general people, places, ideas, or things. Proper nouns refer to specific people, places, ideas, or things.

Common	Proper
college	Triton Community College
town	Westfield
actor	Alec Baldwin
drugstore	Walgreens

Note: Proper nouns are always capitalized. See pages 586–587 for guidelines on capitalization.

KNOWING ENGLISH

Articles

English has three articles:

A and *an* are indefinite articles used with singular nouns to indicate something general:

> Use *a* before a consonant sound—*a* car, *a* girl, *a* loft, *a* wagon.
> Use *an* before a vowel sound or silent letter—*an* apple, *an* error, *an* honest man.

The is the definite article used with singular or plural nouns to indicate something specific: *the* car, *the* apples, *the* girl, *the* girls.

> *The* student borrowed *a* book. [A specific student borrowed some book.]
> *A* student borrowed *the* book. [Some student borrowed a specific book.]

Use articles carefully because they have different meanings:

> "Have *a* teacher sign your request" tells you to get the signature of *any* faculty member.
> "Have *the* teacher sign your request" means you must get the signature of *your* instructor.

What Are Pronouns?

Pronouns take the place of a noun and can be the subject, object, or possessive of a sentence.

Noun	Pronoun
doctor	he *or* she
students	they
computer	it

There are four types of pronouns: *personal, indefinite, relative,* and *demonstrative.*

Personal

Personal pronouns refer to people and have three forms, depending on how they are used in a sentence: **subjective, objective,** and **possessive.** **Subjective** pronouns work as subjects (*He* drove home). **Objective** pronouns work as objects of a verb or preposition (Maria drove *him* home). **Possessive** pronouns show ownership (*His* car is ready). This chart shows the different types of personal pronouns:

	Subjective		Objective		Possessive	
	Singular	**Plural**	**Singular**	**Plural**	**Singular**	**Plural**
1st person	I	we	me	us	my (mine)	our (ours)
2nd person	you	you	you	you	your (yours)	your (yours)
3rd person	he	they	him	them	his (his)	their (theirs)
	she		her		her (hers)	
	it		it		it (its)	

> **She** rented **our** cottage last summer, so **we** trusted **her** to babysit **my** son.
> **He** rented a truck because **it** was cheaper than **your** moving company.

Relative

Relative pronouns introduce noun and adjective clauses:

who, whoever, whom, whose   which, whichever   that, what, whatever

I will help **whoever** applies for the job.
Sara was offered a promotion, **which** she refused to take.

Demonstrative

Demonstrative pronouns indicate the noun they refer to (antecedent):
this, that, these, those

That *book* is fascinating.
These *books* are hard to read.

Indefinite

Indefinite pronouns refer to abstract persons or things:

Singular				Plural	Singular or Plural		
everyone	someone	anyone	no one	both	all	more	none
everybody	somebody	anybody	nobody	few	any	most	some
everything	something	anything	nothing	many			
each	another	either	neither				

Everyone agreed to donate money, but **no one** sent a check.
Someone should do **something**.

Top 20

PRONOUNS
Pronouns should match
the nouns they replace.
See Chapter 30.

Note: Pronouns must clearly refer to specific nouns called ***antecedents*** and agree with or match their singular or plural form.

Incorrect

The school is a disaster. Books are missing from the library. Computer work stations are vandalized. The halls are cluttered with trash. The locker rooms in the gym are strewn with broken equipment and towels. **They** just don't care.

Who does *they* refer to? Teachers, students, administrators, or parents?

Revised

The school is a disaster. Books are missing from the library. Computer work stations are vandalized. The halls are cluttered with trash. The locker rooms in the gym are strewn with broken equipment and towels. **The principal** just doesn't care.

Incorrect

Every student should try **their** best.
Student is a singular noun.

Revised

Every student should try **his or her** best.
Students should try **their** best.

See Chapter 30 for further information about pronouns.

KNOWING ENGLISH

Choosing Subjects

In some languages, a noun and pronoun can be used together as a subject, but in English, you must choose one:

Incorrect:	My **teacher she** wrote the book for our class.
Correct:	My **teacher** wrote the book for our class.

or

She wrote the book for our class.

EXERCISE 1   Locating Subjects

Underline the subject—the main idea—in each sentence. If the subject is plural, underline it twice. If the subject is a pronoun, circle it. To identify the subject, read the sentence carefully. What is the sentence about? What part is connected to an action or linked to other words?

1. The White House is the official residence of the president of the United States.

2. It was designed by the Irish-born architect James Hoban.

3. John Adams became the first president to live in the White House.

4. Since Jefferson's time, visitors have been allowed to tour the building.

5. Built by Theodore Roosevelt, the West Wing contains staff offices.

6. These offices are well known to viewers of the popular TV show *The West Wing.*

7. Over the years, the building fell into disrepair.

8. While Harry Truman was president, a floor collapsed.

9. Steel supports were added during a major renovation in the early 1950s.

10. In 1952 a bunker was added in case of nuclear attack.

Locating "Hidden Subjects"

Subjects don't always appear at the beginning of a sentence, and at first glance they may not look like important words. **Subjects are not possessive nouns, and they are not nouns in prepositional phrases.**

Inverted Sentences

In most sentences the subject comes before the verb:

Mary *sold* her Miami condo.
Last week **my mother** *bought* a new car.
Each week **we** *mail* comment cards to all our customers.

In some sentences this pattern is inverted or reversed so the subject follows the verb:

There *is* **someone** waiting to see you.
At the top of the hill *flies* an **American flag.**
Behind too many of these successful athletes *is* **steroid use.**

Possessives

Many sentences contain a subject that is the object of a possessive:

The school's **policy** angered both parents and students.
Sandy's **house** needs painting.
This spring's **designs** lack originality.

The subject in each sentence appears after a possessive. The subject is not *school* but the *school's* **policy.** One way to keep from being confused is to ask yourself who or what is doing the action or being linked to other ideas. What, for instance, "needs painting?"—*Sandy* or *Sandy's* **house?**

EXERCISE 2   Locating Subjects

Underline the subject in each sentence.

1. Your wallet probably contains a Social Security card.

2. There are Americans who are unaware of the card's history.

3. In 1936 the first cards were issued to track taxes and benefits.

4. The card's uses have expanded over the years.

5. A citizen's Social Security number has become a national identity number.

6. A person's number begins with an "area number" of three digits that indicates where the individual lives or where he or she applied for a card.

7. The highest area number is currently 772.

8. Perhaps because the Bible associates the number 666 with Satan, the Social Security Administration's policy is that 666 is not assigned as an area number.

9. The card's middle two numbers are called a "group number" that simply helps to break up a long number.

10. The last four digits are "serial numbers" issued in a straight sequence from 0001 to 9999.

Top 20

PREPOSITIONS
There are too many prepositions to memorize. Learn to recognize them as words that show relationships between ideas.

Prepositional Phrases

Prepositions are words that express relationships between ideas, usually regarding time and place:

about	before	like	since
above	below	near	to

across	during	of	toward
after	except	off	under
against	for	outside	with
along	from	over	within
around	inside	past	without

Prepositions can begin phrases: *before the play, during the game, down the street, above the clouds, after class, under the sofa, inside the engine, around the house, beyond the stars.* Prepositional phrases appear frequently in English:

> **Before the play** we talked **about the characters. In the last production** I thought the actors overlooked the potential humor **in the first scene.** The director sat **on the stage** and nodded. She agreed that the cast would try **for laughs in the next performance at eight o'clock.**

The only thing you have to remember about prepositional phrases is that **the subject of a sentence will not be found in a prepositional phrase.** The subject of the first sentence is *we,* not *play,* which is part of the prepositional phrase *before the play.*

EXERCISE 3   Locating Subjects and Prepositional Phrases

Underline prepositional phrases once and subjects twice in the following sentences.

1. In 1938 a promotional gimmick by a wallet company caused the newly formed Social Security Administration a major headache.

2. By 1938 forty million cards had been issued throughout the United States.

3. Almost everyone with a job was now expected to carry a card in his or her wallet or purse.

4. The company, based in Lockport, New York, wanted to show how easily the new card would fit into its wallets.

5. They printed fake cards and put them inside each wallet as a promotion and shipped them to department stores around the country.

6. An executive used his secretary's real Social Security number on the fake cards.

7. The word "Specimen" was printed across these cards to indicate they were samples.

8. Across the country, however, thousands of people began using the secretary's number as their own.

9. The Social Security Administration ran ads in major cities informing the public not to use this number.

10. Forty years later, a dozen people in the United States still used the Social Security number they found printed on a fake card in a wallet they bought in a department store.

Verbs

Verbs express action, link ideas, or help other verbs.

Action verbs show what the subject is doing:

The doctor **examined** the X-rays.
We **rejected** the director's proposal.
Italy **introduced** new techniques in motion pictures.

Action verbs also express "invisible" behavior, such as thinking or feeling:

Sara **dreamed** of competing in the Olympics.
Brazil **contains** massive rain forests.
Sean **doubts** the plan will work.

Linking verbs connect the subject to related ideas in the sentence. Linking verbs function much like an = sign. Instead of showing action, they express a relationship between ideas:

The bus **was** late.
Ted **is** a translator.
We **are** hopeful.

Helping verbs assist the main verb by adding information:

The doctor **will** *examine* the X-rays.
Sara **should** *win* at least one medal.
You **might** *assist* me tonight.

Verbs also tell time, explaining when the action or relationship takes place:

Past	She **ran** two miles yesterday.	She **was** a runner.
Present	She **runs** two miles every day.	She **is** a runner.
Future	She **will run** tonight.	She **will be** a runner.

See Chapter 29 for further information on verb tense.

Verbs are either singular or plural:

| **Singular** | She **runs** every day. | She **is** a runner. |
| **Plural** | They **run** every day. | They **are** runners. |

Verbs must **agree with** or **match** their subjects. Many subjects that look like plurals are singular:

Fifty dollars **is** not enough.   The *Senate* **is** debating the new budget.
United Technologies **is** a growth stock.   The *cost of oil* **is** increasing.

See Chapter 28 for further information on subject-verb agreement.

EXERCISE 4 Locating Action, Helping, and Linking Verbs

Underline the action verbs once, underline helping verbs twice, and circle the linking verbs in each of the following sentences.

TO: Pierce Jackson
FROM: Shae Knight

The Southern Car Dealers' Association holds its annual convention in Atlanta next month. Given problems in the credit industry, rising gas prices, and general economic uncertainty, most of our members report declining sales. I was impressed by your appearance at the Bankers of America Council meeting in Chattanooga last month. Your motivational presentation was very inspiring. Our members would benefit from your advice. Car dealers employ a large number of sales personnel who work on commission. Keeping them motivated during an economic downturn is challenging. I will call you next week to see if you are interested in a speaking engagement.

Shae Knight

KNOWING ENGLISH
Verb Phrases

Sometimes a verb consists of more than one word. This type of verb is called a **phrasal verb.** It consists of a verb and an **adverbial particle,** such as *down, on,* or *up.* The adverbial particle may explain that something is completed, as in *finish up* or *close down.* Some phrasal verbs use idioms such as "She *ran up* a huge bill" or "That old building *cries out* for repairs." The literal meaning of *ran up* or *cries out* does not explain the verb's action.

Most phrasal verbs can be separated by pronouns or short noun phrases:

I **picked** Joe's uncle **up** at noon.
I **picked** him **up** at noon.

Some phrasal verbs cannot be separated:

We **went over** the report together.

Standard dictionaries may not include phrasal verbs. If you cannot understand a phrasal verb in context, refer to a dictionary such as the *Longman Dictionary of American English* or the *Collins Cobuild Dictionary.*

EXERCISE 5   Locating Subjects and Verbs

Circle the subject of each sentence. Underline action verbs once, and underline linking verbs twice.

World History   Sean Parker

South American Leaders

Despite historical links to Spain, many of South America's leaders are of non-Spanish origin. Ambrosio O'Higgins, born in Ireland, emigrated to Spain and served as viceroy of Peru from 1796 until his death in 1801. His son, Bernardo O'Higgins, became the first leader of an independent Chile in 1817. Bernardo O'Higgins created the nation's military academy and approved the Chilean flag still in use. His attempts to establish democratic reforms were opposed by wealthy landowners. Overthrown by a revolt, O'Higgins left Chile and died years later in Peru. Alfredo Stroessner, the son of a German immigrant, ruled Paraguay. Stroessner was proud of his German heritage and was accused of turning his country into a safe haven for Nazi war criminals. Alberto Fujimori, the son of Japanese immigrants, served as Peru's president from 1990 to 2000. While visiting Japan in 2000, Fujimori resigned his office and became a Japanese citizen.

Building Sentences with Independent and Dependent Clauses

Sentences are made up of **clauses,** groups of related words that contain both a *subject* and a *verb.* There are two types of clauses: dependent and independent.

Dependent clauses contain a subject and verb but do *not* express a complete thought and are not sentences:

Top 20

FRAGMENTS

Dependent clauses used by themselves are fragments and should be avoided. See Chapter 23.

> Because I take the bus to work
> Before Sara moved to Florida
> After they moved to San Antonio

Dependent clauses have to be joined to an independent clause to create a sentence that expresses a complete thought:

> Because I take the bus to work, **I never pay for parking.**
> **I wanted to have a party** before Sara moved to Florida.
> After they moved to San Antonio, **Sam and Dana opened a restaurant.**

Independent clauses are groups of related words with a subject and verb that express a complete thought. They are sentences:

> I ride the bus.
> Sara moved to Florida.
> They own a restaurant in San Antonio.

Every sentence contains at least one independent clause.

Sentence Length

A sentence can consist of a single word, if it expresses a complete thought:

Run!
Stop!
Go!

In giving commands, the subject, "you," is implied or understood, so it does not have to actually appear in print for a sentence to state a complete thought. Conversely, a long train of words is not necessarily a sentence:

Because the community center, funded by the city, several nonprofit agencies, and hundreds of individual donors, wants to offer day-care services, which are in high demand by local parents.

Although there is a subject (*community center*) and a verb (*wants*), the words do not express a complete thought. If you read the sentence aloud, it sounds incomplete, like the introduction to an idea that does not appear. It leaves us wondering what the issue is about offering day-care services. Incomplete sentences—phrases and dependent clauses—are called **fragments.**

A Note On Fragments

Incomplete sentences that fail to express a complete thought are called *fragments*—a common writing error. Although sometimes written for emphasis, fragments should be avoided in college writing.

See Chapter 23 for help on avoiding fragments.

WORKING TOGETHER

Work with a group of students and revise this e-mail to change linking verbs to action verbs.

Attn: Technical Staff

The new schedule is going to take effect May 1. All employees who are working in the main assembly plant are to start at 7:30 a.m. instead of 8:00. First shift is set to end at 3:30 p.m. Employees in the sales, training, and administration departments are going to follow the old shift schedule from 8:00 a.m. to 4:00 p.m. Carla Fons is in charge of supervising the schedule. If you have any questions about your time or assignments, you are able to call her at ext. 5689.

Sarah Collins

District Supervisor

**Get Thinking
and Writing**

CRITICAL THINKING

If you could eliminate one inconvenience in your life this semester, what would it be and why? Do you need more closet space, better parking, new tires, a day-care center closer to your job, or more time to study? Write a paragraph to explain how solving this one minor inconvenience could make your life easier.

WHAT HAVE YOU WRITTEN?

Read your paragraph carefully. Circle the subjects and underline the verbs in each sentence. If you are unsure if some of your sentences are complete, see Chapter 23.

Choose one of your sentences, and write it below:

_____

Does the sentence clearly express what you were trying to say? Is the subject clearly defined? Is the verb effective? Could more specific words or stronger verbs (see Chapter 21) improve this sentence?

Summarize your points in one sentence. What is the main reason this inconvenience troubles you so much?

_____

Read this sentence carefully. Circle the subject, and underline the verb. How effective is your word choice (see Chapter 21)?

Does this sentence fully express your ideas? Try writing a different version:

_____

Ask a fellow student to read and comment on both sentences. Can your reader understand what you are trying to say?

What Have You Learned?

Underline the subjects (main idea) and circle the verbs (action and linking words) in each sentence. Underline linking verbs twice.

1. My sister's wedding cost $25,000.
2. Movies glamorize violence.
3. The burden of taxes falls on the middle class.
4. Many Americans vacation in Mexico.
5. The team's last play should have worked.
6. The mayor's proposal is being examined by our lawyers.
7. Sandy is nineteen years old.
8. The computers and printers are brand new.
9. It is raining.
10. Smoking is bad for your health.

Answers appear on the following page.

WRITING ON THE WEB

The Internet offers resources on sentence structure and style.

1. Using a search engine such as Yahoo! or Google, enter terms such as *sentence structure, parts of speech,* and *independent clauses* to locate current sites of interest.

2. Review past e-mails you have sent. What changes would you make in your writing? What would make your sentences more effective?

POINTS TO REMEMBER

1. The sentence is the basic unit of written English.

2. Sentences contain a subject and verb and express a complete thought.

3. Subjects explain what the sentence is about.

4. Verbs express action or link the subject to other words.

5. Phrases are groups of related words that form parts of sentences.

6. Dependent clauses are groups of related words with a subject and a verb but do not state a complete thought.

7. Independent clauses are groups of related words that contain a subject and a verb and express a complete thought.

8. All sentences contain at least one independent clause.

Answers to What Have You Learned? on page 408

1. Subject: wedding Verb: cost 2. Subject: Movies Verb: glamorize 3. Subject: burden Verb: falls 4. Subject: Americans Verb: vacation 5. Subject: play Verb: should have worked 6. Subject: proposal Verb: is being examined 7. Subject: Sandy Verb: is 8. Subject: computers and printers Verb: are 9. Subject: It Verb: is 10. Subject: Smoking Verb: is

CHAPTER 23

Avoiding Fragments

CHAPTER GOALS

- Identify Incomplete Sentences
- Repair Fragments

Reuters/Corbis

Get Writing

Do you think that television and movies glamorize crime and violence?

Write a paragraph expressing your views of the way gangsters are portrayed in popular culture. Do you think this is a dangerous influence, or do you think that people are able to separate fantasy from reality?

What Are Sentence Fragments?

In order to communicate, you have to express ideas in **sentences**—*groups of words that have a subject and a verb and express a complete thought:*

The bus arrives at noon.
Rose Fuentes teaches math.
Should we call a cab?

Each of these sentences states a complete thought and can stand on its own. They are **independent clauses.** They make sense all by themselves. Each sentence forms a pattern in which the subject—***bus, Rose Fuentes,*** and *we*—is connected to a verb expressing action—***arrives, teaches,*** *call* (see Chapter 22).

In speaking, we don't always express ourselves with complete sentences, especially when we are talking to people we know. In person, we communicate not only with words but also with gestures, tone, and facial expressions. We may stop mid-sentence and move to the next idea when we recognize that people are following our train of thought. Because our communication is interactive, listeners can interrupt us with questions if they become confused:

"Driving to the game?"
"Going with Al."
"He driving?"
"Sure."
"New car?"
"Got the Mustang Monday."
"He get the red one?"
"What else?"
"He buy or lease?"
"Buy."
"OK, see you at the game."
"Great."

When we write, however, our readers can rely only on the text we give them. If we don't write in complete sentences, we fail to express complete thoughts:

Bought a new car	*Who bought the new car?*
Because I am working second shift	*Then what happens?*
Should Sara and Cindy	*Should they do what?*

Because we often think faster than we can write, it is easy to make mistakes in expressing ideas. We skip words, shift our train of thought mid-sentence, and break off phrases. Instead of stating a complete idea, we leave our readers with partial sentences called **fragments:**

We flew to Chattanooga last weekend. The Chicago airport was crowded. Trying to find a place to park. Took over an hour. We almost missed our flight.

Revised

We flew to Chattanooga last weekend. The Chicago airport was crowded. **Trying to find a place to park took over an hour.** We almost missed our flight.

What Do You Know?

Label each sentence OK for a complete sentence or F for a sentence fragment.

1. _____ The team lagging in last place for the third week.

2. _____ Park behind the building.

3. _____ Attempting to maintain high grades and work overtime was too much for Sara.

4. _____ The mayor, who faces a tough reelection next month.

5. _____ On sale in stores nationwide.

Answers appear on the following page.

WHAT ARE YOU TRYING TO SAY?

Write a brief paragraph describing something you enjoyed in childhood—a favorite television show, a game or hobby, family vacations, or activities with friends.

_____

_____

_____

_____

_____

_____

_____

_____

_____

_____

_____

_____

_____

_____

Top 20

FRAGMENTS

Fragments are a common sentence problem. Learn how to identify and repair them.

WHAT HAVE YOU WRITTEN?

Read each sentence aloud. Does it state a complete thought? Can you underline both the subject and verb?

What Are Fragments?

Fragments are incomplete sentences. They lack a subject or a complete verb, or fail to express a complete thought.

Subject Missing

Danced all night. [Who *danced all night?*]

Revised

She danced all night.

Verb Missing

Jean the new car. [What was Jean doing?]

Revised

Jean washed the new car.

Incomplete Verb

Jean washing the new car. [*-ing* verbs cannot stand alone.]

Revised

Jean is washing the new car.

Incomplete Thought

Although Jean washed the new car. [It has a subject and verb but fails to express a whole idea.]

Revised

Jean washed the new car.

or

Although Jean washed the new car, the fenders were streaked with dirt.

The term **fragment** is misleading because it suggests something small, but length has nothing to do with writing complete sentences. A sentence can consist of a single word:

Duck!

The subject, "you," is understood. Commands express complete thoughts. A long trail of words, even those with subjects and verbs, can be a fragment if it fails to state a whole idea:

After the team won the first game of the playoffs and appeared ready to sweep the series with little chance of facing serious competition.

Although it looks like a long sentence, these words do not express a complete thought. Readers are left wondering. After the team won the first game, then what happened?

KNOWING ENGLISH

Including All Verbs

All parts of the verb phrase must be included to create a complete sentence. Be sure to include helping and linking verbs where needed:

Incorrect

The popularity of basketball **growing.**

Correct

The popularity of basketball **is growing.**

Note: **-ing** verbs cannot stand alone; they need **helping verbs** to create a sentence.

POINT TO REMEMBER

Reading aloud can help identify fragments. Ask yourself, "Does this statement express a complete thought?"

EXERCISE 1   Identifying Fragments

Label each of the following sentences OK for a correct sentence or F for a fragment. Reading a sentence aloud may help you tell whether the sentence expresses a complete idea.

1. _____ Nikola Tesla being born in Croatia in 1856.

2. _____ Emigrating to America in 1884 with just four cents in his pocket.

3. _____ Tesla worked with Thomas Alva Edison and assisted with the inventor's experiments with electricity.

4. _____ Tesla left the Edison organization and formed his own company in 1886.

5. _____ Tesla conducting research on X-rays and formulating ideas about developments such as radar and radio.

6. _____ Tesla became friends with Mark Twain.

7. _____ Although Tesla was a brilliant scientist who made many discoveries years before other researchers.

8. _____ His secretive nature and compulsive disorders led to speculations about his sanity and the nature of his research.

9. _____ Some people claiming Tesla invented a death ray and was communicating with Martians.

10. _____ These stories increased in 1943 when, immediately following his death, his papers were declared top secret by the War Department.

Correcting Fragments

There are two ways to correct fragments:

1. **Turn the fragment into a complete sentence by making sure that it expresses a complete thought:**

Fragments
> Yale being the center for this research.
> Public opinion surveys.
> The mayor designated.

Revised
> Yale **is** the center for this research. [complete verb added]
> **The new study is based on** public opinion surveys. [subject and verb added]

The mayor designated **Sandy Gomez to head the commission.**
[words added to express a complete thought]

2. **Attach the fragment to a sentence to state a complete thought.**
Fragments often occur when you write quickly and break off part of
a sentence:

Fragments

He bought a car. **While living in Florida.**
Constructed in 1873. The old church needs major repairs.

Revised

He bought a car **while living in Florida.**
Constructed in 1873, the old church needs major repairs.

EXERCISE 2 Identifying and Correcting Fragments

*Identify and correct the fragments by adding missing words or connecting
them to another fragment in the exercise. Some items may already be complete sentences.*

1. **Bipolar mood disorder, also known as manic depression.**

   _____

   _____

2. **Typically, sufferers experience mood swings from manic elation to depressed sadness.**

   _____

   _____

3. **In their high or manic states, patients extremely confident, powerful,
   and energetic.**

   _____

   _____

4. **In this hyper state may go on wild spending sprees, abruptly quit a job,
   make rash investments, or engage in high-risk behavior.**

   _____

   _____

5. **Although patients may announce plans to open businesses, launch new
   careers, or discover some invention.**

   _____

   _____

6. **They lacking ability to concentrate and experiencing agitation when
   questioned about the feasibility of their plans.**

   _____

   _____

   _____

   _____

7. While at other times patients slide into deep depression, feeling sad, lost, lonely, and inferior.

_____

_____

8. Leading them to quit jobs or drop out of school, believing they have no chance of success.

_____

_____

_____

9. Can be devastating, especially when patients make impulsive and illogical decisions in manic or depressed states.

_____

_____

10. Drugs and counseling are allowing many people to cope with this serious disorder.

_____

_____

EXERCISE 3   Identifying and Correcting Fragments

Identify and correct the fragments by adding missing words or connecting them to another fragment. Some items may already be complete sentences.

1. The Hollywood Walk of Fame attracting tourists visiting Los Angeles every year.

_____

_____

2. For many this is the highlight of their trip, pointing out the stars dedicated to their favorite actor or actress.

_____

_____

3. The first star on the Hollywood Walk of Fame honoring Joanne Woodward in 1960.

_____

_____

4. In the first year and a half, over 1,500 stars on the walk.

_____

_____

5. Today there are over 2,000 stars decorating the sidewalks along Hollywood Boulevard.

_____

_____

6. **About twenty-five new stars being added each year.**

_____

_____

7. **Because the stars have five categories honoring accomplishments in radio, motion pictures, television, theater, and the recording industry.**

_____

_____

8. **Cowboy star Gene Autry the only person to have been awarded stars in all five categories.**

_____

_____

9. **Not all the stars are dedicated to humans.**

_____

_____

10. **Mickey Mouse and Rin Tin Tin having been honored as well.**

_____

_____

EXERCISE 4   Correcting Fragments

Revise the following paragraph to correct fragments.

Juanita Ramon   World History 101

Zapata

Emiliano Zapata was born in Morelos, Mexico, in 1879, to a family of independent ranchers. Although Zapata was known for wearing flashy clothing in his youth. He always maintained respect for the impoverished peasants. By thirty he had become a spokesperson for his village. Zapata championing the rights of Indians in Morelos. Assisting redistribution of land and defending the villagers' claims in property disputes with wealthy ranchers. Becoming increasingly frustrated by the government's bias in favor of wealthy landowners. Zapata began using force to seize land. Taking a leading role in the 1910 Mexican Revolution, which deposed the Diaz regime. Zapata was disillusioned with the new government's failure to address the needs for effective land reform. Zapata and his followers refused to disarm. The newly reformed Mexican government attempting to bribe Zapata's followers to betray him. Placing a bounty on his head. In April 1919, Mexican General Guajardo offered to meet with Zapata. When Zapata appeared for their meeting, he was shot to death. Although the Zapata movement diminished in influence after his death. Emiliano Zapata remains an honored hero in Mexico. Where his memory still inspires organizations concerned with poverty and Indian rights.

_____

_____

_____

_____

_____

_____

_____

_____

_____

_____

_____

_____

_____

_____

_____

_____

_____

EXERCISE 5   Correcting Fragments

Revise the following letter to correct fragments.

Bianca Jameson Productions
bianca.jameson@bjp.com

April 15, 2009

Sidney Hillerman:

Having read your proposal. I am still concerned about the fall concert tour. I fully understanding your desire to give your band the maximum exposure in the month following the release of their first CD. But I am concerned about the costs this tour might entail. Because the Jersey Girls have never played outside New York. I wonder if they can sell tickets in the cities you list. Chicago, New Orleans, Miami, Dallas, Los Angeles, and San Francisco. Personally, they strike me as a regional group. May I suggest that you reconsider the offer from Trump for a two-month run in Atlantic City? Selling out there providing a lot of exposure and a guaranteed ten thousand a week. While a national tour is always desirable. The cost of travel and accommodations could absorb all your profits if ticket sales are less than expected.

Call me Tuesday, and we can talk.

Bianca Jameson, President

_____

_____

_____

_____

_____

_____

_____

_____

_____

_____

WORKING TOGETHER

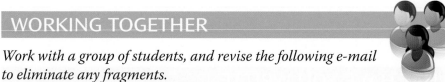

Work with a group of students, and revise the following e-mail to eliminate any fragments.

Attn: All technical staff:

This Monday a seminar being held at Foundation Hall from 9 a.m. to 3 p.m. Concerning the new health-care plan being offered by Empire State Insurance. All employees should plan to attend this important meeting. Medical, dental, and long-term health-care policies being discussed at this meeting. Although Passaic Union will continue to fully pay for your coverage and there will no additional fees. It is important you attend this seminar. You will have to make decisions regarding deductibles and disability options.

Kelly Koberstein
ext. 7878
koberstein.k@passaicunion.org

CRITICAL THINKING

Cheating has always been an issue in college. Today many students use the Internet to download research papers. What action should instructors and administrators take when students are caught cheating? Should the student fail the course or be expelled? Should students be given a second chance?

Get Thinking and Writing

Write a paragraph stating your opinion of how students should be punished for cheating.

When you finish writing, identify and correct any fragments by adding missing elements or attaching the fragment to a related sentence.

1. Select one of your sentences, and write it below:

   _____

   _____

2. Circle the subject, and underline the verb.
3. Why does this sentence state a complete thought? What is the relationship between the subject and the verb?
4. Read the sentence aloud. Could you make the sentence more effective by replacing abstract words with specific nouns and stronger verbs (see Chapter 19)? Try writing a different version of your sentence:

   _____

   _____

WHAT HAVE YOU WRITTEN?

Review writing exercises in this book, papers written for other courses, work you did in high school, and e-mail sent to friends for fragments. Do you have a tendency to forget words or break off phrases to create incomplete sentences? If you discover fragments or continue to make them in upcoming assignments, review this chapter. When you write, refer to pages 675–676 in the handbook.

What Have You Learned?

Label each sentence OK for a complete sentence or F for a sentence fragment.

1. _____ Don't stand there.

2. _____ Although he was running a fever, he hit two home runs.

3. _____ While the Senate was debating the bill on stem-cell research and considering nominees for the federal courts.

4. _____ Before the test, the students rushed to the library to review their notes.

5. _____ Trapped by falling debris after the earthquake struck.

Answers appear on the following page.

WRITING ON THE WEB

Using a search engine such as Yahoo! or Google, enter the terms *sentence fragment, grammar,* and *sentence structure* to locate current sites of interest.

POINTS TO REMEMBER

1. Sentences contain a subject and a verb and express a complete thought.

2. Sentence fragments are incomplete sentences—they lack a subject or a verb or fail to express a complete thought.

3. Reading a sentence aloud is the best way to detect a fragment. If a sentence sounds incomplete or like an introduction to something unstated, it is probably a fragment.

4. Fragments can be corrected in two ways:

   a. create a complete sentence by adding missing elements

   b. attach the fragment to a related sentence to state a complete thought

---

Answers to What Have You Learned? on page 420

1. OK 2. OK 3. F 4. OK 5. F

CHAPTER 24

Building Sentences Using Coordination and Subordination

CHAPTER GOALS

- Join Independent Clauses to Create Compound Sentences

- Join Independent and Dependent Clauses to Create Complex Sentences

- Use Coordination and Subordination to Show the Relationships Between Ideas

Lee Stone/Sygma/CORBIS

Get Writing

Should women serve in combat? Why or why not?

Write one or more paragraphs stating your views.

We communicate in sentences—independent clauses that have a subject and a verb and express a complete thought. Chapter 22 explains the working parts of a **simple sentence,** *a sentence with a single independent clause.* We do not always write in simple sentences. In telling a story, describing a person, or stating an argument, we often **coordinate** ideas, *creating sentences with more than one complete thought.* We place two or three independent clauses in a single sentence to demonstrate how one idea affects another:

> **My car is in the garage,** so **I will take the bus to work.**
> *independent clause   independent clause*

> **The engine plant is in El Paso,** and **the tire factory is in Austin.**
> *independent clause   independent clause*

In other cases we may **subordinate** a less important idea, making it a *dependent clause* connected to an *independent clause* to create a sentence:

> *After we lost the game,* **we were in no mood to go to the party.**
> *dependent clause   independent clause*

> **Sidney quit smoking** *after his doctor told him he had high blood pressure.*
> *independent clause   dependent clause*

Without coordination and subordination, writing can become a list of choppy and repetitive simple sentences:

> My parents moved to Las Vegas last year. I thought I would hate it. I am not interested in nightlife. I do not drink. I do not gamble. I was surprised. I learned that Las Vegas has a lot to offer besides casinos. I had only seen images of the Strip on television. I had no idea that Las Vegas had so many golf courses, parks, and restaurants. I had heard of Lake Mead. I did not know it would be only forty-five minutes from our house. My dad bought a boat. I love it. For me Las Vegas means sailboats, not slot machines.

Joining ideas with coordination and subordination creates writing that is more interesting and easier to follow:

> *When my parents moved to Las Vegas last year,* **I thought I would hate it.** I am not interested in nightlife. **I do not drink,** and **I do not gamble. I was surprised** *when I learned that Las Vegas has a lot to offer besides casinos. Because I had only seen images of the Strip on television,* **I had no idea that Las Vegas had so many golf courses, parks, and restaurants. I had heard of Lake Mead,** but **I did not know it would be only forty-five minutes from our house. My dad bought a boat,** *which I love.* For me Las Vegas means sailboats, not slot machines.

What Are Coordination and Subordination?

Coordination creates **compound sentences** that join **independent clauses** using either semicolons or commas and coordinating conjunctions (*and, or, nor, for, yet, but, so*). You can think of **compound sentences** as double or sometimes triple sentences because they join two or more simple sentences (*independent clauses*) that state complete thoughts:

Simple Sentences (Independent Clauses)
I go to college.   I work full time.

Compound Sentences Created by Coordination
I go to college; I work full time.
I go to college, and I work full time.

Subordination creates **complex sentences** that join an **independent clause** (*simple sentence*) stating a complete thought with **dependent clauses** that add additional information or state a less-important idea:

Simple Sentence (Independent Clause)
I work overtime.

Dependent Clause
when I need money

Complex Sentence Created by Subordination
I work overtime when I need money.
When I need money, I work overtime.*

Note: When the dependent clause begins a sentence, it is set off with a comma.

> *Note:* Subordination is a way of avoiding *fragments* (Chapter 23) by connecting dependent clauses to independent ones.

KNOWING ENGLISH

Choosing The Right Conjunction

You can connect clauses with either **a subordinating conjunction or a coordinating conjunction**—*but not both. Use one or the other:*

Incorrect
Although we returned to campus early, **but** there were long lines at the bookstore.

Correct
Although we returned to campus early, there were long lines at the bookstore.
We returned to campus early, **but** there were long lines at the bookstore.

What Do You Know?

Place a C next to sentences that use coordination to join independent clauses and an S next to sentences that use subordination to join dependent clauses to independent clauses. Mark simple sentences—those with one independent clause—with an X.

1. _____ Although we ran into heavy traffic, we made it to the airport on time.

2. _____ Ted has great speed, but George has greater accuracy.

3. _____ Toronto is the capital of Ontario; Victoria is the capital of British Columbia.

4. _____ Westfield is a popular suburb in Northern New Jersey not far from Manhattan.

5. _____ Frank took the summer off, but the rest of us are going to summer school.

6. _____ It's official; we're getting married!

7. _____ The Chinese are building the biggest dam in the world, which will be the greatest single construction project in human history.

8. _____ The bus takes an hour and a half; the train takes forty-five minutes.

9. _____ Maintaining accurate records of our income and costs is essential if we want to apply for federal funding or attract charitable donations.

10. _____ After we began using recycled products, we discovered that our production costs have fallen almost 15 percent.

Answers appear on the following page.

WHAT ARE YOU TRYING TO SAY?

Get Writing

Write a paragraph that describes your best friend. In addition to providing details about his or her appearance, describe personality qualities that you admire. Why do you consider this person important in your life? How did you meet? How does this person enrich your life?

_____

_____

_____

_____

_____

_____

_____

_____
_____
_____
_____
_____
_____

WHAT HAVE YOU WRITTEN?

Underline the independent clauses in your paragraph—groups of words that have a subject and a verb and express a complete thought. Do some sentences contain more than one complete thought? Did you create any sentences that contained a dependent clause (a group of words with a subject and a verb that does not state a complete thought)?

If all the sentences are single independent clauses or simple sentences, read your paragraph out loud. Would it make your ideas clearer if some of these sentences were combined into a single statement?

Types of Sentences

Just as writers make choices about using different words to express their ideas, they also use different types of sentences. Sentence types are determined by the number and kind of clauses they contain.

A **simple sentence** consists of a single independent clause. A simple sentence is not necessarily short or "simple" to read. Although it may contain multiple subjects and verbs and numerous phrases set off with commas, it expresses a single thought:

Paul drives.
Paul and Nancy drive antique cars in local parades.
Interested in advertising their real estate business, Paul and Nancy drive antique cars in local parades.

A **compound sentence** contains two or more independent clauses but no dependent clauses:

Pacific Mutual sells property insurance; Atlantic Mutual sells life insurance.
(two independent clauses joined by a semicolon)

Jim wants to stay in New York, but **Juanita longs to move to California.**
(two independent clauses joined with a comma and coordinating conjunction)

A **complex sentence** contains one independent clause and one or more dependent clauses:

James is working out twice a day *because he wants to try out for the Olympics.*

Because he wants to try out for the Olympics, **James is working out twice a day.**
(When a dependent clause begins a complex sentence, it is set off with a comma.)

A **compound-complex sentence** contains at least two independent clauses and one or more dependent clauses:

Teachers buy school supplies for their students, and **they often pay for class trips themselves,** *because the new budget has cut funding to elementary schools.*

Because the new budget has cut funding to elementary schools, **teachers buy school supplies for their students,** and **they often pay for class trips themselves.**

The type of sentence you write should reflect your thoughts. Important ideas should be stated in simple sentences to highlight their significance. Equally important ideas can be connected in compound sentences to show cause and effect, choice, or contrast. Minor ideas can be linked to complete thoughts in complex sentences as dependent clauses.

Coordination

Coordination creates *compound sentences* by linking two or more simple sentences (independent clauses). There are two methods of joining simple sentences:

1. **Use a comma [,] and a coordinating conjunction** *(and, or, nor, for, yet, but, so).*

2. **Use a semicolon [;].**

Coordinating Conjunctions

Coordinating conjunctions join simple sentences and show the relationship between the two complete thoughts:

and	adds an idea	We flew to Chicago, **and** we rented a hotel room.
or	shows choice	I will get a job, **or** I will sell the car.
nor	adds an idea when the first is negative	He was neither a scholar, **nor** was he a gentleman.
but	shows contrast	He studied hard, **but** he failed the test.
yet	shows contrast	She never studied, **yet** she got an A.
for	shows a reason	He left town, **for** he had lost his job.
so	shows cause and effect	I had a headache, **so** I left work early.

A simple diagram can demonstrate the way to use coordinating conjunctions:

INDEPENDENT CLAUSE, **and** INDEPENDENT CLAUSE.
or
nor
but
yet
for
so

Note: A comma always comes before the coordinating conjunction.
Parallel independent clauses can also be linked with a semicolon:

Bruno writes about domestic issues; Rosa writes about foreign policy issues.
The mayor supports the plan; the city council is against it.

Semicolons are also used to join independent clauses with adverbial conjunctions (*however, meanwhile,* etc.), which are set off with commas:

Bruno writes about domestic issues; meanwhile, Rosa writes about foreign policy.
The mayor supports the plan; however, the city council is against it.

Adverbial Conjunctions

Adverbial conjunctions link independent clauses, but unlike coordinating conjunctions—*and, or, nor, for, yet, but, so*—they are set off with a comma and require a semicolon:

INDEPENDENT CLAUSE; **adverbial conjunction,** INDEPENDENT CLAUSE

Common Adverbial Conjunctions

To Add Ideas

in addition   likewise   besides
moreover   furthermore

The car needs a muffler; **in addition,** it needs tires.
They won't fix the roof; **furthermore,** they refused to paint the garage.

To Show Choice

instead   otherwise

He did not study; **instead,** he went for coffee.
He went on a diet; **otherwise,** he faced increasing hypertension.

To Show Contrast

however   nonetheless   nevertheless

We rehearsed for two weeks; **however,** we never got the scene right.
The weather was terrible; **nevertheless,** everyone loved the trip.

To Show Time

meanwhile

The teachers asked for more resources; **meanwhile,** the parents looked for other schools.

To Show Cause and Effect

thus   therefore   consequently

accordingly   hence

Our house lost power; **hence,** we canceled the party.
The buses are on strike; **therefore,** we are paying workers to take cabs.

To Show Emphasis

indeed   in fact

The students are angry about the tuition hike; **indeed,** several have transferred.
He did poorly during the World Series; **in fact,** he never got a single hit.

You don't have to memorize all the adverbial conjunctions. Just remember you need to use a semicolon unless independent clauses are joined with *and, or, for, nor, yet, but,* or *so.*

AVOID RUN-ONS
Run-ons are a common writing problem. Learn to identify and repair them.

POINT TO REMEMBER

If you fail to join two independent clauses with a comma and a coordinating conjunction or a semicolon, you create errors called run-ons and comma splices. See Chapter 25 for strategies to spot and repair these errors.

EXERCISE 1   Combining Simple Sentences (Independent Clauses) Using Coordinating Conjunctions and Commas

1. Write two simple sentences joined by *and:*

_____

_____

2. Write two simple sentences joined by *or:*

_____

_____

3. Write two simple sentences joined by *but:*

_____

_____

4. Write two simple sentences joined by *yet*:

_____

_____

5. Write two simple sentences joined by *so*:

_____

_____

EXERCISE 2   Combining Simple Sentences (Independent Clauses) Using Coordinating Conjunctions and Commas

Combine each pair of sentences using a comma and a coordinating conjunction.

1. The Brooklyn Bridge was an engineering triumph.

It claimed the lives of twenty-seven workers.

_____

_____

2. The bridge was dedicated with great ceremony on May 24, 1883.

Tragedy struck a week later.

_____

_____

3. A rumor that the bridge was about to collapse caused a panic.

Twelve people were trampled to death.

_____

_____

4. Robert Odlum jumped off the bridge as a stunt in 1885.

He died of internal injuries from the fall.

_____

_____

5. In 1886 Steve Brodie achieved instant fame when he claimed to have survived a jump from the Brooklyn Bridge.

Most people believe that a dummy was used in the stunt.

_____

_____

_____

EXERCISE 3   Combining Simple Sentences (Independent Clauses) Using Coordinating Conjunctions

Add a second independent clause using the coordinating conjunction indicated. Read the sentence aloud to make sure that it makes sense.

1. The team won the first five games, *but* _____

_____

2. The mayor won an overwhelming victory, *and* _____

_____

3. The largest business in town has gone bankrupt, *so* _____

_____

4. You can fly to Chicago, *or* _____

_____

5. My car needs a lot of work, *yet* _____

_____

EXERCISE 4   Combining Simple Sentences (Independent Clauses) Using Semicolons

Write a sentence joining two independent clauses by a semicolon. Make sure that the statement you add is a complete sentence.

1. _____ **;**

_____

2. _____ **;**

_____

3. _____ **; therefore,**

_____

4. _____ **; however,**

_____

_____

5. _____ **; in fact,**

_____

EXERCISE 5 Combining Simple Sentences (Independent Clauses) with Semicolons

Add a second independent clause to each sentence. Read each sentence aloud to make sure that it makes sense.

1. I love walking to school in the fall; _____

_____

2. Commuting to work can be stressful; _____

_____

3. Math is my toughest course this semester; _____

_____

4. My brother loves the Yankees; _____

_____

EXERCISE 6 Using Compound Sentences to Eliminate Choppy Sentences

Rewrite the following paragraph to eliminate choppy sentences by creating compound sentences using coordination.

NOTICE TO RESIDENTS

The Betz Condominiums are undergoing major repairs this summer. The parking garage will be painted. The driveway will be repaved. This will cause some inconvenience. Parking will be available across the street. Residents will receive a 50-percent discount. The elevators in North Tower will be replaced. The stairwells will be repainted. The work will be done in stages. Residents should not be without elevator service. The pool will be retiled. It will be closed for approximately two weeks. The gym and sauna do not require repairs. They will be open all summer. The rooftop garden will be replanted. New lighting will be installed. We expect all work to be completed by August 15th.

Subordination

Subordination creates *complex* sentences by joining an independent clause with one or more dependent clauses. Dependent clauses contain a subject and a verb but cannot stand alone. They are incomplete thoughts and need to be joined to an independent clause to make sense.

Dependent Clause Stating an Incomplete Thought

Because it started to rain.

After we left the party.

Dependent clauses are **fragments** and should not stand alone (see Chapter 23).

Dependent Clause Linked to an Independent Clause Stating a Complete Thought

Because it started to rain, **we moved the reception to the auditorium.**
A fight broke out after we left the party.

POINT TO REMEMBER

Place a comma after a dependent clause when it comes before an independent clause:

Because I missed the bus, I was late for school.

I was late for school because I missed the bus. [no comma needed]

KNOWING ENGLISH

Using Subordinating Conjunctions in Dependent Clauses

Begin clauses with a subordinating conjunction rather than a preposition.

Incorrect

My mother's family moved to the United States **because of** they wanted a better life.

Correct

My mother's family moved to the United States **because** they wanted a better life.

Because is a subordinating conjunction. *Because of* is a two-word preposition that must be followed by a noun or pronoun:

The flight was delayed **because of** fog.
We were delayed **because of** him.

Subordination helps distinguish between important ideas and minor details. Without subordination, writing can be awkward and hard to follow:

I always loved my brother's Corvette. I should never have bought it. I cannot afford it. I am only working part-time. I earn enough to pay for gas. The insurance is more than I can handle. I drive at least eighty miles a day. I will soon need new tires.

Revised

Although I always loved my brother's Corvette, I should never have bought it. I cannot afford it **because I am only working part-time. While**

I earn enough to pay for gas, the insurance is more than I can handle.
Because I drive at least eighty miles a day, I will soon need new tires.

Dependent clauses can be placed at the beginning, within, and at the end of an independent clause. When they come first or within an independent clause, they are set off with commas:

Primary Idea	*Secondary Idea*
I learned Spanish.	I lived in Cancun.
Sid canceled his vacation.	His mother became ill.
The sanitation workers are on strike.	Their demands have been ignored.

Complex Sentences

Because I lived in Cancun, I learned Spanish.

Sid canceled his vacation when his mother became ill.

The sanitation workers, whose demands have been ignored, are on strike.

EXERCISE 7   Combining Ideas Using Subordination

Create complex sentences by joining the dependent and independent clauses. If the dependent clause comes first, set it off with a comma.

1. **Basil Rathbone became internationally famous.**

   When he played Sherlock Holmes.

   _____

   _____

   _____

   _____

2. **Although the show received good reviews.**

   ***Iron Man* was abruptly canceled.**

   _____

   _____

3. **The boardwalk restaurants do well even in bad weather.**

   Because tourists have to stay indoors when it rains.

   _____

   _____

   _____

   _____

4. I take a cab to work.

When my sister needs the car.

_____

_____

5. Although it will be cheaper to build a new building.

The alumni want to restore Old Main.

_____

_____

_____

_____

EXERCISE 8   Using Coordination and Subordination

The following passage is stated in simple sentences. Revise it, and create compound and complex sentences to make it more interesting and easier to read.

American History 112   Karen Rumski

The Lost Colony

A small North Carolina island holds a secret. It was the site of an early English colony that mysteriously disappeared. Historians and scientists have conducted research for decades. No satisfactory answer has been found. In 1585 colonists were sent to America by Sir Walter Raleigh. They built a settlement on Roanoke Island. More settlers arrived in 1587. Virginia Dare was born on the island that August. She was the first English child born in America. She was the granddaughter of John White. John White was the governor of the colony. John White sailed to England for supplies. His return trip was delayed three years. A war interrupted his plans. He reached the colony. He found it empty. The hundred colonists had disappeared. There was no sign of a battle. There was no sign of violence. The people had just vanished. There was only a single clue. The word "Croatoan" was found carved on a tree. No one could explain what happened to the settlement. It became known as "The Lost Colony." Researchers think they were abducted by Native American tribes or died during a severe drought. No evidence of their fate has been discovered.

After completing your draft, read it aloud. Have you reduced choppy and awkward sentences? Does your version make the essay easier to follow?

WORKING TOGETHER

Work with a group of other students, and reduce the choppy sentences in this business letter by using coordination and subordination.

Dear Ms. Mendoza:

This year the annual convention will be held in Miami. The Miami location is best suited for our needs. We draw attendees from across the country. Our fastest-growing operations are located in Florida.

I would like you to make a presentation about online sales. Many of our new sales representatives have no experience with Internet marketing. As of March 1st we will no longer sell products at Wal-Mart or Target. We will have to rely more on online sales to continue our growth.

You have great experience in developing an online catalog. This makes you a valuable asset to us. I am sure our sales reps can learn a lot from you. They will appreciate any insights you can give them.

Please call me this week. We can discuss details.

Sincerely,

Sid Hussani

Get Thinking and Writing

CRITICAL THINKING

The United States is a superpower that participates in a global economy. To prosper in the twenty-first century, Americans will have to conduct business in dozens of foreign countries. Do you think that every college student should be required to learn a foreign language? Why or why not? Write a paragraph stating your views.

WHAT HAVE YOU WRITTEN?

When you complete your paragraph, read over your work. Underline each independent clause once and each dependent clause twice. Did you create effective compound and complex sentences and punctuate them correctly? Read your sentences aloud. Are there missing words, awkward phrases, or confusing shifts that need revising?

1. Select one of the compound sentences, and write it below:

_____

_____

Are the independent clauses closely related? Do they belong in the same sentence? Could you subordinate one of the ideas to create a complex sentence? Try writing a complex sentence that logically reflects the relationship between the ideas:

_____

_____

Does this complex sentence make sense—or would a compound sentence better express what you are trying to say?

Have you used the best method to join the two ideas? If you used a comma and coordinating conjunction, rewrite the sentence using a semicolon:

_____

_____

How does this version affect meaning? Does it make sense? Why are coordinating conjunctions important?

2. Select one of your complex sentences, and write it below:

_____

_____

Underline the independent clause. Is it the more important idea? Does the dependent clause express only additional or less-important information?

Turn the dependent clause into an independent one, and create a compound sentence—remember to use a semicolon or a comma with and, or, for, nor, yet, but, or so to join the two clauses:

_____

_____

Does the compound sentence better express what you are trying to say, or does it appear illogical or awkward?

Write the two independent clauses as separate simple sentences:

_____

_____

How does stating these ideas in two sentences alter the impact of your ideas? Does it better express what you are trying to say or only create two choppy sentences?

When you are trying to express an important or complex idea, consider writing two or more versions using simple, compound, and complex sentences. Read them aloud, and select the sentences that best reflect your ideas.

What Have You Learned?

Place a C next to sentences that use coordination to join independent clauses and an S next to sentences that use subordination to join dependent clauses to independent clauses. Mark simple sentences—those with one independent clause—with an X.

1. _____ New York is the largest city on the East Coast; Los Angeles is the largest city on the West Coast.
2. _____ Detroit is on Eastern Standard Time.
3. _____ George found that his antique car was difficult to maintain and cost too much to insure.
4. _____ The teachers are willing to donate their time, and some parents have offered money.
5. _____ The buses are slow; the cabs are hard to find.
6. _____ Because it has no calories and can ease hunger pangs, coffee is popular with dieters.
7. _____ I took Advanced Algebra after I got a perfect score on the entrance exam.
8. _____ She has a degree in business and a certificate in accounting, but Deborah lets her brother do the taxes.
9. _____ The governor angered the teachers' union when she claimed teachers deserved only part-time pay for part-time work.
10. _____ Mexico abolished slavery before the United States did.

Answers appear below.

WRITING ON THE WEB

Using a search engine such as Yahoo! or Google, enter terms such as *simple sentence, compound sentence, complex sentence, independent clause,* and *dependent clause* to locate current sites of interest.

POINTS TO REMEMBER

1. Simple sentences contain one independent clause and express a single complete thought.
2. Compound sentences link two or more independent clauses with a semicolon (;) or a comma (,) and a coordinating conjunction (and, or, yet, but, so, for, nor).
3. Complex sentences link one or more dependent clauses with a single independent clause.
4. Compound-complex sentences link one or more dependent clauses to two or more independent clauses.
5. Use compound sentences to coordinate ideas of equal importance.
6. Use complex sentences to link an important idea with a dependent clause adding secondary information.
7. Use sentence structure to demonstrate the relationship between your ideas.

Answers to What Have You Learned?

1. C 2. X 3. X 4. C 5. C 6. S 7. S. 8. C 9. S 10. S

CHAPTER 25

Repairing Run-ons and Comma Splices

Andrew Lichenstein/Sygma/CORBIS

CHAPTER GOAL

■ Identify and Repair Run-ons and Comma Splices

Get Writing

How should the United States cope with illegal immigration? Do we need tighter border security? Should people who hire undocumented workers be punished more severely? Should immigration policy be changed to admit guest workers? What can be done to prevent the deaths of people trying to cross the border? Are those concerned about border security motivated by fears of terrorism or racism?

Write one or more paragraphs expressing your views about illegal immigrants, border security, or the plight of undocumented workers.

What Are Run-ons?

Run-ons are not wordy sentences that "run on" too long. **Run-ons are incorrectly punctuated compound sentences.** Chapter 24 explains how independent clauses are coordinated to create compound sentences that join two or more complete thoughts. You can think of them as "double" or "triple" sentences. Compound sentences demonstrate the relationship between closely related ideas that might be awkward or confusing if stated separately:

> Ted served in the navy for six years.   He never learned how to swim.
> **Ted served in the navy for six years, but he never learned how to swim.**
> (*But* dramatizes the irony of a sailor never learning how to swim.)

> Albany is the capital of New York.   Trenton is the capital of New Jersey.
> *Albany is the capital of New York; Trenton is the capital of New Jersey.*
> (The semicolon links the two matching sentences as an equal pair.)

To be effective, compound sentences have to be accurately punctuated to avoid confusion. There are two methods of joining independent clauses:

Use a semicolon

INDEPENDENT CLAUSE; INDEPENDENT CLAUSE

or

Use a comma with a coordinating conjunction

INDEPENDENT CLAUSE, *and* INDEPENDENT CLAUSE

or
nor
but
yet
so
for

If you don't use the right punctuation, you create a run-on. **Run-on sentences**—also caused **fused sentences**—and a related error called **comma splices,** or **comma faults,** are some of the most common errors found in college writing. Because thoughts occur to us in a stream rather than a series of separate ideas, we can easily run them together in writing if we're not careful:

> **I always thought it would be glamorous to own a restaurant I had no idea how much work is involved. I worked at my aunt's restaurant for just two weeks last summer I could not believe how many hours she put in every day.** Long before the place opened, she was there paying bills, making up schedules, calling vendors, and planning menus. **The last dishwasher left at eleven-thirty she was still at work, counting money and getting ready for the next day.**

Revised

> I always thought it would be glamorous to own a restaurant, **but** I had no idea how much work is involved. I worked at my aunt's restaurant for just two weeks last summer, **and** I could not believe how many hours she put in

every day. Long before the place opened, she was there paying bills, making up schedules, calling vendors, and planning menus. The last dishwasher left at eleven-thirty, **and** she was still at work, counting money and getting ready for the next day.

Run-ons can be of any length. Just as fragments can be long, run-ons can be very short.

She begged no one cared.   He lives in Paris Texas is his birthplace.

Revised

She begged, **but** no one cared.   He lives in Paris; Texas is his birthplace.

What Do You Know?

Label each sentence OK for correct or RO for run-on.

1. _____ Carlos filed his federal taxes on time, but he forgot to submit his state return.

2. _____ Depression is a serious disease too many people dismiss it as a minor ailment.

3. _____ Although they arrived at the airport two hours early and checked in at the express counter, Carol and Steve nearly missed their flight because two of the security scanners were malfunctioning.

4. _____ The online courses are not as popular as we predicted students enjoy the classroom experience.

5. _____ The parents met with the professors, who explained how the new grading system would work.

Answers appear on the following page.

Get Writing and Revising

WHAT ARE YOU TRYING TO SAY?

Describe an upcoming vacation. Do you plan to travel, work, stay at home, or spend time with your family? Explain activities using as many compound sentences as you can to show cause and effect, contrast, or choice.

Example

Over the next break I plan to work. It's a busy time at my uncle's business, and he promised me plenty of overtime that week. I would love to go to Florida with my brother, but I really need money. I don't have much in the bank, but I can no longer put off getting a new car. My Toyota is twelve years old and has over 120,000 miles on it, so it is time to replace it. The $1,500 I can make in one week at my uncle's would really help with a down payment.

_____

_____

_____

_____

Get Writing and Revising

_____

_____

_____

_____

_____

_____

_____

_____

_____

_____

WHAT HAVE YOU WRITTEN?

Read your paragraph carefully. Have you created any compound sentences—sentences that contain two or more independent clauses or two or more complete thoughts? Are the compound sentences properly punctuated? Do you join the independent clauses with commas and coordinating conjunctions (and, or, yet, but, so, for, nor)?

Run-ons: Fused Sentences and Comma Splices

Some writing teachers use the term **run-on** to refer to all errors in compound sentences, whereas others break these errors into two types: **fused sentences** and **comma splices**.

Fused Sentences

Fused sentences lack the punctuation needed to join two independent clauses. The two independent clauses are *fused,* or joined without a comma or semicolon:

Fused Sentence
   I quit smoking cigarettes are expensive.

Revised
   I quit smoking; cigarettes are expensive.

Fused Sentence
   I didn't see the movie but I read the book.

Revised
   I didn't see the movie, but I read the book.

Comma Splices

Comma splices occur when only a comma is used to join independent clauses. Remember, independent clauses must be joined with a **semicolon** or a **comma with a coordinating conjunction** (*and, or, yet, but, so, for, nor*).

Comma splices can be corrected by replacing the comma with a semicolon or by adding a coordinating conjunction.

Comma Splice

The book ends with a funeral, the movie ends with a wedding.

Revised

The book ends with a funeral; the movie ends with a wedding.

Comma Splice

He goes to Vermont to ski, I go to Vermont to paint.

Revised

He goes to Vermont to ski, and I go to Vermont to paint.

Identifying Run-ons

To identify run-ons, do two things:

1. **Read the sentence to determine if it is a compound sentence.**
   Ask yourself if you can divide the sentence into two or more independent clauses (simple sentences):

   Carrie moved to Manhattan but came home   ***Not a compound sentence***
   after two months.

   Carrie moved to Manhattan . . . [independent clause (simple sentence)]
   came home after two months . . . [not a sentence]

   Sara works two shifts she wants another job.   ***Compound sentence***
   Sara works two shifts . . . [independent clause (simple sentence)]
   she wants another job . . . [independent clause (simple sentence)]

2. **If you have two or more independent clauses, determine if they should be connected.** Is there a logical relationship between them? What is the best way of connecting them? Independent clauses can be joined with a comma and *and, or, nor, yet, but, so, for,* or a semicolon:

   Sara works two shifts, but she wants another job.

   But indicates a logical contrast between two ideas. Inserting the missing comma and the word *but* quickly repairs this run-on.

EXERCISE 1   Identifying Run-ons: Comma Splices and Fused Sentences

Label each item OK for correct, CS for comma splice, and RO for run-on.

1. _____ Many towns and states in America were named after places in Europe New York, New Jersey, New London, and Cambridge are obvious examples.

2. _____ There is a region in southern Illinois called Little Egypt, but no one seems exactly sure how it got this rather exotic name.

3. _____ Several towns in the area have Egyptian names, Cairo being the most famous.

4. _____ Anyone who has read *Huckleberry Finn* will remember Cairo, it was Huck and Jim's original destination.

5. _____ Smaller towns also bear exotic names Karnak, Dongola, and Thebes are all named after cities in Egypt.

6. _____ An artificial lake was constructed in southern Illinois and was given the name Lake of Egypt.

7. _____ One explanation for the Egyptian names is geographical; the merging Ohio and Mississippi rivers reminded early settlers of the Nile Delta.

8. _____ Another theory is Biblical, it dates back to 1831 when an early frost killed much of the harvest in northern Illinois.

9. _____ Grain from southern Illinois was shipped north, and the long line of wagons loaded with wheat reminded people of the Old Testament story of Jacob's sons buying grain in Egypt.

10. _____ The origins of the nickname may be lost to history modern residents still enjoy naming stores, schools, and athletic teams after Egyptian sources.

EXERCISE 2   Identifying Run-ons: Comma Splices and Fused Sentences

Underline the comma splices and fused sentences in the following paragraph. If your instructor prefers, you can indicate fused sentences by underlining them twice.

Last summer I learned a valuable lesson it really changed my life. I always wanted to do video production and I applied for several jobs at local TV stations. WPIX had an internship program, and I was lucky to be one of six college students to be selected. I was hired as a production assistant my job was to help a news crew load and unload their equipment and set up remote interviews. Most mornings I would load up the van and ride to City Hall or Wall Street to shoot a press conference. On our way back from taping an interview with a Brooklyn real estate agent, we were sent to cover a house fire. When we got to the location, I began unloading equipment and helping the camera crew get into position. All around us people were screaming. One woman fainted, another sat on the curb crying in her hands. The cameraman stepped over them to get a shot of the paramedics bringing out a stretcher. When the neighbors found out two children were still inside, they began yelling and throwing things at the firefighters. I was upset I felt sick. I did not want to see any more and walked to the back of the van. The reporter asked me to hold up a mirror she had to check her lipstick.

Run-ons Needing Minor Repairs

A fused sentence or comma splice may need only a minor repair. Sometimes in writing quickly you can mistakenly use a comma when a semicolon is needed:

The teachers support the new principal, the parents question her methods.

Revised

The teachers support the new principal; the parents question her methods.

In other cases you may forget a comma or drop one of the coordinating conjunctions:

The teachers support the new principal but the parents question her methods.
Teachers like the new principal, parents have reservations.

Revised

The teachers support the new principal**,** but the parents question her methods.
Teachers like the new principal, **but** parents have reservations.

Run-ons Needing Major Repairs

In other cases run-ons require more extensive repairs. Sometimes you create run-ons when your ideas are not clearly stated or fully thought out:

Hector appeared on *American Dreamer* in 2008 the show won an Emmy.

Adding the needed semicolon eliminates a punctuation error but leaves the sentence awkward and unclear:

Hector appeared on *American Dreamer;* in 2008 the show won an Emmy.

Repairing this kind of run-on requires critical thinking. A compound sentence joins two complete thoughts, and there should be a clear relationship between them. It may be better to revise the entire sentence, changing it from a compound to a simple or complex sentence.

Revised

Hector appeared on *American Dreamer,* which won an Emmy in 2008.

In some instances you may find it easier to break the run-on into two simple sentences, especially if there is no strong relationship between the main ideas:

George Murphy was an actor and singer and he later served in the U.S. Senate.

Revised

George Murphy was an actor and singer. **He** later served in the U.S. Senate.

POINT TO REMEMBER

A compound sentence should join independent clauses that state ideas of equal importance. Avoid using an independent clause to state a minor detail that could be contained in a dependent clause or a phrase:

My sister lives in Chicago, and she is a teacher.

Revised

My sister, who lives in Chicago, is a teacher.   My sister is a teacher in Chicago.

Methods of Repairing Run-ons

There are four methods of repairing run-ons.

1. **Put a period between the sentences.**

    Sometimes in first drafts we connect ideas that have no logical relationship:

    Ken graduated from Salinas Community College, and the school had a famous football team.

    Revised

    Ken graduated from Salinas Community College. The school had a famous football team.

    Even if the two sentences are closely related, your thoughts might be clearer if they were stated in two simple sentences. Blending two sentences into one can weaken the impact of an idea you may want to stress:

    The manager asked for more security guards, but the owner refused.

    Revised

    The manager asked for more security guards. The owner refused.

2. **Insert a semicolon between the sentences to show a balanced relationship between closely related ideas:**

    Los Angeles is the largest city in California; Las Vegas is the largest city in Nevada.

    Commuters demand more roads; residents demand less traffic.

3. **Connect the sentences with a comma and *and, or, nor, yet, but, so, or for* to show a logical relationship between them:**

Ted is tired, ***so*** he is leaving early.	[indicates that one idea causes another]
Ted is tired, ***but*** he will work overtime. Ted is tired, ***yet*** he stays late.	[shows unexpected contrast between ideas]
Ted is tired, ***and*** he feels very weak.	[adds two similar ideas]
Ted will work late tonight, ***or*** he will come in early tomorrow.	[indicates one of two alternatives]

4. **Rewrite the run-on, making it a simple or complex sentence to reduce wordiness or show a clearer relationship between ideas:**

   Wendy bought an SUV and she later sold it to her cousin.
   Carlos took flying lessons in college he hoped to become an airline pilot.

   Revised
   Wendy bought an SUV that she later sold to her cousin. [simple sentence]
   Carlos took flying lessons in college because he hoped to become an airline pilot. [complex sentence]

POINTS TO REMEMBER

In revising a paper, you may wonder, "Should this comma be a semicolon?" To determine which mark of punctuation is correct, apply this simple test:

1. Read the sentence aloud. Ask yourself if you can divide the sentence into independent clauses (simple sentences that can stand alone).
2. Where the independent clauses are joined, you should see a semicolon or a comma with *and, or, nor, yet, but, so,* or *for.*
3. If *and, or, nor, yet, but, so,* or *for* is missing, the comma should be a semicolon.

Remember, a semicolon is a period over a comma—it signals a connection between two complete sentences.

WORKING TOGETHER

Work with a group of students to correct the fused sentences using each method. Have each member provide four solutions; then share your responses. Determine who came up with the most logical, easy-to-read sentence.

1. **Our school may have to suspend its athletic programs the sudden rise in the liability insurance exceeds the budget.**

   Two simple sentences:

   _____

   _____

   Two types of compound sentences:

   _____

   _____

   One complex sentence:

   _____

   _____

2. **The police asked local TV stations to show the photo of a missing girl she is a diabetic and requires immediate medical attention.**

Two simple sentences:

_____

_____

Two types of compound sentences:

_____

_____

_____

One complex sentence:

_____

_____

_____

3. Construction of new housing and a shopping mall has increased the need for expanded public transportation the bus company is announcing additional routes this fall.

Two simple sentences:

_____

_____

Two types of compound sentences:

_____

_____

_____

One complex sentence:

_____

_____

_____

EXERCISE 3   Revising Run-ons: Fused Sentences

Rewrite fused sentences, creating correctly punctuated compound, complex, or simple sentences.

1. Employers try to measure an applicant's personality in a job interview they ask a range of questions.

_____

_____

2. Recent graduates are often surprised by the questions they are asked they expect an interview to be like a college oral exam that tests their knowledge of specific facts and skills.

_____

_____

_____

3. **Employers might ask them about their goals in life or favorite hobbies they want to know if their personalities are suited to the corporate culture.**

   _____

   _____

4. **Applicants may be asked tough questions interviewers want to test how people respond under stress.**

   _____

   _____

5. **In many jobs people work as part of a team employers have to determine if the applicant will fit in with other employees.**

   _____

   _____

EXERCISE 4   Repairing Comma Splices and Fused Sentences with Commas and Semicolons

Revise each of the following sentences to correct run-ons by inserting commas and semicolons.

1. Before leaving home, millions of people slip cell phones into their pockets or purses they are almost as common as credit cards and car keys.

2. Young people have grown up with cell phones and they cannot imagine life without them.

3. The first American cell phone went on the market in 1983 it weighed two pounds and cost four thousand dollars.

4. Today, many companies make money on monthly fees and they give the phones away for free.

5. Cell phones are actually two-way radios they broadcast and receive messages.

6. The word _cell_ does not describe the phone it refers to the system that allows low-power radios to communicate over vast distances.

7. A city, for example, is divided into overlapping cells each cell has a base station with a sending and receiving tower.

8. As a cell phone user drives a car, he or she moves from cell to cell and the signal is passed from one to another.

9. Cell phones can now send text messages and pictures like computers, they can become infected with viruses that steal passwords and address books.

10. The cell phone, which so many people use daily, highlights the differences between rich and poor according to the UN, half the people in the world will never make or receive a telephone call in their lives.

EXERCISE 5   Repairing Comma Splices and Fused Sentences

Edit the following passage for comma splices and fused sentences.

Kerri Andrews   American History 101

The Forgotten Plague

On March 11, 1918, a soldier at Fort Riley, Kansas, went to the base hospital complaining of fever and a sore throat within hours, a hundred other soldiers reported the same symptoms. During the next few days, hundreds more were stricken with high fever, muscle and joint pain, and extreme fatigue. Many died. The disease then appeared in other army camps in California, hundreds of prisoners in San Quentin fell ill. The death toll mounted at an army base near Boston, sixty soldiers died in one day.

By the summer, the disease was spreading across the country and the government became alarmed. The sudden deaths of young men preparing to go to war led to wild rumors many believed German submarines had brought the disease to America. Others blamed terrorists they claimed spies were dispersing germs in movie theaters.

Soon the disease, now named Spanish influenza, infected the civilian population. In Philadelphia 300 people died in a single day in New York the daily death toll reached 700. Hospitals were swamped with patients funeral homes ran out of coffins. Doctors urged people to wear masks and avoid crowds. Schools, churches, and theaters were closed. Parades, sporting events, and bond drives were canceled. Newspapers printed warnings and advertisements for patent medicines. Desperate to avoid the deadly disease, people gargled with strange concoctions made with sugar and kerosene.

As infected American soldiers boarded troop ships bound for Europe, the disease became global. Earlier in the war it was feared that many soldiers would be lost in transit to U-boat attacks. The use of convoys eliminated the U-boat threat and not a single American soldier lost his life to a torpedo thousands would be felled by the flu they contracted in the tightly packed ships. Within months the flu spread throughout war-ravaged Europe it eventually reached India, where millions were infected.

World War I killed 126,000 Americans the Spanish flu killed 675,000. The war that lasted four years and saw some of the deadliest battles in history killed 15 million people but in a single year the flu killed over 20 million. The horror of World War I and political events such as the Russian Revolution overshadowed the deadly epidemic. Today, however, bioterrorism experts view this forgotten epidemic as a warning. The deadliest terrorist weapon is not a nuclear bomb but a flu that could kill 50 million people in a few months.

WORKING TOGETHER

Working with a group of students, revise this e-mail to eliminate fused sentences and comma splices.

OREGON MACHINE TOOL

Attention part-time employees:

As of March 15, part-time employees who work at least twenty hours a week are eligible for health insurance. Atlantic Health Services is holding informational seminars meetings are scheduled every day next week at 4:30 in A220. To enroll you must bring your most recent pay stub and your work schedule. Your supervisor must sign your schedule, you need to supply information about any existing health coverage you may have. This benefit is part of the new contract, it has been supplied to reduce discrepancy in wages and benefits between full- and part-time personnel. Make sure to attend one of the seminars next week, additional information is available on the company website.

Brett Chase
Benefits Manager

CRITICAL THINKING

Get Thinking and Writing

Some nonprofit organizations sell lists of their donors to other charities. Do you think this is fair? When you contribute to an organization, do you think it should sell your name to others? Do you think your record of donations should be kept private? Why or why not?

Write one or more paragraphs expressing your views on the practice of selling donor lists.

WHAT HAVE YOU WRITTEN?

Read your response carefully, and underline the compound sentences—those containing two or more independent clauses. Did you avoid run-ons? Did you join the independent clauses with a semicolon or a comma with and, or, nor, yet, but, so, or for?

Select one of your compound sentences, and write it out below:

_____

_____

1. Why did you place more than one complete idea in this sentence? Are the independent clauses logically related? Does your compound sentence link ideas of equal importance, show cause and effect, demonstrate a choice, or highlight a contrast? Could you improve the impact of your sentence by using a different coordinating conjunction?

2. If the ideas are not of equal importance, would it be better to subordinate one of them?

   My sister lives in Montana, and she won an Olympic medal in skiing.

   Revised
   My sister, who lives in Montana, won an Olympic medal in skiing.

   Select a simple sentence—a single independent clause—and write it out below:

   _____

   Think about the main idea you were trying to express, and write another sentence about the same topic:

   _____

3. Read the two sentences. Should these ideas remain separate, or would it be more effective to join them in a compound sentence to demonstrate their relationship?

   When you are trying to express an important or complex idea, consider writing two or more versions using simple, compound, and complex sentences. Read them aloud, and select the sentence that best reflects your ideas.

What Have You Learned?

Label each sentence OK for correct or RO for run-on.

1. _____ They rented a small apartment, they wanted to save money to buy a house.

2. _____ San Francisco is chilly in the summer but it remains a popular tourist destination.

3. _____ Sandy plays piano and has begun composing her own songs.

4. _____ The cabin lost power during the blizzard we had no heat.

5. _____ Fans surrounded her limo and they demanded autographs.

Answers appear on the following page.

WRITING ON THE WEB

Using a search engine such as Yahoo! or Google, enter terms such as *run-on, comma splice, comma fault, compound sentence, complex sentence,* and *sentence types* to locate current sites of interest.

POINTS TO REMEMBER

1. **Run-ons are common writing errors.**

2. **A run-on is an incorrectly punctuated compound sentence.**

3. **Compound sentences join two or more related independent clauses using semicolons or commas with** *and, or, nor, yet, but, so, or for.*

4. **Run-ons can be corrected in two ways:**

   a. **If the sentence makes sense when you read it out loud and if the independent clauses are related, add the missing words or punctuation.**

Independent Clause; Independent Clause
or
Independent Clause, and Independent Clause
or
nor
yet
but
for
so

   b. **If the sentence does not make sense, reword it or break it into separate simple or complex sentences.**

Answers to What Have You Learned? on Page 452

1. RO (see page 440) 2. RO (see page 440) 3. OK 4. RO (see page 440) 5. RO (see page 440)

CHAPTER 26

Correcting Dangling and Misplaced Modifiers

CHAPTER GOAL

■ Identify and Revise Sentences with Dangling and Misplaced Modifiers

Paul Barton/CORBIS

Get Writing

Is owning a home still part of the American Dream?

Write a paragraph stating your views. Do you own a home? Do you want to own a home? Could you afford to buy a house? Has the mortgage crisis affected anyone you know?

What Are Dangling and Misplaced Modifiers?

Modifiers describe words and phrases. Whether they are **adjectives** (*cold, red, old, inventive, fresh, clear, awkward*), **adverbs** (*quickly, freshly, clearly, awkwardly*), or **participial phrases** (*walking to work, speaking to the angry students, winning the game by one run*), they must be clearly linked to what they describe. **Changing the position of a modifier in a sentence alters the meaning.**

Sentence	*Meaning*
Only Karen takes cabs to work.	Karen is the one person to use a cab to commute to work.
Karen takes **only** cabs to work.	Karen uses cabs as her sole way of commuting to work.
Karen takes cabs **only** to work.	Karen uses cabs to commute to work and uses other means to travel elsewhere.

Top 20

DANGLING AND MISPLACED MODIFIERS
It is easy to put modifiers in the wrong place. Reading papers aloud can help you detect them.

Dangling Modifiers

A **dangling modifier** is a modifier attached to the beginning or end of a sentence that is not clearly linked to what it is supposed to describe.

Dangling Modifier
Running into the street, the truck hit a small boy.

[Who ran into the street—*the truck?*]

Revised
Running into the street, a small boy was hit by the truck.

Dangling Modifier
Hidden by fog, we could not see the island.

[What was hidden by fog—*we?*]

Revised
We could not see the island hidden by fog.

Dangling Modifier
Dripping with barbecue sauce, the girls loved the chicken wings.

[What was dripping with barbecue sauce—*the girls?*]

Revised
The girls loved the chicken wings dripping with barbecue sauce.

Misplaced Modifiers

Misplaced modifiers can occur anywhere in a sentence:

Misplaced Modifier
Tonya searched for her dog **without luck** in the park.

[Who was without luck—*her dog?*]

Revised
Without luck, Tonya searched the park for her dog.

Misplaced Modifier

I remember my father **at six**   [Who was six years old—*my father?*]
taking me to Disney World.

Revised

I remember my father took me at six to Disney World.

What Do You Know?

Write X next to each sentence with a dangling or misplaced modifier and OK for each correct sentence.

1. ____ Losing by three touchdowns, the dejected fans tore up their programs and went home.

2. ____ Elected four times, Franklin Roosevelt became the most influential president since Lincoln.

3. ____ Fulfilling Kennedy's promise to reach the Moon before the 1960s ended, the public watched astronauts land on the lunar surface in July 1969.

4. ____ Jogging four miles a day, Karen's cholesterol level began to drop.

5. ____ Running into sleet and poor visibility, the pilot requested a new course.

6. ____ I missed *American Idol* last night because I was stuck at the airport, which I looked forward to all week.

7. ____ I met the mayor who just resigned in the elevator.

8. ____ I was pulled over and given a speeding ticket by a cop rushing to the final exam.

9. ____ Concerned about the environment, the agency bought a fleet of hybrid cars.

10. ____ Built in 2001, the engineers were shocked by the rust and decay they found under the overpass.

Answers appear on the following page.

Get Writing

WHAT ARE YOU TRYING TO SAY?

Write a paragraph describing the best teacher or boss you have had. How did this person affect your life? What events do you remember most? What lessons did you learn from this person? Provide adjectives that describe this person's characteristics, and provide adverbs to describe this person's actions.

_____

_____

_____

_____

_____

_____

_____

_____

_____

_____

_____

_____

_____

_____

WHAT HAVE YOU WRITTEN?

_Circle each modifying word or phrase, and underline the word or words it
describes. Are they clearly linked? Are any sentences confusing? Could any
sentences be interpreted in different ways? Could your modifiers be located
closer to what they describe?_

Avoiding Dangling Modifiers

We frequently start or end sentences with modifying words, phrases, or
clauses:

> Created by a team of NASA scientists . . .
> Located just outside of Chicago . . .
> Discovered by a passing hiker . . .

These modifiers make sense only if they are correctly linked with what they
are supposed to modify:

> **Created by a team of NASA scientists,** the _lightweight plastic_ is stronger than
> steel.
> Tourists often visit the _Pate Museum,_ **located just outside of Chicago.**
> **Discovered by a passing hiker,** _the wreckage_ is believed by the FAA to be the
> remains of a research balloon lost almost thirty years ago.

In writing, however, it is easy to create sentences that are confusing or
illogical:

> **Created by a team of NASA scientists,** _GM_ wants to use the lightweight
> plastic in its cars.
> The Pate Museum is popular with _tourists_ **located just outside of Chicago.**
> **Discovered by a passing hiker,** _the FAA_ believes the wreckage to be the
> remains of a research balloon lost almost thirty years ago.

Because the ideas are clear in your mind, even reading your sentences
aloud may not help you spot a dangling modifier. Keep this simple diagram
in mind:

modifier, **main sentence**

Think of the comma as a hook or hinge that links the modifier with what it describes:

Costing just three dollars, *these DVDs* are becoming best-sellers.
We stayed at the *Piedmont Hotel,* **first opened in 1876.**

The comma links **Costing just three dollars** with *DVDs* and links **first opened in 1876** with *Piedmont Hotel.*

Testing for Dangling Modifiers

Dangling modifiers can be easily missed in routine editing. When you find a sentence that opens or ends with a modifier, apply this simple test:

1. **Read the sentence, and then turn the modifier into a question, asking** *who* or *what is being described?*

   Question, Answer

2. **The answer to the question follows the comma.** If the answer makes sense, the sentence is probably correct. If the answer does not make sense, the sentence likely contains a dangling modifier and requires revision.

Examples:

Working from noon to midnight, I was tired and hungry.

Question: *Who worked from noon to midnight?*   **Answer:** *I*

Correct

Working double shifts for a month, my check was enormous.

Question: *Who worked double shifts?*   **Answer:** *my check*

Incorrect and needs revision:

Working double shifts for a month, **I** could not believe how enormous my check was.

My check was enormous because **I** *worked double shifts for a month.*

EXERCISE 1   Detecting Dangling Modifiers

Write OK for each correct sentence and DM to indicate those with dangling modifiers.

1. _____ Born to an unwed mother, Eva Peron's career as a radio and movie actress helped her rise from poverty to become a prominent figure in Buenos Aires society.

2. _____ Having married Juan Peron in 1945, she became the First Lady of Argentina when her husband assumed the presidency.

3. _____ Although known for her glamorous appearance, she championed the rights of the poor, especially women, who adoringly called her Evita.

4. _____ Although popular with working people, the aristocratic families of Buenos Aires resented her public adulation and humble origins.

5. _____ Seeking the vice presidency in 1951, the country's military leaders grew increasingly hostile to what they considered her amateurish meddling in state affairs.

6. _____ Bowing to heavy pressure, Juan Peron withdrew his wife's nomination.

7. _____ Stricken with uterine cancer a year later, the public was shocked when their beloved Evita died at thirty-three.

8. _____ Rising to cult status in death, Evita became a symbol of both Argentina and the aspirations of the poor of Latin America.

9. _____ Pointing to her business dealings with former Nazis, many historians are critical of her role in making Argentina a haven for war criminals.

10. _____ Angered by allegations that some of the jewelry Eva Peron wore in public may have been stolen from Holocaust victims, some journalists urged theater-goers to boycott the popular musical *Evita*.

EXERCISE 2   Opening Sentences with Modifiers

Create a complete sentence by adding an independent clause to logically follow the opening modifying phrase. Test each sentence to be sure that you avoid a dangling modifier. Also, make sure that you create a complete sentence and not a fragment (see Chapter 23).

1. Rising in price,

_____

_____

2. Seen by millions on television,

_____

_____

3. Exercising every day,

_____

_____

4. Refusing to change his mind,

_____

_____

5. Facing a tough election,

_____

_____

EXERCISE 3 Ending Sentences with Modifiers

Create a complete sentence by adding an independent clause to logically pre-cede the modifying phrase. Test each sentence to be sure that you avoid a dangling modifier. Make sure that you create a complete sentence and not a fragment (see Chapter 23).

1. _____

_____, **waiting in the rain.**

2. _____

_____, **suffering from a bad cold.**

3. _____

_____, **starring Jennifer Lopez.**

4. _____

_____, **unable to find a place to park.**

5. _____

_____, **written in just ten minutes.**

EXERCISE 4 Eliminating Dangling Modifiers

Rewrite each of the following sentences to eliminate dangling modifiers. Add needed words or phrases, but do not alter the basic meaning of the sentence.

1. **Running out of medical supplies, the UN received calls for an emergency airlift by aid workers.**

_____

_____

2. **Failing to hit a single home run in thirty-five games, sportswriters and comedians began calling him the "Ten Million Dollar Mistake."**

_____

_____

3. Known as spaghetti Westerns, many American movie stars got their start acting in low-budget cowboy movies shot in Italy.

_____

_____

4. Facing rising gas prices, it was harder to get part-time employees to drive all the way to the city for a two-hour shift.

_____

_____

5. Having taught deaf children for years, the day-care center was happy to hire Nadine to work with Shelby and Catherine.

_____

_____

Misplaced Modifiers

Because **misplaced modifiers** can occur anywhere in a sentence and are often not set off by commas, they can be harder to spot:

> I fixed the frame of my bicycle that was hit by a car **in the basement** last night.
> We tried to win approval for the new stadium at the board meeting **the public wants constructed next year.**
> We flew to Miami to see my parents **through the hurricane** last September.

Reading sentences out loud can help you detect some misplaced modifiers, but even this may not help you avoid some of them. Because the ideas are clear in your mind, you may have a hard time recognizing the confusion your sentence creates. You know that you fixed the bicycle in the basement, not that a car hit your bicycle in the basement. You know that the public wants the stadium, not a board meeting, constructed next year. You recall that you flew through a hurricane on your way to Florida last September, not that you wanted to see your parents through a storm. However, readers can rely only on the way that your words appear on the page.

EXERCISE 5   Detecting Misplaced Modifiers

Mark OK for each correct sentence and MM for sentences containing a misplaced modifier.

1. _____ The Jersey Devil is a legendary creature said to live in the desolate pine barrens of southern New Jersey which has terrified and amused residents of the Garden State for over two hundred years.

2. _____ People first sighted the creature in the 1700s said to have large bat-like wings, hoofs, a long neck, and a horselike head.

3. _____ According to one tale, the being was created when a woman cursed her unwanted thirteenth baby worn out from childbirth by saying, "Let it be a devil."

4. _____ This curse instantly transformed the newborn into a winged beast that flew up the chimney.

5. _____ In the 1840s the Jersey Devil was blamed for livestock killings by farmers.

6. _____ In 1909 hysteria swept New Jersey when thousands of people reported seeing the devil throughout Philadelphia suburbs flying over rooftops.

7. _____ Businesses and schools closed, and armed guards were placed on street cars panicked by stories of attacks.

8. _____ The sightings finally stopped, but fifty years later children claimed seeing the devil and hearing the anguished cries of its victims.

9. _____ In 1991 a driver reported seeing the Jersey Devil delivering a pizza.

10. _____ The Jersey Devil inspired the name of the state's hockey team that generated so much hysteria in the Garden State.

EXERCISE 6   Correcting Misplaced Modifiers

Rewrite each of the following sentences to eliminate misplaced modifiers. Add needed words or phrases, but do not alter the basic meaning of the sentence.

1. The coach tried to rally the team after their staggering loss in the locker room by reminding them of last year's upset victory in the playoffs.

_____

_____

2. The manager who was caught shoplifting wrestled the man to the floor until the police arrived.

_____

_____

3. This year my parents wanted their taxes done by an accountant not knowing how to report profits from selling a home.

_____

_____

4. The principal met with the parents whose children vandalized the playground in a parent-teacher conference this afternoon.

_____

_____

5. The hostess served ice cream to her guests dripping with hot chocolate sauce on the patio.

_____

_____

EXERCISE 7 Detecting Dangling and Misplaced Modifiers in Context

Underline dangling and misplaced modifiers in the following announcement:

WestTech

Attention to All Staff:

Predicted to reach four dollars a gallon, WestTech, like all companies, must take steps to conserve fuel. Rising gas prices inflate our overall cost of doing business and make it harder for us to provide health insurance, which continues to rise as well. Because our current contracts do not expire until 2011, we cannot pass these fuel costs on to our customers until next year. Determined to cope with this problem, these recommendations are being made by the transportation committee:

1. Before heading to sales meetings downtown, employees should meet in the lobby to car pool.

2. Wanting to stay in touch with the stores in distant malls, e-mail updates should be used by sales reps.

3. Replacing the need for monthly in-person meetings, managers should make use of video conferencing.

4. Hybrid cars should be reserved by sales reps making long trips, which can get up to forty miles per gallon.

5. Sales reps should phone or e-mail store managers before making a shipment, which can prevent the need for expensive last-minute rush deliveries.

By planning ahead and being creative, rising gas prices won't force us to cut pay or benefits.

Sidney Ballard

EXERCISE 8   Using Modifiers Correctly

Insert the modifier into each sentence by placing it next to the word or words it describes.

1. **Frank drives Karla to the beach every morning.**

   INSERT: *who is a lifeguard* to refer to *Karla*

   _____

   _____

2. **The deans met with faculty members this morning to discuss new course offerings.**

   INSERT: who are concerned about falling enrollments to refer to *the deans*

   _____

   _____

3. **The landlord met with the tenant.**

   INSERT: *who was angry about the broken windows* to refer to *the landlord.*

   _____

   _____

4. **Larry David stars in the HBO hit show *Curb Your Enthusiasm*.**

   INSERT: *who created* Seinfeld.

   _____

   _____

5. **The insurance adjusters met with the homeowners.**

   INSERT: *who refused to pay any repair bills* to refer to *insurance adjusters.*

   _____

   _____

WORKING TOGETHER

Working with a group of students, revise this notice to eliminate dangling and misplaced modifiers.

New Payroll Policies

Beginning March 15, only payroll checks will be issued to employees presenting picture IDs. Direct deposit is available by filling out a request form signed by your supervisor to electronically receive your check. Checks will be sent to the post office if not picked up by 4 p.m.

Employees can contact supervisors who may have questions about these policies.

EXERCISE 9   Cumulative Exercise

Revise each sentence for dangling or misplaced modifiers, fragments, and run-ons.

1. Carefully taped together, the police could read the note the killer had torn to shreds.

   _____

   _____

2. The union decided to strike management's final offer did not meet their minimum demands.

   _____

   _____

3. Shot in just eighteen days, the public loved the low-budget comedy.

   _____

   _____

4. The airline is paying more for fuel but it continues to make a profit because of lucrative government contracts.

   _____

   _____

5. Because the power has still not been restored to the main building.

   _____

   _____

CRITICAL THINKING

Today's children grow up in a world of constant electronic communication through Internet chat rooms, cell phones, and PDAs. How will this influence the way they communicate later in life? Will it prepare them for jobs in the global economy or just lead them to have short attention spans? How will it make them different from previous generations?

Write a paragraph stating your views.

WHAT HAVE YOU WRITTEN?

Underline the modifiers in each sentence. Are they properly placed? Are there any sentences that are confusing or could be interpreted in two ways?

What Have You Learned?

Mark an X next to each sentence with a dangling or misplaced modifier and OK for each correct sentence.

1. ____ Noticing puddles of oil under the car, the mechanic examined the engine for leaks.

2. ____ Caught cheating, the teacher sent the students to the principal's office.

3. ____ Grounded by the blizzard, the agent issued hotel vouchers to the stranded passengers.

4. ____ Driving cross-country in a small car, the five of us were uncomfortable filled with luggage.

5. ____ Suffering from a severe shoulder injury, the quarterback completed only two passes.

6. ____ Having lost her cell phone, Sally had to flag down a passing car to get help.

7. ____ Trying to quit smoking, gaining weight was her greatest fear.

8. ____ She tried to get her children to eat fruits and vegetables concerned about their health.

9. ____ Sealed in plastic, the flood did little damage to the studio's collection of rare audiotapes.

10. ____ Realizing her job was going to be eliminated, Shelly applied for a transfer.

Answers appear on the following page.

WRITING ON THE WEB

Using a search engine such as Yahoo! or Google, enter terms such as *dangling modifiers* and *misplaced modifiers* to locate current sites of interest.

1. Review current online journals or newspapers to see how writers place modifying words and phrases in sentences.

2. Write an e-mail to a friend; then review it for dangling and misplaced modifiers and other errors.

POINTS TO REMEMBER

1. Modifiers are words or phrases that describe other words. To prevent confusion, they must be placed next to what they modify.

2. If sentences begin or end with a modifier, apply this simple test:

   Read the sentence, and then turn the modifier into a question, asking who or what is being described.
   Question, Answer

   If the answer makes sense, the sentence is probably correct.

   > Born on Christmas, I never have a birthday party.
   > *Q: Who was born on Christmas?*   *A: I*
   >
   >   Correct

   If the sentence does not make sense, it probably contains a dangling modifier and needs revision.

   > Filmed in Iraq, critics praise the movie for its realism.
   > *Q: What was filmed in Iraq?*   *A: critics*
   >
   >   Incorrect

   Revisions:
   Filmed in Iraq, the movie was praised by critics for its realism.
   Critics praised the movie, filmed in Iraq, for its realism.

3. In revising papers, underline modifying words and phrases. Circle the words or ideas that they are supposed to modify to test for clear connections.

Answers to What Have You Learned? on page 466

1. OK 2. X (see pages 457–459)
3. X (see pages 457–459)
4. X (see pages 457–459) 5. OK
6. OK 7. X (see pages 457–459)
8. X (see pages 457–459) 9. X (see pages 457–459) 10. OK

CHAPTER 27

Understanding Parallelism

CHAPTER GOAL

■ Identify and Revise
Sentences with Faulty
Parallelism

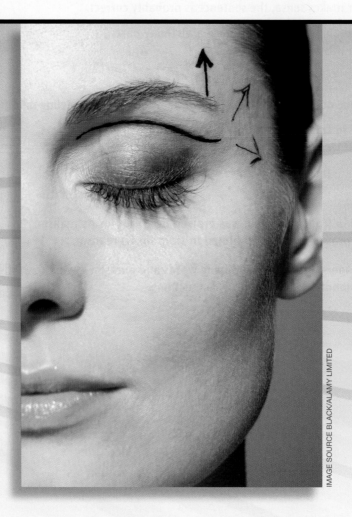

IMAGE SOURCE BLACK/ALAMY LIMITED

Get Writing

Would you ever consider having cosmetic surgery? Why or why not?

Explain your reasons in one or more paragraphs.

What Is Parallelism?

To make sentences easy to understand, pairs and lists of words have to be *parallel* or *match*. They have to be *all nouns, all adjectives, all adverbs, or all verbs in the same form:*

He was known for his **honesty** and **courage.** [both nouns]
The office was **small, dark, dusty,** and **hot.** [all adjectives]
She applied the paint **slowly** and **carefully.** [both adverbs]
You will have to **sell tickets, collect fees,** and **seat the guests.** [all verb phrases matching *will have to*]

In most cases, you probably use parallelism without a problem. When you write a shopping list, you automatically write in parallel form:

We need **bread, cheese, ham,** and **mustard.** [all nouns]

However, it is easy to create sentences with faulty parallelism when you include a list of phrases:

The assistant manager must approve menu changes, schedule waiters, order supplies, and when the manager is unavailable handle customer complaints.

The last item, *when the manager is unavailable handle customer complaints,* does not match the other items in the list:

The assistant manager must . . . **approve** menu changes
                                   . . . **schedule** waiters
                                   . . . **order** supplies
                                   . . . **when the manager is unavailable**
                                         handle customer complaints

Revised

The assistant manager *must* **approve** menu changes, **schedule** waiters, **order** supplies, and **handle** customer complaints when the manager is unavailable.

Not Parallel	*Parallel*
Both **writing** and **to read** are important skills.	Both **writing** and **reading** are important skills.
noun *verb*	*noun* *noun*
He spoke **softly, precisely,** and **with authority**	He spoke **softly, precisely,** and **authoritatively.**
adverb *adverb* *prepositional phrase*	*adverb* *adverb* *adverb*
Hunger, cold, and **fearing more earthquakes**	**Hunger, cold,** and **the fear of more earthquakes**
noun *noun* *adjective*	*noun* *noun* *noun*
drove the refugees farther south.	drove the refugees farther south.
Students can **register for classes, apply for financial aid,**	Students can **register for classes, apply for financial aid,**
verb phrase *verb phrase*	*verb phrase* *verb phrase*
and **textbooks can be ordered online.**	and **order textbooks online.**
independent clause	*verb phrase*

What Do You Know?

Label each sentence OK for correct or FP for faulty parallelism.

1. ____ The movie is fast-paced, colorful, and offers a lot of drama.

2. ____ The car has two flat tires, a missing fender, and a cracked windshield.

3. ____ New Orleans is noted for its history, jazz, shopping, and Mardi Gras celebrations.

4. ____ Providing security and the respect for civil liberties is a difficult balance.

5. ____ She was trained to operate heavy machinery, read blueprints, and supervision of work crews.

Answers appear on the following page.

Get Writing

WHAT ARE YOU TRYING TO SAY?

Describe someone you know well—a friend, co-worker, neighbor, or relative—by writing sentences that list his or her skills, characteristics, or habits.

_____

_____

_____

_____

_____

_____

_____

_____

_____

_____

_____

_____

WHAT HAVE YOU WRITTEN?

Read your sentences aloud. Did you create sentences that contain pairs of words or phrases or lists? If so, are the items parallel—do they match each other?

Overcoming Parallelism Errors

Mistakes in parallelism are easy to make. If you are describing your favorite television show, many ideas, words, or phrases may come to mind. Some may be nouns, adjectives, or verbs:

funny   creative dialogue   great characters

In putting these ideas together, make sure that they are parallel.

Not Parallel

30 Rock has creative dialogue, great characters, and is funny.

Parallel

30 Rock has **creative dialogue, great characters,** and **funny situations.**
[all nouns]

Testing for Parallelism

The simplest way of determining if a sentence is parallel is to test each element to see if it matches the base sentence.

Example: The car is new, well-maintained, and costs very little.

The car is **new.**
The car is **well-maintained.**
The car is **costs very little.**

The last item does not match and should be revised.

The car is new, well-maintained, and inexpensive.

The car is **new.**
The car is **well-maintained.**
The car is **inexpensive.**

A Tip On Revising Faulty Parallelism

Sometimes you may find it difficult to make all the items in a sentence match. You might not be able to think of a suitable noun form of an adjective. In making the sentence parallel, you may find yourself having to change a phrase that you like or create something that sounds awkward. In some cases you may have simply been trying to put too many ideas in a single sentence.

In some instances it may be easier to break up an unparallel sentence. It is easier to make two short sentences parallel than one long one:

Not Parallel

The new dean will be responsible for scheduling courses, expanding student services, upgrading the computer labs, and most important, become a strong advocate for students.

> *Parallel*
> The new dean will be responsible for *scheduling* courses, *expanding* student services, and *upgrading* the computer labs. **Most important, she must become a strong advocate for students.**

EXERCISE 1   Detecting Faulty Parallelism

Write OK by each correct sentence and NP by each sentence that is not parallel.

1. _____ Websites such as My Space, YouTube, and Facebook allow millions of people to post text, share videos, and creating an online presence.

2. _____ However, young people do not always think before they post items that may embarrass or exposing them to danger.

3. _____ Too often they forget that the pages they create in cyberspace can be read by anyone, including future employers and clients, as well as predators and identity thieves.

4. _____ People should think carefully before posting snapshots that reveal house numbers or showing license plates that could be used by stalkers.

5. _____ Teenagers have to consider their futures before they post images showing themselves drinking, engaging in pranks, or events that might later embarrass them.

6. _____ Employers now examine My Space pages and review Facebook entries to check on job applicants.

7. _____ Lawyers search cyberspace to check out potential clients, finding evidence to discredit witnesses, and establish the credibility of people filing claims.

8. _____ Realizing that so many people regret what might be found about them online, new businesses have been created to remove, sanitize, or hide embarrassing information.

9. _____ For a modest fee, these companies can help job applicants and political candidates clean up their online reputations.

10. _____ "I may not be able to take down that video clip of you chugging beer in a funny hat on spring break," one consultant admitted, "but I can flood the Internet with positive images so the embarrassing stuff will be five or ten thousand on the list when someone Googles your name."

EXERCISE 2 Revising Sentences to Eliminate Faulty Parallelism

Rewrite each sentence to eliminate faulty parallelism. You may have to add words or invent phrases, but do not alter the meaning of the sentence. In some cases, you may create two sentences.

1. Few people have heard of Dr. Ignatz Semmelweis, but his work in the 1840s would change medical history, influence scientific thinking, and saving the lives of millions.

   _____

   _____

   _____

2. He noticed that new mothers treated by doctors were more likely to become infected and dying than those attended by midwives.

   _____

   _____

3. At the time, doctors examined patients, performed operations, conducted autopsies, and babies would be delivered without washing their hands.

   _____

   _____

4. He theorized that doctors were transmitting something on their hands that spread infections and causing the high death rate of new mothers.

   _____

   _____

5. Semmelweis ordered caregivers to wash their hands before treating women or to examine their newborns.

   _____

   _____

6. This simple practice dramatically reduced infections and cutting the death rate of mothers and infants.

   _____

   _____

7. Other doctors scoffed at Semmelweis's ideas because they thought hand washing was a needless chore and resenting his suggestion that they were spreading diseases.

   _____

   _____

   _____

8. A conference of leading doctors and scientists rejected Semmelweis's theories, and he was criticized, ridiculed, and became the subject of mockery.

   _____

   _____

9. Discredited and depressing, Semmelweis entered a mental institution, where he died at forty-seven.

   _____

   _____

10. Semmelweis's views are now universally accepted, but patients are still infected by busy doctors who move from patient to patient and failing to wash their hands.

   _____

   _____

   _____

EXERCISE 3   Writing Parallel Sentences

Complete each sentence by adding missing elements, making sure that they create a matched pair or list of matching words or phrases in order to be parallel.

1. The loss of a job leads people to feel depressed, bitter, angry, and
   _____.

2. A skilled football coach must know strategy, evaluate opposing teams, and _____.

3. Anyone wanting to lose weight has to exercise more and _____.

4. To save gas, drivers should consider carpooling, consolidating trips, and _____.

5. Smoking and _____ are major causes of heart disease.

6. He invested in stocks, bonds, rare coins, and _____.

7. To be an effective speaker, maintain good eye contact, speak clearly, and _____.

8. Don't accept a job offer until you know what you will paid, where you will work, who will supervise you, and _____.

9. The rusty, dented, and _____ car could bring only $1,500 at the auction.

10. The comic performed so wildly and _____ that the audience thought he was crazy.

WORKING TOGETHER

Working with a group of students, revise the following announcement to eliminate errors in parallelism. Notice how collaborative editing can help detect errors you may have missed.

Student Grant

Calmex Corporation has announced it will award five ten-thousand-dollar grants to students enrolled in business or technical programs. To be eligible, you must be a full-time student, a resident of California, and U.S. citizenship is required. In order to apply, you need to fill out the required form, submit a current transcript, and two letters of recommendation from instructors or former employers must be obtained. To learn more, view the grant website at www.calmexcorp/studentgrant.com.

CRITICAL THINKING

Write a list of tips to help people lose weight and get in better shape. Create at least five recommendations.

When you complete your writing, review each item in your list for faulty parallelism.

Get Thinking and Writing

What Have You Learned?

Label each sentence OK for correct or FP for faulty parallelism.

1. _____ The trip was long, hot, and dusty.

2. _____ The plan was rejected for three reasons: it cost the city too much, the engineers could not guarantee it would resolve the problems, and refusal by the public to pay more taxes.

3. _____ Dedication, persistence, and being creative helped her keep the business going during the recession.

4. _____ The children lacked warm clothing, clean drinking water, and their diet was not adequate.

5. _____ The riots were blamed on rising tensions between the community and the police and unemployment increased.

Answers appear on the following page.

WRITING ON THE WEB

Using a search engine such as Yahoo! or Google, enter terms such as *faulty parallelism* and *writing parallel sentences* to locate current sites of interest.

1. Review some current online journals or newspapers to see how writers state ideas in parallel form.

2. Write a brief e-mail to a friend describing some recent activities or a person you have met. Review your sentences to see if pairs and lists of words and phrases are parallel.

POINTS TO REMEMBER

1. **Words and phrases that appear as pairs or lists must be parallel—they must match and be nouns, adverbs, adjectives, or verbs in the same form.**

Parallel	*Not Parallel*
Swimming and **fishing** are fun.	**Swimming** and *to fish* are fun.
She is **bright, witty,** and **charming.**	She is **bright, witty,** and *has charm*.
He must **design** the building, **establish** the budget, and **hire** the workers.	He must **design** the building, **establish** the budget, and *workers must be hired*.

2. **You can discover errors in parallelism by testing each element in the pair or series with the rest of the sentence to see if it matches:**

   Whoever we hire will have to collect the mail, file reports, answer the phone, update the website, and accurate records must be maintained.

   Whoever we hire will have to . . . *collect the mail.*
   file reports.
   answer the phone.
   update the website.
   accurate records must be maintained.

   The last item does not match *will have to* and needs to be revised to be parallel with the other phrases in the list:

   Whoever we hire will have to collect the mail, file reports, answer the phone, update the website, and *maintain accurate records.*

3. **If you find it difficult to make a long or complicated sentence parallel, consider creating two sentences. In some instances, it is easier to write two short, parallel lists than a single long one.**

Answers to What Have You Learned? on page 475

1. OK 2. FP (see page 469)
3. FP (see page 469) 4. FP (see page 469) 5. FP (see page 469)

CHAPTER 28

Subject-Verb Agreement

D. HURST/ALAMY LIMITED

CHAPTER GOALS

- Understand Subject-Verb Agreement

- Identify Singular and Plural Subjects

- Locate Hidden Subjects

- Choose the Right Verbs in Sentences with "Either/Or" and Indefinite Pronouns

Get Writing

What report card would you give your high school? Did it adequately prepare you for college or a job?

Write one or more paragraphs expressing your evaluation of your high school. What were its strengths and weaknesses? Would you want your children to attend the same school? Why or why not?

What Is Subject-Verb Agreement?

The most important parts of any sentence are the **subject**—the main idea—and the **verb**—a word or words that express action (*buy, swim, sing*) or link the subject with other ideas (*is, are, was, were*). Both the subject and verb work together to state a **complete thought** and create a sentence:

Suzi jogs four miles a day.   Suzi is in great shape.

For sentences to clearly express ideas, their subjects and verbs must agree—they must match in number. **Singular subjects require singular verbs; plural subjects require plural verbs:**

Singular	*Plural*
The coach **directs** plays.*	The coaches **direct** plays.*
The plane **was** grounded.	The planes **were** grounded.
The book **is** on your desk.	The books **are** on your desk.

*In most cases you add an *-s* or *-es* to a noun to make it plural and add an *-s* or *-es* to a verb to make it singular.

Note: Singular and plural verbs occur only in first and third person.

	Singular	*Plural*
First person:	I **am**	We **are**
Third person:	He **was**	They **were**

In second person, only the plural verb is used:

You **are** a person I can trust.   You **are** people I can trust.
Tom, you **are** late again!   Kids, you **are** late again!

What Do You Know?

Select the correct verb in each sentence.

1. ____ The lawyer, supported by angry homeowners, (talk/talks) to the press at every opportunity.

2. ____ Two hundred dollars (is/are) more than I want to spend.

3. ____ Where (is/are) the letter signed by the teachers and parents?

4. ____ One of our players (is/are) being drafted by the NFL.

5. ____ Henderson Motors (doesn't/don't) deny the allegations.

Answers appear on the following page.

WHAT ARE YOU TRYING TO SAY?

Write a paragraph describing how you prepare for exams.

_____

_____

_____

_____

_____

_____

_____

_____

_____

_____

_____

_____

_____

_____

WHAT HAVE YOU WRITTEN?

Circle the subjects and underline the verbs in each sentence. Do the subjects and verbs match so that your sentences clearly identify which study methods are singular and which are plural?

Grammar Choices and Meaning

Matching subjects and verbs is not just about avoiding grammar mistakes but about making sure your meaning is clear. People commonly use the wrong verbs in speaking. Sometimes the correct verb may sound odd or awkward. But when you write, you have to use the right verb to be precise. Changing a verb from singular to plural changes the meaning of a sentence:

Sentence	**Meaning**
Singular	
My trainer and manager **arranges** my schedule.	_One person is both a trainer and manager._
Plural	
My trainer and manager **arrange** my schedule.	_The trainer and manager are two people._
Singular	
The boat and trailer **goes** on sale Monday.	_The boat and trailer are sold as one item._
Plural	
The boat and trailer **go** on sale Monday.	_The boat and trailer are sold separately._

Answers to What Do You Know? on page 478

1. talks (_lawyer_ is singular; _homeowners,_ set off by commas, is not part of the subject) 2. is (amounts of time and money are singular) 3. is (_Where_ refers to _letter,_ which is singular) 4. is (_One_ is singular) 5. doesn't (_Henderson Motors_ is singular)

Singular
His speed and accuracy **is** amazing.   *His blend of two skills is amazing.*

Plural
His speed and accuracy **are** amazing.   *He has two amazing skills.*

EXERCISE 1   Choosing the Correct Verb

Write out the subject and correct verb in each sentence.

	Subject	Verb
1. Job applicants (use/uses) a number of methods to find employment.	_____	_____
2. Looking at want ads, however, (is/are) not as effective as many think.	_____	_____
3. A leading expert in jobs and employment trends (estimates/estimate) that 80 percent of the jobs, especially the best jobs, are never advertised.	_____	_____
4. A large corporation, such as General Motors or United Airlines, (is/are) likely to use recruiters or employment agencies rather than place want ads.	_____	_____
5. A leading recruiter or headhunter (charge/charges) tens of thousands to locate the right person for the right job.	_____	_____
6. A person with skills in high demand (use/uses) a recruiter as an agent to locate the best job.	_____	_____
7. The method that all employment advisors (recommend/recommends) for anyone looking for a job is networking.	_____	_____
8. Rather than look for jobs, networking (direct/directs) applicants to look for people and organizations that could use their skills or know others who can.	_____	_____
9. One way advisors suggest using networking as a starting point (is/are) by calling friends who have the kind of job you want or know someone who does.	_____	_____
10. If this person (do/does) not know of an opening, he or she may suggest another person who can help.	_____	_____

Special Nouns and Pronouns

In most cases it is easy to tell whether a noun is singular or plural. Most nouns add an *-s* to become plural, but some nouns have separate plural forms:

Singular	*Plural*
woman	women
tooth	teeth
mouse	mice

1. Some nouns that end in *-s* and look like plurals are singular:

   gymnastics   physics   mathematics

   Athletics **takes** discipline.   Economics **relies** on accurate data.

2. Some nouns that may refer to one item are plural:

   pants   fireworks

   My pants **are** torn.   The fireworks **were** canceled.

3. Proper nouns that look plural are singular if they are names of companies, organizations, or titles of books, movies, television shows, or works of art:

   United Nations   *Eight Men Out*   The Teamsters

   The United Nations **attempts**   *Eight Men Out* **tells** the story of
   to prevent war.   a legendary sports scandal.

4. Units of time and amounts of money are generally singular:

   Sixty dollars **is** a nice bonus.   Two hours **is** more than enough time.

   They appear as plurals to indicate separate items:

   The dollars **were** lying on the street.   My first hours in school **were** tough.

Group Nouns

Group nouns—nouns that describe something with more than one unit or member—can be singular or plural, depending on the meaning of the sentence.

Common Group Nouns

audience	committee	faculty	number
board	company	family	public
class	crowd	jury	team

In most sentences, group nouns are singular because they describe a group working as a unit:

"Jury **Declares** Smith Guilty"   [singular verb in a headline describing
                                         a jury acting as one group]

Group nouns are plural when they describe a group working independently:

"Jury **Argue** Over Evidence"　　　　[plural verb in a headline describing
jurors acting individually]

Some group nouns are used as plurals because we think of them as individuals rather than as a single unit:

The Beatles **are** still popular.　　　The Yankees **are** in first place.

EXERCISE 2　Choosing the Correct Verb with Special and Group Nouns

Underline the correct verb in each sentence.

1. These scissors (is/are) very sharp.

2. *Two and a Half Men* (star/stars) Charlie Sheen.

3. The American Federation of Teachers (open/opens) a seminar on distance learning next week.

4. After days of debate, the rules committee (refuses/refuse) to discuss his membership.

5. Thirty thousand dollars (was/were) awarded to each victim by the courts.

6. (Is/Are) your gloves on the table?

7. She was convicted on drug charges, but the public (seem/seems) willing to forgive her.

8. The Lakers (head/heads) to the arena expecting another victory.

9. Thermodynamics (explain/explains) how the process works.

10. The number of students taking online courses (is/are) growing.

Hidden Subjects

In some sentences, the subject is not obvious, so choosing the right verb requires critical thinking. You have to determine what you are trying to say.

- **Subjects followed by prepositional phrases:**

Incorrect
One of the players have the flu.

Correct
One of the players **has** the flu.

[*Players* is plural, but it is not the subject of the sentence; the subject is *One,* which is singular.]

Incorrect
Creation of new products and new markets keep us growing.

Correct
Creation of new products and new markets **keeps** us growing.

[*Products* and *markets* are plural, but the subject is *Creation,* which is singular.]

Remember, the subject of a sentence does not appear in a prepositional phrase. Make sure that you identify the key word of a subject and determine whether it is singular or plural:

The *price* of oil and petroleum products **is** rising.   [singular]
The *prices* of jewelry **are** rising.   [plural]

Prepositions are words that express relationships between ideas, usually regarding time and place:

above	below	near	to
across	during	of	toward
after	except	off	under
against	for	outside	with
along	from	over	within
around	inside	past	without
before	like	since	

- **Subjects followed by subordinate words and phrases:**

  In many sentences, the subject is followed by words or phrases set off by commas. These additional words are subordinate—extra information that is not part of the main sentence. They should not be mistaken for compound subjects:

  The landlord and his tenants **are** suing the contractor for property damage.
    [**Plural:** *and* links *landlord* & *tenants* to create a compound subject]

  The landlord, backed by tenants, **is** suing the contractor for property damage.
    [**Singular:** *is* indicates that the subject, *landlord,* is singular; *tenants,* set off by commas, is subordinate and not part of the subject]

- **Subjects following possessives:**

  It can be easy to choose the wrong verb if the subject follows a possessive noun:

  Incorrect
  The team's best players is injured.

  Correct
  The team's best players **are** injured.
    [The subject is not *team* but *players,* which is plural.]

  Incorrect
  The parents' demand were met.

Correct

The parents' demand **was** met.

[The subject is not *parents* but their *demand,* which is singular.]

POINT TO REMEMBER

The subject is never the word with the apostrophe but what follows it.

- **Inverted subjects and verbs:**

  In some sentences, the usual subject-verb order is inverted or reversed, so the subject follows the verb.

Singular	*Plural*
There **is** *someone* looking for you.	There **are** *people* looking for you.
Here **is** your final *exam.*	Here **are** your final *exams.*
Over the hill **lies** *a refugee camp.*	Over the hill **lie** *refugees.*

EXERCISE 3 Choosing the Correct Verb with Hidden or Complex Subjects

Underline the correct verb in each sentence.

1. **The loss of high-paying factory jobs offering benefits and pensions (lead/leads) workers to pursue new careers.**

2. **Beyond the reach of our most powerful telescopes (lies/lie) distant planets that may contain life.**

3. **The mayor, backed by local business leaders, (demands/demand) that the governor explain the sudden changes in the highway proposal.**

4. **Here (lie/lies) the ruins of the old castle.**

5. **Who (wants/want) to save money on a new house?**

6. **During the hurricane, the loss of radio and telephone communications (was/were) frustrating.**

7. **Voters who supported the mayor's proposal (were/was) stunned by the election results.**

8. **There (is/are) no recommendations or policies about online courses in the dean's annual report.**

9. **Why (is/are) your bills always late?**

10. **The car's sales (is/are) higher than anyone predicted.**

"Either . . . or" Subjects

More than one subject may appear in a sentence, but this does not automatically mean that the verb is plural.

The coach and the manager **are** meeting with reporters.	[*coach* **&** *manager* = two people (plural)]
The coach or the manager **is** meeting with reporters.	[*coach* **OR** *manager* = one person (singular)]

Remember, the conjunctions *or* and *nor* mean "one or the other but not both."

- **If both subjects are singular, the verb is singular:**

  Neither the *book* nor the *website* **helps** me study for the test.
  The *car* or the *truck* **is** available.
  My *brother* or my *cousin* **signs** for the deliveries.

- **If both subjects are plural, the verb is plural:**

  Neither the *players* nor the *owners* **are** happy about the NFL ruling.
  Cars or *trucks* **are** available.
  The *teachers* or *parents* **take** students on field trips.

- **If one subject is singular and one subject is plural, the subject closer to the verb determines whether it is singular or plural:**

  Neither the *players* nor the *owner* **is** happy about the NFL ruling.   [*owner* is singular]
  Cars or a *truck* **is** available.   [*truck* is singular]
  The *teacher* or *parents* **take** students on field trips.   [*parents* is plural]

Pay attention to special and group nouns in "either . . . or" sentences.

Neither the dean nor the faculty **wants** to confront the students.   [*faculty* is singular]
The president or the Senate **has** to take action.   [*Senate* is singular]
Neither the lawyers nor the jury **understands** the judge's rulings.   [*jury* is singular]

Top 20

PRONOUNS
Learn to identify singular and plural pronouns to avoid mistakes. See Chapter 30 for more information about using pronouns.

Indefinite Pronouns

Indefinite pronouns can be singular or plural, but most are singular.

Indefinite Pronouns

Singular Indefinite Pronouns

another	each	everything	nothing
anybody	either	neither	somebody
anyone	everybody	nobody	someone
anything	everyone	no one	something

Everyone *is* invited.   **Something** *seems* wrong.   **Nothing** *was* taken.

Plural Indefinite Pronouns

both	few	many	several

Both *are* late.   **Few** *are* interested.   **Many** *were* broken.

Indefinite Pronouns That Can Be Singular or Plural Depending on Meaning

all	more	none	some
any	most		

Money was stolen. **Some** was recovered.   [*Some* refers to *money* (singular)]
The houses burned. **Some** were destroyed.   [*Some* refers to *houses* (plural)]

EXERCISE 4   Choosing the Right Verb with *Either/Or* and Indefinite Pronouns

Underline the correct verb in each sentence.

1. Filmmakers have always embraced new technologies, but some (is/are) threatening their industry.

2. Anyone who sees movies these days (know/knows) how expensive they are to produce.

3. High-priced stars or a high-tech special effect (drives/drive) up production costs.

4. In order to undertake such costly projects, a producer or a studio (want/wants) exclusive control over sales of the finished product.

5. Since the early 1980s, illegal videotapes have troubled producers, but few (was/were) worried that they would pose a major threat to profits.

6. Bootleg videos were costly to produce and bulky to transport, and most (was/were) of such poor quality that people were willing to pay more for studio-produced versions.

7. However, digital technology and the Internet have changed everything, and many (sees/see) a major threat to their income.

8. Studio executives or a movie critic given advance copies of films on DVD (is/are) often targeted by thieves.

9. A DVD stolen from a messenger or bought from a dishonest employee (is/are) used to make thousands of high-quality copies that are sold illegally all over the world.

10. As computer technology improves, some (fears/fear) that new movies, like music, will be downloaded on personal computers, robbing moviemakers of their ability to make money on their most expensive films.

Relative Pronouns: *Who, Which,* and *That*

The words *who, which,* and *that* can be singular or plural, depending on the noun they replace.

Who
Craig is a comedian who **uses** wit.   [*who* refers to a *comedian* = singular]
They are comedians who **use** wit.   [*who* refers to *comedians* = plural]

Which
He sold a car, which **needs** new tires.   [*which* refers to *a car* = singular]
He sold cars, which **need** new tires.   [*which* refers to *cars* = plural]

That
We love a movie that **has** good music.   [*that* refers to *a movie* = singular]
We love movies that **have** good music.   [*that* refers to *movies* = plural]

It is important to locate the exact noun these words refer to in order to avoid making errors.

Incorrect
The SUV is among the cars that needs new brakes.   [*that* refers to *cars,* not *SUV*]

Correct

The SUV is among the cars that **need** new brakes.   [plural]

Incorrect

General Motors or Ford is joining the   [*that* refers to *companies*,
companies that is supporting tax reform.   not *General Motors or Ford*]

Correct

General Motors or Ford is joining the   [plural]
companies that **are** supporting tax reform.

EXERCISE 5   Choosing the Right Verb with *Who, Which,* and *That*

Underline the correct verb in each sentence.

1. Mulholland Drive is one of several Los Angeles streets that (is/are) well-known to moviegoers around the world.

2. Anyone who (watch/watches) police dramas set in L.A. may recall a detective getting a radio call to follow a car turning onto Mulholland.

3. The drive is a major street in the city, which (is/are) named after William Mulholland, who was born in Belfast in 1855.

4. Mulholland was among a large number of Irish immigrants who (was/were) interested in seeking a better life in the United States.

5. After working in San Francisco and Arizona, he moved to Los Angeles and got a job with the many laborers who (was/were) digging ditches for the city's water department.

6. Although he had no formal education, Mulholland rose from digging ditches to running the Department of Water and Power, which (was/were) a powerful agency for a growing city.

7. Los Angeles is one of several western cities that (has/have) little water.

8. Mulholland directed one of the largest public works projects that (was/were) attempted at that time, a massive 233-mile-long aqueduct that included construction of over a hundred and fifty tunnels.

9. The project drained water from Owen Valley, and farmers who (was/were) in opposition to the aqueduct protested against Mulholland and dynamited installations.

10. However, civic leaders and business owners in Los Angeles supported Mulholland's tactics, which (was/were) seen as necessary to supply the city with water.

EXERCISE 6   Making Subjects and Verbs Agree

Complete each of the following sentences, making sure that the verb matches the subject. Write in the present tense—walk/walks, sing/sings, etc.

1. One of my friends _____

_____.

2. Two of the students _____

_____.

3. Either the parents or the teacher _____

_____.

4. The cost of car repairs _____

_____.

5. The mayor, supported by community leaders, _____

_____.

EXERCISE 7 Making Subjects and Verbs Agree

Revise this e-mail to correct errors in subject-verb agreement.

BATANG ENGINEERING
www.batangeng.com

A N N O U N C E M E N T

MARCH 1, 2009

Batang Engineering, along with its subsidiaries Ballard Productions and GMAX Design, are committed to developing practical, cost-effective solutions to the challenge of rising energy prices that faces our economy. We are proud to announce the development of a new product that revolutionize solar power and provide a highly reliable and low-cost renewable power source:

SUN MAGNET

Sun Magnet is a lightweight, easily folded durable solar panel that are quickly unfolded and used to generate electricity. A one-pound sheet the size of a paperback book can be spread on the ground like a blanket to charge a cell phone, operate a radio, even run a laptop computer. With a retail price of twenty dollars, Sun Magnet are going to be popular with campers, boaters, and hunters. It will be standard survival gear in the military and meet the needs of aid workers in remote areas.

Sun Magnet make its debut at the National Car Show in New York April 25–30th. Commercials begins running April 28th in key markets. Print ads run in *Time, Newsweek, People, Popular Mechanics, Boating,* and *Hunting* in May.

For details, check the Sun Magnet website: www.sunmagnet.com.

Place your orders before March 31st and receive a 15% discount.

CRITICAL THINKING

**Get Thinking
and Writing**

Do you think that high school students take their education seriously? Do they allow sports and social activities to overshadow academics? Do you think that they realize the skills they will need to compete in a global economy? Consider your experiences or those of current high school students, and state your views in one or more paragraphs.

WHAT HAVE YOU WRITTEN?

1. Select two sentences with singular verbs, and write them below:

   _____

   _____

   Read the sentences out loud. Have you identified the right word or words as the subject? Is the subject singular?

2. Select two sentences with plural verbs, and write them below:

   _____

   _____

   _____

   Read the sentences out loud. Have you identified the right word or words as the subject? Is the subject plural?

3. Edit your paragraph for fragments (see Chapter 23), comma splices, and run-ons (see Chapter 25).

EXERCISE 8   Cumulative Exercise

Rewrite this passage to eliminate errors in subject/verb agreement, fragments, and run-ons.

Jacobson-2

The NAACP being formed in 1909 by seven whites and one African American who was concerned about the epidemic of lynching. The organization grew out of the Niagara Movement, headed by W. E. B. DuBois he was opposed to Booker T. Washington's beliefs that was seen as passive and outmoded. DuBois serving as editor of the organization's main publication, *The Crisis*, for almost twenty-five years. The NAACP achieved national attention when it organized boycotts of *Birth of a Nation*, a movie it criticized for its racist portrayals of blacks. The NAACP played a major role during the civil rights movement of the 1950s and 1960s, it sponsored demonstrations and provided legal support for protestors who was arrested. In the 1960s some members suggested changing the name of the organization because of the words "colored people" many people found these terms offensive and old-fashioned. More radical groups, such as the Black Panthers, was challenging the fifty-year-old organization, accusing it of being out of step with the times. The NAACP, however, wishing to honor its early roots in the struggle for equality, decided to maintain the original name. Although the organization has faced declining membership, financial problems, and allegations of being too closely tied to certain politicians. It remains the most well-known and influential civil rights organization in the United States.

_____

_____

_____

_____

_____

_____

_____

_____

_____

_____

_____

_____

_____

_____

_____

_____

_____

_____

WORKING TOGETHER

Working with a group of students, read this letter, and circle any errors in subject-verb agreement. Note how collaborative editing can help detect errors you may have missed on your own.

Dear Ms. Clark:

The hiring committee of the Human Services Department have received your résumé and application. George Peterson, selected by the student body, members of the faculty, and the school board, head the interview team. The team plan to conduct initial interviews April 25–May 3.

Initial interviews are designed to last no more than an hour and a half. We feel that ninety minutes provide enough time for candidates to make a general presentation of their credentials.

Ten candidates have been selected for the initial round of interviews. Three finalists will be chosen to interview with the full board. Each of those who meets with the full board may submit work samples, letters of recommendation, or other written documentation. Powerpoint presentations of less than thirty minutes is also allowed.

To schedule your first interview, please call me no later than April 25.

Sincerely yours,
Carmen Hernandez
Carmen Hernandez

What Have You Learned?

Select the correct verb in each sentence.

1. _____ Each of the parent's requests (demand/demands) a detailed response.

2. _____ The tenants or the landlord (has/have) to be held accountable for the condition of the building.

3. _____ Where (is/are) the committee going to meet this week?

4. _____ The cars that (needs/need) repairs should be parked behind the garage.

5. _____ The price of rare coins (remain/remains) stable.

Answers appear on page 493.

i WRITING ON THE WEB

Using a search engine such as Yahoo! or Google, enter terms such as *subject-verb agreement, verbs,* and *verb agreement* to locate current sites of interest.

1. Read online articles from magazines or newspapers, and notice the number of group words such as *committee, jury,* or *Senate.*

2. Send an e-mail to a friend, and make sure that you choose the right verbs in sentences containing *either . . . or* and *which.*

POINTS TO REMEMBER

1. **Subjects and verb agree—or match—in number.**

   Singular subjects take singular verbs:

   The boy **walks** to school.
   The bus **is** late.

   Plural subjects take plural verbs:

   The boys **walk** to school.
   The buses **are** late.

2. **Verb choice affects meaning:**

   The desk and chair **is** on sale.   [singular—both items sold as a set]
   The desk and chair **are** on sale.   [plural—items are sold separately]

3. **Group nouns, units of time and money, and some words that appear plural are singular:**

   The jury **is** deliberating.
   Fifty dollars **is** not enough.

4. **Some nouns that refer to a single item are plural:**

   My scissors **are** dull.
   The fireworks **are** starting.

5. *Here* and *There* **can precede singular or plural verbs depending on the subject:**

   There is a girl who **wants** to join the team.
   Here are three girls who **want** to join the team.

6. **The subject of a sentence never appears in a prepositional phrase:**

   One of my friends **lives** in Brooklyn.   [*one* is the subject, not *friends*]
   The prices of oil **are** rising.   [*prices* is the subject, not *oil*]

7. **Nouns set off by commas following the subject are not part of the subject:**

   The teacher, supported by students, **is** protesting. [singular]

8. **The subject may follow a possessive:**

   Tom's cars **are** brand-new.   [*cars* is the subject]
   The children's playground **is** open.   [*playground* is the subject]

9. *Either . . . or* **constructions can be singular or plural:**

   If both subjects are singular, the verb is singular:

   Either my aunt or my sister **is** taking me to the airport.

   If both subjects are plural, the verb is plural:

   Either the boys or the girls **are** hosting the party.

   If one subject is singular and the other is plural, the subject closer to the verb determines whether it is singular or plural:

   Either the boy or the girls **are** hosting the party.
   Either the girls or the boy **is** hosting the party.

10. **Some indefinite pronouns are singular:**

    another   each   everything   nothing
    anybody   either   neither   somebody

anyone	everybody	nobody	someone
anything	everyone	no one	something

Anything **is** possible.   Nothing **is** missing.

Some indefinite pronouns are plural:

both	few	many	several

Both **are** missing.   Few **are** available.

Some indefinite pronouns can be singular or plural:

all	more	none	some
any	most		

All the money **is** gone.   All the children **are** gone.

Answers to What Have You Learned? on page 491

1. demands (see page 485)
2. has (see pages 484–485)
3. is (see page 484)   4. need (see page 486)   5. remains (see page 478)

CHAPTER 29

Verbs: Tense, Mood, and Voice

CHAPTER GOALS

- Use Verb Tense to Show Time
- Avoid Illogical Shifts in Tense
- Understand Subjunctive Mood
- Identify Use of Active and Passive Voice
- Avoid Double Negatives

Ashley Cooper/Picmpact/CORBIS

Get Writing

Since 1978 the Exit Glacier in Alaska has retreated half a mile. When it was first discovered, Glacier National Park in Montana had 150 glaciers. Today there are fewer than 50. Some scientists predict that by 2030 the rest will have melted. Do you think our country is doing enough to prevent global warming?

Write one or more paragraphs stating your views.

What Are Verb Tense, Mood, and Voice?

Verbs show action and link ideas. Verbs also use tense (time) to tell readers when an action happened:

We **flew** to San Diego last July.   [*past tense*]
We **fly** to San Diego regularly.   [*present tense*]
We **will fly** to San Diego next month.   [*future tense*]

Timing is critical in many sentences. Explaining *when* something happened can be just as important as telling readers *what* happened.
Verbs also use **mood** to expresses attitudes toward the action or an idea:

The plane **leaves** at noon.   [*Indicative mood* states facts and opinions]
Open a window!   [*Imperative mood* gives orders or commands]
I wish I **were** a boss.   [*Subjunctive mood* states conditions, wishes, requirements, or possible situations]

Voice shows the relationship between the verb and the subject:

The city **repaired** the bridge.   [*Active voice* emphasizes the subject, *city*]
The bridge **was repaired** by the city.   [*Passive voice* emphasizes *the bridge*]

What Do You Know?

Select the correct verb in each sentence

1. _____ Is the city going to (rise/raise) property taxes this year?

2. _____ I was born on Long Island, which (is/was) the site of the 1964 World's Fair.

3. _____ If she (was/were) hired tomorrow, we might finish the job on time.

4. _____ He (lain/laid) his keys on the desk and left the room.

5. _____ Please (set/sit) on the porch, where it is cooler.

Answers appear on the following page.

WHAT ARE YOU TRYING TO SAY?

Get Writing

Write a brief paragraph that describes a change you have observed in a friend, at school or work, in a neighborhood, or in a society. How have television shows changed since you were a child? Has a neighborhood gotten better or worse? How is a team doing this season compared to last year? Explain what is different and what has remained the same.

_____

_____

_____

_____

_____

_____

_____

_____

_____

_____

WHAT HAVE YOU WRITTEN?

Read your paragraph aloud, and underline the verbs. How did you use verbs to tell time? Is it clear what events or actions took place in the past, which began in the past and continue into the present, and which take place only in the present?

Helping Verbs

Top 20

HELPING VERBS

Helping verbs are important to create tense. They explain when something happened.

Top 20

PAST PARTICIPLES

Past-tense verbs can be used as adjectives.

Verb *tenses* tell when events or actions occur. **Helping verbs**—also called **auxiliary verbs**—often appear with verbs to create tense. Common helping verbs are *be, do, have, can, could, may, might, must, shall, should, will, would.* Helping verbs create **past participles** when used with past-tense verbs to show that an action has been completed (The house *was rented.* I *had waxed* the car). Past participles can also be used as adjectives (a *rented* house, a *waxed* car).

TENSES

Tense	Use	Example
present	shows current and ongoing actions	I **run** two miles a day.
simple past	shows actions that occurred in the past and do not continue into the present	I **ran** two miles a day in high school.
future	shows future actions	I **will run** two miles a day when I go to college.
present perfect	shows actions that began in the past and concluded in the present	I **have** just **run** two miles.
past perfect	shows actions concluded in the past before another action occurred	I **had run** two miles before going to practice last Monday.
future perfect	shows future actions preceding an action or event further in the future	I **will have run** 5,000 miles by the time I graduate next May.
present progressive	shows ongoing action	I **am running** two miles a day now.

past progressive	shows actions that were in progress in the past	I **was running** two miles a day in those days.
future progressive	shows ongoing future actions	Next year I **will be running** two miles every day.
present perfect progressive	shows actions that began in the past and continue in the present	I **have been running** two miles a day this semester.
past perfect progressive	shows actions in progress in the past before another past action	I **had been running** two miles a day until I joined the team last fall.
future perfect progressive	shows future ongoing actions taking place before a future event	I **will have been running** two miles a day for a year by the time they reopen the jogging track.

This chart may seem complicated, but we use tense every day to express ourselves. Consider the difference in responses to the question about a friend's travel plans:

She **was** in New York.	**past tense**	indicates *she has returned*
She **is** in New York.	**present tense**	indicates *she is currently in New York*
She **has been** in New York.	**past perfect**	indicates several trips to New York, *suggesting she may be home or still out of town*
She **will be** in New York.	**future**	indicates *she will visit New York in the future*

We use perfect tenses to explain the differences between events in the recent past and distant past or between the near and far future:

Sid **had been looking** for a welding job for two years **when he was hired** last month.
Cara **will owe** twenty thousand dollars **when she finishes** school next year.

Progressive Tense

Progressive verbs show that the action is or was still happening. They end in *-ing*. Verbs that express actions—*look, buy, sell, paint, drive*—can use the progressive form:

I *am searching* for my sister.   They *are restoring* Corvettes.
The city *is paving* the streets.   Juan *was playing* ball that Sunday.

Verbs that express conditions, emotions, relationships, or thoughts—*cost, believe, belong, contain, know, prefer, want*—do not generally use the progressive form:

Incorrect
Citizens of developing countries *are wanting* a higher standard of living.

Correct
Citizens of developing countries *want* a higher standard of living.

Top 20

PROGRESSIVE TENSE
Progressive tense lets readers know that an action is or was ongoing.

Regular and Irregular Verbs

Most verbs are called **regular** because they follow a regular or standard form to show tense changes. They add *-ed* to verbs ending with consonants and *-d* to verbs ending with an *e* to show **past tense** or to form a **past participle** (when a past-tense verb appears with a helping verb):

Present	Past	Past Participle
charge	charged	charged
count	counted	counted
spoil	spoiled	spoiled
wash	washed	washed
watch	watched	watched
work	worked	worked

KNOWING ENGLISH

Verb Endings

The verb endings *-s* and *-ed* may be hard to hear when added to words that end in similar sounds. Some people don't pronounce these verb endings in speaking. Make sure to add them when you are writing:

They were **suppose** to give their presentation yesterday.
She **learn** quickly.

Revised

They were **supposed** to give their presentation yesterday.
She **learns** quickly.

Irregular verbs do not follow the *-ed* pattern.

• **Some irregular verbs make no spelling change to indicate shifts in tense.**

Present	Past	Past Participle
cut	cut	cut
hit	hit	hit
hurt	hurt	hurt
put	put	put
quit	quit	quit
read	read	read
set	set	set

• **Most irregular verbs make a spelling change rather than adding *-ed*.**

Present	Past	Past Participle
awake	awoke	awoken
be	was, were	been
bear	bore	borne (not *born*)

Present	Past	Past Participle
become	became	become
begin	began	begun
blow	blew	blown
break	broke	broken
bring	brought	brought
build	built	built
buy	bought	bought
catch	caught	caught
choose	chose	chosen
come	came	come
dive	dove (or *dived*)	dived
do	did	done
draw	drew	drawn
drink	drank	drunk
drive	drove	driven
eat	ate	eaten
feed	fed	fed
feel	felt	felt
fight	fought	fought
fly	flew	flown
forget	forgot	forgotten
forgive	forgave	forgiven
freeze	froze	frozen
get	got	gotten
go	went	gone
grow	grew	grown
hang (objects)	hung	hung
hang (people)	hanged	hanged
have	had	had
hold	held	held
know	knew	known
lay (place)	laid	laid
lead	led	led
leave	left	left
lie (recline)	lay	lain
lose	lost	lost
make	made	made
mean	meant	meant
meet	met	met
pay	paid	paid
ride	rode	ridden
ring	rang	rung
rise	rose	risen
run	ran	run
say	said	said
see	saw	seen
seek	sought	sought
sell	sold	sold
shine	shone	shone
shoot	shot	shot
sing	sang	sung

Present	Past	Past Participle
sink	sank	sunk
sleep	slept	slept
sneak	sneaked (not *snuck*)	sneaked
speak	spoke	spoken
spend	spent	spent
steal	stole	stolen
sting	stung	stung
strike	struck	struck
strive	strove	striven
swear	swore	sworn
sweep	swept	swept
swim	swam	swum
swing	swung	swung
take	took	taken
teach	taught	taught
tear	tore	torn
tell	told	told
think	thought	thought
throw	threw	thrown
understand	understood	understood
wake	woke	woken
weave	wove	woven
win	won	won
write	wrote	written

EXERCISE 1   Supplying the Right Verb

Complete the following sentences by supplying the correct verb form.

1. Present   I sing in San Antonio clubs.

   Past   I _____ in San Antonio clubs.

   Past participle   I have _____ in San Antonio clubs.

2. Present   I hurt my knee working out.

   Past   I _____ my knee working out.

   Past participle   I have _____ my knee working out.

3. Present   They lie in the sun.

   Past   They _____ in the sun.

   Past participle   They have _____ in the sun.

4. Present   The clothes sell well.

   Past   The clothes _____ well.

   Past participle   The clothes have _____ well.

5. Present   They teach Spanish.

   Past   They _____ Spanish.

   Past participle   They have _____ Spanish.

EXERCISE 2   Choosing the Correct Verb

Underline the correct verb form in each sentence.

1. Most accounts of the Civil War (focus/focused) on the battles that occurred in the South.

2. Few people today (are/were) aware of the impact the war had on California.

3. Though today it (is/was) the most populous state, a hundred and fifty years ago, California (had/has) only a population of 250,000 and was not yet linked with the rest of the country by rail.

4. California's early settlers (mirror/mirrored) the conflict in the rest of the country.

5. The residents of commercial San Francisco identified with Northern business interests, while Californians in the agricultural South (felt/feel) strong ties to the Confederacy.

6. Conflicts between Northern and Southern California (were brewing/ had been brewing) for years when war was declared in 1861.

7. Southern sympathizers in California (planned/had planned) to secede from the United States and form an independent republic by convincing the general in charge of Union troops in the state to support their venture.

8. General Johnston, though he supported the Southern cause, could not bring himself to oppose the Constitution he (swore/had sworn) to defend.

9. The plot to secede failed, but California (became/become) the site of over eighty Civil War battles.

10. Most of the battles consisted of skirmishes and raids by guerillas who (seek/sought) gold to support the Confederacy.

Problem Verbs: *Lie/Lay, Rise/Raise, Set/Sit*

Some verbs are easily confused. Because they are spelled alike and express similar actions, they are commonly misused. In each pair, only one verb can take direct objects. **The verbs *lay, raise,* and *set* take direct objects; *lie, rise,* and *sit* do not.**

Lie/Lay

To lie means to rest or recline. You "lie in bed" or "lie on the floor." *To lay* means to put something down or set something into position. You "lay tile" or "lay cards on a table."

Present	Past	Past Participle
lie	lay	lain
lay	laid	laid

To Lie	*To Lay*
I hate **to lie in the sun.**	I hate **to lay tile floors.**
They **are lying on the beach.**	They **are laying new sod** in the yard.
Yesterday, I **lay in bed** all day with a cold.	Yesterday, I **laid my keys** on the counter.
I have **lain on that sofa.**	We have **laid sod like that** in the past.

Remember: Lie expresses action done by someone or something.

Sid took aspirin, then **lay** on the sofa, hoping that the headache would go away.

Lay expresses action done to someone or something.

We **laid** Sid on the sofa and gave him aspirin.

Rise/Raise

To rise means to get up or move up on your own. You "rise and shine" or "rise to the occasion." *To raise* means to lift something or grow something. You "raise a window" or "raise children."

Present	Past	Past Participle
rise	rose	risen
raise	raised	raised

To Rise	*To Raise*
They **don't rise until ten.**	They **raise the sail** as soon as they leave the dock.
She is **rising to greet** us.	Tom is **raising show horses.**
They **have risen from their naps.**	The agents **have raised insurance rates** again.
He **rose to attention.**	She **raised her arms.**

Remember: Rise can refer to objects as well as people:

The dough **rises** in the oven. Gold prices **are rising.**

Set/Sit

To set means to put something in position or arrange in place. You "set down a cup" or "set down some ideas." *Set* always takes a direct object. *To sit* means to assume a sitting position. You "sit on a sofa" or "sit on a committee."

Present	Past	Past Participle
set	set	set
sit	sat	sat

To Set	*To Sit*
We **set the menu prices.**	We **sit on the menu committee.**
He **is setting a new policy.**	She **is sitting by the window.**

EXERCISE 3   Choosing the Correct Verb

Underline the correct verb in each sentence.

1. Without more rain we cannot hope to (raise/rise) any wheat.

2. You will get a bad burn if you (set/sit) in the sun too long.

3. Don't (set/sit) those plants in direct sunlight.

4. After a brief ceremony she was (lain/laid) to rest beside her husband.

5. I need to (lay/lie) down for a while.

6. I can't (lay/lie) all the responsibility on your shoulders.

7. She is going (to rise/to raise) the flag herself.

8. Let me (raise/rise) the blinds to let in more light.

9. I was so tired I (laid/lay) in bed until noon.

10. The people (rose/raised) when the mayor entered.

Shifts in Tense

Events happen in time. In writing, it is important to avoid illogical shifts in time and to write in a consistent tense.

Illogical

    I **took** the midterm and **miss** only two questions.
     past   *present*

Consistent

    I **took** the midterm and **missed** only two questions.
     past   *past*

        or

    I **take** the midterm and **miss** only two questions.
     present   *present*

You can change tenses to show a logical shift or change in time:

    I **was born** in Fort Worth but **live** in Austin. Next year I **will move** to Denver.
     past   *present*   *future*

You can shift tense to distinguish between past events and subjects that are permanent or still operating:

    I **stayed** at the York Hotel, which **is** one of the largest in Toronto.
     past   *present*

(Using past-*tense was* to refer to the York Hotel might lead readers to believe the hotel no longer exists.)

Changing shifts in tense changes meaning:

    Cindy **worked** for United Express, which **is** the only delivery service used by
       past   *present*
    the FBI.

      [Meaning: *Cindy once worked for the only delivery service used by the FBI.*]

Cindy **works** for United Express, which **was** the only delivery service used by
      present   *past*
the FBI.

> [Meaning: *Cindy is working for a delivery service that used to be the only
> one used by the FBI.*]

Cindy **worked** for United Express, which **was** the only delivery service used by
      past   *past*
the FBI.

> [Meaning: *Cindy once worked for a delivery service that used to be the only
> one used by the FBI.*]

In writing about literature and film, you can relate the plot's events in either past or present tense, as long as you are consistent:

Present	*Past*
In *A Separate Peace,* the hero **is** a shy sixteen-year-old boy at an elite prep school who **feels** a mix of admiration and jealousy for Finny, his roommate. Finny **is** bold, witty, and athletic.	In *A Separate Peace,* the hero **was** a shy sixteen-year-old boy at an elite prep school who **felt** a mix of admiration and jealousy for Finny, is roommate. Finny **was** bold, witty, and athletic.

One of the most common errors that student writers make is beginning a passage in one tense, then shifting when there is no change in time:

The phone **rings,** and I **wake** up. It **is** only five a.m. I **pick** up the phone, expecting bad news about my grandmother, who **is** sick. But it **is** Larry. He **tells** me to meet him at the airport at seven. I *hung* up the phone, *took* a shower, and *got* dressed. I *got* into my car and *was* just pulling out of the driveway when I **remember** he never told me what his flight number **is** or even what airline he **is** on. I **pick** up my cell phone but **get** no response. I **realize** the best thing to do **is** just wait by the baggage claim.

Revised—Present Tense

The phone **rings,** and I **wake** up. It **is** only five a.m. I **pick** up the phone, expecting bad news about my grandmother, who **is** sick. But it **is** Larry. He **tells** me to meet him at the airport at seven. I **hang** up the phone, **take** a shower, and **get** dressed. I **get** into my car and **am** just pulling out of the driveway when I **remember** he never told me what his flight number **is** or even what airline he **is** on. I **pick** up my cell phone but **get** no response. I **realize** the best thing to do **is** just wait by the baggage claim.

Revised—Past Tense

The phone *rang,* and I *woke* up. It *was* only five a.m. I *picked* up the phone, expecting bad news about my grandmother, who *was* sick. But it *was* Larry. He *told* me to meet him at the airport at seven. I *hung* up the phone, *took* a shower, and *got* dressed. I *got* into my car and *was* just pulling out of the driveway when I *remembered* he never told me what his flight number *was* or even what airline he *was* on. I *picked* up my cell phone but *got* no response. I *realized* the best thing to do was just wait by the baggage claim.

Note: The best way to check your work for illogical shifts in tense is to read your essay aloud. It is often easier to hear than see illogical shifts. Remember to shift tense only when there is a clear change in time.

EXERCISE 4   Revising Errors in Tense

Revise this passage from a student essay to eliminate illogical shifts in tense.
NOTE: Some shifts in this passage logically distinguish between past events
and current or ongoing conditions or situations.

English 112   William Bronski

Exposed to a Killer

I was born in Philadelphia, but I grew up in Haddonfield, where my parents
move when I was two. In high school I get a job working on the Jersey shore helping
an old guy sell trinkets on the boardwalk. It was a great job because on my lunch
hour I go swimming and hang out with my friends on the beach. Being sixteen or
seventeen, I felt invincible and never worry about sunscreen and got a bad sunburn
about once a month.

I went to college in San Jose, and my friends and I took weekend trips to Vegas
or the beach. I began to use sunscreen but still forget now and then. At that time all
I worried about was never letting any of my friends drive drunk.

I begin to worry about the sun only when I found out two years ago that my
aunt, who never lie out in the sun, was diagnosed with a serious form of skin cancer. Now I make sure I protect myself with sunscreen. I always keep some in my car
because I live in Southern California and never know when an errand or a call from
a friend will expose me to a killer.

_____

_____

_____

_____

_____

_____

_____

_____

_____

_____

_____

_____

_____

Mood

The mood of a verb expresses the writer's attitude. English has three
moods: **indicative, imperative,** and **subjunctive.** Most people automatically use indicative and imperative moods without a problem.

Indicative mood states facts, questions, actions, and opinions. Probably 95 percent of the sentences that you will ever write will be in the indicative mood:

> Rome is the capital of Italy.
> She drove me to school yesterday.
> The movie is boring.
> Do we have a test this week?

Imperative mood states commands or orders. You write imperative sentences when you give directions or list instructions as in a repair manual or a recipe. The subject ("you") is assumed and usually does not appear in the sentence:

> Run!
> Apply pressure until the bleeding stops.
> See your doctor before starting a diet.

Subjunctive mood indicates a wish, a request, or a hypothetical situation. Subjunctive sentences don't occur very often and sometimes confuse writers because these sentences use *were* instead of *was:*

> I wish I **were** going home today.
> If he **were** here, we'd get the job done on time.

KNOWING ENGLISH

Subjunctive Mood

You use the subjunctive mood only to state a desire or describe a hypothetical situation. Subjunctive sentences don't occur very often, and many people in speaking mistakenly use the indicative mood:

> I wish I *was* going home today.
> If he *was* here, we'd get the job done on time.

Remember, when you state a wish or describe something hypothetical, use *were*—even though it may sound awkward:

> We wish he **were** (not *was*) still on the team.
> If only the coach **were** (not *was*) willing to try something new.

Active and Passive Voice

English has two voices—**active** and **passive. Active voice** emphasizes the subject—who did the act. **Passive voice** emphasizes to whom or to what an act was done.

Active	*Passive*
The **teacher chose** the books.	The **books were chosen** by the teacher.
The **city repaved** the street.	The **street was repaved** by the city.
My **aunt sold** the old house.	The **old house was sold** by my aunt.

Grammar Choices and Meaning

It is important to understand that using active or passive voice is not so much a matter of being right or wrong, but in the meaning you want to express. Active voice is preferred because it is direct, strong, and clear.

Active
> Atlas Electronics developed the new sensor.
> Lisa Montone will direct the film.
> A federal judge authorized the wiretap.

Passive voice tends to reverse the order, emphasizing the object over the subject, sometimes creating a sentence that reports an action without naming a subject.

Passive
> The new sensor was developed by Atlas Electronics.
> The film will be directed by Lisa Montone.
> The wiretap was approved.

Passive voice is used when the act is more significant than its cause.

Passive
> The missing plane was flown by a veteran pilot.
> The museum was destroyed by fire.
> My car was stolen.

Passive Voice in Professional Writing

Police officers and other investigators are trained to use passive voice in writing reports to avoid jumping to conclusions. Because active voice makes a strong connection between subject and verb, it can lead writers to make assumptions. By writing in the passive voice, reporting can be made more objective. Facts are presented and events related without stressing cause and effect or assigning responsibility:

> The security alarm was activated at 3:15 a.m. The window to the rear office was broken. Nothing was reported stolen. Possible data theft has been suggested. No employees have been fired recently. The company has received no threats. The company's insurance company has been informed of the break-in.

However, passive voice can be used to avoid taking responsibility:

> Attempts to repair the roof failed.
> The pump was inspected last year.
> Complaints were made against her.

In all these questions, the "who" is missing. Who attempted to repair the roof? Who inspected the pump? Who made complaints?

EXERCISE 5   Changing Passive Voice to Active Voice

Rewrite these sentences to change them from passive to active voice. In some cases you will have to invent a missing subject.

> **TO ALL MANAGERS:**
>
> The annual Facilities Review was completed last week. Major changes in the way Apex Motors ships and receives spare parts have been suggested. Complaints filed by customers reveal unacceptable turnaround times for replacement of damaged merchandise. Statements made by President Jarmon indicate that he intends to implement the report's recommendations.

Other Verb Problems

Could Have, Must Have, Should Have, Would Have

Because *have* and *of* sound alike when speaking, it is easy to mistakenly write "could *of*" instead of "could *have*." *Have* is used in verb phrases. *Of* is a preposition showing a relationship.

Have	*Of*
She could **have** taken a cab.	The price **of** cabs is rising.
They might **have** called us.	She is the secretary **of** state.
The college should **have** offered tutoring.	I lost my proof **of** purchase.

Double Negatives

Use only one negative to express a negative idea. Don't create **double negatives** with words such as *hardly, scarcely, no, not,* or *never.* Double negatives are illogical. As in mathematics, two negatives make a positive statement. If you ***don't have no money,*** then you are saying that you ***have money.***

Double negative	*Correct*
I **never have no** homework.	I **never have** homework.
She **won't never take** a plane.	She **will never take** a plane.
I **didn't take nothing.**	I **didn't take anything.**

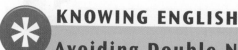

KNOWING ENGLISH

Avoiding Double Negatives

Double negatives are common in some languages and in some English dialects. If you are a native speaker of one of these languages or dialects, be careful to use only one negative word in each clause.

EXERCISE 6 Eliminating Common Verb Problems and Double Negatives

Rewrite the following sentences to eliminate common verb problems or double negatives.

Karen Kincaid   English 112

Failure to Plan

When my roommate offered me a chance to go to San Francisco on spring break, I should of asked her for more details. But I was so excited I did not ask her no questions. I just packed up my bags, helped her load up the car, and hit the ATM. We were on the road less than three hours when we get sidelined by a bad tire. Cindy tells me her credit card is maxed out, so I end up paying for a new tire. She had told me we would stay at her brother's condo. He is supposed to be going to Hawaii with his family and let her stay there. But Cindy never bother to call him to confirm. If I was driving four hundred miles, I would make sure I had a place to sleep. When we get there, we found out that her brother's kids were so sick they canceled their Hawaii trip. Cindy and I end up sleeping on the living room floor, and by the second day we catch the kids' flu and just laid around shivering and coughing. We hardly saw nothing of the city. Our biggest thrill of the whole trip was ordering a pizza and watching *Escape from Alcatraz* the night before we left.

_____

_____

_____

_____

_____

_____

_____

_____

_____

_____

_____

_____

_____

WORKING TOGETHER

Working with a group of students, revise this announcement for verb errors.

Notice to All Employees:

As of March 1, all employees who are working for at least five years will be eligible for inclusion in the expanded benefits program. Federated Insurance, however, has the right to limit coverage with employees who are rejected for health insurance in the last two years because of preexisting conditions. If you are rejected, there is an appeal process. No employees will never lose their basic existing benefits.

Karen Delgado
Human Services Director

**Get Thinking
and Writing**

CRITICAL THINKING

Write a paragraph describing how your career plans have changed since you were in high school. What did you want to be when you were sixteen or seventeen? Did your goals stay the same, or did they change? What career do you dream of pursuing now?

WHAT HAVE YOU WRITTEN?

When you finish writing, review your use of tense, mood, and voice.

1. Write out one of your sentences stated in past tense:

   _____

   _____

   Have you used the proper verb to show past tense?

2. Write out one of your sentences stated in present tense:

   _____

   _____

   Does the verb state the present tense? Does it match the subject?

3. Have you avoided errors with verbs such as *lie* and *lay, raise* and *rise, set* and *sit?*

_____

_____

_____

4. Have you written *of* instead of *have* in *should have* or *would have?*

What Have You Learned?

Select the correct verb in each sentence.

1. ____ If I (was/were) driving, I would have a map.

2. ____ The guests (rose/raised) questions once the cruise started.

3. ____ We could (of/have) rented a limo for the price of a cab.

4. ____ I (lay/laid) the baby down for a nap.

5. ____ The children (spread/spreaded) the blankets for a picnic.

Answers appear on the following page.

WRITING ON THE WEB

Using a search engine such as Yahoo! or Google, enter terms such as *verb tense, past tense, past perfect tense, present progressive tense, irregular verbs, subjunctive,* and *passive voice* to locate current sites of interest.

1. Read online newspaper and magazine articles about an issue that interests you, and notice how writers use tense to show shifts from past to present.

2. Write an e-mail to a friend about what you did last week. Choose verbs carefully to distinguish past events from ongoing ones.

POINTS TO REMEMBER

1. Explaining *when* something happens is as important as explaining *what* happens.

2. Regular verbs add *-d* or *-ed* to show past tense:

call	called	show	showed
talk	talked	want	wanted

3. Irregular verbs do not add *-d* or *-ed* to show past tense:

set	set	thrust	thrust
get	got	make	made

4. *Lie/lay, rise/raise,* and *set/sit* are often confused:

	To lie means *to rest* or *to recline.*		**To lay** means *to place.*	
present	lie	*lie down*	lay	*lay tile*
past	lay		laid	
past participle	lain		laid	

	To raise means *to lift.*		**To rise** means *to get up.*	
present	raise	*raise prices*	rise	*rise up!*
past	raised		rose	
past participle	raised		risen	

	To set means *to place.*		**To sit** means *to recline.*	
present	set	*set prices*	sit	*sit down!*
past	set		sat	
past participle	set		sat	

5. **Avoid illogical shifts in tense or time.**

Illogical
We **drove** to the pier and **see** the whales.

Correct
We **drove** to the pier and **saw** the whales.

6. **Use *were,* not *was,* in subjunctive sentences to state a wish or indicate a hypothetical situation:**

If I *were* you, I would leave now.

7. **Avoid mistaking *of* for *have* in *should have* and *could have.***

I could **have** passed.   *not*   I could **of** passed.

8. *Avoid double negatives.*

I don't have **any cash.**   *not*   I don't have **no cash.**

Answers to What Have You Learned? on page 511

1. were (see page 596) 2. raised (see page 502) 3. have (see page 508) 4. laid (see pages 501–502) 5. spread (see page 498)

CHAPTER 30

Pronoun Reference, Agreement, and Case

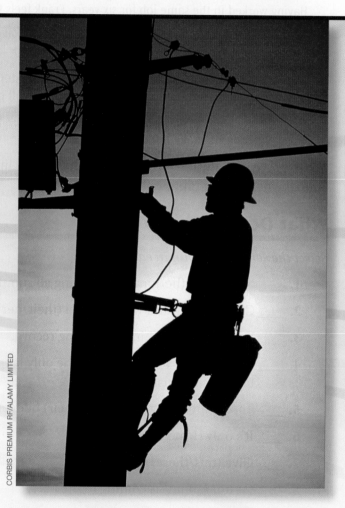

CORBIS PREMIUM RF/ALAMY LIMITED

CHAPTER GOALS

- Understand Pronouns
- Establish Clear Pronoun References
- Repair Errors in Pronoun Agreement
- Avoid Illogical Shifts in Point of View
- Use the Right Pronoun Case

Do you prefer working on your own or as part of a group?
Write a paragraph describing your ideal job.

Get Writing

513

What Are Pronouns?

Pronouns, such as *he, she, they,* and *it,* take the place of nouns. Without pronouns, your writing would be awkward:

Frank gave Frank's presentation to the new employees yesterday. Frank hopes that Frank's system will boost productivity and that Frank's boss will promote Frank.

Having worked in the same job for six years, Frank feels that Frank needs a change in order to make full use of Frank's skills.

Pronouns eliminate needless repetition:

Frank gave *his* presentation to the new employees yesterday. Frank hopes that *his* system will boost productivity and that *his* boss will promote *him.*

Having worked in the same job for six years, Frank feels that *he* needs a change in order to make full use of *his* skills.

To prevent confusion, pronouns must be clearly linked to their **antecedents** (the nouns they represent).

What Do You Know?

Select the correct pronoun in each sentence.

1. ____ Nancy and (he/him) are working all summer.

2. ____ Carmen or Maria will lend you (their/her) coat.

3. ____ We objected to (him/his) voting record.

4. ____ When I went to high school, the only language (I/you) could take was Spanish.

5. ____ The committee votes on (its/their) budget today.

6. ____ It's only (I/me).

7. ____ Give (this/these) discs to Rick.

8. ____ (Who/Whom) is coming to the party?

9. ____ It is (who/whom)?

10. ____ We gave the money to Frank, Jenny, Chris, and (she/her).

Answers appear on the following page.

Get Writing

WHAT ARE YOU TRYING TO SAY?

Describe a historical event that you think changed the United States. Summarize what happened, and explain why you think it was significant.

_____

_____

_____

_____

_____

_____

_____

_____

_____

_____

_____

_____

_____

_____

_____

_____

WHAT HAVE YOU WRITTEN?

Underline all the pronouns in your paragraphs.

1. Can you circle the noun (antecedent) that each pronoun represents?

2. Are plural nouns represented by plural pronouns? Are singular nouns represented by singular pronouns?

3. Are the pronouns in the right case? Do you use *I, we, he, she, they,* and *it* as subjects? Do you use *me, us, him, her,* and *them* as objects? Do you use *my, our, his, hers, their,* and *its* to show possession?

Types Of Pronouns

There are four types of pronouns: **personal, indefinite, relative,** and **demonstrative.**

Personal pronouns refer to people and have three forms, depending on how they are used in a sentence: **subjective, objective,** and **possessive.**

	Subjective		Objective		Possessive	
	Singular	**Plural**	**Singular**	**Plural**	**Singular**	**Plural**
1st person	I	we	me	us	my (mine)	our (ours)
2nd person	you	you	you	you	your (yours)	your (yours)
3rd person	he	they	him	them	his (his)	their (theirs)
	she		her		her (hers)	
	it		it		its	

She bought **our** house, so **we** gave **her** the keys.
They sold the car because **it** was older than **mine**.

Relative pronouns introduce noun and adjective clauses:

who, whoever, whom, whose which, whichever that, what, whatever

> I will help **whoever** asks.
> Tom has a new camera, **which** he won in a contest.

Demonstrative pronouns indicate the noun (antecedent):

this, that, these, those

> **That** book is interesting.
> **These** books are interesting.

Indefinite pronouns refer to abstract persons or things:

Singular				Plural	Singular or Plural		
everyone	someone	anyone	no one	both	all	more	none
everybody	somebody	anybody	nobody	few	any	most	some
everything	something	anything	nothing	many			
each	another	either	neither				

> **Everyone** should cast his or her vote.   **More** security is needed.
> **Both** girls are attending summer school.   **More** security guards are needed.

Using Pronouns

To prevent confusion, pronouns have to be precisely used.

- **Pronouns must be clearly linked to** *antecedents*—**the nouns or other pronouns they represent:**

   Unclear Reference
   The classrooms are half-empty. Test scores are bad. The dropout rate is growing. **They** just don't care.
   > [To whom does *they* refer—*students, teachers, parents?*]

   Clear Reference
   The students skip class, score poorly on tests, and drop out. **They** just don't care.
   > [*They* refers to students]

   Unclear Reference
   Eric asked George to read **his** book.
   > [Whose book is it—*Eric's* or *George's?*]

   Clear Reference
   Eric gave **his** book to George and asked **him** to read it.
   Eric looked at George's book, then asked **him** to read it.

- **Pronouns must agree, or match, the antecedent in number:**

   Incorrect
   Every taxpayer must bring **their** notice to the hearing.
   > [*taxpayer* is singular; *their* is plural]

Singular
Every taxpayer should bring **his or her** notice to the hearing.
  [singular *his or her* refers to singular *taxpayer*]

Plural
Taxpayers should bring **their** notices to the hearing.
  [plural *their* refers to plural *taxpayers*]

- **Pronouns have to agree or match in person:**

Incorrect
We went to the museum, where **you** can see the Picasso collection.
  [awkward shift between *we* (first person) and *you* (second person)]

Revised
We went to the museum, where **we** saw the Picasso collection.

- **Pronouns have to be used in the right case:**

Subjective
They took the train to Chicago.

Objective
We gave **them** the tickets.

Possessive
Ted and Carmen want to visit **their** uncle.

Reflexive
They are traveling by **themselves.**

- **Unnecessary pronouns should be eliminated:**

Unnecessary Pronouns
Carlos **he** should learn to drive.
The movie **it** makes no sense.
The parents **they** are angry.

Revised
Carlos should learn to drive.
The movie makes no sense.
The parents are angry.

Pronoun Reference

To express your ideas clearly, you have to use pronouns accurately. Because you know what you want to say, it is very easy to write sentences that make sense to you but will confuse your readers. For example, the pronoun *he* can refer to any single male. It is easy to create sentences in which the word could refer to more than one person:

> Jack bought a condo last year. When his brother Ted got out of the navy, he moved in to split expenses. At first they got along and enjoyed each other's company. But after a few months, **he** found it hard to live with a roommate.

Top 20

PRONOUN REFERENCE
To prevent confusion, make sure that pronouns are clearly linked to specific nouns.

Who does *he* in the last sentence refer to—Jack or Ted? Inserting the **antecedent**—in this case the proper name—eliminates confusion:

> Jack bought a condo last year. When his brother Ted got out of the navy, he moved in to split expenses. At first they got along and enjoyed each other's company. But after a few months, **Jack** found it hard to live with a roommate.

Without a clear link between the pronoun (*I, we, you, he, she, they,* and *it*) and the antecedent or noun that it represents, sentences can be misleading:

Confusing

The managers met with the employees to discuss their proposal.

Revised

The managers met with the employees to discuss the company's proposal.
The employees discussed their proposal at a meeting with the managers.

In order to correct reference errors, you may have to reword sentences:

Unclear Reference

Jack gave Ted his keys.

Clear Reference

Jack gave his keys to Ted.

Using *They* Without An Antecedent

The pronoun *they* is often used without a clear antecedent. In conversation, we frequently use *they* as an abstract reference to people with authority or power:

> "**They** put too much sex and violence on TV."
> "Can you believe what **they** pay pro athletes these days?"
> "Why don't **they** fix this road?"

In writing, you should be more precise. Make sure that every time *they* appears in your paper it is clearly linked to a specific plural noun. Replace unlinked *theys* with specific nouns:

> Networks put too much sex and violence on TV.
> Too much sex and violence appears on TV.

> Can you believe what owners are paying pro athletes these days?
> Can you believe what pro athletes are paid these days?

> Why doesn't the county fix this road?
> Why isn't this road fixed?

In editing papers, read them aloud. Pause when you see *they,* and determine if it clearly refers to a noun. Revise sentences with unlinked *theys* to eliminate confusion.

EXERCISE 1   Eliminate Unclear Pronoun References

Rewrite the following sentences to eliminate unclear pronoun references. You can revise the sentence to create a clear antecedent (noun) for they *or eliminate the pronoun by supplying a noun.*

1. Carmen suggested that Cindy fix her bicycle.

_____

2. The teachers met with the parents to discuss their concerns.

_____

3. They should repair this street.

_____

4. My sister worked with Karen until she went to college.

_____

5. Why don't they make movies I can take my kids to see?

_____

Pronoun Agreement

Just as singular subjects take singular verbs, **singular nouns take singular pronouns:**

visitor	he *or* she
car	it
Ms. Essex	she
Erica	she
the halfback	he
the nun	she
voter	he *or* she

Ms. Essex left early so **she** would not miss her flight.
The car won't start because **it** needs a battery.
The voter plays an important social role when **he or she** casts a ballot.

Plural nouns take plural pronouns:

visitors	they
cars	they
the Essexes	they
the halfbacks	they
the nuns	they
voters	they

The visitors arrived early because **they** wanted to see the new exhibit.
The cars are ten years old, but **they** are in great condition.
Voters play an important role in shaping society. **They** choose our leaders.

Top 20

PRONOUN AGREEMENT
Pronoun agreement errors are easy to make. Make sure that you match singular pronouns with singular nouns and plural pronouns with plural nouns.

Singular and Plural Nouns and Pronouns

- **Indefinite pronouns refer to no specific person, idea, or object.**
  The following indefinite pronouns are always singular:

another	either	nobody	somebody
anybody	everybody	no one	someone
anyone	everyone	none	something
anything	everything	nothing	
each	neither	one	

  Another house was sold, and **it** was on the market for only two days.
  Someone left **his or her** books in the classroom.
  Neither boy is going to get **his** money on time.

  Some indefinite pronouns are always plural:

both	few	many

  Both of the boys are regretting what **they** did.

  Some indefinite pronouns are singular or plural according to context:

all	any	more	most	none	sum

  Most of the **day** was good.   **Most** of the **people** had gone.

- **Some nouns that end in -s and look like plurals are singular:**

economics	mathematics	athletics	physics

  Economics is tough. **It** demands a lot of math skills.

- **Some nouns that may refer to one item are plural:**

pants	scissors	fireworks	binoculars

  My pants are blue. **They** are made of denim.

- **Proper nouns that look plural are singular if they are names of companies, organizations, or titles of books, movies, television shows, or works of art:**

United Technologies	*Two Women*	Alcoholics Anonymous

  I applied for a job at United Technologies because **it** offers great benefits.

- **Units of time and amounts of money are generally singular:**

  Sixty dollars *is* a fair price; **it** is more than I expected.

  They appear as plurals to indicate separate items:

  Sixty dollars **were** spread on the table. **They** were worn and tattered.

Avoiding Sexism

Because singular pronouns refer to only one sex or the other—*he* or *she*—it can be easy to create sentences that fail to include both males and females. However, it is acceptable to use only *he* or only *she* when writing about a single person or one of a group of people of the same sex:

Sam left work early because **he** has a cold.
Each of the women took **her** children to the clinic.
Kelly is going to night school because **she** wants an associate degree.
The best player in the NFL is one who puts **his** heart into the game.

When writing about people in general, it is important to avoid sexist pronoun use.

Sexist

Every student should do **his** best.	*Aren't women students?*
A doctor must use **his** judgment.	*What about female doctors?*

Methods to Avoid Sexism

1. **Provide both male and female singular pronouns:**
   Every student should do **his or her** best.

2. **Use plural antecedents:**
   Students should do **their** best.

3. **Reword the sentence to eliminate the need for pronouns:**
   Every student must excel.

Using *They* to Avoid Sexism

In speaking, people often use *they* rather than *he or she* to save time:

Incorrect

Every student should do **their** best.
Each employee is required to meet **their** supervisor before **they** can apply for a raise.
A good teacher knows **their** students.

This agreement error is often accepted in speech, but writing requires more formal methods of eliminating sexism. If you find yourself using *they* to refer to a singular noun or pronoun, use these methods to both avoid sexism and an error in agreement:

1. **Use plural nouns and pronouns to match *they:***

   All **students** should do **their** best.
   All **employees** are required to meet **their** supervisors before **they** can apply for raises.
   Good **teachers** know **their** students.

2. **Eliminate the need for pronouns:**

   A student should study hard.
   Every employee must have approval from a supervisor to apply for a raise.
   A good teacher knows the students.

3. **State as commands:**

   Employees—meet with your supervisor before applying for a raise.

EXERCISE 2   Selecting the Right Pronoun

Underline the correct pronoun in each sentence.

1. A chess-playing robot called the Turk caused a sensation when (they/it) first appeared in Europe in the 1770s.

2. The machine, which consisted of a large cabinet containing complex gears and wheels and the upper body of a wooden figure dressed like a Turk with moving arms, was able to play chess, and (it/they) defeated many human opponents.

3. The Turk was constructed by Wolfgang von Kempelen, a court official, and (he/they) exhibited his robot throughout Europe.

4. Benjamin Franklin and Napoleon played the Turk, and (he/they) both lost to the mechanical chess master.

5. Players and observers were amazed when (it/they) saw the machine in action.

6. Johann Maelzel took the Turk on an American tour in the 1800s, where the machine impressed crowds, and many a visitor could not believe (their/his or her) eyes.

7. There were many skeptics, including Edgar Allan Poe, who wrote a popular article explaining (their/his) reasons for believing the machine was a hoax.

8. In fact, the intricate clockwork in the cabinet was just for show, and (they/it) left plenty of room for a person to sit inside the machine and operate the Turk.

9. The public gradually lost interest in the Turk as (their/its) suspicions grew.

10. The Turk and many other exhibits were destroyed when (it/they) were lost in a museum fire in 1854.

Avoiding Illogical Shifts in Point of View

Pronouns express three persons:

	First	Second	Third
Singular	I, me, my	you, you, your	he, him, his/she, her, her
Plural	we, us, our	you, you, your	they, them, their

Avoid making illogical shifts when writing. Maintain consistent point of view.

Illogical Shift
We went to the beach, but **you** couldn't find a place to park.
When **he** went to college, **you** could pay tuition with a part-time job.

Revised

We went to the beach, but **we** couldn't find a place to park.
[consistent use of plural first person]

When **he** went to college, **students** could pay tuition with a part-time job.
[use of *students* eliminates need for second pronoun]

EXERCISE 3   Eliminating Pronoun Shifts in Point of View

Revise the following sentences to eliminate illogical pronoun shifts in point of view.

ATTENTION ALL EMPLOYEES

Until further notice, several important changes will affect hospital admissions:

1. We are moving the admitting nurse's desk to the north corridor, where they can see people entering the main entrance.

2. Outpatients with appointments for lab work should go to the second floor, where you are required to sign in.

3. Until the waiting room is refurbished, family members and visitors can use the doctors' lounge, where you can watch TV and use the vending machines.

_____

_____

_____

_____

_____

_____

Using the Right Case

Nouns serve different functions in sentences. They can be subjects or objects, and they can be possessive. Pronouns appear in different forms to show how they function:

They sold **her** car to **me.**
Subject   possessive   object

These different forms are called *cases.*

Pronoun Cases

	Subjective	Objective	Possessive	Reflexive/Intensive
Singular	I	me	my, mine	myself
	you	you	you, yours	yourself
	he	him	his	himself
	she	her	her	herself
	it	it	its	itself
Plural	we	us	our, ours	ourselves
	you	you	your, yours	yourselves
	they	them	their, theirs	themselves
Singular or Plural	who	whom	whose	

In most sentences we automatically use pronouns in the right case, telling our readers the role that the pronoun plays.

Subjective pronouns serve as the subject of a verb:

We are flying to Chicago tonight.
This month **she** works every other weekend.

Objective pronouns serve as objects:

The hostess made a reservation for **us.**
Help **him** pay the bill.

Possessive pronouns demonstrate that the pronoun owns something:

Our house needs a new roof.
The school changed **her** grades.

Note: Because these pronouns already indicate possession, no apostrophes are needed.

KNOWING ENGLISH

Using Possessive Pronouns

In English, possessive pronouns—*my, your, his, her, our, their*—must agree with the nouns they represent, not the words they modify:

Incorrect
The club members advertised **its** bake sale on TV.

Revised
The club members advertised **their** bake sale on TV.

The possessive pronoun *their* agrees with *club members,* not *bake sale.*

Reflexive pronouns refer to other pronouns:

She moved the furniture **herself.**

Intensive pronouns add emphasis:

I myself ran the fund drive.

However, there are some pronoun uses that can be confusing, including plurals, comparisons, and sentences using certain words.

Plural Constructions

Using a single pronoun as a subject or object is generally easy.

> **She** helped **him** study.
> Sam gave the money to **her.**

However, when pronouns are part of plural subjects and objects, many writers make mistakes.

Incorrect
> Phil, the teachers, the parents, and **him** met with the principal.
> The principal met with Phil, the teachers, the parents, and **he.**

Correct
> Phil, the teachers, the parents, and **he** met with the principal.
> [subjective case]
> The principal met with Phil, the teachers, the parents, and **him.**
> [objective case]

When editing, the quickest method of checking case is to simplify the sentence by eliminating the other nouns:

> . . . **he** met with the principal.
> The principal met with . . . **him.**

Between

Pronouns that serve as objects of prepositions use the objective case—
him, her, me, them. Most constructions give writers few problems—to *him,*
for *them,* with *her.* However, the preposition *between* is often misused:

Incorrect (Subjective Case)	Correct (Objective Case)
between you and **I**	between you and **me**
between you and **he**	between you and **him**
between you and **she**	between you and **her**
between **he** and **she**	between **him** and **her**
between **they** and the teachers	between **them** and the teachers

Although people often used the subjective case with *between* in speaking,
the objective case is correct and should be used in writing.

Comparisons

Comparisons using *than* or *as* use the subjective case:

She is taller than **I**.	*not*	She is taller than **me**.
Tina is smarter than **he**.	*not*	Tina is smarter than **him**.

These constructions are confusing because the second verb is usually omitted. To test which pronoun to use, add the missing verb to see which pronoun sounds correct:

She is taller than **I am**.	*not*	She is taller than **me am**.
Tina is smarter than **he is**.	*not*	Tina is smarter than **him is**.

The Verb *to Be*

Subjective pronouns follow *to be* verbs:

Is it **she** on the phone?	*not*	Is it **her** on the phone?
It is **I**.	*not*	It is **me**.
Was it **they** in the car?	*not*	Was it **them** in the car?

Because we often use phrases such as "It's me" or "Is that her talking?" when we speak, the correct forms can sound awkward. The subjective case is correct and should be used in writing.

If your sentences still sound awkward, rewrite them to alter the *to be* pronoun form:

She is on the phone.
I am at the door.
Did **they** take the car?

Top 20

***TO BE* VERBS**

Remember to use subjective pronouns—*I, we, he, she, they*—after *to be* verbs.

Who and *Whom*

Who and *whom* are easily confused because they are generally used in questions and change the usual word pattern.

Who is subjective and serves as the subject of a verb:

Who is coming?   **Who** bought the house   **Who** is going to the concert?

Whom is objective and serves as the object of a verb or a preposition:

Give the books to **whom?**   To **whom** it may concern.   For **whom** is this intended?

To help choose the right word, substitute *he* and *him*. If *he* sounds better, use *who*. If *him* sounds better, use *whom*.

(Who/Whom) called?	[Use **who**—*He called*]
Take it from (whoever/whomever) can help.	[Use **whoever**—*He can help*]
For (who/whom) are you looking?	[Use **whom**—*I am looking for him*]

This and *That*, *These* and *Those*

***This* and *that* are singular:**

This inspection is not official.   **That** car needs work.   **This** is a fine film.

These and *those* are plural:

These inspections are not official.   **Those** cars need work.   **These** are fine films.

They and *Them*

They is subjective and is used when it is a subject to a verb:

They are working tonight.   You know **they** don't work on weekends.

Them is objective and is used as an object of a preposition or a verb:

Give the papers to **them**.   We can't get **them** *to* work on weekends.

Unnecessary Pronouns

Although in speaking, people sometimes insert a pronoun directly after a noun, these pronouns are unnecessary and should be eliminated.

Unnecessary
Marsha **she is** going to retire early.
The children **they** won't listen.
The book **it** doesn't make sense.

Revised
Marsha is going to retire early.
The children won't listen.
The book doesn't make sense.

EXERCISE 4   Selecting the Right Pronoun

Select the correct pronoun in each sentence.

1. Sandy and (I/me) are going to the concert next week.

2. The supervisor scheduled Sandy and (I/me) to work overtime.

3. That prevents (we/us) from leaving early.

4. I wanted to ask Ted, Carmen, Simon, Sheri, and (she/her) to drive us.

5. But (whom/who) can I ask to get up at four a.m.?

6. (This/These) things happen, I guess.

7. Dion and Carla might be able to help (we/us) out.

8. They get up very early, and we have asked (they/them) for help in the past.

9. I hate to ask Dion and (she/her) for another favor.

10. But Sandy and (I/me) are going to get there one way or another.

Working with a group of students, revise the pronoun errors in the following e-mail.

Attention New Employees:

Every new employee must submit their insurance application to me no later than March 15. Anyone who fails to submit your forms by the deadline risks losing health insurance coverage. Employees who are issued a company car must also fill out his or her vehicle registration slip to make sure you are covered in case of an accident. Great Lakes Mutual representatives will be holding benefits seminars next week. I encourage all new employees to attend one of this seminars so you can get answers to any questions employees may have.

Miranda Rojak

Benefits Manager

EXERCISE 5   Cumulative Exercise

Rewrite this paragraph to correct errors in pronoun use, subject-verb agreement, and run-ons.

Jameson-2

Then Sandy and me faced the problem of telling our parents that we decided to move to Texas because she wanted to go back to college. She needs to get her degree in her field everyone needs formal training unless they want to settle for minimum wage. I knew this made sense but it would be hard to tell her parents we were turning down their offer of giving us a house. Her parents' generosity are amazing. We really owe them a lot. When people go out of their way to help us, you have to consider their feelings. I knew they really wanted Sandy and I to stay in town and we did not want to seem ungrateful. We sat down with them after dinner and during a long conversation between they and we Sandy convinced her parents that her plan made sense.

_____
_____
_____
_____
_____
_____
_____
_____

Get Thinking and Writing

CRITICAL THINKING

Who is the bravest person you know? Write a paragraph describing this person and his or her actions.

WHAT HAVE YOU WRITTEN?

1. Underline all the pronouns, and circle their antecedents. Is there a clear link between pronouns and the nouns or pronouns they represent? Pay attention to uses of *they.*

2. Do nouns and pronouns agree in number? Do plural nouns have plural pronouns? Do singular nouns have singular pronouns?

   • Pay attention to nouns that look plural but are singular, such as *economics, committee,* and *jury.*

   • Remember that indefinite pronouns such as *each, everyone, anyone, someone,* and *somebody* are singular.

3. Review your use of case.

   • Use subjective case in comparisons and with pronouns following *to be* verbs: *taller than I* or *it is I.*

   • Use objective case with *between: between him and me.*

What Have You Learned?

Select the correct pronoun in each sentence.

1. ____ (Who/Whom) can help me change this tire?

2. ____ Kelly, Sandy, Terry, and (she/her) went to practice.

3. ____ (This/These) books are fascinating.

4. ____ Each driver should always carry (his or her/their) license at all times.

5. ____ The teacher told (we/us) students to work harder.

6. ____ How can these systems help the teachers and (we/us) do a better job?

7. ____ Seat (whomever/whoever) arrives first.

8. ____ Between you and (I/me), this budget makes no sense.

9. ____ Take a seat between George and (he/him).

10. ____ I can't pay you and (she/her) until next week.

Answers appear on the following page.

WRITING ON THE WEB

1. Using a search engine such as Yahoo! or Google, enter terms such as *pronoun, pronoun agreement, using pronouns,* and *pronoun cases* to locate current sites of interest.

2. Review e-mails you have sent, and look at your past use of pronouns. Can you locate errors in your writing? Which pronoun constructions have given you the most trouble in the past? Mark pages in this chapter for future reference.

POINTS TO REMEMBER

Pronouns have to be used with precision to prevent confusion.

1. Pronouns must clearly refer to a noun:

Unclear Reference
Sandy gave Vicki **her** keys.

Clear Reference
Sandy gave **her** keys to Vicki.

2. Pronouns and nouns match in number.

Each girl took **her** car.   [singular]
The **girls** took **their** cars.   [plural]

3. Pronouns use consistent point of view.

Inconsistent
When **one** visits New York, **you** have to dine at Sardis.
When **I** work overtime, **it** gets boring.

Consistent
When **you** visit New York, **you** have to dine at Sardis.
When **I** work overtime, **I** get bored.

4. Pronouns must appear in the right case.

Subjective Case
Who is at the door?
She is smarter than **I**.
It is **I**.
Was that **she** on the phone?

Objective Case
To **whom** it may concern.
Between you and **me,** the film is too long.

5. Pronouns directly following nouns they represent are unnecessary.

Unnecessary
The school **it** closed last week.
Frank **he** works weekends.

Revised
The school closed last week.
Frank works weekends.

Answers to What Have You Learned? on pages 529–530

1. Who (see page 526) 2. she (see page 526). 3. These (see pages 526–527) 4. his or her (see pages 519–520) 5. us (see page 524) 6. us (see page 524) 7. whoever (see page 526) 8. me (see page 524) 9. him (see page 524) 10. her (see page 524)

CHAPTER 31

Adjectives and Adverbs

CHAPTER GOALS

- Identify Adjectives and Adverbs

- Use Modifiers Accurately

- Understand Comparisons and Superlatives

ALAN SCHEIN/ALAMY LIMITED

Get Writing

Few employers now provide pensions. More and more workers have to manage their own retirement savings. Do you think that most people know enough about the stock market to make smart decisions? Should schools teach young people about financial planning? Do you feel prepared to save for your retirement?

Write one or more paragraphs explaining how much you know about investing.

What Are Adjectives and Adverbs?

The most important words in any sentence are the subject—the main idea or topic—and the verb—which connects the subject to action or other words. **Adjectives and adverbs add meaning to a sentence by telling us more about nouns and verbs.**

Adjectives are words and phrases that describe nouns and pronouns:

a **new** shirt   he was **tall**   a **unique old** car

Adverbs are words and phrases that describe verbs, adjectives, and other adverbs. They generally end in *-ly:*

she walked *quickly*   *fiercely* debated   a *freshly* painted room

Both add meaning to basic sentences.

Basic Sentence
George bought a car.

Basic Sentence Enhanced with Adjectives
George bought a **battered old** car that was **cheap** and **easy to repair.**

Basic Sentence Enhanced with Adjectives and Adverbs
George *recently* bought a *severely* **battered old** car that was **cheap** and *very* **easy to repair.**

What Do You Know?

Identify the modifiers in each sentence by underlining adjectives and circling adverbs.

1. The former mayor stunned her dedicated supporters by suddenly announcing she was dropping out of the heated Senate race to pursue an acting career.

2. We drove carefully through the thick fog looking for the small cottage.

3. She sang softly while her brother conducted the newly reorganized band.

4. The players cautiously followed the coach's radical training techniques.

5. The old taxi bounced loudly down the winding road.

Answers appear on the following page.

WHAT ARE YOU TRYING TO SAY?

Get Writing

Describe a person you admire in action, such as a quarterback throwing a touchdown pass, a singer performing a hit song, a politician giving a speech, or a parent helping a small child.

_____

_____

_____

_____

_____

_____

_____

_____

_____

_____

_____

_____

WHAT HAVE YOU WRITTEN?

Read through your description, and underline each adjective and circle each adverb. Notice how important modifiers are in expressing your ideas. If you eliminated the adjectives and adverbs, would your writing have the same effect? Would readers be able to appreciate what you are trying to say?

Understanding Adjectives

Some words are clearly adjectives because they describe other words. They add information about nouns and pronouns, telling us about their age, shape, color, quality, quantity, or character.

old	rectangular	green	wealthy	plentiful
new	straight	blue	impoverished	rare
unique	round	violet	firm	few
futuristic	square	orange	broken	numerous

Some adjectives are formed from nouns and verbs and have distinct endings.

Noun Form	Adjective	Verb Form	Adjective
North	northern	rent	rented
law	legal	practice	practiced
navy	naval	slice	sliced
Bible	Biblical	reserve	reserved

Past participles (past-tense verbs) are adjectives—*stolen* cars, *ripped* skirt, *chosen* one, *known* felon, *forgotten* keys.

Answers to What Do You Know? on page 533

1. adj.: former, dedicated, heated, Senate, acting; adv.: suddenly 2. adj.: thick, small; adv.: carefully 3. adj.: reorganized; adv.: softly, newly 4. adj.: radical, training; adv.: cautiously 5. adj.: old, winding; adv.: loudly

Other nouns and verbs appear as adjectives with no spelling change. You can tell they are adjectives only by context, their position in a sentence:

We bought **house** insurance.	Put that in the **book** display.
George gave me a **steel** lock.	We put in a **tile** floor.
They wear **plastic** helmets.	It was found on the **ocean** floor.

These words serve as adjectives because they add meaning to nouns:

What kind of insurance?	**house** insurance	Which display?	**book** display
What kind of lock?	**steel** lock	What kind of floor?	**tile** floor
What kind of helmet?	**plastic** helmet	What kind of floor?	**ocean** floor

KNOWING ENGLISH

Adjectives And Plural Nouns

In many languages, such as Spanish, adjectives must agree with the nouns they modify. In English there is only one adjective form that modifies both singular and plural nouns.

Singular

He wore an **old** suit.

Plural

He wore **old** suits.

EXERCISE 1   Identifying Adjectives

Underline the adjectives in each sentence.

Eastern Security Management

To All Security Staff:

Boston One Bank has contacted us regarding their new ATMs. These electronic machines, installed in retail establishments throughout the city, have been malfunctioning. In rare instances, they have failed to record transactions and dispensed the wrong amount of cash. The original design has been in use nationwide since 2003 with few serious malfunctions. Recent modifications have been limited to strengthening the aluminum exterior to prevent tampering. Bank One security technicians have replaced malfunctioning sensors, but the problems have not been resolved.

Anyone with experience with ATMs should immediately contact Karen Ginzberg.

Tameka Reynolds
Security Analyst

EXERCISE 2   Using Adjectives

Add adjectives in each sentence.

1. I took an exercise class, which was _____ and _____.

2. The _____ dorm was closed for _____ repairs.

3. We stayed at a _____ hotel in the _____ section of the _____ city.

4. Her _____ stories inspired _____ directors to make _____ movies.

5. The _____ car was hard to sell because it was _____.

EXERCISE 3   Using Participles

Past participles are adjectives. Often in speaking, however, people drop the -ed endings and forget to add them in writing. In each sentence, underline the misused past participle and write out the correct adjective form.

1. We made sandwiches with slice cheese and dice ham.   _____

2. I had to wear a borrow suit to the prom.   _____

3. They served corn beef and cabbage and mash potatoes.   _____

4. We have coffee, soda, lemonade, and ice tea.   _____

5. We swam in the *heat* pool all day.   _____

Top 20

PAST PARTICIPLES

Remember to use the *past-tense* form of verbs as adjectives: **broiled** chicken, *not* **broil** chicken.

Top 20

COMMAS

Separate unrelated adjectives with commas.

Commas and Adjectives

Place a comma between two unrelated adjectives describing one noun or pronoun:

We saw a new, fascinating film.   They offered us a nutritious, inexpensive meal.

Do not place a comma between two related adjectives describing one noun or pronoun:

We saw a new Woody Allen film.   They offered us hot apple pie.

Apply this simple test to see if you need commas:

1. Read the sentence aloud, and place the word *and* between the two adjectives. If the sentence sounds OK, ADD a comma.

   We saw a new and fascinating film. = sounds OK, *add comma*

2. If the sentence sounds awkward, DO NOT ADD a comma.

We saw a new **and** Woody Allen film = sounds awkward, *no comma needed*

KNOWING ENGLISH

Order Of Multiple Adjectives

We often use several adjectives to describe a noun. In order to prevent confusion, most writers put adjectives in a common pattern based on their meaning. For example, we typically say "small square box" or "old blue dress" instead of "square small box" or "blue old dress."

When you use more than one adjective, follow the pattern shown below:

• Evaluation	*charming, painful, valid*
• Size	*enormous, large, tiny*
• Shape	*rectangular, round, square*
• Age	*youthful, middle-aged, ancient*
• Color	*orange, blue, brown*
• Nationality	*Libyan, Chinese, Canadian*
• Religion	*Hindu, Catholic, Muslim*
• Material	*concrete, stone, adobe*

Examples:
We rented rooms in a **charming old Spanish** castle.
A **tall young African** gentleman stood behind the pulpit.

Understanding Adverbs

Adverbs describe verbs, adjectives, and other adverbs. They usually add *-ly* to the adjective form:

Adjective	+ *ly*	=	Adverb	Adjective	+ *ly*	=	Adverb
fine	*ly*		finely	intricate	*ly*		intricately
cold	*ly*		coldly	firm	*ly*		firmly
legal	*ly*		legally	scientific	*ly*		scientifically

Other adverbs do not end in *-ly:*

fast	hard	just	right	straight

EXERCISE 4   Identifying Adverbs

Underline the adverbs in each sentence.

Design North

March 31, 2009

RE: Design Changes for Hotel Metro Lobby

Jessica Dana:

I just received your blueprints. Both the architect and builder firmly agree that we need to make changes to the lobby immediately. Because the building will not open until 2012, it will have to meet the newly revised fire code. I like the way you greatly expanded the lobby entrance without sacrificing the sense of intimacy. I fully realize these are not final plans. The architect will have to precisely measure the need for additional marble and brass fittings. The items we selected are widely used and should be readily available. We should have a completely revised price list by mid-April.

I greatly appreciate your hard work.

I will call Friday to set up a meeting next week.

Kentora Jackson

EXERCISE 5   Using Adverbs

Add adverbs in each sentence.

1. He sang so _____ and _____ that the audience applauded _____ .

2. The _____ controversial policy was _____ debated by the school board.

3. Despite all her hard work, the committee _____ rejected her plan and _____ refused to pay for her services.

4. The coach _____ taught the new players to follow the _____ successful techniques that brought the team a/an _____ long string of victories.

5. We drove _____ through the _____ crowded streets on the way to Tiger Stadium.

Grammar Choices and Meaning

Because both adjectives and adverbs modify other words, they can be easily confused. **Changing an adjective to an adverb changes meaning.**

Form		*Meaning*
adjective + adjective		
slow rusting car	=	*a car that is both slow and rusting*
adverb + adjective		
slowly rusting car	=	*a car that is gradually rusting*
adjective + adjective		
new waxed car	=	*a car that is both new and waxed*
adverb + adjective		
newly waxed car	=	*a car (new or old) that has just been waxed*
adjective + adjective		
large fiberglass car	=	*a car that is large and made of fiberglass*
adverb + adjective		
largely fiberglass car	=	*a car (of any size) that is mostly fiberglass*

Use the right adjectives and adverbs to modify verbs of sense—*see, hear, feel, smell, touch,* and *taste.*

Adjective:	I feel **poor** after the accident.	[*poor* modifies the noun *I*, suggesting that the writer feels financially distressed by the accident]
Adverb:	I feel **poorly** after the accident.	[*poorly* modifies the verb *feel;* the writer is injured or in ill health following the accident]

POINT TO REMEMBER

When speaking, people commonly use the shorter adjective form when an adverb is needed:

Incorrect	*Correct*
"Drive careful, now."	"Drive careful**ly**, now."
"Do the tax work accurate."	"Do the tax work accurate**ly**."
"That's real good coffee."	"That's real**ly** good coffee."
"He drove real slow."	"He drove real**ly** slow**ly**."
"She acted crazy."	"She acted craz**ily**."

In writing, make sure that you use adverbs (which often end in *-ly*) to modify verbs, adjectives, and other adverbs.

Good and *Well/Bad* and *Badly*

Two adjective/adverb pairs are commonly confused:

Good and ***bad*** are **adjectives** You look good. [you appear attractive] I feel bad. [I am depressed or sick]	***Well*** and ***badly*** are **adverbs** You look well. [you appear healthy] I feel badly. [I have difficulty sensing touch]
Good and ***bad*** modify **nouns and pronouns** **She** looked *good* despite her accident. She had a ***bad* fracture** in her right arm.	***Well*** and ***badly*** modify **verbs, adjectives, and other adverbs** She **walked** *well* despite injuring her leg. Her right arm was ***badly* fractured.**

Good and *bad* and *well* and *badly* have special comparative and superlative forms:

Basic	Comparative	Superlative
good	better	best
bad	worse	worst
well	better	best
badly	worse	worst

This coffee is **good,** but the **best** coffee is served at Rio's.
The traffic is **bad** this morning, but yesterday it was **worse.**
Keri swims **well,** but Nancy is the **best** swimmer on the team.
That is a **badly** directed movie, but the **worst** has to be *Return to Yonkers*.

EXERCISE 6   Selecting the Correct Adjectives and Adverbs

Select the correct adjective or adverb in each sentence.

1. Operation Bernhardt was an (extreme/extremely) devious plan developed by the Nazis to undermine the British economy during World War II.

2. Bernhardt Kruger, an SS major, assembled engravers, forgers, and printers imprisoned in concentration camps and ordered them to begin the (intricate/intricately) task of forging British pounds.

3. The work was (unbelievably/unbelievable) difficult; the inmates had to make (accurately/accurate) engravings, imitate detailed watermarks, and create special papers.

4. The notes they produced were the (best/better) forgeries ever attempted.

5. The Nazi plan was (devilishly/devilish) and simple.

6. The Germans planned to drop pound notes over English towns, assuming that even the most patriotic Britons would keep the bills and (eventually/eventual) spend them, inflating the British economy.

7. Over 100 million pounds' worth of currency was counterfeited, but it was not ready until the last months of the war, when it was (extremely/extreme) difficult for the Germans to introduce the money into Britain.

8. With the Nazi Reich (totally/total) collapsing, the Germans dumped the currency in a lake, where divers recovered the bills in 1959.

9. Although most of the phony pounds were hidden, some made their way into circulation and (mysteriously/mysterious) appeared in Britain long after the war.

10. SS Major Kruger was imprisoned after the war by the French, who put him to work (secret/secretly) forging documents for France's intelligence agents.

Comparisons

Adjectives and adverbs are often used in comparing two things. There are three basic rules for showing comparisons:

1. Add *-er* for adjectives and adverbs with one syllable.

   Adjectives
Bill is **smart**.	Bill is **smarter** than Ted.
The car is **old**.	The car is **older** than mine.
The house is **cold**.	The house is **colder** than the garage.

   Adverbs
She sang **loudly**.	He sang **louder** than Jane.
She worked **hard**.	She worked **harder** than Ted.
They drive **fast**.	They drive **faster** than I would.

2. Use *more* for adjectives with more than one syllable that do not end in *-y:*

The damage is **extensive**.	The damage is **more extensive** than we expected.
He is **talented**.	He is **more talented** than critics think.

   Use *more* for adverbs, sometimes adding *-er* to the positive form:

He drove **recklessly**.	He drove **more recklessly** than ever.
They worked **fast**.	They worked **faster**.

3. Add *-ier* after dropping the *-y* for adjectives and adverbs ending in *-y:*

   Adjective
The store is **busy**.	The store is **busier** on weekends.
The dorm is **noisy**.	The dorm is **noisier** on weekends.

   Adverb
He felt **sleepy**.	He felt **sleepier** after his nap.
She felt **hungry**.	She felt **hungrier** than usual.

EXERCISE 7 Using Adjectives and Adverbs in Comparisons

Write out the proper comparative form of each adjective and adverb; then use it in a sentence.

1. tired _____

_____

2. warmly _____

_____

3. hotly _____

_____

4. cold _____

_____

5. happy _____

_____

Avoiding Double Comparisons

When speaking, some people use double comparisons:

Sara is **more smarter** than Beth.
This car is **more older** than mine.
The final is **more harder** than the midterm.

Because both *more* and *-er* indicate something greater, only one is needed:

Sara is **smarter** than Beth.
This car is **older** than mine.
The final is **harder** than the midterm.

Superlatives

Comparisons show a difference between two items:

Sam is **taller** than Sean.

To show differences between three or more items, use superlative forms:

Sam is the **tallest** boy in class.

There are three basic rules for creating superlative adjectives and adverbs:

1. Add *-est* to adjectives and adverbs with one syllable.

Basic	Comparative	Superlative
cold	colder	coldest
slow	slower	slowest
cheap	cheaper	cheapest

2. **Add -*iest* after dropping the *y* in adjectives and adverbs that end in -*y*.**

Basic	Comparative	Superlative
witty	wittier	wittiest
easy	easier	easiest
icy	icier	iciest

3. **Use *most* for adjectives and adverbs with two or more syllables that do not end in -*y*.**

Basic	Comparative	Superlative
affordable	more affordable	most affordable
cordial	more cordial	most cordial
depressing	more depressing	most depressing

POINTS TO REMEMBER

Remember that superlatives—which usually end in -*est*—are used only when writing about three or more items. Many people mistakenly use superlatives instead of comparisons when writing about only two items.

Incorrect Use of Superlatives
Sara is the eldest of our two daughters.
In comparing New York and Chicago, New York is the biggest.

Correct Use of Comparison
Sara is the **elder** of our two daughters.
In comparing New York and Chicago, New York is **bigger**.

Do not use superlatives with absolute words such as *impossible, perfect, round, destroyed,* or *demolished.* These terms have no degree. If something is *impossible,* it means that it is not possible, not just difficult. If a building is *destroyed,* it is damaged beyond all repair. To say it is "completely destroyed" is repetitive, like saying someone is "completely dead."

Incorrect
The house was completely demolished.
The room was perfectly round.

Correct
The house was demolished.
The room was round.

EXERCISE 8 Eliminating Adjective and Adverb Errors

Revise each of the following sentences to eliminate errors in using adjectives and adverbs.

1. Born in Alabama, Zora Neale Hurston grew up in Florida and later traveled north to attend Barnard College and Columbia University in the 1920s, when most black women had extreme limited educational opportunities.

   _____

   _____

   _____

2. Hurston collected African American folklore and became one of the most wide published black writers in the 1930s and 1940s.

   _____

   _____

3. Generous supported by patrons, Hurston traveled extensive throughout the South, as well as Haiti, Jamaica, and the Bahamas, to conduct research.

   _____

   _____

4. Hurston became a leading figure in the Harlem Renaissance, making many influential friends and demonstrating her remarkably knowledge of African American folk culture and language.

   _____

   _____

   _____

5. However, some critics found her homey stories about dialect-speaking African Americans unacceptable sentimental.

   _____

   _____

6. They firmly believed that black writers should address the poorly conditions African Americans faced and that it was more better to focus on current political issues rather than old folktales.

   _____

   _____

   _____

7. Hurston's objections to some aspects of the civil rights movement more further alienated her critics.

_____

_____

8. She died poorly and largely forgotten in 1960, her books having gone out of print.

_____

_____

9. Fifteen years later, an article by Alice Walker sparked interest in Hurston, and many scholars began to read this new rediscovered author.

_____

_____

10. Hurston's books, once wide dismissed for being superficial, are now seen as serious works that very accurate captured the life and language of an era.

_____

_____

WORKING TOGETHER

Working with a group of students, review this e-mail for errors in adjective and adverb use. Underline mistakes, and discuss corrections. Note how changing modifiers changes meaning.

Dear Kayla:

I read your report today. I agree we must take immediately action. I was not aware that it was so remarkable easy for people to access our customers' personal data. I feel very badly about any potential loss of extreme sensitive data.

Cindy Diamond in the legal department says that we could face an immensely liability if any data were stolen and our customers became victims of identity theft.

I think the most best thing you can do is talk to Frank Harrison and Sandy Berger tomorrow when you are in New York. I will send them an e-mail tonight and attach your notes. Frank and Sandy have the authority to upgrade security systems throughout the company.

I appreciate you bringing this to my attention so quick.

Dayton Cooper

Get Thinking and Writing

CRITICAL THINKING

In most states, nearly half the inmates who complete their sentences commit crimes when they return to society and end up back in prison. What do you think could make prisons more effective—more job training, drug and alcohol counseling, or tougher policies? Write one or more paragraphs stating your views.

WHAT HAVE YOU WRITTEN?

Read your paragraphs, underlining each adjective and circling each adverb. Review the rules explained in this chapter. Have you used modifiers correctly?

What Have You Learned?

Select the correct adjective or adverb in each sentence.

1. _____ I tripped on the (loose/loosely) gravel on the (bad/badly) maintained driveway.

2. _____ This is the (worse/worst) restaurant in town!

3. _____ California Pacific is the (best/better) of the two insurance companies.

4. _____ It was (impossible/totally impossible) to get to the airport on time.

5. _____ I bought the (new waxed/newly waxed) '87 Corvette.

Answers appear on the following page.

WRITING ON THE WEB

Using a search engine such as Yahoo! or Google, enter terms such as *adjective, adverb,* and *modifier* to locate current sites of interest.

POINTS TO REMEMBER

1. *Adjectives* modify nouns and pronouns; *adverbs* modify verbs, adjectives, and other adverbs.

   Note: Use adjectives and adverbs carefully when referring to verbs such as *see, hear, feel, smell, touch,* and *taste:*

   adjective: I see **good** coming from this.   =   I predict good results.

   adverb: I see **well.**   =   I have good eyesight.

2. **Past participles are adjectives:**

   a **rented** car   a **broken** window   **mashed** potatoes

   Note: In speaking, many people drop the *-ed* ending, but it should always be used in writing. Write *mashed potatoes,* not *mash potatoes.*

3. Most adverbs end in *-ly,* with some exceptions:

hard   fast   right   just   straight

Note: In speaking, many people commonly drop adverb endings, but they should always be used in writing. Write *drive carefully,* not *drive careful.*

4. Adjective and adverb use affects meaning:

fresh sliced bread   = sliced bread that is fresh
freshly sliced bread = bread (fresh or stale) that has just been sliced

5. *Good* and *bad* are adjectives that describe nouns and pronouns:

I feel **good** = I am healthy or happy   I feel **bad** = I am sad

***Well* and *badly* are adverbs that describe verbs, adjectives, or other adverbs:**

I feel **well** = I have a good sense of touch   I feel **badly** = I have a poor sense of touch

6. Use proper comparative form to discuss two items:

Tom is **taller** than Barry.   My car is **more expensive** than hers.

Note: Avoid using double comparisons, such as *more better.*

7. Use proper superlative form to discuss three or more items:

Tom is the **tallest** boy. My car is the **most expensive.**

Note: Avoid using superlatives to compare only two items, such as *eldest of my two girls.*

8. Do not use superlatives with words such as *impossible, destroyed, perfect, demolished,* and *round:*

Incorrect	*Correct*
The house was completely destroyed.	The house was destroyed.
That is totally impossible.	That is impossible.
The room was perfectly round.	The room was round.

Answers to What Have You Learned? on page 546

1. loose (see page 533), badly (see page 533) 2. worst (see page 542) 3. better (see page 541) 4. impossible (see page 543) 5. newly waxed (see page 539)

PART 7

Understanding Punctuation and Mechanics

CHAPTER 32

Commas and Semicolons

CHAPTER GOALS

- Understand Comma and Semicolon Use

- Avoid Common Comma Errors

- Eliminate Unnecessary Commas

SANDRA BAKER/ALAMY LIMITED

Get Writing

What are some of the positive and negative ways that people deal with stress? How do you cope with problems at work or at home?

Write one or more paragraphs describing the best ways that people can overcome stress.

What Are Commas and Semicolons?

Commas [,] and semicolons [;] are two of the most common—and often misused—marks of punctuation. Because they function like road signs, directing the way we read sentences, they are very important.

What Do You Know?

Insert commas and semicolons where needed in the following sentences.

1. Anyone who wants to quit smoking should consider hypnosis.

2. My brother who wants to quit smoking has tried the patch.

3. On April 15 2005 the Akron Ohio office announced it was merging with the offices in Canton Ohio and La Crosse Wisconsin.

4. First we have to start saving money.

5. Washington Lincoln Roosevelt and Reagan were among the most influential and for some the most controversial presidents.

6. Education I have long argued is a lifelong process.

7. Iran exports oil China imports oil.

8. Tom got a job in San Jose Karen got a job in La Jolla.

9. The seminar on countering terrorism included Taylor Gray a former FBI agent Brooke Stefani a security consultant and Sandy Shimi an Iranian dissident.

10. Because a blizzard is predicted for tomorrow we are postponing the board meeting until next Monday.

Answers appear on the following page.

Answers appear on the following page.

Top 20

COMMAS AND SEMICOLONS
Understanding commas and semicolons helps you avoid run-ons and other common sentence errors.

WHAT ARE YOU TRYING TO SAY?

Write a paragraph describing your favorite restaurant. Include details about the atmosphere, the people who dine there, and the menu.

_____

_____

_____

_____

_____

_____

_____

_____

_____

_____

_____

_____

WHAT HAVE YOU WRITTEN?

Circle the commas and semicolons that appear in your paragraph.

1. Can you provide a reason for inserting each comma?

2. Do you insert commas almost on reflex, without thought?

3. Do you sometimes think that you miss needed commas or put them where they don't belong?

4. Do you know if any of your commas should be semicolons?

Answers to What Do You Know? on page 551

1. Anyone who wants to quit smoking should consider hypnosis.
2. My brother, who wants to quit smoking, has tried the patch.
3. On April 15, 2005, the Akron, Ohio, office announced it was merging with the offices in Canton, Ohio, and La Crosse, Wisconsin.
4. First, we have to start saving money.
5. Washington, Lincoln, Roosevelt, and Reagan were among the most influential and, for some, the most controversial presidents.
6. Education, I have long argued, is a lifelong process.
7. Iran exports oil; China imports oil.
8. Tom got a job in San Jose; Karen got a job in La Jolla.
9. The seminar on countering terrorism included Taylor Gray, a former FBI agent; Brooke Stefani, a security consultant; and Sandy Shimi, an Iranian dissident.
10. Because a blizzard is predicted for tomorrow, we are postponing the board meeting until next Monday.

The Comma ,

When we talk, we pause to separate ideas or create emphasis. In writing, we use commas to signal pauses and shifts in sentences. Commas are the most common mark of punctuation used within sentences. By habit, you may automatically insert the commas correctly, just as you remember to capitalize a person's name or place a period at the end of a sentence. However, there are probably times when you are confused about where you should put commas.

Commas work like hooks that attach extra ideas to a basic sentence:

Kim became a citizen.
After studying American history and English, **Kim,** who was born in Korea, **became a citizen,** which enabled him to get a U.S. passport.

(Read this sentence aloud, and notice the pauses you instinctively make to signal shifts in the flow of ideas.)

Comma mistakes, like spelling errors, can seem like minor flaws, but they weaken your writing and make your ideas hard to understand. Remember, when you are writing, you are taking your readers on a journey. If you use commas correctly, they will be able to follow your train of thought without getting lost. Consider how commas change the meaning of these sentences:

The teachers say the students don't care.
The teachers, say the students, don't care.

Let's eat candy.
Let's eat, Candy.

We need coffee, tea, ice water, and soft drinks.
We need coffee, tea, ice, water, and soft drinks.

Saddling up to leave, Nevada Smith took all the gold.
Saddling up to leave Nevada, Smith took all the gold.

The best way to master comma use is to first review all the rules, then concentrate on the ones you do not understand or find confusing.

Comma Uses

Commas have ten basic uses.

1. **Use commas with *and, or, nor, yet, but, for,* or *so* to join independent clauses to create compound sentences and avoid run-ons** (see Chapter 25). When you join two independent clauses (simple sentences), use a comma and the appropriate coordinating conjunction:

   China is a land of ancient culture, **and** it is an emerging industrial power.

   We have to buy a new car, **or** we have to fix the old one.

   Gas prices increased, **yet** sales of SUVs soared.

   She was immensely popular, **but** she decided not to run for reelection.

   I have a headache, **so** I am leaving early.

   Note: In informal writing, some writers omit commas in very short compound sentences:

   I flew but she drove.   Carla jogs and she lifts weights.

POINT TO REMEMBER

Use commas with *and, or, nor, yet, but, for,* or *so* only to join two independent clauses, not pairs of words or phrases.

Unnecessary Commas:
    They served coffee, and tea.

    Outsourcing manufacturing jobs, and declining profits in the banking industry hurt the town's economy.

    Ted was in poor shape when he moved here, but began jogging and lost thirty pounds.

Correct
    They served coffee and tea.

    Outsourcing manufacturing jobs and declining profits in the banking industry hurt the town's economy.

    Ted was in poor shape when he moved here but began jogging and lost thirty pounds.

To see if you need a comma with *and, or, nor, yet, but, for,* or *so,* apply this test:

1. **Replace the coordinating conjunction with a period.** If there is a complete sentence on the left and the right of the period, *add* the comma:

   The film crew spent ten days on location but they shot only two scenes.
   The film crew spent ten days on location. They shot only two scenes. (*two complete sentences*)
   The film crew spent ten days on location, but they shot only two scenes. (*comma needed*)

2. **If placing a period creates a fragment, *omit* the comma:**

   It rained all week and delayed filming the beach scenes.
   It rained all week. Delayed filming the beach scenes. (*one sentence and a fragment*)
   It rained all week and delayed filming the beach scenes. (*no comma needed*)

2. **Use a comma after a dependent clause that opens a complex sentence:**

   Because the school lost power, classes were canceled.
   After she registered for classes, Juanita applied for financial aid.
   While we waited for our flight, we rehearsed our presentations.

   If the dependent clause follows the independent clause, the comma is usually omitted:

   Classes were canceled because the school lost power.
   Juanita applied for financial aid after she registered for classes.
   We rehearsed our presentations while we waited for our flight.

   Writers often omit commas if the opening clause is short and commas are not needed to prevent confusion:

   After he left we celebrated.   Before I run I stretch.

3. **Use a comma after a long phrase or introductory word.** To prevent confusion, commas should follow long phrases that open sentences. There is no clear definition of a "long phrase," so use your judgment. A short opening phrase may not require a comma to prevent confusion:

   After lunch let's go to the beach.

   Longer phrases should be set off with commas to prevent confusion and signal the shift in ideas:

   After lunch with our parents and the new counselors, let's go to the beach.

   Introductory words such as interjections (*hey, wow, yes*) or transitions (*then, later on, next*) are set off with commas to prevent confusion and dramatize a shift in ideas:

   No, I can't take your check.   Amazingly, no one was injured in the accident.

   First, we have to make a plan.   Wait, you forgot your keys!

4. **Use commas to separate words, phrases, and clauses in a series:**

Words

I bought gas, oil, and tires.

Note: Many writers omit the final comma before the conjunction:

I bought gas, oil and tires.

Most editors add the final comma to prevent possible confusion:

We needed salads, soup, ham and cheese sandwiches.
[Do you need *ham and sandwiches made with cheese* or *ham and cheese sandwiches?*]

Phrases

I bought gas, changed the oil, and rotated the tires.

Clauses

I bought gas, Sandy changed the oil, and Jim rotated the tires.

Note: If clauses contain commas, separate them with semicolons (see pages 562–564).

EXERCISE 1   Add Commas Where Needed in Complex and Compound Sentences and to Separate Items in a Series

Add commas where needed in the following e-mail.

FROM: Phil Leotardo
TO: Paul Reles
RE: Brownsville Redevelopment Association

The city has granted us final approval and we plan to begin work on May 15. Because we expect to operate without interruption this summer we anticipate Phase One to be completed by October 30. However we should plan for unexpected delays such as inclement weather labor disputes or late deliveries. In any event if we are to meet our goals we need assurance from you that you can provide us with all the roofing plumbing and electrical supplies by May 1.

I reviewed your current price list and passed it on to the Brownsville Association the contractors and the major investors. After this week's meeting I should be able to send a final materials list. Financially we are in very good shape and we can secure the needed loans without delay. If you offer a cash discount I may be able to convince the board to issue a check upon delivery.

Again thanks for sending over the price list.

Phil Leotardo

5. **Use commas to set off nonrestrictive or parenthetical words or phrases.** In some sentences you will notice a phrase such as *who is my friend* set off with commas, then see the same phrase in another sentence without commas. Whether or not a word or phrase is set off with commas depends on whether it is **nonrestrictive** or **restrictive.** When a word or words simply describe or add extra information about a noun, they are **nonrestrictive** and set off with commas. **Nonrestrictive** words are parenthetical and can be taken out of the sentence without changing the meaning of the noun they describe. If the words limit or define the noun, they are **restrictive** and *not* set off with commas. **Restrictive** words tell us more about a pronoun or abstract noun such as *anyone, someone, student, person,* or *parent:*

Anyone **who wants to lose weight** . . .
Someone **who exercises daily** . . .
The citizen **who fails to vote** . . .
Any student **who takes too many courses** . . .
Each homeowner **who complains about traffic** . . .

These phrases limit or define the subject. Without them the nouns lose much of their meaning. These *restrictive* phrases are part of the noun and therefore are not set off with commas. These same words could be *nonrestrictive* and set off with commas if they followed more specific nouns:

George, **who wants to lose weight,** . . .
Jenna, **who exercises daily,** . . .
My sister, **who fails to vote,** . . .

In each case the phrase adds only extra information about a clearly defined noun. Removing the phrase from the sentence does not change the meaning of the noun:

Nonrestrictive	**Restrictive**
Adds extra information about a noun; commas needed	Defines or limits the noun; no commas
My father, *who wants to quit smoking,* should try hypnosis.	**Anyone** *who wants to quit smoking* should try hypnosis.
My father can refer to only one person; *who wants to quit smoking* adds only EXTRA information about him.	**Anyone** refers to any person; *who wants to quit smoking* defines which person should try hypnosis.
Tina Brown, *who hosts a TV show,* will moderate the debate.	**The editor** *who hosts a TV show* will moderate the debate.
Tina Brown clearly defines the noun, so her hosting a TV show adds only an extra detail about her.	*who hosts a TV show* defines which editor will moderate.

POINT TO REMEMBER

To determine whether a phrase or clause is **restrictive** or **nonrestrictive**, just think of the term "ID." If the phrase or clause "IDs" or identifies the noun, it is **restrictive** and should *not* be set off with commas:

>Will the student who missed the test see me after class?
>Which student? *the student who missed the test*
>The phrase *who missed the test* IDs which student. ***no commas***

If the phrase or clause does *not* "ID" the noun but adds only *extra* information, it is nonrestrictive and should be set off with commas:

>Will Sam, who missed the test, see me after class?
>Which student? *Sam*
>The phrase *who missed the test* adds only *extra* information about *Sam,* who is defined by his name.
>***add commas***

If the phrase or clause IDs the noun—no commas.
If the phrase or clause is *extra*—add commas.

EXERCISE 2   Restrictive and Nonrestrictive Elements

Insert commas where needed to set off nonrestrictive phrases and clauses. Remember, no commas are needed if the phrase or clause defines or IDs the noun.

1. Iran which was known as Persia until 1935 is an important nation in the Middle East.

2. The Iranians who speak Farsi are Persians and not Arabs.

3. The country which is a major oil producer has had complex and often conflicting relations with the West.

4. The United States which sought to contain communism in the 1950s assisted the exiled Shah to regain power in Iran.

5. The Shah who saw himself destined to lead his country onto the international stage launched the White Revolution which expanded women's rights redistributed land and built schools.

6. Many Iranians who objected to the Shah's reforms pro-Western policies and repressive police force supported the Islamic leader Ayatollah Khomeini.

7. The Shah was forced to leave Iran in 1979 by the Islamic Revolution which led to the formation of an Islamic republic that was extremely hostile to the United States.

8. Iranians who did not want to live in a nation ruled by strict Muslim principles fled the country and many settled in the United States.

9. Many Iranians who live in the United States have nicknamed Los Angeles which is now home to as many as half a million Iranian Americans "Tehrangeles."

10. Catherine Bell who appeared on the TV show *JAG* and the entrepreneur who founded eBay are among the growing population of Iranian Americans.

6. **Use commas to set off contrasted elements.** To prevent confusion and highlight contrast, set off words and phrases with commas to signal abrupt or important shifts in a sentence:

   The children, not the parents, want better schools.
   Our dean, unlike the other administrators, wants to limit enrollment.

7. **Use commas after interjections, words used in direct address, and around direct quotations:**

   Hey, you dropped your keys.
   Karen, did you get my e-mail?
   Carlos shouted, "Help, call an ambulance," to Melissa as she came into the room.

8. **Use commas to separate city and state or city and country, items in dates, and every three numerals above 1,000 (such as 4,568,908 dollars or 2,500 students):**

   Cindy was born in Atco, New Jersey, on November 24, 1986, and moved to London, England, where she earned over $100,000 in January 2006 singing in nightclubs.

   Note: A comma goes after states, countries, or dates if followed by other words. No comma is needed if only the month and year are given.

9. **Use commas to set off absolute phrases.** Absolute phrases are groups of words that are not grammatically connected to other parts of sentences. To prevent confusion, they are attached to the main sentence with a comma:

   Unable to compete with discount stores, Housegoods USA increased its catalog operations.
   Frank painted the lobby and trimmed the lawn, **hoping to attract more renters.**

10. **Use commas where needed to prevent confusion or add emphasis.** Writers add commas to create pauses and signal shifts in the flow of words to prevent readers from becoming confused:

    Confusing
    Wherever they ate free coffee was served.
    For Karen Hughes Tool was a great place to work.
    To help the homeless people donate clothes.

    Improved
    Wherever they ate, free coffee was served.
    For Karen, Hughes Tool was a great place to work.
    To help the homeless, people donate clothes.

Note: Reading sentences aloud can help you spot sentences that need commas to prevent confusion. Listen to where you pause.

Writers often use commas for special effect, not to prevent confusion but to emphasize words, phrases, and ideas. Because readers pause when they see a comma, it forces them to slow down and pay additional attention to a word or phrase:

Without Comma
Today I start my diet.

With Comma for Emphasis
Today, I start my diet.

EXERCISE 3   Comma Use

Insert commas where needed in each sentence.

1. The Great Wall of China consists of 1500 miles of fortifications walls guard towers and barracks in northern China.

2. The wall which was built over a thousand years was not a single project but a series of separate defensive fortifications that were connected.

3. Local residents were forced to build the wall and many of them were killed by gangs of attacking bandits.

4. Because so many laborers died during its construction the Great Wall earned a grim nickname "the longest cemetery in the world."

5. The wall was made of mostly stone and brick although some portions in desert regions were constructed of wooden fences and earthworks.

6. Although parts of the Great Wall have been carefully restored much of it has deteriorated over the years.

7. Developers have bulldozed sections to make way for new construction and farmers have taken stones for building materials.

8. It has been often stated that the Great Wall of China is the only man-made object visible from the Moon.

9. In fact shuttle astronauts have reported that they could make out the wall when in orbit a hundred miles or so above the Earth.

10. Because the Moon is over 200000 miles from Earth however it is impossible to see the Great Wall or any other man-made object from its surface without the use of high-powered telescopes.

Avoiding Unnecessary Commas

Because commas have so many uses, it is easy to place them where they are not needed. After reviewing all the rules, you may find yourself putting commas where they don't belong.

Top 20

COMMAS
Avoid unnecessary commas.

Guide to Eliminating Unnecessary Commas

1. ***Don't*** **put a comma between a subject and verb unless setting off nonrestrictive elements or a series:**

   The old car, was stolen.

   Correct
   The car, which was old, was stolen.

2. ***Don't*** **use commas to separate prepositional phrases from what they modify:**

   The van, in the driveway, needs new tires.

   Correct
   The van in the driveway needs new tires.

3. ***Don't*** **use commas to separate two items in a compound verb:**

   They sang, and danced at the party.

   Correct
   They sang and danced at the party.

4. ***Don't*** **put commas around titles:**

   The film opens with, "Love Me Tender," and shots of Elvis.

   Correct
   The film opens with "Love Me Tender" and shots of Elvis.

5. ***Don't*** **put commas after a series unless it ends a clause that has to be set off from the rest of the sentence:**

   They donated computers, printers, and telephones, to our office.

   Correct
   They donated computers, printers, and telephones, and we provided office space.

6. ***Don't*** **set off a dependent clause with a comma when it ends a sentence:**

   The game was canceled, because the referees went on strike.

   Correct
   The game was canceled because the referees went on strike.

   Exception: *Although* clauses are usually set off with a comma.

   He failed the exam, *although he had studied for hours.*

   Note: A comma is needed if a dependent clause opens the sentence:

   Because the referees went on strike, the game was canceled.

EXERCISE 4 Comma Use

Correct comma use in the following passage, adding missing commas where needed and deleting unnecessary commas.

Tony Bergdorf   English 112

A Different Kind of Spring Break

For the past fifty years spring break has meant fun. After a semester and half of college it was a time to find a warm place to party to drink to get away. For decades Florida resorts braced themselves for floods of rowdy college students traffic jams loud parties and underage drinking. In their wake, college kids left behind trashed motel rooms littered beaches and millions of dollars in the cash registers of stores bars and clubs. With cheap flights by the Eighties college students began breaking in Las Vegas Mexico and Jamaica. Some affluent types, even jetted to Rio when spring break coincided with Carnival.

But in the last few years college students have explored other options. Instead of partying these young people, have sought to dedicate a week of their lives to volunteering. Evangelical organizations have sponsored trips to rebuild Mississippi churches ravaged by Katrina. Environmental groups have recruited students to spend a week planting trees installing solar panels on school roofs and cleaning riverbanks. Students have devoted a week repairing the homes of farmworkers serving meals in homeless shelters or helping runaway teens.

The students you see on campus in late April may look tanned and tired. Some are exhausted by a week of partying on the beach but others got sunburnt nailing shingles on a church roof. Some will look back and remember only hangovers silly hats and goofy antics. Others will always remember the week they helped make the world a better place.

_____

_____

_____

_____

_____

_____

_____

_____

_____

_____

_____

_____

Semicolons ;

What Are Semicolons?

You can think of semicolons as capitalized commas. They are used to connect larger items—clauses and complex items in a list.

Semicolons have two uses:

1. **Use semicolons to join independent clauses when** *and, or, nor, yet, but, for,* **or** *so* **are not present:**

   We flew to San Diego; Jack and Jean drove.
   Florida is a popular winter resort; Maine attracts summer visitors.

   Note: Remember to use semicolons even when you use words such as *nevertheless, moreover,* and *however:*

   We missed our flight; however, we arrived at the wedding on time.
   The invention increases fuel efficiency; moreover, it is easy to install.

2. **Use semicolons to separate items in a series that contain commas.** Normally, commas separate items in a list:

   They will arrive in limos, buses, taxis, and rented cars.

   However, if items in the list contain commas, it is difficult to tell which commas are separating items and which commas are separating elements within a single item:

   The governor will meet with Dr. Mendoza, dean of the law school, Dr. Carol Nezgod, dean of health sciences, Professor George Richter, the dean of the business school, and the college auditor.

   How many people will the governor meet? Is Dr. Mendoza the dean of the law school or are Dr. Mendoza and the dean two different people? To prevent confusion, semicolons are inserted to separate items in the series:

   The governor will meet with Dr. Mendoza, dean of the law school; Dr. Carol Nezgod, dean of health sciences; Professor George Richter; the dean of the business school; and the college auditor.

The governor will meet with five people:

1. Dr. Mendoza, dean of the law school

2. Dr. Carol Nezgod, dean of health sciences

3. Professor George Richter

4. the dean of the business school

5. the college auditor

EXERCISE 5 Understanding Semicolons

Underline the items in each list, and enter the number in the right column.

1. The school hired a math teacher; Ted Hines, a web
   designer; Jan Price; and a reading specialist.   _____

2. We read *Death of a Salesman; The Great Gatsby,* the novel by
   F. Scott Fitzgerald; a novel by Camus; a poem by Frost;
   "The Swimmer," an interesting story by John Cheever; and
   my favorite, "The Cask of Amontillado" by Edgar Allan Poe.

3. The class included my sister; Candy, her roommate; Tom
   Drake; Don Bernstein; Tom Price; Tom's sister; Carlos
   Abrams; an exchange student from Chile; a student from
   France; and me.   _____

4. This summer the college will repair the men's dorm;
   Wilson Hall, the senior women's dorm; Tara Hall, the
   Irish genealogy library; the math lab; and Osgood Hall,
   the oldest building on campus.   _____

5. We considered our all-time favorite TV shows and came
   up with a long list, including my favorite soap opera;
   Streets of San Francisco, Sandy's favorite show; *Saturday
   Night Live* with Eddie Murphy; *LA Law; All in the Family;*
   the original *Twilight Zone,* Sid's choice; and, of course,
   Star Trek.

EXERCISE 6 Comma and Semicolon Use

Insert commas and semicolons where needed in each sentence.

1. The names Harry Horwitz Jerry Horwitz and Louis Feinberg are not
   well-known however their stage names Moe Curly and Larry are
   famous the world over.

2. As the Three Stooges the Horwitz brothers and their friend created a
   comedy team that with some cast changes would produce almost two
   hundred comedy films from the early 1930s to the late 1950s.

3. The act got its name from Ted Healy who originally billed them as
   "Ted Healy and his Stooges" in vaudeville houses.

4. In the early days Moe and Curly's brother Samuel who used the name
   Shemp was part of the act but he left to pursue a movie career.

5. The Stooges were immensely popular audiences loved their slapstick comedy wild stage antics and colorful language.

6. Troubled by Healy's drinking and managing style the Stooges left vaudeville to sign a contract with Columbia Pictures which hired the team to make a series of shorts.

7. The Stooges began a long run making films on low budgets within a few days.

8. When the demand for short films dwindled in the 1950s Columbia stopped producing the Stooge films and the comedians were out of work.

9. Columbia however found a new market for its library of old Stooge shorts it sold them to television.

10. Although the Three Stooges made no money when their films appeared on television the renewed interest created a fan base the comics profited from a new career of making public appearances working nightclubs and performing on variety shows.

WORKING TOGETHER

Working with a group of students, edit this e-mail, adding commas and semicolons where needed. Note how adding correct punctuation makes the message easier to read.

Dear Stan:

We are planning next year's convention which will be held July 7–9 in San Diego California. I am putting together the initial plans early next week and I would appreciate your input.

Right now we are anticipating that the main presenters will be George Sims Nancy Houghton and Ted Jackson. According to Frank Taylor all three will be willing to make a general presentation for $4500 apiece and conduct individual seminars for $1500. Because of possible scheduling conflicts George Sims must receive a confirmation by May 30 2009.

Last year's convention drew 12568 attendees and guests this year we expect to draw at least 15000. I am convinced this is a realistic estimate our sales and technical reps are anxious to learn about our new product line.

Stan I look forward to your call. Let's hope we make this convention the best ever.

Lili Holden

CRITICAL THINKING

The president of the United States can serve only two terms. Do you think there should also be term limits for Congress? Would limiting senators and representatives to a few terms allow more people to serve in Washington and open up positions for women and minorities? Would term limits prevent successful politicians from serving again even if they were popular with voters? Write a paragraph stating your views.

Review your writing for comma and semicolon use and other errors. Read your paragraphs aloud. Does this help you discover comma errors, misspelled words, fragments, and awkward phrases?

Get Thinking and Writing

What Have You Learned?

Insert commas and semicolons where needed in the following sentences.

1. In April 1912 the *Titanic* struck an iceberg and sank on April 27 1912 my great-grandmother was officially listed as lost at sea.

2. The museum will sell the painting for $175000 but insists that payments must be by cash money order or bank draft.

3. I grew up in Westfield New Jersey but we moved to Milwaukee Wisconsin when I was sixteen.

4. The player who gets the most votes will be placed in the hall of fame.

5. The president made a quick tour of Latin America hoping to improve trade relationships his visits to Rio Mexico City La Paz and Buenos Aires were highly successful.

6. Africa exports oil wood carvings cocoa beans and handicrafts.

7. Because interest rates and property taxes are difficult to predict the actual cost of this house is hard to estimate.

8. The police FBI and National Guard searched Manhattan the Bronx Staten Island Queens and Brooklyn for the missing diplomat.

9. Well if the summer is hot we may have to raise prices just to pay for the air-conditioning or we may have to eliminate free deliveries.

10. High school students say that dating and parties are their greatest distractions college students report that job and family responsibilities are their greatest distractions.

Answers appear on page 567.

WRITING ON THE WEB

Using a search engine such as Yahoo! or Google, enter terms such as *commas, semicolons, using commas, comma drills, comma rules, understanding commas,* and *punctuation* to locate current sites of interest.

POINTS TO REMEMBER

Commas are used for ten reasons:

1. **Use commas with *and, or, nor, yet, but, for,* or *so* to join independent clauses to create compound sentences and avoid run-ons:**

   I went to the fair, but Margaret drove to the beach.

2. **Use a comma after a dependent clause that opens a complex sentence:**

   Before the game began, the coach spoke to her players.

3. **Use a comma after a long phrase or introductory word:**

   Having waited in the rain for hours, I caught a cold.
   Furthermore, I caught a cold waiting in the rain.

4. **Use commas to separate words, phrases, and clauses in a series:**

   She bought a battered, rusted, and windowless Model A Ford.
   They dug wells, planted crops, and erected new silos.

5. **Use commas to set off nonrestrictive or parenthetical words or phrases:**

   Sid, who lives in Chicago, should know a lot about Illinois politics.
   Anyone who lives in Chicago should know a lot about Illinois politics.

6. **Use commas to set off contrasted elements:**

   Children, not parents, should make this decision.

7. **Use commas after interjections, words used in direct address, and around direct quotations:**

   Nancy, can you work this Saturday?
   Wait, you forgot your keys.
   Rick said, "We must pay cash," every time we wanted to buy something.

8. **Use commas to separate city and state and city and country, items in dates, and every three numerals above 1,000:**

   He moved to Topeka, Kansas, on October 15, 2003, and bought a $125,000 house.

9. **Use commas to set off absolutes:**

   Their plane grounded by fog, the passengers became restless.

10. **Use commas where needed to prevent confusion or add emphasis:**

    Every time I drive, home is my final destination.
    This morning, we play to win.

Semicolons are used for two reasons:

1. **Use semicolons to join independent clauses when *and, or, yet, for, nor, but,* or *so* are not present:**

   We walked to school; they took a limo.

2. **Use a semicolon to separate items in a series that contain commas:**

   I asked Frank, the field manager; Candace, the sales representative; Karla, our attorney; and Erica, the city manager, to attend the budget meeting.

Answers to What Have You Learned? on page 565

1. In April 1912, the *Titanic* struck an iceberg and sank; on April 27, 1912, my great-grandmother was officially listed as lost at sea.
2. The museum will sell the painting for $175,000 but insists that payments must be by cash, money order, or bank draft.
3. I grew up in Westfield, New Jersey, but we moved to Milwaukee, Wisconsin, when I was sixteen.
4. The player who gets the most votes will be placed in the hall of fame.
5. The president made a quick tour of Latin America, hoping to improve trade relationships; his visits to Rio, Mexico City, La Paz, and Buenos Aires were highly successful.
6. Africa exports oil, wood carvings, cocoa beans, and handicrafts.
7. Because interest rates and property taxes are difficult to predict, the actual cost of this house is hard to estimate.
8. The police, FBI, and National Guard searched Manhattan, the Bronx, Staten Island, Queens, and Brooklyn for the missing diplomat.
9. Well, if the summer is hot, we may have to raise prices just to pay for the air-conditioning, or we may have to eliminate free deliveries.
10. High school students say that dating and parties are their greatest distractions; college students report that job and family responsibilities are their greatest distractions.

CHAPTER 33

Other Marks of Punctuation

CHAPTER GOALS

- Understand Uses of Punctuation
- Use Punctuation Correctly
- Overcome Common Punctuation Errors

STEPHEN COBURN/USED UNDER LICENSE FROM SHUTTERSTOCK

Get Writing

Security cameras are now placed in airports, offices, and public spaces all over the world. In Great Britain, for example, it is estimated that the average citizen is videotaped thirty times a day—walking down a street, driving into a parking lot, entering an office building, or getting onto a train. Do you think cameras designed to protect the public can be misused? Do you think we are losing our privacy?

Write one or more paragraphs stating your views. When you see cameras in a public place, do you feel you are being protected or spied on?

What Are the Other Marks of Punctuation?

Writers use punctuation to show when they are quoting other people, presenting parenthetical ideas, posing a question, or creating a contraction. Most students know when to use a question mark or an exclamation point. However, other punctuation marks can be confusing, so they are worth looking at in detail.

What Do You Know?

Add apostrophes, quotation marks, italics, parentheses, question marks, colons, and exclamation points where needed in the following sentences.

1. Alice screamed, Call 911 right now as soon as she saw Tim collapse.

2. Can this really cost $45,000.

3. We need office supplies computer paper, ink, pencils, and stamps.

4. Did you see Miss Saigon on Broadway.

5. Ted and Nancys car wont start because its battery is dead.

6. The mens sale is a big disappointment unless you can wear 48s or 50s.

7. I found her purse on the floor near the womens room.

8. Did you read Can We Save Social Security in Newsweek.

9. I found a boys hat in the childrens library.

10. We drove to Pikes Peak in Sids old Buick.

Answers appear on the following page.

WHAT ARE YOU TRYING TO SAY?

Write a paragraph listing what you consider to be the best and worst television shows, movies, and songs to appear in the last few years. Provide examples of both types.

_____

_____

_____

_____

_____

_____

WHAT HAVE YOU WRITTEN?

Review the punctuation in your paragraph, and circle items that you think are wrong.

The Apostrophe '

Apostrophes are used for three reasons.

1. **Use apostrophes to indicate possession.** The standard way of showing possession, that someone or something owns something else, is to add an apostrophe and an *-s:*

Noun	Tim's house is two miles away.
Acronym	The NFL's rules will change next season.
Indefinite pronoun	Everyone's ticket is canceled.
Endings of *s, x,* or *z* sound	Hollis' [or Hollis's] book is here.

Note: Apostrophes are deleted from some geographical names:

Dobsons Creek   Taylors Pond   Warners Crossing

Note: Apostrophes may or may not appear in possessive names of businesses or organizations:

Marshall Field's   Sears   Tigers Stadium   Sean's Pub

Follow the spelling used on signs, stationery, and business cards.

Because an *-s* is added to make many words plural, apostrophes have to be placed carefully to show whether the noun is singular or plural:

Singular	*Plural*
a boy's bike	the boys' bikes
my girl's hat	my girls' hats
her sister's house	her sisters' house (two or more sisters own one house)
a child's book	children's books*
the woman's coat	women's coats*

*Because *children* and *women* already indicate plurals, the apostrophe is placed before the *-s.*

Compound nouns can indicate joint or individual possession. Jim and Erica, for example, could own and share one car, share the use of several vehicles, or own separate cars they drive individually. The placement of apostrophes demonstrates what you mean:

Jim and Erica's car.	*Jim and Erica both own one car.*
Jim and Erica's cars.	*Jim and Erica both own several vehicles.*
Jim's and Erica's cars.	*Jim and Erica individually own cars.*

2. **Use apostrophes to signal missing letters and numbers in contractions.** When speaking, we often shorten and combine words so that we say "don't" for "do not" and "could've" for "could have." We also shorten numbers, particularly years, so that we talk about "the Spirit of '76" or "a friend having a '99 Mustang." To prevent confusion, apostrophes show that letters or numerals have been eliminated:

shell = an outer casing	she'll = "she will"
well = a source of water	we'll = "we will"
cant = trite opinions	can't = "can not"

Note: Only one apostrophe is used, even if more than one letter is omitted.

Apostrophes are placed over the missing letter or letters, not where the words are joined:

do not = don't   ***not***   do'nt

Deleted numbers are indicated with a single apostrophe:

The roof was damaged in the storm of '97.
He hit two home runs in the '99 World Series.
She is still driving that '82 Toyota.

3. **Use apostrophes to indicate plurals of letters, numbers, or symbols.** Words do not need apostrophes to indicate plurals. An added *-s* or other spelling changes indicate that a noun has been made plural. However, because adding an *-s* could lead to confusion when dealing with individual letters, numbers, or symbols, apostrophes are used to create plurals:

I got all **B**'s last semester and **A**'s this semester.
Do we have any size **7**'s or **8**'s left?
We can sell all the **2005**'s at half price.

Note: Apostrophes are optional in referring to decades, but be consistent:

Inconsistent
The studio was built in the 1970s but was never used until the 1990's.

Consistent
The studio was built in the 1970's but was never used until the 1990's.
or
The studio was built in the 1970s but was never used until the 1990s.

Note: Common abbreviations such as TV and DVD do not need apostrophes to indicate plurals:

We bought new TVs and several DVDs.

POINT TO REMEMBER

It's and *its* are commonly confused:

    it's = contraction of "*it is*"

        It's raining.

        I know **it's** going to be a long day.

    its = possessive of "*it*"

        My car won't start. **Its** battery is dead.

        The house lost **its** roof in the storm.

In editing, use this test to see if you need an apostrophe:

1. Read the sentence out loud, substituting *it is* for *its/it's*.

2. If the sentence sounds OK, use *it's:*
   It is going to be hot.
   It's going to be hot.

3. If the sentence sounds awkward, use *its:*
   I like it is style.
   I like its style.

EXERCISE 1   Using Apostrophes to Show Possession

Use apostrophes to create possessive forms of nouns.

Top 20

COMMONLY CONFUSED WORDS

Understand the difference between *it's* and *its*.

1. **a book belonging to one boy**   _____

2. **money belonging to the people**   _____

3. **the songs of Frank Sinatra**   _____

4. **a fair run by the county**   _____

5. **research conducted by NASA**   _____

6. **cars owned by my brother-in-law**   _____

7. **clothing owned by children**   _____

8. **stories written by Carla Jones**   _____

9. **a store owned by two women**   _____

10. **a house owned by Ted and Jill Jackson** _____

EXERCISE 2   Using Apostrophes to Show Contractions

Use apostrophes to create contractions of each pair of words.

1. **he is**   _____

2. **have not**   _____

3. **he did**   _____

4. who is _____

5. could not _____

6. does not _____

7. I will _____

8. they are _____

9. should have _____

10. have not _____

EXERCISE 3   Using Apostrophes

Revise this notice, adding apostrophes where needed.

KAPLAN PROPERTIES

Notice to Residents

During renovation of the lobbys flooring, we will have to close the main entrance. This will, we realize, cause some inconvenience to both residents and visitors. According to the contractors schedule, this work should take approximately one month to complete. The side entrances on 54th Street will be open, and a security guard will be posted to ensure residents safety. In addition to these repairs, both the mens room and womens room on the lower level will be closed. Visitors can still access restrooms in the heath club. Because well have to shut down the elevators on the west side of the building, the roofs sun deck will not be available until June 30th.

We regret the inconveniences caused by managements redesign plans, but we are confident that residents will appreciate the buildings enhanced look. The last time the lobby was repaired was 82, and we undertook these improvements based on residents concerns.

If you have any questions, contact Sid Grauman at Ext. 125. Hes personally supervising Kaplan Properties renovations.

Quotation Marks " "

Quotation marks—always used in pairs—enclose direct quotations, titles of short works, and highlighted words.

1. **Use quotation marks in direct quotations.** When you copy word for word what someone has said or written, enclose the statement in quotation marks:

   Martin Luther King said, "I have a dream."

   Note: When the final mark of punctuation is a question mark or exclamation point, it precedes the final quotation mark only if it is part of the original text:

   The coach asked her team, "Do you people want to win?"
   Did Martin Luther King say, "I have a dream"?

Remember: Set off with commas identifying phrases that explain whom you are quoting:

Sid argued, "We should ask everyone to vote."
"It won't be fair," Sid insisted, "unless we all have a chance to decide."
"Without a fair election, no one will accept the outcome," Sid argued.

Note: Commas are not used if the quotation is blended into the sentence:

They suggest we adopt a "go slow" approach to urban renewal.

Quotations within quotations are indicated by use of single quotation marks:

Shelly said, "I was only ten when I heard Martin Luther King proclaim, 'I have a dream.'"

Long quotations are indented and not placed in quotation marks:

> For generations, colleges and universities were accustomed to serving single eighteen- to twenty-two-year-olds whose only responsibility was attending class and getting good grades. This began to change in the 1980s: An increasing number of adult students enrolled in college. Women seeking to reenter the workforce sought new skills. Downsized executives and displaced factory workers returned to school to secure jobs in new industries. Others returned to school to learn new skills to secure promotions. To serve the needs of this growing pool of older students, colleges built more parking lots, opened day-care centers, built satellite centers in the suburbs, and offered weekend courses. (Jones 15)

Final commas are placed inside quotation marks:

The e-mail announced, "we will lower prices," but few believed it.

Colons and semicolons are placed outside quotation marks:

The e-mail announced, "The college will lower fees"; few students believed it.

Indirect quotations do not require quotation marks:

Martin Luther King said that he had a dream.

2. **Use quotation marks in titles of short works.** The titles of poems, short stories, chapters, essays, songs, episodes of television shows, and any named section of a longer work are placed in quotation marks. Longer works are underlined or placed in italics:

Did you read "The Bells" by Poe?
You should read "Wall Street Woes" in this week's *Time* magazine.

Note: Do not capitalize articles, prepositions, or coordinating conjunctions (*and, or, yet, for, nor, but, so*) unless they are the first or last words.

Quotation marks and italics (or underlining) distinguish between shorter and longer works with the same title. Many anthologies and albums have title works. Quotation marks and italics indicate whether you are referring to a song or an entire album:

His new CD *Call My Bluff* has two good songs: "Going Home" and "Call My Bluff."

3. **Use quotation marks to highlight words.** Words are placed in quotation marks to draw extra attention:

Instead of laying off employees, the company placed a thousand workers on "unpaid leave."

EXERCISE 4   Quotation Marks and Apostrophes

Add quotation marks and apostrophes where needed.

1. Audrey told us she was getting married in June.

2. I promise I will not raise property taxes, Karen Jackson told voters last night.

3. The courses new reading list includes John Cheevers The Swimmer and Albert Camus The Guest.

4. The crowd could not resist booing when the mayor announced, There is nothing I can do until I receive a final ruling from the court that says, You can proceed.

5. Did you read Jane Mantons story We Cant Go On?

6. Carlos favorite songs are Sinatras My Way and Madonnas Like a Virgin.

7. Franks comments included the remark, Were going to see if hes willing to help us.

8. Building a New World is the first essay in our textbook.

9. I'm going to retire, Tom Watson told us, reminding us of his promise. I will step aside as soon as my daughters internship is completed.

10. Tom told us, Were going to invest when all the economists predictions give us a clear picture where to spend our clients money.

Colon :

Colons are placed after independent clauses to introduce elements and separate items in numerals, ratios, titles, and time references:

Lists   Suki looked for three things in new employees: creativity, discipline, and loyalty.

Note: Colons are placed after independent clauses only to introduce lists:

Incorrect

We need: tires, oil, batteries, and air filters.

Correct

We need auto supplies: tires, oil, batteries, and air filters.

Phrases	The student government saw only one way to deal with Jane: immediate expulsion.
Time references	The plane left at 8:45 this morning.
Ratio	They have a 3:1 advantage.
Title and subtitle	I am reading *Pink Ghetto: Women in the Workplace.*
After salutations in a business letter	Dear Ms. Mendezo:
Scripture reference	Romans 12:1–5
Introduction of block quotations	Karen Meadows remembers the uneasiness the defense workers felt when the radio announced the war was over:

Nancy and I dropped our tools and hugged and kissed. We danced around the engine we were assembling. Older workers were subdued. Some cried. They were glad their sons were coming home, but they were concerned about the future. They feared losing their jobs.

Parentheses ( )

Parentheses ( ) set off nonessential details and explanations and enclose letters and numbers used for inserting numbers:

Nonessential detail	The rules committee (established last year) will supervise the election.
First-time use of acronym	The diagnosis of obsessive compulsive disorder (OCD) is sometimes difficult.
Enumeration	She told us we should (1) paint the bedrooms, (2) carpet the living room, and (3) install a new heating system.

Brackets [ ]

Brackets [ ] set off corrections or clarifications inserted in quotations to prevent confusion and show parentheses within parentheses.

Sometimes quotations taken out of context can be confusing because readers may misunderstand a word or reference. A quotation using the word "Kennedy" in a biography of Robert Kennedy would be clear in context. But if you use this quotation in a paper, readers could easily assume it referred to John, not Robert, Kennedy. If you have to add clarifications or corrections, place them in brackets:

Clarifications to prevent confusion	On the eve of the primary, Lou Harris predicted, "It looks like [Robert] Kennedy will win tonight."

Time noted, "President Bush told Frank Bush [no relation] that he agreed with his tax policies."

The coach said, "I won't talk to them [suspended players] until they apologize."

Corrections	Larry Felber claimed, "I owe only $5,000 [$175,000 according to IRS records] in back taxes."
Parentheses within parentheses	The mayor's committee (headed by Hughes and Habib [both hoping to win city contracts]) will review the budget.

Dash —

Dashes mark a break in thought, set off a parenthetical element for emphasis, and set off an introduction to a series:

Sudden break in thought	She was shocked by the news—who could blame her?
Parenthetical element	The team—which lost ten games straight—became a local joke.
Introduction	She has everything people need to make it in Hollywood—looks, charm, talent, and a good agent.

Note: Create dashes by a continuous line, or hit your hyphen key twice. No spaces separate dashes from the words they connect.

Hyphen -

A hyphen is a short line used to separate or join words and other items:

1. **Use hyphens to break words at the end of a line:**

   She was born in Phila-
   delphia in 1951.

   Note: Break words only between syllables.

2. **Use hyphens to connect words to create adjectives:**

   They made a **last-minute** proposal to save the old school.
   Never pay a **higher-than-average** price.

   Do *not* use hyphens with adverbs ending in -*ly*:

   The city found the hastily written proposal confusing and impractical.

3. **Use hyphens to connect words forming numbers:**

   The school enrolled only **twenty-seven** students last year.

4. **Use hyphens after some prefixes:**

   Kim's **self-reliance** astounded her critics.

5. **Use hyphens between combinations of numbers and words:**

   How can it pull a **50-ton** airplane?

Ellipsis . . .

An ellipsis, composed of three spaced periods [. . .], indicates that words have been deleted from quoted material:

Original text	The report stated, "All schools, including those founded under charter and choice programs, must be held to the highest standards."
With ellipsis	The report stated, "All schools . . . must be held to the highest standards."

Note: Delete only minor ideas or details—never change the basic meaning of a sentence by deleting key words. Don't eliminate a negative word such as *not* to create a positive statement or remove qualifying words:

Original
We must never abandon our support for the public schools.

Incorrect Use of Ellipsis
He said, "We must . . . abandon our support for the public schools."

Note: When deleting words at the end of a sentence, add a period to the ellipsis so that four spaced periods are used:

The report stated, "We depend on schools to build the future. . . ."

Note: Ellipses are not used if words are deleted at the opening of a quotation:

The report stated that "building the future depends on good schools."

Note: If deleting words will create a grammar mistake, insert corrections with brackets:

Original	"Washington, Lincoln, and Roosevelt were among the greatest presidents."
With ellipsis	"Lincoln . . . [was] among the greatest presidents."

Slash /

Slashes separate pairs of words to show alternatives (*rent/own* or *man/woman*) and separate lines in poetry in quotations:

Every citizen should cast his/her vote.
The poem began, "They play / They sing / They dance."

Note: When quoting poems, add spaces around slashes.

Question Mark ?

Question marks are placed at the end of a question and to note questionable items:

When are we leaving?
Did you read, "Who Can Save Us?" in *Time* last week?

Note: Question marks that appear in the original title are placed within quotation marks. If the title does not ask a question, the question mark is placed outside the quotation marks:

Did you like "The Swimmer"?

Question marks in parentheses are used to indicate that the writer questions the accuracy of a fact, number, idea, or quotation:

The report claimed it would cost taxpayers only $50,000 (?) to repair the bridge.

Exclamation Point !

Exclamation points are placed at the end of emphatic or forceful statements:

Help!
You are two hours late!

Note: Exclamation points should be used as special effects. They lose their impact if used too often.

Period .

Periods are used after sentences, in abbreviations, and as decimals:

She went home.
I talked to Ms. Green, who works for Dr. Wilson.
On Jan. 30 the price will be cut from $9.95 to $7.95.

Note: When an abbreviation ends a sentence, only one period is used.
   Note: Widely used abbreviations such as FBI, CIA, ABC, BBC, and UCLA do not require periods.

EXERCISE 5   Punctuation

Add missing punctuation in each sentence.

1. **The Aug 15 flight will leave at 10 25 a.m.**

2. **The womens center is expanding its services to meet the needs of the schools growing number of part time students.**

3. **The college saw three challenges declining enrollments reduced funding from the state and rising health care costs.**

4. **The Look of Love is her favorite song.**

5. **Can I park here**

6. **Dont bother waiting because she wont be off work until 9 30.**

7. **Jane Bush no relation to the president went to Iraq on behalf of the White House.**

8. **To win this game we have to accomplish three goals 1 stop turnovers 2 complete more passes and 3 stay focused.**

9. **Tim and Nans house was the only one damaged by the storm.**

10. **The team made a last ditch attempt to score a touchdown.**

WORKING TOGETHER

Working with a group of students, correct the punctuation in the following announcement.

New Dorm Policy

Beginning Jan 15, the new dorm policy will go into effect. It calls for three major changes:

1. Overnight guests under twentyone must be students. Residents guests must be registered by 900 pm at the dorms front desk.
2. Students are not allowed to operate large appliances refrigerators microwave ovens air conditioners or space heaters.
3. Its no longer acceptable for students vehicles (including motorcycles) to be parked overnight in the librarys north parking lot.

Anyone with questions should speak with hisher resident advisor.

EXERCISE 6 Cumulative Exercise: Punctuation and Coordination and Subordination

Rewrite this passage to correct errors in punctuation and to reduce awkward and repetitive phrasing through coordination and subordination. You may have to reword some sentences, adding or deleting phrases. If you have difficulty revising some of the sentences, review pages 427–429 and 432–434.

```
Murphy-3

Josh Gibson was born on December 21 1911. He was one
of the greatest baseball players in history. He was
often called the Babe Ruth of the Negro Leagues. Be-
cause of segregation Gibson could not try out for
major league teams. He became a star player in black
```

baseball and he broke many records. Lacking accurate statistics historians question some claims made about Gibsons career though most agree he had a lifetime batting average of 350 hit nearly 800 home runs and scored over eighty runs in a single season. Gibsons career contains many legendary moments. Some claim that he was the only player to hit a fair ball out of Yankee Stadium. Although Gibson was one of the players being considered to move into the major leagues along with Jackie Robinson he never made the transition. On January 20 1947 in Pittsburgh Pennsylvania Gibson died at the age of thirty five.

_____

_____

_____

_____

_____

_____

_____

_____

_____

_____

_____

_____

Get Thinking and Writing

CRITICAL THINKING

Do you think that democracy is the best form of government for all countries in the world? Are there exceptions? Write a paragraph stating your views.

WHAT HAVE YOU WRITTEN?

Review your paper for mistakes in punctuation and other errors.

What Have You Learned?

Add apostrophes, quotation marks, italics, parentheses, question marks, colons, and exclamation points where needed in the following sentences.

1. Ted and Ellens favorite car is their 67 VW bug.

2. Its going to rain, according to the 800 am weather report.

3. I turn thirty three on Nov 25.

4. Tom asked Can anyone loan me a dime

5. His Time article Why We Love TV is very interesting.

6. Womens shoes are designed for style mens shoes are designed for comfort.

7. Ms Owens dealership sold 4500 cars last year.

8. Im getting tired of waiting for the deans call.

9. We need to stock winter clothing mens coats childrens mittens and womens gloves.

10. Dont park there because theyre going to spray paint the building.

Answers appear on following page.

WRITING ON THE WEB

Using a search engine such as Yahoo! or Google, enter terms such as *colons, slashes, brackets, parenthesis, ellipsis, question marks, exclamation points, punctuation, understanding punctuation, using punctuation,* and *punctuation rules* to locate current sites of interest.

POINTS TO REMEMBER

1. Apostrophes show possession:

Erica's car   NASA's rocket   someone's hat
Ted and Nancy's cars.   [mutual ownership]
Ted's and Nancy's cars.   [individual ownership]

Apostrophes indicate missing letters or numbers:

Didn't you sell the '97 Thunderbird?
its = possessive of it   it's = it is

Apostrophes indicate plurals of letters, numbers, or symbols:

She got all A's this year.   Get the W-2's at the payroll office.

2. Quotation marks enclose direct quotations, titles of short works, and highlighted words:

He said, "I'll be there."   Can you sing "Blue Eyes"?   Is he "sick" again?

3. Colons are placed after independent clauses to introduce elements and separate items in numerals, titles, ratios, and time references:

We need supplies: gas, oil, and spark plugs.   It is now 10:17 a.m.

4. Parentheses set off nonessential details and explanations and enclose letters and numbers used for enumeration:

We got an apartment ($950 a month) because our State Loan Application (SLA) had not been approved for three reasons: (1) we needed more references, (2) we needed a bigger down payment, and (3) we owed too much on credit cards.

5. **Brackets set off corrections or clarifications in quotations and replace parentheses within parentheses:**

   Time notes, "Frank Bush [no relation to the president] will work for the White House next fall."

6. **Dashes mark breaks in thought, set off parenthetical elements, and set off introductions to a series:**

   She expected help—wouldn't you?

7. **Hyphens separate and join words and other items:**

   He wrote a fast-paced soundtrack for the action film.
   You still owe twenty-eight dollars.

8. **Ellipsis indicates words have been deleted from a direct quotation:**

   The Senator stated, "Our country . . . needs new leadership."

9. **Question marks and explanation points are placed within quotation marks if they appear in the original title or quotation:**

   Her article is called "Can Anyone Lose Weight?"

   Question marks are placed outside quotation marks if they are not part of the original:

   Did you read "The Gold Bug"?

Answers to What Have You Learned? on pages 581–582

 1. Ted and Ellen's favorite car is their '67 VW bug.
 2. It's going to rain, according to the 8:00 a.m. weather report.
 3. I turn thirty-three on Nov. 25.
 4. Tom asked, "Can anyone loan me a dime?"
 5. His *Time* article "Why We Love TV" is very interesting.
 6. Women's shoes are designed for style; men's shoes are designed for comfort.
 7. Ms. Owens' dealership sold 4,500 cars last year.
 8. I'm getting tired of waiting for the dean's call.
 9. We need to stock winter clothing: men's coats, children's mittens, and women's gloves.
10. Don't park there because they're going to spray paint the building.

Capitalization

CHAPTER GOALS

- ■ Understand How Capitalization Affects Meaning

- ■ Use the Rules of Capitalization

Marilyn Monroe after announcing her divorce from Joe Di Maggio, 1954

Get Writing

The average marriage now lasts eight years. Why do so many couples divorce? What causes most marriages to fail?

Write a paragraph stating your views, supporting your points with examples.

What Is Capitalization?

Capital letters are used to begin sentences, indicate special meanings, and prevent confusion.

Words are capitalized to indicate proper nouns and prevent confusion. The word "earth" means soil; "Earth" is the name of a planet. The word "ford" means to cross a river; "Ford" refers to a car or a family name. An "apple" is a fruit; "Apple" is a computer. The word "polish" can be a verb meaning to shine or a noun meaning a protective substance as in "shoe polish"; "Polish" refers to Poland.

Capitalizing words changes their meaning:

Sam likes modern opera.	*indicates an interest in recent opera*
Sam likes Modern Opera.	*indicates an interest in a specific music class*
We flew European airlines.	*indicates several different airlines in Europe*
We flew European Airlines.	*indicates a single airline named European Airlines*
Will used a Dodge to escape.	*indicates using a vehicle to escape*
Will used a dodge to escape.	*indicates using a trick to escape*

What Do You Know?

Underline the letters in each sentence that should be capitalized.

1. He bought a toyota corolla last year because he planned to move south to florida, where he expected to do a lot of driving.

2. He saw a doctor who referred him to dr. green for more tests.

3. She ordered a salad with french dressing, but I stuck with chinese food.

4. I got a's in algebra, history, spanish, and introduction to psychology 101.

5. He spoke at the national bankers association convention last fourth of july.

Answers appear on the following page.

WHAT ARE YOU TRYING TO SAY?

Write a list of things you would like to own—cars, clothes, sound systems, or CDs.

_____

_____

_____

_____

_____

_____

_____

_____

_____

_____

WHAT HAVE YOU WRITTEN?

Review your list for capitalization. Did you capitalize proper nouns, such as names of stores or product brand names? Review the rules on the following pages; then edit your list.

Rules for Capitalization

There are a dozen main rules for capitalizing words. At first the list may seem overwhelming, but if you remember a simple guideline, you can avoid most problems. **Capitalize words that refer to something specific or special—proper names or specific places or things.**

1. **Capitalize the first word of every sentence:**

   They worked hard all week.

2. **Capitalize the first word in direct quotations:**

   Jim said, "We want overtime pay."

3. **Capitalize the first word, last word, and all important words in titles of articles, books, plays, movies, television shows, seminars, and courses:**

   "TV Today"   *Survivor*   *A Chorus Line*
   War of the Worlds   Monday Night Football   Modern History II

4. **Capitalize the names of nationalities, languages, races, religions, deities, and sacred terms:**

   Many Chinese speak English.   The Bible inspires many Catholics.
   I bought a German car.   She was the city's first Latina mayor.

5. **Capitalize the days of the week, months of the years, and holidays:**

   We celebrate Bastille Day every   The party on Saturday is canceled.
   July.
   Muslims celebrate Ramadan.   I went home for Christmas last year.

   Note: The seasons of the year are not capitalized:

   We loved the fall colors.   This summer is very hot.

6. **Capitalize special historical events, documents, and eras:**

   the Civil War   the Monroe Doctrine
   World War I   the Bill of Rights
   the Whisky Rebellion   the French Revolution

**Answers to What Do You Know?
on page 585**

1. He bought a Toyota Corolla last year because he planned to move south to Florida, where he expected to do a lot of driving.
2. He saw a doctor who referred him to Dr. Green for more tests.
3. She ordered a salad with French dressing, but I stuck with Chinese food.
4. I got A's in algebra, history, Spanish, and Introduction to Psychology 101.
5. He spoke at the National Bankers Association Convention last Fourth of July.

7. **Capitalize names of planets, continents, nations, states, provinces, counties, towns and cities, mountains, lakes, rivers, and other geographical features:**

Neptune	South America	Mexico	Ottawa
Lake Erie	Mount McKinley	Michigan	Jersey
the Badlands	Rocky Mountains	Nile	Iraq

8. **Capitalize *north, south, east,* and *west* when they refer to geographical regions:**

   Oil was discovered in the South.
   He wears Western clothes.
   We grew up in the East.

   Note: Do not capitalize *north, south, east,* and *west* when used as directions:

   We drove west for an hour.
   The store is northwest of Albany.

9. **Capitalize brand names:**

Coca-Cola	Pontiac Firebird	a Parker pen

   Note: Some common brand names, such as *Kleenex, Xerox,* and *Coke,* sometimes appear in lowercase, but this generic use of brand names should be avoided in college and professional writing.

10. **Capitalize names of specific corporations, organizations, institutions, and buildings:**

    This plane was built by Boeing.
    The lecture is in Statler Hall at noon.
    We toured the United Nations.
    She works for the Urban League.

11. **Capitalize abbreviations, acronyms, or shortened forms of capitalized words when used as proper nouns:**

FBI	CNN	FOX	ABC
IRA	JFK	LAX	NBC
NRA	GM	IRS	OPEC

12. **Capitalize people's names and nicknames:**

Janet Rossi	Timmy Allen

    Note: Capitalize professional titles when used with proper names:

    Doctor Jackson gave a speech last night.
    We accepted Mayor Wilson's budget.
    Our school president met with President Bush.
    He has to see the president now!

    Note: Capitalize words such as *father, mother, brother, aunt, cousin,* and *uncle* only when used with or in place of proper names:

    My father and I went to see Aunt Jean.
    After the game, I took Father to meet our aunt.

POINT TO REMEMBER

The rules of capitalization sometimes vary. Some publications always capitalize *President* when it refers to the president of the United States; other publications do not. *African American* is always capitalized, but editors vary on whether *blacks* should be capitalized. Some writers capitalize *A.M.* and *P.M.*, whereas others do not.

Follow the standard used in your discipline or career, and be consistent.

EXERCISE 1   Capitalization

Underline letters that should be capitalized.

1. Last april we decided to go to new orleans instead of florida for spring break.

2. I was driving south for almost six hours when my roommate's firebird blew a tire.

3. We almost hit a ups truck before I could park on the shoulder.

4. The car had only a temporary spare, but a mississippi state trooper stopped and told us there was a dealership just off i-60 on western avenue.

5. The service department at southland pontiac was open, so we pulled in and had the tire replaced.

6. While we waited for the car, Jean and I walked over to a country buffet and had lunch, and Karen went to the target across the street to get new sunglasses and more pepsi.

7. We were back on the road within an hour and a half and crossed into louisiana around three o'clock.

8. We made good time until we ran into major construction just outside orleans parish,

9. Traffic crawled along, but Karen popped in a dixieland cd to get us in the mood.

10. I got off the interstate and took a two-lane highway south to the city.

11. New orleans is called america's most fascinating city or the city that care forgot for good reason.

12. We expected to see a lot of damage from katrina, but the old part of the french quarter was not flooded.

13. We parked at the monteleone hotel on royal street, dumped our bags in the room, took showers, changed into fresh clothes, and went out to explore the capital of the old south.

14. Bourbon street was filled with college students from tulane and florida state.

15. We stopped for oysters rockefeller and steamed clams, then went to the napoleon house for drinks.

16. All of us were exhausted, but we could not resist walking around the city, checking out the european-style streets and historic buildings that survived the civil war.

17. We walked through jackson square and the french market, stopping off for some irish coffee before heading back to the hotel.

18. We called room service for a pizza and checked the news on cnn.

19. Our friend jerry, who insisted on going to florida, called from the daytona hyatt.

20. "I should have gone with you," he told us. "It's going to rain every day this week except monday."

EXERCISE 2   Capitalization

Underline letters that should be capitalized.

1. On october 16, 1869, workmen digging a well in cardiff, new york, made an amazing discovery.

2. They informed the farm owner, william newell, that they had found a a giant figure in the earth.

3. Visitors came from all over new york to see the ten-foot-high statue carved from stone.

4. Newell began charging tourists to look at the mysterious artifact that some saw as evidence of the giants mentioned in genesis.

5. Some believed the statue was carved by a jesuit missionary to teach the bible to native americans.

6. Businessmen paid newell for the statue, now called the "cardiff giant," and took it to syracuse, new york, where they planned to charge admission.

7. A yale professor examined the giant, discovered fresh chisel marks, and announced it was a phony.

8. A businessman named hull came forward and explained he had paid stonecutters to make a statue that he buried on the newell farm a year before.

9. Newell, who conspired with hull, then directed workers to dig a well, engineering the giant's "accidental" discovery.

10. The public was so fascinated by the cardiff giant that they paid to seek the fake, now nicknamed "old hoaxy."

11. Always eager to make money with a new exhibit, p. t. barnum offered to lease the giant to display in his museum.

12. When the giant's owners refused, barnum made a plaster replica of the cardiff giant, and people paid to see a copy of a fake.

13. A hundred years later, another great showman, david merrick, came up with another hoax that made broadway history.

14. He was producing a play called *subways are for sleeping,* a show that got poor reviews and sold few tickets.

15. Merrick placed an ad in the *new york herald tribune* announcing that seven of new york's leading critics had raved about his play.

16. The ad featured the names of famous critics and their comments stating how great the show was.

17. The ad was a stunt; the quotations were real but misleading.

18. Merrick found seven new yorkers who shared the same name as seven leading critics and gave them free tickets and treated them to dinner.

19. After enjoying themselves with the famous producer, the seven new yorkers praised his show and agreed to let him use their names and quote their favorable comments.

20. The ad appeared only once but generated enough publicity to keep *subways are for sleeping* running for months and helped phyllis newman win a tony award.

EXERCISE 3   Capitalization

Underline letters that require capitalization.

Rachman Productions

Dear Paul:

I am putting together next season's tour schedules. To make the most of our budget, I think we should skip august and start in late september. The labor day event in st. louis is not suited for any of our acts. So far I worked on three acts: the rocky mountain boys, the gun molls, and rene ruiz.

1. I suggest we send the rocky mountain boys to the west coast. They simply do not draw an eastern audience.

2. The gun molls, on the other hand, should receive maximum exposure. Their last dvd sold 1.2 million. In addition, columbia is releasing a film called *taming the falcon,* which includes two gun molls' songs in the soundtrack. The lead singer, myra long, is scheduled to appear on letterman in september and may do howard stern in october. I see them doing well not only in new york, chicago, and la, but also along the gulf coast and larger cities in the midwest.

3. I agree with you that rene ruiz has to remake herself. Her last cd sold poorly and gets little air play on spanish language stations. She simply has not excited attention casting herself as a latina performer. She is, however, an impressive jazz singer. She should skip pop concerts and continue her act on the piano bar circuit. I have talked with her, and she agrees that smaller venues better suit her voice. She is quite inventive in using the internet to build a loyal fan base. I think we need to work with her this season and devote more time to her costumes, selections, and presentation. She feels, and I agree, that she could succeed as a forties' style latin torch singer.

Let me know what you think of my suggestions,

Jack Rosen

WORKING TOGETHER

Work with a group of students to determine the definition of each word. What difference does capitalization make? You may use a dictionary to check your answers.

1. Bronco _____
   bronco _____

2. Patriots _____
   patriots _____

3. CARE _____
   care _____

4. general motors _____
   General Motors _____

5. prohibition _____
   Prohibition _____

6. new year _____
   New Year _____

7. dial _____
   Dial _____

8. the Gulf _____
   the gulf _____

9. Rolling Stones _____
   rolling stones _____

10. civil war _____
   Civil War _____

CRITICAL THINKING

Write a short paragraph describing recent errands you've run or shopping trips you've been on.

Get Thinking and Writing

WHAT HAVE YOU WRITTEN?

Review your writing for capitalization. Did you remember to capitalize proper nouns—names of people, streets, stores, malls, and specific brands?

What Have You Learned?

Underline letters in each sentence that should be capitalized.

1. I read the article on the internet before the march meeting.

2. The governor met with mayor wilson and suggested that homeland security should assist with protecting the harbor along with the coast guard.

3. I remember her saying, "we must save our public schools" at the pta meeting.

4. We walked south along the hudson river until we reached west point.

5. I hope i get at least a b in dr. smith's introduction to sociology course this spring.

Answers appear on the following page.

WRITING ON THE WEB

Using a search engine such as Yahoo! or Google, enter terms such as *capitalization rules, using capitals,* and *proper nouns* to locate current sites of interest.

POINTS TO REMEMBER

1. Capitalize the first word in each sentence and direct quotation.

2. Capitalize first and important words in titles of books, articles, movies, and works of art.

3. Capitalize names of nationalities, languages, races, and religions.

4. Capitalize days of the weeks, months, holidays, historical events, documents, and eras.

5. Capitalize proper names and nicknames of people, places, products, organizations, and institutions.

6. Capitalize abbreviations such as FBI and NAACP.

7. Capitalize a person's title only when it precedes a name or is used in place of a name:
   "I took Mother to see Dr. Grant."

8. Do not capitalize seasons such as *spring* and *fall* or *north, south, east,* and *west* when used as directions.

Answers to What Have You Learned? on page 591

1. I read the article on the Internet before the March meeting.

2. The governor met with Mayor Wilson and suggested that Homeland Security should assist with protecting the harbor along with the Coast Guard.

3. I remember her saying, "We must save our public schools" at the PTA meeting.

4. We walked south along the Hudson River until we reached West Point.

5. I hope I get at least a B in Dr. Smith's Introduction to Sociology course this spring.

CHAPTER 35

Spelling Errors

BLANEYPHOTO/ISTOCKPHOTO.COM

CHAPTER GOALS

■ Understand Spelling Rules

■ Overcome Common Spelling Errors.

Get Writing

Some people advocate that public school students should wear uniforms. They argue that uniforms reduce differences between rich and poor students and lessen the focus on fashion that distracts young people from their studies. Opponents argue that uniforms inhibit creativity and personal expression. Do you believe public schools should require students to wear uniforms? Why or why not? Would you advocate stricter dress codes instead?

Write a paragraph stating your views.

Spelling influences the way people look at your writing. Consider the impression made by this e-mail:

Dear Mr. Lee:

I heard your talk about oppurtunities in cable telvision in northern California and was very struck by the comments you made. I am compeleting my associate degree this semsester and have two years experince working for to FM radio stations in the Bay Area. I am now seeking a full time job and would interested in meating with you at your convenence to see if you're firm has any openings. You can e-mail me or call me at (415) 555-5442.

Sincerly,
Sid Sadoff

All the student's education and hard work are overshadowed by spelling errors, which make any writer appear careless and uneducated. Not every reader can detect a dangling modifier or faulty parallelism, but almost everyone can identify a misspelled word.

Some people have a photographic memory and need to see a word only once to remember its exact spelling. Others, even professional writers, have difficulty with words. If English is your second language or if you have trouble with spelling, make it a priority. It can be the easiest, most dramatic way of improving your writing and your grades. Make sure that you reserve enough time in the writing process to edit your papers to correct spelling mistakes.

What Do You Know?

Underline the misspelled or misused words in each sentence.

1. Your not conscience of the capitol the bank is loosing, are you?

2. Its starting to snow, so we should leave before it is to late.

3. How will flunking this quiz effect my final grade?

4. It is too quit here.

5. Please except my apology.

6. This problem seems insolveable.

7. She exercices on paralell bars and lifts wieghts.

8. He was sited for fialing to yeild.

9. Her arguements make no cents to me or anyone else.

10. We cannot recieve e-mail for some reason.

Answers appear on page 595.

WHAT ARE YOU TRYING TO SAY?

Do you object to the amount of profanity used in current movies and cable television shows? Directors and writers argue that they are striving for realism by including the language their characters would speak in real life. Critics insist that swearing, especially in popular culture, is unnecessary and cheapens society. Write a paragraph stating your views. Do you think, for instance, that network and cable television shows should have different standards? Why or why not?

Get Writing

_____

_____

_____

_____

_____

_____

_____

_____

_____

_____

WHAT HAVE YOU WRITTEN?

Review what you have written, and check with a dictionary to see if you have misspelled any words.

1. Review assignments you have written in this or any other course for spelling errors. Do see any patterns or any words you repeatedly misspell?

2. List any words you find confusing or have doubts about:

_____ _____

_____ _____

_____ _____

_____ _____

Steps to Improving Spelling

1. Make spelling a priority, especially in editing your papers.

2. Look up new words in a dictionary for correct spelling and meaning. Write them out a few times to help memorize them.

3. Study the glossaries in your textbooks to master new terms.

Answers to What Do You Know? on page 594

1. You're; conscious; capital; losing 2. It's; too 3. affect 4. quiet 5. accept 6. insolvable 7. exercises; parallel; weights 8. cited; failing; yield 9. arguments; sense 10. receive

4. Review lists of commonly misspelled words (see pages 703–704) and commonly confused words (see pages 700–703).

5. Create a list of words you have trouble with. Keep copies of the list next to your computer and in your notebook. Each week try to memorize three or four of these words. Update your list by adding new terms you encounter.

6. Read your writing out loud when editing. Some spelling errors are easier to hear than see.

7. Remember *i* before *e* except after *c,* or when it sounds like *a* as in *neighbor* and *weigh:*

i before *e*

achieve	field	niece	shield
brief	grievance	piece	yield

Except after *c*

ceiling	deceive	perceive	receipt

When it sounds like *a*

eight	freight	rein	vein

Exceptions: either, height, leisure, seize, weird

8. Review rules for adding word endings (see pages 603–604).

9. Learn to use computer spell checks, and understand their limitations. Although spell checks can easily spot typos and commonly misspelled words, not every program will alert you to confusing *there* for *their* or *affect* for *effect* (see pages 700–703).

10. If you are a poor speller, eliminating spelling errors is the fastest and easiest way to improve your grades.

Commonly Misspelled Words

Top 20

COMMONLY MISSPELLED WORDS

Learn to recognize words that you commonly misspell. Check the list on pages 703–704.

Many words are commonly misspelled. They may be foreign words, contain silent letters, or have unusual letter combinations. When speaking, people often slur sounds and fail to pronounce every letter. Because you are accustomed to hearing words mispronounced, you may misspell them when you write.

Incorrect	*Correct*
goverment	gover**n**ment
suppose (past tense)	suppose**d**
ice tea	ice**d** tea

Forty Commonly Misspelled Words

absence	belief	generous	mortgage
achieve	benefit	grammar	necessary
acquire	challenge	guard	obvious
address	committee	height	opinion
among	control	heroes	parallel
analyze	decision	identity	persuade
argument	dying	label	possess
athletic	embarrass	license	privilege
beautiful	enough	marriage	separate
becoming	familiar	material	vacuum

See pages 703–704 for additional words.

EXERCISE 1 Commonly Misspelled Words

Underline the correctly spelled word in each pair.

1. grateful/greatful

2. avalanch/avalanche

3. safety/safty

4. lonelyness/loneliness

5. colum/column

6. disappear/disapear

7. preceed/precede

8. sterotype/stereotype

9. dependant/dependent

10. similar/similiar

Commonly Confused Words

In addition to easily misspelled words, there are easily confused words. The word you put on the page is correctly spelled, but it is the wrong word and has a different meaning from what you are trying to say. Many words look and sound alike but have clearly different meanings:

everyday	*ordinary or common*	"She wore **everyday** clothes."
every day	*each day*	"Take vitamins **every day.**"
any one	*a single person, idea, or item*	"**Any one** of the rooms is open."
anyone	*anybody*	"Can **anyone** help us?"

Top 20

COMMONLY CONFUSED WORDS

Recognize commonly confused words. Check the list on pages 700–703.

| roll | *to turn over/a small bread loaf* | "Let the ball **roll** down the hill." |
| role | *a part in a play or event* | "He played no **role** in the scandal." |

Using the wrong word not only creates a spelling error but also creates confusion by making a statement that means something very different from what you intended:

She will **adopt** our proposal. = She **will *accept*** our proposal.
She will **adapt** our proposal. = She **will *change*** our proposal.

He gave a speech about the **eminent** trial. = He gave a speech about the ***famous*** trial.
He gave a speech about the **imminent** trial. = He gave a speech about the ***upcoming*** trial.

We want to see the **sites.** = We want to see ***specific places*** (example: construction sites).
We want to see the **sights.** = We want to see ***interesting places*** (example: tourist attractions).

Ten Most Commonly Confused Words

accept/except

| accept | to take | "Please ***accept*** my apology." |
| except | but/to exclude | "Everyone ***except*** Tom attended." |

affect/effect

| affect | to change or influence | "Will this ***affect*** my grade?" |
| effect | a result | "What ***effect*** did the drug have?" |

farther/further

| farther | geographical distance | "The farm is ten miles ***farther*** on." |
| further | in addition | "***Further*** negotiations proved useless." |

hear/here

| hear | to listen | "Did you ***hear*** her new song?" |
| here | a place or direction | "Put it over ***here***." |

its/it's

| its | possessive of it | "My car won't start. ***Its*** battery died." |
| it's | "it is" | "Looks like ***it's*** going to rain." |

lay/lie

| lay | to put or place | "***Lay*** the boxes on the table." |
| lie | to recline | "***Lie*** down. You look tired." |

principal/principle

| principal | main/school leader | "Oil is the ***principal*** product of Kuwait." |
| principle | basic law | "This violates all ethical ***principles***." |

than/then		
than	used in comparisons	"Bill is taller *than* Tom."
then	refers to time	"He took the test, *then* went home."

there/their/they're		
there	direction/a place	"**There** he goes." "Put it **there.**"
their	possessive of *they*	"*Their* car won't start."
they're	"they are"	"*They're* taking the bus home."

to/too/two		
to	preposition/infinitive	"Walk *to* school." "He likes *to* dance."
too	excessive/in addition	"It's *too* hot." "I want to go, *too.*"
two	a number	"The dress costs *two* hundred dollars."

See pages 700–703 for a complete list.

EXERCISE 2   Commonly Confused Words

Underline and correct misspelled words in each sentence.

1. He tries to hard to impress people.

2. She was so quite we didn't even now she was there.

3. The employees have little excess to medical care.

4. They were upset when there reservation was canceled.

5. The recent loss really effected the team's moral.

6. I have a great ideal for raising money for the school.

7. The plane truth is I just don't like to see people loose their jobs.

8. The campsite is further from here then I thought.

9. I did not mean my e-mail to infer that you were not working hard enough.

10. We past the gas station half an hour ago.

EXERCISE 3   Commonly Misspelled and Confused Words

Underline each misspelled or misused word, and write the correct spelling over it.

The Grammy Award is the most famous of for discreet music awards in the United

States. The Grammy gets it's name from the award isself, which is a minature replica of an old-fashion gramophone. The award is presented by the Recording Academy, an assocation of professionals in the music industry. Awards are given in thirty generes, including rock, pop, rap, and gospel. These are seperated into over a hundred catagories. Unlike other music awards, the Grammy winners are chosen by voting members of the academy rather then fans. Winners are chosen by there piers in the music industry. The annual awards ceremony is shown on television and recieves very high ratings. Like the Academy Awards, the Grammy Awards have there critics. Some fans belief that its not fare that artists like Elvis and groups like the Rolling Stones received fewer Grammys then Pat Metheny.

Forming Plurals

Words change their spelling to indicate when they are plural. Most nouns simply add an *-s:*

Singular	Plural
pen	pens
coin	coins
paper	papers
bill	bills
cardiologist	cardiologists

However, many nouns use different spellings to indicate plurals. In order to avoid making spelling errors, it is important to understand which words require more than an added *-s* to become plural.

1. **For words ending in *-s, -ss, -x, -z, -sh, or -ch,* add *-es:***

Singular	Plural
hiss	hisses
church	churches
dish	dishes
box	boxes

2. **For words ending in an *-o* preceded by a vowel, add *-s:***

Singular	Plural
stereo	stereos
studio	studios
zoo	zoos
rodeo	rodeos

3. **For words ending in an *-o* preceded by a consonant, add *-es:***

Singular	Plural
hero	heroes
zero	zeroes
echo	echoes
tomato	tomatoes

Exceptions

Singular	Plural
motto	mottos
photo	photos
solo	solos
piano	pianos

4. **For words ending in -f or -fe, change the f to v and add -es:**

Singular	Plural
shelf	shelves
wife	wives
half	halves
thief	thieves

Exceptions

Singular	Plural
safe	safes
roof	roofs
proof	proofs
chief	chiefs

5. **For words ending in -y preceded by a consonant, change the y to i and add -es:**

Singular	Plural
city	cities
story	stories
baby	babies
celebrity	celebrities

6. **For some words, the plural form is irregular:**

Singular	Plural
tooth	teeth
child	children
person	people
woman	women

7. **For some words, the singular and plural spelling are the same:**

Singular	Plural
deer	deer
fish	fish
sheep	sheep
series	series

8. **For Greek and Latin nouns, there are special spellings:**

Singular	Plural
memorandum	memoranda
datum	data
thesis	theses
alumnus	alumni

9. **For compound nouns—made up of two or more words—make the needed change to the main word. For compound nouns written as one word, make the ending plural:**

Singular	*Plural*
mother-in-law	mothers-in-law
stepchild	stepchildren
bookshelf	bookshelves

Exceptions

Singular	*Plural*
passerby	passersby

10. **For compound nouns that appear as separate words or connected by hyphens, make the main word plural:**

Singular	*Plural*
music store	music stores
icebox	iceboxes
water tank	water tanks
brother-in-law	brothers-in-law

EXERCISE 4　Creating Plurals

Write out the correct plural form of each noun.

1. reef　　　　　　_____

2. book　　　　　　_____

3. pop star　　　　_____

4. toss　　　　　　_____

5. wolf　　　　　　_____

6. grandchild　　　_____

7. flurry　　　　　_____

8. employee of the month　_____

9. tax　　　　　　_____

10. stereo　　　　 _____

EXERCISE 5　Plural Spellings

Correct errors in plurals in each sentence.

1. The attorney generals of sixteen states met with representatives of companys concerned about rising bankruptcys.

_____

_____

2. Your cholesterol ratioes would be better if you ate more fishes.

_____

3. Consumer worrys about rising prices are hurting many industrys.

_____

4. These powerful radioes are popular with peoples living in remote areas.

_____

5. These safety features could save many lifes.

_____

Adding Endings

In most instances, suffixes or word endings follow simple rules to indicate past tense or to create an adjective or adverb.

Past-Tense Spellings

Most verbs are called "regular" because they simply add -ed or -d if the word ends with an -e.

Regular Verbs

Present	*Past*
talk	talked
disintegrate	disintegrated
vote	voted
print	printed

1. **If a verb ends in -y, change the y to i + -ed:**

cry	cried
spy	spied
try	tried

2. **If a one-syllable verb ends in a consonant preceded by a vowel, double the last letter + -ed:**

pin	pinned
plan	planned
stop	stopped
grab	grabbed

   Other verbs, called "irregular," have different spellings to indicate past tense.

Irregular Verbs

Present	*Past*
teach	taught
sing	sang
write	wrote
swim	swam
buy	bought

See pages 498–500 for a complete list.

Spelling Other Endings

Endings are added to words to create adjectives, adverbs, or nouns:

sad (*adjective*)	sadly (*adverb*)	sadness (*noun*)
create (*verb*)	creative (*adjective*)	creatively (*adverb*)
motivate (*verb*)	motivation (*noun*)	motivated (*adjective*)
happy (*adjective*)	happily (*adverb*)	happiness (*noun*)

1. **For words ending with a silent *-e,* drop the *-e* if the ending begins with a vowel:**

   arrive + al   = arrival
   come + ing = coming
   fame + ous = famous
   create + ion = creation

   Exceptions: mileage, dyeing

2. **For words ending with a silent *-e,* retain the *-e* if the ending begins with a consonant:**

   elope   + ment = elopement
   safe   + ty   = safety
   like   + ness = likeness
   complete + ly   = completely

   Exceptions: judgment and acknowledgment.

3. **Double the last consonant of one-syllable words if the ending begins with a vowel:**

   rob + ing = robbing
   spot + ed = spotted
   spin + ing = spinning

4. **Double the last consonant of words accented on the last syllable if the ending begins with a vowel:**

   refer   + ing = referring
   admit   + ed = admitted
   technical + ly   = technically

Note

Prefixes do not change spelling of base words. When you add letters before a word, no letters are dropped or added:

un + natural = unnatural	dis + able	= disable
pre + judge = prejudge	il + legal	= illegal
im + moral = immoral	de + mobilize	= demobilize

EXERCISE 6 Past-Tense Spellings

Write the correct past-tense form of each verb.

1. weigh _____

2. walk _____

3. stand _____

4. ram _____

5. capitalize _____

6. think _____

7. double _____

8. rest _____

9. sleep _____

10. broil _____

EXERCISE 7 Adding Endings

Combine the following words and endings.

1. debate + able _____

2. legal + ly _____

3. regret + fully _____

4. force + ing _____

5. attend + ance _____

6. doubt + less _____

7. win + ing _____

8. recycle + able _____

9. make + ing _____

10. fit + ness _____

EXERCISE 8   Identifying and Correcting Misspelled Words

Underline misspelled and misused words, and write the correct spelling below them.

One of the most memorerable peaces of America's passed is the Liberty Bell. More then any other relic of the Revolutionary War, it is immediatly recognized as a symbol of freedom around the world. The bell was cast in England in 1752 and shipped to America to hang in the Pennsylvana State House, later known as Independance Hall.

The first time the bell was rang in 1753, it cracked. It was recast twice, then hanged in the State House. The bell was used to summon members of the Continental Congress in 1775 and 1776. When British solders neared Philadelphia, patriots moved the bell to Allentown and hid it under a church. The bell was returned to Philadelphia in 1778.

The bell tolled at the deaths of Washington, Franklin, Hamilton, Adams, Jefferson, and Lafayette. It was not, however, officaly called the Liberty Bell until the 1830s, when it became a symbol of the antislavery movement. The bell's Biblical inscription, which promised liberty to all, was seen as the perfect emblemn for the abolitionist cause.

The Liberty Bell split when it was rung to celebrate Washington's birthday in 1846. The bell was rung in later years with a rubber mallat. On June 6, 1944, the mayor of Philadelphia tapped the bell twelve times, which was broadcasted on radioes nationwide, to celebrate the liberation of Europe. In 1962 the bell was tapped on the first anniversary of the erection of the Berlin Wall to honor the people of East Germany.

In 2002 the decision to relocate the Liberty Bell stired controversy when it was discovered that the entrance to the new exhibit hall would be placed on the sight of quarters once used to house George Washington's slaves.

EXERCISE 9   Cumulative Exercise

Rewrite these paragraphs to correct spelling errors and missing capitalization and to eliminate fragments and run-ons. To check your revision, see pages 586–587 and 700–704.

Her name was Ann and we met in the port authority bus terminal several januarys ago. I was doing a story on homeless people. She said I wasting my time talking to her she was just passing though, although she'd been passing though for more then too weeks. To prove too me that this was true, she rummaged through a tote bag and a manila envelop and finally unfolded a sheet of typeing paper and bought out her photographs.

They were not pictures of family, or friends, or even a dog or cat, it's eyes brown-red in the flashbulb's light. They were pictures of a house. It was like a thousand houses in a hundred towns, not suburb, not city, but somewhere in between, with aluminun sideing and a chain-link fence, a narrow driveway running up to a one-car garage and a patch of backyard. The house was yellow. I looked on the back for a date or a name but neither was their. There was no need for discussion. I new what what she was trying to tell me for it was something I had often felt. She was not adrift, alone, anonymous, although her bags and her raincoat with the grime shadowing it's creases had made me belief she was. She had a house or at least once upon a time had had one. Inside were curtains, a couch, a stove, potholders. You are where you live. She was somebody.

WORKING TOGETHER

Working with a group of students, correct this ad for spelling errors. Have each member underline misspelled words; then work as a group. Note how collaborative editing helps detect errors you may miss on your own.

COMING THIS SUMMER!

Save you're money . . .
Save time on droped calls . . .
Enjoy the best calling plan in the county . . .

    On July 1, American Horizon starts it's latest and best national calling plan do date.

    7 Cents a Minute Anytime All the Time!

Call 1-800-555-7000, or visit us online at www.americanhorizon.com for details and a free upgrade!

CRITICAL THINKING

How has your writing improved over the semester? What areas of writing still pose challenges? Write a paragraph describing your progress and areas you would like to improve.

Get Thinking and Writing

WHAT HAVE YOU WRITTEN?

Examine your paragraph for spelling errors. If you have listed any areas you would like to improve, bookmark pages in Get Writing *you can use for review and reference on future writing assignments.*

What Have You Learned?

Underline and correct the misspelled or misused words in each sentence.

1. Its later then you think!

2. I stoped there car before it rolled of the ramp.

3. That red-stripped dress is to expensive.

4. The pills had no affect on her blood pressure.

5. Several companys are relocating to Southern California.

6. This will be a causal party, so where every day cloths.

7. We now he is coming later.

8. The principle product of Saudi Arabia is oil.

9. The knew movie casts aging stars in very predictable rolls.

10. You're boxs are in the garage were I left them.

(Check a dictionary to make sure you have successfully identified and corrected all twenty errors.)

WRITING ON THE WEB

Using a search engine such as Yahoo! or Google, enter terms such as *spelling, improving spelling, spelling rules,* and *using spell check* to locate current sites of interest.

POINTS TO REMEMBER

1. **Edit your papers carefully for commonly misspelled words such as** *library, yield, opinion, opportunity,* **and** *separate.* **(See list on pages 703–704.)**

2. **Edit your papers carefully for commonly confused words such as** *anyone* **and** *any one* **or** *implicit* **and** *explicit.* **(See list on pages 700–703.)**

3. **Remember,** *i* **before** *e* **except after** *c,* **or when it sounds like** *a* **such as in** *neighbor* **and** *weigh:*

   achieve   ceiling   freight
   Exceptions: either, height, leisure, seize

4. **Follow the guidelines for creating plurals.**

   For words ending in *-s, -ss, -x, -z, -sh,* **or** *-ch,* **add** *-es:*

   misses   boxes   churches

   For words ending in *-o* **preceded by a vowel, add** *-s:*

   zoos   radios

For words ending in -o preceded by a consonant, add -es:

heroes   zeroes

Exceptions: mottos, photos, pianos, solos

For words ending in -f or -fe, change the f to v and add -es:

shelves   halves   thieves

Exceptions: safes, roofs, proofs, chiefs

Some plural words have irregular forms:

teeth   children   people

Some words have no plural spelling:

sheep   fish   series

Greek and Latin nouns have special plural spellings:

memoranda   data   theses

For compound nouns, make the needed change to the main word:

bookshelves   stepchildren boyfriends

For compound nouns that appear as separate words, change the main word:

brothers-in-law   beer taps   water tanks

5. **Follow guidelines for creating past-tense endings.**

   For regular verbs, add -ed or -d if the word ends in -e:

   walked   created   painted

   For verbs ending in -y, change the y to i + -ed:

   cried   spied   tried

   For a one-syllable verb ending with a consonant preceded by a vowel, double the last letter + -ed:

   pinned   stopped   grabbed

   Some verbs have irregular past-tense forms:

   taught   sang   swam

6. **Follow guidelines for adding suffixes.**

   For words ending with a silent -e, drop the -e if the ending begins with a vowel:

   arrival   coming   creation

   For words ending with a silent -e, keep the -e if the ending begins with a consonant:

   safety   likeness   completely

   Double the last consonant of one-syllable words if the ending begins with a vowel:

   robbing   spotted   spinning

   Double the last consonant of words accented on the last syllable if the ending begins with a vowel:

   referring   admitted   technically

7. **Make and review lists of words you commonly misspell.**

8. **Always budget enough time in the writing process to edit your papers for spelling errors.**

Improving Spelling

Review writing exercises you have completed in this book and papers you have written in this or other courses for errors in spelling. List each word. Add words that you frequently misspell or are unsure of. Check a dictionary, and carefully write out each word correctly. Add definitions to words that are easily confused, such as *conscious* and *conscience* or *then* and *than*.

1. _____   11. _____

2. _____   12. _____

3. _____   13. _____

4. _____   14. _____

5. _____   15. _____

6. _____   16. _____

7. _____   17. _____

8. _____   18. _____

9. _____   19. _____

10. _____   20. _____

PART 8

Readings for Writers

Strategies for Reading

Reading essays can help you improve as a writer because essays demonstrate different ways to develop topics, explore ideas, create a thesis, organize paragraphs, write sentences, and choose words.

When you read for enjoyment, you generally start with the first sentence and let the writer take you on a journey. You allow the writer's words, sentences, and images to tell a story or develop an argument. As a writing student, however, you should read with a "writer's eye." You should examine a reading assignment critically to see what it can teach you about developing ideas, using words, and presenting ideas. Like writing, effective reading takes place in stages.

First Reading

1. **Look ahead and skim entries.** Don't wait for the night before class to read an assignment. Skim upcoming readings to become familiar with them.

2. **Study the title.** Authors often use titles to state a thesis or pose a question. Titles can also give you a clue about the type of essay it is. Titles with the word *how* may indicate a process essay, and titles that present pairs of words may suggest a comparison.

3. **Read the entire work.** Try to get the big picture by reading the entire essay to study its main ideas and organization.

4. **Focus on understanding the writer's main point.** Try to summarize the thesis in your own words.

5. **Jot down your first impressions.** What do you think of this essay? Do you like it? Why or why not? Do you agree with the writer's observations? If you find it dull, silly, or disturbing, ask yourself why. What is missing? How did the author succeed or fail in your view?

6. **Put the essay aside.** If possible, let two or three days pass before returning to the assignment. If the assignment is due tomorrow, try to read the essay in the morning, then return to it in the evening.

Second Reading

1. **Review your first impressions.** Determine if your views are based on your personal reactions or the writer's ability. Don't let personal opinions cloud your critical thinking. Even if you don't like what a writer has to say, you can learn something about writing.

2. **Read with a pen or pencil in your hand.** Make notes in the margin, and underline sentences that express important ideas or make statements that you find interesting, puzzling, or troubling. Writing as you read can make reading an active rather than a passive activity.

3. **Look up unfamiliar words.**

4. **Analyze passages you found difficult or confusing during the first reading.** A second reading can help you understand complex passages. If you still have difficulty understanding part of the essay, ask why. Does the writer use references you do not understand? Search the Internet to find information about phrases, names, or events the writer uses.

5. **Review the questions at the end of the essay. The questions are arranged in three types:**

   - *Understanding Meaning: What Is the Writer Trying to Say?*
     What is the writer's goal?
     What is the thesis?
     What readers is the writer addressing?
     What is the writer trying to share with readers?

   - *Evaluating Strategy: How Does the Writer Say It?*
     How effective is the title?
     How does the writer open the essay?
     What evidence does the writer use?
     How is the essay organized?
     How does the writer end the essay?

   - *Appreciating Language: What Words Does the Writer Use?*
     How does the writer use words?
     Are the words positive or negative?
     How do the words create the writer's tone or express his or her attitude toward the subject?

6. **Summarize your responses in a sentence or two for class discussion.**

7. **Focus on what this essay can teach you about writing.** Noticing how an author states a thesis, organizes details, and presents evidence can help you strengthen your own writing.

Read the following essay by Emily Prager. Notice how a student marked it for a class discussion and made notes for possible writing assignments.

OUR BARBIES, OURSELVES

EMILY PRAGER

Emily Prager is an actress and writer; her books include A Visit from the Footbinder and Other Stories *and* Eve's Tattoo. *In this essay, she analyzes the significance of the Barbie doll.*

AS YOU READ:

Notice how Prager uses several patterns of development, including description, narration, and cause and effect, to develop her essay.

Introduction (obituary as writing prompt)

I read an astounding obituary in the *New York Times* not too long ago. It concerned the death of one Jack Ryan. A former husband of Zsa Zsa Gabor,

1

it said, Mr. Ryan had been an inventor and designer during his lifetime. A man of eclectic creativity, he designed Sparrow and Hawk missiles when he worked for the Raytheon Company, and the notice said, when he consulted for Mattel he designed Barbie.

2   If Barbie was designed by a man, suddenly a lot of things made sense to me, things I'd wondered about for years. I used to look at Barbie and wonder, What's wrong with this picture? What kind of woman designed this doll? Let's be honest: Barbie looks like someone who got her start at the Playboy Mansion. She could be a regular guest on *The Howard Stern Show*. It is a fact of Barbie's design that her breasts are so out of proportion to the rest of her body that if she were a human woman, she'd fall flat on her face.

3   If it's true that a woman didn't design Barbie, you don't know how much saner that makes me feel. Of course, that doesn't ameliorate the damage. There are millions of women who are subliminally sure that a thirty-nine-inch bust and a twenty-three-inch waist are the epitome of lovability. Could this account for the popularity of breast implant surgery?

4   I don't mean to step on anyone's toes here. I loved my Barbie. Secretly, I still believe that neon pink and turquoise blue are the only colors in which to decorate a duplex condo. And like so many others of my generation, I've never married, simply because I cannot find a man who looks as good in clam diggers as Ken.

5   The question that comes to mind is, of course, Did Mr. Ryan design Barbie as a weapon? Because it *is* odd that Barbie appeared about the same time in my consciousness as the feminist movement—a time when women sought equality and small breasts were king. Or is Barbie the dream date of a weapons designer? Or perhaps it's simpler than that: Perhaps Barbie is Zsa Zsa if she were eleven inches tall. No matter what, my discovery of Jack Ryan confirms what I have always felt: There is something indescribably masculine about Barbie—dare I say it, phallic. For all her giant breasts and high-heeled feet, she lacks a certain softness. If you asked a little girl what kind of doll she wanted for Christmas, I just don't think she'd reply, "Please, Santa, I want a hardbody."

6   On the other hand, you could say that Barbie, in feminist terms, is definitely her own person. With her condos and fashion plazas and pools and beauty salons, she is definitely a liberated woman, a gal on the move. And she has always been sexual, even totemic. Before Barbie, American dolls were flat-footed and breastless, and ineffably dignified. They were created in the image of little girls or babies. Madame Alexander was the queen of doll makers in the '50s, and her dollies looked like Elizabeth Taylor in *National Velvet*. They represented the kind of girls who looked perfect in jodhpurs, whose hair was never out of place, who grew up to be Jackie Kennedy—before she married Onassis. Her dolls' boyfriends were figments of the imagination, figments with large portfolios and three-piece suits and presidential aspirations, figments who could keep dolly in the style to which little girls of the '50s were programmed to become accustomed; perhaps what accounts for Barbie's vast popularity is that she was also a '60s woman: into free love and fun colors, anti-class, and possessed a real, molded boyfriend, Ken, with whom she could chant a mantra.

Marginal notes:

description WHY?

female/feminist reaction?

questions cause and effect

Barbie as a weapon?
cause and effect

(modern ideal of a hard body!)

Barbie as role model?

Barbie = adult doll not a baby or child

comparison

Ken sexless? comparison

questions

Barbie's fate
conclusion

final observation

But there were problems with Ken. <u>I always felt weird about him.</u> He had no genitals, and, even at age ten, I found that ominous. I mean, here was Barbie with these humongous breasts, and that was O.K. with the toy company. And then, there was Ken, with that truncated, unidentifiable lump at his groin. I sensed injustice at work. Why, I wondered, was Barbie designed with such obvious sexual equipment and Ken not? Why was he treated as if it were more mysterious than hers? Did the fact that it was treated as such indicate that somehow his equipment, his essential maleness, was considered more powerful than hers, more worthy of the dignity of concealment? And if the issue in the mind of the toy company was obscenity and its possible damage to children, I still object. How do they think I felt, knowing that no matter how many water beds they slept in, or hot tubs they romped in, or swimming pools they lounged by under the stars, Barbie and Ken could never make love? No matter how much sexuality Barbie possessed, she would never turn Ken on. He would be forever withholding, forever detached. There was a <u>loneliness about Barbie's situation that was always disturbing.</u> And twenty-five years later, movies and videos are still filled with topless women and covered men. <u>As if we're all trapped in Barbie's world and can never escape.</u>

7

Student Notes

First Reading

Barbie as symbol of male domination?

What about GI Joe and boys?

Is Prager really serious about this?

Barbie as paradox—a toy that presents a sexist *Playboy* image of women but a toy that is independent and more "liberated" than traditional baby dolls.

Tone: witty but serious in spots, raises a lot of issues but doesn't really discuss many.

Second Reading

Thesis: The Barbie doll, the creation of a male weapons designer, has shaped the way a generation of women defined themselves. (Get other opinions)

Body: spins off a number of topics and observations, a list of associations, suited for general readers.

Approach: a mix of serious and witty commentary, writer appears to entertain as much as inform or persuade.

Organization: use of modes critical to keeping the essay from becoming a rambling list of contradictory ideas. Good use of description, comparison, cause and effect.

Conclusion—"trapped in Barbie's world" good ending.

Prewriting—Possible Topics

Description—childhood toys—models of cars and planes? games—
Monopoly (preparing kids for capitalism?)

Comparison/contrast—boy and girl toys and games, playing house vs.
playing ball (social roles vs. competition, teamwork)

Cause and effect—we are socialized by our toys and games in childhood, affecting how men and women develop (needs support—
Psych class notes)

Example—my daughter's Beanie Baby?

Strategies for Critical Reading

As you read the entries in this chapter, ask yourself these questions:

1. **What is the writer's goal?** What is the purpose of the essay—to
raise questions, motivate readers to take action, or change
people's opinions?

2. **What is the thesis?** What is the writer's main idea? Can you
state the thesis in your own words?

3. **What evidence does the writer provide to support the thesis?** Does the writer use personal observations, narratives, facts,
statistics, or examples to support his or her conclusions?

4. **How does the writer organize the essay?** How does he or she
introduce readers to the topic, develop ideas, arrange information, and conclude the essay? How does the writer use patterns
of development?

5. **Who are the intended readers?** What does the original source
of the document tell you about its intended audience? Does
the writer direct the essay to a particular group or to a general
readership? What terms or references are used? Are technical or
uncommon terms defined? What does the writer seem to expect
readers to know?

6. **How successful is the writing—in context?** Does the writer
achieve his or her goals while respecting the needs of the reader
and the conventions of the discipline or situation? Are there
particular considerations that cause the writer to break the rules
of "good writing"? Why?

7. **What can you learn about writing?** What does this writer
teach you about using words, writing sentences, and developing paragraphs? Are there any techniques you can use in future
assignments?

Description

Description presents details about persons, places, objects, or ideas. It records what you see, hear, feel, taste, and touch.

BORDER STORY

LUIS ALBERTO URREA

In this section from his book Across the Wire, *Luis Alberto Urrea describes the Mexican-American border and the plight of immigrants seeking a new life in the United States.*

AS YOU READ:

Notice how Urrea uses second person—"you"—to dramatize and humanize the illegals by putting his readers in their place.

At night, the Border Patrol helicopters swoop and churn in the air all along the line. You can sit in the Mexican hills and watch them herd humans on the dusty slopes across the valley. They look like science fiction crafts, their hard-focused lights raking the ground as they fly.

Borderlands locals are so <u>jaded</u> by the sight of nightly people-hunting that it doesn't even register in their minds. But take a stranger to the border, and she will *see* the spectacle: monstrous Dodge trucks speeding into and out of the landscape; uniformed men patrolling with flashlights, guns, and dogs; spotlights; running figures; lines of people hurried onto buses by armed guards; and the endless clatter of the helicopters with their harsh white beams. A Dutch woman once told me it seemed altogether "un-American."

But the Mexicans keep on coming—and the Guatemalans, the Salvadorans, the Panamanians, the Colombians. The seven-mile stretch of Interstate 5 nearest the Mexican border is, at times, so congested with Latin American pedestrians that it resembles a town square.

They stick to the center island. Running down the length of the island is a cement wall. If the "illegals" (currently, "undocumented workers"; formerly, "wetbacks") are walking north and a Border Patrol vehicle happens along, they simply hop over the wall and trot south. The officer will have to drive up to the 805 interchange, or Dairy Mart Road, swing over the overpasses, then drive south. Depending on where this pursuit begins, his detour could <u>entail</u> five to ten miles of driving. When the officer finally reaches the group, they hop over the wall and trot north. Furthermore, because freeway arrests would endanger traffic, the Border Patrol has effectively thrown up its hands in surrender.

It seems jolly on the page. But imagine poverty, violence, natural disasters, or political fear driving you away from everything you know. Imagine

Words to Know

jaded used to

entail involve

1

2

3

4

5

how bad things get to make you leave behind your family, your friends, your lovers; your home, as humble as it might be; your church, say. Let's take it further—you've said good-bye to the graveyard, the dog, the goat, the mountains where you first hunted, your grade school, your state, your favorite spot on the river where you fished and took time to think.

6   Then you come hundreds—or thousands—of miles across territory utterly unknown to you, (Chances are, you have never traveled farther than a hundred miles in your life.) You have walked, run, hidden in the backs of trucks, spent part of your precious money on bus fare. There is no AAA or Travelers Aid Society available to you. Various features of your journey north might include police corruption; violence in the forms of beatings, rape, murder, torture, road accident; theft; incarceration. Additionally, you might experience loneliness, fear, exhaustion, sorrow, cold, heat, diarrhea, thirst, hunger. There is no medical attention available to you. There isn't even Kotex.

7   Weeks or months later, you arrive in Tijuana. Along with other immigrants, you gravitate to the bad parts of town because there is nowhere for you to go in the glittery sections where the *gringos* flock. You stay in a rundown little hotel in the red-light district, or behind the bus terminal. Or you find your way to the garbage dumps, where you throw together a small cardboard nest and claim a few feet of dirt for yourself. The garbage-pickers working this dump might allow you to squat, or they might come and rob you or burn you out for breaking some local rule you cannot possibly know beforehand. Sometimes the dump is controlled by a <u>syndicate,</u> and goon squads might come to you within a day. They want money, and if you can't pay, you must leave or suffer the consequences.

syndicate criminal gang

8   In town, you face endless victimization if you aren't streetwise. The police come after you, street thugs come after you, petty criminals come after you; strangers try your door at night as you sleep. Many shady men offer to guide you across the border, and each one wants all your money now, and promises to meet you at a prearranged spot. Some of your fellow travelers end their journeys right here—relieved of their savings and left to wait on a dark corner until they realize they are going nowhere.

9   If you are not Mexican, and can't pass as *tijuanense,* a local, the tough guys find you out. Salvadorans and Guatemalans are routinely beaten up and robbed. Sometimes they are disfigured. Indians—Chinantecas, Mixtecas, Guasaves, Zapotecas, Mayas—are insulted and pushed around; often they are lucky—they are merely ignored. They use this to their advantage. Often they don't dream of crossing into the United States: a Mexican tribal person would never be able to blend in, and they know it. To them, the garbage dumps and street vending and begging in Tijuana are a vast improvement over their former lives. As Doña Paula, a Chinanteca friend of mine who lives at the Tijuana garbage dump, told me, "This is the garbage dump. Take all you need. There's plenty here for *everyone!*"

10   If you are a woman, the men come after you. You lock yourself in your room, and when you must leave it to use the <u>pestilential</u> public bathroom at the end of your floor, you hurry, and you check every corner. Sometimes the lights are out in the toilet room. Sometimes men listen at the door.

pestilential diseased

They call you "good-looking" and "bitch" and *mamacita,*" and they make kissing sounds at you when you pass.

You're in the worst part of town, but you can comfort yourself—at least there are no death squads here. There are no torturers here, or bandit land barons riding into your house. This is the last barrier, you think, between you and the United States—*los Yunaites Estaites.*

11

You still face police corruption, violence, jail. You now also have a wide variety of new options available to you: drugs, prostitution, <u>white slavery,</u> crime. Tijuana is not easy on newcomers. It is a city that has always thrived on taking advantage of a sucker. And the innocent are the ultimate suckers in the Borderlands.

12

white slavery forced prostitution

Get Thinking and Writing

CRITICAL THINKING AND DISCUSSION

Understanding Meaning: What Is the Writer Trying to Say?

1. What dominant impression does Urrea create?
2. What problems do immigrants face on their journey to the border?
3. What special problems do women face along the border?
4. What message is Urrea trying to convey to his readers?

Evaluating Strategy: How Does the Writer Say It?

1. What details does Urrea include to dramatize conditions on the border?
2. How effective is the use of the second person? Does using the pronoun "you" help humanize the illegals? Does "you" have a different impact than the pronoun "they"?

Appreciating Language: What Words Does the Writer Use?

1. Underline words that create Urrea's dominant impression.
2. Throughout the description, Urrea uses lists—"beatings, rape, murder, torture, road accidents. . . ." How effective are lists? Can a writer use too many of them?

Writing Suggestions

1. Write a short essay describing a place that illustrates a social problem. You might describe a traffic jam to highlight the problem of urban congestion or a street of closed stores in a small town to demonstrate the loss of small businesses.
2. *Collaborative writing:* Work with a group of students to respond to Urrea's account. Consider the issues that his description raises. Ask members to suggest what policies could improve conditions along the Mexican border.

UNFORGETTABLE MISS BESSIE

CARL ROWAN

Carl Rowan (1925–2000) was born in Tennessee and received degrees from Oberlin College and the University of Minnesota. He worked as a newspaper columnist for over thirty years and served as the ambassador to Finland.

AS YOU READ:

In this article, published in Reader's Digest, *Rowan recalls a teacher who changed his life. Notice that he describes not only what Miss Bessie looked like but also the influence she had on her students.*

1 She was only about five feet tall and probably never weighed more than 110 pounds, but Miss Bessie was a towering presence in the classroom. She was the only woman tough enough to make me read <u>Beowulf</u> and think for a few foolish days that I liked it. From 1938 to 1942, when I attended Bernard High School in McMinnville, Tenn., she taught me English, history, civics—and a lot more than I realized.

2 I shall never forget the day she scolded me into reading *Beowulf.*

3 "But Miss Bessie," I complained, "I ain't much interested in it."

4 Her large brown eyes became daggerish slits. "Boy," she said, "how dare you say 'ain't' to me! I've taught you better than that."

5 "Miss Bessie," I pleaded, "I'm trying to make first-string end on the football team, and if I go around saying 'it isn't' and 'they aren't,' the guys are gonna laugh me off the squad."

6 "Boy," she responded, "you'll play football because you have guts. But do you know what *really* takes guts? Refusing to lower your standards to those of the crowd. It takes guts to say you've got to live and be somebody fifty years after all the football games are over."

7 I started saying "it isn't" and "they aren't," and I still made first-string end—and class <u>valedictorian</u>—without losing my buddies' respect.

8 During her remarkable 44-year career, Mrs. Bessie Taylor Gwynn taught hundreds of economically deprived black youngsters—including my mother, my brother, my sisters, and me. I remember her now with gratitude and affection—especially in this era when Americans are so wrought-up about a "rising tide of mediocrity" in public education and the problems of finding competent, caring teachers. Miss Bessie was an example of an informed, dedicated teacher, a blessing to children and an asset to the nation.

9 Born in 1895, in poverty, she grew up in Athens, Ala., where there was no public school for blacks. She attended Trinity School, a private institution for blacks run by the American Missionary Association, and in 1911 graduated from the Normal School (a "super" high school) at Fisk University in Nashville. Mrs. Gwynn, the essence of pride and privacy, never talked about her years in Athens; only in the months before her death did she reveal that she had never attended Fisk University itself because she could not afford the four-year course.

Words to Know

Beowulf eighth-century English epic poem

valedictorian student with the highest grades chosen to speak at graduation

At Normal School she learned a lot about Shakespeare, but most of all about the profound importance of education—especially, for a people trying to move up from slavery. "What you put in your head, boy," she once said, "can never be pulled out by the Ku Klux Klan, the Congress, or anybody."

10

Miss Bessie's bearing of dignity told anyone who met her that she was "educated" in the best sense of the word. There was never a discipline problem in her classes. We didn't dare mess with a woman who knew about the Battle of Hastings, the Magna Carta, and the Bill of Rights—and who could also play the piano.

11

This frail-looking woman could make sense of Shakespeare, Milton, Voltaire, and bring to life Booker T. Washington and W. E. B. DuBois. Believing that it was important to know who the officials were that spent taxpayers' money and made public policy, she made us memorize the names of everyone on the Supreme Court and in the President's Cabinet. It could be embarrassing to be unprepared when Miss Bessie said, "Get up and tell the class who Frances Perkins is and what you think about her."

12

Miss Bessie knew that my family, like so many others during the Depression, couldn't afford to subscribe to a newspaper. She knew we didn't even own a radio. Still, she prodded me to "look out for your future and find some way to keep up with what's going on in the world." So I became a delivery boy for the Chattanooga *Times*. I rarely made a dollar a week, but I got to read a newspaper every day.

13

Miss Bessie noticed things that had nothing to do with schoolwork, but were vital to a youngster's development. Once a few classmates made fun of my frayed, hand-me-down overcoat, calling me "Strings." As I was leaving school, Miss Bessie patted me on the back of that old overcoat and said, "Carl, never fret about what you *don't* have. Just make the most of what you *do* have—a brain."

14

Among the things that I did not have was electricity in the little frame house that my father had built for $400 with his World War I bonus. But because of her inspiration, I spent many hours squinting beside a kerosene lamp reading Shakespeare and Thoreau, Samuel Pepys and William Cullen Bryant.

15

No one in my family had ever graduated from high school, so there was no tradition of commitment to learning for me to lean on. Like millions of youngsters in today's ghettos and barrios, I needed the push and stimulation of a teacher who truly cared. Miss Bessie gave plenty of both, as she immersed me in a wonderful world of similes, metaphors and even onomatopoeia. She led me to believe that I could write sonnets as well as Shakespeare, or iambic-pentameter verse to put Alexander Pope to shame.

16

Jim Crow reference to racial segregation in the South

In those days the McMinnville school system was rigidly "Jim Crow," and poor black children had to struggle to put anything in their heads. Our high school was only slightly larger than the once-typical little red schoolhouse, and its library was outrageously inadequate—so small, I like to say, that if two students were in it and one wanted to turn a page, the other one had to step outside.

17

Negroes, as we were called then, were not allowed in the town library, except to mop floors or dust tables. But through one of those secret Old South arrangements between whites of conscience and blacks of stature,

18

Miss Bessie kept getting books smuggled out of the white library. That is how she introduced me to the Brontës, Byron, Coleridge, Keats, and Tennyson. "If you don't read, you can't write, and if you can't write, you might as well stop dreaming," Miss Bessie once told me.

19   So I read whatever Miss Bessie told me to, and tried to remember the things she insisted that I store away. Forty-five years later, I can still recite her "truths to live by," such as Henry Wadsworth Longfellow's lines from "The Ladder of St. Augustine":

> The heights by great men reached and kept
> Were not attained by sudden flight.
> But they, while their companions slept,
> Were toiling upward in the night.

20   Years later, her inspiration, prodding, anger, cajoling, and almost osmotic infusion of learning finally led to that lovely day when Miss Bessie dropped me a note saying, "I'm so proud to read your column in the Nashville *Tennessean*."

21   Miss Bessie was a spry 80 when I went back to McMinnville and visited her in a senior citizens' apartment building. Pointing out proudly that her building was racially integrated, she reached for two glasses and a pint of bourbon. I was momentarily shocked, because it would have been scandalous in the 1930s and '40s for word to get out that a teacher drank, and nobody had ever raised a rumor that Miss Bessie did.

22   I felt a new sense of equality as she lifted her glass to mine. Then she revealed a softness and compassion that I had never known as a student.

23   "I've never forgotten that examination day," she said, "when Buster Martin held up seven fingers, obviously asking you for help with question number seven, 'Name a common carrier.' I can still picture you looking at your exam paper and humming a few bars of 'Chattanooga Choo Choo.' I was so tickled, I couldn't punish either of you."

24   Miss Bessie was telling me, with bourbon-laced grace, that I never fooled her for a moment.

25   When Miss Bessie died in 1980, at age 85, hundreds of her former students mourned. They knew the measure of a great teacher: love and motivation. Her wisdom and influence had rippled out across generations.

26   Some of her students who might normally have been doomed to poverty went on to become doctors, dentists, and college professors. Many, guided by Miss Bessie's example, became public-school teachers.

27   "The memory of Miss Bessie and how she conducted her classroom did more for me than anything I learned in college," recalls Gladys Wood of Knoxville, Tenn., a highly respected English teacher who spent 43 years in the state's school system. "So many times, when I faced a difficult classroom problem, I asked myself, *How would Miss Bessie deal with this?* And I'd remember that she would handle it with laughter and love."

28   No child can get all the necessary support at home, and millions of poor children get *no* support at all. This is what makes a wise, educated, warmhearted teacher like Miss Bessie so vital to the minds, hearts, and souls of this country's children.

CRITICAL THINKING AND DISCUSSION

Understanding Meaning: What Is the Writer Trying to Say?

1. What is Rowan's purpose in describing Miss Bessie? What is he trying to share with readers?
2. What qualities of Miss Bessie's does Rowan admire?
3. How did Miss Bessie influence Rowan and other students?
4. Why do you think so many former students attended her funeral? Why does Rowan describe their professions? How does that support his point?
5. *Critical thinking:* Do you think Rowan sees her as a role model? Could teachers like Miss Bessie change the lives of poor schoolchildren in today's schools? Why or why not?

Evaluating Strategy: How Does the Writer Say It?

1. Rowan opens the description with details about Miss Bessie's appearance. How does this serve his purpose?
2. What dominant impressions does Rowan create about Miss Bessie?
3. How does Rowan blend descriptions of his own life into the essay to demonstrate the effect of Miss Bessie's lessons?

Appreciating Language: What Words Does the Writer Use?

1. Rowan calls Miss Bessie an *asset to the nation.* What does he mean by this phrase?
2. Rowan includes dialogue in his description. What do you notice about Miss Bessie's language? What does this add to the essay?

Writing Suggestions

1. Describe a person you know by focusing on a single positive or negative characteristic or quality. Use brief narratives to illustrate the person's behavior. Include your own reactions to this person's behavior.
2. *Collaborative writing:* Discuss Rowan's description with other students. How did Miss Bessie help generations of disadvantaged children overcome their circumstances? Could her approach help students today? Why or why not? Write a description of how teachers can help at-risk children succeed in life. Your group could write a process essay with numbered suggestions.

Narration

Narration tells stories or relates a series of events, usually in chronological order.

A DOCTOR'S DILEMMA

JAMES DILLARD

James Dillard is a physician who specializes in rehabilitation medicine. In this narrative, first published in the "My Turn" column in Newsweek, *he relates an incident that nearly ended his medical career.*

AS YOU READ:

As you read this essay, consider how people expect doctors to respond in a life-threatening emergency.

Words to Know

Gettysburg Civil War battlefield in Pennsylvania

1   It was a bright, clear February afternoon in Gettysburg. A strong sun and layers of down did little to ease the biting cold. Our climb to the crest of Little Roundtop wound past somber monuments, barren trees, and polished cannon. From the top, we peered down on the wheat field where men had fallen so close together that one could not see the ground. Rifle balls had whined as thick as bee swarms through the trees, and cannon shots had torn limbs from the young men fighting there. A frozen wind whipped tears from our eyes. My friend Amy huddled close, using me as a windbreaker. Despite the cold, it was hard to leave this place.

2   Driving east out of Gettysburg on a country blacktop, the gray Bronco ahead of us passed through a rural crossroad just as a small pickup truck tried to take a left turn. The Bronco swerved, but slammed into the pickup on the passenger side. We immediately slowed to a crawl as we passed the scene. The Bronco's driver looked fine, but we couldn't see the driver of the pickup. I pulled over on the shoulder and got out to investigate.

3   The right side of the truck was smashed in, and the side window was shattered. The driver was partly out of the truck. His head hung forward over the edge of the passenger-side window, the front of his neck crushed on the shattered windowsill. He was unconscious and starting to turn a dusky blue. His chest slowly heaved against a blocked windpipe.

dusky dark

4   A young man ran out of a house at the crossroad. "Get an ambulance out here," I shouted against the wind. "Tell them a man is dying."

5   I looked down again at the driver hanging from the windowsill. There were six empty beer bottles on the floor of the truck. I could smell the beer through the window. I knew I had to move him, to open his airway. I had no idea what neck injuries he had sustained. He could easily end up a quadriplegic. But I thought: he'll be dead by the time the ambulance gets here if I don't move him and try to do something to help him.

quadriplegic totally paralyzed

6   An image flashed before my mind. I could see the courtroom and the driver of the truck sitting in a wheelchair. I could see his attorney pointing at me and thundering at the jury: "This young doctor, with still a year left in his residency training, took it upon himself to play God. He took it upon himself to move this gravely injured man, condemning him forever to this

traction tension
torso upper body

magenta purplish red
stench smell

hyoid bone at base of the
    tongue
cricoid rings cartilage of the
    larynx

wheelchair. . . ." I imagined the millions of dollars in award money. And all the years of hard work lost. I'd be paying him off for the rest of my life. Amy touched my shoulder. "What are you going to do?"

The automatic response from long hours in the emergency room kicked in. I pulled off my overcoat and rolled up my sleeves. The trick would be to keep enough <u>traction</u> straight up on his head while I moved his <u>torso,</u> so that his probable broken neck and spinal-cord injury wouldn't be made worse. Amy came around the driver's side, climbed half in, and grabbed his belt and shirt collar. Together we lifted him off the windowsill.   7

He was still out cold, limp as a rag doll. His throat was crushed and blood from the jugular vein was running down my arms. He still couldn't breathe. He was deep blue-<u>magenta</u> now; his pulse was rapid and thready. The <u>stench</u> of alcohol turned my stomach, but I positioned his jaw and tried to blow air down into his lungs. It wouldn't go.   8

Amy had brought some supplies from my car. I opened an oversize intravenous needle and groped on the man's neck. My hands were numb, covered with freezing blood and bits of broken glass. <u>Hyoid</u> bone—God, I can't even feel the thyroid cartilage, it's gone . . . OK, the thyroid gland is about there, <u>cricoid rings</u> are here . . . we'll go in right here. . . .   9

It was a lucky first shot. Pink air sprayed through the IV needle. I placed a second needle next to the first. The air began whistling through it. Almost immediately, the driver's face turned bright red. After a minute, his pulse slowed down and his eyes moved slightly. I stood up, took a step back, and looked down. He was going to make it. He was going to live. A siren wailed in the distance. I turned and saw Amy holding my overcoat. I was shivering and my arms were turning white with cold.   10

The ambulance captain looked around and bellowed, "What the hell . . . who did this?", as his team scurried over to the man lying in the truck.   11

"I did," I replied. He took down my name and address for his reports. I had just destroyed my career. I would never be able to finish my residency with a massive lawsuit pending. My life was over.   12

The truck driver was strapped onto a backboard, his neck in a stiff collar. The ambulance crew had controlled the bleeding and started intravenous fluid. He was slowly waking up. As they loaded him into the ambulance, I saw him move his feet. Maybe my future wasn't lost.   13

A police sergeant called me from Pennsylvania three weeks later. Six days after successful throat-reconstruction surgery, the driver had signed out, against medical advice, from the hospital because he couldn't get a drink on the ward. He was being arraigned on drunk-driving charges.   14

A few days later, I went into the office of one of my senior professors, to tell the story. He peered over his half glasses and his eyes narrowed. "Well, you did the right thing medically of course. But, James, do you know what you put at risk by doing that?" he said sternly. "What was I supposed to do?" I asked.   15

"Drive on," he replied. "There is an army of lawyers out there who would stand in line to get a case like that. If that driver had turned out to be a   16 quadriplegic, you might never have practiced medicine again. You were a very lucky young man."

17   The day I graduated from medical school, I took an oath to serve the sick and the injured. I remember truly believing I would be able to do just that. But I have found out it isn't so simple. I understand now what a foolish thing I did that day. Despite my oath, I know what I would do on that cold roadside near Gettysburg today. I would drive on.

Get Thinking and Writing

CRITICAL THINKING AND DISCUSSION

Understanding Meaning: What Is the Writer Trying to Say?

1. What was Dillard's goal in publishing this narrative in a national news magazine?
2. Does this narrative contrast ideals and reality? How does Dillard's oath as a doctor conflict with his final decision?
3. Does the fact that the driver was drinking affect your reaction to the doctor's actions?
4. *Critical thinking:* Does this essay suggest there is an undeclared war between doctors and lawyers? Do medical malpractice lawsuits improve or hurt the quality of medicine? Should a doctor responding in an emergency have to worry about being sued?

Evaluating Strategy: How Does the Writer Say It?

1. Can this narrative also be used an argument? Why or why not?
2. Does a first-person account such as this demonstrate the plight a doctor faces in an emergency better than an objective article written in the third person?
3. How do you think Dillard wanted his readers to respond to the essay's last line?

Appreciating Language: What Words Does the Writer Use?

1. What words does Dillard use to dramatize his attempts to save the driver's life? How do they reflect the tension he was feeling? Dillard uses the word *lucky.* Do you think he wants his readers to understand that emergency medicine depends as much on chance as skill?
2. What language does Dillard use to demonstrate what he was risking by trying to save a life?

Writing Suggestions

1. Write a short essay relating an emergency you experienced or describe an event where your job placed you at personal risk.
2. *Collaborative writing:* Discuss Dillard's essay with other students, and write a hypothetical narrative about how doctors should be able to act in an emergency.

CHAMPION OF THE WORLD

MAYA ANGELOU

Maya Angelou (1928–) was a dancer and actress who became best known for her poetry and autobiographical books. In this section from I Know Why the Caged Bird Sings, *Angelou recounts listening to a Joe Louis prizefight on the radio. Known as the Brown Bomber, Joe Louis was the heavyweight champion from 1937 to 1949.*

AS YOU READ:

Notice how Angelou uses dialogue to move the plot of her story. By presenting the words of others, she can show rather than explain how important the fight was. She also demonstrates the importance of Joe Louis by including examples of past racism (paragraph 16).

The last inch of space was filled, yet people continued to wedge themselves along the walls of the Store. Uncle Willie had turned the radio up to its last notch so that youngsters on the porch wouldn't miss a word. Women sat on kitchen chairs, dining room chairs, stools and upturned wooden boxes. Small children and babies perched on every lap available and men leaned on the shelves or each other.   1

The <u>apprehensive</u> mood was shot through with shafts of gaiety, as a black sky is streaked with lightning.   2

"I ain't worried 'bout this fight. Joe's gonna whip that cracker like it's open season."   3

"He gone whip him till that white boy call him Momma."   4

At last the talking was finished and the string-along songs about razor blades were over and the fight began.   5

"A quick jab to the head." In the Store the crowd grunted. "A left to the head and a right and another left." One of the listeners cackled like a hen and was quieted.   6

"They're in a clench, Louis is trying to fight his way out."   7

Some bitter comedian on the porch said, "That white man don't mind hugging that niggah now, I betcha."   8

"The referee is moving in to break them up, but Louis finally pushed the <u>contender</u> away and it's an uppercut to the chin. The contender is hanging on, now he's backing away. Louis catches him with a short left to the jaw."   9

A tide of murmuring <u>assent</u> poured out the doors and into the yard.   10

"Another left and another left. Louis is saving that mighty right. . . ." The mutter in the Store had grown into a baby roar and it was pierced by the clang of a bell and the announcer's "That's the bell for round three, ladies and gentlemen."   11

As I pushed my way into the Store I wondered if the announcer gave any thought to the fact that he was addressing as "ladies and gentlemen" all the Negroes around the world who sat sweating and praying, glued to their "<u>master's voice</u>."   12

Words to Know

apprehensive fearful

contender challenger

assent approval

"master's voice" reference to RCA radios

13   There were only a few calls for RC Colas, Dr. Peppers, and Hire's root beer. The real festivities would begin after the fight. Then even the old Christian ladies who taught their children and tried themselves to practice turning the other cheek would buy soft drinks, and if the Brown Bomber's victory was a particularly bloody one they would order peanut patties and Baby Ruths also.

14   Bailey and I lay the coins on top of the cash register. Uncle Willie didn't allow us to ring up sales during a fight. It was too noisy and might shake up the atmosphere. When the gong rang for the next round we pushed through the near-sacred quiet to the herd of children outside.

15   "He's got Louis against the ropes and now it's a left to the body and a right to the ribs. Another right to the body, it looks like it was low. . . . Yes, ladies and gentlemen, the referee is signaling, but the contender keeps raining the blows on Louis. It's another to the body, and it looks like Louis is going down."

16   My race groaned. It was our people falling. It was another lynching, yet another Black man hanging on a tree. One more woman ambushed and raped. A Black boy whipped and maimed. It was hounds on the trail of a man running through slimy swamps. It was a white woman slapping her maid for being forgetful.

17   The men in the Store stood away from the walls and at attention. Women greedily clutched the babes on their laps while on the porch the shufflings and smiles, flirtings and pinching of a few minutes before were gone. This might be the end of the world. If Joe lost we were back in slavery and beyond help. It would all be true, the accusations that we were lower types of human beings. Only a little higher than the apes. True that we were stupid and ugly and lazy and dirty and unlucky and, worst of all, that God Himself hated us and ordained us to be hewers of wood and drawers of water, forever and ever, world without end.

accusations charges

ordained ordered by God
hewers cutters
drawers carriers

18   We didn't breathe. We didn't hope. We waited.

19   "He's off the ropes, ladies and gentlemen. He's moving towards the center of the ring." There was no time to be relieved. The worst might still happen.

20   "And now it looks like Joe is mad. He's caught Carnera with a left hook to the head and a right to the head. It's a left jab to the body and another left to the head. There's a left cross and a right to the head. The contender's right eye is bleeding and he can't seem to keep his block up. Louis is penetrating every block. The referee is moving in, but Louis sends a left to the body and it's the uppercut to the chin and the contender is dropping. He's on the canvas, ladies and gentlemen."

Carnera Primo Carnera, Louis's opponent

21   Babies slid to the floor as women stood up and men leaned toward the radio.

22   "Here's the referee. He's counting. One, two, three, four, five, six, seven . . . Is the contender trying to get up again?"

23   All the men in the Store shouted, "NO."

24   "—eight, nine, ten." There were a few sounds from the audience, but they seemed to be holding themselves in against tremendous pressure.

ambrosia food of the gods

white lightning homemade
whiskey

"The fight is all over, ladies and gentlemen. Let's get the microphone over to the referee. . . . Here he is. He's got the Brown Bomber's hand, he's holding it up. . . . Here he is. . . ."   25

Then the voice, husky and familiar, came to wash over us—"The winnah, and still heavyweight champeen of the world . . . Joe Louis."   26

Champion of the world. A Black boy. Some Black mother's son. He was the strongest man in the world. People drank Coca-Colas like <u>ambrosia</u> and ate candy bars like Christmas. Some of the men went behind the Store and poured <u>white lightning</u> in their soft-drink bottles, and a few of the bigger boys followed them. Those who were not chased away came back blowing their breath in front of themselves like proud smokers.   27

It would take an hour or more before the people would leave the Store and head for home. Those who lived too far had made arrangements to stay in town. It wouldn't do for a Black man and his family to be caught on a lonely country road on a night when Joe Louis had proved that we were the strongest people in the world.   28

**Get Thinking
and Writing**

CRITICAL THINKING AND DISCUSSION

Understanding Meaning: What Is the Writer Trying to Say?

1. What is the thesis of Angelou's narrative? Why was this fight more than a sporting event?
2. How did Joe Louis's struggle appear to represent the struggle of a people rather than that of a single athlete?
3. How did the people in the store react to the fight?
4. Why did many people decide to stay in town rather than travel home that night?
5. *Critical thinking:* Do you think any athletes today have the same impact on minorities? Why or why not?

Evaluating Strategy: How Does the Writer Say It?

1. How does Angelou use dialogue to advance the narrative and support her main point?
2. How does Angelou re-create the broadcast? Do direct quotations of the announcer work better than summaries or paraphrases? Why or why not?
3. What impact does the last sentence have? How does it reinforce her main point?

Appreciating Language: What Words Does the Writer Use?

1. How does Angelou use the advertising slogan his "master's voice" in this essay? How does it ironically suit a story about race?
2. Angelou uses short sentences in some places: "We didn't breathe. We didn't hope. We waited." What effect do they have? Can a writer use too many short sentences? Why or why not?

Example   631

Writing Suggestions

1. Using Angelou's essay as a model, write a narrative about an experience when you were part of a group responding to a common experience, such as watching a football game, news broadcast, or movie. Did everyone react the same way, or did people behave differently? Try to capture people's responses by using direct quotations or details about their behavior.

2. *Collaborative writing:* Work with a group of students to write a brief essay about the role that athletes play in society today. Do they represent anything more than success in sports? Are they role models? Could any modern athlete have the same significance as Joe Louis did seventy years ago? Why or why not?

Example

Example illustrates ideas, issues, events, or personality types by describing one or more specific events, objects, or people.

HOMELESS

ANNA QUINDLEN

Anna Quindlen (1952–) has written a column for the New York Times *and published several books, including* Living Out Loud, Object Lessons, One True Thing, *and* Black and Blue.

AS YOU READ:

Quindlen uses a single woman to represent the plight of the homeless, whom, she states, are not really homeless but "people without homes."

1   Her name was Ann, and we met in the Port Authority Bus Terminal several Januarys ago. I was doing a story on homeless people. She said I was wasting my time talking to her; she was just passing through, although she'd been passing through for more than two weeks. To prove to me that this was true, she rummaged through a tote bag and a manila envelope and finally unfolded a sheet of typing paper and brought out her photographs.

2   They were not pictures of family, or friends, or even a dog or cat, its eyes brown-red in the flashbulb's light. They were pictures of a house. It was like a thousand houses in a hundred towns, not suburb, not city, but somewhere in between, with aluminum siding and a chain-link fence, a narrow driveway running up to a one-car garage and a patch of backyard. The house was yellow. I looked on the back for a date or a name, but neither was there. There was no need for discussion. I knew what she was trying to tell me, for it was something I had often felt. She was not adrift, alone, anonymous, although her bags and her raincoat with the grime shadowing

its creases had made me believe she was. She had a house, or at least once upon a time had had one. Inside were curtains, a couch, a stove, potholders. You are where you live. She was somebody.

I've never been very good at looking at the big picture, taking the global view, and I've always been a person with an overactive sense of place, the legacy of an Irish grandfather. So it is natural that the thing that seems most wrong with the world to me right now is that there are so many people with no homes. I'm not simply talking about shelter from the <u>elements,</u> or three square meals a day or a mailing address to which the welfare people can send the check—although I know that all these are important for survival. I'm talking about a home, about precisely those kinds of feelings that have wound up in cross-stitch and French knots on <u>samplers</u> over the years.

Home is where the heart is. There's no place like it. I love my home with a <u>ferocity</u> totally out of proportion to its appearance or location. I love dumb things about it: the hot-water heater, the plastic rack you drain dishes in, the roof over my head, which occasionally leaks. And yet it is precisely those dumb things that make it what it is—a place of <u>certainty,</u> stability, predictability, privacy, for me and for my family. It is where I live. What more can you say about a place than that? That is everything.

Yet it is something that we have been edging away from gradually during my lifetime and the lifetimes of my parents and grandparents. There was a time when where you lived often was where you worked and where you grew the food you ate and even where you were buried. When that era passed, where you lived at least was where your parents had lived and where you would live with your children when you became <u>enfeebled.</u> Then, suddenly where you lived was where you lived for three years, until you could move on to something else and something else again.

And so we have come to something else again, to children who do not understand what it means to go to their rooms because they have never had a room, to men and women whose fantasy is a wall they can paint a color of their own choosing, to old people reduced to sitting on molded plastic chairs, their skin blue-white in the lights of a bus station, who pull pictures of houses out of their bags. Homes have stopped being homes. Now they are real estate.

People find it curious that those without homes would rather sleep sitting up on benches or huddled in doorways than go to shelters. Certainly some prefer to do so because they are emotionally ill, because they have been locked in before and they are damned if they will be locked in again. Others are afraid of the violence and trouble they may find there. But some seem to want something that is not available in shelters, and they will not compromise, not for a cot, or oatmeal, or a shower with special soap that kills the bugs. "One room," a woman with a baby who was sleeping on her sister's floor once told me, "painted blue." That was the <u>crux</u> of it; not size or location, but pride of ownership. Painted blue.

This is a difficult problem, and some wise and compassionate people are working hard at it. But in the main I think we work around it, just as we walk around it when it is lying on the sidewalk or sitting in the bus terminal—the problem, that is. It has been customary to take people's pain

Words to Know

elements weather

sampler sembroidered pictures

ferocity intensity

certainty confidence

enfeebled weakened, disabled

crux bottom-line, core

Example   **633**

9   and lessen our own participation in it by turning it into an issue, not a collection of human beings. We turn an adjective into a noun: the poor, not poor people; the homeless, not Ann or the man who lives in the box or the woman who sleeps on the subway grate.

Sometimes I think we would be better off if we forgot about the broad strokes and concentrated on the details. Here is a woman without a bureau. There is a man with no mirror, no wall to hang it on. They are not the homeless. They are people who have no homes. No drawer that holds the spoons. No window to look out upon the world. My God. That is everything.

CRITICAL THINKING AND DISCUSSION

Get Thinking and Writing

Understanding Meaning: What Is the Writer Trying to Say?

1. What is Quindlen's thesis? Can you express it in your own words?
2. What does Quindlen want people to know about the homeless?
3. What kind of person is Ann, the homeless woman Quindlen meets in the bus terminal?

Evaluating Strategy: How Does the Writer Say It?

1. How does Quindlen use the single example of Ann to explain the plight of the homeless? Would an essay without a personal example be as effective?
2. Quindlen focuses on Ann's photo of her old home. Why is this detail important? What does it reveal?

Appreciating Language: What Words Does the Writer Use?

1. What connotations does the word "home" have? What does it mean to be "homeless" besides simply lacking shelter?
2. What does Quindlen mean by the statement "You are where you live"?

Writing Suggestions

1. Use one or more people you have met to serve as examples of a social issue or problem. Your essay could discuss high school dropouts, single parents, people who have overcome a disability, role models, television addicts, or Good Samaritans.
2. *Collaborative writing:* Working with a group of students, develop an essay providing examples of how communities or individuals could assist the homeless.

DEATH OF A DREAM

TONY BROWN

Tony Brown (1933–) is best known for his long-running public television program Tony Brown's Journal *and his book* Black Lies, White Lies: The Truth According to Tony Brown.

AS YOU READ:

Note how Brown uses the failure of a single black-owned supermarket to illustrate his theory "that the most successful economic boycott ever conducted in America is the boycott by Blacks of their own businesses."

Up! Up! You mighty race. You can accomplish what you will.

—MARCUS GARVEY

It was a day of celebration when Rick Singletary opened the largest Black-owned supermarket in the country in Columbus, Ohio—a spectacular $4.4 million operation. He had worked for a major grocery chain for fourteen years and started his own store with his life savings, those of his mother, and a government-insured loan from the Reagan administration. He located Singletary Plaza Mart in the Black community because he knew there was a need for a grocery store there, and because he wanted to create jobs for Blacks.

1

The entrepreneur needed only a $200,000-a-week volume to keep 130 Black people working. And yet, in a tragedy that exemplifies the real reason why Black America has never been able to compete with White America, Singletary's store failed. Although his research had shown that Blacks in Columbus spent $2.5 million per week on groceries, he could not get them to spend even $200,000 of it in the store he had built for them in their own neighborhood.

2

I am familiar with the details because I tried to help Singletary, and I tried to help the Blacks in his community realize what was happening. For three days, I joined others in the Buy Freedom campaign of Black economic empowerment in Columbus. But, sadly, we failed to save his store.

3

This is not simply a neighborhood issue, it is a national disgrace. Rick Singletary, a good man who banked on his community, went bankrupt. He lost his life savings and his mother's savings, and 130 Black people lost their jobs. *This story is repeated somewhere in the Black community every day.* This gives credence to my theory that the most successful economic boycott ever conducted in America is the boycott by Blacks of their own businesses.

4

Making Blacks Competitive

The key to making Black America competitive with White America is really quite simple. Black Americans now earn nearly $500 billion annually, according to economist Andrew F. Brommer. This is roughly equivalent to the gross domestic product of Canada or Australia. And yet Blacks spend only 3 percent of their income with a Black business or Black professional. By spending 97 percent of their money outside of their racial community, they exacerbate their own social and economic problems.

5

This is the reason that Blacks do not keep pace economically or socially with the rest of the country. Since 80 percent of Americans are employed in small businesses, it is common sense that if businesses in the Black neighborhoods do not flourish, job opportunities will be greatly reduced.

6

To succeed as a people, Blacks have to invest in and build their community. Other ethnic groups turn their money over multiple times within their

7

Words to Know

entrepreneur independent
business owner

exemplifies represents

credence acceptance as true

equivalent equal

exacerbate make worse

Example **635**

communities. If money turns over ten times, it means that for every $100 spent by an individual, nine other individuals or businesses will have access to that same $100. This investment increases the community's economic strength by $1,000 instead of just $100.

8   It works this way. You earn $100 a week and I earn $100 a week. You give me ninety-seven of your dollars. I'm living on $197 and you're living on $3. How can your house be as big as mine? How can your car be as new as mine? How, even, can your IQ be as high as mine? Income affects nearly all aspects of life. A higher paycheck means you can afford to live in a better neighborhood with better schools and more opportunities for intellectual development. Studies have found that the group in America with the highest income is the group with the highest IQ. The group with the second-highest income is the group with the second-highest IQ. The overall IQ of Blacks is low in part because the income retained by Blacks is at the bottom.

Take Back Your Mind

9   Rick Singletary knows this all too well. The problem is not that Blacks don't have money. The problem is what we do with it, or don't do with it. Just as we waste our votes by not demanding anything in return, we don't spend our money where it pays off.

10   Over the last twenty-five years, the Black community has had a major thrust in politics and civil rights. We have staged Freedom Marches, but we have never stopped to think about what really buys freedom. It isn't worn-out shoes, and it isn't even civil rights legislation. True freedom springs from economic <u>parity</u> with other Americans.

parity equivalence

11   Money is not everything, but I rate it right up there with oxygen. After almost one hundred years of social engineering, Blacks can sit next to White people in classrooms and restaurants and on airplanes, but can they afford it? *The bottom line is that the only color of freedom is green.* Pride, education, and economic self-sufficiency were the message of Marcus Garvey and Booker T. Washington. But those two great Black men were <u>vilified</u> by the self-serving, self-hating <u>elitists</u> among their own people, and their vital message of <u>self-reliance</u> was blocked. Instead Blacks have spent decades with their arms extended and their hands out, doing the economic death dance to the tune of integration.

vilified slandered, criticized
elitists those with a sense of superiority
self-reliance depending on oneself

CRITICAL THINKING AND DISCUSSION

Understanding Meaning: What Is the Writer Trying to Say?

1. What does the failure of one black business represent to Brown? What makes it significant?
2. Why, in Brown's view, is it important for African Americans to support black-owned businesses?
3. In Brown's view, how can blacks achieve economic parity with the rest of U.S. society?

Get Thinking and Writing

4. Why do blacks, in Brown's view, boycott their own businesses?

5. *Critical thinking:* Where, in Brown's view, has the civil rights movement failed black Americans?

Evaluating Strategy: How Does the Writer Say It?

1. How effective is the example of Singletary's failed supermarket? Would the essay benefit from other examples?

2. Would a hypothetical example be as effective as a real one?

3. Brown includes facts and statistics. Why is this important, especially in an essay with a single example?

4. Where does Brown place the thesis? Is this an effective location in your view?

Appreciating Language: What Words Does the Writer Use?

1. What words and phrases does Brown use to describe Singletary? Does he appear as a hero or role model?

2. Brown uses phrases such as *the color of freedom is green* and *economic death dance.* Are they effective? Why or why not?

Writing Suggestions

1. Write an essay about a person you see as a role model illustrating behavior that other people should imitate or support. Provide details explaining the significance of this person's contribution.

2. *Collaborative writing:* Work with other students, and discuss Brown's essay. Brainstorm and suggest writing a process essay that explains how attitudes can be changed so that minority communities will support minority-owned businesses.

Definition

Definition explains or limits the meaning of a word or idea.

SPANGLISH

JANICE CASTRO

Janice Castro (1949–) is a journalist who became Time *magazine's first health-policy reporter. This essay appeared as part of a* Time *cover story about Hispanics.*

AS YOU READ:

Castro provides a clear definition statement that explains what Spanglish *means and illustrates it with several examples.*

Words to Know

bemused confused or puzzled

In Manhattan a first-grader greets her visiting grandparents, happily exclaiming, "Come here, *siéntate!*" Her <u>bemused</u> grandfather, who does not speak Spanish, nevertheless knows she is asking him to sit down. A Miami

1

personnel officer understands what a job applicant means when he says, "*Quiero un* part time." Nor do drivers miss a beat reading a billboard alongside a Los Angeles street advertising CERVEZA—SIX PACK!

2   This free-form blend of Spanish and English, known as Spanglish, is common linguistic currency wherever concentrations of Hispanic Americans are found in the U.S. In Los Angeles, where 55% of the city's 3 million inhabitants speak Spanish, Spanglish is as much a part of daily life as sunglasses. Unlike the broken-English efforts of earlier immigrants from Europe, Asia, and other regions, Spanglish has become a widely accepted conversational mode used casually—even playfully—by Spanish-speaking immigrants and native-born Americans alike.

3   Consisting of one part Hispanicized English, one part Americanized Spanish and more than a little fractured syntax, Spanglish is a bit like a Robin Williams comedy routine: a crackling line of cross-cultural patter straight from the melting pot. Often it enters Anglo homes and families through the children, who pick it up at school or at play with their young Hispanic contemporaries. In other cases, it comes from watching TV; many an Anglo child watching *Sesame Street* has learned "*uno dos tres*" almost as quickly as "one two three."

4   Spanglish takes a variety of forms, from the Southern California Anglos who bid farewell with the utterly silly "*hasta la* bye-bye" to the Cuban-American drivers in Miami who *parquean* their *carros*. Some Spanglish sentences are mostly Spanish, with a quick detour for an English word or two. A Latino friend may cut short a conversation by glancing at his watch and excusing himself with the explanation that he must "*ir al* supermarket."

5   Many of the English words transplanted in this way are simply handier than their Spanish counterparts. No matter how distasteful the subject, for example, it is still easier to say "income tax" than *impuesto sobre la renta*. At the same time, many Spanish-speaking immigrants have adopted such terms as VCR, microwave, and dishwasher for what they view as largely American phenomena. Still other English words convey a cultural context that is not implicit in the Spanish. A friend who invites you to a *lonche* most likely has in mind the brisk American custom of "doing lunch" rather than the languorous afternoon break traditionally implied by *almuerzo*.

6   Mainstream Americans exposed to similar <u>hybrids</u> of German, Chinese, or Hindi might be mystified. But even Anglos who speak little or no Spanish are somewhat familiar with Spanglish. Living among them, for one thing, are 19 million Hispanics. In addition, more American high school and university students sign up for Spanish than for any other foreign language.

hybrids blends

7   Only in the past ten years, though, has Spanglish begun to turn into a national slang. Its popularity has grown with the explosive increases in U.S. immigration from Latin American countries. English has increasingly collided with Spanish in retail stores, offices and classrooms, in pop music and on street corners. Anglos whose ancestors picked up such Spanish words as *rancho, bronco, tornado* and *incommunicado,* for instance, now freely use such Spanish words as *gracias, bueno, amigo* and *por favor.*

8   Among Latinos, Spanglish conversations often flow more easily from Spanish into several sentences of English and back.

9 Spanglish is a sort of code for Latinos: the speakers know Spanish, but their hybrid language reflects the American culture in which they live. Many lean to shorter, clipped phrases in place of the longer, more graceful expressions their parents used. Says Leonel de la Cuesta, an assistant professor of modern languages at Florida International University in Miami: "In the U.S., time is money, and that is showing up in Spanglish as an economy of language." Conversational examples: *taipiar* (type) and *winshi-wiper* (windshield wiper) replace *escribir a máquina* and *limpiaparabrisas*.

10 Major advertisers, eager to tap the estimated $134 billion in spending power wielded by Spanish-speaking Americans, have ventured into Spanglish to promote their products. In some cases, attempts to sprinkle Spanish through commercials have produced embarrassing <u>gaffes.</u> A Braniff airlines ad that sought to tell Spanish-speaking audiences they could settle back *en* (in) luxuriant *cuero* (leather) seats, for example, <u>inadvertently</u> said they could fly without clothes (*encuero*). A <u>fractured</u> translation of the Miller Lite slogan told readers the beer was "Filling, and less delicious." Similar blunders are often made by Anglos trying to impress Spanish-speaking pals. But if Latinos are amused by mangled Spanglish, they also recognize these goofs as a sort of friendly acceptance. As they might put it, *no problema.*

gaffes mistakes

inadvertently accidentally
fractured mangled or inaccurate

Get Thinking and Writing

CRITICAL THINKING AND DISCUSSION

Understanding Meaning: What Is the Writer Trying to Say?

1. How does Castro define *Spanglish?* Can you define it in your own words and give examples?
2. How does Spanglish differ from broken English spoken by other immigrants?
3. Who speaks Spanglish?
4. *Critical thinking:* What does the growth of Spanglish say about changes in U.S. society and the influence of Hispanics?

Evaluating Strategy: How Does the Writer Say It?

1. How does Castro use examples to explain her definition?
2. Are the opening and closing paragraphs effective?
3. How does Castro organize details?

Appreciating Language: What Words Does the Writer Use?

1. What do the tone and style of Castro's essay suggest about her attitude toward Spanglish?
2. Castro calls Spanglish *slang.* What does the word *slang* suggest to you?

Writing Suggestions

1. Invent a term that defines a behavior, attitude, object, or situation you have observed, such as *blind datism, partyholics, cable TV withdrawal,* or *workphobia.* Develop an essay that explains your term and provides examples.

2. *Collaborative writing:* Work with other students to invent a term for something you have noticed on campus. Write an essay that explains your term and illustrates it with one or more examples.

WHAT IS SUPPORT?

LAURA SCHLESSINGER

Laura Schlessinger is a columnist, talk-show host and author of 11 New York Times best-sellers who comments extensively on ethical and personal issues. In response to a woman's letter, she analyzes the definition of "support."

AS YOU READ:

Consider what people mean when they ask you to "support" them. Do they sometimes want you to approve of or least accept their behavior, even if it is immoral or self-destructive? Can someone be supportive and critical of a friend or family member? Does support, for many people, mean silence?

1   I recently received a letter from a very troubled young woman struggling with the concept of "support." Her married sister is fooling around despite her <u>marital</u> vows, despite the dependent children who love their dad, and despite this young woman's oh-so-careful <u>admonitions.</u>

2   The <u>errant</u> sister, obviously no stranger to <u>expedience</u> in definitions, criticized this young woman for not being supportive.

3   I guess in this case supportive would mean giving <u>alibis</u> for the adulterous sister's whereabouts, maybe even baby-sitting the children so more time would be available for <u>trysts.</u> It would also mean listening to the self-serving complaints that justify the adulterous behavior and generally maintaining a conspiracy of silence against the husband.

4   The young woman was torn between her values, her sense of loyalty to the husband, her fear for the welfare of the children, and her obligation to her sister.

5   One of the first dictionary definitions of "support" is "to sustain without giving way." How might that apply here? How can this woman sustain her relationship with her sister without having her own values give way?

6   Perhaps it would be to affirm the familial love while outlining the devastation being <u>synthesized</u> from her sister's selfish behavior. Perhaps it would be to offer specific resources (religious and/or psychotherapeutic) for the errant sister to use to face her fears, disappointments, personal limitations, frustrations, etc., in a more productive way.

7   Perhaps it would be to inform her sister that without efforts in these more positive directions, she would be <u>obligated</u> to force the issue by speaking the truth in front of the married couple.

8   To stay by people as they endure or struggle with difficult times in their lives is a blessing. To think that support necessarily means to accept,

Words to Know

marital marriage
admonitions warnings
errant misbehaving/wrong
expedience ease
alibis lies/cover stories

trysts romantic encounters

synthesized created

obligated required

blatantly clearly

voyeuristic getting pleasure
    from watching

espouse advocate

scenario story

discern decide

amok frenzy

discernment ability to make
    wise decisions

disdain disapprove of

precludes rules out

advocate or even cooperate in activities that are <u>blatantly</u> wrong is either
weak or <u>voyeuristic</u>—and certainly not in the ultimate best interest of
either person.

And that is where judgment must be brought in. Unfortunately, the term   9
judgment has been distorted into an absolute negative by those who wish
to <u>espouse</u> a life philosophy of "anything goes"—that is, until they are the
loser in someone else's self-centered life <u>scenario.</u>

Making judgments is a necessary part of the life of a creature with free   10
will and a wide range of options. We must <u>discern</u> between choices that are
decent and fair and those that are anything from inappropriate to evil and
self-serving. By our judgments we forge our character; by the integrated
judgments of a people we determine the level of decency of a society.

That some people can run <u>amok</u> with "evil judgment" does not make   11
judgment evil. Judgment is about opinion, evaluation, and <u>discernment.</u> It
is an absolutely necessary quality for an individual who desires to live a decent, admirable, ethical life. Without a decision about right/wrong, noble/
cowardly, charitable/selfish, we'd have no human civilization of merit.

Therefore, it is quite proper for parents to express disappointment and   12
even <u>disdain</u> for their adult child's significant lifestyle choices while keeping the door open for love, change, and growth. However, the parents may
choose not to participate as a "family" with those whose commitment level
<u>precludes</u> that title.

Love does not mean you have to tolerate any behavior whatsoever. Love   13
does mean that you have to offer direction, information, and hope.

Love makes you responsible for conveying concepts such as "ethical,"   14
"right," "good," "moral," "decent," and "polite" because it demands of you
that you take on the risks and challenges of supporting others in the very
human struggle to be more than the animals.

**Get Thinking
and Writing**

CRITICAL THINKING AND DISCUSSION

Understanding Meaning: What Is the Writer Trying to Say?

1. What dilemma does the letter writer face? Has someone ever asked you
   to lie or deceive others to hide his or her behavior?
2. How does the married sister appear to define being "supportive"?
3. How does Schlessinger define *support?* What, in her opinion, is not
   support?
4. In Schlessinger's view, what role should judgment play in offering
   people support?

Evaluating Strategy: How Does the Writer Say It?

1. How does Schlessinger use this example to illustrate her definition of
   support?
2. How does Schlessinger use the dictionary definition of *support* to introduce her own observations?

Appreciating Language: What Words Does the Writer Use?

1. Look up the word *support* in a dictionary. What does it mean? How do people you know define it? If you criticize their behavior or turn down a request to do something you feel is wrong to help them, are they likely to argue that you do not "support" them?

2. Schlessinger also uses the word *judgment,* acknowledging that the word has negative connotations. What does being *judgmental* suggest? Can one be judgmental in a positive way?

Writing Suggestions

1. Write an essay that explores the definition of another quality, such as *bravery, strength, beauty,* or *humor.* Use examples and comparisons to show your opinion of what bravery or beauty is and is not. Consider the standard ways that these qualities are measured in our society.

2. *Collaborative writing:* Working with a group of other students, write an essay that defines your group's view of support. Ask members of the group how they would react if a brother or sister asked them to provide alibis or baby-sit so they could engage in an extramarital affair.

Comparison and Contrast

Comparison and contrast examines similarities and differences.

A FABLE FOR TOMORROW

RACHEL CARSON

Rachel Carson (1907–1964) was a pioneer environmentalist, best known for her 1962 book Silent Spring. *In this section of the book, she uses contrast to demonstrate the effect that pesticides can have on the environment.*

AS YOU READ:

Notice how Carson uses comparison and contrast to create a "before-and-after" view to highlight her concerns about the impact of harmful chemicals.

1   There was once a town in the heart of America where all life seemed to live in harmony with its surroundings. The town lay in the midst of a checkerboard of <u>prosperous</u> farms, with fields of grain and hillsides of orchards where, in spring, white clouds of bloom drifted above the green fields. In autumn, oak and maple and birch set up a blaze of color that flamed and flickered across a backdrop of pines. Then foxes barked in the hills and deer silently crossed the fields, half hidden in the mists of the fall mornings.

2   Along the roads, laurel, <u>viburnum and alder,</u> great ferns and wildflowers delighted the traveler's eye through much of the year. Even in winter the

Words to Know

prosperous wealthy, well-off

viburnum and alder shrubs and trees

abundance large quantity

roadsides were places of beauty, where countless birds came to feed on the berries and on the seed heads of the dried weeds rising above the snow. The countryside was, in fact, famous for the <u>abundance</u> and variety of its bird life, and when the flood of migrants was pouring through in spring and fall, people traveled from great distances to observe them. Others came to fish the streams, which flowed clear and cold out of the hills and contained shady pools where trout lay. So it had been from the days many years ago when the first settlers raised their houses, sank their wells, and built their barns.

maladies diseases

Then a strange blight crept over the area and everything began to change. Some evil spell had settled on the community: mysterious <u>maladies</u> swept the flocks of chickens; the cattle and sheep sickened and died. Everywhere was a shadow of death. The farmers spoke of much illness among their families. In the town the doctors had become more and more puzzled by new kinds of sickness appearing among their patients. There had been several sudden and unexplained deaths, not only among adults but even among children, who would be stricken suddenly while at play and die within a few hours.

3

moribund dying

There was a strange stillness. The birds, for example—where had they gone? Many people spoke of them, puzzled and disturbed. The feeding stations in the backyards were deserted. The few birds seen anywhere were <u>moribund;</u> they trembled violently and could not fly. It was a spring without voices. On the mornings that had once throbbed with the dawn chorus of robins, catbirds, doves, jays, wrens, and scores of other bird voices there was now no sound; only silence lay over the fields and woods and marsh.

4

On the farms the hens brooded, but no chicks hatched. The farmers complained that they were unable to raise any pigs—the litters were small and the young survived only a few days. The apple trees were coming into bloom but no bees droned among the blossoms, so there was no pollination and there would be no fruit.

5

withered wasted, shrunken
anglers fishermen

The roadsides, once so attractive, were now lined with browned and <u>withered</u> vegetation as though swept by fire. These, too, were silent, deserted by all living things. Even the streams were now lifeless. <u>Anglers</u> no longer visited them, for all the fish had died.

6

granular coarse

In the gutters under the eaves and between the shingles of the roofs, a white <u>granular</u> powder still showed a few patches; some weeks before it had fallen like snow upon the roofs and the lawns, the fields and streams.

7

No witchcraft, no enemy action had silenced the rebirth of new life in this stricken world. The people had done it themselves.

8

specter ghost

This town does not actually exist, but it might easily have a thousand counterparts in America or elsewhere in the world. I know of no community that has experienced all the misfortunes I describe. Yet every one of these disasters has actually happened somewhere, and many real communities have already suffered a substantial number of them. A grim <u>specter</u> has crept upon us almost unnoticed, and this imagined tragedy may easily become a stark reality we all shall know.

9

CRITICAL THINKING AND DISCUSSION

Get Thinking and Writing

Understanding Meaning: What Is the Writer Trying to Say?

1. What is Carson trying to explain to her readers? What is the point of her comparison?
2. Can you briefly summarize the before-and-after contrast in your own words? What has happened to this community?
3. What are the major effects of the blight Carson describes?
4. Who is responsible for the changes that occur?
5. *Critical thinking:* Carson published her book more than forty years ago, when many people were not aware of environmental problems. How effective is this comparison in raising concern about pollution?

Evaluating Strategy: How Does the Writer Say It?

1. Carson basically tells a story of mysterious ailments and problems, then announces at the end that the people did it to themselves. Do you think this is an effective approach? Why or why not?
2. How does Carson use a before-and-after contrast to highlight her points?

Appreciating Language: What Words Does the Writer Use?

1. Carson uses terms such as *strange blight, mysterious maladies,* and *evil spell.* What impact do these have?
2. Carson uses the words *silent* and *silence* several times in this short passage. What does *silence* suggest when you think of nature, especially in springtime?

Writing Suggestions

1. Write an essay that uses a before-and-after contrast to show changes in a neighborhood, your workplace, a group of friends, an athletic team, a band, or your college. The changes can be positive or negative.
2. *Collaborative writing:* Work with a group of students and, using Carson's fable as an example, write a similar before-and-after fable to dramatize another problem in a community or single person. You could offer before-and-after views of a person who becomes addicted to drugs, a community after a major employer shuts down, a team after a major victory or defeat, a person who gets a big promotion, or politicians after winning or losing an election.

MAMAN AND AMERICA

AZADEH MOAVENI

Azadeh Moaveni, whose parents left Iran following the fall of the Shah in 1979, was born in Palo Alto, California. In her book Lipstick Jihad: A Memoir of Growing Up Iranian in America and American in Iran, *she describes the complex identity that she developed as someone growing up in a community of exiles trying to make lives in a new country.*

AS YOU READ:

In this passage from Lipstick Jihad, *Moaveni uses comparison and contrast to dramatize the differences between her divorced parents, her teenage conflicts with her mother, whom she calls Maman, and her mother's conflicting opinions of U.S. culture.*

Words to Know

embraced accepted

derived taken from

pilfering stealing

flaunted boldly displayed

disproportionate unequal, exaggerated

allegiance loyalty

prescient prophetic

regressive backward

consistent constant, logical
compromised weakened

physiologically biologically
deprivation going without

When it served her purposes, Maman <u>embraced</u> America and lovingly recited all the qualities that made it superior to our backward-looking Iranian culture. That Americans were honest, never made promises they didn't intend to keep, were open to therapy, believed a divorced woman was still a whole person worthy of respect and a place in society—all this earned them vast respect in Maman's book. It seemed never to occur to her that values do not exist in a cultural vacuum but are knit into a society's fabric; they earn their place, <u>derived</u> from other related beliefs. Maman thought values were like groceries; you'd cruise through the aisles, toss the ones you fancied into your cart, and leave the unappealing ones on the shelf. When I was a teenager we constantly fought over her <u>pilfering</u> through Iranian and American values at random, assigning a particular behavior or habit she felt like promoting to the culture she could peg it to most convincingly.

Our earliest battle on this territory was over Madonna. Maman called her *jendeh,* a prostitute, which I considered an offensive way to describe the singer of "La Isla Bonita." On what grounds, I argued, was she being condemned? Was it because she <u>flaunted</u> her sexuality, and if so, did that make out-of-wedlock sexuality a bad thing? My defense of Madonna seemed to infuriate Maman; her eyes flashed, and her bearing radiated a grave, ominous disappointment. It was the same <u>disproportionate</u> reaction she'd show when I would forget which elder in a room full of aging relatives I should have served tea to first, or when I'd refuse to interrupt an afternoon with a friend to take vitamins to an elderly Iranian lady who couldn't drive. Certain conversations or requests, unbeknownst to me, would become symbolic tests of my <u>allegiance</u> to that Iranian world, and the wrong response would plunge Maman into dark feelings of failure and regret.

At the <u>prescient</u> age of thirteen, I realized our Madonna arguments signaled far more serious confrontations to come. Maman's contempt for Madonna seemed like sheer hypocrisy to me. Was this the same woman who thought it <u>regressive</u> and awful that Iranian culture valued women through their marital status, and rated their respectability according to the success or failure of their marriage? The woman who denounced a culture that considered divorced women criminals? She believed it was only modern to consider women fully equal to men, independent beings with a sacred right to everything men were entitled. Somehow, it became clear through her designation of Madonna as whore, that she also thought it fully <u>consistent</u> to believe premarital sex (for women) was wrong, and that women who practiced it were morally <u>compromised.</u> The men she forgave, offering an explanation worthy of an Iranian villager: "They can't help themselves." Women, it seemed, were <u>physiologically</u> better equipped for <u>deprivation.</u> Often our fights would end with me collapsing in tears, her bitterly condemning my unquestioning acceptance of "this decadent culture's corrupt

1

2

3

ways," and my usual finale: "It's all your fault for raising me here; what did you expect?"

4   In Maman's view, America was responsible for most that had gone wrong in the world. *Een gavhah,* these cows, was her synonym for Americans. She'd established her criticisms early on, and repeated them so often that to this day they are <u>seared</u> on my brain: "Americans have no social skills. . . . They prefer their pets to people. . . . Shopping and sex, sex and shopping; that's all Americans think about. . . . They've figured out how corrupt they are, and rather than fix themselves, they want to force their sick culture on the rest of the world." Since she mostly wheeled out these attitudes to justify why I couldn't be friends with Adam-the-long-haired-guitarist or why I couldn't go to the movies twice in one week, or why I couldn't wear short skirts, I wondered whether they were <u>sincere</u>, or <u>tactical.</u>

5   Her restrictions were futile, and only turned me into a highly skilled liar with a suspiciously heavy backpack. Every morning she would drop me off at a friend's house, <u>ostensibly</u> so we could walk to school together. Once inside I traded the Maman-approved outfit for something tighter, smeared some cherry gloss on my lips, and headed off to class.

6   Knowing I could secretly <u>evade</u> her restrictions helped me endure the sermons, but sometimes the injustice of her moralizing would provoke me, and I would fling <u>jingoistic</u> clichés designed to infuriate her: "Love it or leave it. . . . These colors don't run. . . . No one's keeping you here." At hearing these words come out of my mouth she'd hurl a piece of fruit at me, dissolve into angry tears, and suddenly the fact that I was torturing my poor, exiled single mother filled me with terrible grief, and I would apologize <u>profusely,</u> begging forgiveness in the formal, <u>filial</u> <u>Farsi</u> I knew she craved to hear. In the style of a traditional Iranian mother, she would pretend, for five days, that I did not exist; thaw on the sixth; and by the seventh have forgotten the episode entirely, privately convinced that my rude friends, who didn't even say *salaam* to her when they came over, were responsible for ruining my manners.

7   When we encountered other second-generation Iranians at Persian parties, I was struck by how much less conflicted they seemed over their dueling cultural identities. I decided my own neurotic messiness in this area was the fault of my divorced parents. The only thing they agreed on was the safety record of the Volvo, and how they should both drive one until I finished junior high. But when it came to anything that mattered, for instance how I should be raised, they didn't even bother to carve out an agreement, so vast was the gulf that separated their beliefs. My father was an atheist (Marx said God was dead) who called the Prophet Mohammad a <u>pedophile</u> for marrying a nine-year-old girl. He thought the defining characteristics of Iranian culture—<u>fatalism,</u> political paranoia, social obligations, an enthusiasm for guilt—were responsible for the failures of modern Iran. He wouldn't even <u>condescend</u> to use the term "Iranian culture," preferring to refer, to this day, to "that stinking culture"; he refused to return to Iran, even for his mother's funeral, and wouldn't help me with my Persian homework, a language, he pronounced direly "you will *never* use." When I announced my decision to move to Iran, his greatest fear, I think, was that

seared scorched

sincere genuine
tactical used as a strategy

ostensibly supposedly

evade avoid

jingoistic overly patriotic

profusely abundantly, liberally
filial child/parent relationship
Farsi the language of Iran

salaam traditional greeting

pedophile child molester
fatalism belief that humans are powerless over their destiny
condescend lower oneself, stoop down

hyper-ideologue extremely politically minded person

something sufficiently awful would happen to me that it would require *his* going back. That he had married Maman, a <u>hyper-ideologue,</u> a reactionary as high-strung as they come, was baffling; little wonder they divorced when I was an infant. Daddy was the benevolent father personified; he couldn't have cared less about curfews, dating, a fifth ear piercing, or whether my hair was purple or not.

Get Thinking and Writing

CRITICAL THINKING AND DISCUSSION

Understanding Meaning: What Is the Writer Trying to Say?

1. How does Moaveni use comparison and contrast to explain her mother's conflicted attitude toward the United States?
2. How does Moaveni use comparison and contrast to explain the arguments she had with her mother?
3. Why did they fight over Madonna? What did she represent to Moaveni and her mother?
4. How did Moaveni's mother view men and women?
5. How do Moaveni's parents differ?
6. *Critical thinking:* Do all immigrant parents and their U.S.-born children have clashes over cultural values and identity? Could similar arguments between mothers and daughters occur in a Mexican, Korean, or Vietnamese family?

Evaluating Strategy: How Does the Writer Say It?

1. What role does Madonna play in symbolizing the contrast in Moaveni's attitudes and her mother's?
2. Moaveni states that her mother thought of values like products on a store shelf. Is this an effective comparison? Why or why not?
3. How do her parents' attitudes toward Farsi, the language of Iran, differ? How does Moaveni use this to dramatize their contrasting views of their homeland?

Appreciating Language: What Words Does the Writer Use?

1. What words does Moaveni use to describe her parents?
2. What words does Maman use when she praises the United States? What words does she use when she condemns it? Do you see anything in common? Are they positive and negative ways of describing the same thing, such as personal freedom?

Writing Suggestions

1. Write a comparison essay that describes one or more of your own adolescent conflicts with one or both of your parents. What were points of conflict or challenge? Were the arguments about traditions, values, or parental authority?
2. *Collaborative writing:* Work with other students to develop an essay comparing attitudes that immigrants have about the United States and their own culture. Do some abandon their old values and become fully Americanized while others seek to maintain traditions in a new country?

Division and Classification

Division and classification separates a subject into parts or measures subjects on a scale.

BLACK POLITICAL LEADERSHIP

CORNEL WEST

Cornel West was a religion professor and director of Afro-American studies at Princeton University before being appointed to the faculty of Harvard University. In this passage from his book Race Matters, *West divides black leaders into three distinct types.*

AS YOU READ:

West uses division to discuss types of current black leaders and comparison to suggest that they lack the quality of previous ones.

1   Present-day black political leaders can be grouped under three types: race-effacing managerial leaders, race-identifying protest leaders, and race-transcending prophetic leaders. The first type is growing rapidly. The <u>Thomas Bradleys</u> and <u>Wilson Goodes</u> of black America have become a model for many black leaders trying to reach a large white <u>constituency</u> and keep a loyal black one. This type survives on sheer political savvy and thrives on personal diplomacy. This kind of candidate is the lesser of two evils in a political situation where the only other electoral choice is a conservative (usually white) politician. Yet this type of leader tends to stunt progressive development and silence the prophetic voices in the black community by casting the practical mainstream as the only game in town.

2   The second type of black political leader—race-identifying protest leaders—often view themselves in the tradition of Malcolm X, Martin Luther King, Jr., Ella Baker, and Fannie Lou Hamer. Yet they are usually <u>self-deluded.</u> They actually operate more in the tradition of Booker T. Washington, by confining themselves to the black turf, vowing to protect their leadership status over it, and serving as power brokers with powerful nonblack elites (usually white economic or political elites, though in Louis Farrakhan's case it may be Libyan) to "<u>enhance</u>" this black turf. It is crucial to remember that even in the fifties, Malcolm X's vision and practice were international in scope, and that after 1964 his project was <u>transracial</u>—though grounded in the black turf. King never confined himself to being solely the leader of black America—even though the white press attempted to do so. And Fannie Lou Hamer led the National Welfare Rights Organization, not the Black Welfare Rights Organization. In short, race-identifying protest leaders in the post–Civil Rights era function as figures who white Americans must <u>appease</u> so that the plight of the black poor is overlooked and forgotten. When such leaders move successfully into elected office—as with <u>Marion Barry</u>—they

Words to Know

Thomas Bradley former mayor of Los Angeles

Wilson Goode former mayor of Philadelphia

constituency voters

self-deluded fooling themselves

enhance improve

transracial across racial lines

appease soothe, give into

Marion Barry former mayor of Washington, DC

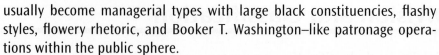

usually become managerial types with large black constituencies, flashy styles, flowery rhetoric, and Booker T. Washington–like patronage operations within the public sphere.

Race-transcending prophetic leaders are rare in contemporary black America. <u>Harold Washington</u> was one. The Jesse Jackson of 1988 was attempting to be another—yet the <u>opportunism</u> of his past weighed heavily on him. To be an elected official and prophetic leader requires personal integrity and political savvy, moral vision and <u>prudential</u> judgment, courageous defiance and organizational patience. The present generation has yet to produce such a figure. We have neither an <u>Adam Clayton Powell, Jr.,</u> nor a <u>Ronald Dellums.</u> This void sits like a festering sore at the center of the crisis of black leadership—and the predicament of the disadvantaged in the United States and abroad worsens.

3

Harold Washington former
    mayor of Chicago
opportunism taking advantage
prudential wise

Adam Clayton Powell, Jr.
    former U.S. Congressman
Ronald Dellums former
    U.S. Congressman

**Get Thinking
and Writing**

CRITICAL THINKING AND DISCUSSION

Understanding Meaning: What Is the Writer Trying to Say?

1. What three types of black leaders does West identify? Can you describe each type in your own words?
2. What does West find lacking in the first two types he describes?
3. What type of leader is rare? Why?
4. Why does West view race-identifying protest leaders as being self-deluded?
5. *Critical thinking:* Can these types of leaders be found in other communities?

Evaluating Strategy: How Does the Writer Say It?

1. In the first paragraph, West announces there are three types of leaders. Is this an effective way to open a division essay? Does giving readers a specific number help them understand important points?
2. How does West use paragraph breaks to organize his essay?
3. How does West define each type of leader? Why are clear definitions important in a division essay?

Appreciating Language: What Words Does the Writer Use?

1. What words does West use to describe each leadership type? Can you find positive and negative terms?
2. Look up the word *patronage* in a dictionary. What does West suggest about race-identifying protest leaders when he uses this term?

Writing Suggestions

1. Describe three types of teachers, coaches, neighbors, roommates, or co-workers. Develop a definition, and supply descriptive details and examples to illustrate each type.
2. *Collaborative writing:* Work with other students to develop an essay that describes three or more types of current local or national political leaders, business leaders, entertainers, or talk-show hosts.

THREE KINDS OF DISCIPLINE

JOHN HOLT

John Holt (1923–1985) wrote several books about children and education, including How Children Fail *and* How Children Learn. *After teaching in public schools for fourteen years, he became an advocate for home schooling.*

AS YOU READ:

Holt classifies three kinds of discipline that children encounter in life. Consider what most parents think of when they hear the word discipline.

1 A child, in growing up, may meet and learn from three different kinds of disciplines. The first and most important is what we might call the Discipline of Nature or of Reality. When he is trying to do something real, if he does the wrong thing or doesn't do the right one, he doesn't get the result he wants. If he doesn't pile one block right on top of another, or tries to build on a slanting surface, his tower falls down. If he hits the wrong key, he hears the wrong note. If he doesn't hit the nail squarely on the head, it bends, and he has to pull it out and start with another. If he doesn't measure properly what he is trying to build, it won't open, close, fit, stand up, fly, float, whistle, or do whatever he wants it to do. If he closes his eyes when he swings, he doesn't hit the ball. A child meets this kind of discipline every time he tries to *do* something, which is why it is so important in school to give children more chances to do things, instead of just reading or listening to someone talk (or pretending to). This discipline is a good teacher. The learner never has to wait long for his answer; it usually comes quickly, often instantly. Also it is clear, and very often points toward the needed correction; from what happened he can not only see that what he did was wrong, but also why, and what he needs to do instead. Finally, and most important, the giver of the answer, call it Nature, is impersonal, <u>impartial,</u> and indifferent. She does not give opinions, or make judgments; she cannot be <u>wheedled,</u> bullied, or fooled; she does not get angry or disappointed; she does not praise or blame; she does not remember past failures or hold grudges; with her one always gets a fresh start, this time is the one that counts.

2 The next discipline we might call the Discipline of Culture, of Society, of What People Really Do. Man is a social, a cultural animal. Children sense around them this culture, this network of agreements, customs, habits, and rules binding the adults together. They want to understand it and be a part of it. They watch very carefully what people around them are doing and want to do the same. They want to do right, unless they become convinced they can't do right. Thus children rarely misbehave seriously in church, but sit as quietly as they can. The example of all those grownups is contagious. Some mysterious ritual is going on, and children, who like rituals, want to be part of it. In the same way, the little children that I see at concerts

Words to Know
impartial fair
wheedled charmed

or operas, though they may fidget a little, or perhaps take a nap now and then, rarely make any disturbance. With all those grownups sitting there, neither moving nor talking, it is the most natural thing in the world to imitate them. Children who live among adults who are habitually courteous to each other, and to them, will soon learn to be courteous. Children who live surrounded by people who speak a certain way will speak that way, however much we may try to tell them that speaking that way is bad or wrong.

The third discipline is the one most people mean when they speak of discipline—the Discipline of Superior Force, of sergeant to private, of "you do what I tell you or I'll make you wish you had." There is bound to be some of this in a child's life. Living as we do surrounded by things that can hurt children, or that children can hurt, we cannot avoid it. We can't afford to let a small child find out from experience the danger of playing in a busy street, or of fooling with the pots on the top of a stove, or of eating up the pills in the medicine cabinet. So, along with other precautions, we say to him, "Don't play in the street, or touch things on the stove, or go into the medicine cabinet, or I'll punish you." Between him and the danger too great for him to imagine we put a lesser danger, but one he can imagine and maybe therefore wants to avoid. He can have no idea of what it would be like to be hit by a car, but he can imagine being shouted at, or spanked, or sent to his room. He avoids these substitutes for the greater danger until he can understand it and avoid it for its own sake. But we ought to use this discipline only when it is necessary to protect the life, health, safety, or well-being of people or other living creatures, or to prevent destruction of things that people care about. We ought not to assume too long, as we usually do, that a child cannot understand the real nature of the danger from which we want to protect him. The sooner he avoids the danger, not to escape our punishment, but as a matter of good sense, the better. He can learn that faster than we think. In Mexico, for example, where people drive their cars with a good deal of spirit, I saw many children no older than five or four walking unattended on the streets. They understood about cars, they knew what to do. A child whose life is full of the threat and fear of punishment is locked into babyhood. There is no way for him to grow up, to learn to take responsibility for his life and acts. Most important of all, we should not assume that having to yield to the threat of our superior force is good for the child's character. It is never good for *anyone's* character. To bow to superior force makes us feel <u>impotent</u> and cowardly for not having had the strength or courage to resist. Worse, it makes us resentful and vengeful. We can hardly wait to make someone pay for our humiliation, yield to us as we were once made to yield. No, if we cannot always avoid using the discipline of Superior Force, we should at least use it as seldom as we can.

There are places where all three disciplines overlap. Any very demanding human activity combines in it the disciplines of Superior Force, of Culture, and of Nature. The <u>novice</u> will be told, "Do it this way, never mind asking why, just do it that way, that is the way we always do it." But it probably *is* just the way they always do it, and usually for the very good reason that it is a way that has been found to work. Think, for example, of ballet training. The student in a class is told to do this exercise, or that; to stand so; to do this or that with his head, arms, shoulders, abdomen,

impotent weak

novice beginner

3

4

hips, legs, feet. He is constantly corrected. There is no argument. But behind these seemingly autocratic demands by the teacher lie many decades of custom and tradition, and behind that, the necessities of dancing itself. You cannot make the moves of classical ballet unless over many years you have acquired, and renewed every day, the needed strength and <u>suppleness</u> in scores of muscles and joints. Nor can you do the difficult motions, making them look easy, unless you have learned hundreds of easier ones first. Dance teachers may not always agree on all the details of teaching these strengths and skills. But no novice could learn them all by himself. You could not go for a night or two to watch the ballet and then, without any other knowledge at all, teach yourself how to do it. In the same way, you would be unlikely to learn any complicated and difficult human activity without drawing heavily on the experience of those who know it better. But the point is that the authority of these experts or teachers stems from, grows out of their greater competence and experience, the fact that what they do *works,* not the fact that they happen to be the teacher and as such have the power to kick a student out of the class. And the further point is that children are always and everywhere attracted to that <u>competence,</u> and ready and eager to submit themselves to a discipline that grows out of it. We hear constantly that children will never do anything unless <u>compelled</u> to by bribes or threats. But in their private lives, or in extracurricular activities in school, in sports, music, drama, art, running a newspaper, and so on, they often submit themselves willingly and wholeheartedly to very intense disciplines, simply because they want to learn to do a given thing well. Our Little-Napoleon football coaches, of whom we have too many and hear far too much, blind us to the fact that millions of children work hard every year getting better at sports and games without coaches barking and yelling at them.

suppleness flexibility

competence ability

compelled forced

CRITICAL THINKING AND DISCUSSION

Understanding Meaning: What Is the Writer Trying to Say?

1. What lessons do children learn from experience? How can even playing teach children discipline?
2. What does Holt mean by the term "Discipline of Culture"? Can you think of examples?
3. What is Holt's opinion of parental authority and direction? When does he believe that strict discipline is justified?
4. *Critical thinking:* What does Holt's view of discipline reveal about his attitude toward children? How much discipline can children learn on their own? Does he think that strict discipline from parents or teachers is effective? Why or why not?

Evaluating Strategy: How Does the Writer Say It?

1. How does Holt organize his classification?
2. What role do paragraph breaks play in organizing the essay?

Get Thinking and Writing

3. How effective are the titles, which Holt capitalizes, in labeling each type of discipline? Can you think of other possible names?

Appreciating Language: What Words Does the Writer Use?

1. What connotations does the word *discipline* have? Do most people associate discipline with punishment?
2. How do Holt's word choices indicate his attitudes toward each type of discipline?

Writing Suggestions

1. Write a short essay that classifies three or more types of college courses, students, stores, radio stations, clubs, or entertainers.
2. *Collaborative writing:* Work with other students to develop an essay that classifies parents from the least to most strict. Supply examples to illustrate each type.

Process

Process explains how something occurs or provides step-by-step instructions to accomplish a specific task.

HOW OUR SKINS GOT THEIR COLOR

MARVIN HARRIS

Marvin Harris (1927–2001) was professor of anthropology who conducted research in Harlem, Africa, Asia, and South America. He published several books for both scholars and general readers, including Cows, Pigs, Wars, and Witches *and* Cannibals and Kings.

AS YOU READ:

In this essay from his book Our Kind: Who We Are, Where We Came From, Where We Are Going, *Harris explains how humans developed different skin colors.*

Words to Know

descendants offspring

adaptations changes

Most human beings are neither very fair nor very dark, but brown. The extremely fair skin of northern Europeans and their <u>descendants,</u> and the very black skins of central Africans and their descendants, are probably special <u>adaptations.</u> Brown-skinned ancestors may have been shared by modern-day blacks and whites as recently as ten thousand years ago.   1

Human skin owes its color to the presence of particles known as melanin. The primary function of melanin is to protect the upper levels of the skin from being damaged by the sun's ultraviolet rays. This radiation poses a critical problem for our kind because we lack the dense coat of hair that acts as a sunscreen for most mammals. Hairlessness exposes us to two kinds of radiation hazards: ordinary sunburn, with its blisters, rashes, and risk   2 of infection; and skin cancers, including <u>malignant</u> melanoma, one of the deadliest diseases known. Melanin is the body's first line of defense against these <u>afflictions.</u> The more melanin particles, the darker the skin, and the lower the risk of sunburn and all forms of skin cancer. This explains why the highest rates for skin cancer are found in sun-drenched lands such as Australia, where light-skinned people of European descent spend a good part of their lives outdoors wearing scanty attire. Very dark-skinned people such as heavily pigmented Africans of Zaire seldom get skin cancer, but when they do, they get it on depigmented parts of their bodies—palms and lips.

malignant deadly

afflictions diseases

3   If exposure to solar radiation had nothing but harmful effects, natural selection would have favored inky black as the color for all human populations. But the sun's rays do not present an <u>unmitigated</u> threat. As it falls on the skin, sunshine <u>converts</u> a fatty substance in the <u>epidermis</u> into vitamin D. The blood carries vitamin D from the skin to the intestines (technically making it a hormone rather than a vitamin), where it plays a vital role in the absorption of calcium. In turn, calcium is vital for strong bones. Without it, people fall victim to the crippling diseases rickets and <u>osteomalacia.</u> In women, calcium deficiencies can result in a deformed birth canal, which makes childbirth lethal for both mother and fetus.

unmitigated total
converts changes
epidermis outer skin layer

osteomalacia bone disease

4   Vitamin D can be obtained from a few foods, primarily the oils and livers of marine fish. But inland populations must rely on the sun's rays and their own skins for the supply of this crucial substance. The particular color of a human population's skin, therefore, represents in large degree a trade-off between the hazards of too much versus too little solar radiation: <u>acute</u> sunburn and skin cancer on the one hand, and rickets and osteomalacia on the other. It is this trade-off that largely accounts for the <u>preponderance</u> of brown people in the world and for the general tendency for skin color to be darkest among <u>equatorial</u> populations and lightest among populations dwelling at higher latitudes.

acute immediate

preponderance prevalence

equatorial near the equator

5   At middle latitudes, the skin follows a strategy of changing colors with the seasons. Around the Mediterranean basin, for example, exposure to the summer sun brings high risk of cancer but low risk for rickets; the body produces more melanin and people grow darker (i.e., they get suntans). Winter reduces the risk of sunburn and cancer; the body produces less melanin, and the tan wears off.

6   The <u>correlation</u> between skin color and latitude is not perfect because other factors—such as the availability of foods containing vitamin D and calcium, regional cloud cover during the winter, amount of clothing worn, and cultural preferences—may work for or against the predicted relationship. Arctic-dwelling Eskimos, for example, are not as light-skinned as expected, but their habitat and economy afford them a diet that is <u>exceptionally</u> rich in both vitamin D and calcium.

correlation relationship

exceptionally especially

7   Northern Europeans, <u>obliged</u> to wear heavy garments for protection against the long, cold, cloudy winters, were always at risk for rickets and osteomalacia from too little vitamin D and calcium. This risk increased sometime after 6000 B.C., when pioneer cattle herders who did not exploit marine resources began to appear in northern Europe. The risk would have been especially great for the brown-skinned Mediterranean peoples who <u>migrated</u> northward along with the crops and farm animals. Samples of

obliged forced

migrated moved

Caucasian skin (infant penile foreskin obtained at the time of circumcision) exposed to sunlight on cloudless days in Boston (42°N) from November through February produced no vitamin D. In Edmonton (52°N) this period extended from October to March. But further south (34°N) sunlight was effective in producing vitamin D in the middle of the winter. Almost all of Europe lies north of 42°N. Fair-skinned, nontanning individuals who could utilize the weakest and briefest doses of sunlight to <u>synthesize</u> vitamin D were strongly favored by natural selection. During the <u>frigid</u> winters, only a small circle of a child's face could be left to peek out at the sun through the heavy clothing, thereby favoring the survival of individuals with <u>translucent</u> patches of pink on their cheeks characteristic of many northern Europeans. . . .

synthesize make
frigid very cold

translucent clear

If light-skinned individuals on the average had only 2 percent more children survive per generation, the changeover in their skin color could have begun five thousand years ago and reached present levels well before the beginning of the Christian era. But natural selection need not have acted alone. Cultural selection may also have played a role. It seems likely that whenever people consciously or unconsciously had to decide which infants to <u>nourish</u> and which to neglect, the advantage would go to those with lighter skin, experience having shown that such individuals tended to grow up to be taller, stronger, and healthier than their darker <u>siblings.</u> White was beautiful because white was healthy.   8

nourish feed

siblings brothers and sisters

To account for the evolution of black skin in equatorial latitudes, one has merely to reverse the combined effects of natural and cultural selection. With the sun directly overhead most of the year, and clothing a <u>hindrance</u> to work and survival, vitamin D was never in short supply (and calcium was easily obtained from vegetables). Rickets and osteomalacia were rare. Skin cancer was the main problem, and what nature started, culture <u>amplified.</u> Darker infants were favored by parents because experience showed that they grew up to be freer of disfiguring and lethal <u>malignancies.</u> Black was beautiful because black was healthy.   9

hindrance obstacle

amplified increased

malignancies cancers

**Get Thinking
and Writing**

CRITICAL THINKING AND DISCUSSION

Understanding Meaning: What Is the Writer Trying to Say?

1. What is the natural color of human skin?
2. What caused people to develop lighter and darker complexions?
3. What role did sunlight play in human evolution? What made white skin beneficial to Northern Europeans and black skin advantageous to Central Africans?
4. *Critical thinking:* What impact could a scientific understanding of skin color have on debates about race and discrimination? Could it change people's attitudes? Why or why not?

Evaluating Strategy: How Does the Writer Say It?

1. How does Harris organize his essay?
2. What research does Harris use to support his observations?

Appreciating Language: What Words Does the Writer Use?

1. How does Harris define *melanin?* What role does it play in determining skin color?
2. Do you detect any bias in Harris's use of the words *white* and *black?* How can someone write about a sensitive topic without using words that might offend readers?

Writing Suggestions

1. Using Harris's essay as a source, write a brief explanation of how humans developed different skin colors for a middle school brochure about race relations. Could understanding the scientific reasons for skin color be the first step in addressing racism?
2. *Collaborative writing:* Work with other students to develop an essay explaining another process, such as how trash is recycled, how elections are conducted, how people are interviewed for jobs, or how winners are chosen on a reality television show.

FENDER BENDERS: LEGAL DO'S AND DON'TS

ARMOND D. BUDISH

Armond D. Budish is an attorney and consumer law reporter. He writes a column on consumer issues for the Cleveland Plain Dealer. *In this article, he explains step by step what drivers should do if they are involved in a minor accident.*

AS YOU READ:

Note that Budish uses numbered steps and bold print to organize his points and present ideas in a way that readers can easily remember.

1   The car ahead of you stops suddenly. You hit the brakes, but you just can't stop in time. Your front bumper meets the rear end of the other car. *Ouch!*

2   There doesn't seem to be any damage, and it must be your lucky day because the driver you hit agrees that it's not worth hassling with insurance claims and risking a <u>premium</u> increase. So after exchanging addresses, you go your separate ways.

3   Imagine your surprise when you open the mail a few weeks later only to discover a letter from your "victim's" lawyer demanding $10,000 to cover car repairs, pain, and suffering. Apparently the agreeable gentleman decided to disagree, then went ahead and filed a police report blaming you for the incident and for his damages.

4   When automobiles meet by accident, do you know how to respond? Here are 10 practical tips that can help you avoid costly legal and insurance hassles.

Words to Know

premium insurance payments

1. Stop! It's the Law.

No matter how serious or minor the accident, stop immediately. If possible, don't move your car—especially if someone has been injured. Leaving the cars as they were when the accident occurred helps the police determine what happened. Of course, if your car is blocking traffic or will cause another accident where it is, then move it to the nearest safe location.

For every rule there are exceptions, though. If, for example, you are rear-ended at night in an unsafe area, it's wisest to keep on going and notify the police later. There have been cases in which people were robbed or assaulted when they got out of their cars.

2. Zip Loose Lips.

Watch what you say after an accident. Although this may sound harsh, even an innocent "I'm sorry" could later be <u>construed</u> as an admission of fault. Also be sure not to accuse the other driver of causing the accident. Since you don't know how a stranger will react to your remarks, you run the risk of making a bad situation worse.

Remember, you are not the judge or jury; it's not up to you to decide who is or is not at fault. Even if you think you caused the accident, you might be wrong. For example: Assume you were driving 15 miles over the speed limit. What you probably were not aware of is that the other driver's blood-alcohol level exceeded the legal limits, so he was at least equally at fault.

3. Provide Required Information.

If you are involved in an accident, you are required in most states to give your name, address and car registration number to: any person injured in the accident; the owner, driver or passenger in any car that was damaged in the accident; a police officer on the scene. If you don't own the car (say it belongs to a friend or your parents), you should provide the name and address of the owner.

You must produce this information even if there are no apparent injuries or damages and even if you didn't cause the accident. Most states don't require you to provide the name of your insurance company, although it's usually a good idea to do so. However, *don't* discuss the amount of your coverage—that might inspire the other person to "realize" his injuries are more serious than he originally thought.

What should you do if you hit a parked car and the owner is not around? The law requires you to leave a note with your name, and the other identifying information previously mentioned, in a secure place on the car (such as under the windshield wiper).

4. Get Required Information.

You should obtain from the others involved in the accident the same information that you provide them with. However, if the other driver refuses to cooperate, at least get the license number and the make and model of the car to help police track down the owner.

construed interpreted

5. Call the Police.

13 It's obvious that if it's a serious accident in which someone is injured, the police should be called immediately. That's both the law and common sense. But what if the accident seems minor? Say you're stopped, another car taps you in the rear. If it's absolutely clear to both drivers that there is no damage or injury, you each can go your merry way. But that's the exception.

14 Normally, you should call the police to <u>substantiate</u> what occurred. In most cities police officers will come to the scene, even for minor accidents, but if they won't, you and the other driver should go to the station (of the city where the accident occurred) to file a report. Ask to have an officer check out both cars.

substantiate prove

15 If you are not at fault, be wary of accepting the other driver's suggestion that you leave the police out of it and arrange a private settlement. When you submit your $500 car-repair estimate several weeks later, you could discover that the other driver has developed "amnesia" and denies being anywhere near the accident. If the police weren't present on the scene, you may not have a legal leg to stand on.

16 Even if you *are* at fault, it's a good idea to involve the police. Why? Because a police officer will note the extent of the other driver's damages in his or her report, limiting your liability. Without police presence the other driver can easily <u>inflate</u> the amount of the damages.

inflate increase

6. Identify Witnesses.

17 Get the names and addresses of any witnesses, in case there's a legal battle some time in the future. Ask bystanders or other motorists who stop whether they saw the accident; if they answer "yes," get their identifying information. It is also helpful to note the names and badge numbers of all police officers on the scene.

7. Go to the Hospital.

18 If there's a chance that you've been injured, go directly to a hospital emergency room or to your doctor. The longer you wait, the more you may <u>jeopardize</u> your health and the more difficult it may be to get <u>reimbursed</u> for your injuries if they turn out to be serious.

jeopardize endanger or risk
reimbursed repaid

8. File a Report.

19 Every driver who is involved in an automobile incident in which injuries occur must fill out an accident report. Even if the property damage is only in the range of $200 to $1,000, most states require that an accident report be filed. You must do this fairly quickly, usually in 1 to 30 days. Forms may be obtained and filed with the local motor vehicle department or police station in the city where the accident occurred.

9. Consider Filing an Insurance Claim.

20 Talk with your insurance agent as soon as possible after an accident. He or she can help you decide if you should file an insurance claim or pay out of your own pocket.

deductible costs not covered by
insurance

For example, let's say you caused an accident and the damages totaled   21
$800. You carry a $250 deductible, leaving you with a possible $550 insur-
ance claim. If you do submit a claim, your insurance rates are likely to
go up, an increase that will probably continue for about three years. You
should compare that figure to the $550 claim to determine whether to file
a claim or to pay the cost yourself. (Also keep in mind that multiple claims
sometimes make it harder to renew your coverage.)

10. Don't Be Too Quick to Accept a Settlement.

If the other driver is at fault and there's any chance you've been injured,   22
don't rush to accept a settlement from that person's insurance company.
You may not know the extent of your injuries for some time, and once you
accept a settlement, it's difficult to get an "upgrade." Before settling, consult with a lawyer who handles personal injury cases.

When you *haven't* been injured and you receive a fair offer to cover the   23
damage to your car, you can go ahead and accept it.

Get Thinking and Writing

CRITICAL THINKING AND DISCUSSION

Understanding Meaning: What Is the Writer Trying to Say?

1. What problems can drivers encounter if they are careless in responding
   to a minor accident?
2. What are the most important things you should do if involved in a
   fender bender?
3. Why does Budish say that you should not offer an apology, even if you
   believe that the accident is your fault?
4. *Critical thinking:* Do you believe most people know what to do if they
   have a minor accident? Should this article be published as a pamphlet
   and distributed at service stations, insurance offices, car rental counters,
   and drivers' training courses?

Evaluating Strategy: How Does the Writer Say It?

1. How does Budish use an opening example to dramatize his point and
   arouse interest?
2. What techniques does Budish use to make his process easy to read and
   remember?
3. Would this essay be less effective if written in standard paragraphs
   without numbers? Why or why not?

Appreciating Language: What Words Does the Writer Use?

1. This article first appeared in *Family Circle.* Does this help explain its
   tone and style?
2. Why does Budish, a lawyer, avoid legal terms?

Writing Suggestions

1. Using this article as a model, write an essay that uses numbered steps to explain how people can avoid heart disease, quit smoking, prepare for a job interview, prevent identity theft, or remove a computer virus.

2. *Collaborative writing:* Work with a group of students to develop a process essay that tells readers how to respond to a specific emergency.

Cause and Effect

Cause and effect explains reasons and results.

WHY SCHOOLS DON'T EDUCATE

JOHN TAYLOR GATTO

John Taylor Gatto taught in New York City public schools for twenty-five years and was named the city's Teacher of the Year three times. He has published several books about public education, including Dumbing Us Down, The Exhausted School, *and* The Empty Child.

AS YOU READ:

As you read Gatto's list of symptoms, consider other causes for childhood behavior. How much of a child's life and future can be shaped by schools, and how much depends on family and cultural influences?

1. Two institutions at present control our children's lives—television and schooling, in that order. Both of these reduce the real world of wisdom, <u>fortitude,</u> temperance, and justice to a never-ending, nonstop <u>abstraction.</u> In centuries past, the time of a child and adolescent would be occupied in real work, real charity, real adventures, and the real search for <u>mentors</u> who might teach what one really wanted to learn. A great deal of time was spent in community pursuits, practicing affection, meeting and studying every level of the community, learning how to make a home, and dozens of other tasks necessary to becoming a whole man or woman.

Words to Know
fortitude strength
abstraction idea
mentors advisors

2. But here is the <u>calculus</u> of time the children I teach must deal with:

calculus schedule

3. Out of the 168 hours in each week, my children must sleep fifty-six. That leaves them 112 hours a week out of which to <u>fashion</u> a self.

fashion create

4. My children watch fifty-five hours of television a week, according to recent reports. That leaves them fifty-seven hours a week in which to grow up.

5. My children attend school thirty hours a week; use about eight hours getting ready, going, and coming home; and spend an average of seven hours a week in homework—a total of forty-five hours. During that time they are under constant surveillance, have no private time or private space, and are disciplined if they try to assert individuality in the use of time or

space. That leaves twelve hours a week out of which to create a unique consciousness. Of course my kids eat, too, and that takes some time—not much, because we've lost the tradition of family dining. If we allot three hours a week to evening meals we arrive at a net amount of private time for each child of nine hours.

It's not enough. It's not enough, is it? The richer the kid, of course, the less television he watches, but the rich kid's time is just as narrowly proscribed by a broader catalogue of commercial entertainments and his inevitable assignment to a series of private lessons in areas seldom of his choice.   6

And these things are, oddly enough, just a more cosmetic way to create dependent human beings, unable to fill their own hours, unable to initiate lines of meaning to give substance and pleasure to their existence. It's a national disease, this dependency and aimlessness, and I think schooling and television and lessons—the entire Chautauqua idea—have a lot to do with it.   7

Think of the things that are killing us as a nation: drugs, brainless competition, recreational sex, the pornography of violence, gambling, alcohol, and the worst pornography of all—lives devoted to buying things—accumulation as a philosophy. All are addictions of dependent personalities and that is what our brand of schooling must inevitably produce.   8

I want to tell you what the effect is on children of taking all their time—time they need to grow up—and forcing them to spend it on abstractions. No reform that doesn't attack these specific pathologies will be anything more than a facade.   9

1. The children I teach are indifferent to the adult world. This defies the experience of thousands of years. A close study of what big people were up to was always the most exciting occupation of youth, but nobody wants to grow up these days, and who can blame them. Toys are us.
2. The children I teach have almost no curiosity, and what little they do have is transitory; they cannot concentrate for very long, even on things they choose to do. Can you see a connection between the bells ringing again and again to change classes, and this phenomenon of evanescent attention?
3. The children I teach have a poor sense of the future, of how tomorrow is inextricably linked to today. They live in a continuous present; the exact moment they are in is the boundary of their consciousness.
4. The children I teach are ahistorical; they have no sense of how the past has predestined their own present, limiting their choices, shaping their values and lives.
5. The children I teach are cruel to each other; they lack compassion for misfortune, they laugh at weakness, they have contempt for people whose need for help shows too plainly.
6. The children I teach are uneasy with intimacy or candor. They cannot deal with genuine intimacy because of a lifelong habit of preserving a secret self inside an outer personality made up of artificial bits and pieces, of behavior borrowed from television or acquired to manipulate teachers. Because they are not who they represent themselves to be, the

proscribed limited
catalogue list
inevitable unavoidable

initiate create/start

Chautauqua 19th-century educational movement

accumulation getting/ consuming

pathologies diseases
facade false front

indifferent uncaring

transitory fleeting

evanescent brief

inextricably definitely
continuous ongoing

predestined already determined

candor honesty

disguise wears thin in the presence of intimacy, so intimate relationships have to be avoided.

7. The children I teach are materialistic, following the lead of schoolteachers who materialistically "grade" everything—and television mentors
who offer everything in the world for sale.

8. The children I teach are dependent, passive, and timid in the presence of new challenges. This timidity is frequently masked by surface
<u>bravado</u> or by anger or aggressiveness, but underneath is a vacuum
without fortitude.

bravado false bravery

10   I could name a few other conditions that school reform will have to tackle if
our national decline is to be arrested, but by now you will have grasped my
thesis, whether you agree with it or not. Either schools, television, or both
have caused these pathologies. It's a simple matter of arithmetic. Between
schooling and television, all the time children have is eaten up. That's what
has destroyed the American family; it no longer is a factor in the education
of its own children.

CRITICAL THINKING AND DISCUSSION

**Get Thinking
and Writing**

Understanding Meaning: What Is the Writer Trying to Say?

1. What is the author's thesis?
2. How has television, in Gatto's view, affected children's lives?
3. Gatto states that children can be both "cruel" and "passive." Can one be
    both cruel and passive? Can pent-up energy and stunted creativity lead
    to children to express themselves in bursts of violence and periods of
    apathy?
4. Gatto observes that children are materialistic. How much of this is
    caused by television and how much by their family's values?
5. *Critical thinking:* Gatto remarks that "children live in a continuous
    present" without a sense of past or future. Is this natural for children or
    something that has been caused by watching television? Doesn't televi-
    sion teach children something about history, even if facts are distorted
    or simplified?

Evaluating Strategy: How Does the Writer Say It?

1. How effective is Gatto's use of numbered points?
2. Gatto begins each of his eight points with "The children I teach." Is this
    an effective use of repetition? Gatto delivered this essay as a speech.
    Does this explain a need to repeat key phrases to a listening audience?
    Can too much repetition become tedious to readers?
3. What risk does Gatto run in criticizing children? How might parents
    respond to his comments?

Appreciating Language: What Words Does the Writer Use?

1. Gatto uses the word *ahistorical.* How would you define this term? What
    does it mean to be "without history"?

2. Gatto calls "being devoted to buying things" the "worst pornography of all." What impact does the word *pornography* have? Is this an effective word choice?

Writing Suggestions

1. Write a similar essay in which you detail the effects that television has had on children you know. Do your observations match Gatto's?

2. *Collaborative writing:* Discuss Gatto's essay with other students. Do they agree with his points? Work together to develop a list of points that would improve public schools.

WHY AMERICA LOVES REALITY TV

STEVEN REISS AND JAMES WILTZ

Steven Reiss teaches at Ohio State University, where James Wiltz is working on his doctorate. In this essay they discuss the results of a survey they conducted to discover why people watch reality TV programs.

AS YOU READ:

First, consider your own experiences and those of your friends. Do you watch reality television shows? Which ones do you like the most? Why do you find them interesting?

Words to Know

salacious scandalous

voyeurs people who get pleasure from watching others

blatant obvious

Even if you don't watch reality television, it's becoming increasingly hard to avoid. The salacious *Temptation Island* was featured on the cover of *People* magazine. *Big Brother* aired five days a week and could be viewed on the Web 24 hours a day. And the *Survivor* finale dominated the front page of the *New York Post* after gaining ratings that rivaled those of the Super Bowl.

Is the popularity of shows such as *Survivor, Big Brother* and *Temptation Island* a sign that the country has degenerated into a nation of voyeurs? Americans seem hooked on so-called reality television—programs in which ordinary people compete in week-long contests while being filmed 24 hours a day. Some commentators contend the shows peddle blatant voyeurism, with shameless exhibitionists as contestants. Others believe that the show's secret to ratings success may be as simple and harmless as the desire to seem part of the in crowd.

Rather than just debate the point, we wanted to get some answers. So we conducted a detailed survey of 239 people, asking them about not only their television viewing habits but also their values and desires through the Reiss Profile, a standardized test of 16 basic desires and values. We found that the self-appointed experts were often wrong about why people watch reality TV.

Two of the most commonly repeated "truths" about reality TV viewers are that they watch in order to talk to friends and coworkers about the show, and that they are not as smart as other viewers. But our survey results show that both of these ideas are incorrect. Although some people may watch because it helps them <u>participate</u> in the next day's office chat, fans and nonfans score almost equally when tested on their sociability. And people who say they enjoy intellectual activities are no less likely to watch reality TV than are those who say they dislike intellectual activities.

5   Another common misconception about *Temptation Island,* a reality program in which couples were <u>enticed</u> to cheat on their partners, is that the audience was watching to see scenes of illicit sex. Some critics were surprised that the show remained popular when it turned out to be much tamer than advertised. In fact, our survey suggests that one of the main differences between fans of the show and everyone else is not an interest in sex but a lack of interest in personal honor—they value <u>expedience,</u> not morality. What made *Temptation Island* popular was not the possibility of watching adultery, but the ethical slips that lead to adultery.

6   One aspect that all of the reality TV shows had in common was their competitive nature: contestants were <u>vying</u> with one another for a cash prize and were engaged in building alliances and betraying allies. The first *Survivor* series climaxed with one contestant, Susan Hawk, launching into a vengeful <u>tirade</u> against a one-time friend and ally before casting the vote that deprived her of the million-dollar prize. It makes sense, then, that fans of both *Survivor* and *Temptation Island* tend to be competitive—and that they are more likely to place a very high value on revenge than are other people. The *Survivor* formula of challenges and voting would seem to embody both of these desired qualities: the spirit of competition paired with the opportunity for payback.

7   But the attitude that best separated the regular viewers of reality television from everyone else is the desire for status. Fans of the shows are much more likely to agree with statements such as, "Prestige is important to me" and "I am impressed with designer clothes" than are other people. We have studied similar phenomena before and found that the desire for status is just a means to get attention. And more attention increases one's sense of importance: We think we are important if others pay attention to us and unimportant if ignored.

8   Reality TV allows Americans to fantasize about gaining status through automatic fame. Ordinary people can watch the shows, see people like themselves and imagine that they too could become celebrities by being on television. It does not matter as much that the contestants often are shown in unfavorable light; the fact that millions of Americans are paying attention means that the contestants are important.

9   And, in fact, some of the contestants have capitalized on their short-term celebrity: Colleen Haskell, from the first *Survivor* series, has a major role in the movie *The Animal,* and Richard Hatch, the scheming contestant who won the game, has been hired to host his own game show. If these former nobodies can become stars, then who couldn't?

10   The message of reality television is that ordinary people can become so important that millions will watch them. And the secret thrill of many of those viewers is the thought that perhaps next time, the new celebrities might be them.

participate take part

enticed lured

expedience using shortcuts to achieve a goal

vying competing

tirade outburst

CRITICAL THINKING AND DISCUSSION

Understanding Meaning: What Is the Writer Trying to Say?

1. What did the survey reveal about why people watch reality TV?
2. What misconceptions do people have about the reasons for the popularity of reality TV programs?
3. What type of people watch reality TV? What is important to them?
4. *Critical thinking:* If you or your friends enjoy reality TV, what reasons can you give for the popularity of these shows?

Evaluating Strategy: How Does the Writer Say It?

1. How do the authors explain the way they conducted their survey?
2. The authors first present misconceptions, then their own findings. Is this effective?

Appreciating Language: What Words Does the Writer Use?

1. What words do the authors use to describe the viewers of reality TV?
2. What words do the authors use to describe the reality shows? What do terms like *alliance* and *contestant* suggest about their appeal?

Writing Suggestions

1. Write an essay that gives reasons why you like another kind of TV program, such as soap operas or sitcoms. Why do you watch them? What appeal do they have?
2. *Collaborative writing:* Discuss reality TV with other students. Do they see other causes for their popularity? For example, did the birth of CNN and other cable news channels create an interest in watching real events rather than fictional dramas? Write an essay summarizing the group's views.

Argument and Persuasion

Argument and persuasion encourages readers to accept a point of view or take action.

WHY I CHANGED MY MIND ON THE DEATH PENALTY

LANCE MORROW

Lance Morrow (1935–) has been a regular contributor to Time *magazine since 1965. In this essay, published in* Time *in 2000, he explains why he now opposes the death penalty.*

AS YOU READ:

Morrow first explains his previous support for the death penalty, then presents his reasons for changing his opinion. The death penalty, he argues, no longer serves a moral purpose, so it has become immoral.

1   Christina Marie Riggs, a nurse in Arkansas and a single mother, killed her two children—Justin, 5, and Shelby Alexis, 2—by giving them injections of <u>potassium chloride</u> and then smothering them with a pillow. She wrote a suicide note, and apparently tried to kill herself with an overdose of 28 antidepressant tablets. She survived.

2   Or she did until last night, when the state of Arkansas put Riggs to death by lethal injection at the state prison in Varner. She was the first woman to be executed in Arkansas since 1845.

3   The state of Arkansas played the part of <u>Jack Kevorkian</u> in a case of assisted suicide. Christina Riggs said she wanted to die. She had dropped all legal appeals. She wanted to be with her children in heaven. Just before Riggs died, she said, "I love you, my babies." Some people said she had killed them because she was severely depressed. The prosecutor, on the other hand, called her "a self-centered, selfish, <u>premeditated</u> killer who did the unspeakable act of taking her own children's lives."

4   So where do we stand on capital punishment now? (And, incidentally, isn't it grand that we seem to be overcoming, at the speed of light, our reluctance to execute women? Bless you, <u>Gloria Steinem</u>.)

5   Review the state of play:

- Deterrence is an unreliable argument for the death penalty, I think because deterrence is unprovable.
- The fear of executing the wrong man (a more popular line of <u>demurral</u> these days) is an unreliable argument against all capital punishment. What if there are many witnesses to a murder? What if it's Hitler? Is capital punishment OK in cases of unmistakable guilt? George W. Bush says that he reviews each case to make sure he is absolutely certain a person did it before he allows a Texas execution to go ahead.

6   I have argued in the past that the death penalty was justified, in certain brutal cases, on the basis of the social contract. That is: Some hideous crimes demand the ultimate punishment in order to satisfy the essentially civilizing deal that we make with one another as citizens. We <u>forgo</u> individual revenge, <u>deferring</u> to the law, but depend upon a certainty that the law will give us a justice that must include appropriate harshness. I favored the Texas folk wisdom: "He needs killing." If the law fails in that task, I said, and people see that evil is fecklessly tolerated, then the social contract disintegrates. Society needs a measure of <u>homeopathic</u> revenge.

7   But I have changed my mind about capital punishment.

8   I think the American atmosphere, the American imagination (news, movies, books, music, fact, fiction, entertainment, culture, life in the streets, zeitgeist) is now so filled with murder and violence (gang wars, random

Words to Know

potassium chloride a poison

Jack Kevorkian a doctor who assisted the terminally ill to commit suicide

premeditated planned

Gloria Steinem feminist who championed equal rights for women

demurral hesitation

forgo give up
deferring accepting

homeopathic referring to a school of medicine that believes a little of what makes one sick can treat or cure

Freudian referring to Sigmund Freud, pioneer psychologist

Superego Freud's term for people's sense of social order and rules

Id Freud's term for instinctual drives and urges

exemplary excellent

nostalgia love of the past

voracious greedy

aesthetic concerning art or beauty

shootings not just in housing projects but in offices and malls and schools) that violence of any kind—including solemn execution—has become merely a part of our cultural routine and joins, in our minds, the passing parade of stupidity/psychosis/chaos/entertainment that Americans seem to like, or have come to deserve. In <u>Freudian</u> terms, the once forceful (and patriarchal) American <u>Superego</u> (arguably including the authority of law, of the presidency, of the military, etc.) has collapsed into a great dismal swamp of <u>Id.</u>

And in the Swamp, I have come to think, capital punishment has lost whatever cautionary social force it had—its <u>exemplary</u> meaning, its power to proclaim, as it once arguably did, that some deeds are, in our fine and virtuous company, intolerable.   9

I think those arguing in favor of capital punishment now are indulging in a form of <u>nostalgia.</u> Capital punishment no longer works as a morality play. Each execution (divorced from its moral meaning, including its capacity to shock and to warn the young) simply becomes part of the great messy pageant, the vast and <u>voracious</u> stupidity, the Jerry Springer show of American life.   10

Maybe most of our moral opinions are formed by emotions and <u>aesthetic</u> reactions. My opinion is this: Capital punishment has lost its moral meaning. Having lost its moral meaning, it has become as immoral as any other expression of violence. And therefore we should stop doing it.   11

Get Thinking and Writing

CRITICAL THINKING AND DISCUSSION

Understanding Meaning: What Is the Writer Trying to Say?

1. What reasons does Morrow give for changing his opinion about the death penalty?
2. Why does Morrow believe that capital punishment does not serve any useful purpose?
3. Morrow opens his essay with the example of Christina Marie Riggs, who was executed for killing her children. Why is this case important in his view?
4. *Critical thinking:* Do you share Morrow's view that our culture has become obsessed with death and violence? If violent crimes and executions become frequent, does capital punishment lose its ability to make a strong statement about the value of life and the severe punishment that murderers deserve?

Evaluating Strategy: How Does the Writer Say It?

1. Why is it effective when trying to persuade people about a controversial issue to explain the merits of both sides?
2. Morrow uses a one-sentence paragraph transition (paragraph 7). Is this effective? Why or why not?
3. Morrow places his thesis in the last sentence rather than the beginning of his essay. Is this effective? Why or why not?

Appreciating Language: What Words Does the Writer Use?

1. What does Morrow mean by the word *swamp?* What does the swamp contain?
2. How does Morrow explain that capital punishment moved from being *moral* to *immoral?* How does he define these terms?

Writing Suggestions

1. Write a persuasive essay about an issue you have changed your mind about. Explain your original views and what led you to change them.
2. *Collaborative writing:* Discuss Morrow's essay with other students, and ask members of the group their opinions of the death penalty. If you are in agreement, develop an essay expressing your views. If members disagree, consider developing opposing essays.

IN PRAISE OF THE F WORD

MARY SHERRY

Mary Sherry, who teaches basic grammar and writing to adults, wrote this essay for Newsweek *that criticizes the public schools for graduating semiliterate students.*

AS YOU READ:

Notice how Sherry uses her own son as evidence to support her view that flunking or threatening to flunk students is a positive teaching tool.

1   Tens of thousands of eighteen-year-olds will graduate this year and be handed meaningless diplomas. These diplomas won't look any different from those awarded their luckier classmates. Their <u>validity</u> will be questioned only when their employers discover that these graduates are semiliterate.

2   Eventually a fortunate few will find their way into educational-repair shops—adult-literacy programs, such as the one where I teach basic grammar and writing. There, high-school graduates and high-school dropouts pursuing graduate-equivalency certificates will learn the skills they should have learned in school. They will also discover they have been cheated by our educational system.

3   As I teach, I learn a lot about our schools. Early in each session I ask my students to write about an unpleasant experience they had in school. No writers' block here! "I wish someone would have had made me stop doing drugs and made me study." "I liked to party and no one seemed to care." "I was a good kid and didn't cause any trouble, so they just passed me along even though I didn't read well and couldn't write." And so on.

4   I am your basic do-gooder, and prior to teaching this class I blamed the poor academic skills our kids have today on drugs, divorce and other <u>impediments</u> to concentration necessary for doing well in school. But, as

Words to Know

validity authority or value

impediments barriers

trump card valuable playing card held until needed

composure calmness

perceive see

I rediscover each time I walk into the classroom, before a teacher can expect students to concentrate, he has to get their attention, no matter what distractions may be at hand. There are many ways to do this, and they have much to do with teaching style. However, if style alone won't do it, there is another way to show who holds the winning hand in the classroom. That is to reveal the <u>trump card</u> of failure.

I will never forget a teacher who played that card to get the attention of one of my children. Our youngest, a world-class charmer, did little to develop his intellectual talents but always got by. Until Mrs. Stifter.

Our son was a high-school senior when he had her for English. "He sits in the back of the room talking to his friends," she told me. "Why don't you move him to the front row?" I urged, believing the embarrassment would get him to settle down. Mrs. Stifter looked at me steely-eyed over her glasses. "I don't move seniors," she said. "I flunk them." I was flustered. Our son's academic life flashed before my eyes. No teacher had ever threatened him with that before. I regained my <u>composure</u> and managed to say that I thought she was right. By the time I got home I was feeling pretty good about this. It was a radical approach for these times, but, well, why not? "She's going to flunk you," I told my son. I did not discuss it any further. Suddenly English became a priority in his life. He finished out the semester with an A.

I know one example doesn't make a case, but at night I see a parade of students who are angry and resentful for having been passed along until they could no longer even pretend to keep up. Of average intelligence or better, they eventually quit school, concluding they were too dumb to finish. "I should have been held back," is a comment I hear frequently. Even sadder are those students who are high-school graduates who say to me after a few weeks of class, "I don't know how I ever got a high-school diploma."

Passing students who have not mastered the work cheats them and the employers who expect graduates to have basic skills. We excuse this dishonest behavior by saying kids can't learn if they come from terrible environments. No one seems to stop to think that—no matter what environments they come from—most kids don't put school first on their list unless they <u>perceive</u> something is at stake. They'd rather be sailing.

Many students I see at night could give expert testimony on unemployment, chemical dependency, abusive relationships. In spite of these difficulties, they have decided to make education a priority. They are motivated by the desire for a better job or the need to hang on to the one they've got. They have a healthy fear of failure.

People of all ages can rise above their problems, but they need to have a reason to do so. Young people generally don't have the maturity to value education in the same way my adult students value it. But fear of failure, whether economic or academic, can motivate both.

Flunking as a regular policy has just as much merit today as it did two generations ago. We must review the threat of flunking and see it as it really is—a positive teaching tool. It is an expression of confidence by both teachers and parents that the students have the ability to learn the material presented to them. However, making it work again would take a dedicated, caring conspiracy between teachers and parents. It would mean facing the tough reality that passing kids who haven't learned the material—while it

5

6

7

8

9

10

11

might save them grief for the short term—dooms them to long-term illiteracy. It would mean that teachers would have to follow through on their threats, and parents would have to stand behind them, knowing their children's best interests are indeed at stake. This means no more doing Scott's assignments for him because he might fail. No more passing Jodi because she's such a nice kid.

12   This is a policy that worked in the past and can work today. A wise teacher . . . gave our son the opportunity to succeed—or fail. It's time we return this choice to all students.

CRITICAL THINKING AND DISCUSSION

Get Thinking and Writing

Understanding Meaning: What Is the Writer Trying to Say?

1. Why does Sherry view flunking as a valuable teaching tool?
2. How do her students recall their high school experiences?
3. How have schools, in Sherry's view, failed students and society?
4. *Critical thinking:* Why does Sherry view flunking as "positive"? What does flunking suggest about student potential? How can it motivate students?

Evaluating Strategy: How Does the Writer Say It?

1. Sherry presents herself both as a teacher and a parent of a student threatened with flunking. Why is this important in persuading readers who might object to flunking students?
2. How does Sherry use her son as evidence for her argument?

Appreciating Language: What Words Does the Writer Use?

1. Sherry calls herself a *do-gooder.* What does this term imply?
2. Sherry suggests what is needed is a "caring conspiracy between teachers and parents." Is *conspiracy* an odd term to use? Do we usually associate it with evil or criminal plots? What impact does this word have?

Writing Suggestions

1. Write an essay about flunking that agrees or disagrees with Sherry's thesis. Use examples from your own high school experiences.
2. *Collaborative writing:* Work with a group of students to develop an essay that persuades readers of other changes that should be made in public schools to motivate students to learn.

A Writer's Guide to Overcoming Common Errors

Basic Sentence Structure

A sentence is a group of words that contains a subject and verb and states a complete thought.

Phrases and Clauses

Phrases are groups of related words that form parts of a sentence:

After the game   Ted and Carlos   are willing to   decorate for the party. the gym

Clauses consist of related words that contain both a subject and a verb:

- Independent clauses contain a subject and verb and express a complete thought. They are sentences:

  I waited for the bus.   It began to rain.

- Dependent clauses contain a subject and verb but do not express a complete thought. They are not sentences:

  While I waited for the bus

  Dependent clauses have to be connected to an independent clause to create a sentence that expresses a complete thought:

  While I waited for the bus, *it began to rain.*

Types of Sentences

Sentence types are determined by the number and kind of clauses they contain. A simple sentence consists of a single independent clause:

Jim sings.
Jim and Nancy sing and dance at the newly opened El Morocco.
Seeking to reenter show business, Jim and Nancy sing and dance at the newly opened El Morocco, located at 55th Street and Second Avenue.

A compound sentence contains two or more independent clauses but no dependent clauses:

Jim studied dance at Columbia; Nancy studied music at Juilliard.
    [two independent clauses joined by a semicolon]

Jim wants to stay in New York, but Nancy longs to move to California.
    [two independent clauses joined with a comma and coordinating conjunction]

A complex sentence contains one independent clause and one or more dependent clauses:

Jim and Nancy are studying drama *because they want to act on Broadway.*
Because they want to act on Broadway, **Jim and Nancy are studying drama.**
    [When a dependent clause begins a complex sentence, it is set off with a comma.]

A compound-complex sentence contains at least two independent clauses and one or more dependent clauses:

> **Jim and Nancy perform Sinatra classics,** and **they often dress in forties clothing** *because the El Morocco draws an older crowd.*

> *Because the El Morocco draws an older crowd,* **Jim and Nancy perform Sinatra classics,** and **they often dress in forties clothing.**

The Parts Of Speech

Nouns	**name persons, places, things, or ideas:**
	teacher, attic, Italy, book, liberty
Pronouns	**take the place of nouns:**
	he, she, they, it, this, that, what, which, hers, their
Verbs	**express action:**
	buy, sell, run, walk, create, think, feel, wonder, hope, dream
	link ideas:
	is, are, was, were
Adjectives	**add information about nouns or pronouns:**
	a **red** car, a **bright** idea, a **lost** cause
Adverbs	**add information about verbs:**
	drove **recklessly,** sell **quickly, angrily** denounced
	add information about adjectives:
	very old teacher, **sadly** dejected leader
	add information about other adverbs:
	rather hesitantly remarked
Prepositions	**link nouns and pronouns, expressing relationships between related words:**
	in the house, **around** the corner, **between** the acts, **through** the evening
Conjunctions	**link related parts of a sentence:**
	Coordinating conjunctions link parts of equal value:
	and, or, yet, but, so, for, nor
	He went to college, **and** she got a job.
	Subordinating conjunctions link dependent or less important parts:
	When he went to college, she got a job.

Interjections	express emotion or feeling that is not part of the basic sentence and are set off with commas or used with exclamation points:
	Oh, he's leaving? **Wow!**

Words can function as different parts of speech:

I bought more **paint** [noun].
I am going to **paint** [verb] the bedroom.
Those supplies are stored in the **paint** [adjective] room.

Parts of speech can be single words or phrases, groups of related words that work together:

Tom and his entire staff [noun phrase]
wrote and edited [verb phrase]
throughout the night. [prepositional phrase]

Sentence Errors

Fragments

Fragments are incomplete sentences. They lack a subject, lack a complete verb, or fail to express a complete thought:

Subject Missing
Worked all night. [Who worked *all night?*]

Revised
He worked all night.

Verb Missing
Juan the new building. [What was *Juan doing?*]

Revised
Juan designed the new building.

Incomplete Verb
Juan designing the new building. [*-ing* verbs cannot stand alone.]

Revised
Juan is designing the new building.

Incomplete Thought
Although Juan designed the building. [It has a subject and verb but fails to express a whole idea.]

Revised
Juan designed the building.
or
Although Juan designed the building, he did not receive any recognition.

Correcting Fragments

There are two ways of correcting fragments.

1. **Turn the fragment into a complete sentence by making sure it expresses a complete thought:**

    Fragments
    Yale being the center for this research
    Based on public opinion surveys

    Revised
    Yale is the center for this research. [complete verb added]
    The new study is based on public opinion surveys. [subject and verb added]

2. **Attach the fragment to a sentence to state a complete thought.**
    (Fragments often occur when you write quickly and break off part of a sentence.)

    Fragments
    He bought a car. While living in Florida.
    Constructed in 1873. The old church needs major repairs.

    Revised
    He bought a car while living in Florida.
    Constructed in 1873, the old church needs major repairs.

POINT TO REMEMBER

Reading out loud can help identify fragments. Ask yourself, "Does this statement express a complete thought?"

Run-ons

Fused Sentences

Fused sentences lack the punctuation needed to join two independent clauses. The two independent clauses are fused, or joined, without a comma and a coordinating conjunction or a semicolon:

Travis entered the contest he won first prize.
Nancy speaks Spanish she has trouble reading it.

Revised
Travis entered the contest; he won first prize.
Nancy speaks Spanish, **but** she has trouble reading it.

Comma Splices

Comma splices are compound sentences where a comma—without a coordinating conjunction—is used instead of a semicolon:

My sister lives in Chicago, my brother lives in New York.
The lake is frozen solid, it is safe to drive on.

Revised

My sister lives in Chicago; my brother lives in New York.

The lake is frozen solid, **so** it is safe to drive on.

Identifying Run-ons

To identify run-ons, do two things:

1. **Read the sentence carefully, and determine if it is a compound sentence. Ask yourself if you can divide the sentence into two or more independent clauses (simple sentences):**

    Sam entered college but dropped out after six months.

    Sam entered college . . . [independent clause (simple sentence)]
    dropped out after six months. [not a sentence]
                        [not a compound sentence]

    Nancy graduated in May she signed up for summer courses.

    Nancy graduated in May . . . [independent clause (simple sentence)]

    she signed up for summer courses. [independent clause (simple sentence)]
                        [compound sentence]

2. **If you have two complete sentences, determine if they should be joined. Is there a logical relationship between them? What is the best way to connect them? Independent clauses can be joined with a comma and *and, or, yet, but, so, for, nor,* or with a semicolon:**

    Nancy graduated in May, **but** she signed up for summer courses.

    But indicates a contrast between two ideas. Be sure to insert a comma before the coordinating conjunction to quickly repair this run-on.

Repairing Run-ons: Minor Repairs

A fused sentence or comma splice may need only a minor repair. Sometimes in writing quickly, we mistakenly use a comma when a semicolon is needed:

The Senate likes the president's budget, the House still has questions.

Revised

The Senate likes the president's budget; the House still has questions.

In other cases we may forget a coordinating conjunction:

The Senate likes the president's budget, the House still has questions.
Senators approve of the budget, they want to meet with the president's staff.

Revised

The Senate likes the president's budget, **but** the House still has questions.
Senators approve of the budget, **and** they want to meet with the president's staff.

Repairing Run-ons: Major Repairs

Some run-ons require major repairs. Sometimes we create run-ons when our ideas are not clearly stated or fully thought out:

> Truman was president at the end of the war the United States dropped the atomic bomb.

Adding the necessary comma and coordinating conjunction eliminates a mechanical error but leaves the sentence awkward and unclear:

> Truman was president at the end of the war, **and** the United States dropped the atomic bomb.

Repairing this kind of run-on requires critical thinking. A compound sentence joins two complete thoughts, and there should be a clear relationship between them. It may be better to revise the entire sentence, changing it from a compound to a complex sentence:

Revised

> Truman was president at the end of the war **when** the United States dropped the atomic bomb.

In some instances you may find it easier to break the run-on into two simple sentences, especially if there is no strong relationship between the main ideas:

> Swansea is a port city in Wales that was severely bombed in World War II Dylan Thomas was born there in 1914.

Revised

> Swansea is a port city in Wales that was severely bombed in World War II. Dylan Thomas was born there in 1914.

POINT TO REMEMBER

A compound sentence should join independent clauses that state ideas of equal importance. Avoid using an independent clause to state a minor detail that could be contained in a dependent clause or a phrase:

Awkward

> My brother lives in Boston, and he is an architect.

Revised

> My brother, who lives in Boston, is an architect.
> My brother in Boston is an architect.

Modifiers

Dangling Modifiers

Modifiers that serve as introductions must describe what follows the comma. When they do not, they "dangle," so it is unclear what they modify:

Grounded by fog, airport officials ordered passengers to deplane.
> [Were airport officials *grounded by fog?*]

Revised
> **Grounded by fog,** *the passengers* were ordered by airport officials to deplane.
> Airport officials ordered passengers to deplane *the aircraft* **grounded by fog.**

Strategy to Detect Dangling Modifiers

Sentences with opening modifiers set off by commas fit this pattern:

Modifier, main sentence

To make sure the sentence is correct, use the following test:

1. Read the sentence; then turn the modifier into a question, asking who or what in the main sentence is performing the action:

   question, answer

2. What follows the comma forms the answer. If the answer is appropriate, the construction is correct:

   Hastily constructed, the bridge deteriorated in less than a year.

   Question: *What was hastily constructed?*
   Answer: *the bridge*
   This sentence is <u>correct.</u>

   Suspected of insanity, the defense attorney asked that her client be examined by psychiatrists.

   Question: *Who was suspected of insanity?*
   Answer: *the defense attorney*
   This sentence is <u>incorrect</u>.

Revised
> **Suspecting her client to be insane,** *the defense attorney* asked that he be examined by psychiatrists.

Misplaced Modifiers

Place modifying words, phrases, and clauses as near as possible to the words they describe:

Confusing

Scientists developed new chips for laptop computers **that cost less than fifty cents.**

[Do laptop computers *cost less than fifty cents?*]

Revised

Scientists developed laptop *computer chips* **that cost less than fifty cents.**

Faulty Parallelism

When you create pairs or lists, the words or phrases must match—they have to be all nouns, all adjectives, all adverbs, or all verbs in the same form:

Nancy is **bright, creative,** and **funny.** [adjectives]
Mary writes **clearly, directly,** and **forcefully.** [adverbs]
Reading and **calculating** are critical skills for my students. [gerunds]
She should **lose weight, stop smoking,** and **limit her intake of alcohol.**
[verbs matching with *should*]

The following sentences are not parallel:

The concert was loud, colorful, and many people attended.
[*many people attended* does not match with the adjectives *loud* and *colorful.*]
John failed to take notes, refused to attend class, and his final exam is unreadable.
[*his final exam is* does not match the verb phrases *failed to take* and *refused to attend.*]
Quitting smoking and daily exercise are important.
[*Quitting,* a gerund, does not match with *daily exercise.*]

Revised

The concert was **loud, colorful,** and **well attended.** [all adjectives]
John **failed** to take notes, **refused** to attend class, and **wrote** an almost unreadable final exam. [all verbs]
Quitting smoking and **exercising** daily are important.
[both gerunds or *-ing* nouns]

Strategies for Detecting and Revising Faulty Parallelism

Apply this simple test to any sentences that include pairs or lists of words or phrases to make sure that they are parallel:

1. Read the sentence and locate the pair or list.

2. **Make sure that each item matches the format of the basic sentence by testing each item.**

Examples:

Students should read directions carefully, write down assignments accurately, and take notes.

> Students should *read directions.*
> Students should *write down assignments accurately.*
> Students should *take notes.*
>
> > [Each item matches *Students should* . . .]
> > *This sentence is* <u>parallel</u>.

Computer experts will have to make more precise predictions in the future to reduce waste, create more accurate budgets, and public support must be maintained.

> Computer experts will have to *make more precise* . . .
> Computer experts will have to *create more accurate* . . .
> Computer experts will have to *public support must be* . . .
>
> > [The last item does not link with *will have to.*]
> > *This sentence is* <u>not parallel</u>.

A Tip On Parallelism

In many cases it is difficult to revise long sentences that are not parallel:

> To build her company, Shireen Naboti is a careful planner, skilled supervisor, recruits talent carefully, monitors quality control, and is a lobbyist for legal reform.

If you have trouble making all the elements match, it may be simpler to break it up into two or even three separate sentences:

> To build her company, Shireen Naboti is a careful planner, skilled supervisor, and lobbyist for legal reform. In addition, she recruits talent carefully and monitors quality control.

The first sentence contains the noun phrases; the second consists of the two verb phrases. It is easier to create two short parallel lists than one long one.

Verbs

Subject-Verb Agreement

Singular subjects require singular verbs:

The **boy** *walks* to school.
Your **bill** *is* overdue.

Plural subjects require plural verbs:

The **boys** *walk* to school.
Your **bills** *are* overdue.

Changing a verb from singular to plural changes the meaning of a sentence:

Singular
The **desk and chair** *is* on sale.   [The desk and chair is sold as one item.]

Plural
The **desk and chair** *are* on sale.   [The desk and chair are sold separately.]

Rules for Forming Plural Nouns

- **Not all nouns add an -s to become plural:**

  The **deer** *run* across the road.   The **women** *play* cards.

- **Some nouns that end in -s and look like plurals are singular:**

  Mathematics *is* my toughest course.   **Economics** *demands* accurate data.

- **Some nouns that may refer to one item are plural:**

  My **scissors** *are* dull.   *Are* these your **pants?**

- **Proper nouns that look plural are singular if they are names of companies, organizations, or titles of books, movies, television shows, or works of art:**

  General Motors *is* building   *The Three Musketeers is* funny.
  a new car.

- **Units of time and amounts of money are generally singular:**

  Twenty-five dollars *is* a lot for   **Two weeks** *is* not enough time.
  a T-shirt.

  They appear as plurals to indicate separate items:

  Three dollars *were* lying on.   **My last weeks** at camp *were*
  the table   unbearable.

- **Group nouns—*audience, board, class, committee, jury, number, team,* and so on—are singular when they describe a group working together:**

  "**Faculty** *Accepts* Offer"   [headline describing teachers
  acting as a group]

  "**Faculty** *Protest* Offer"   [headline describing teachers
  acting individually]

- Verbs in "either . . . or" sentences can be singular or plural. If both subjects are singular, the verb is singular:

Either the **father** or the **mother** *is* required to appear in court.

If both subjects are plural, the verb is plural:

Either the **parents** or the **attorneys** *are* required to appear in court.

If one subject is plural and one is singular, the subject closer to the verb determines whether it is singular or plural:

Either the **parent** or the **attorneys** *are* required to appear in court.
Either the **parents** or the **attorney** *is* required to appear in court.

- Indefinite pronouns can be singular or plural.

Singular indefinite pronouns:

another	each	everything	nothing
anybody	either	neither	somebody
anyone	everybody	nobody	someone

Anything *is* possible.   **Someone** *is* coming.

Plural indefinite pronouns:

both	few	many	several

Both *are* here.   **Many** *are* missing.

Indefinite pronouns that can be singular or plural:

all	some	more	most

Snow fell last night, but **most** *has* melted.   [*Most* refers to the singular *snow.*]

Passengers were injured, but **most** have recovered.   [*Most* refers to the plural *passengers.*]

Verb Tense

Regular Verbs

Most verbs show tense changes by adding *-ed* to words ending with consonants and *-d* to words ending with an *e:*

Present	Past	Past Participle
walk	walked	walked
create	created	created
cap	capped	capped

Irregular Verbs

Irregular verbs do not follow the -ed pattern.

Some irregular verbs make no spelling change to indicate shifts in tense:

Present	Past	Past Participle
cost	cost	cost
cut	cut	cut
fit	fit	fit
hit	hit	hit
hurt	hurt	hurt
put	put	put

Most irregular verbs make a spelling change rather than adding -ed:

Present	Past	Past Participle
arise	arose	arisen
awake	awoke	awoken
be	was, were	been
bear	bore	borne (not *born*)
become	became	become
break	broke	broken
bring	brought	brought
build	built	built
choose	chose	chosen
come	came	come
dive	dove (dived)	dived
do	did	done
draw	drew	drawn
eat	ate	eaten
feed	fed	fed
fly	flew	flown
forgive	forgave	forgiven
freeze	froze	frozen
get	got	gotten
grow	grew	grown
hang (objects)	hung	hung
hang (people)	hanged	hanged
have	had	had
lay (place)	laid	laid
lead	led	led
leave	left	left
lie (recline)	lay	lain
lose	lost	lost
make	made	made
mean	meant	meant
meet	met	met
pay	paid	paid
ride	rode	ridden
ring	rang	rung

rise	rose	risen
run	ran	run
say	said	said
see	saw	seen
sell	sold	sold
shake	shook	shaken
shine	shone	shone
shoot	shot	shot
sing	sang	sung
sink	sank	sunk
sleep	slept	slept
speak	spoke	spoken
spend	spent	spent
steal	stole	stolen
sting	stung	stung
strike	struck	struck
swim	swam	swum
swing	swung	swung
take	took	taken
teach	taught	taught
think	thought	thought
throw	threw	thrown
understand	understood	understood
wake	woke	woken
write	wrote	written

Problem Verbs: Lie/Lay, Rise/Raise, Set/Sit

Lie/Lay

To lie = to rest or recline: "lie down for a nap"
To lay = to put something down or place into position: "lay a book on a table"

Present	Past	Past Participle
lie	lay	lain
lay	laid	laid

Remember: **Lie** *expresses action done by someone or something:*

Tom called 911, then **lay on the sofa** waiting for the paramedics.

Lay *expresses action done to someone or something:*

The paramedics **laid Tom** on the floor to administer CPR.

Rise/Raise

To rise = to get up or move up on your own: "rise and shine" or "rise to the occasion"
To raise = to lift or grow something: "raise a window" or "raise children"

Present	Past	Past Participle
rise	rose	risen
raise	raised	raised

Remember: **Rise** can refer to objects as well as people.

The bread **rises** in the oven.   Oil prices are **rising.**

Set/Sit

To set = to put something in position or arrange in place: "set down a glass" or "set down some notes"

To sit = to assume a sitting position: "sit in a chair" or "sit on a committee"

Present	Past	Past Participle
set	set	set
sit	sat	sat

Remember: **Set** always takes a direct object.

Shifts in Tense

Avoid awkward or illogical shifts in time, and write in a consistent tense:

Awkward

I **drove** to the beach and **see** Karen working out with Jim.
   past   *present*

Consistent

I **drove** to the beach and **saw** Karen working out with Jim.
   past   *past*

    or

I **drive** to the beach and **see** Karen working out with Jim.
   present   *present*

Change tense to show a logical change in time:

I **was born** in Chicago but **live** in Milwaukee. Next year I **will move** to New York.
   past   *present*   *future*

Change tense to distinguish between past events and subjects that are permanent or still operating:

He **was born** in Trenton, which **is** the capital of New Jersey.

Pronouns

Reference

Pronouns should clearly refer to specific antecedents. Avoid unclear references.

- Make sure that pronouns are clearly linked to antecedents—the nouns or other pronouns they represent. Avoid constructions in which a pronoun could refer to more than one noun or pronoun:

  Unclear
  Nancy was with Sharon when she got the news.
     [Who received the news—Nancy or Sharon?]

  Revised
  When Sharon received the news, she was with Nancy.

- Replace pronouns with nouns for clearer references:

  Unclear
  The teachers explained to the students why they couldn't attend the ceremony.
     [Who cannot attend the ceremony—teachers or students?]

  Revised
  The teachers explained to the students why faculty couldn't attend the ceremony.
  The teachers explained to the students why children couldn't attend the ceremony.

- State "either . . . or" constructions carefully:

  Either George or Jim can lend you their key.
     [George and Jim share one key.]

  Either George or Jim can lend you his key.
     [Both George and Jim have keys.]

  Either George or Anna can lend you a key.
     [avoids the need for *his or her*]

- Avoid unclear references with *this, that, it, which,* and *such:*

  Unclear
  Many people think that diets are the only way to lose weight.
  This is wrong.

  Revised
  Many people mistakenly think that diets are the only way to lose weight.

- Avoid unnecessary pronouns after nouns:

  Unnecessary
  Thomas Jefferson **he** wrote the Declaration of Independence.

  Revised
  Thomas Jefferson wrote the Declaration of Independence.

- Avoid awkward use of *you. You* is acceptable for directly addressing readers. Avoid making awkward shifts in general statements:

  Awkward
  Freeway congestion can give **you** stress.

  Revised
  Freeway congestion can be stressful.

Agreement

- **Pronouns agree in number and gender with antecedents:**

  Bill took *his* time.   **Nancy** rode *her* bicycle.   The **children** called *their* mother.

- **Compound nouns require plural pronouns:**

  Both the students and the teachers argue that *their* views are not heard.
  Tom and Nancy announced *they* plan to move to Colorado next year.

- **Collective nouns use singular or plural pronouns:**

  Singular
  The cast played *its* last performance.
    [The cast acts as one unit.]

  Plural
  The cast had trouble remembering *their* lines.
    [Cast members act independently.]

- *Either . . . or* **constructions can be singular or plural. If both nouns are singular, the pronoun is singular:**

  Either **the city council** *or* **the county board** will present *its* budget.
    [Only one group will present a budget.]

  If both nouns are plural, the pronoun is plural:

  The **board members** *or* the **city attorneys** will present *their* report.
    [In both instances, several individuals present a report.]

  If one noun is singular and the other is plural, the pronoun agrees with the nearer noun:

  Either the **teacher** *or* **students** will present *their* findings to the principal.

  Place the plural noun last to avoid awkward statements or having to represent both genders with *he and she, his or her,* or *him and her.*

- **Pronouns should maintain the same person or point of view in a sentence, avoiding awkward shifts:**

  Awkward Shift
  Consumers should monitor *their* use of credit cards to avoid getting in over *your* head in debt.
   third person   *second person*

  Revised
  Consumers should monitor *their* use of credit cards to avoid getting in over *their* heads in debt.

- **In speaking, people often use the plural pronouns *they, them,* and *their* to include both males and females. In formal writing, make sure that singular indefinite pronouns agree with singular pronouns.**

Singular

anybody	either	neither	one
anyone	everybody	nobody	somebody
each	everyone	no one	someone

Anybody can bring *his or her* tax return in for review.
Everybody is required to do the test *himself or herself.*

Plural

If **many** are unable to attend the orientation, make sure to call *them.*

Indefinite pronouns such as *some* may be singular or plural depending on context:

Singular

Some of the ice is losing *its* brilliance.

Plural

Some of the children are missing *their* coats.

Avoiding Sexism in Pronoun Use

Singular nouns and many indefinite pronouns refer to individuals who may be male or female. However, trying to include both men and women can create awkward constructions:

> If **a student** has a problem, *he or she* should contact *his or her* advisor.

In editing your writing, try these strategies to eliminate both sexism and awkward pronoun use:

- **Use plurals:**
  If **students** have problems, *they* should contact *their* advisors.

- **Revise the sentence to limit or eliminate the need for pronouns:**
  Students with problems should contact advisors.
  Advisors assist students with problems.

Adjectives and Adverbs

- **Understand the differences between adjectives and adverbs:**

She gave us **freshly** *sliced* peaches.
> [The adverb **freshly** modifies the adjective *sliced,* meaning that the peaches, whatever their freshness, have just been sliced.]

She gave us *fresh sliced* peaches.
> [The adjectives *fresh* and *sliced* both describe the noun, *peaches,* meaning that the peaches are both fresh and sliced.]

- Review sentences to select the most effective adjectives and adverbs. Adjectives and adverbs add meaning. Avoid vague modifiers:

  Vague
  The concert hall was **totally inappropriate** for our group.

  Revised
  The concert hall was **too informal** for our group.
  The concert hall was **too large** for our group.

- Use adverbs with verbs:

  Incorrect
  Drive careful. [adjective]

  Revised
  Drive **carefully**.

- Avoid unnecessary adjectives and adverbs:

  Unnecessary
  We drove down the old, winding, potholed, dirt road.

  Revised
  We drove down the winding, potholed road.

- Use *good* and *well,* and *bad* and *badly* accurately. *Good* and *bad* are adjectives and modify nouns and pronouns:

  The cookies taste **good**. [**Good** modifies the noun *cookies*.]
  The wine is **bad**. [**Bad** modifies the noun *wine*.]

  Well and *badly* are adverbs and modify verbs, adjectives, and adverbs:

  She sings **well**. [**Well** modifies the verb *sings*.]
  He paid for **badly** needed repairs. [**Badly** modifies the adjective *needed*.]

Comma ,

- Use commas with *and, or, yet, but, for, nor,* or *so* to join independent clauses to create compound sentences and avoid run-ons:

  Chinatown is a popular tourist attraction, and it serves as an important cultural center.

- Use a comma after a dependent clause that opens a complex sentence:

  Because the parade was canceled, we decided to go to the shore.

  If the dependent clause follows the independent clause, the comma is usually deleted:

  We decided to go to the shore because the parade was canceled.

- **Use a comma after a long phrase or an introductory word:**

  After breakfast with the new students and guest faculty, we are going to the museum.
  Yes, I am cashing your check today.

- **Use commas to separate words, phrases, and clauses in a series:**

  ### Words
  We purchased computer paper, ink, pens, and pencils.

  ### Phrases
  We purchased computer paper, ordered fax supplies, and photocopied the records.

  ### Clauses
  We purchased computer paper, Sarah ordered fax supplies, and Tim photocopied the records.

  If clauses contain commas, separate them with semicolons (see page 693).

- **Use commas to set off nonrestrictive or parenthetical words or phrases. Nonrestrictive words or phrases describe or add extra information about a noun and are set off with commas:**

  George Wilson, who loves football, can't wait for the Super Bowl.

  Restrictive words or phrases limit or restrict the meaning of abstract nouns and are not set off with commas:

  Anyone who loves football can't wait for the Super Bowl.

- **Use commas to set off contrasted elements:**

  The teachers, not the students, argue that the tests are too difficult.

- **Use commas after interjections, words used in direct address, and around direct quotations:**

  Hey, get a life.
  Paul, help Sandy with the mail.
  George said, "Welcome to the disaster," to everyone arriving at the party.

- **Use commas to separate city and state or city and country, items in dates, and every three numerals 1,000 and above (such as 4,568,908 dollars or 2,500 students):**

  I used to work in Rockford, Illinois, until I was transferred to Paris, France.
    [A comma goes after the state or country if followed by other words.]
  She was born on July 7, 1986, and graduated high school in May 2004.
    [A comma goes after the date if followed by other words. No comma is needed if only month and year are given.]
  The new bridge will cost the state $52,250,000.

- **Use commas to set off absolute phrases:**

  Her car unable to operate in deep snow, Sarah borrowed Tim's Jeep.
  Wilson raced down the field and caught the ball on one knee, his heart pounding.

- Use commas where needed to prevent confusion or add emphasis:

Confusing
Whenever they hunted people ran for cover.
To Sally Madison was a good place to live.
To help feed the hungry Jim donated bread.

Improved
Whenever they hunted, people ran for cover.
To Sally, Madison was a good place to live.
To help feed the hungry, Jim donated bread.

Reading sentences out loud can help you spot those sentences that need commas to prevent confusion.

Guide to Eliminating Unnecessary Commas

1. **Don't put a comma between a subject and verb unless setting off nonrestrictive elements or a series:**

   Incorrect
   The old car, was stolen.

   Correct
   The car, which was old, was stolen.

2. **Don't use commas to separate prepositional phrases from what they modify:**

   Incorrect
   The van, in the driveway, needs new tires.

   Correct
   The van in the driveway needs new tires.

3. **Don't use commas to separate two items in a compound verb:**

   Incorrect
   They sang, and danced at the party.

   Correct
   They sang and danced at the party.

4. **Don't put commas around titles:**

   Incorrect
   The film opens with, "Love Me Tender," and shots of Elvis.

   Correct
   The film opens with "Love Me Tender" and shots of Elvis.

5. **Don't put commas after a series unless it ends a clause that has to be set off from the rest of the sentence:**

Incorrect
They donated computers, printers, and telephones, to our office.

Correct
They donated computers, printers, and telephones, and we provided office space.

6. **Don't set off a dependent clause with a comma when it ends a sentence:**

Incorrect
The game was canceled, because the referees went on strike.

Correct
The game was canceled because the referees went on strike.

A comma is needed if a dependent clause opens the sentence:

Because the referees went on strike, the game was canceled.

Semicolon ;

Semicolons have two uses.

1. **Use semicolons to join independent clauses when *and*, or, *yet*, *but, for, nor,* or *so* are not present:**

   Olympia is the capital of Washington; Salem is the capital of Oregon.

   Remember to use semicolons even when you use words such as *nevertheless, moreover,* and *however*:

   They barely had time to rehearse; however, opening night was a success.

2. **Use semicolons to separate items in a series that contain commas:**

   The governor will meet with Vicki Shimi, the mayor of Bayview; Sandy Bert, the new city manager; the district attorney; Peter Plesmid; and Al Leone, an engineering consultant.

Apostrophe '

Apostrophes are used for three reasons:

1. **Apostrophes indicate possession:**

   | Noun | Erica's car broke down. |
   | Acronym | NASA's new space vehicle will launch on Monday. |

| Indefinite pronoun | Someone's car has its lights on. |
| Endings of *s, x,* or *z* sound | Phyllis' car is stalled. [or Phyllis's] |

Apostrophes are omitted from most geographical names:

Pikes Peak   Taylors Meadows   Warners Pond

Apostrophes may or may not appear in possessive names of businesses or organizations:

Marshall Field's Sears   Tigers Stadium Sean's Pub

Follow the spelling used on signs, stationery, and business cards.

2. **Apostrophes signal missing letters and numbers in contractions:**

Ted can't restore my '67 VW.

3. **Apostrophes indicate plurals of letters, numbers, or symbols:**

I got all B's last semester and A's this semester.
Do we have any size 7's or 8's left?
We can sell all the 2009's at half price.

Apostrophes are optional in referring to decades, but be consistent:

She went to high school in the 1990's but loved the music of the 1960's.

or

She went to high school in the 1990s but loved the music of the 1960s.

Common abbreviations such as TV and UFO do not need apostrophes to indicate plurals:

We bought new TVs and several DVDs.

POINT TO REMEMBER

it's	=	contraction of *it is*
		It's raining.
its	=	possessive of **it**
		My car won't start. Its battery is dead.

Quotation Marks " "

Quotation marks—always used in pairs—enclose direct quotations, titles of short works, and highlighted words:

• **For direct quotations:**

Martin Luther King said, "I have a dream."

Question marks and exclamation points precede the final quotation mark unless they do not appear in the original text:

Did Martin Luther King say, "I have a dream"?

Set off identifying phrases with commas:

Shelly insisted, "We cannot win unless we practice."
"We cannot win," Shelly insisted, "unless we practice."
"We cannot win unless we practice," Shelly insisted.

Commas are not used if the quotation is blended into the sentence:

They exploited the "cheaper by the dozen" technique to save a fortune.

Quotations within quotations are indicated by use of single quotation marks:

Shelly said, "I was only ten when I heard Martin Luther King proclaim, 'I have a dream.'"

Final commas and periods are placed inside quotation marks:

The letter stated, "The college will lower fees," but few students believed it.

Colons and semicolons are placed outside quotation marks:

The letter stated, "The college will lower fees"; few students believed it.

Indirect quotations do not require quotation marks:

Martin Luther King said that he had a dream.

- **For titles of short works:**

Titles of short works—poems, stories, articles, and songs—are placed in quotation marks:

Did you read "When Are We Going to Mars?" in *Time* this week?

Do not capitalize articles, prepositions, or coordinating conjunctions (*and, or, yet, but, so, for, nor*) unless they are the first or last words. (Titles of longer works—books, films, magazines, and albums—are underlined or placed in italics.)

- **To highlight words:**

Highlighted words are placed in quotation marks to draw extra attention:

I still don't know what "traffic abatement" is supposed to mean.
This is the fifth time this month Martha has been "sick" when we needed her.

Colon :

Colons are placed after independent clauses to introduce elements and separate items in numerals, ratios, titles, and time references:

The coach demanded three things from his players: loyalty, devotion, and teamwork.

The coach demanded one quality above all others: attention to detail.
The coach says the team has a 3:1 advantage.
I am reading *Arthur Miller: Playwright of the Century.*
The play started at 8:15.

Parentheses ( )

Parentheses set off nonessential details and explanations and enclose letters and numbers used for enumeration:

The Senate committee (originally headed by Warner) will submit a report to the White House.
The Federal Aviation Administration (FAA) has new security policies.
The report stated we must (1) improve services, (2) provide housing, and (3) increase funding.

Brackets [ ]

Brackets set off corrections or clarifications in quotations and replace parentheses within parentheses:

Eric Hartman observed, "I think [Theodore] Roosevelt was the greatest president."
Time noted, "President Bush told Frank Bush [no relation] that he agreed with his tax policies."
The ambassador stated, "We will give them [the Iraqi National Congress] all the help they need."
The company faced problems (sales dropped 50 percent in two years [2005–2006]).

Dash —

Dashes mark a break in thought, set off a parenthetical element for emphasis, and set off an introduction to a series:

Ted was angry after his car was stolen—who wouldn't be?
The movie studio—which faced bankruptcy—desperately needed a hit.
They had everything needed to succeed—ideas, money, marketing, and cutting-edge technology.

Hyphen -

A hyphen is a short line used to separate or join words and other items.

- **Use hyphens to break words at the end of a line:**

We saw her on tele-
vision last night.

Break words only between syllables.

- **Use hyphens to connect words to create compound adjectives:**

  We made a last-ditch attempt to score a touchdown.

  Do not use hyphens with adverbs ending in *-ly:*

  We issued a quickly drafted statement to the press.

- **Use hyphens to connect words forming numbers:**

  The firm owes nearly thirty-eight million dollars in back taxes.

- **Use hyphens after some prefixes:**

  His self-diagnosis was misleading.

- **Use hyphens between combinations of numbers and words:**

  She drove a 2.5-ton truck.

Ellipsis . . .

An ellipsis, three spaced periods [. . .], indicates that words are deleted from quoted material:

Original Text

   The mayor said, "Our city, which is one of the country's most progressive, deserves a high-tech light-rail system."

With Ellipsis

   The mayor said, "Our city . . . deserves a high-tech light-rail system."

Delete only minor ideas or details—never change the basic meaning of a sentence by deleting key words. Don't eliminate a negative word such as *not* to create a positive statement or remove qualifying words:

Original

   We must, only as a last resort, consider legalizing drugs.

Incorrect

   He said, "We must . . . consider legalizing drugs."

When deleting words at the end of a sentence, add a period before the ellipsis:

   The governor said, "I agree we need a new rail system. . . ."

An ellipsis is not used if words are deleted at the opening of a quotation:

   The mayor said "the city deserves a high-tech light-rail system."

If deleting words will create a grammar mistake, insert corrections with brackets:

Original

   "Poe, Emerson, and Whitman were among our greatest writers."

With Ellipsis

   "Poe . . . [was] among our greatest writers."

Slash /

Slashes separate words when both apply and show line breaks when quoting poetry:

The student should study his/her lessons.
Her poem read in part, "We hope / We dream / We pray."

Note: Place spaces around slashes when separating lines of poetry.

Question Mark ?

Question marks are placed at the end of a question and are used to note questionable items:

Did Adrian Carsini attend the auction?
Did you read "Can We Defeat Hunger?" in *Newsweek* last week?

Question marks that appear in the original title are placed within quotation marks. If the title does not ask a question, the question mark is placed outside the quotation marks:

Did you read "The Raven"?

Question marks in parentheses are used to indicate that the writer questions the accuracy of a fact, number, idea, or quotation:

The children claimed they waited two hours (?) for help to arrive.

Exclamation Point !

Exclamation points are placed at the end of emphatic statements:

Help!
We owe her over ten million dollars!

Exclamation points should be used as special effects. They lose their impact if overused.

Period .

Periods are used at the ends of sentences, in abbreviations, and as decimals:

I bought a car.
We gave the car to Ms. Chavez, who starts working for Dr. Gomez on Jan. 15.
The book sells for $29.95 in hardcover and $12.95 in paperback.

When an abbreviation ends a sentence, only one period is used. Common abbreviations such as FBI, CIA, ABC, BBC, and UCLA do not require periods.

Capitalization

- **Capitalize the first word of every sentence:**

  We studied all weekend.

- **Capitalize the first word in direct quotations:**

  Felix said, "The school should buy new computers."

- **Capitalize the first word, last word, and all important words in titles of articles, books, plays, movies, television shows, seminars, and courses:**

  "Terrorism Today"   *Gone with the Wind*   *Death of a Salesman*

- **Capitalize the names of nationalities, languages, races, religions, deities, and sacred terms:**

  Many Germans speak English.
  The Koran is the basic text in Islam.

- **Capitalize the days of the week, months of the year, and holidays:**

  We celebrate Flag Day every June 14.
  The test scheduled for Monday is canceled.
  Some people celebrate Christmas in January.
  We observed Passover with her parents.

  The seasons of the year are not capitalized:

  We loved the spring fashions.   Last winter was mild.

- **Capitalize special historical events, documents, and eras:**

  Battle of the Bulge   Declaration of Independence

- **Capitalize names of planets, continents, nations, states, provinces, counties, towns and cities, mountains, lakes, rivers, and other geographic features:**

  Mars   North America   Canada   Ontario

- **Capitalize *north, south, east,* and *west* when they refer to geographic regions:**

  The convention will be held in the Southwest.

  Do not capitalize *north, south, east,* and *west* when used as directions:

  The farm is southwest of Rockford.

- **Capitalize brand names:**

  Coca-Cola   Ford Thunderbird   Cross pen

- **Capitalize names of specific corporations, organizations, institutions, and buildings:**

  This engine was developed by General Motors.
  After high school, he attended Carroll College.
  We visited the site of the former World Trade Center.

- **Capitalize abbreviations, acronyms, or shortened forms of capitalized words when used as proper nouns:**

FBI	CIA	NOW	ERA
IRA	JFK	LAX	NBC

- **Capitalize people's names and nicknames:**

  Barbara Roth   Timmy Arnold

  Capitalize professional titles when used with proper names:

  Last week Doctor Ryan suggested that I see an eye doctor.
  Our college president once worked for President Carter.
  This report must be seen by the president.
     [The word *president* is often capitalized to refer to the president of the United States.]

  Capitalize words such as *father, mother, brother, aunt, cousin,* and *uncle* only when used with or in place of proper names:

  My mother and I went to see Uncle Al.
  After the game, I took Mother to meet my uncle.

POINT TO REMEMBER

A few capitalization rules vary. *African American* is always capitalized, but editors vary whether *blacks* should be capitalized. Some writers capitalize *a.m.* and *p.m.,* but others do not. Follow the standard used in your discipline or career, and be consistent.

Spelling

Commonly Confused Words

accept	*to take*	Do you **accept** checks?
except	*but/to exclude*	Everyone **except** Joe went home.
adapt	*to change*	We will **adapt** the army helicopter for civilian use.
adopt	*to take possession of*	They want to **adopt** a child.
adverse	*unfavorable*	**Adverse** publicity ruined his reputation.
averse	*opposed to*	I was **averse** to buying a new car.
advice	*a noun*	Take my **advice.**
advise	*a verb*	Let me **advise** you.
affect	*to influence*	Will this **affect** my grade?
effect	*a result*	What is the **effect** of the drug?
all ready	*prepared*	We were **all ready** for the trip.
already	*by a certain time*	You are **already** approved.

allusion	*a reference*	She made a biblical **allusion.**
illusion	*imaginary vision*	The mirage was an optical **illusion.**
all together	*unity*	The teachers stood **all together.**
altogether	*totally*	**Altogether,** that will cost $50.
among	*relationship of three or more*	This outfit is popular **among** college students.
between	*relationship of two*	This was a dispute **between** Kim and Nancy.
amount	*for items that are measured*	A small **amount** of oil has leaked.
number	*for items that are counted*	A large **number** of cars are stalled.
any one	*a person, idea, item*	**Any one** of the books will do.
anyone	*anybody*	Can **anyone** help me?
brake	*to halt/a stopping mechanism*	Can you fix the **brakes?**
break	*an interruption*	Take a coffee **break.**
	to destroy	Don't **break** the window.
capital	*money*	She needs venture **capital.**
	government center, a city	Trenton is the **capital** of New Jersey.
capitol	*legislative building*	He toured the U.S. **Capitol.**
cite	*to note or refer to*	He **cited** several figures in his speech.
site	*a location*	We inspected the **site** of the crash.
sight	*a view, ability to see*	The **sight** from the hill was tremendous.
complement	*to complete*	The jet had a full **complement** of spare parts.
compliment	*express praise, a gift*	The host paid us a nice **compliment.**
conscience	*moral sensibility*	He was a prisoner of **conscience.**
conscious	*aware of*	Is he **conscious** of these debts?
	awake	Is the patient **conscious?**
continual	*now and again*	We have **continual** financial problems.
continuous	*uninterrupted*	The brain needs a **continuous** supply of blood.
council	*a group*	The student **council** will meet Tuesday.
counsel	*to advise/advisor*	He sought legal **counsel.**
discreet	*tactful*	He made a **discreet** hint.
discrete	*separate/distinct*	The war had three **discrete** phases.

elicit	*evoke/persuade*	His hateful remarks will **elicit** protest.
illicit	*illegal*	Her use of **illicit** drugs ruined her career.
emigrate	*to leave a country*	They tried to **emigrate** from Germany.
immigrate	*to enter a country*	They were allowed to **immigrate** to the United States.
eminent	*famous*	She was an **eminent** eye specialist.
imminent	*impending*	Disaster was **imminent.**
everyday	*ordinary*	Wear **everyday** clothes to the party.
every day	*daily*	We exercise **every day.**
farther	*distance*	How much **farther** is it?
further	*in addition*	He demanded **further** investigation.
fewer	*for items counted*	There are **fewer** security guards this year.
less	*for items measured*	There is **less** security this year.
good	*an adjective*	She has **good** eyesight.
well	*an adverb*	She sees **well.**
hear	*to listen*	Can you **hear** the music?
here	*a place/direction*	Put the table **here.**
imply	*to suggest*	The president **implied** that he might raise taxes.
infer	*to interpret*	The reporters **inferred** from his comments that the president might raise taxes.
its	*possessive of* it	The car won't start because **its** battery is dead.
it's	*contraction of* it is	**It's** snowing.
lay	*to put/to place*	**Lay** the books on my desk.
lie	*to rest*	**Lie** down for a nap.
loose	*not tight*	He has a **loose** belt or **loose** change.
lose	*to misplace*	Don't **lose** your keys.
moral	*dealing with values*	She made a **moral** decision to report the crime.
morale	*mood*	After the loss, the team's **morale** fell.
passed	*successfully completed*	She **passed** the test.
past	*history*	That was in my **past.**
personal	*private/intimate*	She left a **personal** note.
personnel	*employees*	Send your résumé to the **personnel** office.

plain	simple/open space	She wore a **plain** dress.
plane	airplane/geometric form	They took a **plane** to Chicago.
precede	to go before	A film will **precede** the lecture.
proceed	go forward	Let the parade **proceed.**
principal	main/school leader	Oil is the **principal** product of Kuwait.
principle	basic law	I understand the **principle** of law.
raise	to lift	**Raise** the window!
rise	to get up	**Rise** and shine!
right	direction/correct	Turn **right.** That's **right.**
rite	a ritual	She was given last **rites.**
write	to inscribe	They **write** essays every week.
stationary	unmoving	The disabled train remained **stationary.**
stationery	writing paper	The hotel **stationery** was edged in gold.
than	used to compare	I am taller **than** Helen.
then	concerning time	We ate lunch **then** headed to class.
their	possessive of they	**Their** car has stalled.
there	direction/place	Put the chair over **there.**
they're	contraction of they are	**They're** coming to dinner.
to	preposition/infinitive	I went **to** school **to** study law.
too	in excess/also	It was **too** cold to swim.
two	a number	We bought **two** computers.
wear	concerns clothes/damage	We **wear** our shoes until they **wear** out.
where	a place in question	**Where** is the post office?
weather	climatic conditions	**Weather** forecasts predict rain.
whether	alternatives/no matter what	You must register, **whether** or not you want to audit the class.
who's	contraction of who is	**Who's** on first?
whose	possessive of who	**Whose** book is that?

Commonly Misspelled Words

absence	across	anonymous	athletic	believe
accept	address	apparent	attention	benefit
accident	adolescence	appreciate	attitude	breakfast
accommodate	advertisement	approach	basically	business
accumulate	a lot	arctic	basis	calendar
achieve	amateur	argument	beautiful	candidate
achievement	analysis	article	becoming	career
acquaint	analyze	assassination	beginning	carrying
acquire	annual	assistance	belief	celebrate

cemetery	field	libel	politician	situation
challenge	finally	library	positive	skillfully
characteristic	foreign	license	possession	sociology
column	forgotten	lightning	possible	sophisticated
coming	forty	loneliness	precede	sophomore
commitment	fourth	luxury	preference	special
committee	frequent	lying	prejudice	specimen
competition	friend	magazine	presence	stereotype
completely	frighten	maintenance	primitive	straight
complexion	fulfill	maneuver	probably	strict
conceive	fundamental	marriage	procedure	studying
consistent	further	martial	prominent	success
continually	generally	material	psychic	summary
control	generous	mathematics	psychology	surprise
controversial	government	meant	publicly	synonymous
criticism	gradually	mechanical	qualify	technique
curious	grammar	medieval	quality	temperament
dealt	grateful	mere	quantity	tenable
decision	guarantee	miniature	query	tendency
definite	guard	mischief	quiet	thorough
deliberate	guidance	misspell	quizzes	thought
dependent	happiness	mortgage	realize	throughout
description	height	necessary	recede	tomorrow
difficult	heroes	ninety	receive	tragedy
disappear	holocaust	noticeable	reception	tremendous
disappoint	huge	obligation	recognition	truly
discipline	humorous	obvious	recommend	unfortunate
discuss	hypocrite	occasionally	refer	uniform
dominant	identically	occupation	regulation	unique
dying	identity	occurred	relation	until
efficient	immediately	omit	religious	unusual
eighth	importance	operate	remember	useful
eligible	incidental	opinion	repetition	using
embarrass	independence	opportunity	responsible	usually
enough	influence	oppose	restaurant	vacillate
environment	intelligence	optimism	rhythm	vacillation
equipment	interest	ordinarily	ridicule	vacuum
essential	interpret	original	roommate	valuable
exaggerate	interrupt	paid	sacrifice	various
excellent	involvement	pamphlet	safety	vengeance
existence	irrelevant	parallel	scene	villain
experience	irresistible	particularly	schedule	violence
explanation	irresponsible	perform	seize	vulnerable
extremely	judgment	permanent	separate	weird
fallacy	judicial	permission	sergeant	whole
familiar	judicious	persistent	severely	writing
fantasy	knowledge	persuade	significance	yield
fascination	label	persuasion	significant	
favorite	laboratory	philosophy	similar	
February	language	physical	simplify	
feminine	leisure	playwright	sincerely	

List other words you often misspell:

_____   _____
_____   _____
_____   _____
_____   _____
_____   _____
_____   _____
_____   _____
_____   _____
_____   _____
_____   _____
_____   _____
_____   _____
_____   _____
_____   _____
_____   _____

Two Hundred Topics for College Writing

best friends	hobbies	MySpace	voting
gangs	foreign aid	goal for this year	adoption
fad diets	airport security	SAT	celebrity justice
job interviews	cruise ships	day care	favorite movie
athletes as role	blind dates	taxes	teen eating habits
models	exploring Mars	AIDS	cable TV bills
bad habits	being "in"	cults	minimum wage
child support	used cars	lawsuits	the president
NBA salaries	Osama bin Laden	sweatshops	health insurance
doctors	democracy	chat rooms	images of women
terrorism	being religious	drunk drivers	taking the bus
military spending	freeways	school prayer	discrimination
solar power	televised trials	commercials	TV moms
right to die	sitcoms	student housing	the Super Bowl
best teacher	cheating	wearing fur	pensions
car insurance	today's comics	work ethic	welfare reform
health clubs	drug prevention	eating disorders	the United Nations
shopping malls	ethnic stereotypes	insanity defense	being downsized
fashion models	lotteries	Internet	favorite singer

prenatal care
workaholics
cable news
parties
reality TV
school loans
women in combat
secondhand smoke
spring break
drinking age
coffee bars
outsourcing jobs
labor unions
married priests
nightclubs
gas prices
car repairs
plea bargaining
banks
lying
fast food
cable TV
fatherhood
racism
study skills
immigration
the Olympics
cell phones
property taxes
bilingual
    education
world hunger
slavery reparations
worst boss
binge drinking

the pope
college instructors
cyberspace
best restaurant
profanity in public
reporters
your mayor
Wall Street
shopping till you
    drop
overcoming de-
    pression
fraternities and
    sororities
racial profiling
casinos
prisons
hunting
online dating
steroids
YouTube
single parents
religion in public
    schools
animal testing
life after death
Hollywood
school choice
hate speech
suburbs
public schools
birth control
credit cards
funerals
toughest course

working out
Social Security
talk shows
heating bills
drug testing
aging population
summer jobs
stereotypes
car prices
affirmative action
moving
animal rights
living wills
marriage vows
reading
grandparents
plastic surgery
passion
dreams
family values
hospitals
best jobs
stalking
gay marriage
NFL
death penalty
pets
divorce
domestic violence
Iraq
gay bashing
MTV
Islam
sex on television
hip-hop music

glass ceiling
remembering 9/11
gun control
the homeless
soap operas
learning English
being in debt
relationships
dorm life
person you admire
surveillance
    cameras
sexual harassment
Letterman or Leno
rape shield laws
mortgage crisis
right to privacy
Internet pornog-
    raphy
biological weapons
downloading
    music
teaching methods
coping with illness
sexist or racist
    jokes
definition of
    success
drug busts
final exams
raising boys and
    girls

Odd-Numbered and Partial-Paragraph Answers to the Exercises in Chapters 3–35

CHAPTER 3

Exercise 1

1. People must take responsibility for their own health.
3. Throughout history, adults have identified popular culture as the cause of juvenile delinquency.

Exercise 2

1. c
3. a
5. a

Exercise 3

Answers vary.

Exercise 4

Answers vary.

Exercise 5

Today, college students have many alternatives to the traditional three-day-a-week lecture. Across the country, a growing number of students are taking advantage of new delivery systems.

Many of these students are working adults with families whose schedules prevent them from taking standard courses. Some work during the day or travel, making it difficult to even sign up for night school courses. Other students live at great distance from the nearest college offering the programs they need.

To meet the needs of these nontraditional students, colleges offer a variety of distance-learning opportunities. For decades many colleges have broadcast telecourses on cable or local PBS stations, allowing students to watch educational programs and mail in assignments. These courses are being supplemented with newer television technology that lets students interact with the instructor or other students. . . .

Exercise 6

Last summer I had what I thought would be an ideal summer job, working at a local cable TV station. I was fascinated with the high-tech control room and seeing

the reporters and sportswriters for the evening news.
I even hoped to see some athletes and celebrities who
did interviews on *News at Nine*. But I had no idea I
would have a boss like Cynthia Peterson to work with.

"Just do what I say, when I say it, and everything
will work out," she told me sternly at our interview.

"Great," I told her. "I've never worked in TV and
want to learn as much as I can."

"Good," she told me with a tight-lipped smile.
"First thing, take the webcast footage down to the
control room for me," she said, handing me a CD and
walking out of the room. . . .

CHAPTER 4

Exercise 1
Answers vary.

Exercise 2
1. b, c, d
3. a, b
5. a, c, d

Exercise 3
Answers vary.

Exercise 4
Answers vary.

Exercise 5
Answers vary.

CHAPTER 5

Exercise 1
Answers vary.

Exercise 2
Answers vary.

Exercise 3
Answers vary.

Exercise 4
Answers vary.

Exercise 5
Answers vary.

Chapter 6

Exercise 1
Answers vary.

Exercise 2
Within a few decades . . . as it was reaching its peak . . .
At that time . . . By the turn of the century . . .

Exercise 3
Answers vary.

Exercise 4
Answers vary.

Chapter 7

Exercise 1
1. Laws often have unintended consequences.
3. A law to ban smoking in the workplace, for instance . . .

Exercise 2
Answers vary.

Exercise 3
Answers vary.

Exercise 4
Answers vary.

Chapter 8

Exercise 1
Answers vary.

Exercise 2
Answers vary.

Exercise 3
Answers vary.

Chapter 9

Exercise 1
Answers vary.

Exercise 2
Answers vary.

CHAPTER 10

Exercise 1
Answers vary.

Exercise 2
Answers vary.

Exercise 3
Answers vary.

CHAPTER 11

Exercise 1
Answers vary.

Exercise 2
Answers vary.

Exercise 3
Answers vary.

CHAPTER 12

Exercise 1
1. X
3. X
5. X
7. X
9. C

Exercise 2
1. We can expect oil prices to increase over the next decade.

Exercise 3
1. The likely increase in oil prices will have dramatic effects on the economy, consumer behavior, and scientific research.

Exercise 4
Answers vary.

CHAPTER 13

Exercise 1

1. The college must overhaul its obsolete registration software if it wants to serve its students, project a good image to the community, and achieve President Neiman's enrollment goals.
3. a. [N]early one-third of students who registered off campus never appeared on official college rosters.
   b. Many were mailed packets of forms that arrived too late to sign up for needed courses.
   c. Twenty-six nursing students who received e-mail confirmations discovered they were never actually registered in clinical programs and had to delay graduation.
5. Student provides evidence that off-campus registration defeats President Neiman's enrollment goals.

Exercise 2

Answers vary.

Exercise 3

1. Facts, examples. Very reliable.
3. Testimony. Somewhat reliable. Lacks objectivity, biased.

Exercise 4

Answers vary.

Exercise 5

Answers vary.

CHAPTER 14

Exercise 1

Answers vary.

Exercise 2

1. High school football benefited the writer and made him a better student.
3. Provides evidence that football improved his health habits, taught him discipline, and increased his energy.
5. Most valuable lesson football taught him was maturity and responsibility.

Exercise 3

Answers vary.

CHAPTER 16

Exercise 1

Answers vary.

Exercise 2

Answers vary.

CHAPTER 17

Exercise 1

The most widely reproduced photograph in history is the flag raising on Iwo Jima taken by Joe Rosenthal on February 23, 1945. This photograph **inspired** the Marine Corps War Memorial in Washington, D.C. Initial confusion about how the picture **was** taken **caused** controversy that **lasts** to this day. Some people have discredited the photograph, insisting that the picture was posed and not really a news photo of a genuine historical event. They point out that it is not a picture of the original flag raising but a reenactment. Others insist that the photograph is genuine.

Much of the confusion **stems** from the photographer's initial comments. On February 23, 1945, a small American flag **was** flying atop Mt. Suribachi on the embattled island of Iwo Jima. The sight of the flag rallied the Marines locked in the bloodiest campaign in their history. It was decided to replace this flag with a larger one.

Joe Rosenthal, an AP photojournalist, **trudged** up the mountain with military photographers, one of whom carried a color movie camera. The Marines carefully **timed** the changing of the flags so that the second, larger one would be raised just as the smaller flag **was** lowered. Five Marines and a Navy corpsman began to raise the bigger flag, and Rosenthal **scrambled** to catch the moment. He **swung** his bulky camera into position and snapped a picture without having time to look through the viewfinder. Thinking he **missed** shooting the event, he **asked** the Marines to pose at the base of the flagpole. The Marines **clustered** around and **waved** at the camera. . . .

Exercise 2

Last month outbreaks of food-borne illnesses struck three Atlanta restaurants. In order to prevent problems in our outlets, I am reminding all managers to follow company food safety procedures. Yesterday fresh food **was** found left on loading docks for up to four hours. This is unacceptable. Fresh produce must be refrigerated on delivery. Last week inspectors **found** employees preparing food without washing their hands after clearing dirty dishes. When asked, the workers **explained** no one told them they had to wash their hands before entering food prep areas. . . .

Exercise 3

For fifty years, television news was dominated **by network** evening broadcasts. Tens of millions of Americans rushed home from work to see the day's events reported on television. With only three **networks**, **anchormen** such as Walter Cronkite and Huntley and Brinkley were popular and highly influential. Their coverage of civil rights demonstrations, assassinations, and moon landings shaped the way Americans thought of the country and themselves. The power of news anchors was summed up by President Johnson's comment: "If I've lost Cronkite, I've lost middle America." Infuriated by Cronkite's coverage of the Vietnam War, Johnson sometimes called CBS, demanding to speak to Cronkite during a commercial break. Cronkite was so powerful that he refused to take calls from the White House. . . .

Exercise 4

We reached San Francisco by noon and checked in to our hotel. We walked to Chinatown, where **we found** silk dresses, inlaid boxes, Chinese coins, and exotic prints at great prices. We then took a cab to Fisherman's Wharf. **Tourists** can take a boat to Alcatraz, where **they** can tour the old prison, which is now a national park. The trip is so popular that **visitors** should make reservations. We were lucky because it was a weekday, and we could get tickets. The trip is worth it. . . .

Exercise 5

Three of the most significant black leaders to emerge following the emancipation of the slaves were Frederick Douglass, Booker T. Washington, and W. E. B. DuBois.

Frederick Douglass was best known for his impassioned oratory against slavery. He was born a slave in 1817 and fled to freedom in 1838. He began a career in public speaking, denouncing not only slavery but also discrimination and segregation in the North. After publishing his autobiography, *Narrative of the Life of Frederick Douglass*, he went to England, where he continued to campaign against slavery. Friends raised money to purchase his freedom. Douglass returned to America and founded an anti-slavery newspaper called *The North Star*. During the Civil War, Douglass met with Lincoln several times and helped recruit blacks to serve in the Union Army. He served as the U.S. Minister to Haiti from 1889 to 1891. He died in 1895.

   Booker T. Washington is best known for his interest in education. Washington was born a slave in 1856 and taught himself to read. He founded the Tuskegee Institute, which stressed vocational skills, and the National Negro Business League, which encouraged black enterprise. Washington advised several presidents and addressed Southern politicians, urging them to provide jobs for blacks. His position that economic opportunities were more important than civil rights led to criticism from other black leaders. His organizations began to lose support after 1910. Washington died in 1915. . . .

Exercise 6

Answers vary.

CHAPTER 18

Exercise 1

1. Desi Arnaz was a band leader, singer, actor, and the husband of Lucille Ball.
3. At that time, TV comedies were broadcast live from studios in New York.
5. They suggested recording the show on film like a motion picture.
7. Desi helped pioneer a new way of recording a live performance using three cameras.
9. Desi agreed in exchange for owning the rights to the films.
11. Television was so new that few people understood the value of reruns.
13. A few years later, Lucy and Desi sold the films back to CBS for four million dollars.
15. For a while, Desilu was the largest studio in the world until Lucy and Desi divorced in 1960 and split the company.

Exercise 2

   Almost thirty years before 9/11, Samuel Byck planned to hijack a jet and use it as a weapon. Samuel Byck was a failed salesman. Emotionally unbalanced, he

blamed President Nixon for his personal problems. He
made threats against the president and sent strange
tapes to celebrities. The Secret Service took notice.
He picketed the White House and was arrested. When he
was denied a small business loan, Byck blamed Nixon.
He tape-recorded an elaborate plan called Operation
Pandora's Box. He obtained a gun and made a gasoline
bomb. He planned to hijack a commercial airliner and
force the pilot to fly over Washington. . . .

Exercise 3

1. Science fiction writers have imagined inventions long before they became practical realities. Jules Verne wrote about submarines and moon rockets in the nineteenth century. H. G. Wells described nuclear weapons in 1914.
3. In his 1932 novel *Public Faces,* Harold Nicholson envisioned rockets, much like modern cruise missiles, delivering atomic bombs. The blasts create tidal waves that cause global climate change.
5. In April 1944, *Astounding Science Fiction* published a story about an atom bomb. Readers rated it the worst story in that issue, but the story's details so closely resembled the top-secret atom bomb being developed by the Manhattan Project that the author was investigated by military intelligence.

Exercise 4

When it first appeared, the Internet was simply another way that news organizations broadcast their stories to the public. **By the** mid-1990s even small-town newspapers had online editions, which allowed them to reach a worldwide audience. The change was dramatic, and it presented publishers and broadcasters with a financial challenge. People could now read stories and see video online rather than buy a newspaper or watch a TV broadcast. **Media** owners are dependent on advertising revenue, and they feared a loss of income. Now there is another challenge, and it has to do with content. Blogs have turned regular citizens into columnists and journalists. **Popular** sites such as YouTube have become alternative networks where average citizens can post their camcorder clips of events. . . .

Exercise 5

Cinco de Mayo is widely celebrated by Mexican Americans throughout the United States. But what does it celebrate? It is not Mexican Independence Day! Mexico's equivalent of the Fourth of July is not the Fifth of May (Cinco de Mayo) but the Sixteenth of September. . . .

Exercise 6

1. Always put your name at the top of the page.
3. Reluctantly, Terry placed her badge and gun on the chief's desk.
5. Bravely, he clung to the raft, waiting for help.
7. Slowly, the overloaded plane lifted off the ground.
9. Thoughtlessly, the editor failed to check the facts of the story.

Exercise 7

Answers vary.

Exercise 8

1. Throughout history, world leaders have been concerned about their public image.
3. Beneath his heavy uniforms, Stalin hid a deformed arm.
5. By leaning on the arm of an aide and using a cane, he created the illusion that he could walk.
7. Before leaving his car or *Air Force One,* he would slip the lit cigar into his pocket.
9. Among other things, Kennedy hid his reading glasses from the public because he felt they detracted from his image of youth and strength.

Exercise 9

Answers vary.

Exercise 10

Every child in America has probably played with Crayola crayons. Edward Binney and Harold Smith founded the brand in 1903. Previously, they had developed dustless chalk that became a hit with schoolteachers and even received a gold medal at the St. Louis World's Fair. They visited schools and noticed the poor quality of wax crayons that children used for coloring. They added color to industrial wax markers and created an improved crayon for artwork. By combining the French word craie ("chalk") and *oleaginous* ("oily"), Binney's wife came up with the name "Crayola." . . .

Exercise 11

1. Having worked in my father's waste management company for four years, I have learned a lot about business.
3. Knowing that my father wanted to expand, I thought I would help him get new accounts.
5. Wanting to surprise my dad with a new account, I decided to work fast.
7. Writing up the offer, I hoped my dad would be proud of me.
9. Looking over my shoulder, he tapped the screen.

Exercise 12

1. Born in 1860, Charles Goodyear is credited with developing vulcanization, the process that revolutionized the use of rubber.
3. Subjected to cold or heat, rubber became brittle or melted.
5. Imprisoned for not paying bills after the store failed, Goodyear sought a new venture.
7. Obsessed with rubber, Goodyear endured poverty and illness to devote his time to experiments.
9. Brokenhearted by the death of his daughter and legal battles over his discovery, Goodyear died deeply in debt.

Exercise 13

1. The 1919 World Series and eight players became embroiled in scandal.
3. Chick Gandil, the first baseman for the Chicago White Sox, and Joseph Sullivan, a professional gambler, decided to fix the games.
5. Gandil and many other Chicago players resented White Sox owner Charles Comiskey, who was known for paying low salaries.
7. Eight White Sox players and gamblers conspired to fix the games so the underdog Reds would win an upset victory.
9. Shoeless Joe Jackson, the most famous player charged with throwing the games, and Eddie Cicotte first confessed, then retracted their confessions.

Exercise 14

1. Many scientific developments do not rely on a single person or depend on a single discovery.
3. Without a safe way of rendering a patient unconscious, however, doctors were limited to simple procedures and had to operate fast to prevent shock.
5. In the 1840s the discovery of ether allowed doctors to put patients to sleep and take time to perform complicated operations.
7. However, doctors at the time had no knowledge of germs and rarely bothered to wash their hands between operations.
9. Doctors began to accept the germ theory of disease in the late nineteenth century, introduced sanitary operating procedures, and sterilized their instruments.

Exercise 15

1. The Academy of Motion Pictures Arts and Sciences, a professional honorary organization, has some 6,000 members.
3. The organization is best known for awarding the Academy Award of Merit, the Oscar, to directors, actors, writers, and technicians.
5. Frederic Hope, Gibbons's assistant, designed the original black marble base.
7. There are many stories about how the award began to be called Oscar, a nickname.
9. From 1942 to 1944, the Academy presented winners with Oscars made of plaster, a wartime substitute.

Exercise 16

1. Daylight saving time, which is sometimes called Summer Time, is designed to extend daylight during working hours.
3. Advocates, who included economists, business leaders, and politicians, argued that daylight saving time would help farmers and reduce traffic accidents.
5. Daylight saving time, which was introduced during World War I, was unpopular.
7. Daylight saving time, which was again signed into law in 1942, was supposed to save energy for the war effort.
9. Japanese citizens, who greatly resented being forced to change their clocks, ended its use as soon as the U.S. occupation ended.

Exercise 17

Few moviegoers have heard of Oscar Micheaux, a pioneer African American filmmaker. Born in Illinois in 1884 to former slaves, he overcame many odds. Moving to South Dakota, Micheaux operated a homestead farm. He began writing stories. When no one was interested in publishing his work, Micheaux created his own publishing company, selling his books door to door. In 1919 he became the first African American to make a movie, *The Homesteader*, which was based on his novel of the same name. In 1924 he produced *Body and Soul*, starring Paul Robeson. Over the next three decades, Micheaux made forty movies. . . .

Exercise 18

1. Answers vary.

CHAPTER 19

Exercise 1

1. wear
3. illicit
5. raise
7. lose
9. already

Exercise 2

1. explanation
3. sarcastic
5. criminal
7. related to marriage
9. traditional

Exercise 3

Answers vary.

Exercise 4

1. During the Great Depression, people sought escape from unrelenting unemployment and business failures.
3. Charles Darrow developed a board game he called Monopoly, which allowed players to fantasize about wheeling and dealing properties like the Rockefellers and Vanderbilts.
5. Undaunted, Darrow manufactured Monopoly sets himself, which sold well in a local department store.
7. Parker Brothers purchased Darrow's game, and soon Monopoly was being played coast to coast.
9. Seventy years after its debut, Monopoly remains a popular pastime.

Exercise 5

1. After a long shift, I was tired and could not wait to get home to relax and cook dinner.
3. Sara and Andy were painting the room, but they ran out of paint and had to quit.
5. They were driving to work when they got a flat tire and had to hitchhike the rest of the way.

Exercise 6

1. In 1976 the Ebola virus **appeared** in the Sudan, signaling the presence of a previously unknown infectious agent.
3. NASA engineers reported consistent computer failures in the Mars rover that will cost **a great deal** to repair.
5. All **phone calls and e-mails** to customers may be monitored for adherence to **company rules.**

Exercise 7

Answers vary.

CHAPTER 20

Exercise 1

1. 155,554 (U.S. Census, 2000)
3. No. www.uwm.edu
5. Answers vary.

Exercise 2

1. F
3. T
5. T

Exercise 3

Answers vary.

Exercise 4

Answers vary.

CHAPTER 21

Exercise 1

Answers vary.

CHAPTER 22

Exercise 1

1. White House
3. John Adams
5. West Wing
7. building
9. Steel supports (plural)

Exercise 2

1. wallet
3. cards
5. number
7. number
9. numbers

Exercise 3

1. In 1938 . . . gimmick (subject) by a wallet company.
3. everyone (subject) . . . with a job . . . in his or her wallet or purse.
5. They (subject) inside each wallet . . . as a promotion . . . to department stores . . . around the country.
7. "Specimen" (subject) . . . across these cards.
9. The Social Security Administration (subject) . . . in major cities.

Exercise 4

The Southern Car Dealers' Association <u>holds</u> its annual convention in Atlanta next month. Given problems in the credit industry, rising gas prices, and general economic uncertainty, most of our members <u>report</u> declining sales. I (was) impressed by your appearance at the Bankers of America Council meeting in Chattanooga last month. Your motivational presentation (was) very inspiring. . . .

Exercise 5

Despite historical links to Spain, (many) of South America's leaders <u>are</u> of non-Spanish origin. (Ambrosio O'Higgins), born in Ireland, <u>emigrated</u> to Spain and <u>served</u> as viceroy of Peru from 1796 until his death in 1801. His (son), Bernardo O'Higgins, <u>became</u> the first leader of an independent Chile in 1817. (Bernardo O'Higgins) <u>created</u> the nation's military academy and <u>approved</u> the Chilean flag still in use. . . .

CHAPTER 23

Exercise 1
1. F
3. OK
5. F
7. F
9. F

Exercise 2
1. Bipolar disorder is also known as manic depression.
3. In their high or manic states, patients feel extremely confident, powerful, and energetic.
5. Although patients may announce plans to open businesses, launch new careers, or discover some new invention, they lack the ability to concentrate and experience agitation when questioned about the feasibility of their plans.
7. At other times patients slide into deep depression, feeling sad, lost, lonely, and inferior, leading them to quit jobs or drop out of school, believing they have no chance of success.
9. Bipolar disorder can be devastating, especially when patients make impulsive and illogical decisions in manic or depressed states.

Exercise 3
1. The Hollywood Walk of Fame attracts tourists visiting Los Angeles every year.
3. The first star on the Hollywood Walk of Fame honored Joanne Woodward in 1960.
5. Correct
7. The stars have five categories honoring accomplishments in radio, motion pictures, television, theater, and the recording industry.
9. Correct

Exercise 4
Emiliano Zapata was born in Morelos, Mexico, in 1879 to a family of independent ranchers. Although Zapata was known for wearing flashy clothing in his youth, he always maintained respect for the impoverished peasants. By thirty he had become a spokesperson for his village. Zapata championed the rights of Indians in Morelos. He assisted in the redistribution of land and defended the villagers' claims in property disputes with wealthy ranchers. Becoming increasingly frustrated by the government's bias in favor of wealthy landowners, Zapata began using force to seize land. He took a leading role in the 1910 Mexican Revolution, which deposed the Diaz regime, but was disillusioned with the new government's failure to address the needs for effective land reform. . . .

Exercise 5

```
   Having read your proposal, I am still concerned
about the fall concert tour. I fully understand your
desire to give your band the maximum exposure in the
month following the release of their first CD. But
I am concerned about the costs this tour might entail.
Because the Jersey Girls have never played outside
New York, I wonder if they can sell tickets in the
cities you list: Chicago, New Orleans, Miami, Dallas,
Los Angeles, and San Francisco. Personally, they
strike me as a regional group. . . .
```

CHAPTER 24

Exercise 1

Answers vary.

Exercise 2

1. The Brooklyn Bridge was an engineering triumph, but it claimed the lives of twenty-seven workers.
3. A rumor that the bridge was about to collapse caused a panic, and twelve people were trampled to death.
5. In 1886 Steve Brodie achieved instant fame when he claimed to have survived a jump from the Brooklyn Bridge, but most people believe that a dummy was used in the stunt.

Exercise 3

Answers vary.

Exercise 4

Answers vary.

Exercise 5

Answers vary.

Exercise 6

Answers vary.

Exercise 7

1. Basil Rathbone became internationally famous when he played Sherlock Holmes.
   When he played Sherlock Holmes, Basil Rathbone became internationally famous.
3. The boardwalk restaurants do well even in bad weather because tourists have to stay indoors when it rains.
   Because tourists have to stay indoors when it rains, the boardwalk restaurants do well even in bad weather.

5. Although it will be cheaper to build a new building, the alumni want to restore Old Main.

The alumni want to restore Old Main although it will be cheaper to build a new building.

Exercise 8

Answers vary.

CHAPTER 25

Exercise 1

1. RO
3. OK
5. RO
7. OK
9. OK

Exercise 2

<u>Last summer I learned a valuable lesson it really changed my life. I always wanted to do video production and I applied for several jobs at local TV stations</u>. WPIX had an internship program, and I was lucky to be one of six college students to be selected. <u>I was hired as a production assistant my job was to help a news crew load and unload their equipment and set up remote interviews</u>. Most mornings I would load up the van and ride to City Hall or Wall Street to shoot a press conference. On our way back from taping an interview with a Brooklyn real estate agent, we were sent to cover a house fire. . . .

Exercise 3

1. Employers try to measure an applicant's personality in a job interview by asking a range of questions.
3. Employers might ask them about their goals in life or favorite hobbies. They want to know if their personalities are suited to the corporate culture.
5. In many jobs people work as part of a team, and employers have to determine if the applicant will fit in with other employees.

Exercise 4

1. Before leaving home, millions of people slip cell phones into their pockets or purses; they are almost as common as credit cards and car keys.
3. The first American cell phone went on the market in 1983; it weighed two pounds and cost four thousand dollars.
5. Cell phones are actually two-way radios; they broadcast and receive messages.

7. A city, for example, is divided into overlapping cells; each cell has a base station with a sending and receiving tower.

9. Cell phones can now send text messages and pictures; like computers, they can become infected with viruses that steal passwords and address books.

Exercise 5

On March 11, 1918, a soldier at Fort Riley, Kansas, went to the base hospital complaining of fever and a sore throat; within hours, a hundred other soldiers reported the same symptoms. During the next few days, hundreds more were stricken with high fever, muscle and joint pain, and extreme fatigue. Many died. The disease then appeared in other army camps; in California hundreds of prisoners in San Quentin fell ill. The death toll mounted. At an army base near Boston, sixty soldiers died in one day.

By the summer, the disease was spreading across the country, and the government became alarmed. The sudden deaths of young men preparing to go to war led to wild rumors; many believed German submarines had brought the disease to America. Others blamed terrorists; they claimed spies were dispersing germs in movie theaters. . . .

CHAPTER 26

Exercise 1

1. DM
3. OK
5. DM
7. DM
9. OK

Exercise 2

Answers vary.

Exercise 3

Answers vary.

Exercise 4

Answers vary.

Exercise 5

1. MM
3. MM

5. MM
7. MM
9. MM

Exercise 6

Answers vary.

Exercise 7

<u>Predicted to reach four dollars a gallon</u>, WestTech, like all companies, must take steps to conserve fuel. Rising gas prices inflate our overall cost of doing business and make it harder for us to provide health insurance, which continues to rise as well. Because our current contracts do not expire until 2011, we cannot pass these fuel costs on to our customers until next year. <u>Determined to cope with this problem</u>, these recommendations are being made by the transportation committee:

1. Before heading to sales meetings downtown, employees should meet in the lobby to car pool.
2. <u>Wanting to stay in touch with the stores in distant malls</u>, e-mail updates should be used by sales reps. . . .

Exercise 8

1. Frank drives Karla, who is a lifeguard, to the beach every morning.
3. The landlord, who was angry about the broken windows, met with the tenant.
5. The insurance adjusters, who refused to pay any repair bills, met with the homeowners.

Exercise 9

Answers vary.

CHAPTER 27

Exercise 1

1. NP
3. OK
5. NP
7. NP
9. OK

Exercise 2

1. Few people have heard of Dr. Ignatz Semmelweis, but his work in the 1840s would change medical history, influence scientific thinking, and save the lives of millions.
3. At the time, doctors examined patients, performed operations, conducted autopsies, and delivered babies without washing their hands.

5. Semmelweis ordered caregivers to wash their hands before treating women or examining their newborns.
7. Other doctors scoffed at Semmelweis's ideas because they thought hand washing was a needless chore and resented his suggestion that they were spreading diseases.
9. Discredited and depressed, Semmelweis entered a mental institution, where he died at forty-seven.

Exercise 3

Answers vary.

CHAPTER 28

Exercise 1

1. applicants (subject)	use (verb)
3. expert (subject)	estimates (verb)
5. recruiter or headhunter (subject)	charges (verb)
7. advisors (subject)	recommend (verb)
9. way (subject)	is (verb)

Exercise 2

1. are
3. opens
5. was
7. seems
9. explains

Exercise 3

1. leads
3. demands
5. wants
7. were
9. are

Exercise 4

1. are
3. drives
5. were
7. see
9. is

Exercise 5

1. are
3. is
5. were
7. have
9. were

Exercise 6

Answers vary.

Exercise 7

Batang Engineering, along with its subsidiaries Ballard Productions and GMAX Design, is committed to developing practical, cost-effective solutions to the challenge of rising energy prices that faces our economy. We are proud to announce the development of a new product that revolutionizes solar power and provides a highly reliable and low-cost renewable power source:

SUN MAGNET

Sun Magnet is a lightweight, easily folded durable solar panel that is quickly unfolded and used to generate electricity. A one-pound sheet the size of a paperback book can be spread on the ground like a blanket to charge a cell phone, operate a radio, even run a laptop computer. . . .

Exercise 8

Answers vary.

CHAPTER 29

Exercise 1

 1. sang, sung
 3. lay, lain
 5. taught, taught

Exercise 2

 1. focus
 3. is, had
 5. felt
 7. planned
 9. became

Exercise 3

 1. raise
 3. set
 5. lie
 7. to raise
 9. lay

Exercise 4

I was born in Philadelphia, but I grew up in Haddonfield, where my parents moved when I was two. In high school I got a job working on the Jersey shore

```
helping an old guy sell trinkets on the boardwalk. It
was a great job because on my lunch hour I went swim-
ming and hung out with my friends on the beach. Being
sixteen or seventeen, I felt invincible and never wor-
ried about sunscreen and got a bad sunburn about once
a month.
    I went to college in San Jose, and my friends and
I took weekend trips to Vegas or the beach. I began to
use sunscreen but still forgot now and then. At that
time all I worried about was never letting any of my
friends drive drunk. . . .
```

Exercise 5

Answers vary.

Exercise 6

```
    When my roommate offered me a chance to go to San
Francisco on spring break, I should have asked her
for more details. But I was so excited I did not ask
her any questions. I just packed up my bags, helped
her load up the car, and hit the ATM. We were on the
road less than three hours when we were sidelined by
a bad tire. Cindy told me her credit card was maxed
out, so I ended up paying for a new tire. She had told
me we would stay at her brother's condo. He was sup-
posed to be going to Hawaii with his family and let
her stay there. But Cindy never bothered to call him
to confirm. . . .
```

CHAPTER 30

Exercise 1

1. Carmen showed her bicycle to Cindy and suggested that she fix it.
3. This street needs repairs.
5. Why doesn't Hollywood make movies I can take my kids to see?

Exercise 2

1. it
3. he
5. they
7. his
9. its

Exercise 3

1. We are moving the admitting nurse's desk to the north corridor, where the nurse can see people entering the main entrance.
2. Outpatients with appointments for lab work should go to the second floor, where they are required to sign in. . . .

Exercise 4

1. I
3. us
5. whom
7. us
9. her

Exercise 5

Then Sandy and I faced the problem of telling our
parents that we decided to move to Texas because she
wanted to go back to college. She needs to get her
degree; in her field everyone needs formal training
unless he or she wants to settle for minimum wage. I
knew this made sense, but it would be hard to tell her
parents we were turning down their offer of giving us
a house. Her parents' generosity is amazing. . . .

CHAPTER 31

Exercise 1

Boston One Bank has contacted us regarding their
<u>new</u> ATMs. These <u>electronic</u> machines, installed in
<u>retail</u> establishments throughout the city, have been
malfunctioning. In <u>rare</u> instances, they have failed
to record transactions and dispensed the <u>wrong</u> amount
of cash. The <u>original</u> design has been in use nationwide since 2003 with <u>few</u> <u>serious</u> malfunctions. . . .

Exercise 2

Answers vary.

Exercise 3

1. sliced, diced
3. corned, mashed
5. heated

Exercise 4

I <u>just</u> received your blueprints. Both the architect
and builder <u>firmly</u> agree that we need to make changes
to the lobby <u>immediately</u>. Because the building will
not open until 2012, it will have to meet the <u>newly</u>
revised fire code. I like the way you <u>greatly</u> expanded
the lobby entrance without sacrificing the sense of
intimacy. . . .

Exercise 5

Answers vary.

Exercise 6

1. extremely
3. unbelievably, accurate
5. devilish
7. extremely
9. mysteriously

Exercise 7

1. more tired
3. more hotly
5. happier

Exercise 8

1. Born in Alabama, Zora Neale Hurston grew up in Florida and later traveled north to attend Barnard College and Columbia University in the 1920s, when most black women had extremely limited educational opportunities.
3. Generously supported by patrons, Hurston traveled extensively throughout the South, as well as Haiti, Jamaica, and the Bahamas, to conduct research.
5. However, some critics found her homey stories about dialect-speaking African Americans unacceptably sentimental.
7. Hurston's objections to some aspects of the civil rights movement further alienated her critics.
9. Fifteen years later, an article by Alice Walker sparked interest in Hurston, and many scholars began to read this newly rediscovered author.

CHAPTER 32

Exercise 1

The city has granted us final approval, and we plan to begin work on May 15. Because we expect to operate without interruption this summer, we anticipate Phase One to be completed by October 30. However, we should plan for unexpected delays such as inclement weather, labor disputes, or late deliveries. In any event, if we are to meet our goals, we need assurance from you that you can provide us with all the roofing, plumbing, and electrical supplies by May 1. . . .

Exercise 2

1. Iran, which was known as Persia until 1935, is an important nation in the Middle East.
3. The country, which is a major oil producer, has had complex and often conflicting relations with the West.
5. The Shah, who saw himself destined to lead his country onto the international stage, launched the White Revolution, which expanded women's rights, redistributed land, and built schools.

7. The Shah was forced to leave Iran in 1979 by the Islamic Revolution, which led to the formation of an Islamic republic that was extremely hostile to the United States.

9. Many Iranians who live in the United States have nicknamed Los Angeles, which is now home to as many as half a million Iranian Americans, "Tehrangeles."

Exercise 3

1. The Great Wall of China consists of 1,500 miles of fortifications, walls, guard towers, and barracks in northern China.

3. Local residents were forced to build the wall, and many of them were killed by gangs of attacking bandits.

5. The wall was made of mostly stone and brick, although some portions in desert regions were constructed of wooden fences and earthworks.

7. Developers have bulldozed sections to make way for new construction, and farmers have taken stones for building materials.

9. In fact, shuttle astronauts have reported that they could make out the wall when in orbit a hundred miles or so above the Earth.

Exercise 4

For the past fifty years spring break has meant fun. After a semester and half of college, it was a time to find a warm place to party, to drink, to get away. For decades Florida resorts braced themselves for floods of rowdy college students, traffic jams, loud parties, and underage drinking. In their wake, college kids left behind trashed motel rooms, littered beaches, and millions of dollars in the cash registers of stores, bars, and clubs. With cheap flights, by the Eighties college students began breaking in Las Vegas, Mexico, and Jamaica. Some affluent types even jetted to Rio when spring break coincided with Carnival.

But in the last few years, college students have explored other options. Instead of partying, these young people have sought to dedicate a week of their lives to volunteering. Evangelical organizations have sponsored trips to rebuild Mississippi churches ravaged by Katrina. Environmental groups have recruited students to spend a week planting trees, installing solar panels on school roofs, and cleaning riverbanks. . . .

Exercise 5

1. The school hired a math teacher; Ted Hines, a web designer; Jan Price; and a reading specialist.   4

3. The class included my sister; Candy, her roommate; Tom Drake; Don Bernstein; Tom Price; Tom's sister; Carlos Abrams; an exchange student from Chile; a student from France; and me.   10

5. We considered our all-time favorite TV shows and came up with a long list, including <u>my favorite soap opera; Streets of San Francisco</u>, Sandy's favorite show; <u>Saturday Night Live</u> with Eddie Murphy; <u>LA Law; All in the Family</u>; the original <u>Twilight Zone</u>, Sid's choice; and, of course, <u>Star Trek</u>.

_____7_____

Exercise 6

1. The names Harry Horwitz, Jerry Horwitz, and Louis Feinberg are not well-known; however, their stage names, Moe, Curly, and Larry, are famous the world over.
3. The act got its name from Ted Healy, who originally billed them as "Ted Healy and his Stooges" in vaudeville houses.
5. The Stooges were immensely popular; audiences loved their slapstick comedy, wild stage antics, and colorful language.
7. The Stooges began a long run, making films on low budgets within a few days.
9. Columbia, however, found a new market for its library of old Stooge shorts; it sold them to television.

CHAPTER 33

Exercise 1

1. a boy's book
3. Frank Sinatra's songs
5. NASA's research
7. children's clothing
9. two women's store

Exercise 2

1. he's
3. he'd
5. couldn't
7. I'll
9. should've

Exercise 3

During renovation of the lobby's flooring, we will have to close the main entrance. This will, we realize, cause some inconvenience to both residents and visitors. According to the contractor's schedule, this work should take approximately one month to complete. The side entrances on 54th Street will be open, and a security guard will be posted to ensure residents' safety. In addition to these repairs, both the men's room and women's room on the lower level will be closed. Visitors can still access restrooms in the heath club. Because we'll have to shut down the

```
elevators on the west side of the building, the roof's
sun deck will not be available until June 30th. . . .
```

Exercise 4

1. Audrey told us she was getting married in June.
3. The course's new reading list includes John Cheever's "The Swimmer" and Albert Camus' "The Guest."
5. Did you read Jane Manton's story "We Can't Go On"?
7. Frank's comments included the remark, "We're going to see if he's willing to help us."
9. "I'm going to retire," Tom Watson told us, reminding us of his promise. "I will step aside as soon as my daughter's internship is completed."

Exercise 5

1. The Aug. 15 flight will leave at 10:25 a.m.
3. The college saw three challenges: declining enrollments, reduced funding from the state, and rising health-care costs.
5. Can I park here?
7. Jane Bush (no relation to the president) went to Iraq on behalf of the White House.
9. Tim and Nan's house was the only one damaged by the storm.

Exercise 6

```
    Josh Gibson, who was one of the greatest baseball
players in history, was born on December 21, 1911. He
was often called the "Babe Ruth of the Negro Leagues."
Because of segregation, Gibson could not try out for
major league teams. He became a star player in black
baseball, and he broke many records. Lacking accurate
statistics, historians question some claims made about
Gibson's career, though most agree he had a lifetime
batting average of .350, hit nearly 800 home runs, and
scored over eighty runs in a single season. . . .
```

CHAPTER 34

Exercise 1

1. Last April we decided to go to New Orleans instead of Florida for spring break.
3. We almost hit a UPS truck before I could park on the shoulder.
5. The service department at Southland Pontiac was open, so we pulled in and had the tire replaced.
7. We were back on the road within an hour and a half and crossed into Louisiana around three o'clock.
9. Traffic crawled along, but Karen popped in a Dixieland CD to get us in the mood.

11. New Orleans is called America's Most Fascinating City or the City That Care Forgot for good reason.

13. We parked at the Monteleone Hotel on Royal Street, dumped our bags in the room, took showers, changed into fresh clothes, and went out to explore the capital of the Old South.

15. We stopped for oysters Rockefeller and steamed clams, then went to the Napoleon House for drinks.

17. We walked through Jackson Square and the French Market, stopping off for some Irish coffee before heading back to the hotel.

19. Our friend Jerry, who insisted on going to Florida, called from the Daytona Hyatt.

Exercise 2

1. On October 16, 1869, workmen digging a well in Cardiff, New York, made an amazing discovery.

3. Visitors came from all over New York to see the ten-foot-high statue carved from stone.

5. Some believed the statue was carved by a Jesuit missionary to teach the Bible to Native Americans.

7. A Yale professor examined the giant, discovered fresh chisel marks, and announced it was a phony.

9. Newell, who conspired with Hull, then directed workers to dig a well, engineering the giant's "accidental" discovery.

11. Always eager to make money with a new exhibit, P. T. Barnum offered to lease the giant to display in his museum.

13. A hundred years later, another great showman, David Merrick, came up with another hoax that made Broadway history.

15. Merrick placed an ad in the *New York Herald Tribune* announcing that seven of New York's leading critics had raved about his play.

17. The ad was a stunt; the quotations were real but misleading.

19. After enjoying themselves with the famous producer, the seven New Yorkers praised his show and agreed to let him use their names and quote their favorable comments.

Exercise 3

```
    I am putting together next season's tour schedules.
To make the most of our budget, I think we should
skip August and start in late September. The Labor Day
event in St. Louis is not suited for any of our acts.
So far I worked on three acts: The Rocky Mountain
Boys, The Gun Molls, and Rene Ruiz.

    1. I suggest we send The Rocky Mountain Boys to the
       West Coast. They simply do not draw an Eastern
       audience.
    2. The Gun Molls, on the other hand, should receive
       maximum exposure. Their last DVD sold 1.2 mil-
       lion. In addition, Columbia is releasing a film
       called Taming the Falcon which includes two
       Gun Molls' songs in the soundtrack. The lead
```

singer, Myra Long, is scheduled to appear on
Letterman in September and may do Howard Stern
in October. . . .

CHAPTER 35

Exercise 1

1. grateful
3. safety
5. column
7. precede
9. dependent

Exercise 2

1. too
3. access
5. affected, morale
7. plain, lose
9. imply

Exercise 3

The Grammy Award is the most famous of <u>for</u> [four]
<u>discreet</u> [discrete] music awards in the United States.
The Grammy gets <u>it's</u> [its] name from the award <u>isself</u>
[itself], which is a <u>minature</u> [miniature] replica of
an <u>old-fashion</u> [old-fashioned] gramophone. The award
is presented by the Recording Academy, an <u>assocation</u>
[association] of professionals in the music industry.
Awards are given in thirty <u>generes</u> [genres], including
rock, pop, rap, and gospel. These are <u>seperated</u> [sepa-
rated] into over a hundred <u>catagories</u> [categories].
Unlike other music awards, the Grammy winners are
chosen by voting members of the academy rather <u>then</u>
[than] fans. . . .

Exercise 4

1. reefs
3. pop stars
5. wolves
7. flurries
9. taxes

Exercise 5

1. The attorneys general of sixteen states met with representatives of
companies concerned about rising bankruptcies.
3. Consumer worries about rising prices are hurting many industries.
5. These safety features could save many lives.

Exercise 6

1. weighed
3. stood
5. capitalized
7. doubled
9. slept

Exercise 7

1. debatable
3. regretfully
5. attendance
7. winning
9. making

Exercise 8

One of the most <u>memorerable</u> [memorable] <u>peaces</u> [pieces] of America's <u>passed</u> [past] is the Liberty Bell. More <u>then</u> [than] any other relic of the Revolutionary War, it is <u>immediatly</u> [immediately] recognized as a symbol of freedom around the world. The bell was cast in England in 1752 and shipped to America to hang in the <u>Pennsylvana</u> [Pennsylvania] State House, later known as <u>Independance</u> [Independence] Hall.

The first time the bell was <u>rang</u> [rung] in 1753, it cracked. It was recast twice, then <u>hanged</u> [hung] in the State House. The bell was used to summon members of the Continental Congress in 1775 and 1776. When British <u>solders</u> [soldiers] neared Philadelphia, patriots moved the bell to Allentown and hid it under a church. The bell was returned to Philadelphia in 1778. . . .

Exercise 9

See page 631.

CREDITS

This page constitutes an extension of the copyright page. We have made every effort to trace the ownership of all copyrighted material and to secure permission from copyright holders. In the event of any question arising as to the use of any material, we will be pleased to make the necessary corrections in future printings. Thanks are due to the following authors, publishers, and agents for permission to use the material indicated.

Text Credits

60: From "Makes Me Wanna Holler" by Nathan McCall; **60:** From "Unforgettable Miss Bessie" by Carl Rowan; **61:** From "The Power Broker" by Robert Caro; **62:** From "An Idea Whose Time Has Come" by Manning Marable; **62:** From "Vietnam: A History" by Stanley Karnow; **361:** The Prize: The Epic Quest for Oil, Money & Power by Daniel Yergin. (NY: Simon & Schuster, 1991, 1992); **372:** From "University of Wisconsin Takes Up the Issue of Student Credit Card Debt" in 'Cardline' (June 11, 2004) vol. 4:24; **373:** From "How to Survive College" by Nancy Hughes (Academic Press, 2005); **373:** Reprinted with permission of InCharge® Education Foundation, Inc. Fall 2002 issue of YOUNG MONEY, www.youngmoney.com. All rights reserved.; **614:** "Our Barbies, Ourselves" by Emily Prager, originally published in INTERVIEW Magazine, December 1991, Brant Publications, Inc. Reprinted by permission.; **618:** "The Border Story" from Across the Wire: Life & Hard Times by Luis Alberto Urrea copyright © 1993 by Luis Alberto Urrea. Used by permission of Doubleday, division of Random House, Inc.; **621:** "Unforgettable Miss Bessie" by Carl Rowan. Reprinted with permission from the March 1985 Readerýs Digest. Copyright © 1985 by The Readerýs Digest Assn., Inc.; **625:** "A Doctor's Dilemma" by James Dillard from NEWSWEEK, June 12, 1995. Copyright © 1995 Newsweek, Inc. All rights reserved. Reprinted by permission. Reprinted by permission.; **628:** "Champion of the World", copyright © 1969 and renewed 1997 by Maya Angelou, from I KNOW WHY THE CAGED BIRD SING by Maya Angelou. Used by permission of Random House, Inc. and Little Brown Book Group Limited.; **631:** "Homeless" copyright © 1987 by Anna Quindlen, from LIVING OUT LOUD by Anna Quindlen. Used by permission of Random House, Inc.; **633:** "Death of a Dream" by Tony Brown from "Black Lives, White Lies: The Truth According to Tony Brown" by Tony Brown (William Morrow and Company). Copyright © 1995 by Tony Brown.; **636:** "Spanglish" by Janice Castro, Dan Cook and Christina Garcia. Copyright © 1988 Time, Inc. Reprinted by permission.; **639:** : Does Cheating Wife Deserve Her Sister's Support? by Dr. Laura Schlessinger as appeared in STAR TRIBUNE, May 11, 1997. Reprinted by permission of the author.; **641:** "A Fable for Tomorrow" by Rachel Carson from "Silent Sprint" by Rachel Carson

Revising for Style

Have I avoided shifts in tense and point of view? (p. 288)

Have I maintained parallel structures? (p. 297)

How can I add variety to my sentences? (p. 306)

How can I avoid writing too many short, choppy sentences? (p. 307)

Does my choice of words convey exactly the meaning I want? (p. 336)

Revising for Grammatical Correctness

Can I readily identify the subjects and verbs in all of the independent and dependent clauses of my sentences? (pp. 397–407)

Have I avoided or corrected all sentence fragments? (pp. 412–415)

Have I avoided or corrected all run-on sentences and comma splices? (pp. 440–447)

Do I have any dangling or misplaced modifiers? (pp. 455–461)

Have I written any sentences with faulty parallelism? (pp. 469–472)

Have I avoided passive voice except where appropriate? (p. 506)

Do my pronouns clearly refer to the correct antecedents? (pp. 516–518)

Do my pronouns and their antecedents agree in number? (p. 520)

Do my adjectives use the correct forms for comparatives and superlatives? (p. 534)

Proofreading for Punctuation and Mechanics

Have I inserted commas where necessary to clarify meaning in the sentence? (pp. 552–561)

Have I used semicolons appropriately? (p. 562)

Have I proofread to make sure all marks of punctuation are correctly used? (pp. 569–579)

Have I correctly capitalized quotations, titles, names, historical events, etc.? (pp. 585–587)

Have I made sure that all of my words are spelled correctly, especially commonly confused words? (pp. 596–599)

Have I correctly formed the plurals of words? (pp. 600–602)

Where is the Handbook in this textbook located?

(pp. 671–706)

Selected
Readings

Brief Contents

For

SELECTED READINGS

Analysis, Argument & Persuasion

Unless you're an educator (and even if you are an educator), you may never have heard of Paulo Freire (1921–1997). Yet he is one of the most influential education theorists of the twentieth century. At the center of his theories of education is the notion that schooling should be about becoming "fully human," which means understanding that

THE *Banking* Concept OF Education

reality is not fixed but is a process in which individual human beings participate. In other words, we don't simply live in the world as it is; we create it. Being fully human is knowing that we have the capacity to change the world through our active participation. But conventional schooling, according to Freire, teaches students to be passive components of the status quo and in doing so it "dehumanizes" them. This conventional approach to schooling, which Freire calls the "banking concept of education," thus helps maintain the status quo, with all its inequalities and injustices.

Now, if this seems abstract to you, consider that Freire was jailed in his native Brazil in the 1960s for the "subversive" act of developing literacy programs for rural peasants. He was subsequently exiled by the military dictatorship that ruled Brazil at the time, but his ideas about "liberatory" education began

PAULO FREIRE

A careful analysis of the teacher-student relationship at any level, inside or outside the school, reveals its fundamentally *narrative* character. This relationship involves a narrating Subject (the teacher) and patient, listening objects (the students). The contents, whether values or empirical dimensions of reality, tend in the process of being narrated to become lifeless and petrified. Education is suffering from narration sickness.

The teacher talks about reality as if it were motionless, static, compartmentalized, and predictable. Or else he expounds on a topic completely alien to the existential experience of the students. His task is to "fill" the students with the contents of his narration—contents which are detached from reality, disconnected from the totality that engendered them and could give them significance. Words are emptied of their concreteness and become a hollow, alienated, and alienating verbosity.

The outstanding characteristic of this narrative education, then, is the sonority of words, not their transforming power. "Four times four is sixteen; the capital of Pará is Belém." The student records, memorizes, and repeats these phrases without perceiving what four times four really means, or realizing the true significance of "capital" in the affirmation "the capital of Pará is Belém," that is, what Belém means for Pará and what Pará means for Brazil.

Narration (with the teacher as narrator) leads the students to memorize mechanically the narrated content. Worse yet, it turns them into "containers," into "receptacles" to be "filled" by the teacher. The more completely she fills the receptacles, the better a teacher she is. The more meekly the receptacles permit themselves to be filled, the better students they are.

5   Education thus becomes an act of depositing, in which the students are the depositories and the teacher is the depositor. Instead of communicating, the teacher issues communiqués and makes deposits which the students patiently receive, memorize, and repeat. This is the "banking" concept of education, in which the scope of action allowed to the students extends only as far as receiving, filing, and storing the deposits. They do, it is true, have the opportunity to become collectors or cataloguers of the things they store. But in the last analysis, it is the people themselves who are filed away through the lack of creativity, transformation, and knowledge in this (at best) misguided system. For apart from inquiry, apart from the praxis, individuals cannot be truly human. Knowledge emerges only through invention and re-invention, through the restless, impatient, continuing, hopeful inquiry human beings pursue in the world, with the world, and with each other.

In the banking concept of education, knowledge is a gift bestowed by those who consider themselves knowledgeable upon those whom they consider to know nothing. Projecting an absolute ignorance onto others, a characteristic of the ideology of oppression, negates education and knowledge as processes of inquiry. The teacher presents himself to his students as their necessary opposite; by considering their ignorance absolute, he justifies his own existence. The students, alienated like the slave in the Hegelian dialectic, accept their ignorance as justifying the teacher's existence—but, unlike the slave, they never discover that they educate the teacher.

The *raison d'être* of libertarian education, on the other hand, lies in its drive towards reconciliation. Education must begin with the solution of the teacher-student contradiction, by reconciling the poles of the contradiction so that both are simultaneously teachers *and* students.

This solution is not (nor can it be) found in the banking concept. On the contrary, banking education maintains and even stimulates the contradiction through the following attitudes and practices, which mirror oppressive society as a whole:

a. the teacher teaches and the students are taught;

b. the teacher knows everything and the students know nothing;

c. the teacher thinks and the students are thought about;

to influence other educators. The publication of his now-famous book Pedagogy of the Oppressed, *which appeared in English in 1970 and in which the following essay first appeared, brought his ideas to a worldwide audience. By the time he returned to Brazil in the 1980s as an internationally prominent voice for education reform, Brazil was once again under civilian rule, and he became minister of education for the city of São Paulo. He remained in Brazil and continued to push for education reform until his death.*

The first time I read the following essay, I don't think I fully understood his complicated ideas. Maybe that's because Freire's essay is less about schooling and more fundamentally about how we understand ourselves as beings in the world. In that sense, it is really a philosophical text that addresses age-old questions: Who are we? How do we know the world? What is our relationship to the world? What is reality? Don't be put off by some of the difficulties of Freire's essay. His ideas are sometimes hard to understand, and his writing can be challenging as well. So you may need to work through his essay carefully. But I think you'll find that it's worth the effort. As you read, ask yourself whether Freire's ideas, which grew out of his experiences in South America, are valid for American schools. That's a question that many educators— those who agree with Freire and those who don't—have asked. In trying to answer it, you will be joining one of the most vigorous conversations about education that continues today, so many years after Freire first presented his ideas in this essay. ◪

d. the teacher talks and the students listen—meekly;

e. the teacher disciplines and the students are disciplined;

f. the teacher chooses and enforces his choice, and the students comply;

g. the teacher acts and the students have the illusion of acting through the action of the teacher;

h. the teacher chooses the program content, and the students (who were not consulted) adapt to it;

i. the teacher confuses the authority of knowledge with his or her own professional authority, which she and he sets in opposition to the freedom of the students;

j. the teacher is the Subject of the learning process, while the pupils are mere objects.

It is not surprising that the banking concept of education regards men as adaptable, manageable beings. The more students work at storing the deposits entrusted to them, the less they develop the critical consciousness which would result from their intervention in the world as transformers of that world. The more completely they accept the passive role imposed on them, the more they tend simply to adapt to the world as it is and to the fragmented view of reality deposited in them.

10   The capability of banking education to minimize or annul the students' creative power and to stimulate their credulity serves the interests of the oppressors, who care neither to have the world revealed nor to see it transformed. The oppressors use their "humanitarianism" to preserve a profitable situation. Thus they react almost instinctively against any experiment in education which stimulates the critical faculties and is not content with a partial view of reality but always seeks out the ties which link one point to another and one problem to another.

Indeed, the interests of the oppressors lie in "changing the consciousness of the oppressed, not the situation which oppresses them";[1] for the more the oppressed can be led to adapt to that situation, the more easily they can be dominated. To achieve this end, the oppressors use the banking concept of education in conjunction with a paternalistic social action apparatus, within which the oppressed receive the euphemistic title of "welfare recipients." They are treated as individual cases, as marginal persons who deviate from the general configuration of a "good, organized, and just" society. The oppressed are regarded as the pathology of the healthy society, which must therefore adjust

---

CONVERSATIONS: THE PROBLEMS WITH SCHOOLS

Freire's criticisms of formal schooling have influenced many well-known educational theorists, including Henri Giroux, Peter McLaren, and bell hooks. (Essays by bell hooks appear on page 256 and page 515 in this book.) If those names don't ring any bells for you, it's probably because you haven't read the kind of educational theory that they write. Their articles and books—and the articles and books of their critics—amount to a lively but specialized conversation about education among academics and theorists. It's worth asking whether that conversation is different from the larger public conversations about education reform that are always occurring in the popular media and in political campaigns. We always seem to be hearing about crises in our schools and about various government programs to improve education. For example, in 2001, President George W. Bush signed into law a sweeping education reform bill that has come to be known as No Child Left Behind. But what supporters of that law say is wrong with schools seems very different from Freire's list. Why? If Freire is such an internationally known and influential education theorist and reformer, why do his ideas seem to have been left out of the public discussions about education reform efforts such as No Child Left Behind? What might that tell us about how different ideas reach different audiences at different times?

these "incompetent and lazy" folk to its own patterns by changing their mentality. These marginals need to be "integrated," "incorporated" into the healthy society that they have "forsaken."

The truth is, however, that the oppressed are not "marginals," are not people living "outside" society. They have always been "inside"— inside the structure which made them "beings for others." The solution is not to "integrate" them into the structure of oppression, but to transform that structure so that they can become "beings for themselves." Such transformation, of course, would undermine the oppressors' purposes; hence their utilization of the banking concept of education to avoid the threat of student *conscientização*.[o]

The banking approach to adult education, for example, will never propose to students that they critically consider reality. It will deal instead with such vital questions as whether Roger gave green grass to the goat, and insist upon the importance of learning that, on the contrary, *Roger gave green grass to the rabbit*. The "humanism" of the banking approach masks the effort to turn women and men into automatons—the very negation of their ontological vocation to be more fully human.

Those who use the banking approach, knowingly or unknowingly (for there are innumerable well-intentioned bank-clerk teachers who do not realize that they are serving only to dehumanize), fail

CONVERSATIONS: CLASSROOMS AND LEARNING

This photograph depicts a typical college classroom. Consider how this scene might help illustrate some of Freire's criticisms of what he calls the "banking concept of education." What does it reveal about schooling?

Cartoons are often used to critique public education. Consider whether the criticism of schooling made by Mike Keefe's cartoon coincides with Freire's critique of formal schooling. Consider, too, whether the medium of a cartoon can convey such criticisms as effectively as a conventional academic essay.

[o]**conscientização** According to Freire's translator, "The term *conscientização* refers to learning to perceive social, political, and economic contradictions, and to take action against the oppressive elements of reality."

to perceive that the deposits themselves contain contradictions about reality. But, sooner or later, these contradictions may lead formerly passive students to turn against their domestication and the attempt to domesticate reality. They may discover through existential experience that their present way of life is irreconcilable with their vocation to become fully human. They may perceive through their relations with reality that reality is really a *process,* undergoing constant transformation. If men and women are searchers and their ontological vocation is humanization, sooner or later they may perceive the contradiction in which banking education seeks to maintain them, and then engage themselves in the struggle for their liberation.

15   But the humanist, revolutionary educator cannot wait for this possibility to materialize. From the outset, her efforts must coincide with those of the students to engage in critical thinking and the quest for mutual humanization. His efforts must be imbued with a profound trust in people and their creative power. To achieve this, they must be partners of the students in their relations with them.

The banking concept does not admit to such partnership—and necessarily so. To resolve the teacher-student contradiction, to exchange the role of depositor, prescriber, domesticator, for the role of student among students would be to undermine the power of oppression and serve the cause of liberation.

Implicit in the banking concept is the assumption of a DICHOTOMY BETWEEN HUMAN BEINGS AND THE WORLD: a person is merely *in* the world, not *with* the world or with others; the individual is spectator, not re-creator. In this view, the person is not a conscious being (*corpo consciente);* he or she is rather the possessor of *a* consciousness: an empty "mind" passively open to the reception of deposits of reality from the world outside. For example, my desk, my books, my coffee cup, all the objects before me—as bits of the world which surrounds me—would be "inside" me, exactly as I am inside my study right now. This view makes no distinction between being accessible to consciousness and entering consciousness. The distinction, however, is essential: the objects which surround me are simply accessible to my consciousness, not located within it. I am aware of them, but they are not inside me.

It follows logically from the banking notion of consciousness that the educator's role is to regulate the way the world "enters into" the students. The teacher's task is to organize a process which already occurs spontaneously, to "fill" the students by mak-

---

CONVERSATIONS: THE NATURE OF REALITY

In paragraph 17, when Freire refers to a "dichotomy between human beings and the world," he is participating in an age-old philosophical conversation about the nature of reality and how (or if) we can come to know that reality. This conversation has been occurring at least since the time of the ancient Greek philosophers and has preoccupied some of the world's greatest minds ever since. To anyone who has studied philosophy, Freire's discussion of "consciousness" may sound familiar. If his discussion seems abstract to you, it may help to keep in mind that what Freire calls the "banking concept of education" is based on the assumption that knowledge exists separately from the knower. In other words, reality is "out there," separate from us, and we can know it only through careful observation—for example, through science. We can only describe what is real; we can't create or change it. Although this may sound abstract, it's actually the idea on which modern science—and modern education—is based. And part of what Freire is trying to do in this essay is to challenge this way of thinking about knowledge. For Freire, believing that reality is "objective," as modern science asks us to do, makes it possible for all kinds of injustices to seem "natural" or "inevitable." But understanding reality as something we can change means that we can eliminate those injustices. You might think about it in this way: This is where philosophy meets real life.

ing deposits of information which he or she considers to constitute true knowledge.[2] And since people "receive" the world as passive entities, education should make them more passive still, and adapt them to the world. The educated individual is the adapted person, because she or he is better "fit" for the world. Translated into practice, this concept is well suited to the purposes of the oppressors, whose tranquility rests on how well people fit the world the oppressors have created, and how little they question it.

The more completely the majority adapt to the purposes which the dominant minority prescribe for them (thereby depriving them of the right to their own purposes), the more easily the minority can continue to prescribe. The theory and practice of banking education serve this end quite efficiently. Verbalistic lessons, reading requirements,[3] the methods for evaluating "knowledge," the distance between the teacher and the taught, the criteria for promotion: everything in this ready-to-wear approach serves to obviate thinking.

The bank-clerk educator does not realize that there is no true security in his hypertrophied role, that one must seek to live *with* others in solidarity. One cannot impose oneself, nor even merely co-exist with one's students. Solidarity requires true communication, and the concept by which such an educator is guided fears and proscribes communication.

Yet only through communication can human life hold meaning. The teacher's thinking is authenticated only by the authenticity of the students' thinking. The teacher cannot think for her students, nor can she impose her thought on them. Authentic thinking, thinking that is concerned about *reality*, does not take place in ivory tower isolation, but only in communication. If it is true that thought has meaning only when generated by action upon the world, the subordination of students to teachers becomes impossible.

Because banking education begins with a false understanding of men and women as objects, it cannot promote the development of what Fromm calls "biophily," but instead produces its opposite: "necrophily."

> While life is characterized by growth in a structured, functional manner, the necrophilous person loves all that does not grow, all that is mechanical. The necrophilous person is driven by the desire to transform the organic into the inorganic, to approach life mechanically, as if all living persons were things. . . . Memory, rather than experience; having, rather than being, is what counts. The necrophilous person can relate to an object—a flower or a person—only if he possesses it; hence a threat to his possession is a threat to himself; if he loses possession he loses contact with the world. . . . He loves control, and in the act of controlling he kills life.[4]

Oppression—overwhelming control—is necrophilic; it is nourished by love of death, not life. The banking concept of education, which serves the interests of oppression, is also necrophilic. Based on a mechanistic, static, naturalistic, spatialized view of consciousness, it transforms students into receiving objects. It attempts to control thinking and action, leads women and men to adjust to the world, and inhibits their creative power.

When their efforts to act responsibly are frustrated, when they find themselves unable to use their faculties, people suffer. "This suffering due to impotence is rooted in the very fact that the human equilibrium has been disturbed."[5] But the inability to act which causes people's anguish also causes them to reject their impotence, by attempting

> . . . to restore [their] capacity to act. But can [they], and how? One way is to submit to and identify with a person or group having power. By this symbolic participation in another person's life, [men have] the illusion of acting, when in reality [they] only submit to and become part of those who act.[6]

Populist manifestations perhaps best exemplify this type of behavior by the oppressed, who, by identifying with charismatic leaders, come to feel that they themselves are active and effective. The rebellion they express as they emerge in the historical process is motivated by that desire to act effectively. The dominant elites consider the remedy to be more domination and repression, carried out in the name of freedom, order, and social peace (that is, the peace of the elites). Thus they can condemn—logically, from their point of view—"the violence of a strike by workers and [can] call upon the state in the same breath to use violence in putting down the strike."[7]

Education as the exercise of domination stimulates the credulity of students, with the ideological intent (often not perceived by educators) of indoctrinating them to adapt to the world of oppression. This accusation is not made in the naïve hope that the dominant elites will thereby simply abandon the practice. Its objective is to call the attention of true humanists to the fact that they cannot use banking educational methods in the pursuit of liberation, for they would only negate that very pursuit. Nor may a revolutionary society inherit these methods from an oppressor society. The revolutionary society which practices banking education is either misguided or mistrusting of people. In either event, it is threatened by the specter of reaction.

Unfortunately, those who espouse the cause of liberation are themselves surrounded and influenced by the climate which generates the banking concept, and often do not perceive its true significance or its dehumanizing power. Paradoxically, then, they utilize this same instrument of alienation in what they consider an effort to liberate. Indeed, some "revolutionaries" brand as "innocents," "dreamers," or even "reactionaries" those who would challenge this educational practice. But one does not liberate people by alienating them. Authentic liberation—the process of humanization—is not another deposit to be made in men. Liberation is a praxis: the action and reflection of men and women upon their world in order to transform it. Those truly committed to the cause of liberation can accept neither the mechanistic concept of consciousness as an empty vessel to be filled, nor the use of banking methods of domination (propaganda, slogans—deposits) in the name of liberation.

Those truly committed to liberation must reject the banking concept in its entirety, adopting instead a concept of women and men as conscious beings, and consciousness as consciousness intent upon the world. They must abandon the educational goal of deposit-making and replace it with the posing of the problems of human beings in their relations with the world. "Problem-posing" education, responding to the essence of consciousness—*intentionality*—rejects communiqués and embodies communications. It epitomizes the special characteristic of consciousness: being *conscious of,* not only as intent on objects but as turned in upon itself in a Jasperian "split"—consciousness as consciousness *of* consciousness.

Liberating education consists in acts of cognition, not transferrals of information. It is a learning situation in which the cognizable object (far from being the end of the cognitive act) intermediates the cognitive actors—teacher on the one hand and students on the other. Accordingly, the practice of problem-posing education entails at the outset that the teacher-student contradiction be resolved. Dialogical relations—indispensable to the capacity of cognitive actors to cooperate in perceiving the same cognizable object—are otherwise impossible.

Indeed, problem-posing education, which breaks with the vertical   30 patterns characteristic of banking education, can fulfill its function as the practice of freedom only if it can overcome the above contradiction. Through dialogue, the teacher-of-the-students and the students-of-the-teacher cease to exist and a new term emerges: teacher-student with students-teachers. The teacher is no longer merely the-one-who-teaches, but one who is himself taught in dialogue with the students, who in turn while being taught also teach. They become jointly responsible for a process in which all grow. In this process, arguments based on "authority" are no longer valid; in order to function, authority must be *on the side of* freedom, not *against* it. Here, no one teaches another, nor is anyone self-taught. People teach each other, mediated by the world, by the cognizable objects which in banking education are "owned" by the teacher.

The banking concept (with its tendency to dichotomize everything) distinguishes two stages in the action of the educator. During the first, he cognizes a cognizable object while he prepares his lessons in his study or his laboratory; during the second, he expounds to his students about that object. The students are not called upon to know, but to memorize the contents narrated by the teacher. Nor do the students practice any act of cognition, since the object towards which that act should be directed is the property of the teacher rather than a medium evoking the critical reflection of both teacher and students. Hence in the name of the "preservation of culture and knowledge" we have a system which achieves neither true knowledge nor true culture.

The problem-posing method does not dichotomize the activity of the teacher-student: she is not "cognitive" at one point and "narrative" at another. She is always "cognitive," whether preparing a project or engaging in dialogue with the students. He does not regard cognizable objects as his private property, but as the object of reflection by himself and the students. In this way, the problem-posing educator constantly re-forms his reflections in the reflection of the students. The students—no longer docile listeners—are now critical co-investigators in dialogue with the teacher. The teacher presents the material to the students for their consideration, and reconsiders her earlier considerations as the students express their own. The role of the problem-posing educator is to create, together with the students, the conditions under which knowledge at the level of the *doxa* is superseded by true knowledge, at the level of the *logos*.

Whereas banking education anesthetizes and inhibits creative power, problem-posing education involves a constant unveiling of reality. The former attempts to maintain the *submersion* of consciousness; the latter strives for the *emergence* of consciousness and *critical intervention* in reality.

Students, as they are increasingly posed with problems relating to themselves in the world and with the world, will feel increasingly challenged and obliged to respond to that challenge. Because they apprehend the challenge as interrelated to other problems within a total context, not as a theoretical question, the resulting comprehension tends to be increasingly critical and thus constantly less alienated. Their response to the challenge evokes new challenges, followed by new understandings; and gradually the students come to regard themselves as committed.

35   Education as the practice of freedom—as opposed to education as the practice of domination—denies that man is abstract, isolated, independent, and unattached to the world; it also denies that the world exists as a reality apart from people. Authentic reflection considers neither abstract man nor the world without people, but people in their relations with the world. In these relations consciousness and world are simultaneous: consciousness neither precedes the world nor follows it.

> La conscience et le monde sont dormés
> d'un même coup: extérieur par essence à la

conscience, le monde est, par essence relatif
à elle.[8]

In one of our culture circles in CHILE, the group was discussing (based on a codification) the anthropological concept of culture. In the midst of the discussion, a peasant who by banking standards was completely ignorant said: "Now I see that without man there is no world." When the educator responded: "Let's say, for the sake of argument, that all the men on earth were to die, but that the earth itself remained, together with trees, birds, animals, rivers, seas, the stars . . . wouldn't all this be a world?" "Oh no," the peasant replied emphatically. "There would be no one to say: 'This is a world.'"

The peasant wished to express the idea that there would be lacking the consciousness of the world which necessarily implies the world of consciousness. *I* cannot exist without a *non-I*. In turn, the *not-I* depends on that existence. The world which brings consciousness into existence becomes the world *of* that consciousness. Hence, the previously cited affirmation of Sartre: *"La conscience et le monde sont dormés d'un même coup."*

As women and men, simultaneously reflecting on themselves and on the world, increase the scope of their perception, they begin to direct their observations towards previously inconspicuous phenomena:

> In perception properly so-called, as an explicit awareness [*Gewahren*], I am turned towards the object, to the paper, for instance. I apprehend it as being this here and now. The apprehension is a singling out, every object having a background in experience. Around and about the paper lie books, pencils, ink-well, and so forth, and these in a certain sense are also "perceived," perceptually there, in the "field of intuition"; but whilst I was turned towards the paper there was no turning in their direction, nor any apprehending of them, not even in a secondary sense. They appeared and yet were not singled out, were not posited on their own account. Every perception of a thing has such a zone of background intuitions or background awareness, if "intuiting" already includes the state of being turned towards, and this also is a "conscious experience," or more briefly a "consciousness of" all indeed that in point of fact lies in the co-perceived objective background.[9]

That which had existed objectively but had not been perceived in its deeper implications (if indeed it was perceived at all) begins to "stand out," assuming the character of a problem and therefore of challenge. Thus, men and women begin to single out elements from their "background awarenesses" and to reflect upon them. These elements are now objects of their consideration, and, as such, objects of their action and cognition.

CONVERSATIONS: CHILE IN THE 1960S
In paragraph 36, Freire refers to his literacy work with peasants in Chile in the 1960s. At the time, Chile was experiencing political tensions, which worsened after socialist leader Salvadore Allende was elected president in 1970. In 1973, Allende was killed in a coup led by Chile's military. Subsequently, the military leader who took control of the nation, Augusto Pinochet, declared martial law. Many people believed that Allende's overthrow was orchestrated in a plot that involved the U.S. CIA. In the years that followed, many Allende supporters and others who criticized or opposed the government were persecuted; thousands disappeared or were executed in what the Chilean government claimed was an effort to protect the nation from communist subversion. How might this context have shaped Freire's ideas about education and freedom? And how might this context lead some of Freire's critics to complain that his education theories are too political?

STRATEGIES: TALKING PHILOSOPHY
In paragraph 38, Freire includes a long quotation from well-known twentieth century German philosopher Edmund Husserl. Elsewhere, Freire includes quotations from other famous philosophers, including Jean-Paul Sartre, Reinhold Niebuhr, and Erich Fromm. What does Freire accomplish with these quotations and references? What do these quotations suggest about Freire's sense of his audience? Who might be familiar with such philosophers? What do these references reveal about Freire's sense of his purpose in writing this essay?

In problem-posing education, people develop their power to perceive critically *the way they exist* in the world *with which* and *in which* they find themselves; they come to see the world not as a static reality, but as a reality in process, in transformation. Although the dialectical relations of women and men with the world exist independently of how these relations are perceived (or whether or not they are perceived at all), it is also true that the form of action they adopt is to a large extent a function of how they perceive themselves in the world. Hence, the teacher-student and the students-teachers reflect simultaneously on themselves and the world without dichotomizing this reflection from action, and thus establish an authentic form of thought and action.

40   Once again, the two educational concepts and practices under analysis come into conflict. Banking education (for obvious reasons) attempts, by mythicizing reality, to conceal certain facts which explain the way human beings exist in the world; problem-posing education sets itself the task of demythologizing. Banking education resists dialogue; problem-posing education regards dialogue as indispensable to the act of cognition which unveils reality. Banking education treats students as objects of assistance; problem-posing education makes them critical thinkers. Banking education inhibits creativity and domesticates (although it cannot completely destroy) the *intentionality* of consciousness by isolating consciousness from the world, thereby denying people their ontological and historical vocation of becoming more fully human. Problem-posing education bases itself on creativity and stimulates true reflection and action upon reality; thereby responding to the vocation of persons as beings who are authentic only when engaged in inquiry and creative transformation. In sum: banking theory and practice, as immobilizing and fixating forces, fail to acknowledge men and women as historical beings; problem-posing theory and practice take the people's historicity as their starting point.

Problem-posing education affirms men and women as beings in the process of *becoming*—as unfinished, uncompleted beings in and with a likewise unfinished reality. Indeed, in contrast to other animals who are unfinished, but not historical, people know themselves to be unfinished; they are aware of their incompletion. In this incompletion and this awareness lie the very roots of education as an exclusively human manifestation. The unfinished character of human beings and the transformational character of reality necessitate that education be an ongoing activity.

Education is thus constantly remade in the praxis. In order to *be,* it must *become*. Its "duration" (in the Bergsonian meaning of the word) is found in the interplay of the opposites *permanence* and *change*. The banking method emphasizes permanence and becomes reactionary; problem-posing education—which accepts neither a "well-behaved" present nor a predetermined future—roots itself in the dynamic present and becomes revolutionary.

Problem-posing education is revolutionary futurity. Hence, it is prophetic (and, as such, hopeful). Hence, it corresponds to the historical nature of humankind. Hence, it affirms women and men as beings who transcend themselves, who move forward and look ahead, for whom immobility represents a fatal threat, for whom looking at the past must only be a means of understanding more clearly what and who they are so that they can more wisely build the future. Hence, it identifies with the movement which engages people as beings aware of their incompletion—an historical movement which has its point of departure, its Subjects and its objective.

The point of departure of the movement lies in the people themselves. But since people do not exist apart from the world, apart from reality, the movement must begin with the human-world relationship. Accordingly, the point of departure must always be with men and women in the "here and now," which constitutes the situation within which they are submerged, from which they emerge, and in which they intervene. Only by starting from this situation—which determines their perception of it—can they begin to move. To do this authentically they must perceive their state not as fated and unalterable, but merely as limiting—and therefore challenging.

Whereas the banking method directly or indirectly reinforces   45
men's fatalistic perception of their situation, the problem-posing method presents this very situation to them as a problem. As the situation becomes the object of their cognition, the naïve or magical perception which produced their fatalism gives way to perception which is able to perceive itself even as it perceives reality, and can thus be critically objective about that reality.

A deepened consciousness of their situation leads people to apprehend that situation as an historical reality susceptible of transformation. Resignation gives way to the drive for transformation and inquiry, over which men feel themselves to be in control. If people, as historical beings necessarily engaged with other people in a movement of inquiry, did not control that movement, it would be (and is) a violation of their humanity. Any situation in which some individuals prevent others from engaging in the process of inquiry is one of violence. The means used are not important; to alienate human beings from their own decision-making is to change them into objects.

This movement of inquiry must be directed towards humanization—the people's historical vocation. The pursuit of full humanity, however, cannot be carried out in isolation or individualism, but only in fellowship and solidarity; therefore it cannot unfold in the antagonistic relations between oppressors and oppressed. No one can be authentically human while he prevents others from being so. Attempting *to be more* human, individualistically, leads to *having more,* egotistically, a form of dehumanization. Not that it is not fundamental *to have* in order *to be* human. Precisely because it *is* necessary, some men's *having* must not be allowed to constitute an obstacle to others' *having*, must not consolidate the power of the former to crush the latter.

Problem-posing education, as a humanist and liberating praxis, posits as fundamental that the people subjected to domination must fight for their emancipation. To that end, it enables teachers and students to become Subjects of the educational process by overcoming authoritarianism and an alienating intellectualism; it also enables people to overcome their false perception of reality. The world—no longer something to be described with deceptive words—becomes the object of that transforming action by men and women which results in their humanization.

Problem-posing education does not and cannot serve the interests of the oppressor. No oppressive order could permit the oppressed to begin to question: Why? While only a revolutionary society can carry out this education in systematic terms, the revolutionary leaders need not take full power before they can employ the method. In the revolutionary process, the leaders cannot utilize the banking method as an interim measure, justified on grounds of expediency, with the intention of *later* behaving in a genuinely revolutionary fashion. They must be revolutionary—that is to say, dialogical—from the outset.

NOTES

[1] Simone de Beauvoir, *La pensée de droite, aujourd'hui* (Paris); ST, *El pensamiento político de la derecha* (Buenos Aires, 1963), p. 34.

[2] This concept corresponds to what Sartre calls the "digestive" or "nutritive" concept of education, in which knowledge is "fed" by the teacher to the students to "fill them out." See Jean-Paul Sartre, "Une idée fundamentale de la phénomenologie de Husserl: L'intentionalité," *Situations* I (Paris, 1947).

[3] For example, some professors specify in their reading lists that a book should be read from pages 10 to 15—and do this to "help" their students!

[4] Erich Fromm, *The Heart of Man* (New York, 1966), p. 41.

[5] Ibid., p. 31.

[6] Ibid.

[7] Reinhold Niebuhr, *Moral Man and Immoral Society* (New York, 1960), p. 130.

[8] Sartre, op. cit., p. 32. [The passage is obscure but could be read as "Consciousness and the world are given at one and the same time: the exterior world as it enters consciousness is relative to our ways of seeing and understanding that world."—Editors' note]

[9] Edmund Husserl, *Ideas—General Introduction to Pure Phenomenology* (London, 1969), pp. 105–06.

Understanding the Text

1. Summarize the "banking concept of education," as Freire understands it. What are the main features of this kind of education?

2. What is the "teacher-student contradiction," according to Freire? Why is it important for his criticism of conventional schooling? Do you agree with him? Why or why not?

3. In what ways is education "the exercise of domination," as Freire sees it?

4. What is "liberating education" or "problem-posing education" according to Freire? How is this kind of education different from the banking concept of education that Freire criticizes? Do you think problem-posing education, as Freire describes it, would solve the problems he sees with conventional education? Explain.

5. What does Freire mean when he says that problem-posing education should foster a "critical intervention in reality"? In what sense can students "intervene" in reality, as Freire sees it? Why is this intervention so important to him?

6. Why does Freire's problem-posing approach to education describe people as "beings in the process of becoming"? What exactly does that mean? Why is that important in his approach to education?

Exploring the Issues

1. What does Freire mean when he describes students as "oppressed" and teachers as "oppressors"? Using Freire's ideas, explain how you as a student might be described as oppressed within formal schooling. Cite specific passages from his essay to support your answer.

2. Review Freire's list of the ten "attitudes and practices" of conventional education listed in paragraph 8. Does this list sound at all familiar to you? Do you think it accurately describes schools you have attended? Explain.

3. In paragraph 41, Freire discusses *permanence* and *change*. He claims that conventional education, which he describes as the "banking model of education," emphasizes permanence, whereas his problem-posing approach to education is based on the possibility of change. Based on your own experiences as a student and your own knowledge of education, do you think Freire is right on this point? Why or why not? Refer to your own experiences as well as to specific passages from Freire's essay to support your answer.

4. What would Freire's problem-posing method of education mean for American schools? What exactly do you think it would look like if it were applied to American schools? What specific changes would it lead to? Do

you think it would work? Why or why not?

5. Freire's educational theories and proposed reforms have been criticized as too political. Based on this essay, do you think those criticisms are justified? Explain.

6. Why do you think Freire's ideas about education have been so influential? What appeal do you see in his theories? What might the appeal of his ideas in Western nations like the United States suggest to you about the problems facing the educational systems in those nations?

Entering the Conversations

1. Write a conventional essay in which you explain Freire's ideas about education. In your essay, summarize his criticisms of what he calls the "banking concept of education" and describe his "problem-posing" method. Explain his basic ideas regarding knowledge and reality and how those ideas figure into his criticisms of conventional education. Draw your own conclusions about the effectiveness of his proposed method of education.

2. Rewrite the essay you wrote for Question 1 for a general audience, such as readers of a publication such as *USA Today* or the readers of your local newspaper.

3. Using Freire's ideas about education, write an analysis of your own school (you can choose to analyze your high school or your college). In your essay, summarize what you believe are the most important of Freire's ideas. Then apply those ideas to your own experiences in your school. In what ways might Freire's ideas help explain your experiences? What do his ideas reveal about the school you attended? On the basis of your critique, draw conclusions about any changes that you believe should be made to your school.

4. In a group of classmates, compare the essays you wrote for Question 3. In what ways do your essays describe similar or different problems in the schools you attended? On the basis of your discussion, try to draw conclusions about the usefulness of Freire's ideas about education or about problems you see with his ideas.

INFOTRAC

5. Using InfoTrac College Edition, the Internet, your library, and any other relevant sources, try to determine whether Freire's ideas have been applied to schools in the United States or elsewhere. Examine how those schools have used Freire's ideas. Try to find reviews or criticisms of Freire's work that might help you gain a better understanding of some of the benefits or drawbacks of using his ideas about education in an American school setting. Then write a report for your classmates in which you describe these efforts and evaluate their effectiveness.

6. Using appropriate technology and working with several classmates, create a video or photo collage that illustrates Freire's criticisms of the banking concept of education. Alternatively, create a web site with the same purpose.

Most Americans accept majority rule as the way things should be. In the U.S. political system, for example, the party that wins more seats in the House of Representatives or the Senate controls that body. If more Republicans win seats, then all Senate committees are chaired by Republicans and the Senate is effectively run by Republicans. This

THE Tyranny OF THE Majority

winner-take-all approach to political power is a basic principle of the American style of democracy—so basic that many Americans assume that democracy is equivalent to majority rule. But some democracies distribute power proportionally, assigning a portion of political power to each party based on the percentage of votes that party received in an election. In parliamentary democracies like Canada or Israel, several parties will compete in elections, and the percentage of the vote that each party receives determines how much power that party will have in the government. Such a system requires that the party with the largest percentage of votes form coalitions with other parties in order for the government to function.

Some political scientists and legal scholars believe that such parliamentary democracies avoid some of the problems associated with the winner-take-all process in the

LANI GUINIER

I have always wanted to be a civil rights lawyer. This lifelong ambition is based on a deep-seated commitment to democratic fair play—to playing by the rules as long as the rules are fair. When the rules seem unfair, I have worked to change them, not subvert them. When I was eight years old, I was a Brownie. I was especially proud of my uniform, which represented a commitment to good citizenship and good deeds. But one day, when my Brownie group staged a hatmaking contest, I realized that uniforms are only as honorable as the people who wear them. The contest was rigged. The winner was assisted by her milliner mother, who actually made the winning entry in full view of all the participants. At the time, I was too young to be able to change the rules, but I was old enough to resign, which I promptly did.

To me, fair play means that the rules encourage everyone to play. They should reward those who win, but they must be acceptable to those who lose. The central theme of my academic writing is that not all rules lead to elemental fair play. Some even commonplace rules work against it.

United States. In her carefully reasoned essay, Lani Guinier (b. 1950) explains how American-style majority rule is not always fair and does not necessarily best serve the needs and interests of the minority, especially in a diverse society. Guinier reminds us that some of the founding fathers expressed concerns about the possibility that the American political process could result in a "tyranny of the majority," and she suggests some steps to make the American political process fairer. Her essay is part of an ongoing debate in American society about how to interpret the Constitution and how best to manage the process of power.

Lani Guinier, a distinguished legal scholar, taught at the University of Pennsylvania before becoming the first black woman tenured professor at Harvard Law School in 1998. She has written extensively about political and legal issues and has published several books, including The Tyranny of the Majority *(1994), in which the following essay first appeared.* ▾

The professional milliner competing with amateur Brownies stands as an example of rules that are patently rigged or patently subverted. Yet, sometimes, even when rules are perfectly fair in form, they serve in practice to exclude particular groups from meaningful participation. When they do not encourage everyone to play, or when, over the long haul, they do not make the losers feel as good about the outcomes as the winners, they can seem as unfair as the milliner who makes the winning hat for her daughter.

Sometimes, too, we construct rules that force us to be divided into winners and losers when we might have otherwise joined together. This idea was cogently expressed by my son, Nikolas, when he was four years old, far exceeding the thoughtfulness of his mother when she was an eight-year-old Brownie. While I was writing one of my law journal articles, Nikolas and I had a conversation about voting prompted by a *Sesame Street Magazine* exercise. The magazine pictured six children: four children had raised their hands because they wanted to play tag; two had their hands down because they wanted to play hide-and-seek. The magazine asked its readers to count the number of children whose hands were raised and then decide what game the children would play.

Nikolas quite realistically replied, "They will play both. First they will play tag. Then they will play hide-and-seek." Despite the magazine's "rules," he was right. To children, it is natural to take turns. The winner may get to play first or more often, but even the "loser" gets something. His was a positive-sum solution that many adult rule-makers ignore.

The traditional answer to the magazine's problem would have been a zero-sum solution: "The children—all the children—will play tag, and only tag." As a zero-sum solution, everything is seen in terms of "I win; you lose." The conventional answer relies on winner-take-all majority rule, in which the tag players, as the majority, win the right to decide for all the children what game to play. The hide-and-seek preference becomes irrelevant. The numerically more powerful majority choice simply subsumes minority preferences.

In the conventional case, the majority that rules gains all the power and the minority that loses gets none. For example, two years ago Brother Rice High School in Chicago held two senior proms. It was not planned that way. The prom committee at Brother Rice, a boys' Catholic high school, expected just one prom when it hired a disc jockey, picked a rock band, and selected music for the prom by consulting student preferences. Each senior was asked to list his three favorite songs, and the band would play the songs that appeared most frequently on the lists.

Seems attractively democratic. But Brother Rice is predominantly white, and the prom committee was all white. That's how they got two proms. The black seniors at Brother Rice felt so shut out by the

5

"democratic process" that they organized their own prom. As one black student put it: "for every vote we had, there were eight votes for what they wanted. . . . [W]ith us being in the minority we're always outvoted. It's as if we don't count."

Some embittered white seniors saw things differently. They complained that the black students should have gone along with the majority: "The majority makes a decision. That's the way it works."

In a way, both groups were right. From the white students' perspective, this was ordinary decisionmaking. To the black students, majority rule sent the message: "we don't count" is the "way it works" for minorities. In a racially divided society, majority rule may be perceived as majority tyranny.

That is a large claim, and I do not rest my case for it solely on the actions of the prom committee in one Chicago high school. To expand the range of the argument, I first consider the ideal of majority rule itself, particularly as reflected in the writings of James Madison and other founding members of our Republic. These early democrats explored the relationship between majority rule and democracy. James Madison warned, "If a majority be united by a common interest, the rights of the minority will be insecure." The tyranny of the majority, according to Madison, requires safeguards to protect "one part of the society against the injustice of the other part."

For Madison, majority tyranny represented the great danger to our early constitutional democracy. Although the American revolution was fought against the tyranny of the British monarch, it soon became clear that there was another tyranny to be avoided. The accumulations of all powers in the same hands, Madison warned, "whether of one, a few, or many, and whether hereditary, self-appointed, or elective, may justly be pronounced the very definition of tyranny."

As another colonist suggested in papers published in Philadelphia, "We have been so long habituated to a jealousy of tyranny from monarchy and aristocracy, that we have yet to learn the dangers of it from democracy." Despotism had to be opposed "whether it came from Kings, Lords or the people."

The debate about majority tyranny reflected Madison's concern that the majority may not represent the whole. In a homogeneous society, the interest of the majority would likely be that of the minority also. But in a heterogeneous community, the majority may not represent all competing interests. The majority is likely to be self-interested and ignorant or indifferent to the concerns of the minority. In such case, Madison observed, the assumption that the majority represents the minority is "altogether fictitious."

10

STRATEGIES: SUMMARY
Notice how Guinier uses her summary of James Madison's political ideas to help explain the problems with majority rule. In these paragraphs and for much of the rest of her essay, she relies on Madison's ideas to lay out her own position on this issue, using quotations from his writings. She also relies on Madison's status as one of the founding fathers, which gives his words more weight with many American readers than the words of a less revered political figure or scholar.

CONVERSATIONS: TYRANNY IN HISTORY
The quotation Guinier includes here from a colonist in the late eighteenth century indicates that the historical context within which James Madison and the other founding fathers were writing the U.S. Constitution was very different from our own time. This colonist's concerns about tyranny were based on the many examples of powerful monarchs who ruled European nations at the time of the American Revolution. As Americans formed their own government, the world had many tyrannical governments but no examples of the kind of democracy Americans were trying to create. As a result, the idea of the "tyranny of the majority," which may seem odd to many contemporary readers, would have been a very real concern at the time Madison and his colleagues were debating how to form a new government. Today, few Americans have such concerns, which makes Guinier's argument in this essay a little harder to make. Consider how she uses historical information to help her modern readers appreciate the significance of her concerns about majority rule.

15   Yet even a self-interested majority can govern fairly if it cooperates with the minority. One reason for such cooperation is that the self-interested majority values the principle of reciprocity. The self-interested majority worries that the minority may attract defectors from the majority and become the next governing majority. The Golden Rule principle of reciprocity functions to check the tendency of a self-interested majority to act tyrannically.

So the argument for the majority principle connects it with the value of reciprocity: You cooperate when you lose in part because members of the current majority will cooperate when they lose. The conventional case for the fairness of majority rule is that it is not really the rule of a fixed group—The Majority—on all issues; instead it is the rule of shifting majorities, as the losers at one time or on one issue join with others and become part of the governing coalition at another time or on another issue. The result will be a fair system of mutually beneficial cooperation. I call a majority that rules but does not dominate a Madisonian Majority.

The problem of majority tyranny arises, however, when the self-interested majority does not need to worry about defections. When the majority is fixed and permanent, there are no checks on its ability to be overbearing. A majority that does not worry about defectors is a majority with total power.

In such a case, Madison's concern about majority tyranny arises. In a heterogeneous community, any faction with total power might subject "the minority to the caprice and arbitrary decisions of the majority, who instead of consulting the interest of the whole community collectively, attend sometimes to partial and local advantages."

"What remedy can be found in a republican Government, where the majority must ultimately decide," argued Madison, but to ensure "that no one common interest or passion will be likely to unite a majority of the whole number in an unjust pursuit." The answer was to disaggregate the majority to ensure checks and balances or fluid, rotating interests. The minority needed protection against an overbearing majority, so that "a common sentiment is less likely to be felt, and the requisite concert less likely to be formed, by a majority of the whole."

20   Political struggles would not be simply a contest between rulers and people; the political struggles would be among the people themselves. The work of government was not to transcend different interests but to reconcile them. In an ideal democracy, the people would rule, but the minorities would also be protected against the power of majorities. Again, where the rules of decisionmaking protect the minority, the Madisonian Majority rules without dominating.

But if a group is unfairly treated, for example, when it forms a racial minority, *and* if the problems of unfairness are not cured by conventional assumptions about majority rule, then what is to be done?

The answer is that we may need an *alternative* to winner-take-all majoritarianism. In this book, a collection of my law review articles, I describe the alternative, which, with Nikolas's help, I now call the "principle of taking turns." In a racially divided society, this principle does better than simple majority rule if it accommodates the values of self-government, fairness, deliberation, compromise, and consensus that lie at the heart of the democratic ideal.

In my legal writing, I follow the caveat of James Madison and other early American democrats. I explore decisionmaking rules that might work in a multi-racial society to ensure that majority rule does not become majority tyranny. I pursue voting systems that might disaggregate The Majority so that it does not exercise power unfairly or tyrannically. I aspire to a more cooperative political style of decisionmaking to enable all of the students at Brother Rice to feel comfortable attending the same prom. In looking to create Madisonian Majorities, I pursue a positive-sum, taking-turns solution.

Structuring decisionmaking to allow the minority "a turn" may be necessary to restore the reciprocity ideal when a fixed majority refuses to cooperate with the minority. If the fixed majority loses its incentive to follow the Golden Rule principle of shifting majorities, the minority never gets to take a turn. Giving the minority a turn does not mean the minority gets to rule; what it does mean is that the minority gets to influence decisionmaking and the majority rules more legitimately.

Instead of automatically rewarding the preferences of the monolithic majority, a taking-turns approach anticipates that the majority rules, but is not overbearing. Because those with 51 percent of the votes are not assured 100 percent of the power, the majority cooperates with, or at least does not tyrannize, the minority.

25   The sports analogy of "I win; you lose" competition within a political hierarchy makes sense when only one team can win; Nikolas's intuition that it is often possible to take turns suggests an alternative approach. Take family decisionmaking, for example. It utilizes a taking-turns approach. When parents sit around the kitchen table deciding on a vacation destination or activities for a rainy day, often they do not simply rely on a show of hands, especially if that means that the older children always prevail or if affinity groups among the children (those who prefer movies to video games, or those who prefer baseball to playing cards) never get to play their activity of choice. Instead of allowing the majority simply to rule, the parents may pro-

CONVERSATIONS: TURN-TAKING AND THE 2004 U.S. PRESIDENTIAL ELECTION

Ten years after Guinier's essay was published, one of the closest and most controversial presidential elections in U.S. history ended with George W. Bush being reelected by historically slim margins. His party controlled both the U.S. House of Representatives and the U.S. Senate, also by slim margins. In many ways, the 2004 election illustrates some of Guinier's concerns about the winner-take-all approach in American politics: A very small majority effectively gained full power to rule everyone. But circumstances in 2004 were different from 1994, when Guinier's essay was first published. In 2004, many groups who felt that their concerns were being ignored by both the Republican and Democratic Parties began to use alternative ways of voicing their concerns and participating in the political process. One way was the use of alternative media like the Internet to mobilize opposition to the two main political parties, as MoveOn.org, one of the most visible of such groups, did. Consider how the emergence of groups like MoveOn.org might complicate—or lend support to—Guinier's argument for an alternative to simple majority rule in the United States. Consider, too, how the rise of new technologies like the Internet might affect her proposals.

pose that everyone take turns, going to the movies one night and playing video games the next. Or as Nikolas proposes, they might do both on a given night.

Taking turns attempts to build consensus while recognizing political or social differences, and it encourages everyone to play. The taking-turns approach gives those with the most support more turns, but it also legitimates the outcome from each individual's perspective, including those whose views are shared only by a minority.

In the end, I do not believe that democracy should encourage rule by the powerful—even a powerful majority. Instead, the idea of democracy promises a fair discussion among self-defined equals about how to achieve our common aspirations. To redeem that promise, we need to put the idea of taking turns and disaggregating the majority at the center of our conception of representation. Particularly as we move into the twenty-first century as a more highly diversified citizenry, it is essential that we consider the ways in which voting and representational systems succeed or fail at encouraging Madisonian Majorities.

To use Nikolas's terminology, "it is no fair" if a fixed, tyrannical majority excludes or alienates the minority. It is no fair if a fixed, tyrannical majority monopolizes all the power all the time. It is no fair if we engage in the periodic ritual of elections, but only the permanent majority gets to choose who is elected. Where we have tyranny by The Majority, we do not have genuine democracy.

Understanding the Text

1. What specific problems does Guinier see with majority rule in American politics? How serious are these problems, in your view?

2. What is a "Madisonian Majority," according to Guinier? Why are James Madison's ideas about democracy and specifically about majority rule so important, in her view?

3. How would Guinier's alternative "turn-taking" approach to government and political power be fairer to political minorities than the current

"winner-take-all majoritarianism" in U.S. politics, in her view? Under what circumstances does Guinier believe that we might need such an alternative? Do you agree with her that these circumstances would require such an alternative? Why or why not?

4. What fundamental values does Guinier hold that shape her view of how government should work? Do you think most Americans share these values? Explain.

Exploring the Issues

1. Guinier uses several examples to illustrate the problems with majority rule and to sup-

port her argument for changes in the American political process. How effective do you think these examples are in helping her make her case? What might her examples suggest about her sense of her audience?

2. In 1993, when President Bill Clinton nominated Guinier to serve on the U.S. Supreme Court, her nomination was strenuously opposed by many critics who disagreed with her views about affirmative action and "proportional representation," which is the belief that power should be distributed proportionally according to the percentage of the vote received by each party. Based on this essay, why do you think some Americans would have such severe objections to a person with Guinier's views serving on the U.S. Supreme Court? To what extent do you think this essay might address—or worsen—the concerns of such critics?

3. Guinier includes several anecdotes from her personal life in this essay. How do you think these anecdotes might affect a reader's sense of Guinier as a person and as an authority on the legal issues she is addressing in this essay? Do you think these anecdotes make her essay more or less effective? What might your answer to that question reveal about you as a reader?

4. How would you sum up Guinier's view of democracy? Do you think most Americans share her view? Why or why not?

Entering the Conversations

1. Write an essay for an audience of your classmates in which you discuss your basic concerns about the current American political process. In your essay, draw on Guinier's ideas and on any other essays in this cluster to explain or support your position.

2. Visit the web sites of several active political groups, such as MoveOn.org. Try to get a sense of their political views and what their organizations seem to believe about the American political process. Then write a report about what you learned about these groups and their uses of the Internet to participate in the political process. Alternatively, create a web site on the basis of your research.

INFOTRAC

3. In this essay, Guinier is calling for reforms to the American political process. In recent years, a number of related political reforms have been proposed and debated, including changes to the rules governing campaign funding and even abandoning the electoral college for U.S. presidential elections. Using InfoTrac College Edition and any other relevant resources, investigate current proposals for political reform in the United States, perhaps focus-

ing on one particular reform, such as campaign finance reform or changes in the electoral college system. Try to get a sense of what kinds of reforms are being proposed, by whom, and why. What advantages or disadvantages might the proposed reforms have compared to the current political process? Then write a report for an audience of your classmates in which you discuss what you learned through your research and offer your conclusions about political reform.

4. On the basis of your research for Question 3, write a letter to the editor of your local newspaper (or another appropriate publication) in which you make an argument for or against a specific political reform. In your letter, identify what you believe is the basic problem with the political process today and propose your reform as a way to address that problem.

5. Create a pamphlet (or a web site) whose purpose is to explain what you believe to be the most important aspects of the process of political power in the United States today.

As Bakari Kitwana writes in the following essay, the well-known rapper Chuck D of the rap group Public Enemy declared in 1988 that rap music is "the Black CNN." Chuck D may have been making a point about rap music's role in describing the realities of life facing Black people in contemporary society. But by the turn of the new century, it became

THE Challenge OF *Rap* Music

clear that rap music had become something even bigger than the Black CNN. Its influence seems to be far-reaching. The sounds of rap music blare from everywhere on the radio dial, from hip-hop stations to mainstream top 40 stations. Rappers themselves are no longer exclusively Black but reflect a diversity of racial and ethnic categories. Eminem, who is White, is among the world's most popular rappers, and rappers from Africa, Asia, and South America have found success. Young people of every color and income level now wear hip-hop clothing styles that were once seen only in a few Black neighborhoods in a few big cities. Big mainstream corporations like McDonald's and Coca-Cola use rap music in their television commercials. All of these developments seem to give strength to Kitwana's description of rap music as a cultural movement. Kitwana helps us see that music can communicate and influence in ways that go well beyond the lyrics of

BAKARI KITWANA

*Mr. Mayor, imagine this was your backyard
Mr. Governor, imagine it's your kids that starve
imagine your kids gotta sling crack to survive,
swing a Mac to be live . . .*

—Nas, *"I Want to Talk to You"*

In June 2001, Rush Communications CEO Russell Simmons convened a hip-hop summit in New York City. With the theme "Taking Back Responsibility," the summit focused its agenda on ways to strengthen rap music's growing influence. The 300 participants included major rap artists and industry executives as well as politicians, religious and community leaders, activists, and scholars. Few forces other than rap music, now one of the most powerful forces in American popular culture, could bring together such a diverse gathering of today's African American leaders. In many ways, the summit signaled hip-hop as the definitive cultural movement of our generation.

As the major cultural movement of our time, hip-hop (its music, fashion, attitude, style, and language) is undoubtedly one of the core

songs. He shows us that hip-hop as a musical style sends larger messages about race, gender, and social issues as well as about money and success. It has also emerged in film, television, and clothing styles, revealing that music can work in connection with other media to communicate effectively to many different audiences. Kitwana's arguments about hip-hop thus help us gain insight into the many different ways we can communicate with and beyond words.

Writer and editor Bakari Kitwana has written about hip-hop culture for a variety of publications, including the Village Voice, The Source, *and the* Progressive. *He is the author of* The Rap on Gangsta Rap *(1994),* Why White Kids Love Hip Hop *(2005), and* The Hip Hop Generation *(2002), in which this essay first appeared.* ◪

influences for young African Americans born between 1965 and 1984. To fully appreciate the extent to which this is true, think back for a moment about the period between the mid-1970s and the early 1980s, before rap became a mainstream phenomenon. Before MTV. Before BET's Rap City. Before the Fresh Prince of Bel Air. Before *House Party* I or II. It is difficult now to imagine Black youth as a nearly invisible entity in American popular culture. But in those days, that was the case. When young Blacks were visible, it was mostly during the six o'clock evening news reports of crime in urban America.

In contrast, today it is impossible not to see young Blacks in the twenty-first century's public square—the public space of television, film, and the Internet. Our images now extend far beyond crime reports. For most of our contemporaries, it's difficult to recall when this was not the case. Because of rap, the voices, images, style, attitude, and language of young Blacks have become central in American culture, transcending geographic, social, and economic boundaries.

To be sure, professional athletes, especially basketball players, have for decades been young, Black, highly visible, and extremely popular. Yet, their success just didn't translate into visibility for young Blacks overall. For one thing, the conservative culture of professional sports, central to their identity, was often at odds with the rebellious vein inherent in the new Black youth culture. While household-name ball players towed the generic "don't do drugs and stay in school" party line, rappers, the emissaries of the new Black youth culture, advocated more anti-establishment slogans like "fuck the police." Such slogans were vastly more in synch with the hard realities facing young Blacks—so much so that as time marched on and hip-hop culture further solidified its place in American popular culture, basketball culture would also come to feel its influence.

Largely because of rap music, one can tune in to the voices and find the faces of America's Black youth at any point in the day. Having proven themselves as marketable entertainers with successful music careers, rappers star in television sit-coms and film and regularly endorse corporate products (such as Lil' Kim—Candies, Missy Elliot—the Gap, and Common, Fat Joe, and the Goodie Mob—Sprite). In the mid-1980s, a handful of corporations began incorporating hip-hop into their advertisement spots. Most were limited to run-of-the-mill product endorsements. By the late 1990s, however, ads incorporating hip-hop—even those promoting traditionally conservative companies—became increasingly steeped in the subtleties of hip-hop culture. Setting the standard with their extremely hip-hop savvy 1994 Voltron campaign, Sprite broke away from the straight-up ce-

5

CONVERSATIONS: RAP AS A CULTURAL MOVEMENT

The idea that a form of music can be thought of as a "cultural movement" is not new. In the 1950s and 1960s, rock-n'-roll music was seen as a youth movement in reaction to some of the values of their parents' generation. Rock-n'-roll music seemed to express the rebellious views of young people at the same time that it also seemed to influence their views. Certain styles of dress, slang, and social practices (such as popular dances called "sock hops") came to be associated with rock-n'-roll. This is the sense in which Kitwana describes hip-hop as a cultural movement. In this essay, Kitwana is joining an expanding conversation among scholars, critics, and others about the importance of hip-hop as such a movement. But this ongoing conversation has often been contentious, too, with some critics offering harsh condemnations of what they believe is the glorification of violence, sexism, and even racism by hip-hop artists.

lebrity endorsement format. Says Coca-Cola global marketing manager Darryl Cobbin, who was on the cutting edge of this advertising strategy: "I wanted to usher in a real authenticity in terms of hip-hop in advertising. We wanted to pay respect to the music *and* the culture. What's important is the value of hip-hop culture, not only as an image, but as a method of communication."

By the late 1990s, advertisers like the Gap, Nike, AT&T, and Sony soon followed suit and incorporated hip-hop's nuances into their advertising campaigns. As a result, the new Black youth culture resonates throughout today's media, regardless of what companies are selling (from soft drinks and footwear to electronics and telecommunications).

Of course, none of this happened overnight. In fact, more important than the commercialization of rap was the less visible cultural movement on the ground in anyhood USA. In rap's early days, before it became a thriving commercial entity, dj party culture provided the backdrop for this off-the-radar cultural movement. What in the New York City metropolitan area took the form of dj battles and MC chants emerged in Chicago as the house party scene, and in D.C. it was go-go. In other regions of the country, the local movement owed its genesis to rap acts like Run DMC, who broke through to a national audience in the early 1980s. In any case, by the mid-1980s, this local or underground movement began to emerge in the form of cliques, crews, collectives, or simply kids getting together primarily to party, but in the process rhyming, dj-ing, dancing, and tagging. Some, by the early 1990s, even moved into activism. In large cities like Chicago, San Francisco, Houston, Memphis, New Orleans, Indianapolis, and Cleveland and even in smaller cities and suburban areas like Battle Creek, Michigan, and Champaign, Illinois, as the '80s turned to the '90s, more and more young Blacks were coming together in the name of hip-hop.

In the early 1980s, the "in" hip-hop fashion for New York City Black youth included Gazelles (glasses), sheepskins and leather bombers (coats), Clarks (shoes), nameplates, and name belts. In terms of language, Five Percenter expressions like "word is bond" were commonplace. These hip-hop cultural expressions in those days were considered bizarre by Black kids from other regions of the country. A student at the University of Pennsylvania at the time, Conrad Muhammad, the hip-hop minister, speaks to this in reminiscing on the National Black Students Unity Conference he organized in 1987:

> Jokers were getting off buses with shower caps on, perms and curls. MTV and BET had not yet played a role in standardizing Black youth culture the way they do today. Young people from different cities weren't all dressing the same way. Brothers

CONVERSATIONS: HIP-HOP FASHION
Images like this one showing young people in hip-hop fashions have become commonplace in recent years, especially in advertisements for clothing. Consider what images like this suggest about hip-hop as a cultural movement. Does this image convey the same kinds of messages about hip-hop that Kitwana argues for in this essay?

© Brand X Pictures/Alamy

CHAPTER 8: **COMMUNICATION** • Beyond Words

and sisters were stepping off buses saying "we're from the University of Nebraska, Omaha." "We're from University of Minnesota." "We're from Cal Long Beach."

But by the early to mid-1990s, hip-hop's commercialized element had Black kids on the same page, regardless of geographic region. In this hip-hop friendly national environment, hip-hop designers like Enyce, Mecca, and FUBU were thriving, multi-platinum sales for rap artists were routine (and dwarfed the 1980s mark of success: gold sales), and hip-hop expressions like "blowin' up," "representin'," and "keepin' it real" worked their way into the conversational language of Black youth around the country. Contrast this to the mid-1980s when even those deep into hip-hop didn't see the extent to which a national cultural movement was unfolding.

10   "Before the Fresh Fest Tour of 1984, few folks were defining hip-hop culture as hip-hop culture," says Hashim Shomari, author of *From the Underground: Hip-Hop as an Agent of Social Change.* "That was a relatively 1990s phenomenon." Practitioners like Africa Bambaataa, Grandmaster Flash, Fab-Five Freddy, Chuck D, and KRS-One were on the frontlines of those who saw the need to flesh out the definitions. Also, it wasn't until the early 1990s that breakthrough books like Joseph Eure and James Spady's *Nation-Conscious Rap* (1991), Michael Gonzales and Havelock Nelson's *Bring the Noise: A Guide to Rap Music and Hip-Hop Culture* (1991), and Tricia Rose's *Black Noise: Rap Music and Black Culture in Contemporary America* (1994) began to discuss hip-hop as an influential culture that went beyond the commercial.

Without question, rap's national exposure played a key role in the uniform way in which the local cultural manifestations evolved. More recently, given rap's commercial success, alongside limited employment options beyond minimum wage-jobs for young Blacks, hip-hop's cultural movement at the local level is increasingly marked by an entrepreneurial element. On the West Coast, East Coast, in southern and northern cities, and in rural and suburban areas in between, young Blacks are pressing their own CDs and selling them "out the trunk" regionally.° many of them are hoping to eventually put their city on the hip-hop map. What all this around the way activity has in common is that kids are tuned in to the same wavelength via hip-hop, some aspiring to be the next Air Jordan of hip-hop, others engaging in what is to them a way of life without commercial popular culture

---

°My emphasis here is on Black youth—no disrespect to the countless folks of other racial and ethnic groups down with hip-hop. This is not to say that Latino and to a lesser extent Asian and Native American youth have not been influential in and touched by hip-hop culture. Neither is it meant to ignore the distinctiveness of Caribbean Americans. More recently white kids, a large segment of hip-hop's listening audience, are jumping into the fray. Nevertheless, rap music indisputably remains dominated by Black youth in both its commercial and local manifestations. [Author's note]

aspirations, and still others tuning in as a basic engagement with the youth culture of our time.

The commercialized element of this cultural movement and the off-the-radar one fuel each other. The underground element provides a steady stream of emerging talent that in turn gets absorbed into commercialization. That new voice and talent again inspires more discussion (about the art form, new styles, trends, language, and larger issues and themes) and more talent at the local level, which later infuses the commercial manifestation of the cultural movement. Case in point: the more recent wave of talent (say, Master P out of New Orleans, Eve from Philly, and Nelly from St. Louis) is similar to the much earlier waves like the Geto Boys out of Houston and Compton's NWA. Those earlier waves of talent (the Geto Boys, NWA, Too Short, E-40, and others) most certainly provided inspiration for the No Limit Soldiers and Ruff Ryders, who came later. Like the earliest waves of artists, each group represents its distinct region, while tapping into the national movement. In turn, Master P, Eve, and Nelly will influence the next wave of talent breaking from the margins into the mainstream.

It's not exactly a chicken-or-egg question, however. Hip-hop as a culture indisputably emerged in the South Bronx in the late 1970s, and in other parts of the northeast shortly thereafter, before branching out around the country in the early 1980s. What's arguable is the extent to which hip-hop would have become the national cultural movement that it is today without commercialization.

In 1988, rapper Chuck D of the rap group Public Enemy described rap music as "the Black CNN." This was certainly true at the grassroots level at the time. However, the decade of the 1990s proved even more profound as rap music became thoroughly accepted and promoted in mainstream American popular culture. As such, rap provided the foundation for a resounding young Black mainstream presence that went far beyond rap music itself.

Understanding the degree to which the local and commercial are   15
deeply entrenched and interdependent, one can begin to grasp the far-reaching effects of hip-hop on young Blacks. As the primary vehicle through which young Blacks have achieved a national voice and presence, rap music transmits the new Black youth culture to a national audience. And in the same way as the mainstream media establishes the parameters for national discussion for the nation at large, rap music sets the tone for Black youth. As the national forum for Black youth concerns and often as the impetus for discussion around those issues, rap music has done more than any one entity to help our generation forge a distinct identity.

Another important aspect of what makes rap so substantive in the lives of young Blacks is its multilingual nature. In addition to beaming out hip-hop culture, rap also conveys elements of street culture, prison culture, and the new Black youth culture. Often all of these elements overlap within rap's lyrics and visual images. In the process, images and ideas that define youth culture for this generation—such as designer clothes, like Sean Jean, Phat Farm, and Tommy Hilfiger, ever-changing styles of dress, and local colloquialisms—are beamed out to a captive national audience. Also transmitted are cues of personal style, from cornrows and baby dreads to body piercing and tattoos.

And finally, even more important than fashion, style, and language, the new Black culture is encoded within the images and lyrics of rap and thus help define what it means to be young and Black at the dawn of the millennium. In the process, rap music has become the primary vehicle for transmitting culture and values to this generation, relegating Black families, community centers, churches, and schools to the back burner.

To be sure, rap marked a turning point, a shift from practically no public voice for young Blacks—or at best an extremely marginalized one—to Black youth culture as the rage in mainstream popular culture. And more than just increasing Black youth visibility, rap articulated publicly and on a mass scale many of this generation's beliefs, relatively unfiltered by the corporate structures that carried it. Even when censored with bleeps or radio-friendly "clean" versions, the messages were consistent with the new Black youth culture and more often than not struck a chord with young Blacks, given our generation's unique collective experiences. At the same time, the burgeoning grassroots arts movement was underway. All was essential to rap's movement into the mainstream and its emergence as the paramount cultural movement of our time.

* * *

Although hip-hop has secured its place as a cultural movement, its biggest challenge lies ahead. In the late 1980s when gangsta rap first emerged, community activists and mainstream politicians of the civil rights generation began to challenge rap's content. This criticism forced a dialogue that revealed one of the Black community's best kept secrets, the bitter generational divide between hip-hop generationers and our civil rights/Black power parents.

20   The key concern was Black cultural integrity: how have the very public images of young Blacks in hip-hop music and culture affected the larger Black community? Central to this discussion was the pervasive use of offensive epithets in rap lyrics, such as "nigga," "bitch," and "ho," all of which reinforce negative stereotypes about Blacks. What was the price of this remarkable breakthrough in the visibility of young Blacks in the mainstream culture? Had young rappers simply transferred images of young Black men as criminals from news reports to entertainment? And finally, had the growing visibility of

young Black entertainers further marginalized young Black intellectuals and writers, who have remained nearly invisible?

A handful of responses emerged. The response from the rap industry was unanimous: free speech is a constitutional right. The predominant response from rap artists themselves was a proverbial head in the sand. Most reasoned that the older generation was out of touch with the concerns of hip-hop generationers. Just as our parents' generation was unfamiliar with the music, the thinking went, when it came to other matters of our generation, particularly issues involving hip-hop, they, likewise, didn't know what they were talking about. By and large, the question of rap's attack on Black cultural integrity went unaddressed. In fact, the use of incendiary words like "nigga" and "bitch" has become so commonplace in rap's lyrics that today even those in rap's growing white audience routinely use them when referring to each other and often their Black peers (a matter Spike Lee vaguely touched on in the film *Bamboozled*).

Lately, as the theme of the Simmons summit "Taking Back Responsibility" suggests, hip-hop is again undertaking the critical task of questioning its relationship to the community. David Mays, publisher of the hip-hop magazine *The Source*, and Reverend Al Sharpton held a series of summits eight months prior to the Simmons summit, which called for a code of conduct in light of arrests of numerous rappers and the growing association of rappers with criminality. Minister Conrad Muhammad, dubbed the hip-hop minister for the moral voice he's long brought to the hip-hop community, felt the Mays-Sharpton gathering didn't go far enough. Muhammad called for a summit of Black rap artists, rap industry executives, and activists to discuss ways of holding the hip-hop industry accountable to the Black community. Appalled by Muhammad's moral challenge to the rap industry, Simmons countered Muhammad with a call for his own summit to be held within a few weeks of the Muhammad one.

Simmons, a major player in the rap industry who earlier began flexing his political muscle by reaching out to Democratic party insiders like Hillary Clinton in her bid for the U.S. Senate, brought together the largest and most media-celebrated summit to date. Joining rap industry insiders were African American notables like minister Louis Farrakhan, NAACP-head Kweisi Mfume, U.S. Representative Cynthia McKinney, and scholars Cornel West and Michael Eric Dyson.

The Simmons event was impressive in terms of sheer numbers and diverse backgrounds. But where it most seriously came up short was in its failure to incorporate the grassroots segment of hip-hop's cultural movement, especially hip-hop generation activists. When hip-hop's true influence as a cultural movement is finally understood, events like these will recognize that the very same synergy at the heart of hip-hop's commercial success has also informed our generation's activists and political theorists. Just as some record executives can

CONVERSATIONS: OFFENSIVE LYRICS
In this passage, Kitwana refers to some of the criticisms of hip-hop music by parents' groups, religious organizations, and women's groups. As Kitwana suggests, these criticisms have focused on what many people consider offensive lyrics, including obscenities, racial epithets, and language that denigrates women. Some advocates for hip-hop have argued that these lyrics reflect the realities of contemporary Black life and call attention to the injustices many Blacks face. In acknowledging these criticisms here, Kitwana might be seen to be offering his response to such criticisms and to encourage advocates for hip-hop to address those criticisms. Consider how your own sense of this debate might influence the way you read this passage and react to Kitwana's view.

give us a blueprint for blowin' up rap acts, the ideas that our generation's activists hold about maximizing rap's potential for social change have been seasoned in their day-to-day work and experience. If our generation's cultural movement is to evolve to have a meaningful political impact, the local segments of hip-hop's cultural movement—from hip-hop generation activists to local entrepreneurs to the everyday hip-hop kids on the block—must not only be brought to the table, but must have a major voice.

*   *   *

25   Furthermore, rather than centering the discussion within our own generation—*and*, yes, including the expertise and insight of our parents' generation—the invitation-only Simmons summit turned to the mostly liberal-integrationist civil rights leadership and music industry executives. The result was predictable: a combination of the traditional music industry call for free speech, which allows for continued blockbuster sales without disrupting the minstrel-esque proven formula for success, and the traditional civil rights activist call for young voters to support Democratic candidates for public office. Neither of these same-game-with-another-name reforms challenge civil righters or industry insiders to do anything different than what they are already doing. Moreover, pushing activists of the civil rights generation to the forefront of this effort is tantamount to casting older-generation R&B singers like Dionne Warwick and Lionel Richie as leads in a 'hood film or featuring them at a concert alongside ODB or Lil' Kim.

Until hip-hop is recognized as a broad cultural movement, rather than simply an influential moneymaker, those who seek to tap into hip-hop's potential to impact social change should not expect substantive progress. A unified front between hip-hop's commercial and grassroots sectors on the issue of sociopolitical action would change the nature of the dialogue. For example, in the same way that the hip-hop community as a cultural movement inherently answered the question, "what is hip-hop culture?" a new inclusive framework inevitably would answer the question, "what do we mean by politicizing the hip-hop generation?" Is our goal to run hip-hop generationers for office, to turn out votes for Democrats and Republicans, to form a third party, or to provide our generation with a more concrete political education?

Understanding the Text

1. Why does Kitwana believe that hip-hop is "the definitive cultural movement of our generation," as he puts it? What evidence does he provide to support that statement? Do you agree with him? Why or why not?

2. What factors does Kitwana identify as important in the rise of hip-hop? What do you think these factors and the rise of hip-hop suggest about the role of music in contemporary society?

3. What specific effects has the rise of hip-hop as a national movement had on contemporary society, according to Kitwana? Why are these effects important, in his view? Do you think he's right? Explain.

4. What does Kitwana see as the challenges facing hip-hop music today? What goals does he believe hip-hop should seek to achieve? What does Kitwana's discussion of these challenges and goals suggest about his view of hip-hop and of Black America in general?

Exploring the Issues

1. Throughout this essay, Kitwana uses the first person. For example, in paragraph 3 he writes that "it is impossible not to see young Blacks in the twenty-first century's public square," and he then goes on to state that "our images now extend far beyond crime reports." Who is Kitwana referring to here when he mentions "*our* images"? What might his use of the first person suggest about his sense of his intended audience? How did you react to his use of the first person in this essay? What might your answer to that question suggest about you as a reader?

2. Throughout this essay, Kitwana includes quotations from books and articles as well as from statements by various artists and critics. Examine these quotations. Who are the people that Kitwana quotes? Do they have anything in common? What might his choices of quotations suggest about his sense of his audience? How effective do you think these specific quotations are in helping Kitwana make his argument about hip-hop as a cultural movement?

3. In paragraphs 22–25, Kitwana criticizes the meeting organized by Russell Simmons (first described in par. 1). Examine these criticisms. What exactly concerns Kitwana about this event? What significance does he see in the event? To whom does Kitwana seem to be addressing his criticisms in this passage? What might this passage suggest about Kitwana's sense of purpose for this essay? How effectively do you think he accomplishes that purpose? Explain.

Entering the Conversations

1. Write an essay in which you describe the influence of hip-hop music on contemporary society from your perspective. In your essay, describe the role of hip-hop in your own life and the lives of your friends, family, or others you know. Draw on Kitwana's essay and any other relevant sources to discuss this role and what you see as the impact that hip-hop music has had.

2. Select several popular hip-hop artists that you believe have been influential in the current music scene. Write an essay in which you analyze their songs for their themes and messages. In your essay, identify what you see as the main themes that these artists address in their music and discuss what those themes might suggest about hip-hop as a musical form and as a cultural movement.

3. Create a photo essay or a web site that defines hip-hop as a cultural movement. Use any images, sounds, and text that you think best reflect your view of hip-hop as a cultural movement and its influence on contemporary society.

4. Write an essay intended for your local newspaper (or another appropriate publication) in which you express your view about the debates over the lyrics of some hip-hop songs. In your essay, discuss your position about lyrics that some people consider offensive and explain why you believe they should or should not be subject to any form of censorship (such as banning songs from some radio stations or preventing the sale of CDs to children or teens).

5. Many colleges now offer courses in hip-hop culture. With a group of classmates, write a proposal for such a course at your school. (If your school already has such a course, you might write a proposal to change it in some way or to add an additional course.) In your proposal, identify the topics or issues your course on hip-hop would address and describe the assignments, readings, activities, and other features of the course. In addition, write a rationale or justification for the course that explains why you believe your school should offer such a course and what benefits it would offer students.

Shortly after the war in Iraq began in March *2003, a number of slogans began appearing on bumper stickers, in newspapers and magazines, on the Internet, and on billboards throughout the United States. Perhaps the most common of these slogans was "Support Our Troops," but other slogans were also popular: "Home of the Brave," "United We Stand,"*

Sleuthing *Patriotic* Slogans

"God Bless America." At the time, these slogans were obviously referring to the war in Iraq and what President George W. Bush called "the war on terror." They were usually interpreted as expressions of patriotism. But writer Gary Sloan wondered just what these slogans really mean. Writing a few months after the United States and its allies invaded Iraq, Sloan offered a careful, if lighthearted, analysis of some of the most common patriotic slogans at the time. His essay is a good example of the use of irony in political writing. But it has a special twist: Sloan is a retired English professor, and he draws on his expertise as a grammarian to analyze political slogans. His analysis calls attention to the ways in which the larger political meanings of slogans often have little to do with grammar or the technical definitions of words. And he helps us see how language acquires meaning in specific historical and cultural contexts.

GARY SLOAN

In this best of times and worst of times, the American landscape is dotted with signs, billboards, posters and stickers emblazoned with patriotic slogans. In my hometown, merchants have scrawled on their display windows a smorgasbord of venerable shibboleths: "United We Stand," "Support the Troops," "Pray for the Troops," "Let Freedom Ring," "Home of the Brave," "God Bless America." Taped on many windows is a flyer that reads: "Pro-America Rally in Railroad Park. Bring lawn chairs, flags, and snacks. Dress patriotic."

When I read the flyer, I thought: Shouldn't that be "Dress *patriotically*?"

Because I have spent much of my life studying and teaching language, I respond inappropriately to patriotic slogans: I parse them grammatically and try to explicate them the way I would an obscure fragment in an essay. Like Hamlet, I sometimes become sicklied over with the pale cast of thought when I shouldn't be thinking at all. The slogans are designed to evoke warm feelings of camaraderie and unity, not grimaces and cocked brows.

Yet I persist in my folly. To wit: Many patriotic slogans are in the imperative mood. They issue a command ("Support the Troops,"

GARY SLOAN, "SLEUTHING PATRIOTIC SLOGANS." FROM *ALTERNET*, APRIL 10, 2003. REPRINTED BY PERMISSION.

As you read this essay, it's worth remembering that it was originally published in Alternet.org, an Internet site that describes itself as a progressive news source. The intended audience for this essay, then, very likely had specific political views about the war in Iraq that Sloan certainly was aware of (and perhaps shared). You might consider how the political views of an audience might shape the meaning of a slogan. Consider, too, how well the irony in Sloan's essay would work with a more conservative audience as compared to a liberal one. ▾

CONVERSATIONS
CLICHÉS AND QUOTATIONS
In the opening sentence, Sloan recalls a famous line from Charles Dickens's novel *A Tale of Two Cities* (1859): "It was the best of times, it was the worst of times." Many readers will recognize this reference to that famous novel about politics and self-sacrifice that takes place during the French Revolution in the late eighteenth century. In the novel, the main character, Sydney Carton, gives up his life so that the woman he loves can be with her husband, whose life is spared by Carton's sacrifice. But many readers may not recognize this reference to Dickens's novel. Consider how Sloan's use of this reference (which is technically called an *allusion*) might enhance the meaning of this paragraph. What might Sloan wish to suggest with such an allusion? What would his paragraph lose if he had not included this allusion? Will his point be clear to readers who don't recognize the allusion? Sloan makes allusions to other well-known literary works in this essay. Consider the effects of those allusions as well.

GRAMMAR
In paragraph 4, Sloan uses a technical grammar term, the *imperative mood,* which refers to statements that are commands. In paragraph 7, he uses another grammar term, the *subjunctive mood,* which is a verb form that describes a possible or desired action or state, not a factual or actual one. (A typical example of subjunctive mood is a statement like this one: "I wish I were home right now.") Sloan is a retired English professor, so he can be expected to be familiar with such technical terms. But he wrote this essay for a much broader audience, not for linguists or grammarians. Consider what purposes his use of these technical terms might serve in this essay. What might they accomplish that less technical terms would not?

GLOSS: THE DELPHI ORACLE
The Oracle at Delphi was Pythia, priestess of the god Apollo in ancient Greek mythology, who resided at the city of Delphi around 1400 B.C. and gave predictions about the future that her listeners often could not make sense of and interpreted in various ways.

"Pray for the Troops"). Commands are risky. They create resistance in natural-born rebels and in patriophobes (those with an excessive fear of patriotism).

Are "Let Freedom Ring" and "United We Stand" logically compatible? If everyone exercises freedom of speech and conscience, will we all stand united? Instead of assenting to the war against Iraq, some may opt to ring their dissent. How does one "Support the Troops"? Letters? Pep rallies? Boxes of homemade cookies? Can one support the troops by urging them to obey their consciences even if their consciences conflict with their orders?

"Home of the Brave." Hmm. Brave in what sense? Obviously, many Americans aren't physically brave. Millions are afraid to walk the streets at night or open their doors to strangers. If "brave" refers to moral courage, might the bravest Americans be those who resist the will of the majority? Might it require more bravery to protest Operation Iraqi Freedom than to support it?

"God Bless America" is almost as inscrutable as the utterances of a **DELPHI ORACLE**. Grammatically, the words are in the subjunctive mood. They express a wish or a prayer: "Please, God, bless America," or "May God bless America."

The real conundrum: What do the words mean? In what sense is God to bless America? With good health, bouncing babies, supportive spouses? Good schools? High IQs? Philosophical wisdom? Fat paychecks, sirloin steaks, sport utility vehicles, faster computers, more cable channels, bigger boom boxes? Competitive Superbowls? Better face lifts and liposuction? Speedier cruise missiles, smarter smart bombs, stealthier stealth bombers? Continued monopoly of the planet's natural resources?

And does "America" mean Americans? If so, does it comprise all Americans, including murderers, rapists, thieves, swindlers, embezzlers, muggers, liars, cheats, bullies, pederasts, pornographers, conceited airheads, slobs, slum lords, domestic tyrants, bigots and racists?

Or does "America" refer to land, spacious skies and amber waves of grain? Or to some platonic ideal of government embodied in the Declaration of Independence and the Constitution, worthy of being blessed even if some Americans aren't?

Now, if I can just figure out how to dress patriotic.

CONVERSATIONS: SLOGANS
In all these photographs, the slogan "Support Our Troops" is used, but consider how the meaning of the slogan might differ in each case. How might Sloan's analysis of such slogans help us understand how their meaning can change depending on the context of their use?

Understanding the Text

1. What does Sloan mean when he writes that he "responds inappropriately to patriotic slogans"? Why does he describe his responses as "folly"? Do you believe him? Why or why not?

2. In paragraph 8, Sloan asks "What do the words mean?" What do you think his answer is? Do you think he really does not know? Do you agree with him?

3. How would you summarize Sloan's main point about slogans?

Exploring the Issues

1. How does Sloan present himself in this essay? What kind of person does he seem to be? What authority does he seem to have for making these kinds of statements about slogans? Do you think he wishes to be taken seriously? Explain, citing specific passages to support your answer.

2. Sloan's essay is a careful analysis of the way language is used in political slogans. His analysis rests on a knowledge of formal grammar and linguistic concepts. How effective do you find his analysis of these common slogans? Does his careful reading of such slogans offer us insights into language use that we could not otherwise gain? Does Sloan's grammatical analysis lead to a useful understanding of the political uses of language? Does it make us aware of aspects of our language use that we would otherwise miss?

3. How would you describe Sloan's strategy in making his point about political slogans and about political language in general? Does he state his position explicitly? If so, where do you see that statement in his essay? If not, how do you know what his point is? How effective do you think this essay is in conveying Sloan's point? To what extent do you think your answer to that question depends on your own political beliefs? Explain.

Entering the Conversations

1. Write a response to Sloan's essay about political slogans.

2. With a group of classmates, write several slogans related to what you believe are the most important current political issues.

3. Listen to a political speech. (You can find transcripts or audiotapes of major speeches from the most recent presidential election on the Internet or in your school library.) Identify any statements that you

would describe as political slogans and analyze the way the candidate uses those slogans in his or her speech. What do you think the candidate means by those slogans? Are the slogans being directed to a particular audience?

4. Each of these images shows a vehicle sporting bumper stickers. Consider what overall message each driver might be sending by the selection of specific bumper stickers. What conclusions can you draw about the driver? What purposes do you think each driver might have had in placing these particular bumper stickers on the vehicle? How effective are these bumper stickers in conveying specific messages to others?

© Dave G. Houser/Corbix

© Richard Hamilton Smith/Corbis

Classification

Dagoberto Gilb (b. 1950) has focused much of his writing on his Chicano identity. One critic noted that what he found most impressive about Gilb's essays is "his measured indignation at the inability of white America to grasp Chicano beliefs or culture." I was struck by that comment not only because it so nicely describes the distinctive quality of Gilb's writing,

You Know Him by His Labors, but Not His Face

but also because it says something interesting about how people understand others from backgrounds that differ from their own. In a sense, Gilb's writing is an effort to define his Chicano identity and to resist the ways in which mainstream America defines that identity. That is not a straightforward task because for many people, Chicano is associated with other kinds of identities, such as immigrant or migrant worker, that can be thought of as negative—as "Other" (a term discussed in the introduction to this cluster on page 86). In the following essay, as in much of his writing, Gilb challenges such attitudes. Here, he asks his readers to go beyond the surface, to consider the humanity that can be hidden behind labels like "immigrant." As you read this thoughtful and unusual essay, you might consider whether Gilb is

DAGOBERTO GILB

The one who left wasn't the only one sleeping on a stained twin mattress under a carpet remnant in the room near the stench of sewage, wasn't the only one making shadows from a single light bulb dangling by a wire, who laughed at that old snoring dog, who liked to praise that dinner of beans and rice and chiles, not the only one who shared a torn love seat to watch a fuzzy TV with so many brothers drinking beer and soda and sisters getting married and having babies, that crowd of aunts, uncles, cousins, nephews and nieces, not the only one with unfaded scars and bad teeth, not the only one who complained about that so-loud radio always somewhere, not the only one who could pick out the best used retread tires.

He wasn't the only one loving a mother who wore that same house-dress and apron, warming tortillas in the morning and early evening, who was still a beautiful woman.

He was the one who left and he will never stop loving her either. He had to leave behind a wife. The one who left had to leave behind his children. It was as though where he was going was a distant uncle's place, a man not blood, on his father's side, or it was the ex-husband of his godmother.

Somebody close to somebody else, somebody known but who is not in the family. That rich man has a successful construction business, or is a landowner, or he is just from "the States." He is the one many have seen drinking, laughing, talking loud in his language. He wouldn't live in even the nicest house in Mexico.

5   In "the States," there is work that pays and that is what the one who left needs and wants and he knows how to work, he is not afraid of any work, of earning. He is the one who left and he met good people, and bad people, and it was always dirty and mean, the same clothes no matter where or when or what. And that rich man does have lots of work. The one who left sweeps the sawdust and scrubs the cement and masonry tools and coils the hoses.

He stoops low for the cinder blocks and he lifts a beam that has to be set high. He pushes the wheelbarrow and pounds spikes with a flattened waffle-face metal hammer and he pulls out pins with its claws. He hauls the trash scraps and he digs the plumbing trench.

He always says yes and he means yes. He is a CHEAP WAGE, and he is quiet because he is far from home, AS PAPERLESS AS BIRTH, and he not only acts grateful, he is grateful, because there is always worse at home.

The one who left is nobody special, and he knows it himself.

There are so many others just like him, hungry, even hungrier once they've been paid. His only home is work and job. His only trust, his only confidence, is the work, the job.

10   The one who left lives near streets in the States that were the first and are now the last. He shops at markets where others who left go.

He does not go to banks, but of course he wants to. He does not have a driver's license, but of course he wants one. He does not have a phone, but of course he wants one. He wants his family to be with him.

He learned early to live like a shadow watching a single light bulb and now he moves with almost a natural invisibility, carefully crossing into the light of night, not really seen when he's working in the sun.

He is someone who left his mother to get work.

He left his wife to find work.

15   He left his children to get work.

His citizenship is not in Mexico or in "the States" but is at a job.

He is not a part-time citizen, a temporary citizen.

He is loyal to work, and he is a patriot of its country.

He does not want to leave it in three years, or in six years. Like everyone else, he wants to become wealthy in his country.

challenging your own attitudes about people who may be different from you.

Dagoberto Gilb is the author of Gritos: Essays *(2003), which was a finalist for the National Book Critics Circle Award, as well as three other books of fiction. The following essay was first published in the* Los Angeles Times *in 2004.* ▾

STRATEGIES: DESCRIPTION WITH A PURPOSE
The scene Gilb describes in the opening paragraphs of this essay is detailed and vivid, but it is not identified as a specific place at a particular time. Why? What do you think Gilb tries to accomplish with this description? What do the details he includes suggest about the people being described? In what ways might this description be different if it were given a specific place and time? Keep these questions in mind as you read the rest of this essay, and consider how this description helps convey Gilb's message.

CONVERSATIONS: ILLEGAL IMMIGRATION
In paragraph 7, Gilb describes the "one who left" as a "cheap wage" and "as paperless as birth." The descriptions might seem vague, but they have significance in the context of the ongoing debates about illegal immigration in the United States. Such debates have a long history in the United States, but they intensified in the years since 2000, as the U.S. economy struggled through a recession. Some Americans believe that illegal immigrants take jobs away from U.S. citizens. Others argue that immigrants do work that most Americans refuse to do. In recent decades, several plans to grant an amnesty to some illegal immigrants have been proposed. In early 2004, for example, President George W. Bush announced plans to reform immigration laws so that some illegal immigrant workers could acquire legal status. But many people opposed the plan. As these debates continue, many immigrants remain "paperless," like the man Gilb describes here—that is, they have no papers to document their status as legal immigrants and are therefore often referred to as "undocumented immigrants." Consider how the meaning of Gilb's essay is shaped by this context and by the ongoing conversations about immigration. Consider as well how he relies on that context as he chooses his words and develops his ideas in this essay.

Understanding the Text

1. Who is "the one who left" that Gilb describes in the opening paragraph? What is noteworthy about him, if anything? Why does Gilb describe him as "nobody special" later in the essay (par. 8)?

2. Who is the "somebody close to somebody else" that Gilb describes in the fourth paragraph? In what ways is he different from the people described elsewhere in this essay? Why are these differences important?

3. What is the significance of work to the people described in this essay? Why does Gilb write that the "person who left" is "loyal to work, and he is a patriot of its country"? What does this suggest about immigrant workers?

Exploring the Issues

1. Examine Gilb's decision not to identify the people in this essay in more specific terms. What effect do you think this decision has on Gilb's essay? What effect did it have on you as a reader? Do you think the essay would have been more or less effective if Gilb had identified specific people in specific locations? Explain.

2. Notice how Gilb ends this essay: "Like everyone else, he wants to become wealthy in his country." Why do you think he ends with this line? What point do you think he is making? What might this line suggest about the similarities and differences between the immigrant worker described in this essay and the people in the United States that he works for? Do you agree with Gilb that "everyone else" wants to become wealthy? Why or why not?

3. What do you think this essay suggests about the United States and about Americans? What do you think it suggests about Mexico? Do you think Gilb is criticizing one or both of these countries? Explain, citing specific passages from the essay to support your answer.

Entering the Conversations

1. Write an essay in which you express your views about immigration. Be sure to support your position appropriately. (You may wish to do some research about immigration for this assignment, as described in Question 4.)

2. In a group of classmates, share the essays you wrote for Question 1. What main arguments do you and your classmates present regarding immigration? What do these arguments suggest about how you define *American* and *immigrant*? In what ways might Gilb's essay influence your position on immigration or the positions of your classmates?

3. Try to find a friend or family member who is an immigrant or whose ancestors immigrated to the United States. Or visit the office for international students on your campus to meet someone from another country who might be willing to talk to you about his or her experiences. Interview this person and try to get a sense of what it has been like to come to the United States from somewhere else. Or get a sense of how the fact that their parents or grandparents were immigrants has affected their sense of who they are. Then write an essay on the basis of this interview in which you explore the identity of *immigrant*. If you are yourself an immigrant, write an essay about your experiences in coming to the United States.

INFOTRAC

4. Search InfoTrac College Edition, the Internet, and other relevant resources for information and viewpoints regarding immigration in the United States. (Currently, many advocacy groups both for and against greater restrictions on immigration to the United States maintain web sites, so be aware that much information about immigration on the web is presented from these viewpoints.) Try to identify the main arguments for and against greater or fewer restrictions on immigration, and focus specifically on illegal immigrant workers and their role in these arguments. Then write a report on the basis of your research. In your report, provide an overview of these debates about immigration, and try to draw conclusions about how attitudes toward people of certain races, ethnicity, cultural backgrounds, religious beliefs, and national origin seem to influence the ongoing debates about immigration.

5. On the basis of your research for Question 4, write a letter to the editor of your local newspaper or another appropriate publication in which you express your views about immigration.

Alternatively, create a blog or web site devoted to this issue.

Compare & Contrast

A few years ago, a student of mine wrote an *essay in which she made a very persuasive argument against eating meat. In her essay, she cited many statistics to support her claim that eating meat was not only less healthy than a vegetarian diet but also contributed to environmental damage because of the way cattle, chickens, and pigs are raised and*

Should We *All* Be Vegetarians?

processed. She concluded that becoming a vegetarian was therefore an ethical matter as well as a matter of health. Not long ago, that student, who is now a high school English teacher, contacted me, and we met at a local restaurant to talk about teaching. For her dinner, she ordered a large hamburger.

You might call my former student a hypocrite, but I think the matter is more complicated. I have no doubt that she believed what she wrote in her essay, but I also think she learned how challenging it can be to give up eating meat if you live in the United States. The following article helps explain why. As writer Richard Corliss (b. 1944) points out in this article, meat is not only a major part of the American diet, but it is also part of American culture. Think hamburgers on the Fourth of July and hot dogs at the baseball park. Moreover, despite health risks associated with eating meat, becoming a vegetarian has risks of

RICHARD CORLISS

FIVE REASONS TO EAT MEAT:

1) It tastes good

2) It makes you feel good

3) It's a great American tradition

4) It supports the nation's farmers

5) Your parents did it

Oh, sorry . . . those are five reasons to smoke cigarettes. Meat is more complicated. It's a food most Americans eat virtually every day: at the dinner table; in the cafeteria; on the barbecue patio; with mustard at a ballpark; or, a billion times a year, with special sauce, lettuce, cheese, pickles, onions on a sesame-seed bun. Beef is, the TV commercials say, "America's food"—the Stars and Stripes served up medium rare—and as entwined with the nation's notion of its robust frontier heritage as, well, the Marlboro Man.

But these days America's cowboys seem a bit small in the saddle. Those cattle they round up have become politically incorrect: for many, meat is an obscene cuisine. It's not just the additives and ailments connected with the consumption of beef, though a dish of hormones, E. coli bacteria or the scary specter of mad-cow disease might be effective enough as an appetite suppressant. It's that more and more Americans, particularly young Americans, have started engaging in a practice that would once have shocked their parents. They are eating their vegetables. Also their grains and sprouts. Some 10 million Americans today consider themselves to be practicing vegetarians, according to a *Time* poll of 10,000 adults; an additional 20 million have flirted with vegetarianism sometime in their past.

To get a taste of the cowboy's ancient pride, and current defensiveness, just click on South Dakota cattleman Jody Brown's web site, www.ranchers.net, and read the new meat mantras: "Vegetarians don't live longer, they just look older"; and "If animals weren't meant to be eaten, then why are they made out of meat?" (One might ask the same of humans.) For Brown and his generation of unquestioning meat eaters, dinner is something the parents put on the table and the kids put in their bodies. Of his own kids, he says, "We expect them to eat a little of everything." So beef is served nearly every night at the Brown homestead, with nary a squawk from Jeff, 17, Luke, 13, and Hannah, 11. But Jody admits to at least one liberal sympathy. "If a vegetarian got a flat tire in my community," he says, "I'd come out and help him."

For the rancher who makes his living with meat or the vegetarian whose diet could someday drive all those breeder-slaughterers to bankruptcy, nothing is simple any more. Gone is the age of American innocence, or naiveté when such items as haircuts and handshakes, family names and school uniforms, farms and zoos, cowboys and ranchers, had no particular political meaning. Now everything is up for rancorous debate. And no aspect of our daily lives—our lives as food consumers—gets more heat than meat.

5   For millions of vegetarians, beef is a four-letter word; veal summons charnel visions of infanticide. Many children, raised on hit films like *Babe* and *Chicken Run*, recoil from eating their movie heroes and switch to what the meat defeaters like to call a "nonviolent diet." Vegetarianism resolves a conscientious person's inner turf war by providing an edible complex of good-deed-doing: to go veggie is to be more humane. Give up meat, and save lives!

Of course, one of the lives you could save or at least prolong is your own. For vegetarianism should be about more than not eating; it's also about smart eating. You needn't be a born-again foodist to think this. The American Dietetic Association, a pretty centrist group, has proclaimed that "appropriately planned vegetarian diets are healthful, are nutritionally adequate and provide health benefits in the prevention and treatment of certain diseases."

So, how about it? Should we all become vegetarians? Not just teens but also infants, oldsters, athletes—everyone? Will it help us live lon-

its own. Corliss's article explores these complexities and helps us see that a basic necessity like food is not always as basic as it might seem.

Richard Corliss writes about popular culture for Time *magazine, in which the following article appeared in 2002. (Corliss was assisted in writing this article by reporters Melissa August, Matthew Cooper, David Bjerklie, Lisa McLaughlin, Wendy Cole, and Jeffrey Ressner.)* ⬛

CONVERSATIONS: POPULAR CULTURE AND OUR FRONTIER HERITAGE

Corliss makes several references (par. 1) that are probably familiar to most Americans. For example, the phrase "special sauce, lettuce, cheese, pickles, onions on a sesame-seed bun" is a reference to a popular advertisement for McDonald's restaurants from several years ago; "America's food" is a reference to an advertising campaign by U.S. producers of beef. These references suggest that writers like Corliss rely on their readers' familiarity with various aspects of popular culture, such as well-known advertisements. They also assume that readers are familiar with certain ideas that are part of the culture. For example, later in this paragraph (par. 1), Corliss associates meat with what he calls "the nation's notion of its robust frontier heritage," which is reflected in the image of the famous Marlboro Man in cigarette advertisements. Here, Corliss assumes his readers understand the idea of the frontier, which is well established in American culture. This brief paragraph provides a good example of how much knowledge readers and writers bring to a text; it also shows how that knowledge helps shape the meaning that readers and writers make in a piece of writing.

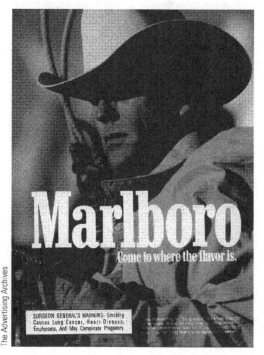

The Advertising Archives

ger, healthier lives? Does it work for people of every age and level of work activity? Can we find the right vegetarian diet and stick to it? And if we can do it, will we?

There are as many reasons to try vegetarianism as there are soft-eyed cows and soft-hearted kids. To impressionable young minds, vegetarianism can sound sensible, ethical and—as nearly 25% of adolescents polled by Teenage Research Unlimited said—"cool." College students think so too. A study conducted by Arizona State University psychology professors Richard Stein and Carol Nemeroff reported that, sight unseen, salad eaters were rated more moral, virtuous and considerate than steak eaters. "A century ago, a high-meat diet was thought to be health-favorable," says Paul Rozin of the University of Pennsylvania. "Kids today are the first generation to live in a culture where vegetarianism is common, where it is publicly promoted on health and ecological grounds." And kids, as any parent can tell you, spur the consumer economy; that explains in part the burgeoning sales of veggie burgers (soy, bulgur wheat, cooked rice, mushrooms, onions and flavorings in Big Mac drag) in supermarkets and fast-food chains.

Children, who are signing on to vegetarianism much faster than adults, may be educating their parents. Vegetarian food sales are savoring double-digit growth. Top restaurants have added more meatless dishes. Trendy "living foods" or "raw" restaurants are sprouting up, like Roxanne's in Larkspur, Calif., where no meat, fish, poultry or dairy items are served, and nothing is cooked to temperatures in excess of 118°F. "Going to my restaurant," says Roxanne Klein, "is like going to a really cool new country you haven't experienced before."

Like any country, vegetarianism has its hidden complexities. 10 For one thing, vegetarians come in more than half a dozen flavors, from sproutarians to pesco-pollo-vegetarians. The most notorious are the vegan (rhymes with intriguin' or fatiguin') vegetarians. The Green Party of the movement, vegans decline to consume, use or wear any animal products. They also avoid honey, since its production demands the oppression of worker bees. TV's favorite vegetarian, the cartoon 8-year-old **LISA SIMPSON**, once had a crush on a fellow who described himself as "a Level Five vegan—I don't eat anything that casts a shadow." Among vegan celebrities: the rock star Moby and Ohio Congressman Dennis Kucinich, who swore off steak for breakfast and insists he feels much better starting his day with miso soup, brown rice or oat groats.

To true believers—who refrain from meat as an A.A. member does from drink and do a spit-take if told that there's gelatin in their soup—a semivegetarian is no vegetarian at all. A phrase like pesco-pollo-vegetarian, to them, is an oxymoron, like "lapsed Catholic" or "semivirgin." *Vegetarian Times*, the bible of this particular congregation, lays down the dogma: "For many people who are working to become vegetarians, chicken and fish may be transitional foods, but they are not vegetarian foods . . . the word 'vegetarian' means someone who eats no meat, fish or chicken."

Clear enough? Not to many Americans. In a survey of 11,000 individuals, 37% of those who responded "Yes, I am a vegetarian" also reported that in the previous 24 hours they had eaten red meat; 60% had eaten meat, poultry or seafood. Perhaps those surveyed thought a vegetarian is someone who, from time to time, eats vegetables as a side dish—say, alongside a prime rib. If more than one-third of people in a large sample don't know the broadest definition of vegetarian, one wonders how they can be trusted with something much more difficult: the full-time care and picky-picky feeding of their bodies, whatever their dietary preferences.

We know that fruits, vegetables, grains, legumes and nuts are healthy. There are any number of studies that show that consuming more of these plant-based foods reduces the risk for a long list of chronic maladies (including coronary artery disease, obesity, diabetes and many cancers) and is a probable factor in increased longevity in the industrialized world. We know that on average we eat too few fruits and vegetables and too much saturated fat, of which meat and dairy are prime contributors. We also know that in the real world, real diets—vegetarian and nonvegetarian—as consumed by real people range from primly virtuous to pig-out voracious. There are meat eaters who eat more and better vegetables than vegetarians, and vegetarians who eat more artery-clogging fats than meat eaters.

The International Congress on Vegetarian Nutrition, a major conference on the subject, was held this spring at Loma Linda (Calif.) University. The research papers presented there included some encouraging if tentative findings: that a predominantly vegetarian diet may have beneficial effects for kidney and nerve function in diabetics, as well as for weight loss; that eating more fruits and vegetables can slow, and perhaps reverse, age-related declines in brain function

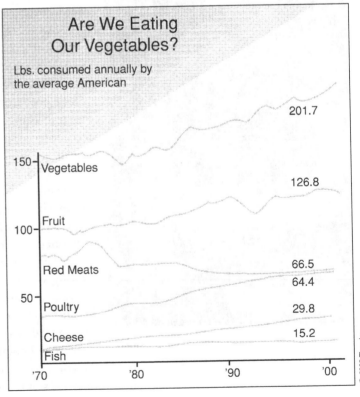

Are We Eating Our Vegetables?

Lbs. consumed annually by the average American

- Vegetables — 201.7
- Fruit — 126.8
- Red Meats — 66.5
- Poultry — 64.4
- Cheese — 29.8
- Fish — 15.2

'70 '80 '90 '00

© 2002 Time Inc.

and in cognitive and motor performance—at least in rats; that vegetarian seniors have a lower death rate and use less medication than meat-eating seniors; that vegetarians have a healthier total intake of fats and cholesterol but a less healthy intake of fatty acids (such as the heart-protecting omega-3 fatty acids found in fish oil).

15   But one paper suggested that low-protein diets (associated with vegetarians) reduce calcium absorption and may have a negative impact on skeletal health. And although several studies on Seventh-Day Adventists (typically vegetarians) indicated that they have a longer-than-average life expectancy, other studies found that prostate-cancer rates were high in Adventists, and one study found that Adventists were more likely to suffer hip fractures.

Can it be that vegetarianism is bad for your health? That's a complex issue. There's a big, beautiful plant kingdom out there; you ought to be able to dine healthily on this botanical bounty. With perfect knowledge, you can indeed eat like a king from the vegetable world. But ordinary people are not nutrition professionals. While some vegetarians have the full skinny on how to watch their riboflavin and vitamins D and B12, many more haven't a clue. This is one reason that vegetarians, in a study of overall nutrition, scored significantly lower than nonvegetarians on the USDA's Healthy Eating Index, which compares actual diet with USDA guidelines.

Another reason is that vegans skew the stats, because their strict avoidance of meat, eggs and dairy products can lead to deficiencies in iron, calcium and vitamin B12. "These nutrients are the problem," says Johanna Dwyer, a professor of nutrition and medicine at Tufts University. "At least among the vegans who are also philosophically opposed to fortified foods and/or vitamin and mineral supplements."

Debates about the efficacy of vegetarianism follow us from cradle to wheelchair. In 1998 child-care expert Dr. Benjamin Spock, who became a vegetarian late in life, stoked a stir by recommending that children over the age of 2 be raised as vegans, rejecting even milk and eggs. The American Dietetic Association says it is possible to raise kids as vegans but cautions that special care must be taken with nursing infants (who don't develop properly without the nutrients in mother's milk or fortified formula). Other researchers warn that infants breast-fed by vegans have lower levels of vitamin B12 and DHA (an omega-3 fatty acid), important to vision and growth.

And there is always the chance of vegetarian theory gone madly wrong in practice. A Queens, N.Y., couple were indicted last May for first-degree assault, charged with nearly starving their toddler to death on a strict diet of juices, ground nuts, herbal tea, beans, flaxseed and cod-liver oils. At 16 months, the girl weighed 10 lbs., less than half the normal weight of a child her age. Their lawyer's defense: "They felt that they have their own lifestyle. They're vegetarians." The couple declined to plea bargain, and are still in jail awaiting trial.

Many children decide on their own to become vegetarians and are declaring their preference at ever more precocious ages; it's often their first act of domestic rebellion. But a youngster is at a disadvantage insisting on a rigorous cuisine before he or she can cook food—or buy it or even read—and when the one whose menu is challenged is the parent: nurturer, disciplinarian and executive chef. Alicia Hurtado of Oak Park, Ill., has been a vegetarian half her life—she's 8 now—and mother Cheryle mostly indulges her daughter's diet. Still, Mom occasionally sneaks a little chicken broth into Alicia's pasta dishes. "When she can read labels," Cheryle says, "I'll be out of luck."

By adolescence, kids can read the labels but often ignore the ingredients. Research shows that calcium intake is often insufficient in American teens. By contrast, lacto-ovo teens usually have abundant calcium intake. For vegans, however, consuming adequate amounts of calcium without the use of fortified foods or supplements is difficult without careful dietary planning. Among vegan youth who do not take supplements, there is reason for concern with respect to iron, calcium, vitamins D and B12, and perhaps also selenium and iodine.

For four years Christina Economos has run the Tufts longitudinal health study on young adults, a comprehensive survey of lifestyle habits among undergraduates. In general, she finds that "kids who were most influenced by family diet and health values are eating healthy vegetarian or low-meat diets. But there is a whole group of students who decide to become vegetarians and do it in a poor way. The ones who do it badly don't know how to navigate in the vegetarian world. They eat more bread, cheese and pastry products and load up on salad dressing. Their saturated-fat intake is no lower than red-meat eaters, and they are more likely to consume inadequate amounts of vitamin B12 and protein. They may think they are healthier because they are some sort of vegetarian and they don't eat red meat, but in fact they may be less healthy."

Jenny Woodson, 20, now a junior at Duke, has been a vegetarian from way back. At 6, on a trip to McDonald's, she ordered a tossed salad. When Jenny lived in a dorm at high school, she quickly realized that teens do not live on French fries and broccoli alone. "We ended up making vegetarian sandwiches with bagels and ingredients from the salad bar, cheese fries and stuffed baked potatoes with cottage cheese." Jenny and her friends were careful to avoid high-fat, calorie-laden fare at the salad bar, but for those who don't exercise restraint, salad-bar fixings can become vegetarian junk food.

Maggie Ellinger-Locke, 19, of the St. Louis, Mo., suburb of University City, has been a vegetarian for eight years and went vegan at 15. Since then she has not worn leather or wool products or slept under

STRATEGIES: EXAMPLES
Notice the examples of two young people who are vegetarians described in paragraphs 23 and 24. Both are women. One attended Duke, a prestigious university; the other lives in a suburb of St. Louis. Consider how the author uses these examples to convey specific ideas about being a vegetarian. Consider, too, whether these two people are in any way typical of Americans.

a down comforter. She has not used cups or utensils that have touched meat. "It felt like we were keeping kosher," says Maggie's mother Linda, who isn't Jewish. At high school Maggie was ridiculed, even shoved to the ground, by teen boys who apparently found her eating habits threatening. She found a happy ending, of sorts, enrolling at Antioch College, where she majors in ecofeminism. "Here," she says, "the people on the defensive are the ones who eat meat."

Maggie hit a few potholes on the road to perfection. Until recently, she smoked up to two packs of cigarettes a day (cigarettes, after all, are plants fortified with nicotine), quitting only because she didn't want to support the tobacco business. And she freely admits to an eating disorder: for the past year she has been bulimic, bingeing and vomiting sometimes as much as once a day to cope with stress. But she insists she is true to her beliefs: even when bingeing, she remains dedicated to vegan consumption. 25

The American Dietetic Association found that vegetarian diets are slightly more common among adolescents with eating problems but that "recent data suggest that adopting a vegetarian diet does not lead to eating disorders." It can be argued that most American teens already have an eating disorder—fast food, soft drinks and candy are a blueprint for obesity and heart trouble. Why should teens be expected to purge their bad habits just because they have gone veggie? Still, claims Simon Chaitowitz of the pro-vegetarian and animal-rights group Physicians Committee for Responsible Medicine, "Kids are better off being junk-food vegetarians than junk-food meat eaters."

Maybe. According to Dr. Joan Sabate, chairman of the Loma Linda nutrition conference, there are still concerns over vegetarian diets for growing kids or lactating women. When you are in what he calls "a state of high metabolic demand," any diet that excludes foods makes it harder to meet nutrient requirements. But he is quick to add that "for the average sedentary adult living in a Western society, a vegetarian diet meets dietary needs and prevents chronic diseases better than an omnivore diet."

Like kids and nursing moms, athletes need to be especially smart eaters. Their success depends on bursts of energy, sustained strength and muscle mass, factors that require nutrients more easily obtained from meat. For this reason, relatively few top athletes are vegetarians. Besides, says sports nutritionist Suzanne Girard Eberle, the author of *Endurance Sports Nutrition*, "lots of athletes have no idea how their bodies work. That's why fad diets and supplements are so attractive to them."

Eberle notes that vegetarian diets done correctly are high in fiber and low in fat. "But where are the calories?" she asks. "World-class endurance athletes need in excess of 5,000 or 6,000 calories a day. Competition can easily consume 10,000. You need to eat a lot of plant-based food to get those calories. Being a vegetarian athlete is hard, really hard to do right."

It's not that easy for the rest of America, either. Middle-aged to el-   30
derly adults can also develop deficiencies in a vegetarian diet (as they
can, of course, with a poor diet that includes meat). Deficiencies in
vitamins D and B12 and in iodine, which can lead to goiter, are common. The elderly tend to compensate by taking supplements, but
that approach carries risks. Researchers have found cases in which
vegetarian oldsters, who are susceptible to iodine deficiency, had dan-
gerously high and potentially toxic levels of iodine in their bodies
because they overdid the supplements.

Meat producers acknowledge that vegetarian diets can be healthy.
They also have responded to the call for leaner food; the National
Pork Board says that, compared with 20 years ago, pork is on average
31% lower in fat and 29% lower in saturated fat, and has 14% fewer
calories and 10% less cholesterol. But the defenders of meat and
dairy can also go on the offensive. They mention the need for B12.
And then they ratchet up the fear factor. Kurt Graetzer, CEO of the
Milk Processor Education Program, scans the drop in milk consumption (not only by vegans but by kids who prefer soda, Snapple and
Fruitopia) and declares, "We are virtually developing a generation of
osteoporotic children."

Dr. Michelle Warren, a professor of medicine at New York Presbyte-
rian Medical Center in New York City—and a member of the Council
for Women's Nutrition Solutions, which is sponsored by the National
Cattlemen's Beef Association—expresses concern about calcium deficiency connected with a vegan diet: "The most serious consequences
are low bone mass and osteoporosis. That is a permanent condition."
Warren says that in her practice, she has seen young vegetarians with
irregular periods and loss of hair. "And there's a peculiar color, a yellow tinge to the skin," that occurs in people who eat a lot of vegetables
rich in beta carotene in combination with a low-calorie diet. "I think
it's very unattractive." She also is troubled by the reasons some young
vegetarians give for their choice of diet. One female patient, Warren
says, wouldn't eat meat because she was told it was the reason her father had a heart attack.

Michael Jacobson, executive director of the Center for Science in
the Public Interest in Washington, sees most of the meat and dairy
lobby's arguments as desperate, disingenuous scare stories. "It un-
masks the industry's self-interest," he says, "when it voices concern
about B12 while hundreds of thousands of people are dying prema-
turely because of too much saturated fat from meat and dairy products." Indeed, according to David Pimentel, a Cornell ecologist, the
average American consumes 112 grams of protein a day, twice the
amount recommended by the National Academy of Sciences. "This
has implications for cancer risks and stress on the urinary system,"
says Pimentel. "And with this protein comes a lot of fat. Fully 40% of
our calories—and heavy cardiovascular risks—come from fat."

Pimentel argues that vegetarianism is much more environment-friendly than diets revolving around meat. "In terms of caloric content, the grain consumed by American livestock could feed 800 million people—and, if exported, would boost the U.S. trade balance by $80 billion a year." Grain-fed livestock consume 100,000 liters of water for every kilogram of food they produce, compared with 2,000 liters for soybeans. Animal protein also demands tremendous expenditures of fossil-fuel energy—eight times as much as for a comparable amount of plant protein. Put another way, says Pimentel, the average omnivore diet burns the equivalent of a gallon of gas per day—twice what it takes to produce a vegan diet. And the U.S. livestock population—cattle, chickens, turkeys, lambs, pigs and the rest—consumes five times as much grain as the U.S. human population. But then there are 7 billion of them; they outnumber us 25 to 1.

35   In the spirit of fair play to cowboy Jody Brown and his endangered breed, let's entertain two arguments in favor of eating meat. One is that it made us human. "We would never have evolved as large, socially active hominids if we hadn't turned to meat," says Katharine Milton, an anthropologist at the University of California, Berkeley. The vegetarian primates (orangutans and gorillas) are less social than the more omnivorous chimpanzees, possibly because collecting and consuming all that forage takes so darned much time. The early hominids took a bold leap: 2.5 million years ago, they were cracking animal bones to eat the marrow. They ate the protein-rich muscle tissue, says Milton, "but also the rest of the animal—liver, marrow, brains—with their high concentrations of other nutrients. Evolving humans ate it all."

Just as important, they knew why they were eating it. In Milton's elegant phrase, "Solving dietary problems with your head is the trajectory of the primate order." Hominids grew big on meat, and smart on that lovely brain-feeder, glucose, which they got from fruit, roots and tubers. This diet of meat and glucose gave early man energy to burn—or rather, energy to play house, to sing and socialize, to make culture, art, war. And finally, about 10,000 years ago, to master agriculture and trade—which provided the sophisticated system that modern humans can use to go vegetarian.

The other reason for beef eating is, hold on, ethical—a matter of animal rights. The familiar argument for vegetarianism, articulated by Tom Regan, a philosophical founder of the modern animal-rights movement, is that it would save Babe the pig and *Chicken Run*'s Ginger from execution. But what about Bugs Bunny and Mickey Mouse? asks Steven Davis, professor of animal science at Oregon State University, pointing to the number of field animals inadvertently killed during crop production and harvest. One study showed that simply mowing an alfalfa field caused a 50% reduction in the gray-tailed vole population. Mortality rates increase with each pass of the tractor to plow, plant and harvest. Rabbits, mice and pheasants, he says, are the indiscriminate "collateral damage" of row crops and the grain industry.

By contrast, grazing (not grain-fed) ruminants such as cattle produce food and require fewer entries into the fields with tractors and other equipment. Applying (and upending) Regan's least-harm theory, Davis proposes a ruminant-pasture model of food production, which would replace poultry and pork production with beef, lamb and dairy products. According to his calculations, such a model would result in the deaths of 300 million fewer animals annually (counting both field animals and cattle) than would a completely vegan model. When asked about Davis' arguments, Regan, however, still sees a distinction: "The real question is whether to support production systems whose very reason for existence is to kill animals. Meat eaters do. Ethical vegetarians do not."

The moral: there is no free lunch, not even if it's vegetarian. For now, man is perched at the top of the food chain and must live with his choice to feed on the living things further down. But even to raise the question of a harvester Hiroshima is to show how far we have come in considering the humane treatment of that which is not human. And we still have a way to go. "It may take a while," says actress and vegetarian Mary Tyler Moore, "but there will probably come a time when we look back and say, 'Good Lord, do you believe that in the 20th century and early part of the 21st, people were still eating animals?'"

It may take a very long while. For most people, meat still does taste good. And can "America's food" ever be tofu?   40

Understanding the Text

1. Why is the matter of eating meat or being a vegetarian no longer simple, according to Corliss? Do you think it ever was? Explain.

2. What are the main reasons for becoming a vegetarian, according to this article? What do you think these reasons suggest about Americans' eating habits and attitudes toward food?

3. What are some of the challenges of having a true vegetarian diet? Why are these challenges important, according to the author? What do you think these challenges reveal about our habits and attitudes relating to food?

4. What are the reasons for eating meat, according to this article? Do you think these reasons are persuasive? Why or why not? What might your answer to that question suggest about your own values regarding food and lifestyle?

Exploring the Issues

1. How would you characterize the writing style in this article? What specific features of the writing style—such as word choice, figures of speech, sentence structure, or rhythm—are most distinctive in your view? Do you find this writing style effective? Explain.

2. Corliss cites many statistics, refers to scientific studies of nutrition, provides examples, and quotes food researchers. Examine his use of information and evidence in this article. What kinds of information seem to be emphasized? How effectively do you think the specific points raised in the article are supported by information and evidence?

3. This article originally appeared in *Time* magazine, a large-circulation weekly news magazine that reaches a general audience. *Time* is known for informative articles that present an in-depth discussion of timely issues or events. This was intended to be such an article rather than an editorial that presents an opinion about an issue or event. To what extent do you think this article succeeds in presenting its subject fairly and objectively? Do you think the author favors one side or another in the debates about whether or not to eat meat? Explain, citing specific passages to support your answer.

4. Corliss depicts representatives of various groups in this article, including cattle ranchers and beef producers, nutritionists and scientists, and vegetarians. Examine the picture he paints of these groups. What does he seem to emphasize about each? Do you think his picture of these groups is accurate and fair? Why or why not?

Entering the Conversations

1. Write an essay in which you make a case for or against becoming a vegetarian. Base your argument on your own principles for living and for using resources.

2. In a group of classmates, share the essays you wrote for Question 1. Identify the main arguments for and against becoming a vegetarian. Try to draw conclusions about what these arguments might reveal about your attitudes regarding food.

3. Create a web site, PowerPoint presentation, flyer, or some other appropriate kind of document in which you educate a general audience about the pros and cons of eating meat or becoming a vegetarian. Draw on this article and other appropriate resources in creating your document.

4. Write a letter to the editor of your local newspaper indicating why you believe people who live in your region should or should not eat meat.

5. Watch television to find advertisements about food—for example, advertisements for fast-food restaurants, certain snack foods or other food products, or food stores. (Or look for similar advertisements in newspapers, magazines, or on the Internet.) Select several common ads for popular products or restaurants and analyze them for the messages they seem to convey about food in general. Then write a report on the basis of your analysis. Try to draw conclusions about American attitudes regarding food.

Definition

One of the most influential Black women *scholars in the United States today, bell hooks (b. 1952) is well known for her provocative and unconventional writing about race, gender, education, and culture in well-received books like* Talking Back *(1989) and* Teaching to Transgress *(1994). She is perhaps less well known as a prominent*

ON Building A Community OF Love

student of Buddhism who has written widely on Buddhist ideas about love, relationships, and community. In the following essay, hooks presents a dialogue with Thich Nhat Hanh, one of the world's foremost teachers of Zen Buddhism, who first gained international attention in the 1960s for his peace activism against the Vietnam War. As hooks tells us in this essay, Thich Nhat Hanh's writings profoundly influenced her own writing, especially her book All about Love *(2001). In this dialogue, she invites Nhat Hanh to explore with her the concepts of love and community from a Buddhist perspective. In doing so, she and Nhat Hanh raise questions about the nature of love among people in a community—questions that go beyond any single religious or cultural perspective. Their examination of Buddhist ideas about love and community can help us think more broadly about what*

BELL HOOKS

As teacher and guide Thich Nhat Hanh has been a presence in my life for more than twenty years. In the last few years I began to doubt the heart connection I felt with him because we had never met or spoken to one another, yet his work was ever-present in my work. I began to feel the need to meet him face to face, even as my intuitive self kept saying that it would happen when the time was right. My work in love has been to trust that intuitive self that kept saying that it would happen when the time was right. My work in love has been to trust that intuition knowledge.

Those who know me intimately know that I have been contemplating the place and meaning of love in our lives and culture for years. They know that when a subject attracts my intellectual and emotional imagination, I am long to observe it from all angles, to know it inside and out.

In keeping with the way my mind works, when I began to think deeply about the metaphysics of love I talked with everyone around me about it. I talked to large audiences and even had wee one-on-one

BELL HOOKS, "ON BUILDING A COMMUNITY OF LOVE: BELL HOOKS MEETS WITH THICH NHAT HANH TO ASK: HOW DO WE BUILD A COMMUNITY OF LOVE?" FROM *SHAMBHALA SUN ONLINE*, JANUARY 2000. FROM THE *SHAMBHALA SUN* MAGAZINE: WWW.SHAMBHALA-SUN.COM. REPRINTED BY PERMISSION.

conversations with children about the way they think about love. I talked about love in every state. Indeed, I encouraged the publishers of my new book *All About Love: New Visions* to launch it with postcards, t-shirts, and maybe even a calendar with the logo "Love in every state." I talked about love everywhere I traveled.

To me, all the work I do is built on a foundation of loving-kindness. Love illuminates matters. And when I write provocative social and cultural criticism that causes readers to stretch their minds, to think beyond set paradigms, I think of that work as love in action. While it may challenge, disturb and at times even frighten or enrage readers, love is always the place where I begin and end.

5   A central theme of all about love is that from childhood into adulthood we are often taught misguided and false assumptions about the nature of love. Perhaps the most common false assumption about love is that love means we will not be challenged or changed. No doubt this is why people who read writing about racism, sexism, homophobia, religion, etc. that challenges their set assumptions tend to see that work as harsh rather than loving.

Of all the definitions of love that abound in our universe, a special favorite of mine is the one offered in *THE ROAD LESS TRAVELED* BY PSYCHOANALYST M. SCOTT PECK. Defining love as "the will to extend one's self for the purpose of nurturing one's own or another's spiritual growth," he draws on the work of Erich Fromm to emphasize again and again that love is first and foremost exemplified by action—by practice—not solely by feeling.

FROMM'S *THE ART OF LOVING* was published when I was four years old. It was the book I turned to in my late teens when I felt confused about the nature of love. His insistence that "love is the active concern for the life and growth of that which we love" made sense to me then and it still does. Peck expands this definition. Knowing that the world would be a paradise of peace and justice if global citizens shared a common definition of love which would guide our thoughts and action, I call for the embrace of such a common understanding in all about love: new visions. That common understanding might be articulated in different words carrying a shared meaning for diverse experiences and cultures.

Throughout the more than twenty years that I have written on the subject of ending domination in whatever form it appears (racism, sexism, homophobia, classism), I have continually sought those paths that would lead to the end of violence and injustice. Since so much of my thinking about love in my late teens revolved around familial and romantic love, it was not until I was in my early twenties writing feminist theory that I began to think deeply about love in relation to domination.

we mean when we talk about love among members of a community.

This essay can also help us think about how we talk and write about love. The form of the dialogue, which hooks has used in many of her academic books, is as old as Plato's famous dialogues, written more than 2,500 years ago, in which the great philosopher Socrates offers his wisdom by engaging in dialogue with his peers or his students. hooks's dialogues do not follow a strict question-and-answer format but involve a give-and-take by two people interested in understanding a complicated idea. As you read, consider how this form might help hooks accomplish her goals as a writer. Consider, too, how the non-Western cultural perspective that she and Nhat Hanh take might complicate your own ideas about love and community.

Born Gloria Watkins, bell hooks is currently distinguished professor of English at City College of the City University of New York. The following dialogue first appeared in 2000 in Shambhala Sun Online, *a publication devoted to Buddhism.* ▼

CONVERSATIONS: LOVE
In Chapter 1 of *All about Love* (2001), bell hooks writes, "Imagine how much easier it would be for us to learn how to love if we began with a shared definition. The word 'love' is most often defined as a noun, yet all the more astute theorists of love acknowledge that we would all love better if we used it as a verb." In this dialogue with Thich Nhat Hanh, hooks refers to definitions of love from M. Scott Peck and Erich Fromm, two very popular writers whose work focuses on love and emotional well-being. In doing so, she not only helps her readers better understand her way of defining love, but she also places her essay in the context of a much larger conversation about love and relationships.

STRATEGIES: PERSONAL VOICE
hooks is well known for the way she draws on personal experience and adopts a personal voice in her writing, even when she is writing about complicated theoretical topics for an academic audience. In her book *Talking Back,* she argues that "if we are to reach our people and all people . . . we must understand that the telling of one's personal story provides a meaningful example, a way for folks to identify and connect." Here in paragraph 9, as she often does in her writing, hooks shares some of her own experiences to introduce her dialogue with Thich Nhat Hanh. Some scholars have criticized hooks for this personal writing style. Consider the potential impact of this personal approach on readers. What do you think this approach might help hooks achieve in her writing? What problems do you see with her personal style?

CONVERSATIONS: THE CIVIL RIGHTS MOVEMENT AND THE WOMEN'S MOVEMENT
In this section of her essay, hooks explains how two important social and political movements in the United States in the 1960s and 1970s shaped her ways of thinking about love and relationships. She traces a pendulous swing of people involved in the Civil Rights and the women's movements from love to hate and back to love. It might be difficult for us today to understand the intense debates within these movements about how to relate to one's opponents. For example, some Black leaders openly called for violence against Whites to combat the violence of White racism. Some, including Martin Luther King, Jr., disagreed, promoting instead a nonviolent approach based on a belief in equality, justice, and love. Obviously, this experience deeply affected hooks and helped shape her ideas about love and hate. Do you think hooks speaks effectively about these issues to readers who were not alive during the social movements she describes in this passage?

During my first years in college Martin Luther King's message of love as the path to ending racism and healing the wounds of racial domination had been replaced by a black power movement stressing militant resistance. While King had called for nonviolence and compassion, this new movement called on us to harden our hearts, to wage war against our enemies. Loving our enemies, militant leaders told us, made us weak and easy to subjugate, and many turned their backs on King's message.

Just as the energy of a racially-based civil rights liberation struggle was moving away from a call for love, the women's movement also launched a critique of love, calling on females to forget about love so that we might seize power. When I was nineteen participating in feminist consciousness-raising groups, love was dismissed as irrelevant. It was our "addiction to love" that kept us sleeping with the enemy (men). To be free, our militant feminist leaders told us, we needed to stop making love the center of our imaginations and yearnings. Love could be a good woman's downfall.

These two movements for social justice that had captured the hearts and imagination of our nation—movements that began with a love ethic—were changed by leaders who were much more interested in questions of power. By the late seventies it was no longer necessary to silence discussions of love; the topic was no longer on any progressive agenda.

Those of us who still longed to hold on to love looked to religions as the site of redemption. We searched everywhere, all around the world, for the spiritual teachers who could help us return to love. My seeking led me to Buddhism, guided there by the Beat poets, by personal interaction with Gary Snyder. At his mountain home I would meet my first Buddhist nun and walk mindfully with her, all the while wondering if my heart could ever know the sweet peace emanating from her like a perfume mist.

My seeking led me to the work of a Buddhist monk Martin Luther King had met and been touched by—Thich Nhat Hanh. The first work I read by this new teacher in my life was a conversation book between him and Daniel Berrigan, *The Raft Is Not the Shore.*

At last I had found a world where spirituality and politics could meet, where there was no separation. Indeed, in this world all efforts to end domination, to bring peace and justice, were spiritual practice. I was no longer torn between political struggle and spiritual practice. And here was the radical teacher—a Vietnamese monk living in exile—courageously declaring that "if you have to choose between Buddhism and peace, then you must choose peace."

Unlike white friends and comrades who were often contemptuous   15
of me because I had not traveled to the East or studied with important teachers, Thich Nhat Hanh was calmly stating: "Buddhism is in
your heart. Even if you don't have any temple or any monks, you can
still be a Buddhist in your heart and life." Reading his words I felt an
inner rapture and could only repeat, "Be still my heart." Like one
wandering in the desert overcome by thirst, I had found water. My
thirst was quenched and my spiritual hunger intensified.

For a period of more than ten years since leaving home for college
I had felt pulled in all directions by anti-racist struggle, by the feminist movement, sexual liberation, by the fundamentalist Christianity
of my upbringing. I wanted to embrace radical politics and still know
god. I wanted to resist and be redeemed. *The Raft Is Not the Shore*
helped strengthen my spiritual journey. Even though I had not met
with Thich Nhat Hanh he was the teacher, along with Chögyam
Trungpa Rinpoche, who were my chosen guides. Mixing the two was
a fiery combination.

As all became well with my soul, I began to talk about the work of
THICH NHAT HANH in my books, quoting from his work. He helped me
bring together theories of political recovery and spiritual recovery.
For years I did not want to meet him face to face for fear I would be
disappointed. Time and time again I planned to be where he was and
the plan would be disrupted. Our paths were crossing but we were
never meeting face to face.

Then suddenly, in a marvelous serendipitous way, we were meeting.
In his presence at last, I felt overwhelmed with gratitude that not only
was I given the blessing of meeting him, but that a pure spirit of love
connected us. I felt ecstatic. My heart jumped for joy—such union
and reunion to be in the presence of one who has tutored your heart,
who has been with you in spirit on your journey.

The journey is also to the teacher and beyond. It is always a path to
the heart. And the heart of the matter is always our oneness with divine spirit—our union with all life. As early as 1975, Thich Nhat Hanh
was sharing: "The way must be in you; the destination also must be in
you and not somewhere else in space or time. If that kind of self-
transformation is being realized in you, you will arrive."

Walking on love's path on a sunny day on my way to meet my teach-   20
er, I meet Sister Chan Khong. She too has taught me. She felt my
heart's readiness. Together we remembered the teacher who is everywhere awakening the heart. As she writes at the end of *Learning True
Love*, "I am with you just as you have been with me, and we encourage
each other to realize our deepest love, caring and generosity . . . together on the path of love."

* * *

GLOSS: THICH NHAT HANH
In 1966, Thich Nhat Hanh, a Buddhist monk, was forced to leave his native Vietnam because of his activism against the war then raging in his homeland. He has since become one of the world's foremost Buddhist teachers and peace activists. He established Plum Village in France, a center for the study and practice of what he calls "engaged Buddhism," which has several satellite centers around the world. He is author of dozens of books about Buddhism and about working toward peace.

bell hooks: I began writing a book on love because I felt that the United States is moving away from love. The civil rights movement was such a wonderful movement for social justice because the heart of it was love—loving everyone. It was believing, as you taught us yesterday, that we can always start anew; we can always practice forgiveness. I don't have to hate any person because I can always start anew, I can always reconcile. What I'm trying to understand is why are we moving away from this idea of a community of love. What is your thinking about why people are moving away from love, and how we can be part of moving our society towards love?

Thich Nhat Hanh: In our own Buddhist **SANGHA,** community is the core of everything. The sangha is a community where there should be harmony and peace and understanding. That is something created by our daily life together. If love is there in the community, if we've been nourished by the harmony in the community, then we will never move away from love.

The reason we might lose this is because we are always looking outside of us, thinking that the object or action of love is out there. That is why we allow the love, the harmony, the mature understanding, to slip away from ourselves. This is, I think, the basic thing. That is why we have to go back to our community and renew it. Then love will grow back. Understanding and harmony will grow back. That's the first thing.

The second thing is that we ourselves need love; it's not only society, the world outside, that needs love. But we can't expect that love to come from outside of us. We should ask the question whether we are capable of loving ourselves as well as others. Are we treating our body kindly—by the way we eat, by the way we drink, by the way we work? Are we treating ourselves with enough joy and tenderness and peace? Or are we feeding ourselves with toxins that we get from the market—the spiritual, intellectual, entertainment market?

So the question is whether we are practicing loving ourselves? Because loving ourselves means loving our community. When we are capable of loving ourselves, nourishing ourselves properly, not intoxicating ourselves, we are already protecting and nourishing society. Because in the moment when we are able to smile, to look at ourselves with compassion, our world begins to change. We may not have done anything but when we are relaxed, when we are peaceful, when we are able to smile and not to be violent in the way we look at the system, at that moment there is a change already in the world.

So the second help, the second insight, is that between self or no-self there is no real separation. Anything you do for yourself you do for the society at the same time. And anything you do for society you do for yourself also. That insight is very powerfully made in the practice of **NO-SELF.**

bell hooks: I think one of the most wonderful books that Martin Luther King wrote was *Strength to Love*. I always liked it because of the word "strength," which counters the Western notion of love as easy. Instead, Martin Luther King said that you must have courage to love, that you have to have a profound will to do what is right to love, that it does not come easy.

Thich Nhat Hanh: Martin Luther King was among us as a brother, as a friend, as a leader. He was able to maintain that love alive. When you touch him, you touch a **BODHISATTVA,** for his understanding and love was enough to hold everything to him. He tried to transmit his insight and his love to the community, but maybe we have not received it enough. He was trying to transmit the best things to us—his goodness, his love, his nonduality. But because we had clung so much to him as a person, we did not bring the essence of what he was teaching into our community. So now that he's no longer here, we are at a loss. We have to be aware that crucial transmission he was making was not the transmission of power, of authority, of position, but the transmission of the dharma. It means love.

bell hooks: Exactly. It was not a transmission of personality. Part of why I have started writing about love is feeling, as you say, that our culture is forgetting what he taught. We name more and more streets and schools after him but that's almost irrelevant, because what is to be remembered is that strength to love.

That's what we have to draw courage from—the spirit of love, not [30] the image of Martin Luther King. This is so hard in the West because we are such an image and personality driven culture. For instance, because I have learned so much from you for so many years of my life, people kept asking me whether I had met you in person.

Thich Nhat Hanh: (laughs) Yes, I understand.

bell hooks: And I said yes, I have met him, because he has given his love to me through his teachings, through mindfulness practice. I kept trying to share with people that, yes, I would like to meet you some day, but the point is that I am living and learning from his teaching.

Thich Nhat Hanh: Yes, that's right. And that is the essence of interbeing. We had met already in the very non-beginning (laughs). Beginning with longing, beginning with blessings.

bell hooks: Except that you have also taught that to be in the presence of your teacher can also be a moment of transformation. So people say, is it enough that you've learned from books by him, or must you meet him, must there be an encounter?

Thich Nhat Hanh: In fact, the true teacher is within us. A good teacher [35] is someone who can help you to go back and touch the true teacher within, because you already have the insight within you. In Buddhism we call it buddhanature. You don't need someone to transfer buddhanature to you, but maybe you need a friend who

---

GLOSS: BODHISATTVA
In Buddhism, a *bodhisattva* is a being that, while not yet fully enlightened, is actively striving toward that goal. Conventionally, the term is applied to hypothetical beings with a high degree of enlightenment and power, but as hooks and Nhat Hanh use it in this dialogue, it also refers to people who have made a formal commitment to Buddhist practice and study. Bodhisattva literally means "enlightenment being" in Sanskrit.

can help you touch that nature of awakening and understanding working in you.

So a good teacher is someone who can help you to get back to a teacher within. The teacher can do that in many different ways; she or he does not have to meet you physically. I feel that I have many real students whom I have not met. Many are in cloisters and they never get out. Others are in prison. But in many cases they practice the teachings much better than those who meet me every day. That is true. When they read a book by me or hear a tape and they touch the insight within them, then they have met me in a real way. That is the real meeting.

bell hooks: I want to know your thoughts on how we learn to love a world full of injustice, more than coming together with someone just because they share the same skin or the same language as we do. I ask this question of you because I first learned about you through Martin Luther King's homage to your compassion towards those who had hurt your country.

Thich Nhat Hanh: This is a very interesting topic. It was a very important issue for the Buddha. How we view justice depends on our practice of looking deeply. We may think that justice is everyone being equal, having the same rights, sharing the same kind of advantages, but maybe we have not had the chance to look at the nature of justice in terms of no-self. That kind of justice is based on the idea of self, but it may be very interesting to explore justice in terms of no-self.

bell hooks: I think that's exactly the kind of justice Martin Luther King spoke about—a justice that was for everyone whether they're equal or not. Sometimes in life all things are not equal, so what does it mean to have justice when there is no equality? A parent can be just towards a child, even though they're not equal. I think this is often misunderstood in the West, where people feel that there can be no justice unless everything is the same. This is part of why I feel we have to relearn how we think about love, because we think about love so much in terms of the self.

40 **Thich Nhat Hanh:** Is justice possible without equality?

bell hooks: Justice is possible without equality, I believe, because of compassion and understanding. If I have compassion, then if I have more than you, which is unequal, I will still do the just thing by you.

Thich Nhat Hanh: Right. And who has created inequality?

bell hooks: Well, I think inequality is in our minds. I think this is what we learn through practice. One of the concepts that you and Daniel Berrigan spoke about in *The Raft Is Not the Shore* is that the bridge of illusion must be shattered in order for a real bridge to be constructed. One of the things we learn is that inequality is an illusion.

Thich Nhat Hanh: Makes sense (laughs).

bell hooks: Before I came here I had been struggling with the ques- 45 tion of anger toward my ex-boyfriend. I have taken my vows as a bodhisattva, and so I always feel very depressed when I have anger. I had come to a point of despair because I had so much difficulty with my anger in relation to this man. So yesterday's dharma talk about embracing our anger, and using it, and letting it go, was very essential for me at this moment.

Thich Nhat Hanh: You want to be human. Be angry, it's okay. But not to practice is not okay. To be angry, that is very human. And to learn how to smile at your anger and make peace with your anger is very nice. That is the whole thing—the meaning of the practice, of the learning. By taking a look at your anger it can be transformed into the kind of energy that you need—understanding and compassion. It is with negative energy that you can make the positive energy. A flower, although beautiful, will become compost someday, but if you know how to transform the compost back into the flower, then you don't have to worry. You don't have to worry about your anger because you know how to handle it—to embrace, to recognize, and to transform it. So this is what is possible.

bell hooks: I think this is what people misunderstand about Martin Luther King saying to love your enemies. They think he was just using this silly little phrase, but what he meant was that as Black Americans we need to let our anger go, because holding on to it we hold ourselves down. We oppress ourselves by holding on to anger. My students tell me, we don't want to love! We're tired of being loving! And I say to them, if you're tired of being loving, then you haven't really been loving, because when you are loving you have more strength. As you were telling us yesterday, we grow stronger in the act of loving. This has been, I think, a very hurting thing for Black Americans—to feel that we can't love our enemies. People forget what a great tradition we have as African-Americans in the practice of forgiveness and compassion. And if we neglect that tradition, we suffer.

Thich Nhat Hanh: When we have anger in us, we suffer. When we have discrimination in us, we suffer. When we have the complex of superiority, we suffer. When we have the complex of inferiority, we

CONVERSATIONS: ANGER AND ACTIVISM
Throughout this dialogue, Thich Nhat Hanh refers to the importance of love and compassion in dealing with anger and conflict. During the Vietnam War, he preached this same message of love in his activism against the war, even in the face of violence. But other Buddhists took a different path in opposing the war. In 1963, hundreds of newspapers around the world published images like this one depicting a Buddhist monk after he set himself on fire to protest the war. Consider how such a form of protest, which received a great deal of attention at the time, might complicate Thich Nhat Hanh's ideas about the path to peace. How might this historical context have influenced Nhat Hanh's ideas? How might it affect the way you read this essay? Consider, too, the impact of such an image as compared to the written or spoken words of an activist like Thich Nhat Hanh.

Buddhist monk committing ritual suicide, 1963

suffer also. So when we are capable of transforming these negative things in us, we are free and happiness is possible.

If the people who hurt us have that kind of energy within them, like anger or desperation, then they suffer. When you see that someone suffers, you might be motivated by a desire to help him not to suffer anymore. That is love also, and love doesn't have any color. Other people may discriminate against us, but what is more important is whether we discriminate against them. If we don't do that, we are a happier person, and as a happier person, we are in a position to help. And anger, this is not a help.

50 **bell hooks:** And lastly, what about fear? Because I think that many white people approach black people or Asian people not with hatred or anger but with fear. What can love do for that fear?

Thich Nhat Hanh: Fear is born from ignorance. We think that the other person is trying to take away something from us. But if we look deeply, we see that the desire of the other person is exactly our own desire—to have peace, to be able to have a chance to live. So if you realize that the other person is a human being too, and you have exactly the same kind of spiritual path, and then the two can become good practitioners. This appears to be practical for both.

The only answer to fear is more understanding. And there is no understanding if there is no effort to look more deeply to see what is there in our heart and in the heart of the other person. The Buddha always reminds us that our afflictions, including our fear and our desiring, are born from our ignorance. That is why in order to dissipate fear, we have to remove wrong perception.

bell hooks: And what if people perceive rightly and still act unjustly?

Thich Nhat Hanh: They are not able yet to apply their insight in their daily life. They need community to remind them. Sometimes you have a flash of insight, but it's not strong enough to survive. Therefore in the practice of Buddhism, **SAMADHI** is the power to maintain insight alive in every moment, so that every speech, every word, every act will bear the nature of that insight. It is a question of cleaning. And you clean better if you are surrounded by sangha—those who are practicing exactly the same.

55 **bell hooks:** I think that we best realize love in community. This is something I have had to work with myself, because the intellectual tradition of the West is very individualistic. It's not community-based. The intellectual is often thought of as a person who is alone and cut off from the world. So I have had to practice being willing to leave the space of my study to be in community, to work in community, and to be changed by community.

Thich Nhat Hanh: Right, and then we learn to operate as a community and not as individuals. In Plum Village, that is exactly what we try to do. We are brothers and sisters living together. We try to operate like cells in one body.

GLOSS: SAMADHI
A Sanskrit term for "meditative absorption," *samadhi* refers to a state of mind that Buddhists try to achieve through meditation.

bell hooks: I think this is the love that we seek in the new millennium, which is the love experienced in community, beyond self.

Thich Nhat Hanh: So please, live that truth and disseminate that truth with your writing, with your speaking. It will be helpful to maintain that kind of view and action.

bell hooks: Thank you for your open-hearted example.

Thich Nhat Hanh: You're welcome. Thank you.   60

Understanding the Text

1. How does hooks define love? How does her understanding of love play a role in her own writing and in her work as a teacher and a cultural critic? How might your own understanding of love differ from hooks's? In what ways might your understanding of love influence your reaction to this essay?

2. What experiences did hooks have as a young woman that shaped her thinking about love? In what ways did those experiences influence her?

3. Why, according to hooks, was her encounter with the writings of Thich Nhat Hanh, Chögyam Trungpa Rinpoche, and other Buddhist teachers so important in the development of her thinking about social justice and her involvement in the Civil Rights and women's movements?

4. How does Thich Nhat Hanh define *community*? How does he understand the relationship between individuals and communities? What role does love play in that relationship, according to him?

Exploring the Issues

1. How would you describe the voices of bell hooks and Thich Nhat Hanh in this dialogue? What role does each voice play? What similarities and differences can you "hear" in their voices? How do you think these similarities or differences might strengthen or weaken this essay?

2. How effective do you think the form of a dialogue is to convey a point or examine an idea? Cite specific passages to support your answer.

3. In paragraph 26, Thich Nhat Hanh refers to "the practice of no-self," which is explained in *Gloss: No-Self* on page 260. Some scholars have pointed out that it is similar to the Christian idea of the Holy Trinity of God the Father, Jesus, and the Holy Spirit. Consider how a reader's religious beliefs and upbringing might shape his or her response to this dialogue between bell hooks and Thich Nhat Hanh. In what ways do you think Nhat Hanh's references to Buddhist beliefs might help him achieve his goals with readers? What obstacles might his references to Buddhist beliefs present for non-Buddhist readers? How did you react to these references? What might your answer to that question reveal about you as a reader?

4. This essay was originally published in *Shambhala Sun,* a Buddhist magazine. Throughout their dialogue, both hooks and Nhat Hanh use many specialized terms from Buddhist teachings, such as *sangha* and *samadhi,* which would be familiar to readers of *Shambhala Sun.* Examine the effect of these terms on you as a reader. Do you need to understand these terms if you are to understand the basic points that hooks and Nhat Hanh make about love and community? If you are unfamiliar with these terms, did you find the essay difficult to follow? If hooks and Nhat Hanh had their discussion without using these terms, would the essay have been different in any way? Explain. What might this essay help us understand about the role of specialized language in a piece of writing? What might it suggest about what readers need to know to make sense of any piece of writing?

Entering the Conversations

1. In the opening section of this essay, hooks writes about the great influence of the writings of Thich Nhat Hanh and other Buddhist teachers on her. In an essay intended for an audience of your classmates, describe the effect of a book or writer that was especially important to you in some way.

INFOTRAC

2. Search InfoTrac College Edition as well as the Internet for resources on Buddhism and especially on Buddhist ideas about love. Then, drawing on these sources as well as on this essay by bell hooks, write a report in which you examine how love is understood by

Buddhism and by Christianity (or another religious tradition of interest to you). What similarities and differences can you identify in how these religious traditions understand love? How does the understanding of love in each tradition seem to affect its religious practices? What conclusions can you draw about religious or cultural differences when it comes to the idea of love?

3. Drawing on this essay and any other relevant sources, write an essay in which you discuss the power of love. Alternatively, create a visual representation (such as a web site or a photo essay) of the power of love.

4. Several films in recent years have focused on the encounter of Westerners with Buddhism. In the film *Beyond Rangoon* (1995), two American women are traveling in Myanmar (formerly Burma), where protests, led by internationally famous activist Aung San Suu Kyi (whose es-

say appears in Chapter 9), against the military government were violently suppressed. The film examines Buddhist ideas about life and death and is based in part on the notion that a Westerner can learn about life and love by seeing the world as a Buddhist. *Seven Years in Tibet* (1997), based on the famous book of that same title by Heinrich Harrer, tells the story of a German climber trapped in Tibet at the start of World War II. He develops a close relationship with the Dalai Lama and through that relationship comes to understand the world differently. Focusing on these or similar films, write an analysis of how Buddhist ideas are portrayed in contrast to a Western perspective. What do the films suggest about Buddhism? About Western culture? What questions do they raise about culture and community? In your analysis, draw conclusions about how culture affects the way we talk about love.

Description

I have seen a weasel in the wild only once in my life, while I was sitting on the shore of a remote lake in the Adirondack Mountains in New York. The weasel appeared suddenly on a brush pile near the shore. Like Dillard, I found that brief encounter exhilarating. It was an unexpected moment of wonder when I was close to a wild creature that I had previously seen only in photographs—an opportunity to experience the wild more intimately than most of us usually do. But for

Living LIKE Weasels

ANNIE DILLARD

Dillard, the chance encounter with a weasel takes on much greater meaning. It prompts her to reflect on her life in a profound way and to raise questions about the choices she has made about how to live. These seem to be weighty issues to ponder as a result of a brief glimpse of a wild creature. But perhaps that's part of what makes Dillard such a respected and popular writer. If you read carefully, you'll see that her vivid descriptions are more than descriptions; they are part of her efforts to explore complex ideas with seemingly simple prose. With careful choices of words, Dillard directs our attention to seemingly obvious things in which she sees great significance. Just as Dillard's observations of her surroundings can reveal surprises and insights, paying careful attention to her words can reward you with surprises and insights as

A weasel is wild. Who knows what he thinks? He sleeps in his underground den, his tail draped over his nose. Sometimes he lives in his den for two days without leaving. Outside, he stalks rabbits, mice, muskrats, and birds, killing more bodies than he can eat warm, and often dragging the carcasses home. Obedient to instinct, he bites his prey at the neck, either splitting the jugular vein at the throat or crunching the brain at the base of the skull, and he does not let go. One naturalist refused to kill a weasel who was socketed into his hand deeply as a rattlesnake. The man could in no way pry the tiny weasel off, and he had to walk half a mile to water, the weasel dangling from his palm, and soak him off like a stubborn label.

And once, says Ernest Thompson Seton—once, a man shot an eagle out of the sky. He examined the eagle and found the dry skull of a weasel fixed by the jaws to his throat. The supposition is that the

well. Her essay reminds us that learning can happen unexpectedly and in the most mundane circumstances.

Annie Dillard (b. 1945) is the author of a number of books, including the award-winning Pilgrim at Tinker Creek *(1974) and* Teaching a Stone to Talk *(1982), in which the following essay was first published.* ▼

STRATEGIES: DESCRIPTION
In paragraphs 4 and 5, Dillard describes the area around her home, which she tells us is in "suburbia." Notice the kinds of details she includes in this description. Consider how these details focus your attention on specific aspects of her surroundings and how they convey a sense of Dillard's suburbia.

STRATEGIES: RHYTHM
Dillard begins paragraph 6 with a single word: *So.* That one-syllable word, which is not a complete sentence by itself, slows down the pace of this passage and changes the rhythm of her prose. It also serves as a transition from the description of the area around her home (par. 4 and 5) to the narrative about her encounter with the weasel. Notice that Dillard uses the word by itself again at the end of paragraph 10. Compare these two uses of the word. Do they accomplish the same things in each case? Dillard's use of the word *so* is a good example of a writer manipulating rhythm to achieve an effect or signal an important shift in a passage.

eagle had pounced on the weasel and the weasel swiveled and bit as instinct taught him, tooth to neck, and nearly won. I would like to have seen that eagle from the air a few weeks or months before he was shot: was the whole weasel still attached to his feathered throat, a fur pendant? Or did the eagle eat what he could reach, gutting the living weasel with his talons before his breast, bending his beak, cleaning the beautiful airborne bones?

*   *   *

I have been reading about weasels because I saw one last week. I startled a weasel who startled me, and we exchanged a long glance.

Twenty minutes from my house, through the woods by the quarry and across the highway, is Hollins Pond, a remarkable piece of shallowness, where I like to go at sunset and sit on a tree trunk. Hollins Pond is also called Murray's Pond; it covers two acres of bottomland near Tinker Creek with six inches of water and six thousand lily pads. In winter, brown-and-white steers stand in the middle of it, merely dampening their hooves; from the distant shore they look like miracle itself, complete with miracle's nonchalance. Now, in summer, the steers are gone. The water lilies have blossomed and spread to a green horizontal plane that is terra firma to plodding blackbirds, and tremulous ceiling to black leeches, crayfish, and carp.

5   This is, mind you, suburbia. It is a five-minute walk in three directions to rows of houses, though none is visible here. There's a 55 mph highway at one end of the pond, and a nesting pair of wood ducks at the other. Under every bush is a muskrat hole or a beer can. The far end is an alternating series of fields and woods, fields and woods, threaded everywhere with motorcycle tracks—in whose bare clay wild turtles lay eggs.

So. I had crossed the highway, stepped over two low barbed-wire fences, and traced the motorcycle path in all gratitude through the wild rose and poison ivy of the pond's shoreline up into high grassy fields. Then I cut down through the woods to the mossy fallen tree where I sit. This tree is excellent. It makes a dry, upholstered bench at the upper, marshy end of the pond, a plush jetty raised from the thorny shore between a shallow blue body of water and a deep blue body of sky.

The sun had just set. I was relaxed on the tree trunk, ensconced in the lap of lichen, watching the lily pads at my feet tremble and part dreamily over the thrusting path of a carp. A yellow bird appeared to my right and flew behind me. It caught my eye; I swiveled around—and the next instant, inexplicably, I was looking down at a weasel, who was looking up at me.

                                   *   *   *

Weasel! I'd never seen one wild before. He was ten inches long,
thin as a curve, a muscled ribbon, brown as fruitwood, soft-furred,
alert. His face was fierce, small and pointed as a lizard's; he would
have made a good arrowhead. There was just a dot of chin, maybe two
brown hairs' worth, and then the pure white fur began that spread
down his underside. He had two black eyes I didn't see, any more
than you see a window.

The weasel was stunned into stillness as he was emerging from beneath an enormous shaggy wild rose bush four feet away. I was stunned
into stillness twisted backward on the tree trunk. Our eyes locked,
and someone threw away the key.

Our look was as if two lovers, or deadly enemies, met unexpectedly   10
on an overgrown path when each had been thinking of something
else: a clearing blow to the gut. It was also a bright blow to the brain,
or a sudden beating of brains, with all the charge and intimate grate
of rubbed balloons. It emptied our lungs. It felled the forest, moved
the fields, and drained the pond; the world dismantled and tumbled
into that black hole of eyes. If you and I looked at each other that way,
our skulls would split and drop to our shoulders. But we don't. We
keep our skulls. So.

He disappeared. This was only last week, and already I don't remember what shattered the enchantment. I think I blinked, I think I
retrieved my brain from the weasel's brain, and tried to memorize
what I was seeing, and the weasel felt the yank of separation, the ca-
reening splashdown into real life and the urgent current of instinct.
He vanished under the wild rose. I waited motionless, my mind suddenly full of data and my spirit with pleadings, but he didn't return.

Please do not tell me about "approach-avoidance conflicts." I tell you
I've been in that weasel's brain for sixty seconds, and he was in mine.
Brains are private places, muttering through unique and secret tapes—
but the weasel and I both plugged into another tape simultaneously,
for a sweet and shocking time. Can I help it if it was a blank?

What goes on in his brain the rest of the time? What does a weasel
think about? He won't say. His journal is tracks in clay, a spray of
feathers, mouse blood and bone: uncollected, unconnected, loose-
leaf, and blown.

                                   *   *   *

I would like to learn, or remember, how to live. I come to Hollins
Pond not so much **TO LEARN HOW TO LIVE** as, frankly, to forget about it.
That is, I don't think I can learn from a wild animal how to live in
particular—shall I suck warm blood, hold my tail high, walk with my
footprints precisely over the prints of my hands?—but I might learn

---

CONVERSATIONS: LEARNING TO LIVE
In his classic book, *Walden,* Henry David
Thoreau (1817–1862) explains his reasons
for living alone in a small cabin in the
forest this way: "I went into the woods
because I wished to live deliberately, to
front only the essential facts of life, and
see if I could not learn what it had to
teach, and not, when I came to die,
discover that I had not lived." I wondered
if Dillard had this passage in mind when
she wrote, "I would like to learn, or
remember, how to live" (par. 14). If so, she
would be joining a longstanding
conversation in Western culture about our
relationship to the land.

something of mindlessness, something of the purity of living in the physical senses and the dignity of living without bias or motive. The weasel lives in necessity and we live in choice, hating necessity and dying at the last ignobly in its talons. I would like to live as I should, as the weasel lives as he should. And I suspect that for me the way is like the weasel's: open to time and death painlessly, noticing everything, remembering nothing, choosing the given with a fierce and pointed will.

15   I missed my chance. I should have gone for the throat. I should have lunged for that streak of white under the weasel's chin and held on, held on through mud and into the wild rose, held on for a dearer life. We could live under the wild rose wild as weasels, mute and uncomprehending. I could very calmly go wild. I could live two days in the den, curled, leaning on mouse fur, sniffing bird bones, blinking, licking, breathing musk, my hair tangled in the roots of grasses. Down is a good place to go, where the mind is single. Down is out, out of your ever-loving mind and back to your careless senses. I remember muteness as a prolonged and giddy fast, where every moment is a feast of utterance received. Time and events are merely poured, unremarked, and ingested directly, like blood pulsed into my gut through a jugular vein. Could two live that way? Could two live under the wild rose, and explore by the pond, so that the smooth mind of each is as everywhere present to the other, and as received and as unchallenged, as falling snow?

We could, you know. We can live any way we want. People take vows of poverty, chastity, and obedience—even of silence—by choice. The thing is to stalk your calling in a certain skilled and supple way, to locate the most tender and live spot and plug into that pulse. This is yielding, not fighting. A weasel doesn't "attack" anything; a weasel lives as he's meant to, yielding at every moment to the perfect freedom of single necessity.

I think it would be well, and proper, and obedient, and pure, to grasp your one necessity and not let it go, to dangle from it limp wherever it takes you. Then even death, where you're going no matter how you live, cannot you part. Seize it and let it seize you up aloft even, till your eyes burn out and drop; let your musky flesh fall off in shreds, and let your very bones unhinge and scatter, loosened over fields, over fields and woods, lightly, thoughtless, from any height at all, from as high as eagles.

Understanding the Text

1. How does Dillard encounter the weasel? Why is this encounter unusual or remarkable to her? What was it about this encounter that made such an impression on Dillard?

2. What do you think Dillard learns about herself in thinking about her encounter with the weasel?

3. What does Dillard believe she can learn from an animal like a weasel? Why does she believe that she missed her chance to live like a weasel? What does this reveal about her and her views about modern living?

Exploring the Issues

1. Dillard begins this essay with a description of weasels. What does this description suggest about weasels? Why do you think Dillard begins in this way? What ideas are introduced in this beginning that will become important in her essay?

2. In paragraph 10, Dillard describes in detail the look she exchanged with the weasel. Examine this description for what it seems to suggest about the weasel and about Dillard. Look especially at the figures of speech she uses in her description (for example, she describes the encounter as if "two lovers, or deadly enemies, met unexpectedly"). What do you think she is trying to convey through such figures of speech and through her choice of details?

3. Assess Dillard's use of metaphor in this essay—not only the specific metaphors she uses to describe scenes she has witnessed

but also the metaphor of living like a weasel. What ideas does that metaphor allow Dillard to convey? How effectively do you think that metaphor conveys her ideas?

4. How would you describe the tone of this essay? In additional to her detailed descriptions of her surroundings and her encounter with the weasel, Dillard also includes thoughts about how she lives her life and raises questions about how she should do so. What impact do these thoughts and questions have on the essay? How did you react to them? What might your reaction suggest about you as a reader?

Entering the Conversations

1. In an essay intended for your classmates, describe an encounter you had with wildlife or something else that struck you as special in some way. Write your essay in a way that might convey an idea or insight you gained from that encounter. Try also to convey a sense of what you learned about yourself.

2. Writers have long examined the idea that we humans can learn a great deal from nature. Dillard's essay can be seen as an example of such learning. Drawing on her essay and on any other essays that seem appropriate, write an essay in which you discuss how these writers understand nature and how and what they learn from their encounters with the natural world. (For this assignment, you might consider using the following essays: Scott Russell Sanders, "Stillness"; M. Scott Momaday, "The Way to Rainy Mountain"; E. B. White,

"Once More to the Lake"; or Melissa Pierson, "Losing Home."

INFOTRAC

3. Many educators argue that environmental education should be a required part of the school curriculum. One justification they offer for this requirement is that through environmental education students not only can learn more about preserving the environment but they can also learn about themselves, as Dillard did in this essay. Using InfoTrac College Edition and any other relevant resources, find out what environmental education is and how its proponents justify it. Try to find examples of schools and colleges where environmental education is a part of the curriculum. If possible, interview people in your own school who are involved in environmental education. Then, on the basis of your research, write a proposal in which you make a case for or against an environmental education curriculum at your school. (If your school already has such a curriculum, you can make a proposal for changing it in ways that you believe would improve it.) In your proposal, draw on your research to support your specific recommendations. Draw also on Dillard's essay and others like it.

4. Visit one or more blogs that focus on the environment in some way. Analyze the discussion on the blogs for how they seem to address our interactions with the natural world. Then, write an essay reporting on these blogs and what they seem to suggest about the lessons we learn as a result of our interactions with nature.

A few years ago, I had the opportunity to teach a writing class in a prison. My students ranged in age from their teens to their fifties; they were incarcerated for all kinds of crimes, from auto theft and drug trafficking to murder. Many of them could hardly write a correct sentence. But all of them worked hard on their writing, and some of

Becoming A Poet

them took advantage of the assignments I gave to tell the stories of their often sad and difficult lives. I often felt that the power of their writing did not lie so much in what they wrote about but in the fact that for a few hours each week they could escape the dull yet dangerous lives they led in prison and become something other than inmates. Writing gave them a way to feel human again.

Maybe because of that experience I have found this essay by Jimmy Santiago Baca (b. 1952) to be especially powerful. In this essay, which is taken from his autobiography, Working in the Dark: Reflections of a Poet of the Barrio *(1992), Baca describes his own difficult life growing up in the American Southwest, a life characterized by crime and trouble with the law. His descriptions of his horrific experiences while in prison are especially powerful, and they sometimes make me wonder*

JIMMY SANTIAGO BACA

On weekend graveyard shifts at St. Joseph's Hospital I worked the emergency room, mopping up pools of blood and carting plastic bags stuffed with arms, legs, and hands to the outdoor incinerator. I enjoyed the quiet, away from the screams of shotgunned, knifed, and mangled kids writhing on gurneys outside the operating rooms. Ambulance sirens shrieked and squad car lights reddened the cool nights, flashing against the hospital walls: gray—red, gray—red. On slow nights I would lock the door of the administration office, search the reference library for a book on female anatomy and, with my feet propped on the desk, leaf through the illustrations, smoking my cigarette. I was seventeen.

One night my eye was caught by a familiar-looking word on the spine of a book. The title was *450 Years of Chicano History in Pictures*. On the cover were black-and-white photos: Padre Hidalgo exhorting Mexican peasants to revolt against the Spanish dictators; Anglo vigilantes hanging two Mexicans from a tree; a young Mexican woman with rifle and ammunition belts crisscrossing her breast; César Chávez and field workers marching for fair wages; Chicano railroad workers

JIMMY SANTIAGO BACA, "BECOMING A POET." FROM *WORKING IN THE DARK: REFLECTIONS OF A POET OF THE BARRIO* (1992). PUBLISHER: RED CRANE BOOKS. REPRINTED BY PERMISSION.

laying creosote ties; Chicanas laboring at machines in textile facto-ries; Chicanas picketing and hoisting boycott signs.

From the time I was seven, teachers had been punishing me for not knowing my lessons by making me stick my nose in a circle chalked on the blackboard. Ashamed of not understanding and fearful of ask-ing questions, I dropped out of school in the ninth grade. At seven-teen I still didn't know how to read, but those pictures confirmed my identity. I stole the book that night, stashing it for safety under the slop sink until I got off work. Back at my boardinghouse, I showed the book to friends. All of us were amazed; this book told us we were alive. We, too, had defended ourselves with our fists against hostile Anglos, gasping for breath in fights with the policemen who outnum-bered us. The book reflected back to us our struggle in a way that made us proud.

Most of my life I felt like a target in the cross hairs of a hunter's ri-fle. When strangers and outsiders questioned me I felt the hang-rope tighten around my neck and the trapdoor creak beneath my feet. There was nothing so humiliating as being unable to express myself, and my inarticulateness increased my sense of jeopardy, of being en-dangered. I felt intimidated and vulnerable, ridiculed and scorned. Behind a mask of humility, I seethed with mute rebellion.

5   Before I was eighteen, I was arrested on suspicion of murder after refusing to explain a deep cut on my forearm. With shocking speed I found myself handcuffed to a chain gang of inmates and bused to a holding facility to await trial. There I met men, prisoners, who read aloud to each other the works of Neruda, Paz, Sabines, Nemerov, and Hemingway. Never had I felt such freedom as in that dormitory. Lis-tening to the words of these writers, I felt that invisible threat from without lessen—my sense of teetering on a rotting plank over swamp water where famished alligators clapped their horny snouts for my blood. While I listened to the words of the poets, the alligators slum-bered powerless in their lairs. Their language was the magic that could liberate me from myself, transform me into another person, transport me to other places far away.

And when they closed the books, these Chicanos, and went into their own Chicano language, they made barrio life come alive for me in the fullness of its vitality. I began to learn my own language, the bilingual words and phrases explaining to me my place in the uni-verse. Every day I felt like the paper boy taking delivery of the latest news of the day.

Months later I was released, as I had suspected I would be. I had been guilty of nothing but shattering the windshield of my girlfriend's car in a fit of rage.

Two years passed. I was twenty now, and behind bars again. The fed-eral marshals had failed to provide convincing evidence to extradite me to Arizona on a drug charge, but still I was being held. They had ninety

about the men in my prison writing class and what they went through. But Baca's essay is really more about writing than it is about his hard life as a young criminal and an inmate. His essay includes some of the most provocative descriptions of writing that I have ever encountered. Thankfully, few of us have known the degradation and humiliation that Baca suffered in prison, so perhaps we have not experienced the power of writing in the way he has. Yet, I think most of us have known moments when we can feel some of that power. And certainly Baca's essay might help us think about what writing can mean in a person's life. I selected this essay for this cluster partly because I hope it will help you gain a sense of what writing might mean in your life.

In addition to his autobiography, Working in the Dark: Reflections of a Poet of the Barrio *(1992), Jimmy Santiago Baca has written several volumes of poetry, including* Black Mesa Poems *(1987), and has received numerous awards for his writing.* ▼

days to prove I was guilty. The only evidence against me was that my girlfriend had been at the scene of the crime with my driver's license in her purse. They had to come up with something else. But there was nothing else. Eventually they negotiated a deal with the actual drug dealer, who took the stand against me. When the judge hit me with a million-dollar bail, I emptied my pockets on his booking desk: twenty-six cents.

One night in my third month in the county jail, I was mopping the floor in front of the booking desk. Some detectives had kneed an old drunk and handcuffed him to the booking bars. His shrill screams raked my nerves like a hacksaw on bone, the desperate protest of his dignity against their inhumanity. But the detectives just laughed as he tried to rise and kicked him to his knees. When they went to the bathroom to pee and the desk attendant walked to the file cabinet to pull the arrest record, I shot my arm through the bars, grabbed one of the attendant's university textbooks, and tucked it in my overalls. It as the only way I had of protesting.

10   It was late when I returned to my cell. Under my blanket I switched on a pen flashlight and opened the thick book at random, scanning the pages. I could hear the jailer making his rounds on the other tiers. The jangle of his keys and the sharp click of his boot heels intensified my solitude. Slowly I enunciated the words . . . p-o-n-d, ri-pple. It scared me that I had been reduced to this to find comfort. I always had thought reading a waste of time, that nothing could be gained by it. Only by action, by moving out into the world and confronting and challenging the obstacles, could one learn anything worth knowing.

Even as I tried to convince myself that I was merely curious, I became so absorbed in how the sounds created music in me and happiness, I forgot where I was. Memories began to quiver in me, glowing with a strange but familiar intimacy in which I found refuge. For a while, a deep sadness overcame me, as if I had chanced on a long-lost friend and mourned the years of separation. But soon the heartache of having missed so much of life, that had numbed me since I was a child, gave way, as if a grave illness lifted itself from me and I was cured, innocently believing in the beauty of life again. I stumblingly repeated the author's name as I fell asleep, saying it over and over in the dark: Words-worth, Words-worth.

Before long my sister came to visit me, and I joked about taking her to a place called Kubla Khan and getting her a blind date with this *vato* named Coleridge who lived on the seacoast and was *malías* on morphine. When I asked her to make a trip into enemy territory to buy me a grammar book, she said she couldn't. Bookstores intimidated her, because she, too, could neither read nor write.

Days later, with a stub pencil I whittled sharp with my teeth, I propped a **RED CHIEF NOTEBOOK** on my knees and wrote my first words. From that moment, a hunger for poetry possessed me.

STRATEGIES: USING DETAILS
Throughout this essay, Baca uses physical details to convey a sense of his experiences. But sometimes the details he selects do more than describe the scene. Here, for example, he tells us that the notebook he was writing in was a Red Chief notebook, which was a common brand of notebook often used in schools. Consider what message that detail might convey in this scene and how it might relate to Baca's larger point about literacy and identity. What would he lose in this passage if he had simply mentioned that he had a notebook without specifying that it was a Red Chief notebook?

Until then, I had felt as if I had been born into a raging ocean where I swam relentlessly, flailing my arms in hope of rescue, of reaching a shoreline I never sighted. Never solid ground beneath me, never a resting place. I had lived with only the desperate hope to stay afloat; that and nothing more.

But when at last I wrote my first words on the page, I felt an island   15 rising beneath my feet like the back of a whale. As more and more words emerged, I could finally rest: I had a place to stand for the first time in my life. The island grew, with each page, into a continent inhabited by people I knew and mapped with the life I lived.

I wrote about it all—about people I had loved or hated, about the brutalities and ecstasies of my life. And, for the first time, the child in me who had witnessed and endured unspeakable terrors cried out not just in impotent despair, but with the power of language. Suddenly, through language, through writing, my grief and my joy could be shared with anyone who would listen. And I could do this all alone; I could do it anywhere. I was no longer a captive of demons eating away at me, no longer a victim of other people's mockery and loathing, that had made me clench my fist white with rage and grit my teeth to silence. Words now pleaded back with the bleak lucidity of hurt. They were wrong, those others, and now I could say it.

Through language I was free. I could respond, escape, indulge; embrace or reject earth or the cosmos. I was launched on an endless journey without boundaries or rules, in which I could salvage the floating fragments of my past, or be born anew in the spontaneous ignition of understanding some heretofore concealed aspect of myself. Each word steamed with the hot lava juices of my primordial making, and I crawled out of stanzas dripping with birth-blood, reborn and freed from the chaos of my life. The child in the dark room of my heart, that had never been able to find or reach the light switch, flicked it on now; and I found in the room a stranger, myself, who had waited so many years to speak again. My words struck in me lightning crackles of elation and thunderhead storms of grief.

*   *   *

When I had been in the county jail longer than anyone else, I was made a trustee. One morning, after a fistfight, I went to the unlocked and unoccupied office used for lawyer-client meetings, to think. The bare white room with its fluorescent tube lighting seemed to expose and illuminate my dark and worthless life. And yet, for the first time, I had something to lose—my chance to read, to write; a way to live with dignity and meaning, that had opened for me when I stole that scuffed, secondhand book about the Romantic poets. In prison, the abscess had been lanced.

"I will never do any work in this prison system as long as I am not allowed to get my G.E.D." That's what I told the reclassification panel.

The captain flicked off the tape recorder. He looked at me hard and said, "You'll never walk outta here alive. Oh, you'll work, put a copper penny on that, you'll work."

20   After that interview I was confined to deadlock maximum security in a subterranean dungeon, with ground-level chicken-wired windows painted gray. Twenty-three hours a day I was in that cell. I kept sane by borrowing books from the other cons on the tier. Then, just before Christmas, I received a letter from Harry, a charity house samaritan who doled out hot soup to the homeless in Phoenix. He had picked my name from a list of cons who had no one to write to them. I wrote back asking for a grammar book, and a week later received one of Mary Baker Eddy's treatises on salvation and redemption, with Spanish and English on opposing pages. Pacing my cell all day and most of each night, I grappled with grammar until I was able to write a long true-romance confession for a con to send to his pen pal. He paid me with a pack of smokes. Soon I had a thriving barter business, exchanging my poems and letters for novels, commissary pencils, and writing tablets.

One day I tore two flaps from the cardboard box that held all my belongings and punctured holes along the edge of each flap and along the border of a ream of state-issue paper. After I had aligned them to form a spine, I threaded the holes with a shoestring, and sketched on the cover a hummingbird fluttering above a rose. This was my first journal.

Whole afternoons I wrote, unconscious of passing time or whether it was day or night. Sunbursts exploded from the lead tip of my pencil, words that grafted me into awareness of who I was; peeled back to a burning core of bleak terror, an embryo floating in the image of water, I cracked out of the shell wide-eyed and insane. Trees grew out of the palms of my hands, the threatening otherness of life dissolved, and I became one with the air and sky, the dirt and the iron and concrete. There was no longer any distinction between the other and I. Language made bridges of fire between me and everything I saw. I entered into the blade of grass, the basketball, the con's eye, and child's soul.

At night I flew. I conversed with floating heads in my cell, and visited strange houses where lonely women brewed tea and rocked in wicker rocking chairs listening to sad Joni Mitchell songs.

Before long I was frayed like a rope carrying too much weight, that suddenly snaps. I quit talking. Bars, walls, steel bunk, and floor bristled with millions of poem-making sparks. My face was no longer familiar to me. The only reality was the swirling cornucopia of images in my mind, the voices in the air. Mid-air a cactus blossom would appear, a snake-flame in blinding dance around it, stunning me like a guard's fist striking my neck from behind.

25   The prison administrators tried several tactics to get me to work. For six months, after the next monthly prison board review, they

CONVERSATIONS: WRITING AND IMAGINATION
In this and the following paragraphs, Baca offers vivid descriptions of how he felt when he was writing. Consider what these images might suggest about writing and about the connections between writing and thinking. Compare Baca's descriptions with Min Zhan Lu's account of writing in her essay on page 371. How does each writer complicate our views of the power of writing?

sent cons to my cell to hassle me. When the guard would open my cell door to let one of them in, I'd leap out and fight him—and get sent to thirty-day isolation. I did a lot of isolation time. But I honed my image-making talents in that sensory-deprived solitude. Finally they moved me to death row, and after that to "nut-run," the tier that housed the mentally disturbed.

As the months passed, I became more and more sluggish. My eyelids were heavy, I could no longer write or read. I slept all the time.

One day a guard took me out to the exercise field. For the first time in years I felt grass and earth under my feet. It was spring. The sun warmed my face as I sat on the bleachers watching the cons box and run, hit the handball, lift weights. Some of them stopped to ask how I was, but I found it impossible to utter a syllable. My tongue would not move, saliva drooled from the corners of my mouth. I had been so heavily medicated I could not summon the slightest gesture. Yet inside me a small voice cried out, I am fine! I am hurt now but I will come back! I am fine!

Back in my cell, for weeks I refused to eat. Styrofoam cups of urine and hot water were hurled at me. Other things happened. There were beatings, shock therapy, intimidation.

Later, I regained some clarity of mind. But there was a place in my heart where I had died. My life had compressed itself into an unbearable dread of being. The strain had been too much. I had stepped over that line where a human being has lost more than he can bear, where the pain is too intense, and he knows he is changed forever. I was now capable of killing, coldly and without feeling. I was empty, as I have never, before or since, known emptiness. I had no connection to this life.

But then, the encroaching darkness that began to envelop me 30 forced me to reform and give birth to myself again in the chaos. I withdrew even deeper into the world of language, cleaving the diamonds of verbs and nouns, plunging into the brilliant light of poetry's regenerative mystery. Words gave off rings of white energy, radar signals from powers beyond me that infused me with truth. I believed what I wrote, because I wrote what was true. My words did not come from books or textual formulas, but from a deep faith in the voice of my heart.

I had been steeped in self-loathing and rejected by everyone and everything—society, family, cons, God, and demons. But now I had become as the burning ember floating in darkness that descends on a dry leaf and sets flame to forests. The word was the ember and the forest was my life.

*　*　*

I was born a poet one noon, gazing at weeds and creosoted grass at the base of a telephone pole outside my grilled cell window. The

CONVERSATIONS: THE PRISON WRITER

Baca writes compellingly about how he discovered writing while in prison. His story is not unique. A number of others have earned fame either by discovering writing while in prison or by writing about their experiences while there. Perhaps the most famous is Malcolm X, the controversial Black leader during the Civil Rights Movement whose book *The Autobiography of Malcolm X* (1965) describes how he learned to read and write in prison and then used his language skills to advance his political causes. More recently, a few cases of prison writers have provoked controversy. For example, in his book *Monster: The Autobiography of an L.A. Gang Member* (1993), Sanyika Shakur describes his disturbing, violent life as a gang member and his transformation while in prison, where he educated himself and rejected his former life of crime. Shakur's book was criticized by some who argued that it not only glorified violence but also enabled Shakur to profit from his crimes. Baca's essay might be considered another version of this story of someone who changed his or her life as a result of being imprisoned. It might also be seen as part of a never-ending conversation about the power of writing.

words I wrote then sailed me out of myself, and I was transported and metamorphosed into the images they made. From the dirty brown blades of grass came bolts of electrical light that jolted loose my old self; through the top of my head that self was released and reshaped in the clump of scrawny grass. Through language I became the grass, speaking its language and feeling its green feelings and black root sensations. Earth was my mother and I bathed in sunshine. Minuscule speckles of sunlight passed through my green skin and metabolized in my blood.

Writing bridged my divided life of prisoner and free man. I wrote of the emotional butchery of prisons, and of my acute gratitude for poetry. Where my blind doubt and spontaneous trust in life met, I discovered empathy and compassion. The power to express myself was a welcome storm rasping at tendril roots, flooding my soul's cracked dirt. Writing was water that cleansed the wound and fed the parched root of my heart.

I wrote to sublimate my rage, from a place where all hope is gone, from a madness of having been damaged too much, from a silence of killing rage. I wrote to avenge the betrayals of a lifetime, to purge the bitterness of injustice. I wrote with a deep groan of doom in my blood, bewildered and dumbstruck; from an indestructible love of life, to affirm breath and laughter and the abiding innocence of things. I wrote the way I wept, and danced, and made love.

Understanding the Text

1. What role do books play in Baca's life? To what extent do you think the impact of books on Baca was related to his circumstances? In other words, would books have meant as much to him if he had not been in prison and suffered abuse there? Explain.

2. What does Baca mean when he writes, "Through language I was free"? In what sense was he free, even when he was in prison? What kind of freedom did his writing give him? What do you think Baca's experiences might suggest about writing in general?

3. Why was Baca subject to such terrible abuse while in prison? Why did his demand about getting a GED result in such harsh treatment? What do you think this experience might suggest about learning? About writing?

4. How does Baca use writing to pull himself out of the terrible state he was in while in prison? What changed in him as a result of his writing? Do you find his descriptions of how he used writing believable? Explain, citing specific passages to support your answer.

Exploring the Issues

1. Assess Baca's writing style in this essay. What features of his writing stand out for you? How effective do you find his writing? How might Baca's writing style reflect his own beliefs about writing and its importance in his life?

2. In paragraph 24, Baca describes his mental state in solitary confinement as one in which his "only reality was the swirling cornucopia of images in my mind, the voices in the air." Given his description, his condition could easily be taken as mental illness. However, his earlier descriptions of his writing (for example, in par. 22), which he presents as happy moments, sound very similar to the description in paragraph 24. Examine the way Baca describes his mental state when he was writing and at other times as well. What metaphors and images does he use? What ideas do you think he is trying to convey about writing? What might his experience suggest about language and our sense of self in general? Do you find his descriptions effective? Do you think they accurately convey a sense of the experience of writing?

3. Baca has been acclaimed as a writer who speaks powerfully for Chicanos and for people of color in general. In what ways do you think this essay reflects Baca's desire to speak for his people? Based on this essay, do you think Baca's reputation as a poet of Chicanos and people of color is justified? Why or why not?

4. Baca describes his experiences and his writing as deeply connected to his identity as a Chicano who grew up in a barrio in the south-western United States. Do you think he imagined his primary audience for this essay to be Chicanos? In what ways might he have been trying to address a wider audience? Do you think you are part of the audience that Baca imagined for this essay? Explain, citing specific passages to support your answers.

Entering the Conversations

1. Write an essay describing an experience in which writing somehow made a difference in your life. Alternatively, write an essay in which you discuss the role that writing has played in your life.

2. In a group of classmates, share the essays you wrote for Question 1. What similarities and differences can you identify among your classmates regarding the role of writing in your lives? What might your essays suggest about writing?

3. In his essay, Baca describes learning about Chicano history through reading and through conversations with other inmates. This passage suggests the importance of telling the story of a people. Write an essay in which you tell your version of the story of your family or some other group or community that you identify with.

4. Write an essay in which you compare Baca's ideas about the connections between writing and identity with the ideas of Gloria Anzaldúa, whose essay begins on page 337.

5. Write an essay that explains how writing can be a means to freedom. Alternatively, create a web site or some other visual document that reflects your sense of how writing can make a person free.

6. Locate a blog or online discussion group devoted to writing and follow the conversations there for a time. Then, write an essay presenting an analysis of those conversations. Draw conclusions about how the people in those conversations understand the power of writing.

Narrative

I can remember as a young child asking my grandmother, who was a very religious person, questions about religious matters that puzzled me. Often, her response was, "You just have to have faith." I'm sure many people have heard such a comment. It seems natural to question some of the things we are taught to believe as children, and it is not unusual

Salvation

for people to experience great doubt about what they have been taught as they get older and learn more about themselves and the world. In the following essay, Langston Hughes (1902–1967) writes about that kind of doubt. But for Hughes, the religious doubt he experienced was dramatic and frightening. He writes of a time in his church when he was asked to declare his faith publicly as a Christian. It was an agonizing moment for Hughes, who was just twelve years old at the time, for he was not sure what he was supposed to be feeling. He was unable to wholeheartedly embrace the faith that everyone else in the church seemed to embrace. And the consequences of that inability were profound.

In a sense, this brief excerpt from Hughes's autobiography, The Big Sea *(1940), is about the public and private aspects of religious faith. It seems likely that Hughes would not have experienced this*

LANGSTON HUGHES

I was saved from sin when I was going on thirteen. But not really saved. It happened like this. There was a big revival at my Auntie Reed's church. Every night for weeks there had been much preaching, singing, praying, and shouting, and some very hardened sinners had been brought to Christ, and the membership of the church had grown by leaps and bounds. Then just before the revival ended, they held a special meeting for children, "to bring the young lambs to the fold." My aunt spoke of it for days ahead. That night I was escorted to the front row and placed on the mourners' bench with all the other young sinners, who had not yet been brought to Jesus.

My aunt told me that when you were saved you saw a light, and something happened to you inside! And Jesus came into your life! And God was with you from then on! She said you could see and hear and feel Jesus in your soul. I believed her. I had heard a great many old people say the same thing and it seemed to me they ought to know. So I sat there calmly in the hot, crowded church, waiting for Jesus to come to me.

The preacher preached a wonderful rhythmical sermon, all moans and shouts and lonely cries and dire pictures of hell, and then he sang a song about the ninety and nine safe in the fold, but one little lamb was left out in the cold. Then he said: "Won't you come? Won't you come to Jesus? Young lambs, won't you come?" And he held out his arms to all us young sinners there on the mourners' bench. And the little girls cried. And some of them jumped up and went to Jesus right away. But most of us just sat there.

A great many old people came and knelt around us and prayed, old women with jet-black faces and braided hair, old men with work-gnarled hands. And the church sang a song about the lower lights are burning, some poor sinners to be saved. And the whole building rocked with prayer and song.

5   Still I kept waiting to *see* Jesus.

Finally all the young people had gone to the altar and were saved, but one boy and me. He was a rounder's son named Westley. Westley and I were surrounded by sisters and deacons praying. It was very hot in the church, and getting late now. Finally Westley said to me in a whisper: "God damn! I'm tired o' sitting here. Let's get up and be saved." So he got up and was saved.

Then I was left all alone on the mourners' bench. My aunt came and knelt at my knees and cried, while prayers and song swirled all around me in the little church. The whole congregation prayed for me alone, in a mighty wail of moans and voices. And I kept waiting serenely for Jesus, waiting, waiting—but he didn't come. I wanted to see him, but nothing happened to me. Nothing! I wanted something to happen to me, but nothing happened.

I heard the songs and the minister saying: "Why don't you come? My dear child, why don't you come to Jesus? Jesus is waiting for you. He wants you. Why don't you come? Sister Reed, what is this child's name?"

"Langston," my aunt sobbed.

10   "Langston, why don't you come? Why don't you come and be saved? Oh, Lamb of God! Why don't you come?"

Now it was really getting late. I began to be ashamed of myself, holding everything up so long. I began to wonder what God thought about Westley, who certainly hadn't seen Jesus either, but who was now sitting proudly on the platform, swinging his knickerbockered legs and grinning down at me, surrounded by deacons and old women on their knees praying. God had not struck Westley dead for taking his name in vain or for lying in the temple. So I decided that maybe to save further trouble, I'd better lie, too, and say that Jesus had come, and get up and be saved.

So I got up.

Suddenly the whole room broke into a sea of shouting, as they saw me rise. Waves of rejoicing swept the place. Women leaped in the air.

wrenching moment if he had not been among believers in church, who set certain expectations regarding faith and salvation. His story asks us to think about the relationship between religion as a social institution, with its doctrines that shape what we believe, and our individual faith. To what extent is our faith our own? To what extent is it a function of social convention and upbringing? These are not easy questions, and Hughes's essay may prompt you to wrestle with them.

Hughes was a prolific poet, essayist, fiction writer, and playwright who is considered one of the key figures in the great American literary movement of the 1920s called the Harlem Renaissance. The experience described in the following essay took place in Missouri, where Hughes was born. ◪

CONVERSATIONS: REVIVAL MEETINGS
The meeting that Hughes attended at his Auntie Reed's church was part of a much larger movement in the late nineteenth and early twentieth centuries in the United States that some historians call the Second Great Awakening. This movement was characterized by an increase in religious activity in response to concerns about the immoral state of society. An important component of this movement was "revival meetings," such as the one Hughes describes in this essay, which were often organized by traveling preachers and sometimes attracted thousands of people for several days of preaching and worship. Today, religion remains as important—and controversial—as it was in Hughes's lifetime, and you might consider what Hughes's essay contributes to our longstanding debates about religion and faith.

My aunt threw her arms around me. The minister took me by the hand and led me to the platform.

When things quieted down, in a hushed silence, punctuated by a few ecstatic "Amens," all the new young lambs were blessed in the name of God. Then joyous singing filled the room.

That night, for the first time in my life but one for I was a big boy twelve years old—I cried. I cried, in bed alone, and couldn't stop. I buried my head under the quilts, but my aunt heard me. She woke up and told my uncle I was crying because the Holy Ghost had come into my life, and because I had seen Jesus. But I was really crying because I couldn't bear to tell her that I had lied, that I had deceived everybody in the church, that I hadn't seen Jesus, and that now I didn't believe there was a Jesus anymore, since he didn't come to help me. 15

Understanding the Text

1. What expectations does Hughes have about the revival meeting that he was attending with his aunt? Where did these expectations come from? What might they suggest about religious faith and religious events like the meeting at his aunt's church?

2. What prevents Hughes from going up to the preacher during the revival meeting? What do you think Hughes's hesitation reveals about him as a person?

3. What role does Westley play in this experience? In what ways do you think Westley helps Hughes convey his perspective on faith and religion?

Exploring the Issues

1. What main ideas about religion and faith do you think Hughes is trying to convey in this essay? Do you agree with him? Why or why not?

2. In this essay, Hughes describes an experience that happens during a relatively short time—a few hours at most. Examine how he conveys a sense of time. What

moments during the experience does he emphasize? How does he describe those moments? How does his manipulation of time in this essay help him convey his ideas about faith?

3. How would you describe Hughes's voice in this essay? He is describing an experience he had when he was twelve years old, but he wrote this passage when he was nearly forty. Do you think he tries to capture the voice of a twelve-year-old boy? Explain, citing specific passages to support your answer.

Entering the Conversations

1. Write an essay in which you describe your own understanding of faith. In your essay, define faith as you understand it, drawing on your own experiences and on Hughes's essay (or any other relevant essay or book) to support your explanation.

2. In a group of classmates, share your essays from Question 1. How does each of you define faith? What similarities and differences can you identify among your respec-

tive ideas about faith? What questions about faith might be raised by the essays that each of you wrote?

3. Write an essay in which you describe an important experience you have had involving your faith or religion.

4. Interview several people you know about their views regarding religion and faith. Try to determine whether they see any distinction between religion and faith. Then write a report for your classmates about what you learned through your interviews.

5. Create a visual document (such as a web site or photo essay) that reflects your view of faith.

6. In recent years, several popular television shows have focused on issues of faith. Shows like *Touched by an Angel,* for example, assume a certain kind of understanding of faith and spirituality. Select one or more such shows and examine how they present faith, spirituality, or religion. Then write an essay in which you discuss these shows and what they seem to suggest about faith in contemporary culture.

All of Amy Tan's novels have something to do with China, where her mother was born, and in each one, the Chinese language and cultural heritage are central to the story. The following essay may help explain why. In this essay, Tan (b. 1952) describes her struggles as a student whose mother's "broken" English wasn't spoken in schools and often caused problems

Mother Tongue

for both Tan and her mother. It quickly becomes clear that despite the difficulties she experienced with her mother, Tan sees something special in her mother's language. It also becomes clear that Tan appreciates the complexities of the different "Englishes" that she learned. She understands, for example, that people can suffer discrimination because they speak in a dialect that is not Standard English. And she knows that a person's language can send different messages to different people, some of which arise from bias and prejudice. Tan's experiences can help us understand why the charged debates about Standard English and bilingual education can have such important consequences for individuals. In a sense, her essay is a vivid personal portrayal of the politics of language. But this essay is also a statement of her own love affair with her language heritage—and with language in general.

AMY TAN

I am not a scholar of English or literature. I cannot give you much more than personal opinions on the English language and its variations in this country or others.

I am a writer. And by that definition, I am someone who has always loved language. I am fascinated by language in daily life. I spend a great deal of my time thinking about the power of language—the way it can evoke an emotion, a visual image, a complex idea, or a simple truth. Language is the tool of my trade. And I use them all—all the Englishes I grew up with.

Recently, I was made keenly aware of the different Englishes I do use. I was giving a talk to a large group of people, the same talk I had already given to half a dozen other groups. The nature of the talk was about my writing, my life, and my book, *The Joy Luck Club*. The talk was going along well enough, until I remembered one major difference that made the whole talk sound wrong. My mother was in the room. And it was perhaps the first time she had heard me give a lengthy speech, using the kind of English I have never used with her. I was saying things like, "The intersection of memory upon imagination"

Award-winning writer Amy Tan is the author of four novels, including The Joy Luck Club *(1989), which was a* New York Times *bestseller that was translated into twenty-five languages and made into a movie. The following essay first appeared in the* Threepenny Review *in 1990.* ▣

STRATEGIES: USING DIALECT
In paragraph 6, Tan quotes her mother, whose first language is Chinese, to give us an example of what Tan calls her "family talk." Fiction writers often use dialects like this to help convey a sense of their characters. Such uses of dialect are less common in nonfiction writing, in part because writers often try to avoid embarrassing the people they are quoting, who may feel they sound unintelligent by speaking in dialect. (Tan expresses this view in par. 8 and 9.) In fact, many newspapers and magazines edit quotations so that they do not contain dialects. Consider what messages Tan is sending about dialects by quoting her mother as she does here.

and "There is an aspect of my fiction that relates to thus-and-thus"—a speech filled with carefully wrought grammatical phrases, burdened, it suddenly seemed to me, with nominalized forms, past perfect tenses, conditional phrases, all the forms of standard English that I had learned in school and through books, the forms of English I did not use at home with my mother.

Just last week, I was walking down the street with my mother, and I again found myself conscious of the English I was using, the English I do use with her. We were talking about the price of new and used furniture and I heard myself saying this: "Not waste money that way." My husband was with us as well, and he didn't notice any switch in my English. And then I realized why. It's because over the twenty years we've been together I've often used that same kind of English with him, and sometimes he even uses it with me. It has become our language of intimacy, a different sort of English that relates to family talk, the language I grew up with.

5   So you'll have some idea of what this family talk I heard sounds like, I'll quote what my mother said during a recent conversation which I videotaped and then transcribed. During this conversation, my mother was talking about a political gangster in Shanghai who had the same last name as her family's, Du, and how the gangster in his early years wanted to be adopted by her family, which was rich by comparison. Later, the gangster became more powerful, far richer than my mother's family, and one day showed up at my mother's wedding to pay his respects. Here's what she said in part:

"Du Yusong having business like fruit stand. Like off the street kind. He is Du like Du Zong—but not Tsung-ming Island people. The local people call putong, the river east side, he belong to that side local people. That man want to ask Du Zong father take him in like become own family. Du Zong father wasn't look down on him, but didn't take seriously, until that man big like become a mafia. Now important person, very hard to inviting him. Chinese way, came only to show respect, don't stay for dinner. Respect for making big celebration, he shows up. Mean give lots of respect. Chinese custom. Chinese social life that way. If too important won't have to stay too long. He come to my wedding. I didn't see, I heard it. I gone to boy's side, they have YMCA dinner. Chinese age I was nineteen."

You should know that my mother's expressive command of English belies how much she actually understands. She reads the *Forbes* report, listens to *Wall Street Week*, converses daily with her stockbroker, reads all of Shirley MacLaine's books with ease—all kinds of things I can't begin to understand. Yet some of my friends tell me they understand 50 percent of what my mother says. Some say they understand 80 to 90 percent. Some say they understand none of it, as if she were speaking pure Chinese. But to me, my mother's English is perfectly clear, perfectly natural. It's my mother tongue. Her language, as I hear it, is vivid, direct, full of observation and imagery. That was the language that helped shape the way I saw things, expressed things, made sense of the world.

*   *   *

Lately, I've been giving more thought to the kind of English my mother speaks. Like others, I have described it to people as "broken" or "fractured" English. But I wince when I say that. It has always bothered me that I can think of no way to describe it other than "broken," as if it were damaged and needed to be fixed, as if it lacked a certain wholeness and soundness. I've heard other terms used, "limited English," for example. But they seem just as bad, as if everything is limited, including people's perceptions of the limited English speaker.

I know this for a fact, because when I was growing up, my mother's "limited" English limited *my* perception of her. I was ashamed of her English. I believed that her English reflected the quality of what she had to say. That is, because she expressed them imperfectly her thoughts were imperfect. And I had plenty of empirical evidence to support me: the fact that people in department stores, at banks, and at restaurants did not take her seriously, did not give her good service, pretended not to understand her, or even acted as if they did not hear her.

My mother has long realized the limitations of her English as well. 10 When I was fifteen, she used to have me call people on the phone to pretend I was she. In this guise, I was forced to ask for information or even to complain and yell at people who had been rude to her. One time it was a call to her stockbroker in New York. She had cashed out her small portfolio and it just happened we were going to go to New York the next week, our very first trip outside California. I had to get on the phone and say in an adolescent voice that was not very convincing, "This is Mrs. Tan."

And my mother was standing in the back whispering loudly, "Why he don't send me check, already two weeks late. So mad he lie to me, losing me money."

And then I said in perfect English, "Yes, I'm getting rather concerned. You had agreed to send the check two weeks ago, but it hasn't arrived."

Then she began to talk more loudly. "What he want, I come to New York tell him front of his boss, you cheating me?" And I was trying to calm her down, make her be quiet, while telling the stockbroker, "I can't tolerate any more excuses. If I don't receive the check immediately, I am going to have to speak to your manager when I'm in New York next week." And sure enough, the following week there we were in front of this astonished stockbroker, and I was sitting there red-faced and quiet, and my mother, the real Mrs. Tan, was shouting at his boss in her impeccable broken English.

CONVERSATIONS: SECOND-LANGUAGE LEARNERS
Like many second-language learners, Tan sometimes struggled with language in school, as she describes in paragraph 15. In the past few decades, educators have paid much more attention to the challenges facing students whose first language is other than English or who live in households where other languages are spoken. Bilingual education programs, in which students are taught in their first language rather than in English, are intended to address the needs of such students, but they have long been controversial and have recently been abandoned by many states. Tan's description in this paragraph provides a vivid example of some of the difficulties facing second-language learners.

We used a similar routine just five days ago, for a situation that was far less humorous. My mother had gone to the hospital for an appointment, to find out about a benign brain tumor a CAT scan had revealed a month ago. She said she had spoken very good English, her best English, no mistakes. Still, she said, the hospital did not apologize when they said they had lost the CAT scan and she had come for nothing. She said they did not seem to have any sympathy when she told them she was anxious to know the exact diagnosis, since her husband and son had both died of brain tumors. She said they would not give her any more information until the next time and she would have to make another appointment for that. So she said she would not leave until the doctor called her daughter. She wouldn't budge. And when the doctor finally called her daughter, me, who spoke in perfect English—lo and behold—we had assurances the CAT scan would be found, promises that a conference call on Monday would be held, and apologies for any suffering my mother had gone through for a most regrettable mistake.

15   I think my mother's English almost had an effect on limiting my possibilities in life as well. Sociologists and linguists probably will tell you that a person's developing language skills are more influenced by peers. But I do think that the language spoken in the family, especially in immigrant families which are more insular, plays a large role in shaping the language of the child. And I believe that it affected my results on achievement tests, IQ tests, and the SAT. While my English skills were never judged as poor, compared to math, English could not be considered my strong suit. In grade school I did moderately well, getting perhaps B's, sometimes B-pluses, in English and scoring perhaps in the sixtieth or seventieth percentile on achievement tests. But those scores were not good enough to override the opinion that my true abilities lay in math and science, because in those areas I achieved A's and scored in the ninetieth percentile or higher.

This was understandable. Math is precise; there is only one correct answer. Whereas, for me at least, the answers on English tests were always a judgment call, a matter of opinion and personal experience. Those tests were constructed around items like fill-in-the-blank sentence completion, such as, "Even though Tom was _____, Mary thought he was _____." And the correct answer always seemed to be the most bland combinations of thoughts, for example "Even though Tom was shy, Mary thought he was charming," with the

CONVERSATIONS: TESTING ENGLISH
Few educational issues have been more controversial than standardized testing, and in this section of her essay, Tan provides a glimpse into that controversy. The examples of test items that Tan includes in these two paragraphs (16 and 17) suggest some of the complexities of standardized testing that critics have often cited. When this essay was first published in 1990, standardized testing was becoming more widespread as many states tried to address concerns about low standards in public education. In the late 1990s and the first few years of the twenty-first century, the trend accelerated as federal education policy encouraged states to require standardized testing in core subjects, including English. Consider what Tan's experiences with tests might suggest about the challenges of testing students' language knowledge and skill.

grammatical structure "even though" limiting the correct answer to some sort of semantic opposites, so you wouldn't get answers like, "Even though Tom was foolish, Mary thought he was ridiculous." Well, according to my mother, there were very few limitations as to what Tom could have been and what Mary might have thought of him. So I never did well on tests like that.

The same was true with word analogies, pairs of words in which you were supposed to find some sort of logical, semantic relationship—for example, "*Sunset* is to *nightfall* as _____ is to _____." And here you would be presented with a list of four possible pairs, one of which showed the same kind of relationship: *red* is to *spotlight, bus* is to *arrival, chills* is to *fever, yawn* is to *boring*. Well, I could never think that way. I knew what the tests were asking, but I could not block out of my mind the images already created by the first pair, "*sunset* is to *night-fall*"—and I would see a burst of colors against a darkening sky, the moon rising, the lowering of a curtain of stars. And all the other pairs of words—red, bus, spotlight, boring—just threw up a mass of confusing images, making it impossible for me to sort out something as logical as saying: "A sunset precedes nightfall" is the same as "a chill precedes a fever." The only way I would have gotten that answer right would have been to imagine an associative situation, for example, my being disobedient and staying out past sunset, catching a chill at night, which turns into feverish pneumonia as punishment, which indeed did happen to me.

*   *   *

I have been thinking about all this lately, about my mother's English, about achievement tests. Because lately I've been asked, as a writer, why there are not more Asian Americans represented in American literature. Why are there few Asian Americans enrolled in creative writing programs? Why do so many Chinese students go into engineering? Well, these are broad sociological questions I can't begin to answer. But I have noticed in surveys—in fact, just last week—that Asian students, as a whole, always do significantly better on math achievement tests than in English. And this makes me think that there are other Asian American students whose English spoken in the home might also be described as "broken" or "limited." And perhaps they also have teachers who are steering them away from writing and into math and science, which is what happened to me.

Fortunately, I happen to be rebellious in nature and enjoy the challenge of disproving assumptions made about me. I became an English major my first year in college, after being enrolled as pre-med. I started writing nonfiction as a free-lancer the week after I was told by my former boss that writing was my worst skill and I should hone my talents toward account management.

20   But it wasn't until 1985 that I finally began to write fiction. And at first I wrote using what I thought to be wittily crafted sentences, sentences that would finally prove I had mastery over the English language. Here's an example from the first draft of a story that later made its way into *The Joy Luck Club,* but without this line: "That was my mental quandary in its nascent state." A terrible line, which I can barely pronounce.

Fortunately, for reasons I won't get into today, I later decided I should envision a reader for the stories I would write. And the reader I decided upon was my mother, because these were stories about mothers. So with this reader in mind—and in fact she did read my early drafts—I began to write stories using all the Englishes I grew up with: the English I spoke to my mother, which for lack of a better term might be described as "simple"; the English she used with me, which for lack of a better term might be described as "broken"; my translation of her Chinese, which could certainly be described as "watered down"; and what I imagined to be her translation of her Chinese if she could speak in perfect English, her internal language, and for that I sought to preserve the essence, but neither an English nor a Chinese structure. I wanted to capture what language ability tests can never reveal: her intent, her passion, her imagery, the rhythms of her speech, and the nature of her thoughts.

Apart from what any critic had to say about my writing, I knew I had succeeded where it counted when my mother finished reading my book and gave me her verdict: "So easy to read."

Understanding the Text

1. What are "all the Englishes" that Tan grew up with? What exactly does Tan mean by Englishes? What differences are there among the different Englishes she uses? Why are these differences important to her?

2. Tan shares several anecdotes about her mother's use of "broken" or "limited" English in dealing with bankers, doctors, and other professional people. What do these anecdotes reveal about what Tan calls the "limitations" of her mother's English? Why are these limitations important to Tan? What do they suggest about our uses of language? What do they suggest about our attitudes toward language differences?

3. Why is the fact that Asian American students seem to do better in math and science than in other school subjects important to Tan? What does it suggest to her about the role of language in the learning of such students? Do you think she is right? Why or why not?

4. Why does Tan believe that her mother is the best reader for her stories and novels?

What might this suggest about a writer's audience?

Exploring the Issues

1. In the first two paragraphs, Tan identifies herself as "someone who has always loved language," and not as "a scholar of English or literature." Why do you think Tan begins her essay in this way? How did this beginning affect your view of Tan as the author of this essay? Did it give her more or less credibility, in your view? Explain.

2. In paragraph 3, Tan describes a talk she was giving about her novel *The Joy Luck*

Club, and she describes the language she was using in that talk as the "standard English that I had learned in school and through books." Do you think Tan is criticizing "school English" in her essay? If so, do you think her criticism is valid? Explain, citing specific passages from the text and drawing on your own experience with English to support your answer.

3. Examine Tan's descriptions of her mother. What kind of person is Tan's mother? What characteristics does Tan focus on in her descriptions of her mother? Why do you think Tan emphasizes these characteristics? How might her descriptions of her mother contribute to her main point in this essay?

4. In paragraph 20, Tan shares the following sentence from a draft of one of her stories: "That was my mental quandary in its nascent state." Tan calls this sentence a "terrible line." What do you think she finds terrible about this sentence? Do you agree with her? Why or why not? What might Tan's opinion of this sentence suggest about her views about writing style?

Entering the Conversations

1. Write an essay for an audience of your classmates describing an experience in which your use of language was important. The experience can be a time when your use of language was problematic or troubling, a time when your language put you at some kind of advantage or disadvantage, or a time when language played a central role in some event. Describe the experience in a way that helps your readers understand what you might have learned about language through that experience.

2. In a group of classmates, share the essay you wrote for Question 1. Discuss what the experiences you and your classmates described might suggest about language. What was political about the way language was used in your experiences? What conclusions can you draw from your discussion?

INFOTRAC

3. Using InfoTrac College Edition and any other relevant resources, investigate the challenges facing second-language learners in schools today and the programs that educators are developing to address those challenges. Find out what educators have learned about how best to help second-language learners. Write a report on the basis of your research.

4. Try to find someone who is a second-language learner.

(See *Conversations: Second Language-Learners* on page 326.) Interview this person about his or her experiences with language in school as well as outside school. How has that language affected schoolwork or social activities that are done in English? What problems or difficulties has this person experienced? Then write an essay in which you describe the person you interviewed and his or her experiences as a second language-learner. Draw conclusions about the politics of language from your interview.

5. Write an essay in which you present your position on the question of requiring only English in schools, workplaces, government meetings, and elsewhere. (The movement to adopt such requirements is known as the English Only movement. You may want to learn more about it by visiting the web sites of groups that support such requirements.) Explain why you think English should be (or should not be) the exclusive language used in certain circumstances. What are the advantages of requiring (or not requiring) English only? What problems do you see with having different languages in school or the workplace? Try to address such questions in your essay.

When I was in the seventh grade, I bought a paperback copy of Battle Cry, *a novel by Leon Uris about the experiences of a group of young American marines fighting in the Pacific theater during World War II. I enjoyed reading military history and fiction, and I often read novels like* Battle Cry. *In school one day, during a study*

THE Library Card

period, my teacher noticed me reading and asked about the book. She borrowed it from me, returning it at the end of the day. As she gave it back to me, she asked, "Do you think you can handle this?" At the time, I assumed she was referring to the graphic descriptions of violence and sex in the book. But as I look back on that incident, I see that she was monitoring my reading. If she considered the book inappropriate for me, she may have contacted my parents. It's possible that the school might have tried to prevent me from reading the book.

I thought of that incident as I read the following excerpt from Richard Wright's autobiography, Black Boy *(1945). In this compelling passage, Wright describes his efforts to obtain books from a library at a time when it was risky for Blacks to do so. His story is about the impact of racism on the lives of Black Americans, which affected even what and how they*

RICHARD WRIGHT

One morning I arrived early at work and went into the bank lobby where the Negro porter was mopping. I stood at a counter and picked up the Memphis *Commercial Appeal* and began my free reading of the press. I came finally to the editorial page and saw an article dealing with one **H. L. MENCKEN.** I knew by hearsay that he was the editor of the *American Mercury*, but aside from that I knew nothing about him. The article was a furious denunciation of Mencken, concluding with one, hot, short sentence: Mencken is a fool.

I wondered what on earth this Mencken had done to call down upon him the scorn of the South. The only people I had ever heard denounced in the South were Negroes, and this man was not a Negro. Then what ideas did Mencken hold that made a newspaper like the *Commercial Appeal* castigate him publicly? Undoubtedly he must be advocating ideas that the South did not like. Were there, then, people other than Negroes who criticized the South? I knew that during the Civil War the South had hated northern whites, but I had not encountered such hate during my life. Knowing no more of Mencken than I did at that moment, I felt a vague sympathy for him. Had not the

read. But it is also about the impact that reading can have on a person. Wright explores the effects of his reading on his sense of who he was as a Black man, and he describes how his reading helped him learn some difficult lessons. In many ways, his reading—as well as the writing he eventually did—changed him dramatically; it helped him gain a new understanding of himself. And it represented a challenge to the Whites who controlled the southern communities like the one where Wright grew up. In this regard, Wright's passage helps us understand why there have always been attempts to control what people read and write. It also helps us see why people will resist efforts to control their reading and writing.

Richard Wright (1908–1960) is considered one of the foremost American writers of the twentieth century. In addition to his autobiography, Black Boy, *he was author of a number of collections of stories, works of nonfiction, and novels, including* Native Son *(1940) and* Uncle Tom's Children *(1938). He was a passionate voice for the victims of oppression and a controversial figure in part because of his sympathies for the Communist Party.* ◪

GLOSS: H. L. MENCKEN
Henry Louis Mencken (1880–1956), who is mentioned in the first paragraph, was one of the best-known writers and political observers of his time. A prolific author of newspaper columns as well as poetry and books of social commentary, he was known for his sharp wit and often biting criticisms of public figures and human nature. In paragraph 61, Wright offers his own description of Mencken's writing.

South, which had assigned me the role of a non-man, cast at him its hardest words?

Now, how could I find out about this Mencken? There was a huge library near the riverfront, but I knew that Negroes were not allowed to patronize its shelves any more than they were the parks and playgrounds of the city. I had gone into the library several times to get books for the white men on the job. Which of them would now help me to get books? And how could I read them without causing concern to the white men with whom I worked? I had so far been successful in hiding my thoughts and feelings from them, but I knew that I would create hostility if I went about the business of reading in a clumsy way.

I weighed the personalities of the men on the job. There was Don, a Jew; but I distrusted him. His position was not much better than mine and I knew that he was uneasy and insecure; he had always treated me in an offhand, bantering way that barely concealed his contempt. I was afraid to ask him to help me get books; his frantic desire to demonstrate a racial solidarity with the whites against Negroes might make him betray me.

Then how about the boss? No, he was a Baptist and I had the suspicion that he would not be quite able to comprehend why a black boy would want to read Mencken. There were other white men on the job whose attitudes showed clearly that they were Kluxers or sympathizers, and they were out of the question. 5

There remained only one man whose attitude did not fit into an anti-Negro category, for I had heard the white men refer to him as a "Pope lover." He was an Irish Catholic and was hated by the white southerners. I knew that he read books, because I had got him volumes from the library several times. Since he, too, was an object of hatred, I felt that he might refuse me but would hardly betray me. I hesitated, weighing and balancing the imponderable realities.

One morning I paused before the Catholic fellow's desk.

"I want to ask you a favor," I whispered to him.

"What is it?"

"I want to read. I can't get books from the library. I wonder if you'd let me use your card?" 10

He looked at me suspiciously.

"My card is full most of the time," he said.

"I see," I said and waited, posing my question silently.

"You're not trying to get me into trouble, are you, boy?" He asked, staring at me.

"Oh, no sir." 15

"What book do you want?"

"A book by H. L. Mencken."

"Which one?"

"I don't know. Has he written more than one?"

"He has written several."

"I didn't know that."

"What makes you want to read Mencken?"

"Oh, I just saw his name in the newspaper," I said.

"It's good of you to want to read," he said. "But you ought to read the right things."

I said nothing. Would he want to supervise my reading?

"Let me think," he said. "I'll figure out something."

I turned from him and he called me back. He stared at me quizzically.

"Richard, don't mention this to the other white men," he said.

"I understand," I said. "I won't say a word."

A few days later he called me to him.

"I've got a card in my wife's name," he said. "Here's mine."

"Thank you, sir."

"Do you think you can manage it?"

"I'll manage fine," I said.

"If they suspect you, you'll get in trouble," he said.

"I'll write the same kind of notes to the library that you wrote when you sent me for books," I told him. "I'll sign your name."

He laughed.

"Go ahead. Let me see what you get," he said.

That afternoon I addressed myself to forging a note. Now, what were the names of books written by H. L. Mencken? I did not know any of them. I finally wrote what I thought would be a foolproof note: *Dear Madam: Will you please let this nigger boy*—I used the word "nigger" to make the librarian feel that I could not possibly be the author of the note—*have some books by H. L. Mencken?* I forged the white man's name.

I entered the library as I had always done when on errands for whites, but I felt that I would somehow slip up and betray myself. I doffed my hat, stood a respectful distance from the desk, looked as unbookish as possible, and waited for the white patrons to be taken care of. When the desk was clear of people, I still waited. The white librarian looked at me.

"What do you want, boy?"

As though I did not possess the power of speech, I stepped forward and simply handed her the forged note, not parting my lips.

"What books by Mencken does he want?" she asked.

"I don't know, ma'am," I said, avoiding her eyes.

"Who gave you this card?"

"Mr. Falk," I said.

"Where is he?"

"He's at work, at the M—— Optical Company," I said. "I've been in here for him before."

"I remember," the woman said. "But he never wrote notes like this."

20

25

30

35

40

45

CONVERSATIONS: RACIAL SLURS
Wright tells us in paragraph 39 that when he forged the note to the librarian, he used the word "nigger." Notice how that racially charged word, which we consider a slur, carries several meanings in this scene. What are those meanings? Consider what that word might have meant in 1945, when Wright's book was published, compared to today. Consider, too, how Wright uses the word as a tool in this context. What might this scene reveal about the way political and historical context influences the meaning of words?

50   Oh, God, she's suspicious. Perhaps she would not let me have the books? If she had turned her back at that moment, I would have ducked out the door and never gone back. Then I thought of a bold idea.

"You can call him up, ma'am," I said, my heart pounding.

"You're not using these books, are you?" she asked pointedly.

"Oh, no, ma'am. I can't read."

"I don't know what he wants by Mencken," she said under her breath.

55   I knew now that I had won; she was thinking of other things and the race question had gone out of her mind. She went to the shelves. Once or twice she looked over her shoulder at me, as though she was still doubtful. Finally she came forward with two books in her hand.

"I'm sending him two books," she said. "But tell Mr. Falk to come in next time, or send me the names of the books he wants. I don't know what he wants to read."

I said nothing. She stamped the card and handed me the books. Not daring to glance at them, I went out of the library, fearing that the woman would call me back for further questioning. A block away from the library I opened one of the books and read a title: *A Book of Prefaces*. I was nearing my nineteenth birthday and I did not know how to pronounce the word "preface." I thumbed the pages and saw strange words and strange names. I shook my head, disappointed. I looked at the other book; it was called *Prejudices*. I knew what that word meant; I had heard it all my life. And right off I was on guard against Mencken's books. Why would a man want to call a book *Prejudices*? The word was so stained with all my memories of racial hate that I could not conceive of anybody using it for a title. Perhaps I had made a mistake about Mencken? A man who had prejudices must be wrong.

When I showed the books to Mr. Falk, he looked at me and frowned.

"That librarian might telephone you," I warned him.

60   "That's all right," he said. "But when you're through reading those books, I want you to tell me what you get out of them."

That night in my rented room, while letting the hot water run over my can of pork and beans in the sink, I opened *A Book of Prefaces* and began to read. I was jarred and shocked by the style, the clear, clean, sweeping sentences. Why did he write like that? And how did one write like that? I pictured the man as a raging demon, slashing with his pen, consumed with hate, denouncing everything American, extolling everything European or German, laughing at the weaknesses of people, mocking God, authority. What was this? I stood up, trying to realize what reality lay behind the meaning of the words . . . Yes, this man was fighting, fighting with words. He was using words as a weapon, using them as one would use a club. Could words be weapons? Well, yes, for here they were. Then, maybe, perhaps, I could use them as a weapon? No. It frightened me. I read on and what amazed

STRATEGIES: DETAILS
Notice the details in the first sentence of paragraph 61. Writers often use details not only to describe a scene or event but also to convey messages about that scene or event. What messages do these details convey?

me was not what he said, but how on earth anybody had the courage to say it.

Occasionally I glanced up to reassure myself that I was alone in the room. Who were these men about whom Mencken was talking so passionately? Who was Anatole France? Joseph Conrad? Sinclair Lewis, Sherwood Anderson, Dostoevski, George Moore, Gustave Flaubert, Maupassant, Tolstoy, Frank Harris, Mark Twain, Thomas Hardy, Arnold Bennett, Stephen Crane, Zola, Norris, Gorky, Bergson, Ibsen, Balzac, Bernard Shaw, Dumas, Poe, Thomas Mann, O. Henry, Dreiser, H. G. Wells, Gogol, T. S. Eliot, Gide, Baudelaire, Edgar Lee Masters, Stendhal, Turgenev, Huneker, Nietzsche, and scores of others? Were these men real? Did they exist or had they existed? And how did one pronounce their names?

I ran across many words whose meanings I did not know, and I either looked them up in a dictionary or, before I had a chance to do that, encountered the word in a context that made its meaning clear. But what strange world was this? I concluded the book with the conviction that I had somehow overlooked something terribly important in life. I had once tried to write, had once reveled in feeling, had let my crude imagination roam, but the impulse to dream had been slowly beaten out of me by experience. Now it surged up again and I hungered for books, new ways of looking and seeing. It was not a matter of believing or disbelieving what I read, but of feeling something new, of being affected by something that made the look of the world different.

As dawn broke I ate my pork and beans, feeling dopey, sleepy. I went to work, but the mood of the book would not die; it lingered, coloring everything I saw, heard, did. I now felt that I knew what the white men were feeling. Merely because I had read a book that had spoken of how they lived and thought, I identified myself with that book. I felt vaguely guilty. Would I, filled with bookish notions, act in a manner that would make the whites dislike me?

I forged more notes and my trips to the library became frequent. 65 Reading grew into a passion. My first serious novel was Sinclair Lewis's *Main Street*. It made me see my boss, Mr. Gerald, and identify him as an American type. I would smile when I saw him lugging his golf bags into the office. I had always felt a vast distance separating me from the boss, and now I felt closer to him, though still distant. I felt now that I knew him, that I could feel the very limits of his narrow life. And this had happened because I had read a novel about a mythical man called George F. Babbitt.

The plots and stories in the novels did not interest me so much as the point of view revealed. I gave myself over to each novel without reserve, without trying to criticize it; it was enough for me to see and feel something different. And for me, everything was something different. Reading was like a drug, a dope. The novels created moods in which I lived for days. But I could not conquer my sense of guilt, my

CONVERSATIONS: FAMOUS NOVELS
Wright refers to two novels by Theodore Dreiser, one of the best-known American novelists in the first half of the twentieth century. Dreiser's novels, especially *Sister Carrie* and *An American Tragedy,* are considered sharp criticisms of American capitalism. Wright himself came to sympathize with the anticapitalist views of the Communist Party. In a sense, Wright's reading helped shape his political and social views—as well as his own novels. His descriptions of the novels he read can be seen as an example of how fiction can be part of the broader discussions of social and political issues that are carried on in our society through the political process and the press.

CONVERSATIONS: JIM CROW
In the brief scene in paragraph 76, Wright describes some of the risks he faced as his anger about the way he was treated by Whites increased because of his reading. This scene gives us a glimpse into what life was like in the American South in the 1930s and 1940s, when Jim Crow laws (which Wright mentions earlier in par. 74) were in effect. These laws prohibited Blacks from certain activities and rights (such as voting) and created a climate of tension and fear, as Wright suggests in this passage. It's worth considering how Wright's reading was a challenge to the Jim Crow culture of the American South and how it might therefore be seen as subversive. This is what writers sometimes mean when they discuss the power of literacy.

feeling that the white men around me knew that I was changing, that I had begun to regard them differently.

Whenever I brought a book to the job, I wrapped it in newspaper—a habit that was to persist for years in other cities and under other circumstances. But some of the white men pried into my packages when I was absent and they questioned me.

"Boy, what are you reading those books for?"

"Oh, I don't know, sir."

"That's deep stuff you're reading, boy."   70

"I'm just killing time, sir."

"You'll addle your brains if you don't watch out."

I read **DREISER'S JENNIE GERHARDT AND SISTER CARRIE** and they revived in me a vivid sense of my mother's suffering; I was overwhelmed. I grew silent, wondering about the life around me. It would have been impossible for me to have told anyone what I derived from these novels, for it was nothing less than a sense of life itself. All my life had shaped me for the realism, the naturalism of the modern novel, and I could not read enough of them.

Steeped in new moods and ideas, I bought a ream of paper and tried to write; but nothing would come, or what did come was flat beyond telling. I discovered that more than desire and feeling were necessary to write and I dropped the idea. Yet I still wondered how it was possible to know people sufficiently to write about them? Could I ever learn about life and people? To me, with my vast ignorance, my Jim Crow station in life, it seemed a task impossible of achievement. I now knew what being a Negro meant. I could endure the hunger and I had learned to live with hate. But to feel that there were feelings denied me, that the very breath of life itself was beyond my reach, that more than anything else hurt, wounded me. I had a new hunger.

In buoying me up, reading also cast me down, made me see what   75
was possible, what I had missed. My tension returned, new, terrible, bitter, surging, almost too great to be contained. I no longer *felt* that the world about me was hostile, killing; I *knew* it. A million times I asked myself what I could do to save myself, and there were no answers. I seemed forever condemned, ringed by walls.

I did not discuss my reading with Mr. Falk, who had lent me his library card; it would have meant talking about myself and that would have been too painful. I smiled each day, fighting desperately to maintain my old behavior, to keep my disposition seemingly sunny. But some of the white men discerned that I had begun to brood.

"Wake up there, boy!" Mr. Olin said one day.

"Sir!" I answered for the lack of a better word.

"You act like you've stolen something," he said.

80   I laughed in the way I knew he expected me to laugh, but I resolved to be more conscious of myself, to watch my every act, to guard and hide the new knowledge that was dawning within me.

If I went north, would it be possible for me to build a new life then? But how could a man build a life upon vague, unformed yearnings? I wanted to write and I did not even know the English language. I bought English grammars and found them dull. I felt that I was getting a better sense of the language from novels than from grammars. I read hard, discarding a writer as soon as I felt that I had grasped his point of view. At night the printed page stood before my eyes in sleep.

Mrs. Moss, my landlady, asked me one Sunday morning:

"Son, what is this you keep on reading?"

"Oh, nothing. Just novels."

85 "What you get out of 'em?"

"I'm just killing time," I said.

"I hope you know your own mind," she said in a tone which implied that she doubted if I had a mind.

I knew of no Negroes who read the books I liked and I wondered if any Negroes ever thought of them. I knew that there were Negro doctors, lawyers, newspapermen, but I never saw any of them. When I read a Negro newspaper I never caught the faintest echo of my preoccupation in its pages. I felt trapped and occasionally, for a few days, I would stop reading. But a vague hunger would come over me for books, books that opened up new avenues of feeling and seeing, and again I would forge another note to the white librarian. Again I would read and wonder as only the naïve and unlettered can read and wonder, feeling that I carried a secret, criminal burden about with me each day.

That winter my mother and brother came and we set up housekeeping, buying furniture on the installment plan, being cheated and yet knowing no way to avoid it. I began to eat warm food and to my surprise found that regular meals enabled me to read faster. I may have lived through many illnesses and survived them, never suspecting that I was ill. My brother obtained a job and we began to save toward the trip north, plotting our time, setting tentative dates for departure. I told none of the white men on the job that I was planning to go north; I knew that the moment they felt I was thinking of the North they would change toward me. It would have made them feel that I did not like the life I was living, and because my life was completely conditioned by what they said or did, it would have been tantamount to challenging them.

I could calculate my chances for life in the South as a Negro fairly clearly now. 90

I could fight the southern whites by organizing with other Negroes, as my grandfather had done. But I knew that I could never win that way; there were many whites and there were but few blacks. They were strong and we were weak. Outright black rebellion could never win. If I fought openly I would die and I did not want to die. News of lynchings were frequent.

CONVERSATIONS: THE DECLINE OF READING
In 2004, A National Endowment for the Arts (NEA) released a report indicating that fewer Americans were reading novels, stories, plays, and poems. According to the NEA report, 10 percent fewer Americans were reading such literature in 2002 than in 1982. When the report was released, many observers and educators expressed alarm at these figures, suggesting that a decline in reading literature was detrimental to American society, which requires an educated citizenry to keep democracy healthy. It is interesting to consider the reaction to the NEA report in the context of this passage (par. 88) from Richard Wright's autobiography, which shows how reading literature could be risky in some ways and has also been controlled in our own country.

I could submit and live the life of a genial slave, but that was impossible. All of my life had shaped me to live by my own feelings, and thoughts. I could make up to **BESS** and marry her and inherit the house. But that, too, would be the life of a slave; if I did that, I would crush to death something within me, and I would hate myself as much as I knew the whites already hated those who had submitted. Neither could I ever willingly present myself to be kicked, as Shorty had done. I would rather have died than do that.

I could drain off my restlessness by fighting with **SHORTY AND HARRISON.** I had seen many Negroes solve the problem of being black by transferring their hatred of themselves to others with a black skin and fighting them. I would have to be cold to do that, and I was not cold and I could never be.

I could, of course, forget what I had read, thrust the whites out of my mind, forget them; and find release from anxiety and longing in sex and alcohol. But the memory of how my father had conducted himself made that course repugnant. If I did not want others to violate my life, how could I voluntarily violate it myself?

95 I had no hope whatever of being a professional man. Not only had I been so conditioned that I did not desire it, but the fulfillment of such an ambition was beyond my capabilities. Well-to-do Negroes lived in a world that was almost as alien to me as the world inhabited by whites.

What, then, was there? I held my life in my mind, in my consciousness each day, feeling at times that I would stumble and drop it, spill it forever. My reading had created a vast sense of distance between me and the world in which I lived and tried to make a living, and that sense of distance was increasing each day. My days and nights were one long, quiet, continuously contained dream of terror, tension, and anxiety. I wondered how long I could bear it.

GLOSS: BESS, SHORTY, AND HARRISON
Bess was a woman with whom Wright was in love and whom he describes elsewhere in his autobiography, *Black Boy,* from which this passage is excerpted. Shorty and Harrison are friends of his who are also described elsewhere in *Black Boy.*

Understanding the Text

1. What prompted Wright to try to obtain books from the library? What might this episode reveal about Wright as a person?

2. What is Wright's reaction to the books he reads by H. L. Mencken (par. 61–63)? Why do you think he focuses attention on Mencken's writing? What does Wright mean when he writes that reading Mencken's book convinced him that he "had somehow overlooked something terribly important" in his life? What was it that he had overlooked?

3. Why does Wright say that "reading was like a drug, a dope" for him? What does this simile suggest about reading? Do you think this is an appropriate simile to describe the effects of reading on him? Why or why not?

4. What dilemma does reading lead to for Wright? What does he realize as a result of confronting this dilemma? How does he resolve it? What does his dilemma suggest about the circumstances within which Blacks lived in the American South?

Exploring the Issues

1. In a sense, this excerpt from Wright's autobiography is a description of the effect of reading on one person. Examine the sections in this passage (par. 63–65 or par. 73, for example) in which Wright describes how he was affected by the specific books he read. What were the effects of these books on him? How did they change his thinking? Were there similarities in the way the different books he read affected him? Explain.

2. Imagine if you were prevented from having access to books, newspapers, the Internet, or other sources of information you use regularly. What impact might that have on your life? What might Wright's difficulties obtaining books tell us about reading and writing and their roles in our society?

Entering the Conversations

1. In paragraph 63, Wright tells us that after reading H. L. Mencken's book, he "hungered for books, new ways of looking and seeing." Write an essay about a time you experienced new ways of looking and seeing as a result of reading a book or having a profound experience.

2. Given Wright's descriptions about the power that Whites had over Blacks during the time he was growing up, I might have put this essay in Chapter 9 on power. Using Wright's essay and any of the essays in Chapter 9 that seem appropriate, write an essay in which you discuss the relationship between power and learning. In what ways did the power dynamics between Whites and Blacks affect Wright's learning? What do his experiences tell us about how such dynamics can hinder learning or result in certain kinds of learning?

INFOTRAC

3. Throughout history, there have been many attempts to control what people read and even whether they can read. Today, we continue to see efforts to control reading and writing—from attempts by totalitarian governments to ban certain kinds of books to efforts by individuals and groups in the United States to prohibit schools from assigning certain books to students. Using InfoTrac College Edition and other appropriate resources, examine previous and current efforts to control writing and reading. Try to find examples of attempts to ban certain kinds of reading materials, and examine those examples to understand the reasons for them. Write a report in which you describe such efforts to control reading and writing. Describe these situations and explain the views of the people involved.

Draw conclusions about reading and writing on the basis of the examples you discuss.

4. This painting by Jacob Lawrence (1917–2000), an African American artist interested in the struggles of freedom during the Civil Rights Movement, depicts a scene entitled *The Library* (1960). Write an essay in which you analyze the messages this painting communicates about libraries and reading.

Jacob Lawrence, *The Library*, 1960

Humor / Satire

Political humor has a long tradition in American culture. Americans have always used humor to criticize the foibles of those in power, perhaps to defuse some of the anxiety we feel about how political power is used by those who hold it. In fact, some of the most revered writers in American literary history were famous in their day for their political satire, most

Bill of Rights Pared Down to a Manageable Six

notably Mark Twain. You can get a sense of his brand of political humor in some sections of his best-known novel, The Adventures of Huckleberry Finn, *in which minor characters serve as vehicles for Twain's biting criticisms of political officials. Today, the stand-up monologue, in which a comedian pokes fun at current political events, is a standard part of the acts of popular television comedians like David Letterman and Jay Leno. And the growing popularity of comedians like Jon Stewart and Stephen Colbert, whose humor focuses on politics, indicates that Twain's spirit is alive and well today.*

The following article, taken from the satiric newspaper The Onion, *is a good example of the kind of political humor that seems to have*

THE ONION

Washington, DC

Flanked by key members of Congress and his administration, President Bush approved Monday a streamlined version of the Bill of Rights that pares its 10 original amendments down to a "tight, no-nonsense" six.

A Republican initiative that went unopposed by congressional Democrats, the revised Bill of Rights provides citizens with a "more manageable" set of privacy and due-process rights by eliminating four amendments and condensing and/or restructuring five others. The Second Amendment, which protects the right to keep and bear arms, was the only article left unchanged.

Calling the historic reduction "a victory for America," Bush promised that the new document would do away with "bureaucratic impediments to the flourishing of democracy at home and abroad."

resurged in popularity in recent years. Like Jon Stewart and Stephen Colbert, The Onion *relies on satire and irony for its humor. But what lies beneath the barbs and tongue-in-cheek lines are serious ideas about what is wrong with the way power is used in the United States today. Perhaps it takes this kind of offbeat but unflinching humor to make us more aware of the consequences of power. In that regard, humor, and especially satire, is an important kind of power itself. It is no coincidence that satirists, from Twain to Jon Stewart, can profoundly influence the political views of Americans. In fact, polls show that among many younger Americans, Stewart's TV show,* The Daily Show, *is the primary source of political information. That is surely a reflection of the power of political satire.*

The following article appeared in The Onion *in December 2002.* ▼

© AP/Wide World Photos/Ron Edmonds/STF

As supporters look on, Bush signs the Bill of Rights Reduction and Consolidation Act

"It is high time we reaffirmed our commitment to this enduring symbol of American ideals," Bush said. "By making the Bill of Rights a tool for progress instead of a hindrance to freedom, we honor the true spirit of our nation's forefathers."

The Fourth Amendment, which long protected citizens' homes against unreasonable search and seizure, was among the eliminated amendments. Also stricken was the Ninth Amendment, which stated that the enumeration of certain Constitutional rights does not result in the abrogation of rights not mentioned.

"Quite honestly, I could never get my head around what the Ninth Amendment meant anyway," said outgoing House Majority Leader Dick Armey (R-TX), one of the leading advocates of the revised Bill of Rights. "So goodbye to that one."

Amendments V through VII, which guaranteed the right to legal counsel in criminal cases, and guarded against double jeopardy, testifying against oneself, biased juries, and drawn-out trials, have been condensed into Super-Amendment V: The One About Trials.

Attorney General John Ashcroft hailed the slimmed-down Bill of Rights as "a positive step."

"Go up to the average citizen and ask them what's in the Bill of Rights," Ashcroft said. "Chances are, they'll have only a vague notion. They just know it's a set of rules put in place to protect their individual freedoms from government intrusion, and they assume that's a good thing."

Ashcroft responded sharply to critics who charge that the Bill of Rights no longer safeguards certain basic, inalienable rights.

"We're not taking away personal rights; we're increasing personal *security*," Ashcroft said. "By allowing for greater government control over the particulars of individual liberties, the Bill of Rights will now offer expanded personal freedoms whenever they are deemed appro-

5

10

STRATEGIES: USING STYLE TO CREATE HUMOR
This article is written in a way that mimics standard journalistic writing style. This paragraph, for example, seems to report the elimination of two amendments from the Bill of Rights in the straightforward, objective style of a newspaper article. Consider how this writing style contributes to the satiric humor of this article. Do you need to know that the statements in this paragraph aren't true for this writing style to be effective as humor? Consider, too, how the authors of this article rely on their readers' background knowledge—for example, about the Bill of Rights and about the presidency of George W. Bush—to make their "fake" journalism humorous.